School Counseling for the Twenty-First Century

Stanley B. Baker
North Carolina State University

Edwin R. Gerler, Jr.
North Carolina State University

PEARSON

Merrill
Prentice Hall

Upper Saddle River, New Jersey
Columbus, Ohio

Library of Congress Cataloging-in-Publication Data

Baker, Stanley B.
  School counseling for the twenty-first century / Stanley B. Baker, Edwin R. Gerler, Jr.—5th ed.
    p. cm.
  Includes bibliographical references and index.
  ISBN-13: 978-0-13-189037-4
  ISBN-10: 0-13-189037-9
  1. Student counselors—Training of—United States.   2. Educational counseling—United
States.   I. Gerler, Edwin R.   II. Title.
  LB1731.75.B35 2008
  371.4—dc22   2007010734

Vice President and Executive Publisher: Jeffery W. Johnston
Publisher: Kevin M. Davis
Editor: Meredith D. Fossel
Senior Editorial Assistant: Kathleen S. Burk
Production Editor: Mary Harlan
Production Coordinator: Kelly Ricci/Aptara, Inc.
Design Coordinator: Diane C. Lorenzo
Text Design: Aptara, Inc.
Cover Design: Candace Rowley
Production Manager: Susan W. Hannahs
Director of Marketing: David Gesell
Marketing Manager: Autumn Purdy
Marketing Coordinator: Brian Mounts

This book was set in Garamond by Aptara, Inc. It was printed and bound by Courier/
Westford. The cover was printed by Phoenix Color Corp.

Photo Credits for Chapter Openers: Stanley B. Baker, p. 1; all other, Edwin R. Gerler, Jr.

Pearson Education Ltd.   Pearson Education Australia Pty. Limited
Pearson Education Singapore Pte. Ltd.   Pearson Education North Asia Ltd.
Pearson Education Canada, Ltd.   Pearson Educación de Mexico, S.A. de C.V.
Pearson Education–Japan   Pearson Education Malaysia Pte. Ltd.

PEARSON
Merrill
Prentice Hall

10 9 8 7 6 5 4 3 2 1
ISBN-13: 978-0-13-189037-4
ISBN-10:   0-13-189037-9

To our wives and best friends—
Mary Esther Clark Baker
Muffin Padgett Gerler

PREFACE

If you are reading this, you may be intent on becoming a school counselor, or you may already be a school counselor or another educator wanting to learn more about counseling in schools. School counselors make a difference in the lives of many people—students, parents, teachers, and school administrators. Even though we have spent most of our lives teaching and helping graduate students enter the profession, we have memories from early in our careers (when we worked as school counselors), memories that we have carried throughout our professional and personal lives and that have profoundly affected our teaching, research, and writing. The calls we received late at night from students in trouble and from distressed parents remain in our minds as if they happened yesterday. The words of thanks we received from those we helped are embedded in our thinking, as are the times we failed in our attempts to help.

When you open this textbook for the first time and glance at the table of contents, you will see chapter titles that reflect crucial subject matter about what it takes to be a school counselor. As you read, you will see examples of national models and paradigms, all designed to make the profession manageable and understandable. We have tried to incorporate the human side of school counseling into the core of every chapter, hoping not to block the spirit of caring for people by what at first glance might appear to be academic jargon.

We are old enough to remember when Gilbert Wrenn (1962) wrote his famous little book, *The Counselor in a Changing World*. One of our graduate students recently came across the book in our university library. She had heard about Professor Wrenn at a conference program focused on pioneers in counseling, so she decided to page through the book. She quickly noticed that most of the 1960s issues raised in the book were still issues in the 21st century. She wondered aloud, "Why haven't school counselors made more progress on these issues?" She speculated, without waiting for our response, that maybe graduate students, new counselor education graduates, and practicing school counselors need to raise their voices a bit to get the profession moving in new directions—and to lead the way to counseling innovations.

After subtly noting that some of us old people in the profession have done some innovative thinking about school counseling and about the issues raised by Gilbert Wrenn, we applauded our graduate student's initiative and, in fact, decided to use our book as means for graduate students and others to lend their voices to the issues confronting school counselors—and most important, to chart the course for invention in school counseling. We believe that the school counseling profession is enriched when the voices of aspiring professionals meet the voices of experience, with the aim of creating new ways to serve.

You will note, in particular, that chapter 13 (the shortest in the book) is your chapter to write. It is a living chapter that will change from week to week, month to month, and year to year as you contribute your thinking at http://www.genesislight.com/scan21st/newdirections/. We have created a place at the School Activities Network for the 21st Century (SCAN21st) Web site for us to record your creative thinking about school counseling: www.scan21st.com.

In addition, the end of each chapter offers you the opportunity to share your voice on the material we presented. We will incorporate your thinking as best we can at the SCAN21st Web site. Be patient with us, as we will be with you. We are inventing together.

One last thought—and a moment of self-disclosure. This textbook has given us, two longtime colleagues and friends, the opportunity to take a journey that offered surprises. When we began this new edition of our book, we believed that we knew exactly where we were headed. But, as Robert Frost (1920) said long ago, "way leads on to way" and "that has made all the difference." We hope our journey makes a difference for you—and for counseling in schools.

ONLINE INSTRUCTOR'S MANUAL

The *Online Instructor's Manual with Test Items* is free to adopters of this text. This electronic material includes chapter goals and content outlines, in addition to a solid test bank with multiple-choice and essay questions. Adopting professors can access this supplement with an access code by searching www.prenhall.com under the ISBN 0-13-189037-9.

ACKNOWLEDGMENTS

The authors want to thank the following reviewers for their helpful comments and suggestions: Michael J. Karcher, University of Texas–San Antonio; Michael J. Scheel, University of Nebraska–Lincoln; Hemla Singaravelu, Saint Louis University; and Toni Tollerud, Northern Illinois University.

REFERENCES

Frost, R. (1920). *Mountain interval.* New York: Henry Holt.

Wrenn, G. (1962). *The counselor in a changing world.* Washington, DC: American Personnel and Guidance Association.

DISCOVER THE COMPANION WEBSITE
ACCOMPANYING THIS BOOK

THE PRENTICE HALL COMPANION WEBSITE:
A VIRTUAL LEARNING ENVIRONMENT

Technology is a constantly growing and changing aspect of our field that is creating a need for content and resources. To address this emerging need, Prentice Hall has developed an online learning environment for students and professors alike—Companion Websites—to support our textbooks.

In creating a Companion Website, our goal is to build on and enhance what the textbook already offers. For this reason, the content for each user-friendly website is organized by chapter and provides the professor and student with a variety of meaningful resources.

Common Companion Website features for students include:

- **Chapter Objectives**—outline key concepts from the text.
- **Interactive Self-quizzes**—complete with hints and automatic grading that provide immediate feedback for students. After students submit their answers for the interactive self-quizzes, the Companion Website **Results Reporter** computes a percentage grade, provides a graphic representation of how many questions were answered correctly and incorrectly, and gives a question-by-question analysis of the quiz. Students are given the option to send their quiz to up to four email addresses (professor, teaching assistant, study partner, etc.).
- **Essay Questions**—these questions allow students to respond to themes and objectives of each chapter by applying what they have learned to real classroom situations.
- **Web Destinations**—links to www sites that relate to chapter content.

To take advantage of the many available resources, please visit the *School Counseling for the Twenty-First Century*, Fifth Edition, Companion Website at

www.prenhall.com/baker

BRIEF CONTENTS

CONTENTS

CHAPTER 5
Legal and Ethical Responsibilities in School Counseling   93

CHAPTER 6
Advocacy in School Counseling   126

CHAPTER 7
Leadership and Collaboration in School Counseling 154

CHAPTER 8
Prevention Programming in School Counseling: Serving All Students Proactively 167

CHAPTER 11
School Counselor Consulting: A Bridge Between Prevention and Intervention   264

CHAPTER 12
Assessment in School Counseling   288

CHAPTER 13
Inventing a School Counseling Program Online   323

CHAPTER 14
Beyond the Training Program: A School Counseling Career   330

APPENDIX A
Standards for School Counseling Programs   347

APPENDIX B
Lesson Outlines for Succeeding in School   349

APPENDIX C
Key Components of the National Standards for School Counseling Programs   352

APPENDIX D
Presidential High School: MEASURE of Success   358

NOTE: Every effort has been made to provide accurate and current Internet information in this book. However, the Internet and information posted on it are constantly changing, so it is inevitable that some of the Internet addresses listed in this textbook will change.

CHAPTER 1

The School Counseling Profession

Goal: To introduce readers to the school counseling profession and present our ideas for technology-enhanced learning that will complement this text.

During our years as counselor educators, we have heard hundreds of stories about the lives of people who have become school counselors. This story is one of the most compelling.

In mid-August, when I was 18 years old, I had my bags packed and ready to head out to college. I had been salutatorian of my high school class and had been recruited heavily by colleges across the United States. It seemed that everyone wanted me. I chose Cornell—I wanted to go there since I'd never been east of the Mississippi. My dad's cousin had gone to Cornell but never finished due to a life-threatening illness.

On the day I was scheduled to leave home, my parents—along with my five brothers and two sisters—had a party for me at Lemon Grove Baptist Church. Everyone in Lemon Grove came, even folks from the Catholic Church down the street. The minister at Lemon Grove was even friendly with the Catholic priest that day. Usually they didn't get along too well.

While we were partying and everyone was wishing me a safe trip to the East, we heard the beginnings of a typical, summer afternoon thunderstorm. As the rain began, we thought nothing of it. We were all kind of glad to have the rain. The summer had been dry, and August had been hot, so the rain promised to cool the day.

My mom and I poked our heads out the door to get away from the noise of the party. We sat down on a bench under a covered porch at the side of the church. We wanted to have a few moments to ourselves before leaving the party and heading out to the airport. She told me how much she loved me, and she hugged me. I, of course, had tears in my eyes and was already getting homesick. We were a very close family.

Just as we were turning to go back inside the church, a bolt of lightening hit the wall of the church and knocked me to the ground. My mother screamed and cried out for help. I could not move. They rushed me to the hospital, where I stayed for almost 5 weeks. From that day to this, I have not been able to walk. My upper body has functioned normally all my life, but I've been wheelchair bound. My family and the folks from Lemon Grove have been a constant source of support.

I eventually graduated from Cornell, married, worked for a newspaper for about 30 years, and decided to apply to graduate school in counseling about a year after my wife died. I thought it was about time that I help some kids. My wife and I never had kids. And I thought children could learn something from me and the challenges I faced and overcame. I was 55 years old when I received the letter accepting me into a counselor education program. I'm now 66 and will retire from my school counseling job at the end of this school year. The kids all say they are sorry to see me leave.

I've decided to move back to Lemon Grove and write a book for school counselors—a book filled with ideas about helping kids. I'm not going to write a textbook because textbooks are too boring!

Individuals give many other reasons for wanting to join the school counseling profession. In this chapter, we help aspiring counselors understand this profession and the challenges they face in preparing to become outstanding counseling professionals in the schools. This textbook is unique in that it is the foundation for an evolving online network, the School Counseling Activities Network (SCAN; www.scan21st.com), whereby graduate students, their professors, and practicing school counselors can work together to bring the graduate classroom and the practice of school counseling into closer harmony. We are excited about the prospects for this network and about working with school counseling graduate students, counselor educators, and professional school counselors around the world. We hope this network will bring the perspectives of many cultures to the practice of school counseling. We describe the potential for this network later in the chapter.

You will also note that chapter 13 is your chapter to write. It is a living chapter that will change from week to week, from month to month, and from year to year as you contribute your thoughts at http://www.genesislight.com/scan21st/newdirections/. We have created a place at the School Counseling Activities Network for the 21st Century for us to record your creative thinking about school counseling: www.scan21st.com.

In addition, at the end of every chapter, you will also have the opportunity to share your thoughts on the material we present. We will incorporate your input as best we can on the SCAN Web site. Be patient with us, as we will be with you. We are inventing together.

Each chapter of this textbook is also supplemented by online lessons that encourage professors and graduate students to reflect on the material presented in print and to generate ideas for the SCAN. The online lessons appear at http://www.prenhall.com/baker.

INTRODUCTION

"Positions to Programs"

This textbook is a tale about professional school counseling. The profession began as an individual manifestation of the Progressive Reform Movement in the late 19th and early 20th centuries and is perhaps most clearly depicted today by the American School Counselor Association's (ASCA's) National Model for School Counseling Programs (ASCA, 2005). Gysbers and Henderson (2000) referred to this century-long transition as "positions to programs" (p. 3). Just who determines what school counselors do has not been clear over the past century. School boards and administrators, state departments of education or public instruction, counselor educators, textbook authors, parents and students, and school counselors themselves have had their say but have not spoken with a unified voice. Consequently, the role of professional school counselors still lacks clarity. We applaud the efforts of the ASCA to achieve clarity through the development and presentation of the National Standards for School Counseling Programs (Campbell & Dahir, 1997) and subsequently of the National Model for School Counseling Programs (ASCA, 2005), although the latter has not yet achieved universal acceptance.

School Counseling for the Twenty-First Century is designed for an introductory course in school counseling, but it may be useful in other academic settings as well. Virtually all higher education programs for training school counselors must meet the standards established by respective state departments of education/public instruction in order for their graduates to receive school counseling licenses or certificates. These minimum standards vary from state to state. Among the universal requirements these standards present is coursework designed to socialize the students to the school counseling profession. Enhancing that socialization process is the general goal of this textbook.

Standards of the Council for the Accreditation of Counseling and Related Educational Programs

Although licenses or certification standards vary among states, the Council for the Accreditation of Counseling and Related Educational Programs (CACREP; 2001) provided a universal set of standards for training school counselors, as well as those preparing

Table 1.1
CACREP core areas for entry-level programs and professional identity core areas.

Core Areas for Entry-Level Programs
- Professional identity
- Social and cultural diversity
- Human growth and development
- Career development
- Helping relationships
- Group work
- Assessment
- Research and program evaluation

Professional Identity Core Areas
- History and philosophy of the counseling profession, including significant factors and events
- Professional roles, functions, and relationships with other human service providers
- Technological competence and computer literacy
- Professional organizations, primarily ACA, its divisions, branches, and affiliates, including membership benefits, activities, services to members, and current emphases
- Professional credentialing, including certification, licensure, and accreditation practices and standards, and the effects of public policy on these issues
- Public and private policy processes, including the role of professional counselor in advocating on behalf of the profession
- Advocacy processes needed to address institutional and social barriers that impede access, equity, and success for clients
- Ethical standards of ACA and related entities, and application of ethical and legal considerations in professional counseling

Note. CACREP = Council for the Accreditation of Counseling and Related Educational Programs, ACA = American Counseling Association.

for such fields a community/agency, college, and mental health counseling. The CACREP Standards for School Counseling Programs are equal to or more comprehensive than those established by the state departments of education/public instruction.

For example, Section II.k.1 of the 2001 CACREP standards for entry-level programs (i.e., master's degree programs) requires all students to have curricular experiences and demonstrated knowledge in their respective identity core areas (http://www.cacrep.org). Table 1.1 presents the eight common core areas of the 2001 CACREP standards and the eight standards in the Professional Identity core area. This textbook is designed to highlight the eight standards in the Professional Identity core area so students have the desired curricular experience and acquire "demonstrated knowledge."

The 2001 CACREP standards also present a section devoted to the standards for school counseling programs (http://www.cacrep.org). The four primary standards are

- Foundation for school counseling
- Contextual dimensions of school counseling
- Knowledge and skill requirements for school counseling
- Clinical instruction

Appendix A presents the CACREP Standards for School Counseling Programs in detail. This book addresses many of these standards, either in depth or via an overview. Some state departments of education/public instruction use the CACREP standards completely or as an option in the school counselor licensure/certification process. Those individuals who have completed CACREP-accredited programs or state-approved programs not accredited by CACREP (who have acquired 2 years of post-graduate experience) and who have received acceptable scores on the National Counselor Examination (NCE) can become national certified counselors (NCC) by the National Board for Certified Counselors (NBCC). In some states, successful completion of the NCE is one of the criteria for becoming a licensed professional counselor. We view this book as a vehicle for providing information and exercises in support of instruction in courses designed to meet the professional identity goals established by CACREP and state departments of education/public instruction. In addition, the book will help individuals prepare for the NCE and for the Educational Testing Service's School Guidance and Counseling (#20420) PRAXIS test, which is required in some states as part of the licensure/certification process.

Our Background

Although we attempt to be even-handedly objective in our treatment of ideas and information, the content covered and the point of view presented in this book is influenced by the experiences and philosophy of the coauthors. We have both been associated with the school counseling profession for a number of years, and this text has a history of four editions dating back to 1992. The first author (SBB) began his entry-level program at the University of Minnesota, Minneapolis, in 1960 and his career as a high school counselor at a Janesville, Wisconsin, senior high school in 1964. His higher education career as a counselor educator spans over three decades from 1971 (doctoral degree from the State University of New York at Buffalo) to the present at both the Pennsylvania State and North Carolina State universities. The second author (ERG) began his entry-level program at Bucknell University (Lewisburg, Pennsylvania) in 1969 and his career as an elementary/middle school counselor in Millville, Pennsylvania, in 1972. His higher education career spans three decades from 1975 (when he received his doctorate from Penn State) to the present at the University of Wisconsin, Whitewater, and North Carolina State universities. In the remainder of this opening chapter, we present information that students enrolled in an introductory course should be aware of at the beginning of the course and the training program so they can carefully process the meaning of that information throughout their learning experience.

PROFESSIONALS WITH MIXED ALLEGIENCES

Ascribing Professional Status to School Counselors

Are school counselors professionals? If they are professionals, what defines them as such? *Professional* is a term used frequently and somewhat loosely in American society because it seems to create an aura of respectability. Some individuals do not deserve that respectability, whereas others truly do. Some professionals assume the respectability and accompanying status without giving much thought to the real meaning of the word *professional* and to the responsibilities it implies, whereas others are fully aware of these responsibilities. Ideally, all professionals would fit into the latter category.

A *profession* is a vocation requiring special knowledge or education in some department of learning or science; a *professional* is one belonging to a learned or skilled profession; and *professionalism* is the character, spirit, or methods of a professional or the standing, practice, or methods of a professional as distinguished from an amateur, according to the *American College Dictionary*. If school counselors are professionals, then school counseling is a vocation requiring special knowledge or education in some department of learning or science. What is the department of learning or science from which school counselors receive their special knowledge? This is a somewhat difficult question to answer. The historical information presented in chapter 2 reveals that the guidance field from which school counseling evolved had several influences, including vocational guidance, psychometrics, mental health, and clinical psychology. The evolution of school counseling as a profession has not been clear-cut or even.

School counseling is part of two larger applied professions: counseling and education. These broader fields draw from the behavioral sciences such as anthropology, political science, psychology, and sociology. They have developed their own knowledge bases, and both have influenced school counseling. However, school counseling has been developing its own knowledge base over the years, which also influences practicing and emerging school counseling professionals. Consequently, school counseling is a profession with the behavioral sciences and the applied fields of counseling and education as its foundational departments of learning, and a profession in the process of developing its own knowledge base.

Drawing on the work of Barber (1965) and Greenwood (1957), Herr and Cramer (1987) suggested additional criteria for attributing professional status to a vocation. In summary, those criteria are

- The members have a service orientation (they are educated to serve community rather than self-interests).
- The degree of self-control is high (practitioner behaviors are regulated via community sanctions, ethical codes, etc.).
- Systems of rewards (monetary and honorary) are included that not only are symbols of work-related achievements but are also ends in themselves.
- A professional culture is perpetrated by consistent training programs.

It is the authors' contention that school counselors have a service orientation, are regulated by community sanctions and ethical codes, derive their monetary and honorary rewards from work-related achievements, and have consistent training programs. Therefore, the evidence indicates that school counseling is a profession and that school counselors are professionals who should be expected to behave in a professional manner.

Competing Professional Loyalties

A common practice among professionals is to band together in professional associations or societies. There are a number of reasons for doing so. Among the more prominent are unity, status, influence, services, standards and guidelines, continuing education opportunities, self-regulation, and economic enhancement. School counselors, as members of the broader professional fields of education and counseling, find themselves encouraged to join professional societies in both fields. The choices are difficult because each offers different advantages, and membership in both is more expensive than in one. This is an important issue for school counselors, many of whom earn relatively modest salaries, compared with members of other professional groups.

Opportunities in the Field of Education.   The major general educational professional organization to which school counselors belong is the National Education Association (NEA), which is subdivided into state, regional, and local organizations. Administrators, teachers, school counselors, college professors, and other people with an interest in education are welcome as members. It is a relatively large professional society that provides the member benefits cited previously. At the national and state levels, the NEA and its state divisions have a significant impact on legislation and executive-level policy making. At the community level, NEA local chapters are often recognized by school boards as the bargaining units for their members. In this regard, the NEA, which is a professional organization, takes on the attributes of a union, making it unique as a professional organization. In other communities, the bargaining unit is the American Federation of Teachers (AFT), a true labor union affiliated with the American Federation of Labor.

The economic services the NEA and AFT provide their members are perhaps the main reason school counselors join either organization. In many instances, it is expected or required that all members of the bargaining unit belong to the local, regional, state, and national organizations. Dues may be deducted from one's wages by arrangement with the school district. When there is a choice, not joining may place one in a potentially unpopular minority position—deemed willing to benefit from the efforts of the organization but too selfish to support it. This is a very compelling argument to join these organizations. Dues for the package of memberships usually amount to several hundred dollars; they can be more than $1,000 per year in urban and suburban areas where salaries and benefits are greater.

Although NEA or AFT membership has benefits for school counselors, some of them are limited. Status as an educator is shared with all members. Within the educational community, school counselors are several steps down the hierarchy, just as they are in most schools. In addition, they are a relatively small subgroup within the organization, compared to teachers. Therefore, school counselors have little influence on policy making, and few services are directed toward the special needs of school counselors. In fact, school counselors are members of an organization that includes other professionals—administrators—who assign duties to school counselors that sometimes make it difficult for them to achieve the goals of their professional training. The largest subgroup of professionals in these organizations—teachers—includes some who hold school counselors in contempt and low esteem.

Ethical codes, publications, and conference programs reflect the responsibilities and interests of the broad field of education and the guildlike issues of professionals rightly concerned about their economic welfare. These issues are important to school counselors because they work in the same environment as their colleagues, yet few of these presentations are specific to the responsibilities and interests of school counselors.

Belonging to a general educational professional organization such as the NEA provides school counselors with several of the advantages associated with membership in such organizations. Chief among these advantages for school counselors is economic enhancement, an important consideration that explains why most school counselors belong to the NEA or AFT. For those school counselors desiring to fulfill higher-order professional needs, professional organizations in the broad field of counseling have more to offer than those in education. Unfortunately, professional counseling organizations have little or nothing to offer that matches the effect of the educational profession's unions on salaries and benefits.

Opportunities in the Counseling Field.   In 1952, four independent professional organizations in the broad field of counseling joined forces to create an umbrella association in which all four maintained their identity and autonomy but through which they worked together to achieve higher levels of professionalism. The umbrella organization was known as the American Personnel and Guidance Association (APGA); the groups that joined together to found the APGA were the National Vocational Guidance Association (NVGA), the American College Personnel Association (ACPA), the National Association for Guidance Supervisors and Counselor Trainers (NAGSCT), and the Student Personnel Association for Teacher Education (SPATE). Within a year, the ASCA joined the original four APGA divisions. In analyzing the original structure of the APGA, Super (1953) referred to the ACPA, SPATE, and ASCA as institutionally oriented divisions because they represented the interests of persons employed as personnel workers in the colleges and schools. The NVGA was viewed as an interest division because members working in a variety of institutions could share a common interest in vocational guidance problems, principles, procedures, and programs. The NAGSCT was seen as a functional or job-oriented division because its members were interested in the supervision and training of school counselors. In the beginning, the APGA was a counseling organization whose members were employed mainly in educational settings, including school counseling.

The APGA grew in size and gradually incorporated divisions representing counseling professionals from a broader range of institutional settings (rehabilitation counselors, employment counselors, public offender counselors, mental health counselors, and military counselors) and interest areas (assessment in counseling, marriage and family counseling, multicultural concerns, religious and value issues, and group work). State and regional branches of the APGA and its divisions were also created. The APGA changed its name to the American Association for Counseling and Development (AACD) in 1983 to more accurately reflect the goals and membership of the organization. Some of the original divisions had changed their names earlier, or did so in the 1980s, for similar reasons. The National Vocational Guidance Association became the National Career Development Association, the National Association for Guidance Supervisors and Counselor Trainers became the Association for Counselor Education and Supervision (ACES), and the Student Personnel Association for Teacher Education became the Association for Humanistic Education and Development.

By the 1980s, the AACD had become the primary general professional association for counselors, including school counselors. At that time, the membership of the AACD was more than 50,000, with the ASCA having perhaps 8,000 or 9,000 members. Not as large and influential as the NEA or AFT, the AACD had nevertheless become influential in its own right, and its influence was focused on the needs and services of counselors.

In 1992, the AACD changed its name to the American Counseling Association (ACA), once again stating that the change more accurately reflected the organization's goals and membership. Not all members and divisions agreed with this viewpoint, and one of the founding divisions, the ACPA, withdrew from the association, believing that its goals and mission were no longer compatible with those of the ACA. Many ASCA members became dissatisfied with their relationship with the ACA during the 1990s, leading them to consider withdrawing from the ACA as well. A compromise was arranged between the ASCA and ACA, and although the ASCA remains a division of the ACA, it is more autonomous than was previously the case (i.e., the ASCA handles its own membership functions).

The ACA and ASCA offer professional services that respond to the higher-order needs of school counselors better than the NEA or AFT. Among those services are codes of ethics and policy statements specifically directed to counselors or school counselors and developed by counseling colleagues, training standards for counselors, accreditation for counselors, conferences and workshops directed primarily to the needs of counselors, placement services, lobbying for legislation that enhances the counseling profession, and publications and media directed toward counseling audiences. Members of the ACA receive the newsletter *Counseling Today* and the professional journal *Journal of Counseling & Development*. Members of the ASCA receive the newsletter *The ASCA Counselor* and the journal *Professional School Counseling*. These benefits are covered by the membership dues. These journals provide more substantive, discursive, and empirical content for counseling professionals than do the journals of the NEA. Members also have access to the information-rich Web sites of the two organizations (ACA: www.counseling.org, ASCA: www.schoolcounselor. org). Approximate membership figures for the ACA and ASCA in mid-2006 were 45,000 and 19,000, respectively.

The ACA and its divisions have been responsible for two initiatives that, although currently autonomous from the professional organizations, provide important influences on professional counseling. They are the CACREP and NBCC. The CACREP provides the counseling profession with what are currently the highest standards for accrediting training programs, and the NBCC provides national credentials, both generic and specific, for professional counselors.

Although unable to provide the economic clout that the NEA and AFT do, the ACA and ASCA offer services that appeal to the higher-order needs of professionals and that are not provided by the NEA and AFT. Because membership in the NEA or AFT is semivoluntary and relatively expensive, the decision to join the ACA and ASCA and many of the other divisions is affected by the fact that one may have already paid dues to one professional organization; that is, the dues for a counseling professional organization, although considerably less, have to be taken from what is left over for discretionary expenses. Under these circumstances, allegiance to a professional counseling organization such as the ACA or ASCA occurs less often for school counselors than it otherwise might. Consequently, the membership of the ASCA is much smaller than it could be. Individuals who join at a lower cost when they are graduate students sometimes drop out because the dues increase as they become working professionals and are faced with joining a bargaining unit (Herr, 1985). Others may not find jobs in the field immediately and allow their memberships to lapse. They may or may not rejoin later.

The preferred scenario would be for school counselors to belong to important professional organizations in the fields of both education and counseling. Economic realities give the advantage to professional organizations in the field of education. This creates a situation in which many school counselors have no direct affiliation with a professional counseling organization. Individually, they suffer because they become isolated professionally and are less likely to behave according to the standards of their counseling profession. The counselors, their stakeholders, and the profession suffer as a result. Collectively, school counseling suffers because only a fraction of its members share in the unity and influence a professional organization can achieve. The ACA and ASCA are less influential as a result. This unfortunate circumstance is an ongoing problem the profession is challenged to address if school counseling is to survive and blossom. If the competition for professional loyalties is resolved successfully, other issues remain for school counseling to address (e.g., the ASCA National Model for School Counseling Programs).

COUNSELORS IN SCHOOLS

According to Holland (1997), persons and environments interact, and both individuals and working environments may have personality types or structures. Of the six Holland personality types, school counselors tend to be primarily Social. Social types value helping others, and tend to be friendly, enthusiastic, understanding, receptive, warm, and generous. They function best in predominantly social environments. In many schools, the predominant environment is not social. Unfortunately, the dominant environment in many schools is conventional, and conventional environments tend to be conservative and dogmatic. Preferred traits in conventional environments are conformity, conscientiousness, practical-mindedness, neatness, obedience, and docility.

The primary actors in creating and maintaining the school's environment are the administrators and teachers, in that order. Principals clearly influence the environment in their schools. What they value most will influence their own behavior and what they reinforce positively or negatively in the values and behaviors of their subordinates, in the school rules, and in the assignment of responsibilities within their purview. Teachers will influence the environment because they are the largest single group of professionals in a school. Depending on the circumstances, the teachers may or may not reflect the environmental preferences of the principal, especially if the principal was not involved in hiring them. Although teachers and counselors may differ from their principal(s) with respect to personality type, Holland (1997) believed that the most powerful individual in the environment will have the greatest influence. A principal can influence the environment as a model or by force of personality and will.

What does this mean for school counselors in training? Most prospective school counselors enthusiastically look forward to a career of applying the values, knowledge, and competencies acquired from their training in an environment that is conducive to achieving their goals. Unfortunately, many school administrators and teachers have other ideas about what counselors should do. Fitch, Newby, Ballestero, and Marshall (2001) found that, although many of the future school administrators they surveyed were aware of and appreciated roles and duties for school counselors that were commensurate with their training, some of them also rated noncounseling functions such as discipline, record keeping, and registration as important.

Two factors about school administrators and their training have been and will continue to be challenges for school counselors. First, many individuals who become school administrators are more conventional than social types of people. Second, programs that train school administrators rarely attempt to inform trainees about the roles and functions of school counselors according to either the content of the counselor education training programs or the content of the standards for training school counselors of the respective states. Although counselor educators have attempted to address the second challenge both individually and collectively, their efforts have not been very successful, and we do not envision a breakthrough in that domain in the near future. Therefore, the brunt of trying to do something constructive about this challenge seems to fall on the shoulders of individual school counselors at the grassroots level—each trying to make an impact on his or her own environment to make it more congruent. Perhaps the availability of the ASCA National Model for School Counseling Programs may be the resource school counselors can use to meet this challenge.

Some beginning school counselors experience the challenge of incongruent environments as interns and others do so in their first jobs. Not all school counselors will experience this incongruence. Some will find themselves in a school environment that is congruent with their type and goals. Others will not, and we do not know the exact probabilities. Regarding this challenge, Fitch et al. (2001) highlighted the importance of the job interview. They recommended using the first interview to present a summary of one's programmatic plans and goals to the chief school administrator. The administrator's response to this introduction is an important indicator of what the environment is and will be like for the prospective counselor. Thus, one way to deal with the possibility of environmental incongruence is to avoid it if possible. For those who cannot or did not, we next discuss some of the challenges that school counselors may have to face when working in incongruent environments.

CHALLENGES TO THE PROFESSIONAL IDENTITY OF SCHOOL COUNSELORS

You Never Told Us About . . .

Occasionally, interns and former students challenge us about not preparing them for the often onerous noncounseling functions they encounter on the job as school counselors. The implicit message is that, somehow, we should have included preparation for those functions in the training program. Should we write chapters about, and teach units on, how to build and monitor master schedules; coordinate testing programs; discipline misbehaving students; set up filing systems; and conduct lunchroom, hall, and bus duty? We think not! These are not functions that are included in role statements by the ASCA, CACREP, and state departments of education/public instruction. We view our role as ensuring that the training program meets the standards of the relevant professional and educational oversight organizations. We must prepare school counselors to be proficient at what they are supposed to do. Yet, we are very aware that many school counselors are assigned noncounseling tasks. Therefore, we do feel responsible for preparing school counseling students to cope with the noncounseling challenges. Our formula for meeting the challenges is as follows.

First, school counselors must know what they should be doing and be proficient at the requisite competencies. Proficiency leads to demonstrated competence that garners support from significant stakeholders, such as parents, students, teachers, and administrators. Second, school counselors will be challenged to advocate for themselves and their profession, as are counselor educators. Third, school counselors, as advocates, are challenged to provide leadership in helping colleagues and administrators discover better ways to get things done and use counselor time and talents wisely.

Our role as counselor educators then is to make students aware of the noncounseling challenges and prepare them to cope successfully—not train them to be proficient at noncounseling tasks. The remainder of this section of the chapter addresses some of the most prevalent noncounseling functions that school counselors may be requested to perform.

Dealing With Responsibility for Noncounseling Functions

Because of its diverse origins, school counseling has experienced greater identity problems than other professions in the field of education. On the one hand, most laypeople and professional educators have clear and relatively similar ideas about the roles of schoolteachers and administrators. On the other hand, those same people have widely differing opinions about the role of school counselors. Counselor education and training programs for school counselors have gradually reached the point where they have more similarities than differences; the differences often reflect the experiences and preferences of the counselor educators more than radical differences in the training programs. Professional organizations dedicated to promoting the counseling professions (the ACA, ACES, and ASCA) have developed and promoted role statements such as "Role Statement: The School Counselor" (ASCA, 1990) and developed training standards. In addition, the CACREP is an accrediting agency whose attention is focused on counselor training programs. A relatively new accrediting agency, the CACREP may have considerable influence in the 21st century.

Although counselor education and the ASCA have gradually developed a somewhat uniform identity for school counselors through its training programs and professional literature, the message has not reached the decision makers in the schools; many school counselors still find themselves engaging in functions that are unrelated or only remotely related to their training. These noncounseling functions, often highly regarded by individual principals and teachers, receive higher priority than counseling functions, leaving counselors to attend to noncounseling duties first and to engage in counseling functions in the remaining time. These conditions discourage some from entering the school counseling field; cause others to leave early, defeated and disappointed; cause some to adjust and become pseudocounselors; confuse students, parents, and colleagues about the roles and functions of counselors; and leave many counselors disappointed in their training and trainers because they were not properly prepared for the noncounseling responsibilities and because their mentors cannot relieve them of the onerous responsibilities.

Because role senders are individuals in positions of authority or influence, they send messages both directly and implicitly to other individuals in institutional settings that influence the behaviors of those individuals (Haettenschwiller, 1970). Those who receive and react to the messages are boundary people who have little or no authority in the institutions. School counselors tend to be boundary people who have weak power status because they are a relatively small contingent of professionals and because they often differ from their teaching and administrating colleagues with regard to priorities. For example, Willower, Hoy, and Eidell (1967) found that administrators and teachers have high regard for custodial goals (or maintaining order), whereas counselors have high regard for humanistic goals (or those focused on promoting an environment for interaction and experience). As boundary people, school counselors traditionally receive messages from role senders that cause them to have responsibility for some custodial, noncounseling tasks. Cumulatively, these have considerable influence on determining an image of school counselors that is some distance from the ideal established by professional role statements and training standards. Until this situation is changed, school counselors will be unable to achieve either professional autonomy or the promise implied in the content and emphases of their training programs.

Clark and Amatea (2004) offered recommendations for school counselors and counselor educators that may help them address these challenges. Teachers in elementary, middle, and secondary school settings were interviewed, and the themes derived from those interviews suggest that school counselors can be most effective and accepted if they communicate and collaborate in the process of helping students achieve success academically. Being visible and involved in the total school were additional themes. Interestingly, a majority of the teachers did not perceive the custodial tasks mentioned previously as important to the counselors' mission in the schools.

Lest readers believe that the findings of Willower, Hoy, and Eidell (1967) are dated, note that Perusse, Goodenough, Donegan, and Jones (2004) found that most of the principals in their study "continue to believe that appropriate tasks for school counselors include clerical tasks such as registration and scheduling of all new students, administering cognitive aptitude and achievement tests, and maintaining student records" (p. 189).

Scheduling. School counselors have traditionally acquired some noncounseling functions. The most onerous and time-consuming functions are the gatekeeping and custodial tasks associated with scheduling. These administrative functions have become traditional responsibilities of counselors in most secondary schools. Secondary school counselors, responding to a survey from Tennyson, Miller, Skovholt, and Williams (1989), reported that as a group they are involved more frequently in scheduling than in any other activity. Although it is a lesser task in middle and elementary schools, scheduling may still be among the responsibilities of middle and elementary school counselors. Gatekeeping occurs when counselors must determine which students will be allowed to enroll in specific classes and which ones will be allowed to change classes. These responsibilities place counselors in potentially adversarial relationships with students and teachers, groups who should view counselors in more positive ways for counseling services to be received favorably. Students, and sometimes their parents, view counselors as adversaries who they must cajole or entreat in order to receive limited resources (e.g., oversubscribed courses) or exceptions to the rules (e.g., making a course change after a course-drop deadline has passed). These encounters are hardly conducive to healthy helping relationships outside the scheduling domain. For some students, these are the only or initial encounters, and their impressions are colored unfavorably thereafter.

Teachers may view counselors as adversaries because, as gatekeepers, the counselors are directly responsible for fluctuating class enrollments. All teachers want class enrollments that are both consistent and sufficient. Receipt of additional students after the term has started creates stress for teachers, as does having students leave classes suddenly. Not having enough students in an elective course is threatening to teachers whose jobs are vulnerable. The number of students in their classes and the amount of student traffic into and out of their classes are annoyances that teachers attribute to the scheduling gatekeepers. When they are unhappy with the results of gatekeeping efforts, they blame the gatekeepers. These authors' experiences as school counselors, counselor educators, and consultants have led to the conclusion that the opinions of most secondary school teachers about the value and competence of their counselors are heavily influenced by the way counselors are perceived to deal with scheduling gatekeeping chores. Not being able to please teachers as scheduling gatekeepers may condemn many school counselors to eternal disfavor, negating their counseling accomplishments in the minds of these important colleagues.

Custodial tasks associated with scheduling include correcting mistakes on individual students' schedules and on master schedules; organizing, filing, and distributing student schedules; and screening individual student schedule requests for mistakes. These are tasks that can be performed by clerical personnel or mechanically (via computer) but are often done manually by school counselors. When schools begin their academic year, they are captive to the activities and abilities of a handful of counselors who are trying to fit all students into the master schedule. Doing such work on a large scale is a demeaning and wasteful misuse of the time and expertise of professionals trained to deliver much different services. Students and teaching colleagues, observing counselors performing these custodial functions, conclude that counselors are essentially professional clerks. Therefore, they, too, often dismiss counselors as having few worthy services to offer or as being too busy with clerical tasks to be bothered with the higher-order needs of students and colleagues.

Scheduling is an administrative function, but principals, usually fewer in number than counselors, do not have the time or the inclination for most gatekeeping or custodial tasks. Interestingly, however, they usually control scheduling policies tightly. If scheduling is an administrative function and if the role of administrators is making policy, then they do need help with such gatekeeping and custodial responsibilities.

Our position is that using counselors as gatekeepers and custodians is a mistake. If counselors are not the appropriate choice, who is? Even though scheduling is an administrative function, it serves teachers as well, providing them with a system that controls enrollments, assigns students to appropriate courses, and indicates where the participants are to meet. Therefore, because teachers benefit so greatly from the scheduling function, one can argue that they should be involved in the process. They should be involved in scheduling but not in the gatekeeping and custodial tasks any more than counselors should. Placing these responsibilities on teachers will have the same negative effects on them as it has on counselors.

Because the master schedule is an essential component of basic education and touches the lives of everyone in the schools, a team approach to making it work seems appropriate and fair. Baker (1982) offered an idea for implementing the team approach that provides basic responsibilities and leaves the details to those who might adapt the idea to specific settings. Specific task categories are identified. Adapted from that idea, five task categories are recommended:

1. *Instruction* consists of administrators informing counselors, teachers, students, parents and guardians, and other interested persons about the purposes, procedures, and content of the schedule and the scheduling process.
2. *Direction and control*, or gatekeeping, is an administrative function, so this can be the responsibility of administrators with the assistance of teachers, counselors, and clerical and paraprofessional personnel as consultants.
3. *Consultation* involves teachers, counselors, and students in the process of advising administrators about the strengths and weaknesses of the scheduling process and about the needs of individuals and the system. For example, teachers can suggest that students be assigned to certain classes, counselors can provide information about student problems associated with scheduling, and students can make their own needs and opinions known. Administrators can serve as clearinghouses for this information with the assistance of clerical and paraprofessional personnel.
4. *Counseling* occurs when counselors, administrators, and teachers help students make decisions that affect their choices and schedules. In a system managed by administrators who make the policies, it stands to reason that they should also be the gatekeepers, setting rules about entering and leaving courses and making decisions when the rules are appealed or challenged. Teachers and counselors may provide counsel when asked.
5. *Custodial tasks* (e.g., processing and filing documents) are to be performed by clerical and paraprofessional personnel responsible to administrators.

This plan places the gatekeeping responsibilities in the administrative domain where they should be, recommends that clerical and paraprofessional personnel perform the custodial tasks they have been trained to do, and places teachers and counselors in the active and professional roles of fulfilling the consultation and counseling functions they have been trained to provide. If implemented, plans of this nature will free counselors from some undesirable noncounseling responsibilities and offer enhanced opportunities to provide professional services more attuned to their training.

Discipline.   Many counselors find that students they have requested to come to their office for service-oriented reasons often arrive displaying symptoms of tension and anxiety. The more assertive students want to know what they did wrong, and others behave reticently until put at ease by a quieting explanation or simply by an opportunity to experience a friendly, empathic atmosphere. Why do so many children and adolescents approach appointments with school counselors with tension and anxiety? Why do they think they are in trouble if a counselor has asked to see them? To attribute these reactions to one cause would be an oversimplification of what is probably a complex set of reasons. Two very real and important reasons are that some counselors have disciplinary responsibilities and that others are assumed to have them. In either case, school counselors are viewed as disciplinarians by many students.

Discipline and guidance may have been linked through the concept of deans of men and women that was popular in student services before the influence of client-centered counseling ideas and before the counseling professions developed clear statements of roles and functions. Early, simpler models of guidance viewed student services workers (e.g., deans) as wise, caring, and authoritarian individuals who were parent figures, providing support, advice, and discipline as needed. Currently, discipline is an administrative function in elementary, middle, and secondary schools. All disciplinary actions are subject to the scrutiny of school administrators. The schools that have assistant principals recognize them as having student discipline among their responsibilities. Discipline and counseling are antithetical when students are to be lectured, scolded, punished, interrogated, or accused. If counselors engage in such negative interactions with students, no matter how deserving, it will be difficult to also establish empathic, unconditional helping relationships with them. Students will then view going to the counselor's office as an aversive experience—one to be avoided if at all possible.

If discipline is an administrative function, how did counselors get involved? One reason is history. Because of the way it was, some expect the situation to continue or assume it is continuing. Another reason is guilt by association. Counselors work in offices that are often near the principal's; thus, the activities of administrators, including discipline, are attributed to counselors, too. Another reason is the outright assignment of disciplinary responsibilities to counselors. This is more likely to occur in schools where principals do not have assistants, and many of the more onerous disciplinary responsibilities are assigned to counselors. It can also occur in schools where discipline has been assigned to school counselors by principals because those principals believe that counselors should be involved.

One of the best solutions to this dilemma will be recognition by the school administrators' profession, trainers of school administrators, and individual administrators that school counselors are professionals with their own definite and valuable programs to offer (e.g., the ASCA National Model for School Counseling Programs); they are not administrative assistants. Although individual counselors may contribute to this change, most are too isolated and powerless to do so; those who are successful may only have local or regional influence. A solution to this problem and to the other noncounseling responsibilities that interfere with counseling services will probably have to come at a national level, through the efforts of professional organizations such as the NEA, ACA, ACES, and ASCA. These organizations may influence members of other professional organizations such as the National Association of Secondary School Principals, and perhaps legislators and the public. In the meantime, counselors are left with the challenge to devise solutions at the local and area levels.

School counselors who balk at the assignment of disciplinary responsibilities will probably have to determine ways to change the thinking of those who assign them such responsibilities. Successful attention-getting approaches may range from diplomacy to confrontation. Whatever approach is used, it will probably have to be accompanied by efforts to educate those who make the decisions. In short, school counselors need to be advocates for themselves and their profession. Professional counseling associations have helpful resources, primarily publications and media, and counselor educators may also be willing to offer consultation services.

Overcoming the image of being a disciplinarian requires more subtle efforts. Proactive strategies seem in order. The best way to change an undesirable image is to create a desired one. For example, elementary school counselors can engage in programmatic activities in the classroom that help them achieve counseling and developmental goals while introducing them to students as the kinds of professionals they want to be known as—caring, empathic, helpful, nonthreatening, and knowledgeable. Middle and secondary school counselors can engage in similar activities. All school counselors may also be able to use individual counseling contacts to introduce themselves appropriately. Get-acquainted interviews allow counselors to reach out to prospective student clients proactively and to establish a preferred agenda. Included in topics for get-acquainted interviews can be open-ended questions about interests and hobbies, future plans, progress in school, recreational activities, and perceptions of the counseling services. Responses to open-ended questions may lead to specific topics on which students want to work once they accept the counselor as someone to trust who may be helpful (e.g., "What things interest you?" "What else would you like to talk about today?"). Personal topics (e.g., "Tell me about your family") and questions that focus the response on other individuals (e.g., "Who is your favorite teacher?") may be too threatening for students to handle in get-acquainted interviews.

The way invitations to students are made may prevent students from assuming the worst before learning the truth. Students who are invited with an advance explanation of the purpose of the interview, oral or printed, are less likely to think they have been summoned to the office for a threatening purpose. Get-acquainted interviews provide students with accurate perceptions of the kinds of people counselors are and the reasons why students might visit them again, either by appointment or self-referral. Additional proactive activities include newsletters for adults and older students, in-service programs for adults, and presentations for children—all designed to communicate accurate and understandable information about counselors and their services. A proactive approach to image management requires advance planning and assertiveness in gaining opportunities to meet with those whose favorable impressions are desired.

Secretarial and Clerical Tasks. Secretaries and clerks perform noble and useful work. They choose to do so and prepare themselves accordingly before beginning their careers. School counselors, in contrast, receive specialized training at the graduate level to perform tasks other than secretarial and clerical work. School counselors need secretarial and clerical support because of the nature of their work. They must request or provide college transcripts, letters of recommendation to prospective employers, cumulative records, lesson plans and handouts for prevention programming activities, individualized educational plans, newsletters, informational flyers and memos, drop-in requests for appointments, incoming telephone calls, media and materials for the information service, tests and testing reports, and various other items. These tasks are all reasons why school counselors need clerical and secretarial support to carry out their professional responsibilities successfully. Noncounseling tasks, such as scheduling, create additional needs for clerical and secretarial support.

Despite these legitimate reasons, many school counselors have either no secretarial and clerical support or too little. One result is that counselor time and energy that should be devoted to legitimate professional activities are spent on such support tasks. Another result is that the tasks are not done at all, or not done well, because there is too little time, interest, or talent for them. The first situation leads to making counselors into under-trained, part-time clerk-secretaries, and the second leads to diminished effectiveness and negative impressions by students, colleagues, and administrators. These people are influenced by their first impressions of the obvious components of a professional's services—neatness, punctuality, availability, responsiveness, dependability, and organization.

The advent of computers with useful word processing, record keeping, and printing capabilities has provided technological assistance to counselors for both counseling and noncounseling tasks. Although technological advances may make better secretaries and clerks out of counselors, counselors are still doing secretarial and clerical work. Advanced technology is not the solution. An appropriate level of secretarial and clerical support is the solution. Providing this support is another challenge for national professional organizations such as the NEA, ACA, ACES, and ASCA. By doing so, school counselors will be able to achieve their professional potential.

Paraprofessional Tasks.   For some counselors, responsibilities include selling lunch tickets, monitoring bus schedules, determining whether students have met graduation requirements, organizing and monitoring student fund-raising activities, monitoring prom and banquet planning, planning and conducting award ceremonies, and monitoring the distribution of diplomas at graduation ceremonies. These are time-consuming noncounseling functions, administrative in nature, that have been assigned to counselors by their administrators. The implication is that these tasks are as important as the counseling functions for which the counselors were trained. Few can argue that these tasks are unimportant in the life of the school, but the counseling profession argues that they are not appropriate assignments for school counselors (ASCA, 1990). Based on a survey of school counselors, Astramovich and Holden (2002) reported that the participants supported the employment of paraprofessionals. They also found that secondary school counselors were more likely to make this recommendation than elementary school counselors, probably because they were more inundated with paraprofessional tasks.

Assigning such tasks to counselors places them in a role best identified as an administrative assistant—not only conducting paraprofessional tasks but also having their competence judged largely on the performance of these tasks. A widely held assumption in educational administration is that school counselors are supposed to serve primarily as administrative assistants to principals. How else can one explain the widespread assignment of so many noncounseling duties to school counselors? This mistaken assumption must be altered if school counseling is to achieve its necessary professional identity. In the authors' opinion, the only way this assumption and the actions it inspires will be changed is through a concerted effort by all national professional organizations that represent these professionals. School counselors, in turn, can unite and work through their professional organizations and take leadership responsibilities for this undertaking, something that has not occurred on a large enough scale thus far.

Changes may require assertive and provocative actions by school counselors and their colleagues to get the attention of stakeholders, who may offer sympathetic support, and in educating administrators, who may respond in an adversarial fashion to proposals that threaten their assumptions about the role of school counselors. To do little or nothing about this will support the status quo; counselors in the 21st century, although possibly better prepared than their predecessors, will still be administrative assistants performing many noncounseling tasks.

Substitute Teaching.　Administrators sometimes find it convenient and cost effective to call on school counselors to substitute for missing teachers and school nurses. The false assumptions and negative outcomes stated previously apply in these instances as well. In addition, students are likely to receive lower quality instruction than from a qualified substitute teacher, and counselors engaging in substitute teaching or nursing are more vulnerable to accusations of negligence or malpractice than are qualified substitutes or than the counselors would be if they were engaging in responsibilities for which they have been trained and certified/licensed. Perhaps counselors will serve themselves and the profession better by playing the devil's advocate when asked to help out in this manner.

Challenges From Individuals and Groups Outside the School System.　In the 1990s, school counseling experienced challenges to elements of and entire school counseling programs. For example, a disagreement over materials and methods led to the cancellation of an entire school counseling program in Clackamas, Oregon, and self-esteem programs in the Capistrano, California, school district were challenged as unlawful (McCullough, 1994). Although it is difficult to predict exactly what might be challenged in the future, previous challenges seem to have focused on materials, programs, and practices that are viewed by some individuals and groups as invasions of privacy or religious in nature; as unlawful psychotherapeutic interventions or sacrilegious in nature; and as in opposition to the values of the dissenting groups or individuals. The issues become emotional and tend to polarize communities, leading to nastiness, attempts at censorship, political pressuring, and bad publicity for professionals and communities.

McCullough (1994) cited prevention advice from Greg Brigman, a counselor educator who recommends the following responses:

- Contact the ASCA for information on resources and procedures.
- Develop district policies for reviewing curriculum materials and follow them.
- Keep the educational community informed about programs and materials.
- Obtain a clear idea of what the national and local communities want children to learn in schools.

McCullough's (1994) article provides additional specific advice to counselors. Although it is tempting to view the challengers as reactionaries, these events contain an important message for all school counselors. A careful examination of the teaching/ instruction domain of the schools will usually lead one to discover that the content of courses taught in English, social studies, mathematics, science, kindergarten, third grade, and the like is the result of a curriculum development process and that the content is based on foundational principles and guidelines, studied, and approved by committees, administrators, and school boards before it is implemented. Sometimes large group guidance programming by school counselors has gone through much less rigorous planning and scrutiny, leaving the programs and the counselors more vulnerable when challenged. Therefore, an important message the challenges seem to provide for school counselors is that their group guidance programming should be developed with as much care and scrutiny as are the academic curricula in their schools. Doing so will help make school counselors less vulnerable to outside challenges.

THE IMPORTANCE OF TEACHING EXPERIENCE

In the early years of the profession, most school counselors came from the teaching ranks. School systems and counselor educators preferred it that way. Therefore, a teaching certificate or license and 1 to 2 years of successful teaching experience became

The Internet helps school counselors collaborate across the world at www.scan21st.com.

requirements for school counselor licensure or certification across the states. Changing times and circumstances led to expansion of eligibility for licensure/certification to individuals outside the teaching profession on a state-by-state basis. Concern over whether these newcomers would know how to function in schools was often alleviated by school-based internships during their training programs. These changes were accompanied by controversy over whether teaching experience should be required. This led to a spate of studies in the 1960s and 1970s.

In a review of these studies, Baker (1994) reported

> When effectiveness of counselors was operationalized as characteristics that are important to counseling relationships, the data sometimes indicated that teaching experience could be detrimental, or there were no differences among counselors. There were no findings indicating that those lacking teaching experience might have difficulty in counseling relationships. When the dependent measures represented effectiveness as a school counselor, broad "guidance" skills, and attitudes, the findings seemed to suggest that there were no differences, or they were limited to a short period of time when counselors without teaching experience were adjusting to the school systems. (p. 321)

The controversy seemed dormant during the 1980s and then heated up again as echo baby boomers increased school enrollments significantly and as fewer teachers showed interest in becoming school counselors. As states that still held to the teaching experience requirement removed it or felt pressure to do so, more research on the topic was published.

Olson and Allen (1993) found that principals discovered no differences between high school and elementary school counselors with and without teaching experience. There were perceived differences at the middle school level on 3 of the 13 functions covered in the study. In a study of the perceptions of counselor educators, Smith, Crutchfield, and Culbreth (2001) found that many more of today's counselor educators, as opposed to those in the mid-1960s, believe that teaching experience, although potentially helpful, is not necessary for success in school counseling.

In the most recent study of which we are aware, Peterson, Goodman, Keller, and McCauley (2004) compared former school counseling interns with and without teaching experience via an in-depth analysis of their responses to four open-ended questions across 16 categories of school counselor functions. The four questions focused on their recollections of the greatest challenges and difficulties, what they wished they had known, what they appreciated about the training, and what they appreciated about themselves. Peterson et al. (2004) found that all interns experienced significant adjustments during the first 2 years of employment as school counselors, and the adjustments of former teachers differed from those of nonteachers. This study seems to shed light on the controversy because it points out that former teachers, as well as those without teaching experience, face challenges when beginning careers as school counselors.

Documents dating back more than 30 years highlight challenges faced by counselors when adapting to the school culture because they did not advance through the teaching ranks and learn about the folkways and mores (Baker, 1994). Peterson et al.

(2004) discovered that, even though teachers knew the folkways and mores of teaching, being a school counselor introduced them to new roles in the established folkways and mores. For example, former teachers had to cope with (a) having to earn credibility again; (b) being on the receiving end of negative comments from teachers about the credibility and effectiveness of counselors; (c) learning to adjust to fragmented, disjointed days and lack of closure; (d) having no break or preparation periods; (e) needing to be less directive and content oriented; (f) feeling unfamiliar with age levels other than those previously taught; and (g) lacking a clear place in the school hierarchy.

Thus, the evidence indicates that all school counseling students have adjustments to make when starting careers as school counselors. In our opinion, regulations that restrict the school counseling profession to former teachers are outdated and uninformed. The profession and those it serves will benefit from access to all caring and competent prospects. Enlightened counselor education training programs will realize that comprehensive internship experiences, such as those recommended by the CACREP, are important in the preparation of all trainees, not just those without teaching experience.

It is hoped that this introduction to school counseling provides readers with a realistic perspective of working conditions and challenges. Chapter 2 presents important historical background information about the development of the school counseling profession and about current paradigms that hold promise for enhancing the school counseling profession. We conclude this chapter with introductions to our technology-enhanced learning opportunities.

HOW SCHOOL COUNSELORS USE NETWORKING TECHNOLOGY

The evolving SCAN (www.scan21st.com) associated with this textbook encourages the invention of online projects focused on helping students succeed in school. An example is the online program Succeeding in School (Gerler, 2001), designed to help students focus on behaviors, attitudes, and human relations skills that lead to improved academic achievement. Graduate students and school counselors are invited to use and to contribute lessons to the topics covered in this program. The Web site for Succeeding in School is http://genesislight.com/web%20files/index.htm.

The initial research on a paper-and-pencil version of this program was conducted with 900 children across North Carolina and produced promising results (Gerler & Anderson, 1986). Several subsequent studies have been conducted (Gerler, 1990; Gerler, Drew, & Mohr, 1990; Gerler & Herndon, 1993), including one in Long Beach, California, that found statistically significant improvement in children's math achievement as a result of participation in the program (Lee, 1993). The current Web version of the program allows upper elementary and middle school students to complete interactive program activities online and to complete pre- and postprogram measures of school success online. This feature encourages studies of the program across the United States and elsewhere. The online version of Succeeding in School incorporates ten sections: Models of Success, Being Comfortable in School, Being Responsible in School, Listening in School, Asking for Help in School, Improving at School, Cooperating With Peers, Cooperating With Teachers, The Bright Side of School, and The Bright Side of Me. An outline of each section appears in appendix B.

The paper-and-pencil version of the Succeeding in School program has had important effects on the educational process in elementary and middle schools. The SCAN (www.scan21st.com) will offer counselor educators, graduate students, and school counselors the opportunity to coordinate their efforts in implementing and testing the Succeeding in School program as well as in creating new approaches toward enhancing students' performance in school.

INTRODUCTION TO SCAN21ST: THE WEB SITE FOR SCHOOL COUNSELING FOR THE 21ST CENTURY

We have created a place on the School Counseling Activities Network for the 21st Century Web site for us to record your creative thinking about school counseling. This site also provides a set of online resources and activities that may help you as you learn about school counseling. The site can be found at www.scan21st.com.

One of the special features of this textbook is the opportunity to access online activities associated with each chapter in the text. To see an overview of these online activities go to http://www.genesislight.com/scan21st/tell_us/.

These activities allow graduate students to reflect on the material presented in this textbook and to generate innovative ideas that may appear on the SCAN. It is hoped that graduate students will challenge the material they read in the textbook and send us innovative ideas to share with school counselors around the world.

The next section includes the first of the featured online opportunities to express your perspectives on the material you have read.

FEATURED ACTIVITY: GRADUATE STUDENT PERSPECTIVES ON INNOVATION IN SCHOOL COUNSELING

We were recently visiting with a creative, energetic student who was taking her first graduate course, "Introduction to School Counseling." She spoke first about the bewildering array of professional bureaucracies associated with school counseling. She wondered aloud how much benefit school counselors and the people they serve derive from these bureaucracies. She posed the questions: "What gets in the way of school counseling's future?" "How can graduate students, before they get mired in professional bureaucracy, help school counseling evolve?" "How can graduate students help invent effective, interesting, and creative solutions to the social and psychological challenges young people face in the 21st century?"

We were initially taken aback by the seeming arrogance of this graduate student and defended much of the organizational structure that embodies school counseling as a profession. After a bit of reflection, however, we recognized the value of her questions, and we asked ourselves: "How can graduate students who have relatively little investment in school counseling's status quo contribute to the evolution of the profession?" We are determined to find out.

After you read this chapter, go to http://www.genesislight.com/scan21st/tell_us/innovation.html and complete the form. With your permission, we will periodically post some of your creative thinking for the world to read.

OTHER SUGGESTED ACTIVITIES

1. Debate the merits of joining or not joining a professional organization.
2. Debate the merits of joining the NEA, ACA, or ASCA.
3. Debate the merits of becoming a licensed professional counselor.
4. Survey a sample of school counselors about their attitudes toward scheduling.
5. Discuss the merits, limits, and cautions associated with computer-assisted counseling and using the Internet in school counseling.
6. Ask the counselor educator responsible for coordinating your program to elaborate on the most important influences during his or her master's and doctoral training programs.
7. Go to the SCAN Web site (www.scan21st.com) to participate in online counseling exercises.

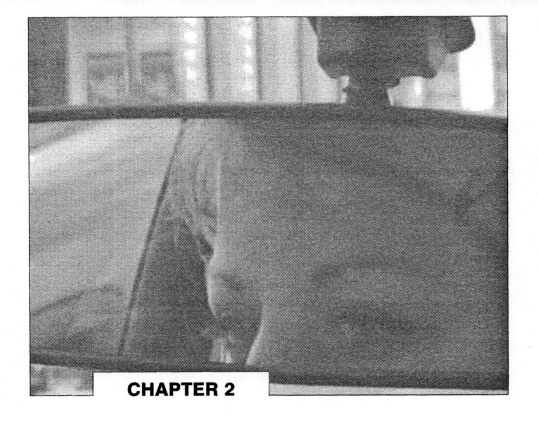

CHAPTER 2

School Counseling and the Challenge of History

Goals: To provide a historical survey of the development of the school counseling profession, cite current challenges to the profession, and present current paradigms designed to meet the challenges and move school counseling into the mainstream of school reform.

Most school counselors have read something about the history of counseling and understand the contributions of recognized leaders in the profession. During a recent panel discussion on changes in school counseling, however, we listened carefully to the following remarks from a former English teacher (who is now a high school counselor), and we were surprised by how changes in language may have influenced school counseling:

> *The school counseling profession is best understood in the context of its past and as part of an ever-changing and evolving society. The landmarks of our past are found in words. Here are some of the words that emerged during the 20th century.*
>
> > *1940s: A-bomb, bikini, cheeseburger, jet plane, tape recorder, TV*
> >
> > *1950s: beatnik, desegregate, hash browns, junk mail, weirdo*
> >
> > *1960s: cable television, crib death, doofus, jet lag, pantsuit, sitcom, sexism*
> >
> > *1970s: chairperson, consciousness-raising, detox, in vitro fertilization, personal computer, space cadet, video game, X-rated*
> >
> > *1980s: ATM, compact disc, designer drug, glass ceiling, mall rat, palmtop, Twelve Step, virtual reality*
> >
> > *1990s: bad hair day, buffalo wing, designated driver, granny dumping, intranet, McJob, personal trainer, superchurch, V-chip, Web site*
>
> *These words reflect the evolution of society, and they indicate the continually changing world that young people bring to their interactions with school counselors in the classrooms, hallways, and counseling offices of schools around the world. New language will continue to emerge throughout the 21st century. School counselors will hear the language, use the language, and face the challenges of young people whose lives are marked by the changes symbolized in new language.*
>
> *School counseling offers professionals a wide choice of options for improving life at school among students, parents, teachers, and school administrators. Counselors need to find some balance in their work and establish priorities based on the foundation of the past that are also focused on a rapidly changing world that expects schools to prepare young people who are inventive, adaptable, productive, and excellent.*

The talented counselors who work in our schools seldom have time to reflect on the historical context from which their services have emerged. Nevertheless, the context is important and will help future school counselors thoughtfully consider what lies ahead in helping clients meet the challenges of an ever-changing world.

INTRODUCTION

The following historical overview provides a context from which to understand, appreciate, and reflect on the circumstances and challenges facing professional school counselors early in the 21st century. As is the case with surveys of this nature, we highlight events while trying to indicate their importance, yet we do not cover them extensively. The overview relates a story about how school counseling was transformed from "positions to programs" (Gysbers & Henderson, 2000). We also identify three paradigms that appear to hold promise for helping the profession to resolve its historical role confusion and be recognized as integral to the mission of its school system.

One way in which the historical role confusion manifests itself is through discontinuity in terminology. Readers who are unfamiliar with the profession may find that the terms *guidance* and *school counseling* appear to be used interchangeably. However, *guidance* is a generic term covering all functions in which professional school counselors might engage. Counseling is one of those functions, whereas others include consulting and assessing. The current preference of the profession is to use one of the functions, counseling, as the generic term as well. We see examples of this preference in the ASCA National Model for School Counseling Programs and in the name of the ASCA's journal *Professional School Counseling*. Therefore, *school counseling* is preferred to *guidance counseling*. Both *school counseling* and *guidance* are used to refer to essentially the same activities in this textbook because guidance has not been completely purged from the professional vernacular. An example of this is the popularity of developmental guidance programs that are introduced in this chapter.

HISTORICAL OVERVIEW

Pioneers

Seen as a "series of learning experiences complementing the existing curriculum" (Aubrey, 1977, p. 289), guidance first appeared in the schools like any other subject. Guidance had a curriculum, the goals of which evolved from the social reform movements of the late 19th and early 20th centuries. Guidance teachers also sought to have a positive impact on the moral development of their charges. One such program was established by Jesse B. Davis, a high school principal in Grand Rapids, Michigan, who, in 1907, had one period per week set aside in English composition classes for vocational and moral guidance. The goals for this early guidance curriculum were to help high school students better understand their own characters, emulate good role models, and develop into socially responsible adults.

What we think of currently as school counseling did not begin with a formal design consisting of established goals, assumptions, and functions. It evolved to what it is today. Davis and other pioneers were responding to local needs. His ideas led to a school guidance curriculum. Others, such as David S. Hill, Anna Y. Reed, and Eli W. Weaver, founded their guidance services on different ideas, such as making students employable, helping them find suitable employment, and responding to their individual differences (Rockwell & Rothney, 1961). Additional influences outside education were integrated into the structure of guidance and gradually reshaped its features. For example, those involved in the vocational guidance movement created an interest in assessing individual differences and making personal, educational, and vocational decisions based on the resulting data. What have become known as the psychometric and mental health movements also had an impact on the guidance movement.

Vocational Guidance Movement

Near the end of a long career as a social reformer, Frank Parsons (1909) established a Vocation Bureau in Boston in 1908, the purpose of which was to provide vocational guidance for out-of-school youths. Parsons believed that individuals must have dependable information about occupations and about themselves to make good occupational choices. He also believed that the role of the vocational counselor was to make such information available and to help individuals comprehend and use it.

At about the same time, programs that would later be categorized as representing vocational guidance were being introduced in a few metropolitan school districts. For example, selected elementary and secondary teachers in Boston were appointed to *positions* as vocational counselors (Gysbers & Henderson, 2000). Some universities offered courses in vocations, and the federal government passed legislation that subsidized vocational education and teacher training (e.g., the Smith-Hughes Vocational Education Act of 1917). Yet, in the first quarter of the 20th century, the influence of vocational guidance on school guidance was minimal, there were no accredited training programs and no widely accepted theoretical underpinnings (Aubrey, 1977).

Psychometric Movement

A series of events in the first quarter of the 20th century led to the use of psychometric principles and techniques in applied settings. Psychometric principles, such as reliability theory and test validity, as well as techniques for standardizing psychometric instruments and making them precise, had previously been used by academicians and researchers to enhance their scholarly efforts. In 1905, Alfred Binet and T. Simon developed a scale to measure mental ability to help the school system in Paris, France, classify students for educational instruction. Binet's scale popularized the idea of using psychometrics to solve practical problems and was the forerunner of modern intelligence testing.

In response to the federal government's need to classify millions of young men eligible for the military when the United States entered World War I in 1917, several eminent psychologists produced a group-administered intelligence test. The success of the military use of the tests, known as Army Alpha (paper-and-pencil administration) and Beta (performance administration), popularized the idea of using group testing in education. In addition, vocational guidance workers found testing attractive as an apparently scientific means of determining a person's interests, strengths, and limitations.

Psychometrics offered school guidance not only the tools for assessment but also corresponding respectability because the tools seemed so precise and scientific. Psychometrics emphasized objectivity, individual differences, prediction, classification, and placement. With these emphases came tendencies for some school guidance workers to engage in testing and telling—relying on testing and information giving as the basis for guidance. As was the case with vocational guidance, because no uniform national guidance program existed, some were more influenced than others by the psychometric movement.

Mental Health Movement

Several parallel movements in the early 20th century ushered in what has been called the mental health movement. In 1908, Clifford Beers, a former mental patient, published a book called *A Mind That Found Itself*, which brought about reforms in the treatment of mental illness and fostered widespread interest in mental hygiene and the early identification and treatment of mental illness. Sigmund Freud's psychoanalytic ideas focusing on the importance of individual development and the influence of the mind on one's mental health became popular in the treatment of mental health problems and in mental health studies. These activities led to a newfound interest in the importance of the formative years as the foundation of personality and development. This interest in the promotion of healthy individual adjustment eventually influenced early school guidance workers.

Emergence of a School Guidance Profession

In the 1920s and 1930s, the number of guidance specialists in the schools increased, although no widely accepted standards for training or practice existed. School administrators, circumstances, and the training and beliefs of the specialists combined to influence the philosophies and practices in those early school guidance programs. Often, the secondary school guidance programs that emerged in the 1920s were imitations of college student personnel programs that emphasized discipline and attendance (Gibson & Mitchell, 1981). Like college and university deans of students, high school guidance counselors acquired some administrative responsibilities and often concerned themselves with remedial goals. One outcome was that guidance counselors became responsive to the day-to-day wishes of their school administrators and were more likely to be identified with them (Shaw, 1973).

The advent of compulsory school attendance and the influence of the vocational guidance and mental health movements helped shape school guidance in the direction of a specialty. Compulsory school attendance increased the number of students who were unsure about their future plans and who had difficulty adjusting to the school environment. Proctor (1925) advocated guidance as a means of helping students cope with life forces by providing help in the selection of school subjects, extracurricular activities, colleges, and vocational schools. Through the end of World War II in 1945, school guidance was characterized by a relatively narrow focus on vocational guidance, adjustment to one's environment, and accompanying administrative duties. Between 1924 and 1946, four states required guidance counselors to have special certificates (Smith, 1955), indicating that school guidance was largely a function of local influences. In the few instances where guidance was offered at the elementary school level, it was most often a transplanted version of the secondary school program (Zaccaria, 1969).

What emerged as the dominant school guidance model in the 1930s and early 1940s has been labeled *trait and factor*, or directive, guidance (Aubrey, 1977). Publications by E. G. Williamson (1950; Williamson & Darley, 1937) had considerable influence at this time. Williamson (1950) promoted enhancing normal adjustment, helping individuals set goals and overcome obstacles to those goals, and assisting individuals to achieve satisfying lifestyles. Influenced by the medical model for treating individuals, Williamson recommended that counseling competencies include analysis, synthesis, diagnosis, prognosis, counseling, and follow-up (Ewing, 1975; Smith, 1955). Techniques were suggested for forcing conformity, changing the environment, selecting the appropriate environment, teaching needed skills, and changing attitudes (Williamson, 1950). The descriptor *trait and factor* was applied to these techniques because diagnostic data derived from standardized tests, and case studies emphasizing individual differences were used to advise students about vocational and adjustment issues.

The directive approach to guidance eventually proved to be too narrow in the changing times following World War II. Aubrey (1977) believed the changes were influenced by an increasing desire for personal freedom and autonomy. Into this setting came Carl Rogers (1942, 1951, 1961), whose nonmedical approach to counseling had an impact on the field unlike the work of any person before him. His ideas transferred the focus of counseling away from problems and onto the individuals receiving counseling. Rogers emphasized the counseling relationship and climate. His general goal was to help individuals grow so they might resolve their own problems and have the strength to function effectively.

Individual counseling had gradually emerged as the dominant guidance function in the 1930s and 1940s. The changing social environment after World War II and the addition of Rogers's ideas led Smith (1955) to conclude that counseling had become the central secondary school guidance function, with all other functions in supplementary roles. Smith observed that the nondirective and directive approaches each had proponents, as did an eclectic approach that occupied the middle of the road but was more directive in practice. Rogers's influence had moved school counselors away from being highly directive toward being eclectic. In addition, group counseling was emerging as a relatively new idea with some merit for school counseling (Smith, 1955).

The creation of the American Personnel and Guidance Association (APGA) in 1952 (now the ACA), the passage of the George-Barden Vocational Education Act of 1946 (PL 586) and the National Defense Education Act (NDEA) of 1958, and the increased school enrollments caused by the baby boomers all caused the training of school counselors to become more standardized and increased their number in the 1960s. This was the boom era in school counseling, and Rogers's theory and techniques dominated the training programs and practices of school counselors. Reflecting back on these times, authors of the ASCA National Model for School Counseling Programs (ASCA, 2005) seemed to regret the infusion of psychological and clinical paradigms into training programs once rooted in education paradigms because it caused role confusion for school counselors and their constituents.

Two divisions of the APGA—the ASCA and ACES—led the way to developing and promoting standards for the training of school counselors that strongly emphasized counseling theory and practicum training. Practicum training often focused on the development of skills for one-to-one counseling relationships and occurred at the end of the training program, leaving the impression that the counseling function was very important. Although the standards tended to fortify the importance of counseling, other functions, such as record keeping, information dissemination, placement, follow-up, and evaluation, were also identified as important. In addition, uniformity was introduced to collegiate training programs and state certification standards. In the years after World War II and into the 1960s, the remaining states adopted certification standards for school counselors. In 1957, the ASCA, recognizing a need, initiated a study on elementary school counseling.

The George-Barden Act of 1946 ruled that federal funds could be used to support such activities as (a) state supervision programs, (b) salaries for counselor trainees, (c) research in the guidance field, and (d) salaries for local counselors and supervisors (Gysbers & Henderson, 2000). The NDEA was passed after the Soviets successfully launched the space satellite named *Sputnik* in 1957. On the basis of this perceived threat of Soviet educational superiority and the subsequent desire to identify academically talented students and guide them into careers in strategic fields, the

NDEA provided federal funds to the states for the enhancement of school counseling programs and to colleges and universities to update working school counselors and train new ones. Even though the primary purpose of the funding was rather narrow, it was used to achieve goals of a much broader scope. New and improved counselor education programs proliferated. The demand for graduates was immense because of the need for counselors to serve the growing number of students in the schools as a result of the birth rate explosion after World War II.

In 1959, James B. Conant recommended a ratio of one full-time high school counselor for every 200 to 300 students in his widely read book *The American High School Today*. Conant's focus on the importance of guidance helped create an impression that all high school students should have access to school counselors. The following year, the 1960 White House Conference on Children and Youth emphasized the importance of extending counseling services to preadolescents. Consultants to the U.S. Secretary of Health, Education, and Welfare recommended that the NDEA be extended to elementary schools. The 1964 amendments to the NDEA gave impetus to elementary school counseling by providing funds for training to extend the search for talent to elementary schools. This instigated a period of debate over models for elementary school guidance that extended into the 1970s.

In *The Counselor in a Changing World*, 60,000 copies of which were printed between 1962 and 1966, C. Gilbert Wrenn (1962) chided secondary school guidance counselors for having allowed themselves to become narrowly focused on the remedial needs of a few students. He recommended that the newly evolving population of elementary school counselors learn from the mistaken decision by secondary school counselors to build crisis-oriented programs and instead emphasize responding to the developmental needs of the wide range of students in their programs. Wrenn's advocacy of developmental rather than remedial goals for elementary and secondary school guidance came at a time when others were voicing similar opinions. Dinkmeyer (1967) advocated helping children to know, understand, and accept themselves. Also emphasizing the importance of promoting positive individual growth and development, Zaccaria (1969) pointed out that the emphasis of developmental guidance should be on preventing problems. Writing that the major emphasis among authorities publishing papers and books about guidance programs seemed to be on a developmental approach, Shaw (1973) concluded that the term *developmental guidance* was being used so globally that it had yet to be defined precisely. As the 1970s approached, the number of school counseling professionals being trained and employed had grown significantly, elementary school counseling was emerging and seeking an identity, and the traditional service delivery model was being challenged.

After the Boom

An era of declining enrollments in the schools and economic problems across the United States led to reductions of personnel in numerous school districts during the 1970s and into the 1980s. Many school counseling positions were eliminated, significantly fewer jobs were available for newly trained school counselors, and the thrust for elementary school guidance programs initiated in the 1960s was muted. At the same time, several themes about the appropriate roles for school counselors were championed. Influenced by the turbulent 1960s and the problems of the inner-city schools, Menacker (1974, 1976) called for counselors working in metropolitan areas to become more active in the schools and communities and to rely more on the fields of sociology, political science, and economics than on psychology for helping models. The developmental guidance approach was also gaining momentum at this time. One reason for this was the compatibility of the idea with elementary school guidance. The enhancement of self-understanding and adjustment, and the importance of consulting and collaboration for elementary school counselors, were already emphasized. A second reason for the momentum was the interest generated by career education proponents. Emphasizing the importance of work and careers to healthy human adjustment, career education advocates recommended integrating general and vocational education, instruction, and guidance around a career development theme from kindergarten to 12th grade (Hoyt, Evans, Mackin, & Mangum, 1974). Some federal funds were made available for career education programming in basic education during the 1970s. A third reason was the attention given to psychological education after Mosher and Sprinthall (1970) introduced psychologically based curriculum interventions for counselors to offer students in an effort to persuade guidance programs to help the schools focus more on personal development.

Shaw (1973) advocated what Zaccaria (1969) classified as a *services approach* to guidance. Shaw believed that guidance programs should be founded on clearly stated goals and objectives. He also believed that guidance workers should be able to provide a set of functions as needed, depending on where guidance goals belonged on a continuum ranging from primary prevention to diagnosis and therapy. The functions, or services, included counseling, consultation, testing, curriculum development, provision of information, in-service training, use of records, articulation, referral, and evaluation and research. Others, such as Keat (1974), advocated eclectic models. Keat's eclecticism, designed for elementary school counselors, was summarized in a blended set of roles. Group and individual counseling, collaboration and consultation with teachers, and coordination with school district and community resources were taken from the recommendations of professional organizations (APGA, 1969); communication with children and adults and offering an effective curriculum were borrowed from Stamm and Nissman (1971); and fostering child growth and development and teaching coping behaviors were added to the set by Keat.

In an increasing number of states, counseling students who had no teaching experience were trained and certified, creating greater diversity among the new generation of school counselors. At this time, school counseling was still a field without a central unifying theme. It was, in fact, experiencing an increasing number of themes, all having varying degrees of influence across training programs and among counselors. The newer activist, developmental, service-oriented, and eclectic themes mixed with remnants of the trait and factor, adjustment, administrative, and counseling themes that were still very much alive. In times of job shortages and threats to existing jobs, school counseling was at a loss to define itself uniformly. The winds of change led the APGA to rename itself the AACD in the mid-1980s and the ACA in the early 1990s. Divisions and state organizations followed suit or had already initiated similar changes (Herr, 1985). Officially, the words *guidance* and then *development* had become archaic. The term *counseling* now represented the goals of the organized members of the profession more accurately. Table 2.1 presents a summary of many of these important events in chronological order.

Table 2.1
Highlights of the evolution of school counseling in the 20th century.

Date	Event
1905	Binet and Simon develop mental ability scale.
1907	Jesse B. Davis conducts guidance classes in Grand Rapids, Michigan.
1908	Frank Parsons establishes Vocation Bureau in Boston.
1908	Clifford Beers publishes *A Mind That Found Itself.*
1917	Army Alpha and Beta developed.
1920s	Number of school guidance specialists increases; however, no widely accepted training or practice standards are developed.
1920	Sigmund Freud's ideas begin to influence mental health professionals.
1924	State certification of guidance counselors begins.
1925	Proctor advocates guidance program to help students make educational and vocational choices.
1937	Williamson and Darley publish *Student Personnel Work: An Outline of Clinical Procedures* and begin *trait and factor* approach.
1942	Carl Rogers publishes *Counseling and Psychotherapy* and begins the era of individual counseling.
1945	Changing social environment after World War II and influence of Rogers's writings cause counseling to become the dominant school guidance service.
1946	George-Barden Act passed.
1952	American Personnel and Guidance Association (APGA) created.
1953	American School Counselor Association (ASCA) joins the APGA.
1958	National Defense Education Act (NDEA) passed.
1959	Conant publishes *The American High School Today.*
1960	Boom decade in school guidance and counseling and in counselor education begins.
1962	C. Gilbert Wrenn publishes *The Counselor in a Changing World.*
1964	NDEA amended to provide funds for enhancing elementary school guidance.
1970	Decade of declining enrollments in the schools and corresponding reductions in school counselors begins.
1970	Mosher and Sprinthall introduce their deliberate psychological education curriculum.
1974	Hoyt, Evans, Mackin, and Mangum include guidance in the career education theme.
1976	Menacker publishes *Toward a Theory of Activist Guidance.*
1985	APGA changes its name to the American Association for Counseling and Development (AACD).
1987	AACD task force on school counseling as a profession at risk publishes its report.
1988	Gysbers and Henderson publish *Developing and Managing Your School Guidance Program.*
1990	Interdivisional task force (AACD, ACES, ASCA) begins working on plans to improve school counseling.

(continued)

Date	Event
1991	"Multiculturalism as a Fourth Force in Counseling" is introduced in a special issue of the AACD journal.
1992	ASCA publishes *Children Are Our Future, School Counseling 2000.*
1992	AACD changes its name to the American Counseling Association (ACA).
1993	ASCA, ACA, and others reintroduce the Elementary School Counseling Demonstration Act.
1996	Effects of baby boom echo generation begin to take effect.
1996	Alger report indicates that youths' perception of school counseling is improving.
1997	ASCA proposes the National Standards for School Counseling Programs.
1997	DeWitt Wallace Reader's Digest Fund provides the Education Trust with funding to initiate a transformation of school counseling.
1998	Strong U.S. economy indicates potential for enhanced educational expenditures and an improving employment market.
1999–2000	Funding achieved for the Elementary and Secondary School Counseling Demonstration Program under the Elementary and Secondary Education Act.
2000	Application of School–Community Collaboration Model selected by U.S. Department of Education is 1 of 22 outstanding model schools are encouraged to support.
2001	No Child Left Behind initiative becomes legislation.
2002	ASCA presents the National Model for School Counseling Programs.
2002	The Education Trust receives funds from Met Life for the Transforming School Counseling Initiative.
2003	*ASCA National Model Workbook* published.
2004	ASCA announces that five schools had met the criteria for becoming Recognized ASCA Model Programs.

Challenges of the Late 20th Century

Generally, basic education and school counseling in the United States have been bombarded by a range of challenges that, when evaluated closely, seem to place increasing responsibility on elementary, middle, and secondary school educators to respond to the nation's problems and to prepare future generations of students to cope with economic competitors. These challenges include demands that the school curriculum be made more rigorous, drug abuse be prevented, drug users be treated and rehabilitated, exceptional students and culturally different populations be integrated and their differences appreciated, dropout rates be reduced, children of working parents be cared for, students be prepared for more complex and challenging jobs, gender equity be promoted, and local and state taxes for supporting the schools be reduced or maintained at existing levels.

Profession at Risk. Depicting school counseling as a profession at risk, a task force constituted by the AACD in 1987 pointed out that standards varied widely across the 333 training programs in the United States and that only 70 programs had been accredited by the CACREP, which had existed since 1981. In addition, the task force reported that standards for certifying counselors varied widely across the United States and that, as individual members of the task force, they had mixed feelings about whether school counseling was truly a profession.

Data from a U.S. Department of Education survey of 333 heads of public high school guidance programs suggested that school counseling faced significant challenges as the 20th century entered its last decade (Moles, 1991). The survey data indicated that, on average, counselors in these schools spent 16% of their time on various nonguidance activities; the average ratio of students to counselors was 350 to 1 (250 to 1 is recommended; College Board, 1986) (the ACA and ASCA recommend 250 to 1 as well), 41% of schools had no guidance-related courses or units (proactive programming), and students who continued their education beyond high school received considerably more career planning assistance from counselors than did those who ended their formal education with high school. These findings indicated that school counseling services may have been unbalanced, unevenly provided, and diluted by intrusive nonguidance responsibilities and large caseloads.

Competitors have appeared from several arenas, none apparently because of a desire to replace school counselors. Instead, more global issues seem to underscore the situations that lead to competition. Some competitors are hired to replace or supplement counselors, performing some functions traditionally in the domain of school counselors. Roberts, Coursol, and Morotti (1997) described circumstances in Minnesota that led to employment of school social workers because school districts could use federal special education funds to pay their salaries. In an article on privatization of school counseling functions, Dykeman (1995) identified six approaches that vary according to whether the school and the school counseling programs are partially or completely privatized and whether the contractors are nonprofit or for-profit entities. Thus, some privatization schemes lead to replacing school counselors, whereas others lead to sharing caseloads. Among the issues that privatization creates are job erosion, unequal pay scales, caseload inequity, insufficient supervision, and decreased confidentiality. The school counseling profession is also challenged by competitors that provide other services. For example, some school systems faced with limited funds may hire reading specialists in place of school counselors to meet the demand for improved academic performance of students, concluding that even though both programs are worthwhile, one is more important at the moment and both cannot be afforded at once.

Multicultural Competence.   From within the general field of counseling came a call for multicultural competence (AACD, 1991). Professional counselors are challenged to (a) know about and be able to establish relationships with individuals in all cultural groups (Westbrook & Sedlacek, 1991), (b) be able to conceptualize client concerns from their perspective or worldview (Ibrahim, 1991), and (c) provide proactive programming that is culturally sensitive (Dobbins & Skillings, 1991). Knowledge of differing worldviews is incomplete unless accompanied by corresponding knowledge of one's own feelings, thoughts, and experiences, according to Speight, Myers, Cox, and Highlen (1991).

Educational Reform.   President George W. Bush's No Child Left Behind Act (PL 107-110) is, according to Herr (2002), the latest national educational reform movement, and the school counseling profession finds itself assessing its role—collectively and individually. "Each time there is a change of national presidential administrations, there is likely to be a proposed shift in the emphasis that national policy and practice should address, creating a constant process of 'starting over,' looking for new solutions to enduring problems" (p. 220). Herr's paper was among several articles published in the April 2002 issue of *Professional School Counseling,* the goal of which was to address the role of school counseling in the latest school reform movement. Herr carefully addresses school reform from a historical perspective and presents viewpoints on why previous reform movements have had limited success. One is left with the belief that school counselors need to be careful not to become caught up in reform efforts that focus only on restructuring schools via increased academic rigor. That school counselors and school reform should also focus on alleviating the circumstances that prevent some children and youths from being successful in school seems clear.

Increasing Enrollments.   Information from the U.S. Department of Education indicates that school enrollment has increased dramatically at some levels of education and in some regions of the United States during the decade of 1996/1997 to 2006/2007. The impact of this *baby boom echo generation* will be felt the most in high schools (15% enrollment increases) and in the southern and western parts of the country (Goetz, 1997; Morrissey, 1996). Although at lower levels, the increases will also occur in the middle and elementary schools and in other regions of the United States. These demographics indicate that this decade of transition from one century to the next will present opportunities and challenges ranging from increased employment for school counselors to larger caseloads than were previously experienced.

Four possible causes of the rising enrollment are (a) many baby boomers delayed marriage and childbearing, (b) more children enrolled in preschools and are remaining in school to earn diplomas, (c) birth rates are high among ethnic minority populations, and (d) immigration to the United States increased. The latter two factors indicate an increased need for multicultural counseling competence. The 21st-century schools are likely to be in settings where school counselors and their student clients have increasingly diverse cultural and economic backgrounds. Therefore, counselors will be challenged to focus on student clients' presenting problems while also being comfortable exploring cultural and dispositional sources of resistance to the helping process (Coleman, 1995). School counselors will also be challenged to respond to competing individual and community needs. As an example of this dual challenge, Coleman cited a hypothetical case of a counselor seeking to help student clients who perform less well on college and university admissions tests. The hypothetical counselor contacts colleges to inquire about admissions policies that do not discriminate (individual needs) and joins others in an effort to lobby for culturally sensitive admissions tests (community needs).

The 1990s were good times in the United States economically. Unfortunately, a variety of circumstances, such as increasing enrollments coupled with decreasing revenues, led to an economic downturn beginning in 2000 and 2001 that continued into the early years of the 21st century. Historically, school counseling has been affected negatively by such economic developments through reductions in staff and declining opportunities for graduates of counselor education programs. In 2004, the economy began to recover and then leveled off. A national state of macroeconomic confusion caused Samuelson (2005) to suggest that it was time to reconsider the state of knowledge in economics.

Emerging Themes.   Several themes seem to emerge from these challenges. First, external circumstances such as growing enrollments and decreasing revenues indicate that school counselors will be challenged to demonstrate their worth and cost effectiveness in the schools. Second, national, state, and local governments recognize the importance of education in the future health of the United States, and are concerned about viable outcomes and accountability. Third, these circumstances lead to national school reform efforts, such as the No Child Left Behind initiative. Fourth, as was the case in early school reform efforts, school counseling has not been included as an important participant in the reform's response. Fifth, there is widespread belief that many school counseling programs have been and remain marginalized ancillary services that are endangered in economic hard times (ASCA, 1996; Baker, 2001; Campbell & Dahir, 1997; House & Hayes, 2002). Sixth, without a designed program, a clear mission, and an identified role or vision, counselors will continue to function at the discretion of others (Borders & Drury, 1992; Gysbers & Henderson, 2000; House & Hayes, 2002; Paisley & Borders, 1995). Seventh, a well-conceived effort by school counselors to address the needs of all students seems to be essential for the future good health of individual school counselors, school counseling programs, and the school counseling profession (Bowers, Hatch, & Schwallie-Giddis, 2001).

Responding to the Challenges

Federal Funding.   The ASCA, ACA, and other sister professional organizations reintroduced the Elementary School Counseling Demonstration Act (ESCDA) in 1992. Their activity had potential for responding constructively to the challenges listed in the previous section. The prospective legislation called for funding to schools that proposed promising and innovative approaches to expanding elementary school counseling programs. Included among the criteria for funding programs under the legislation were recommendations that school counselors work cooperatively with school psychologists and social workers in integrated teams, that student-to-counselor ratios be not more than 250 to 1, that 85% of the team members' time be devoted to providing direct services with no more than 15% devoted to administrative tasks, and that the program be developmental and preventive.

Working cooperatively, ACA, ASCA, the National Association of School Psychologists, the National Association of Social Workers, the American Psychological Association, and the School Social Work Association of America convinced Congress to reauthorize/rewrite the ESCDA as part of a larger Elementary and Secondary Education Act (ESEA) bill and to fund it as part of an appropriations bill in 1998 (Urbaniak, 2000). Funding victories were accomplished in 1999 and 2000 (Urbaniak, 2000). Since 2000, school counselors, school psychologists, school social workers, and other interested professionals have worked independently and through respective professional organizations to enhance the ESCDA/ESEA legislation (e.g., provide

The school counseling pro-
fession has met challenges
by forging new models for
counseling services.

Edwin R. Gerler, Jr.

for counseling programs in secondary schools), get ESEA authorized, and acquire funding.

Comprehensive Guidance Programs. Reports by Lapan, Gysbers, and Sun (1997); Neukrug, Barr, Hoffman, and Kaplan (1993); and Sink and MacDonald (1998) indicated that the number of states adopting comprehensive guidance programs had been increasing steadily. This development suggested a growing awareness of, and appreciation for, the concept of guidance for everyone and corresponding emphases on planned, sequential, and flexible guidance curricula integrated into the general curriculum. In turn, deemphasis of the importance of administrative and clerical-centered response modes is suggested.

Multicultural Competence. A concerted effort to enhance the multicultural counseling competence of counselors in general and school counselors in particular has been under way for more than a decade. In 1991, the Association for Multicultural Counseling and Development approved a rationale for multicultural counseling that led to a proposed set of multicultural competencies (Sue, Arredondo, & McDavis, 1992). Although these and other efforts appear to have had an effective impact, both evidence and opinion suggest that the goals have yet to be achieved (Nuttal, Webber, & Sanchez, 1996). Counselor education programs are challenged to continue transforming their curricula to integrate multicultural perspectives, and professional counselors are challenged to become culturally competent counselors.

National Standards for School Counseling. In an attempt to respond to Goals 2000: Educate America Act (EAA) of 1994, the ASCA adopted School Counseling

2000, a set of goals for school counseling derived from the six broad goals for achieving success in American education in the EAA. The general theme of the school counseling goals is to work directly and collaboratively with students, parents, teachers, community members, and employers to develop policies and programs that address the challenging problems that have been widely identified.

Consequently, the ASCA governing board committed to developing national standards for school counseling programs (Dahir, 2001). The National Standards for School Counseling Programs (Campbell & Dahir, 1997) were completed in 1997. The standards are designed to (a) shift the focus from counselors to school counseling programs, (b) create a framework for a national school counseling program model, (c) establish school counseling as an integral part of the academic mission of the schools, (d) lead to equal access to school counseling services for all students, (e) highlight the key ingredients of developmental school counseling, (f) identify the knowledge and skills to which all students should have access from comprehensive school counseling programs, and (g) ensure comprehensive school counseling programs are delivered in a systematic manner (Dahir, 1997). Emphasis is on the role of counseling in student achievement, on collaboration with teachers and school administrators toward helping students be successful in school, and on program content standards that specify what students should know and be able to do (Dahir, 2001).

An analysis of survey data from more than 2,000 members of ASCA led to the conclusion that the content of school programs focuses on academic, career, and personal-social development (Dahir, 2001). Key components of the National Standards for School Counseling Programs are found in appendix C. As presented in this appendix, there are nine national standards, three in each of the content areas listed earlier in this paragraph. The academic development standards focus on implementing programs and strategies that maximize student learning. Dahir pointed out that, in this way, the National Standards correspond to the school reform agenda.

The goal of the career development component of the National Standards is to guide school counselors toward helping students make transitions from grade to grade, from school to postsecondary education, and from school to the world of work. The personal-social component standards are designed to assist counselors in developing personal and social growth-producing experiences that lead to a successful transition to adulthood. These personal-social development experiences should also contribute to achieving the academic and career success goals. The competencies found in the National Standards are viewed as resources for counselors to use in developing program strategies and measurable criteria for assessing outcomes and achieving accountability (Dahir, 2001).

Dahir (2001) stated: "More than 400 schools or districts throughout the 50 states have established comprehensive school counseling programs based on the National Standards with full statewide adoption currently under way in Delaware and New Jersey" (p. 325). Furthermore, she notes that the standards have been supported or endorsed by the ACA, the American College Testing Program, the Association for Career and Technical Education, the Association for Counselor Education and Supervision, the College Board, the CACREP, the National Alliance of Business, the National Association of Elementary Principals, the National Association of Secondary School Principals, the NBCC, the National Association of College Admissions

Counseling, the National Career Development Association, and the National Parent Teacher Association. Finally, Dahir noted that 69% of the counselor education programs were using the standards in some way (Perusse, Goodnough, & Noel, 2000), and some of the programs funded by the Education Trust (1997) initiative were using the standards in pre- and in-service professional development programming (House & Martin, 1998).

Findings from a survey of 1,127 ASCA members indicated strong support for the National Standards (82%), especially that they may help clarify the scope and practice of school counseling (Dahir, 2004). They appreciated the goal of having school counseling programs become integral components of the academic missions of their respective schools. There also seemed to be a preference for basing standards on envisioned practice rather than either theory or current practice. Dahir concluded: "The school counseling community has never been in a better situation to position itself at the forefront of school improvement and educational change" (p. 352).

Best Paradigms Currently Available

Three well-articulated conceptualizations of how school counseling can be structured to be effective for all students were underway before President Bush's No Child Left Behind initiative was proposed. They now seem to be the best visions the profession has to offer for school counseling in the 21st century. Although their origins and primary thrusts differ, they have much in common. For example, they all stress (a) the importance of school counseling being an integral part of the educational program rather than a set of ancillary services, (b) leadership by school counselors directed toward enhancing the academic achievement of all students, (c) advocacy for students and families, (d) collaboration within and outside the schools, and (e) school counselors being well positioned to play a proactive role in the school reform initiatives.

Here, we provide a survey of each initiative and demonstrate how the basic competencies for school counseling presented in this textbook are universal and lend themselves to preparing school counselors to carry out the goals, roles, and functions of each of these initiatives as well as others. We do not promote one initiative over any of the others. As individuals who do not have a vested interest in any of the three initiatives, we believe that they have more to offer collectively than any one does individually. For example, the National Model for School Counseling Programs appears to emphasize a broad range of school counseling functions within a clearly defined program, and promotes school counselors being leaders in their schools and in responding to school reform initiatives. It also presents competencies devoted to enhancing student academic, career, and personal-social development directed toward success in school and life. The Transforming School Counseling Initiative (TSCI) emphasizes leadership and advocacy functions for school counselors, and presents a mission that all students have access to and success in a rigorous academic curriculum in order to be successful in their lives. The School–Community Collaboration Model emphasizes the collaboration function for school counselors while following a mission to meet the social, emotional, and health needs of all students so they can be successful in school.

The ASCA National Model. The National Model (ASCA, 2005) is sponsored by the ASCA and incorporates the ASCA National Standards for School Counseling Programs (Campbell & Dahir, 1997). Details about the National Standards were provided earlier in this chapter and additional information is found in appendix C. The process of developing and implementing this model began in 2001 and continues today (Bowers et al., 2001; Hatch & Bowers, 2002). The general goal is that comprehensive school counseling must be integral to student academic achievement and must help set high standards for student achievement. It is believed that school counselors must be trained to inform administrators of the contributions they plan to make rather than asking them what to do.

It is also believed that the National Model maximizes the full potential of the National Standards and reflects the current education reform movements, including the No Child Left Behind initiative. In so doing, the National Model incorporates school counseling standards and competencies for all students. The National Standards serve as a foundation for the National Model and lead to an organized, planned, sequential, and flexible school counseling program. Interventions will be intentional and designed to meet the needs of all students. A primary objective of intentional planning will be to close the gap between academically disadvantaged students and their advantaged peers.

The National Model is perceived as a flexible template that individual school districts can use to create programs that reflect their own needs and accountability expectations. The components of the model include, but are not limited to, (a) the ASCA National Standards; (b) implementation of a districtwide delivery system that includes a guidance curriculum, individual planning, responsive services, and system support; (c) a management system that ensures programs are based on student needs; (d) a data-driven evaluation system; (e) intentional services for academically underperforming students; and (f) infusion of systemic change, leadership, and advocacy throughout all components. The National Model was tested by seven school districts in Riverside, California, in 2001 and reviewed by school counseling leaders. In 2004, five schools in California, Oregon, and Arizona were declared Recognized ASCA Model Programs (ASCA, 2004). Survey research data reported by Foster, Young, and Hermann (2005) indicated that school counselors believe that work activities that promote the academic, career, and personal/social development of students are important. These findings provide support for the ASCA National Standards and the National Model. For further information, see www.SchoolCounselor.org.

The ASCA National Standards are viewed as complementing the comprehensive school guidance and counseling program concept, and the ASCA National Model is strongly influenced by that concept as well. Sink and McDonald (1998) reported that 35 state departments of education or school counseling associations have promoted the implementation of comprehensive school counseling models. Herr (2001) believed the concept, originally depicted as comprehensive guidance programs, has its roots in the 1960s when a systems approach in guidance was being advocated. The concept of planned, comprehensive, systematic guidance programs emerged in the 1980s and has received support from national professional associations, such as the ASCA, and from federal legislation, such as the Carl D. Perkins Vocational and Applied Technology Education Act of 1984 and the School-to-Work Opportunities Act of 1994 (Herr, 2001).

Currently, many advocates are voicing their support of this concept in the professional literature, and we have selected Gysbers and Henderson (2000) to represent them here. According to Gysbers and Henderson (2001), a comprehensive guidance and counseling program consist of three elements: content, organizational framework, and resources. Content refers to the competencies students achieve through participation in components of a comprehensive guidance and counseling program. The organizational framework consists of a K–12 curriculum of guidance activities designed to help students achieve the competencies. For example, the curriculum might include a classroom guidance program designed to help students investigate the world of work, acquire a better understanding of themselves in the world of work, and eventually make wise career decisions.

Furthermore, the organizational framework includes delivery modes for the organized curriculum such as classroom and schoolwide activities and individual planning. Individual planning is a comprehensive process designed to help students learn about themselves and plan accordingly, and it calls on counselors to possess appraisal, advisement, placement, and follow-up competencies. The organizational framework also includes services needed to respond to student problems that deter academic, career, and personal-social development. These services are identified as personal counseling, diagnostic and remediation activities, consultation, and referral. Finally, it is important not to overlook the necessity for an ongoing support system consisting of (a) program evaluation leading to continued program development, (b) continuous professional development of school counselors, (c) public relations thrusts to keep all stakeholders informed, (d) service on advisory boards, (e) community outreach, and (f) continuous program planning and management.

The resource element of a comprehensive program refers to the importance of human, financial, and political resources. School counselors, teachers, administrators, parents, students, community members, and business and labor representatives all have important contributions to make in a comprehensive guidance and counseling program. Adequate financial support is also needed. Finally, political resources need to be mobilized appropriately to achieve full endorsement by school district boards of education. Gysbers and Henderson (2001) believed that "The program's organizational structure not only provides the means and a common language for ensuring guidance for all students and counseling for students that need it, it also provides a foundation for the accountable use of an ever-broadening spectrum of resources" (p. 256). Finally, Gysbers and Henderson (2001) viewed the comprehensive school guidance and counseling program approach as the best vehicle for achieving the convergence of the currently incongruent goals of providing an academically rigorous education while including all students.

According to Rowley, Stroh, and Sink (2005), variations of the comprehensive guidance and counseling programs (CGCPs) are being implemented throughout the United States. Rowley et al. (2005) surveyed a national sample of school counselors working within CGCPs and found that, although implementation methods were varied, the guidance curriculum component of the model was viewed as fruitful. That is, many counselors believed that their implementation of the curriculum was helping students attain developmental competence, and they were using a wide range of curriculum materials in support of achieving their program goals.

The Transforming School Counseling Initiative.   Supported by a 1996 grant from the DeWitt Wallace Reader's Digest Fund, the Education Trust set out to bring about dramatic changes in the training of school counselors in order to transform school counseling by causing school counselors to become more responsive to student needs (Guerra, 1998). Six counselor education programs were selected to receive funding for developing model school counseling training programs. Advocates of the trust's initiative believe that the programs for training school counselors must change if constructive changes are to occur in school counseling (Sears & Granello, 2002). New funding from the Met Life Foundation allowed the Education Trust to initiate the National School Counselor Training Initiative (Stone & House, 2002). This funding allows the Education Trust to deliver workshops to school counselors and administrators that focus on transforming the work of counselors. For more information, contact rhouse@edtrust.org.

An underlying theme of this initiative is that school counselors need to be integral participants in closing the gap between poor students and students of color and their more advantaged peers (House & Hayes, 2002). Therefore, school counselors must believe that all students can achieve at a high level and act accordingly. House and Hayes believe that school counselors are in the best position to assess their schools for barriers to academic success for all students and to use that information to be advocates for equity and entitlement. Although not negating the importance of traditional school counselor roles such as counselor, coordinator, and consultant, this initiative emphasizes the roles of leader, advocate, and collaborator. According to Sears and Granello (2002), the traditional roles and their corresponding skills remain necessary, yet they are no longer sufficient for school counselors to be effective in today's schools. In summary, the TSCI recommends that school counselors and counselor education training programs move away from an overemphasis on providing mental health services to an academic/student achievement focus ("The New Vision"), that is, from individual concerns to whole school and system concerns (Perusse, Goodenough, Donegan, & Jones, 2004).

School counselors attempting to achieve the goals of this initiative will develop, coordinate, and implement well-articulated developmental counseling programs with attention to equity, access, and support services (House & Hayes, 2002). These programs will be designed to improve the learning success of all students, especially those who experience difficulty in rigorous academic programs. School counselors will provide leadership and collaborate in building teams of students, professional and support staff members, parents, and individuals in the community in order to accomplish a communitywide effort to achieve the goals of educational reform.

If school counselors proactively emphasize and implement the educational leader, advocate, and collaborator roles and are successful, then they will move school counseling from the periphery to a central position in the schools (Education Trust, 1997; House & Hayes, 2002). In so doing, they will make a significant contribution to closing the achievement gap between poor students and students of color and their more advantaged peers.

House and Hayes (2002) offered examples of how school counselors can take advantage of their unique position in the schools to achieve the goals of this initiative. These proactive leaders can present themselves to the students as caring and committed adult advocates and mentors. They are in a position to determine what barriers to academic success exist in their schools and communities and to engage in proactive efforts to alleviate them through leadership, advocacy, and collaboration. In so doing, they will be at the forefront of promoting high expectations and standards.

The School–Community Collaboration Model. A basic principle of this initiative is that external barriers—such as poverty, violence, gangs, drugs, language and culture differences, and inadequate health care—lead to emotional, behavior, and learning problems in schools (Adelman & Taylor, 2002). Unless these are addressed successfully, efforts to leave no student behind academically will fail. This approach seems to respond to the criticism Herr (2002) shared about previous school reform movements having a focus that was too narrow.

In recent years, several writers in the counseling profession have published articles promoting this approach (Green & Keys, 2001; Hobbs & Collison, 1995; Keys & Bemak, 1997; Keys, Bemak, & Lockhart, 1998). Adelman and Taylor (2002) reported that various forms of school–community collaboration have been tested. Although these programs had limited focus and ran into many challenges, Adelman and Taylor believed that there is sufficient inferential evidence that these programs can be successful and cost effective over time.

Adelman and Taylor (2002) believed that few schools currently have the resources needed and that educational reform has ignored the importance of reforming and restructuring the work of those school professionals who are responsible for psychosocial and health programs. They recommended that new strategies for coordinating, integrating, and redeploying resources should be implemented to increase the comprehensiveness of school-based responses to social, emotional, and physical health problems.

The proposed model espouses the following recommendations. First, because student problems are usually complex in terms of causes and needed interventions, a comprehensive, multifaceted continuum of braided interventions is needed. These braided interventions would employ strategies that may be categorized as primary prevention, early identification and treatment, and treatment of severe and chronic problems. Second, efforts must be linked to the basic mission of schools: to educate children and youths. Therefore, "the current emphasis on improving instruction and school management should also include a comprehensive component for addressing barriers to learning" (Adelman & Taylor, 2002, p. 242).

Six arenas are offered through which coordination and eventually integration of a myriad of school and community resources might be achieved. They are all focused on addressing barriers to learning and enhancing healthy development in the school sites: (a) increase the effectiveness of classroom instruction; (b) support students and families in coping with a variety of transitions; (c) help families become involved successfully in the education of their children; (d) provide a systematic program for crisis assistance and prevention; (e) integrate and personalize social, mental health, and physical health assistance for students and their families; and (f) create and maintain collaborative connections with public and private agencies, higher education, business and professional organizations, churches, and volunteer organizations.

Adelman and Taylor (2002) recommended trying to achieve school–community collaboration at the school and neighborhood levels first and then pursuing central restructuring thereafter. They believed that, if school counselors engage in school–community collaboration endeavors, "the roles of school counselors as advocates, catalysts, brokers, leaders, and facilitators of systemic reform will expand in order to engage in an increasingly wide array of activity to promote academic achievement and healthy development and address barriers to student learning" (p. 244).

Adoptions of the model have occurred in the California Department of Education, the Los Angeles Unified School District, and the Hawaii Department of Education. The New American Schools Urban Learning Center, an application of this approach, has been selected by the U.S. Department of Education as 1 of 22 outstanding models schools are encouraged to adopt.

Critics of this initiative might note that the emphasis on academic rigor may overlook two important concepts. First, there may be evidence that, even with all barriers removed, some individuals are simply not suited for or interested in rigorous academic curricula or a college education. Second, the seemingly narrow focus on preparation for college ignores the ideas that education should be preparation for work and that there is dignity in all work.

Integrating the Three Paradigms.   These initiatives seem to offer considerable promise for enhancing the school counseling profession, making it part of the mainstream of education, providing recommendations for the competencies school counselors need to be successful in the 21st century, and ensuring comprehensive and helpful interventions for America's students. In another publication, one of us shared an opinion that, historically, ideas that were introduced from the top down did not seem to take hold at the grassroots level of school counseling (Baker, 2001). Time will tell with these initiatives. Those promoting them seem to be willing to undertake the hard work necessary for achieving understanding and approval at the grassroots levels. It is hoped that they are all successful in some way and that the good that each has to offer may find its way into a mixture of all three initiatives.

Should these initiatives not succeed in achieving their important goals, the ASCA, ACES, and ACA, through their efforts to serve school counselors in particular and counselors in general, probably remain the organizations best positioned to help counselors respond to current and future challenges. As demonstrated, they offer potential for counselors to respond collectively to the challenges that face the nation, the schools, and the profession. School counselors, in turn, are challenged to become members of one or more of these organizations to strengthen them and to work within them.

The CACREP provides a vehicle for uniformity in training standards. In that vein, in 1990, an interdivisional task force representing the ACES, ACA, and ASCA began planning to improve school counseling. Specifically, the task force recommended uniform state certification/licensure standards and adoption of CACREP standards as minimum requirements for certification/licensure as a school counselor. The task force was thus attempting to enhance the preparation of school counselors (Cecil, 1990). Their goals have not yet been fully achieved. Seem (2002) depicted program accreditation as "a hallmark for defining a profession. . . . Its accreditation standards are the major reference for defining what is known as the counseling core" (p. 7).

This historical overview traces the development of school counseling from "positions to programs." It also provides a context from which we have developed a paradigm for school counseling that is presented in chapter 3.

FEATURED ACTIVITY: GRADUATE STUDENT PERSPECTIVES ON THE EVOLUTION OF SCHOOL COUNSELING

As society has changed and education evolved, school counselors have been asked to apply various paradigms in their work. Among the most recent paradigms are

The ASCA National Model for School Counseling Programs
The Transforming School Counseling Initiative
The School–Community Collaboration Model

These are presented and discussed in chapter 2.

We recently discussed these paradigms (in the context of the history of school counseling) with a group of school counseling graduate students. One of our most diligent students (who was browsing in the university library) happened upon Gilbert Wrenn's (1962) classic book, *The Counselor in a Changing World*. After quickly reviewing the book's table of contents and leafing through the book, she commented

Except for a few changes in terminology, much of Wrenn's book could be applied to school counseling in the 21st century; so, why all the rush for new paradigms?

After you read this chapter, go to http://www.genesislight.com/scan21st/tell_us/directions.html and complete the form. With your permission, we will periodically post some of your creative thinking for the world to read.

OTHER SUGGESTED ACTIVITIES

1. Discuss the merits of the following statements:
   a. School counseling was not born, it evolved.
   b. The greatest periods of growth and support for guidance have occurred when the federal government was responding to a national crisis.
2. Ask the counselor educator responsible for coordinating your program to elaborate on the most important influences during his or her master's and doctoral training programs.
3. Discuss the merits of the three "best paradigms." Which one appeals to you? Why?
4. Go to the SCAN Web site (www.scan21st.com) to participate in online counseling exercises.

CHAPTER 3

A Comprehensive Model for Professional School Counseling: A Balanced Approach

Goal: To promote comprehensive, balanced K–12 school counseling programs conducted by counselors capable of meeting both responsive and developmental goals for children and adolescents living in a pluralistic society.

School counselors often reflect on the large responsibilities they encounter daily and over the course of a school year. Here are samples of what they say:

"The children who are leaving elementary school for middle school have no idea what they are about to face. We try our best to help them prepare, but we have neither the time nor the resources to reach all the children. I think effective, transition-to-middle-school programs should be a top priority for all school counselors."

"What am I going to do if a natural disaster hits my school—like a tornado, or heaven forbid, a disaster like Hurricane Katrina in New Orleans? How can I pre-pare myself and the teachers at my school to deal with the horrendous psychologi-cal consequences of disasters. I've read lots of good ideas in counseling articles, but, somehow, I just don't think these articles provide a realistic flavor for what occurs during these events. How can I help children through a disaster when, in all like-lihood, I'm trying to survive the event myself—perhaps, even the destruction of my own house."

"I had a father tell me that I had no business running groups for parents since I'm not a parent and have no idea what it's really like to raise a child, and, in his words, 'am hardly more than a child myself.' I am defensive about his comments but don't want to alienate him and hurt my chances to work with other parents who are more accept-ing of me. Unfortunately, he is a prominent citizen and may turn others against me. How can I work with him and win him over?"

"Some of the migrant workers in my community, who have children at my school, have asked me to help them stay in the United States. I think they've come to me because I speak Spanish, and no one else at my school understands any Spanish. I am really conflicted over their request. I hardly have enough time to do what I need to do at school, much less spend spare time in the evenings wrestling with their problems—which seem so insurmountable."

"A few days ago one of my favorite students, who has already been accepted to an Ivy League school, was accused of date rape by his former girlfriend. She made this accu-sation during our meeting to prepare her for spending her junior year abroad in France. She wanted to talk nothing about her plans for France. She doesn't think it's fair for her ex-boyfriend to receive all the glory for his admission to an Ivy League institution while she spends all her time in guilt and anger resulting from the way he treated her. I can't even sleep; I'm so worried about what I need to do."

"I have all these ideas about how we can use computer technology to improve the counseling services we offer our students. But, no one seems to want to listen to me; they are all too busy with their own work, and they have no time to learn the technology necessary for planning and implementing new programs that integrate technology."

School counseling offers professionals a wide choice of options for improving life at school among students, parents, teachers, and school administrators. Counselors need to explore a balanced approach to their work and to consider how to establish priorities.

INTRODUCTION

Earlier editions of this textbook proposed a balanced approach to school counseling based on the principle that both prevention and treatment goals need to be equally addressed. Although this principle remains important, circumstances that evolved since the previous edition was published demand that we also address the three best programmatic paradigms currently available (presented in chapter 2), as well as the relevant CACREP standards, when employing the balanced approach principle. This chapter is devoted to presenting our thoughts on a comprehensive, balanced model for school counseling programs and its potential implications.

The final chapter of the previous edition of this textbook concluded with a section entitled "Beyond the Present: What Does the Future Hold for School Counselors?" Although the publication date for the previous edition was 2004, the contingencies associated with publication lag led to the most recent material therein actually being produced in 2002. In the meantime, the future we presented in 2002 became part of the present. Therefore, the ending of our previous edition becomes part of the presentation of the model we are recommending in the current edition.

BEYOND THE PRESENT: WHAT DOES THE FUTURE HOLD FOR SCHOOL COUNSELORS?

As editors of *The Handbook of Counseling,* Locke, Myers, and Herr (2001) contributed their own chapter on "counseling in the future." Their thoughts were based in part on a review of the material in the 43 chapters from contributors to their handbook, including the authors of this textbook (Baker & Gerler, 2001). Among their concluding comments were the following thoughts:

> Professional counselors will need a broad knowledge base to deliver comprehensive counseling services and also will need specialized knowledge to cope with changes in client conditions. . . . These changes are assumed to affect all areas of the counseling profession. . . . Counselors will be functioning on a more professional level as a result of changes in practice environments and will expect to be treated as colleagues rather than the subordinates of the past. . . . Commonly understood descriptions of what counselors do for clients are essential if counseling is to be recognized as a principal contributor to mental health care. Counselors need to work in collaboration, not competition, with other mental health care providers to increase the effectiveness of the mental health delivery system. (Locke et al., 2001, p. 691)

The focus of the thinking of Locke et al. (2001) is on the broad field of professional counseling. More specific to school counseling, Schmidt (2003) stated that

> Traditional guidance and counseling services will no longer meet the needs of future students and families. School counselors at all levels—elementary, middle, and high school—can be expected to adjust their goals, create expanded services, develop new skills, and serve broader populations in the years to come. To meet these challenges,

future counselors will 1. Develop a broader knowledge of human development throughout the life span. . . . 2. Adapt to new technology. . . . 3. Increase the use of group practices. . . . 4. Expand their professional development. . . . 5. Measure the outcome of their services. . . . 6. Become professionally and perhaps politically active through state and national counseling associations to ensure the integrity of the school counseling profession. (p. 308)

In a special issue of *Professional School Counseling* on the past, present, and future of school counseling, one of us wrote

These are not the comments of a pessimist. I am by nature an optimist. My view of school counseling is probably most appropriately labeled as realistic optimism. . . . As a realistic optimist, I predict that improvements will occur slowly and inconsistently over the decades to come if circumstances remain as they are. . . . Is the glass half full or half empty? For this realistic optimist, it is half full. . . . How does the profession implement these wonderful ideas expeditiously and systematically? In my opinion, this is the question that raises the primary challenge to the school counseling profession at the present time. (Baker, 2001, p. 82)

Other writers contributed to this special issue of *Professional School Counseling* devoted to the future of school counseling. Gysbers (2001) advocated "fully implemented comprehensive guidance and counseling programs in every school district in the United States, serving all students and their parents, staffed by active, involved school counselors" (p. 103). He continued by pointing out that fully implemented comprehensive guidance programs would place school counselors and their programs in the center of education rather than on the periphery. Paisley and McMahon (2001) described the ideal school counselor of the future as one who completed a CACREP accredited program, was familiar with the larger school community, and was committed to lifelong learning. The ideal counselor would "be equally grounded in the three domains of academic, career and personal/social development" (p. 113). Finally, the ideal counselor would demonstrate the areas of competence covered in this textbook. Green and Keys (2001) pointed out that, although the comprehensive developmental model had aligned the profession more closely with the needs of students, there remained the need to address the contextual factors that hinder the promotion of healthy development for those students who have little access to the benefits of a good education.

Note that these presentations address some of the ideas advocated in the three "best paradigms" presented in chapter 2. Gysbers (2001) spoke directly about comprehensive school counseling programs, and Paisley and McMahon (2001) mentioned the importance of counselors being grounded in academic, career, and personal/social development. These ideas are crucial components of the ASCA's National Model for School Counseling Programs (ASCA, 2005). In addition, Green and Keys's (2001) attention to those students who have little access to the benefits of a good education addressed a central theme for both the Education Trust's TSCI and the School–Community Collaboration Model. Further analysis of the Green and Keys (2001) article will indicate that they are strong proponents of the School–Community Collaboration Model.

Critiquing the Predictions

A second issue of *Professional School Counseling* presented reactions to the four presentations just cited. From his position as a school counselor and former president of the ASCA, Kuranz (2002) agreed with the views that promoted comprehensive school counseling programs and stated that "real success requires change . . . to develop and move forward" (p. 178). In her presentation, Whitson (2002) wondered whether the existing comprehensive developmental programs were indeed truly comprehensive—a point similar to that made by Green and Keys (2001). She also pointed out that none of the writers in the first issue had addressed "a significant dearth of research on school counseling" (Whitson, 2002, p. 154). She concluded this theme by suggesting that the future of school counseling may hinge on the profession being able to document evidence of its effectiveness (a.k.a. accountability).

As spokespersons for TSCI, Sears and Granello (2002) expressed concern about inconsistency in language and failure to espouse alternative views in the four articles. They believe school counselors will need additional skills that empower them to be advocates for change, and that this will best occur via significant changes in the preparation of school counselors. Those additional skills will allow school counselors to provide leadership, collaboration, coordination, and advocacy.

After digesting the four articles, Sink (2002) concluded that the school counseling profession had "made significant strides forward and its future is bright" (p. 161). He also discerned from the four articles a theme suggesting that

> the profession cannot simply rest, so to speak, on its laurels; rather, school counselors must actively engage in dialogue with their advocates and detractors, learning what they can about pertinent and effective educational and counseling innovations, and disagreeing respectfully with those notions that depart substantially from the profession's core beliefs and goals. (p. 161)

Applauding the Paradigms

Although clearly not in full agreement, the writers just cited have a passion for the school counseling profession—past, present, and future. Although unable to predict and arbitrarily mold the future, they were trying to influence it in a positive way. Despite their efforts, our concern about how effectively ideas from professional association leaders and counselor educators will influence school counseling programs remained. School counselors and other stakeholders such as administrators, teachers, parents, and communities will clearly influence what happens. Yet, we were very impressed with the efforts of the ASCA National Model for School Counseling Programs, the TSCI of the Education Trust, and the school–community collaboration model.

We applauded what had been accomplished within each initiative thus far and have highlighted their positions throughout the previous edition. Spokespersons for all three initiatives had specified the connections with current educational reform initiatives, and that seemed to be a strategically wise decision. Yet, as Borders (2002) pointed out, many of the goals of these initiatives were important in school counseling before the current reform movement, and "riding the wave of educational reform, however (whatever the reform movement focus of a particular time may be), does subject school counseling to the tides of public opinion and legislative decision making" (p. 183).

Blending the Paradigms

Remembering the influence of the NDEA of 1958, we understand the importance of riding the wave of the current educational reform movement. We also agree with Borders's (2002) point, viewing it as a recommendation to accept the current initiatives as something more than responses to the current educational reform movement. We believe the value of the three initiatives extends well beyond the focus of the current educational reforms and holds promise for strengthening the school counseling profession well into the 21st century. We also believe that the initiatives have promise for achieving grassroots support from school counselors across the land and from their administrators, teachers, students and families, and communities.

Having offered our support for the initiatives individually, we also want to state our belief that together they offer much more than any of them offers alone. The ASCA National Model for School Counseling Programs provides the performance-based ASCA National Standards and advocacy for comprehensive school counseling programs. The emphasis on performance-based comprehensive programs is important because it focuses on school counseling as a program with a curriculum and provides a basis for accountability. In addition, the ASCA linkage with Norman Gysbers and colleagues offers the strength of building on their work across the United States over two decades. These counselor educators and professional counselors know how to build consensus among grassroots school counselor groups and how to negotiate successfully with state departments of education and local school boards. They have already prompted several states to adopt the comprehensive guidance model and several schools to adopt the National Model. They have mastered important networking competencies.

The Education Trust's TSCI provides strength through its focus on upgrading the training of school counselors, especially in the leadership, collaboration, and advocacy domains. The trust has established training prototypes in several counselor education programs. In addition, the initiative has captured the attention of decision makers at the federal level, especially for its focus on school counselors as leaders within the No Child Left Behind reform activities and on making rigorous, high-quality educational opportunities available to all students.

In our opinion, the School–Community Collaboration Model provides the missing piece in this design for the future of school counseling. Although access to the benefits of a good education for all students is a noble cause, some students will not benefit from merely being placed in more rigorous courses of study. We draw on Maslow's (1954) hierarchy of needs to make this point. If the basic needs of students are not met, then they will be unable to respond to enhanced educational opportunities. In recognition of the mental health, physical health, and social service needs of students from impoverished and dysfunctional circumstances, proponents of the School–Community Collaboration Model promote collaborations between school systems and community services systems within and outside the schools. These collaborations will improve the potential for students and their families to receive needed services that will allow the students to attend to the higher-order needs that rigorous academic offerings present, and school counselors are viewed as key players in coordinating such collaborations.

The Importance of Competence

Our position on the future of school counseling thus stated, we closed with a comment about competencies, a subject highlighted throughout the previous edition. We believe the competencies presented in this textbook are generic to any model for school counseling. We also believe these competencies will remain important in the future. Therefore, we encourage all school counseling students and school counselors to be skillful across these competency domains. Whatever the circumstances, competent, flexible school counselors are better positioned to provide high-quality services to their constituencies and make their programs relevant than are those who are inadequately competent and inflexible. This appears to be one important way that each school counselor can have an impact on his or her own future.

GOALS OF A BALANCED APPROACH TO SCHOOL COUNSELING

Here, we specifically state the goals of our balanced approach to professional school counseling. In the remainder of this chapter, we elaborate on the goals, using that information to set the stage for the remainder of the textbook. We believe that school counseling is best viewed as a program within a school system and that professional school counselors should be trained for competence and motivation to achieve the following goals:

- Attend to the affective and cognitive development of all students.
- Be an advocate for all students.
- Be an integral part of the academic mission and total education program of the schools.
- Collaborate with families, other human service providers, and communities.
- Provide both prevention programming and responsive services.
- Conform with applicable laws, regulations, and guidelines, and the appropriate professional ethical standards.
- Achieve accountability.
- Be an advocate for the school counseling profession.

Attend to the Affective and Cognitive Development of All Students

Most school counselors believe that human learning is the product of development in a variety of areas. Carl Rogers, Rudolph Dreikurs, and William Glasser are among the counseling theorists whose writing has helped school counselors and others in education understand that learning involves more than cognitive activity, and that education involves emotional, social, and other factors as well.

The affective domain of human existence encompasses the whole range of human feelings and emotions, including feelings about self, fear, anxiety, joy, and many others. This domain is important in the learning process. No one more clearly spelled out the relationships between emotions and learning than did Brown (1971) in his book

Human Teaching for Human Learning: An Introduction to Confluent Education. He noted that "the relationship between intellect and affect is indestructibly symbiotic . . . it is the passion of the scholar that makes for truly great scholarship" (p. 11). Brown's view about the coming together of the affective and cognitive domains, however, is only one of many attempts at explaining the role of emotions and feelings in learning. The whole notion of affective education, which gained popularity in the late 1960s and early 1970s, reflects the importance with which many educators regard the affective domain.

The most studied and discussed aspect of the affective domain is self-concept (i.e., how students view themselves). Many other affective variables, such as anxiety, motivation, and interest, also influence learning. As is the case with self-concept, the degree to which these factors affect learning is uncertain. Factors of this kind cannot be neglected in the classroom if learning opportunities are to be maximized.

Be an Advocate for All Students

The ASCA National Model (ASCA, 2005) recommends that the majority of a school counselor's time be spent in direct service to all students. Advocates of the TSCI believe that school counselors should position themselves to advocate for equity and entitlement for all students. Proponents of both the TSCI and the School–Community Collaboration Model view school counselors as integral players in removing barriers to academic success of all students.

As advocates, school counselors are committed to helping students achieve their goals. Helping students achieve their goals may require active responses to those conditions that may impede goal achievement (e.g., coordinating community mental health services for students who need them). Advocacy requires a sense of social responsibility (Lee & Sirch, 1994), and suggests collaboration and leadership competencies. We elaborate more on advocacy, collaboration, and leadership in chapters 6 and 7.

Be an Integral Part of the Academic Mission and Total Education Program of the Schools

The ASCA National Model (ASCA, 2005) highlights this goal succinctly, stating that professional school counselors support the academic mission of the schools by "promoting and enhancing the learning process for all students through an integration of academic, career, and personal/social development" (p. 15). Requisite competencies for achieving these objectives include (a) having specialized knowledge in child and adolescent development, (b) coordinating a developmental school counseling program, (c) calling attention to conditions in the schools that prevent academic success, and (d) providing leadership and collaboration in the process of resolving the conditions preventing academic success.

According to Gysbers and Henderson (2000), school counseling becomes part of the total education program when it is viewed as "a program that is an integral part of the educational process with a content base of its own" (p. viii). The ASCA national model is structured to achieve the goals established by the proponents of developmental guidance (a.k.a. developmental school counseling). Ways to achieve this goal are integrated into many of the remaining chapters of this textbook.

Collaborate With Families, Other Human Service Providers, and Communities

The importance of this goal was introduced in the supporting material for the student advocacy and academic mission goals. That is, professional school counselors are uniquely positioned to identify impediments that prevent students from achieving academic success and are also strategically positioned to serve as coordinators of community and human service resources that may help students overcome the impediments (e.g., substance abuse, homelessness, dysfunctional families, poverty). Luongo (2000) pointed to overwhelming evidence indicating that core social institutions (including schools) have a constant need for behavioral health services. He emphasized: "If partnerships at the service delivery level are to make the best use of existing resources, they need to reflect not only collaboration among service institutions and providers, but also an actual integration of basic services" (p. 308). Luongo cited data that indicate a 30% to 40% overlap in services to children by core social institutions. That is, many children, while receiving special services in schools, are also receiving special services in the community. In addition to partnering multiple social institutions, he states that the home must be involved as a "critical partner." Luongo concluded:

> The execution of the function of schools, however, must change . . . schools will take on an even greater collaborative and integrative relationship to other core social institutions. . . . Onsite collaboratives within schools . . . have rapidly spread throughout the country. . . . Schools redefining school counselors as school–community counselors is a critical component. . . professional practice does not end at the school house door. . . . Effective practice requires familiarity and expertise in the workings and methods of other disciplines. (p. 313)

We elaborate more on this in chapters 6, 7, and 10.

Provide Both Prevention Programming and Responsive Services

The ASCA National Model (ASCA, 2005) and the comprehensive guidance paradigm (Gysbers & Henderson, 2000) highlight the importance of a school counseling program founded on proactive planning. Such planning requires (a) goals based on knowledge of basic developmental needs of children and adolescents and academic expectations of schools, (b) measurable objectives for achieving those goals, (c) deliverable programs designed to achieve the goals and objectives, (d) requisite competencies needed to achieve those goals, (e) a place in the school's curriculum to provide the programs, and (f) evaluation of the effects of delivering the programs in order to achieve accountability.

Because the programs are based on knowledge of the developmental needs of children and adolescents, they are preventive in nature. That is, they are designed to prevent recipients from encountering negative experiences such as floundering and indecisiveness in career development, as well as choice and anxiety that prevent achievement of academic success. These programs are developmental and preventative. We agree that prevention programming is an important component of a school counseling program.

Of equal importance is responding to and providing intervention for students who are already experiencing many of the challenges that prevention programming is designed to address. Through student self-referrals, referrals from others, such as teachers and parents, and initiation of contacts by counselors based on observation of documents, school counselors find themselves expected to address the needs of students who are at risk in some way. The list of reasons to be responsive is quite long. A short list, for example, includes divorce, grief, abuse, school phobia, depression, sexuality, and peer relationships. These issues demand reactive rather than proactive programming. School counselors are confronted with these issues and challenged to respond in a helpful way.

A study of the articles published in the *Elementary School Guidance and Counseling* journal (last three volumes), *The School Counselor* (last three volumes), and *Professional School Counseling* (first five volumes) covering the years 1994 to 2002 revealed that out of 537 articles, 40.4% focused on mental health issues (i.e., addressed psychosocial needs of students with primary focus on personal and social functioning). The nature of the data collection did not indicate why articles devoted to mental health issues were more prevalent than those to educational achievement (i.e., preparation of all students for academic success [18.9%] or neither topic [25.1%]). However, one possible explanation the researchers offered was

> That mental health articles reflect the needs and professional development interest of practitioners. Specifically, school counselors continue to express concerns about the increasing level of emotional and behavioral problems evidenced in the students with whom they are working. [They] programmatically need to know how to conduct suicide assessments, make accurate diagnostic assessments, and develop appropriate intervention plans within school settings. (Alexander, Kruczek, Zagelbaum, & Ramirez, 2003, p. 32)

A balanced school counseling program is designed to provide both proactive prevention programming and reactive intervention/responsive/treatment services. The different nature of these two approaches, that is, proactive versus reactive, presents unique challenges. Demands occur for responsive intervention services. They do not have to be planned, developed, and delivered systematically as is the case with prevention programming. Therefore, it is highly likely that many school counselors and school counseling programs are overwhelmed by intervention service demands and find themselves pressed for time to either engage in prevention programming or opt out of it voluntarily. Consequently, many current school counseling programs are not balanced because of an overemphasis on intervention services.

Proponents of the TSCI are especially critical of these circumstances because school counseling programs focusing primarily on intervention services serve only a small percentage of the students in their schools and therefore cannot be advocates for all students. The ASCA National Model and the comprehensive guidance paradigm present well-conceived ideas for changing school counseling programs that are out of balance in favor of intervention. As well, the School–Community Collaboration Model offers a way to achieve balance by using community resources efficiently in response to demands for intervention services. We elaborate more on these two elements of a balanced program in chapters 8 and 9.

Conform With Applicable Laws, Regulations, and Guidelines and the Appropriate Professional Ethical Standards

In chapter 1, we ascribed professional status to school counselors. One of the criteria for ascribing professional status to professions is that they practice a degree of self-control via community sanctions, ethical codes, and the like. Both the ACA and ASCA have had codes of ethics in place for quite some time. Copies of the latest versions of these codes are found in appendices E and F of this textbook. Chapter 5 covers this topic in further detail.

School counselors are employed in positions of public trust. Parents in particular and communities in general entrust counselors and their professional colleagues with the education and care of their children. The general expectations of that trust are that counselors and their colleagues will obey the laws and regulations that relate to their activities and abide by the ethical guidelines of their professions. State departments of education/public instruction establish standards that determine the minimum competencies that counselors and their professional colleagues must meet to be eligible for employment in the schools. The standards usually include expectations that counselors and their professional colleagues be familiar with pertinent legal codes and concepts, governmental regulations, and ethical standards. Therefore, at the level of basic counseling training, school counselors are challenged to become grounded in these important competencies and to adopt the appropriate frame of mind toward legal and ethical responsibilities. "Appropriate frame of mind" means simply that school counselors recognize the responsibilities they have assumed, strive to acquire the requisite knowledge, and endeavor to act responsibly and in good faith. These concerns are important in all facets of a balanced approach to school counseling.

Herlihy and Remley (2001) depicted laws as the "musts" components in our professional behavior. Laws "dictate the minimum standards of behavior that society will tolerate" (p. 71). They depicted ethics as the "shoulds" of our professional behavior. Ethics "represent the ideals or aspirations of the counseling profession" (p. 71).

Achieve Accountability

Achieving accountability is a systematic process that incorporates evaluation of one's programmatic efforts. As presented in this textbook, the words *evaluation* and *accountability* are neither interchangeable nor synonymous. Each represents an important ingredient of the accountability domain, and both functions are important. Each complements the other. *Evaluation* is the act of gathering information about the attributes of one's program; *accountability* is the act of sharing the results of the evaluation. Evaluation precedes accountability. Translating evaluative data into accountability information completes the process and leads to accomplishing the goals of the accountability process.

The ASCA National Model (ASCA, 2005) is especially adamant about the importance of accountability: "The accountability system answers the question: 'How are students different as a result of the program?'" (p. 23). The model emphasizes the importance of evaluating and immediate, intermediate, and long range impacts of school counselor programming and using the information to inform stakeholders and to improve the programs.

Although evaluation and accountability are relatively easy concepts to understand and champion, they require competencies that are especially challenging to master and use successfully. The competencies associated with evaluation and accountability are challenging for most individuals with master's degrees in counseling. With that challenge in mind, chapter 4 on accountability provides recommendations for applying the information presented therein throughout the remaining chapters where appropriate.

Be an Advocate for the School Counseling Profession

Confusion about the role of school counselors was once referred to as an "old ghost" (Shertzer & Stone, 1963). Comments in chapter 2 attributed to contributors to a special issue of *Professional School Counseling* in 2001 (past, present, and future of school counseling) and 2002 (reactions to the first group of articles) indicate that the confusion remains. In many schools, counselors find themselves outside the mainstream, looking inward for direction from various stakeholders such as administrators, teachers, students, parents, and other interested citizens/taxpayers. These stakeholders often send messages to counselors about their roles and the program goals that are deemed important. These messages are sometimes inconsistent with the training counselors received and the standards established by accrediting agencies and professional associations (e.g., expecting counselors to perform clerical and administrative functions and be responsible for disciplining students). To counter these misperceptions and corresponding inappropriate expectations, professional counselors are challenged to advocate for themselves and for balanced school counseling programs both as individuals and collectively through participation in and support of their respective professional associations. We present more on this topic in chapters 6 and 7.

DIRECT AND INDIRECT PROGRAMMING

In most instances, the demands on and expectations of school counselors challenge or exceed their ability to respond in a manner that results in their clientele always receiving desired responses. The somewhat open-ended nature of the school counselor's role and the relatively small size of counseling staffs create settings in which a systematic and careful approach is necessary both for effective programming and for protecting the mental health of the counselors themselves.

This textbook is designed to help counselors become systematic and organized. An important step in that direction is to understand that all programming need not be direct to be effective. Direct programming is provided when counselors interact with the people they are helping; indirect programming is provided when counselors influence or serve third parties such as teachers, parents, and principals, who, in turn, interact with the person being helped. A balanced counseling program may include both direct and indirect programming.

Prevention offers a vehicle for both direct and indirect programming. On the one hand, counselors may offer prevention programs directly by designing the programs and leading the groups. On the other hand, counselors may offer prevention programs indirectly by helping classroom teachers design and/or deliver prevention programs.

Direct and indirect options are available in interventions, too. The traditional one-to-one counseling relationship is a common example of direct intervention: Counselors meet directly with clients to help them in making decisions, resolving problems, changing their behaviors, or changing environmental circumstances. Consultation relationships, in contrast, are indirect interventions. That is, counselors help clients through others who have responsible relationships directly with the clients (e.g., a counselor helps a teacher design and implement a plan for helping a child interact more successfully with classmates).

A careful analysis of the National Model for School Counseling Programs, the TSCI, and the School–Community Collaboration Model indicates that all three advocate a blend of direct and indirect programming. Otherwise, it would be impossible for school counselors to meet the goals of any of the three initiatives.

Realizing the importance of direct and indirect helping leads counselors to more efficient programming than would occur with an overreliance on one type. Balanced programs require balanced counselors who envision a place for both direct and indirect helping in their plans and who possess the competencies to provide both kinds.

BENEFICIARIES OF A BALANCED PROGRAM

School counseling programs exist to help a clientele ranging from kindergarten through senior high school students (K–12). Although not all school systems have K–12 counseling programs, professional counseling associations, the CACREP, and state departments of education/public instruction recognize the importance of continuous, developmental programming and have designed training programs and developed certification criteria accordingly. In balanced, comprehensive programming, K–12 counseling programs will be designed around developmental concepts and organized so all activities are coordinated across administrative levels (elementary, middle, and secondary). Conversely, allowing elementary, middle, and secondary school units to develop their own programs independently may lead to duplicated and disjointed programs, lost opportunities, elitism, and estrangement among counselors in the different units, as well as to negative opinions by parents, teachers, and administrators.

Much has been discovered and written about human development, but there is still much to learn. Generally, writers view human development as a somewhat linear process. For the sake of clarity, categories or stages of development across what is essentially a continuous life span are identified. Age groupings or ranges, often called *stages*, are the most common categories. Scholarly studies reveal common variables shared by those within a particular developmental stage (e.g., physical changes, cognitive changes, societal expectations). Finding that differences exist among individuals within any stage (e.g., adolescence), developmentalists assume that those differences are distributed normally. Thus, characteristics of the average members of a

Edwin R. Gerler, Jr.; photos from Getty Images

A balanced school counseling program benefits all students.

developmental stage are depicted as typical, although experts fully realize that variation occurs within the group. For example, if hypothetically the available data about the height of 12-year-old boys indicate that the average height is 5 feet, boys around that height will be considered normal for 12-year-olds even though some are as short as 4 feet and as tall as 6 feet. Not all 12-year-old boys will be at the average or "normal" height, nor should they be expected to be. The range of heights for 12-year-old boys provides information about the distribution of their heights and indicates that most of them are around 5 feet tall.

Counselors who understand the attributes of developmental stages and the concepts of normality and variability can have a better sense of what to expect of children or adolescents in a particular age group. Powers, Hauser, and Kilner (1989) suggested that individual differences may vary dramatically, not only within a developmental sphere but also across spheres. For example, a child may have average height, above-average intelligence, and below-average social skills, compared with others in his or her age group. Therefore, practitioners are encouraged to assess the performances and experiences of individuals within each developmental sphere, rather than try to impose global developmental expectations.

Erikson's (1963) stages of psychosocial development is one developmental theory with credibility among educators and psychologists, and it is offered as the foundation for several suggestions on how counselors may use developmental theory in their prevention and intervention programming efforts. Figure 3.1 presents a summary of Erikson's developmental stages.

School counselors, when developing prevention programs for secondary school students or intervening with those who are experiencing parental conflicts, may base their programs or interventions on Erikson's principle for the adolescent stage—that is, an individual's need to achieve a separate identity based on understanding both

---

Note. The titles stated as adversarial relationships represent desired general goals for the stages. The first term identifies the positive goal of the stage; the second labels negative outcomes that may occur if individuals fail to achieve the desired positive goal. Such failure may lead to unresolved issues that interfere with healthy ego development.

I. **Trust versus Basic Mistrust (Infancy)**
   The infant learns to trust adults and to be alone at different times.

II. **Autonomy versus Shame and Doubt (Early Childhood)**
   The child begins to assume some responsibility for basic behavior (e.g., bowel control) and gains self-confidence.

III. **Initiative versus Guilt (Late Childhood)**
   The child begins to take initiative, particularly in terms of becoming educated.

IV. **Industry versus Inferiority (Early Adolescence)**
   The individual begins to acquire a basic skill related to achieving economic independence.

V. **Identity versus Role Confusion (Adolescence)**
   The individual must have achieved a separate identity based on an understanding of personal strengths and weaknesses.

VI. **Intimacy versus Isolation (Early Adulthood)**
   The individual begins to reach out to members of the opposite gender and develops close relationships.

VII. **Generativity versus Stagnation (Middle Adulthood)**
   Individuals assume responsibility for others through their contribution to society and their children.

VIII. **Ego Integrity versus Despair (Maturity)**
   Individuals recognize the inevitability of death and gain a sense of quality in their lives.

Figure 3.1
Erikson's stages of psychosocial development.

Source: Data from *Childhood and Society,* 2nd ed., by E. H. Erikson, 1963, New York: Norton. Used with permission.

strengths and weaknesses. Yet, these counselors, although making the best assumption at the outset, are also challenged to be aware that some members of their prevention groups and some clients receiving interventions may be struggling with tasks or expectations associated with earlier Eriksonian stages (e.g., failure to learn basic reading and writing skills from Stage III) or may have achieved identity successfully and be working on challenges associated with the next Eriksonian stage (developing close relationships from Stage VI).

Although a widely respected theory of ego identity development, Erikson's position seems to be more applicable to contemporary White male rather than female development or to the development of persons of color. Josselson (1987) offered an explanation of the identity development of women that seems to reflect contemporary circumstances, the central theme of which is commitment to self in relation, rather than to an independent self. Josselson's position is also restricted—to White, college-age women. Support for Josselson's position is found in Gilligan's (1982) emphasis on interconnections and relationships in the identity development of women. Although not proposing her own developmental stages, Gilligan suggested that women may fuse Erikson's identity (Stage V) and intimacy (Stage VI) stages.

People of color may be dealing with issues related to their racial status that influence their development differently. Helms (1995) believed that people of color in the United States have acquired and internalized racism that may cause them to have to cope with such issues as devaluing their own race, being confused about their racial identity, and learning to embrace their own culture while attempting to achieve a positive racial identity. These issues, coupled with the general issues offered by Erikson's model, indicate that children and youth of color may have additional developmental challenges.

School counselors are challenged to be aware of the values and assumptions that influence development differentially across the various worldviews that are represented in our multicultural society. Failing to do so may lead to what Sue (1992) describes as cultural oppression—that is, imposing one's values on culturally different student clients.

Acknowledging developmental changes and stages while recognizing the existence of individual and worldview differences within stages and across spheres enhances the balanced counseling program concept. In a comprehensive counseling program, counselors work cooperatively across grade levels to provide direct and indirect prevention and intervention programming appropriate for the developmental needs of average students while remaining cognizant of the possibility of developmental and cultural variations among individuals.

SUMMARY

In these three introductory chapters, we presented information about challenges school counselors experience, an historic overview of the profession, and our conception of a comprehensive balanced program. In the remaining chapters, we address and elaborate on the goals presented in this chapter, with an emphasis on the competencies professional school counselors need to achieve the goals. Chapter 4 covers the increasingly important accountability concept.

FEATURED ACTIVITY: GRADUATE STUDENT PERSPECTIVES ON BALANCE IN SCHOOL COUNSELING

In this chapter, we recommend that school counselors adopt a balanced approach to their work that includes the following elements:

1. Attend to the affective and cognitive development of all students.
2. Be an advocate for all students.
3. Be an integral part of the academic mission and total education program of the schools.
4. Collaborate with families, other human services providers, and communities.
5. Provide both prevention programming and treatment services.
6. Conform with applicable laws, regulations, and guidelines and the appropriate professional ethical standards.
7. Achieve accountability.
8. Be an advocate for the school counseling profession.

One of our busy graduate students (who is taking one class per semester toward a master's degree) commented that "balanced equals overwhelmed." And, "I'm not good at all that is included in a balanced approached." She asked, "How in the world can school counselors balance their own professional and personal lives and try to manage a balanced approach to school counseling?"

How would you answer this student's question?

After you read this chapter, go to http://www.genesislight.com/scan21st/tell_us/balance.html and complete the form. With your permission, we will periodically post some of your creative thinking for the world to read.

OTHER SUGGESTED ACTIVITIES

1. Analyze the counselor education program where you are being trained or were trained in terms of its balance between emphases on intervention responses and prevention programming.
2. Discuss the claim that prevention programming and intervention responses are both manifestations of developmental guidance.
3. Establish teams and debate prevention versus intervention goals as dominant themes of your school counseling program.
4. Discuss the relative merits of the goals for school counseling presented in this chapter.
5. Debate the merits of the theme presented in this chapter: School counseling programs should have a *balance* between intervention and prevention.
6. Go to the SCAN Web site (www.scan21st.com) to review online programs for prevention and intervention.

CHAPTER 4

Accountability in School Counseling

Goal: To promote comprehensive evaluation strategies and understandable, informative accountability information.

At school counseling conferences across the United States, we have the opportunity to listen to a variety of case examples that shed light on the challenges that counselors face. Here is an interesting case example on the topic of accountability.

> *I have been at Greenstone High School for 15 years. I have spent most of my time helping kids with taking the right classes and getting our seniors into the right colleges. I have occasionally helped a pregnant girl break the news to her parents and have sometimes helped kids who are drinking too much—or abusing drugs. I've enjoyed my work and have experienced the rewards of being a counselor.*

Yesterday, my principal asked me to justify my job. I asked him what that meant. He said, "How does your work improve our dropout rate and influence the academic success of our students?" He added, "I need you to quantify your contribution to our school." When I reminded him of what I do and told him that I didn't have any numbers, he said, "Get the numbers, Eric. We're living in a new world of education. Numbers are the name of the game."

I'm now sitting here in my office on Saturday afternoon learning how to create an Excel spreadsheet full of numbers that will translate into bar graphs with lots of color. I'm accounting for how many students I've mentored through the college admission process and how many students I've consulted with about getting into appropriate classes. How in the world am I going to show my influence on the dropout rate at our school—which has been steadily increasing. I think I will ask 20 or 30 students to write testimonials about how I have helped them get into college. That's not numbers, but sometimes a few good stories help the cause.

I am so tired of trying to satisfy the higher-ups. Wouldn't it be just as easy to sell insurance? I might even make more money.

I will never forget, however, the time I spent with Marcia's mother last year, helping her cope with Marcia's alcoholism. We got Marcia into treatment, into recovery, and into college. Her mother was so grateful. Marcia has had a great first year in college. I love my job, but how do I translate Marcia's story (and all the others) into a spreadsheet. This is worrisome.

I woke up in the middle of the night (on a Friday night of all things), and here I sit wasting a Saturday on inventing a spreadsheet. How can I show what I do in a spreadsheet? My work just doesn't lend itself to numbers, tables, and graphs.

I'm going home. I've been here for 4 hours—on Saturday. I'll talk with the principal on Monday. I need to convince him that numbers are not appropriate for my work. I've got stories—not numbers.

Professional educators across the United States are being asked to account for what they do. School counselors, in particular, must attend to documenting their value as partners in the community of educators.

INTRODUCTION

Definitions and Standards

One of the goals of a balanced approach to school counseling presented in chapter 3 was to "achieve accountability." When elaborating on this goal, we pointed out that evaluation (i.e., gathering information about the attributes of one's program) and accountability (i.e., sharing the results of the evaluation process) complement each other. Therefore, both topics are covered in this chapter.

We also highlighted the importance of accountability in the ASCA National Model for School Counseling Programs (ASCA, 2005), particularly the concept of being accountable to stakeholders in the same way as are school teachers and

Table 4.1
ASCA School Counselor Performance Standards relevant to accountability.

Standard 8: The PSC collects and analyzes data to guide program direction and emphasis.
    8.1 Data are used to make decisions regarding student choice of classes and special programs.
    8.2 Data are used to make decisions regarding program revisions.
    8.3 Data are analyzed to ensure every student has equity and access to a rigorous academic program.
    8.4 Data are understood and used to establish goals and activities to close the gap.

Standard 9: The PSC monitors the students on a regular basis as they progress in school.
    9.1 Every student's progress is to be monitored.
    9.2 Monitoring systems are appropriate for individual schools.
    9.3 Appropriate interventions for students are developed as needed and progress is monitored.

Standard 11: The PSC develops a results-based evaluation for the program.
    11.1 Data are acquired from the school guidance curriculum and closing the gap activities.
    11.2 Counseling team members and principals are consulted in order to determine how programs are evaluated and results shared.
    11.3 The PSC knows how to collect process, perception, and results data.

Standard 12: The PSC conducts a yearly program audit.
    12.1 The audit determines the degree to which the program is being implemented.
    12.2 Result of the audit are shared with the advisory board.
    12.3 The yearly audit is used to make changes in the program and calendar for the following year.

Note. ASCA = American School Counselor Association, PSC = professional school counselor, closing the gap = closing the achievement gap between students.
Source: Data from *The ASCA National Model: A framework for school counseling programs,* 2nd ed., by American School Counselor Association (ASCA), 2005, Alexandria, VA: Author. Used with permission.

administrators. This data-driven, results-based accountability concept stresses the importance of demonstrating that school counselors share in being held accountable for student academic achievement. Both the ASCA and the CACREP emphasize the importance of evaluation and accountability in their standards. Table 4.1 presents the relevant ASCA Standards for Professional School Counselors (ASCA, 2005) and Table 4.2 the relevant CACREP (2001) Standards. We have presented them in an abbreviated form due to space considerations. The complete text can be found in the previously cited references.

A Pervasive Challenge

We are reminded of the historical importance of accountability in professional school counseling by recent publications written by two venerable scholars in our field, Norman Gysbers (2004) and Robert Myrick (2003). Gysbers's (2004) historical presentation covers "the evolution of accountability from the 1920s to 2003" (p. 10), including summaries of classic studies of the impact of school counseling published in the 1940s and 1950s. Gysbers views accountability as an ongoing challenge: "I believe the topic keeps reappearing because accountability is not a one time phenomenon. Accountability is an ongoing responsibility of the profession at the national, state, and local levels"

Table 4.2
CACREP Standards relative to accountability.

General Entry-Level Standards
Section II: Program Objectives and Curriculum
  K. Curricular Experiences
    1. Professional Identity: Studies provide an understanding of
      g. advocacy programs needed to address barriers to equity and success for students.
    7. Assessment
      c. statistical concepts, including scales of measurement.
      g. strategies for selecting, administering, and implementing assessment and evaluation instruments.
    8. Research and Program Evaluation
      a. the importance of research and opportunities and difficulties in conducting research.
      b. research methods.
      c. use of technology and statistical methods in conducting research and evaluation.
      d. principles, models, and applications of needs assessments, program evaluation, and use of findings to effect program modifications.

Standards for School Counseling Programs
  A. Foundations of School Counseling
    8. Knowledge and understanding of variables that enhance and impede student academic, career, and social development.
  B. Contextual Dimensions of School Counseling
    6. Methods of planning, developing, implementing, monitoring, and evaluating comprehensive developmental counseling programs.
  C. Knowledge and Skill Requirements of School Counselors
    1. Program development, implementation, and evaluation
      a. management analysis; presentation of data from school-based information, surveys, interviews, focus groups, and needs assessments to improve student outcomes.
      b. design, implementation, monitoring, and evaluation of school counseling programs (e.g., ASCA National Standards) including various systems that affect students, schools, and homes.
      c. implementation and evaluation of strategies that meet program goals and objectives.
      d. identify student academic, career, and personal/social competencies and implement processes and activities to help students achieve the competencies.
      e. prepare action plans and school counseling calendars that reflect appropriate commitments and priorities.
      f. strategies for seeking and securing alternative funding for program expansion.
      g. use of technology in design, implementation, monitoring, and evaluation of a school counseling program.

Note. CACREP = Council for the Accreditation of Counseling and Related Educational Programs.
Source: Data from *CACREP Accreditation Manual,* by Council for the Accreditation of Counseling and Related Educational Programs (CACREP), 2001, Alexandria, VA: Author. Used with permission.

(p. 11). His recommendations for professional school counseling are (a) create a mind-set that engaging in activities that demonstrate effectiveness and identifying areas that can be improved is something to be done in schools daily rather than to be avoided, (b) focus on goals and data that are important in school improvement plans, and (c) accept the challenges and respond to them actively.

Although recognizing that accountability is a sign of the times, Myrick (2003) also pointed out that it has been with us for decades. He stressed the importance of designing school counseling programs based on measurable written goals, interventions or activities designed to achieve the goals, and data reporting the results of having implemented the goal-driven procedures and made a difference. Several classic resistance to evaluation themes are recognized as real concerns that need to be addressed: (a) "don't have time," (b) "don't have the knowledge and skills," (c) "accountability is confronting," and (d) "results are difficult to measure." Myrick suggests that the avenue to successful accountability efforts may be to focus on student success, collaborate with others, and begin with a well-designed accountability system.

The Current Scene

Two recent publications appear to have had a significant impact on the current approach to accountability in professional school counseling. They are *The ASCA National Model: A Framework for School Counseling Programs* (ASCA, 2005) and *School Counseling Accountability: A Measure of Student Success* (Stone & Dahir, 2007). The content of these publications supports the basic ideas of the accountability model presented in earlier editions of this textbook while also offering new ideas and a new vocabulary. Viewing these publications as perhaps the most important current work on accountability in professional school counseling, we refer to them considerably both in this chapter and throughout the text.

Accountability and Action Research

Evaluation and *research* are terms that tend to be used separately and interchangeably, depending on the user. Unfortunately, research has too often been associated with recollections by many school counseling program students and graduates of struggling to comprehend and pass required courses in descriptive statistics. In that regard, note Myrick's (2003) "don't have the knowledge and skills" theme presented previously. For many, these are valid feelings of being overwhelmed. If one defines *research* as "forms of inquiry historically associated with scientific method . . . where the purpose is to establish verifiable facts as a basis for explanations of events" (Stringer & Dwyer, 2005, p. 19), then most school counselors are out of their element and rightly experiencing feelings of being overwhelmed. These traditional research paradigms are for professional researchers, investigators, and scholars and need not be considered by professional school counselors in their evaluation and accountability endeavors.

Like the traditional paradigm, practitioner and action research "may be defined as a process of systematic investigation leading to increased understanding of a phenomenon or issue of interest" (Stringer & Dwyer, 2005, p. 3). We believe that both practitioner and action research are appropriate paradigms for professional school counselors, are within their domain of competence, and will get the job done for them in the evaluation/accountability arena. *Practitioner research* occurs when professionals use a variety of methods to obtain objective factual information related to their program delivery interventions, and *action research* is engaging in a collaborative process with stakeholders to solve program delivery challenges (Stringer & Dwyer, 2005). Therefore, data from practitioner research may support the action research process,

When school counselors are the decision-makers themselves, objectivity is of the utmost importance.

and the action research process may identify desired practitioner research projects. The participatory feature of action research focuses on (a) changing and improving practices and behaviors, (b) thinking about and reflecting on practices and behaviors, (c) including all stakeholders, (d) sharing perspectives with others, (e) achieving clarity and understanding of various perspectives, (f) testing new understandings as a basis for constructive changes, and (g) building a community of stakeholders (Stringer & Dwyer, 2005).

Read the following components of the action research paradigm presented by Stringer and Dwyer (2005). Then compare them to the information in this chapter as well as the ideas presented by the ASCA National Model for School Counseling Programs (ASCA, 2005) and Stone and Dahir (2007).

- Define the issue, formulate a research question, plan a systematic inquiry process, and check the ethics and validity of the plan.
- Collect data from all relevant sources.
- Analyze the data according to the research goals.
- Communicate the outcomes to relevant stakeholders.
- Act based on the goals of the research and the goals derived from the data.

INGREDIENTS OF THE EVALUATION/ACCOUNTABILITY FUNCTION

Given the busy environment in which school counselors find themselves, evaluation activities need to be convenient and efficient. Also, given the press of external demands for accountability, supporting data need to be comprehensive, informative, and understandable to stakeholders. Finally, accountability data are most helpful when used constructively.

Convenient and Efficient Evaluation

Accountability activities will be less burdensome and aversive if they fit in with other counseling activities. One important factor to be controlled is the amount of time devoted to evaluation and accountability activities; it would be ridiculously cost inefficient to spend an inordinate amount of time collecting and reporting information about one's own performance. It would also be cost inefficient and demoralizing for counselors to have to engage in antiquated, burdensome, and time-consuming data collecting behaviors. Time can be better managed and convenience enhanced if data collection and reporting are streamlined and systematic.

A second important factor to be controlled is the procedure for collecting data. To avoid demoralization and increase efficiency, the procedures can be made convenient by streamlining the process and using systems that are not overly sophisticated and confusing. The systems and procedures should be commensurate with the training that school counselors at the master's level have received.

Comprehensive Accountability Data

Comprehensiveness is a desirable characteristic of the evaluation/accountability function because the programs provided by school counselors have many facets, and school counselors have a varied set of stakeholders to serve. Therefore, no one approach to evaluation is broad enough to be all encompassing. Indeed, to rely on a narrow repertoire of evaluation approaches is to risk missing important information, underserving one's stakeholders, and being judged unfairly. Following is an inventory of recommended categories of evaluation/accountability data that together represent a comprehensive set of approaches.

We believe that our emphasis on comprehensiveness conforms with the positions taken by the ASCA (2005) and Stone and Dahir (2004). However, we are aware of differences in terminology and of additional important emphases that these two resources provide. A listing of important evaluation/accountability data components taken from these resources and the previous edition of this textbook is presented in Table 4.3. In the next section, we elaborate on important competencies associated with each data component.

Table 4.3
Important evaluation/accountability data components.

Needs assessment data
Process data
Time-on-task data
Perception data
Results-based data
Impact on school improvement/student achievement data

BASIC DATA COMPONENT COMPETENCIES

Not all competencies are perceived to be equally important. The data components presented in Table 4.3 provide data of a different nature than the others. Although each may be deemed important enough to include in statements of standards and training programs, they are not perceived as being equally important by spokespersons for the ASCA National Model (ASCA, 2005) and others in the profession. Traditional evaluation strategies such as time-on-task, process, and needs assessment data are perceived as less important than results-based and student outcome data by Stone and Dahir (2007) because "This traditional practice of counting will not demonstrate to our colleagues and community stakeholders that we are powerful contributors to our schools" (p. 2). Stone and Dahir based their position on the work of Johnson and Johnson (2003) who believe that the best approach to accountability is through results-based program evaluations that emphasize (a) the number of students who demonstrate having learned competencies versus the number of students receiving help (i.e., process data), (b) the amount of time devoted to offering services to students who need help (i.e., time-on-task data), and (c) how students feel about those services (i.e., perception data). Essentially, this position strongly states that without results-based data there is no real accountability for professional school counselors in the present high-stakes educational climate.

Our position in previous editions of this textbook was that time-on-task (a.k.a. enumerative), perception (a.k.a. satisfaction), and results-based (a.k.a. outcome) data each provided different information about school counseling programs, and a comprehensive accountability process needs to include all three components because they complement each other. For example, a counseling program goal may be to help all students use effective communication skills (ASCA National Personal/Social Standard A.2.6). A prevention program is designed to achieve this goal and others. At the end of the program, student performance in a simulated communications skills test provides outcome/results-based data, a record of how much counselor time was involved in planning and delivering the program provides enumerative/time-on-task data, and participant responses to a survey instrument about the program provides satisfaction/perception data. If the evaluators find that the outcome data were favorable, then the results-based accountability goal would have been met, and this is the domain most favored by the ASCA National Model (ASCA, 2005), Johnson and Johnson (2003), and Stone and Dahir (2007). Yet, what if the participants gave the program low satisfaction ratings (e.g., "It was boring" "It took too much time") and the amount of time devoted to preparing and delivering the program was not cost effective? These questions seem to make the results-based stance less compelling than its advocates claim. However, the case they make for results-based accountability is an important one, and we want to give their position full support in this textbook—with reservations about their attitude toward "traditional" accountability strategies. Therefore, our presentation in this chapter includes the accountability components in Table 4.3, and we consider each of them important enough for counselors to acquire the requisite knowledge and skills. This textbook, of course, is introductory and survey in nature and cannot devote sufficient space to the comprehensive training associated with acquiring the required competencies. Comprehensive training is the grist for more domain-specific courses in a training program (e.g., counseling theories and method).

BASIC EVALUATION COMPETENCIES

Needs Assessment Data

Needs Assessment. *Needs assessment* is a common term referring to activities designed to acquire information about consumer needs. Cook (1989) summed up the needs assessment process as identifying those to be assessed, determining a method for reaching them, devising a measuring plan, and interpreting the results to those stakeholders who will make relevant decisions.

Whose Needs Should Be Assessed? Needs assessments are best conducted with a broad brush. It is good to know the expectations and perceived needs of a wide range of potential consumers, including minority and special populations. Knowing the needs of all prospective consumers, however, is not synonymous with guaranteeing delivery to all of them or even with agreeing that their expectations are legitimate. Eventually, school counselors learn that they cannot be all things to all people. Program delivery is best approached from a realistic perspective. Knowledge of the range of expectations and needs allows counselors to make informed decisions about using limited time and resources.

How Should Needs Be Assessed? Needs can be assessed in several ways, some of which are more challenging and time consuming than others. Comprehensiveness is an important guiding principle. Possibilities include the following:

- Publications about child and adolescent development offer suggestions about the common needs that individuals have in various stages of life.
- Key stakeholders in the school and the community can share what they know about the setting. One has to guard against views representing only a particular bias when gathering this kind of information or when receiving unsolicited offerings (Cook, 1989).
- Community forums provide access to groups that have garnered consensus about some needs and expectations. Care must be taken to achieve true representation or to recognize that it has not been achieved (Cook, 1989).
- Stakeholders can be surveyed to learn about their needs and expectations.

A survey is probably the most popular and common approach to assessing needs. It is also probably the most time-consuming, challenging, and expensive approach. The challenge, in addition to time and expense, is in having the requisite skills to design a survey, administer it, and evaluate the results. Fortunately, others have designed and published needs assessment surveys (see Thompson, Loesch, & Seraphine, 2003), and consultants are able to assist in designing and conducting needs assessments or in providing surveys to share.

Needs assessment surveys can take one of two approaches: Ask respondents what their needs are, or offer them a predetermined list of possibilities from which to choose (Cook, 1989). Each approach has advantages and disadvantages. Open-ended surveys may be easier to design. They also allow respondents to state their own thoughts and opinions, volunteering ideas that surveyors using a predetermined list might not think of asking. Results, however, may be more difficult to understand. Respondents are limited to immediate needs and often cannot forecast future needs whose importance they do not realize at the time. Surveys based on predetermined lists often include topics that counselors know are important but that might not have been thought of by naive respondents. These surveys are more difficult and time consuming to develop. Fortunately, once developed, they are easier to interpret than open-ended surveys and can be used repeatedly. They are limited to the range of questions the designers think to ask, however, and the potential range of needs is enormous.

Which Needs Assessment Strategy Should Be Used?

The information presented in the preceding section paints a picture of two incomplete approaches, which may leave the impression that the best approach is to use both the open-ended and predetermined listing methods to get comprehensive coverage of the consumers' needs. Development of surveys representing either approach or a combination begins with goals and objectives. The surveyors then develop survey questions that reflect those goals and objectives. Specifying objectives helps surveyors design questions, open ended or specific, that address the issues. The basic competencies required are stating goals and objectives in measurable terms, designing survey items that measure those objectives appropriately, and conducting surveys scientifically. If these skills were not developed adequately in one's counselor training program, they can be learned through continued education efforts. An alternative is to acquire the consultant services of others who already possess the requisite competencies.

Additionally, those who would employ the needs assessment survey approach must keep in mind the differences in students. Plans for surveying children differ from those for surveying adolescents. Goals and objectives may remain similar, but methods are different. Younger respondents will be less able to answer in writing, for example, and oral responses may be necessary in some cases. Finding that the professional literature did not provide any needs assessment surveys that had useful formats for primary-age children, Kelly and Ferguson (1984) developed their own instrument. The survey was administered orally to a randomly selected sample of children from grades 1 through 5 to determine whether the children understood the questions and could complete the survey in 30 to 40 minutes. Kelly and Ferguson reported engaging in the following steps:

1. Determine what you want to know.
2. Decide on the best approach for acquiring the desired information.
3. Develop survey items, paying attention to language levels.
4. Have the items reviewed by colleagues, change the items as necessary, and then pilot-test them with a sample of children to determine the adequacy.

5. When the items are given orally to young children, the authors recommend
   - Opening with an overview of the survey and its purpose
   - Explaining each item in detail and encouraging discussion to uncover mis-understandings
   - Reviewing the items to allow children to mark the ones they want to learn more about
   - Allowing children to review their answers if time permits to identify incorrect responses

Surveying teachers, parents, and the professional literature, which are indirect needs assessment approaches, may be more productive than direct assessments. An example of what might be learned from teachers is provided by Schmidt (1986). In a survey inviting teachers to rate an elementary school counselor in different performance categories (opinion data), one item asked for additional comments and suggestions. Schmidt learned that some teachers want help in understanding achievement test results and that others have concerns with school record keeping. These needs assessment data serve as reference points when the counselor engages in consulting with teachers who have responded to the survey.

How Will the Results Be Interpreted to Stakeholders? Because the ultimate purpose of assessing consumer needs is to determine the best ways to serve those consumers, stakeholders should be involved in the process at the outset. If this is done, they can become informed of the assessment's intentions and are better able to respond to the results intelligently. Working with stakeholders in this manner helps school counselors know their expectations. Counselors can then plan for those expectations throughout the assessment process. When school counselors are the decision makers themselves, objectivity is of the utmost importance.

Advisory committees may be beneficial in the decision-making process (Fairchild & Seeley, 1995). Said committees, having representation from various publics (e.g., parents, community members, faculty members, students), can provide useful feedback and be helpful in the needs assessment process. Because of their commitment, advisory committee members are likely to become knowledgeable about the program and supportive of its efforts to respond to consumer needs. All this, in turn, has the potential for enhancing public relations.

Johnson and Johnson (2003) value needs assessment as a tool for gathering data that identify the gap between achieved and desired student achievement. From this position, we assumed that, in their opinion, it is important for professional school counselors to possess basic needs assessment competencies.

Process Data

Previous editions of this textbook introduced the term *process data* as that information used to determine effect of one's program delivery efforts. For example, in the prevention program designed to teach communication skills (presented in a previous example), process data would be collected while the training program was under way in order to acquire information about the intermediate effects of the program and formulate the necessary changes. Acquiescing to the newer vocabulary of the ASCA

National Model (ASCA, 2005), we are now referring to process data as *intermediate results-based data*.

The ASCA National Model (ASCA, 2005) presents process data as "what services are provided to students" (p. 16). From this description, we surmised that process data include listings or inventories of the varied services or functions that school counselors provide in their programs. A sample listing of process data for a school counseling program might include the following program services or functions, which are represented in the chapters in this textbook: individual and group counseling, prevention programming, consultation, program evaluation, and referral and coordination. Process data inventories, to be more complete, should include definitions or descriptions of the specific functions or services. The process of listing and defining services or functions will help professional school counselors make their role more clear to stakeholders.

Time-on-Task Data

Counselors inventory their activities to acquire time-on-task data. Enumerating these data usually takes the form of keeping records of how individuals use their time. Targeted behaviors are identified, and their frequency and duration are tallied.

Consider the following simulation. The evaluation stage has two parts:

1. Counselors in a school district make a list of the activities they engage in when carrying out their responsibilities and when trying to achieve program goals. Some activities are general, and some are specific to elementary, middle, and high school levels. This process data (ASCA, 2005).
2. Individual counselors keep records of how often the activities are performed and how much time is devoted to each activity. The time-on-task data are recorded as hours per activity (e.g., for one counselor in 1 week: individual counseling = 5 hours, scheduling = 15 hours).

The accountability stage also has two parts:

1. The hours-per-activity data are then multiplied by the hourly pay rate of the respective counselors to acquire evidence of cost effectiveness. If the hourly pay rate for the counselor is $20, for example, then the amount of money spent on individual counseling services and scheduling is $100 for the 5 hours of counseling and $300 for the 15 hours of scheduling.
2. Stakeholders will have time-on-task data that indicate how much time and money are devoted to each activity, and this information can be used in making cost-effectiveness decisions. The decisions will be based on the goals and priorities of the stakeholders and those they represent.

In the example, the amount of money spent on scheduling is three times that devoted to individual counseling. Determining whether the expenditures of time and money are cost effective is based on a variety of factors important to those making the cost-effectiveness decisions. Following are questions that counselors must answer when establishing a foundation for making cost-effectiveness decisions:

- What is the relative importance of the individual counseling and scheduling functions? (If one is more important than the other, it seems that more time and money should be spent on it.)
- What is being accomplished during the time devoted to each function?
- Is the money spent on each function worth the results being achieved?

Notice that time-on-task data do not provide qualitative information. Data that answer such questions as "How much?" or "How many?" are quantitative and objective; they are not qualitative unless outcome goals have been determined. Therefore, time-on-task data cannot be used to provide qualitative information unless accompanied by results-based data. Using the time-on-task data from this example, results-based data are added to provide an example of the previous point.

Results-based data were reported for each client who received individual counseling and scheduling assistance as follows: In the 5 hours devoted to individual counseling, two students made decisions with which they were satisfied, one received needed support for anxieties associated with enrolling in a new school, and two believed that the counselor understood them well enough to make appointments for follow-up interviews. In the 15 hours devoted to scheduling, 10 schedules were changed as requested, 3 could not be changed as requested but alternatives were determined, and 2 remained unchanged.

The combination of time-on-task and results-based data provides information about how much time is used and what goals are accomplished. The addition of perception data may complete the picture when trying to determine the cost effectiveness of the counselor's activities. In Gibson's (1990) report, teachers ranked individual counseling as the most important activity. Scheduling or administrative duties ranked 10th of 10 activities.

Given all this information, a stakeholder's thoughts might be as follows:

- The amount of time and money devoted to the lowest ranked activity is three times that devoted to the highest ranked activity.
- The results associated with individual counseling seem clearer and more important than those associated with scheduling.
- Therefore, it appears that the counselors' time is not being used in a cost-effective manner.

This is one of many possible responses to the data. However, responses differ, depending on the goals and biases of individual stakeholders.

Perception Data

Knowledge of stakeholder satisfaction comes directly from the stakeholders. Asking for their opinions is a relatively common practice in the business world, where corporations employ experts to determine what customers want and how much they value the services they have received, and in politics where the opinions of prospective voters are highly valued. When school districts evaluate their programs, stakeholder opinions are also a popular source of information. Because formally assessing consumer satisfaction is not a routine counseling function, the process can be onerously time consuming and frustrating, especially if the people involved have little experience and expertise with surveys. School counselors are challenged to know how to identify their stakeholders, what to ask them, and how to acquire the desired information.

Identifying Stakeholders. Who are the consumers of the counselor's services? The authors prefer a broad definition, believing that individuals who are influenced both directly and indirectly should be included. Also, stakeholders with perceptions about the program services, even though they are not students, should be surveyed. Categorically, then, this broad definition of stakeholders includes currently enrolled students, former students, members of the teaching faculty, members of the administration, members of the school board, parents and guardians, and citizens without direct ties with the schools.

Determining What Information Should Be Asked of Stakeholders. A popular saying in the computer sciences is "Garbage in, garbage out." A poorly conceived perception survey generates information that will haunt those who developed it and who depend on that information. The key principles are that surveys must contain questions that elicit relevant information and that items must be constructed and phrased so the desired results are achieved. Accomplishing these goals requires direct involvement of those who can provide the relevant information. They pay close attention to how the items are worded and constructed.

School counselors are most likely to know the relevant information. Therefore, it will be to their advantage to have direct involvement in the construction of perception surveys. Committees can be established to work on developing surveys for specific stakeholders, and representatives of those stakeholder populations can be invited to participate in the survey construction. For example, school counselors working on surveys for teachers and parents may invite representatives of those groups to join their committee.

Item construction requires some sophistication about wording questions so their intent is clear to the readers, they are easy to score objectively, and they generate information that is constructive while not being unwittingly deceptive. Clarity is enhanced by proper grammar, simple sentence structure, jargon-free terminology, and sequencing of items according to a logical system.

Open-ended questions are useful for finding out what is on the respondents' minds. Therefore, a place is included for a limited number of open-ended questions at the close of the survey. (Be sure to leave enough room on the paper for responses.) Used as the primary item strategy for opinion surveys, open-ended questions create problems that mitigate the initial advantage of generating them more quickly than closed-end questions. First, open-ended questions are difficult to score collectively and objectively, presenting surveyors with interpretation, tabulation, and presentation difficulties. Second, such questions limit the range of provided information to that which is in the front of the respondents' minds.

Closed-end questions, although more time consuming to develop, have advantages that make them preferred for use in the bulk of perception surveys. One advantage is that they can be scored objectively. There are several common types of objective scoring systems for perception and attitude surveys, all of which are easy to tabulate and generate information easily understood by professionals and laypeople. For instance, questions that can be answered yes or no can be tabulated so the percentages of affirmative and negative responses are reported. In an example, student responses to the survey item "Do you think that counselors are available to the students?" were Yes = 75%, No = 25%. Another common tactic is to employ a numbers-based rating system. One example is asking respondents to rate the career counseling program on a scale from 1 to 10, with 10 being the most positive. The average of the individual ratings can be reported. For instance, the average rating of the career counseling in the program was 6.76 on a 10-point scale. A simple scoring system is to have respondents check or leave blank items according to predetermined instructions. For example, "Check the activities listed below that you knew existed before you received this survey." The total number of students who checked each activity can be reported, as well as the percentage of all students who completed the questionnaire.

Another advantage to using closed-end questions is that survey constructors can ensure that they have developed items to represent the topics they want to cover. This forces respondents to think about the topics the designers deem important, some of which the respondents would not have known prior to the survey. Also, it is easier to report the results of surveys with closed-end questions. In the previous examples, percentages and totals were cited as tabulating methods that can be used to report the results. These methods and others like them allow perception surveyors to report simply the collective results of surveys given to groups of respondents.

Acquiring Desired Information.   After developing the surveys, the next step is to use them in the field. Decision making focuses on whether to survey the targeted population or to sample it; whether to have the respondents fill in their own answers or to have the questions presented by others who may also have to fill in the answers; whether to mail the surveys, use e-mail to send them, or use another delivery system; and whether to make responding a requirement or a voluntary act. If a survey program is comprehensive, all of these decisions are made. Additional decisions are as follows: When the number of administrators in a school system is small, all will be surveyed; because many adults are in the school district, an arbitrarily determined percentage of them will be surveyed randomly; older children, adolescents, and adults will complete their own survey, but primary-grade teachers will read the questions to their students and fill in the answers for them if necessary; and all administrators will be expected to complete a survey, whereas students and other adults will be allowed to do so voluntarily.

After such decisions have been made, perception surveying skills have to be employed. For instance, respondent anonymity must be protected, appropriate sample sizes determined, and strategies for obtaining adequate responses from mailed surveys developed. Some of these competencies are within the range of professional school counselors and their colleagues, and some may have to be acquired from professional

School counselors are challenged to be competent in translating evaluative data to meaningful accountability information.

literature or from consultants. *Surveys, Polls, and Samples: Practical Procedures* by Parten (1966) is one classic source of information. It includes planning strategies, sampling ideas, survey construction suggestions, procedures for mailing questionnaires, and techniques for tabulating data.

Getting started may seem like a monumental task. Indeed, it is a lot of work; however, most of the work is at the beginning. Once surveys have been designed, they can be used again with necessary modifications. In addition, not all stakeholders need to be surveyed every time, nor do all members of a targeted group need to be surveyed at once. Samples can be selected and surveyed periodically according to a predetermined schedule. Therefore, getting started represents a major time commitment, one that must be made if there is a desire or a need to acquire meaningful perception data.

Results-Based Data

Results-based data focus on outcomes from programs and interventions. A basic result-based question is "What was the impact of the program or intervention on the participants?" Four important stages for collecting results-based data are available to evaluators. They are (a) preprogram presentation data (Answers the question: What knowledge, skills, or attitudes exist among the participants at the outset of the program?); intermediate data (Answers the question: How well is the program doing as it progresses, and what may need to be changed?); (b) immediate data (Answers the question: What are the effects at the end of the program?); and long-range data (Answers the question: How well have the effects held over time?). An important basic ingredient of results-based data is formulating goals/objectives for programs and interventions that can be measured to determine whether the desired outcomes were realized. For example, ASCA National Standards A.1.5 and A.1.6 state that students will learn to make decisions and set goals. The minimum outcome to be assessed for a program designed to achieve these objectives would need to include procedures for determining how many participants acquired the competence at the intermediate re-sults-based stage. Long-range results would be even more convincing. Preprogram data would help the evaluators learn how much change may have occurred during the program, and intermediate data would provide helpful data during the program de-livery process.

Determining Outcome Goals and Objectives.

For the sake of simplicity, the word *goals* is used in the remainder of this chapter as a global term representing goals and objectives. We do this because of the tendency for the terms to be used dif-ferently in the professional literature. Determining what outcome data to collect and how to collect them depends on the goals one is trying to achieve. Therefore, the collection and reporting of outcome data depend on the identification of outcome goals. Sometimes the goals and the means of assessing them are clear. On other oc-casions, the goals may be clear but the means of assessing them are difficult to iden-tify. At still other times, both the goals and the means of assessing them are difficult to discern. Two important skills emerge. School counselors are challenged, first, to be able to identify goals for their professional endeavors that can be assessed objec-tively and, second, to identify outcomes that measure whether those goals were achieved.

Often, counselors engage in activities for which the goals are implied or deter-mined by others. In responding to the demands for such activities, counselors find themselves proceeding without fully realizing the underlying goals. Instead, they sim-ply do what they are expected to do. For example, many secondary school counselors find themselves involved in the gatekeeping and clerical chores associated with sched-uling, such as determining whether students should be allowed to make schedule changes, recording the changes, and monitoring the master schedule. On the surface, the goals appear to have been imposed by the school's administration. Indeed, some implied administrative goals are measurable: Is the system running smoothly? Has everyone who desired services been served? Is the paperwork in order? Are the class sizes balanced? Additionally, each student who seeks scheduling-related counseling services has his or her own goals. In these individual cases, counselors and clients can determine goals cooperatively, providing counselors with a foundation for determining the outcomes for which to strive.

On some occasions, counselors can set goals in advance of their activities. For ex-ample, an elementary school counselor planned a primary prevention program that was to be delivered in selected classrooms by basing the activity on predetermined goals. On still other occasions, counselors set goals after engaging in activities. This is often the case when counselors engage in individual counseling. Goal setting usually follows time spent exploring and clarifying the presentation of issues and feelings with student clients.

The underlying principle here is that goals exist for all programs and interventions that counselors render. Some are predetermined by clients, administrators, and teachers. Some are determined by counselors. Others are negotiated. Realizing that all their ac-tivities are goal directed is the first step counselors can take to understand how to assess the final effects of their efforts. The next step is actively interpreting these goals as desired outcomes of their programs. For example, a middle school student was miserable because her friends were shunning her. She did not know what to do. The goal was to help her determine a plan of action. The outcome was a workable plan. Once counselors make the identification of goals a conscious behavior, they are in a position to consider methods for assessing outcomes. Perhaps another way to state this belief in the importance of goals is to put it in terms of job satisfaction. A clear understanding of goals will lead to a clear job description, whereas a lack of goals or unclear goals will, in turn, lead to an unclear job description.

Assessing Results.   Having mastered the art of identifying goals and translating them into results, counselors then need results-based measures. Although not limitless, the universe of possible outcome measures is large and impossible to inventory in this textbook. Essentially, the desired results dictate the measures to be used in assessing those outcomes. For example, in the cases cited previously in which counselors helped students make decisions about their schedules, whether a decision was made is an example of results-based data for one client. In the case of the middle school student who was being shunned, whether a plan for responding was developed would be results data. Whether the plan worked successfully would be results-based data for another goal—to carry out the plan. In such cases, the results data are unique to one student client and do not lend themselves to summarizing and categorizing across student clients.

In the situation of the elementary school counselor planning a prevention program with goals determined in advance, means for measuring the results can also be planned in advance, allowing the counselor to choose one or more measures to be given at strategic times during the program. For example, if the purpose of the program is to make children aware of nontraditional careers, the counselor might present an inventory of pictures or titles of careers to participants at the outset to determine how many of the nontraditional careers presented in the inventory are familiar to them. The same inventory can be given at the close of the program to determine how much was learned. The same inventory can also be presented to students not in the program at the same time to compare results and to rule out reasons other than the program for changes in participants' performances. If changes in the program participants are greater than changes in nonparticipants, then the results-based data are evidence of program effectiveness. Another measure the counselor can use in the same manner is to assess whether the attitudes of participants toward the nontraditional careers become more favorable after the program.

Impact on School Improvement/Student Achievement Data

An important contribution of the approach to accountability advocated by the ASCA National Model for School Counseling Programs (ASCA, 2005), Johnson and Johnson (2003), and Stone and Dahir (2007) is their focus on reporting direct benefits to students. More specifically, these advocates for results-based accountability believe that professional school counselors must demonstrate to stakeholders that they are equal participants with teachers and principals in the school improvement process and in closing the gap between academically successful and unsuccessful students. The latter goal (i.e., closing the gap) is a primary theme of the TSCI. The recommended behaviors through which professional school counselors participate in the school improvement process should lead to their being perceived as advocates, leaders, and collaborators—also TSCI goals.

Stone and Dahir (2007) provided detailed recommendations for collecting school improvement/school achievement data that are presented in an abbreviated format in this textbook. They introduce a six-step process for collecting evaluation data and achieving accountability that is identified by the acronym MEASURE. MEASURE provides a process for organizing one's efforts, targeting critical data elements, and reporting results. The MEASURE process is a valid manifestation of the action research model presented previously in this chapter.

Step 1: Mission (M).
The mission is to align the school counselor's role with the school's mission and objectives of the annual school improvement plan. Stone and Dahir (2007) offered a sample school mission statement: "To promote the conditions necessary so that each student experiences academic success. Each student will have the coursework required to choose from a wide array of options after high school" (p. 23).

Steps 2 and 3: Element (E) and Analyze (A).
School counselors are directed to identify and examine critical elements of available data that are important to the school's mission. These data should be found in the school district or building report card and are usually stored in a retrievable format. An important skill for school counselors to acquire for this process is the ability to *disaggregate* data. School districts collect and report student achievement data about attendance, promotion rates, number of suspensions, graduation rates, postsecondary attendance, and standardized testing results. School counselors are encouraged to collect these *aggregated data* and separate (i.e., disaggregate) them according to important *equity variables* such as ethnicity, gender, socioeconomic status, and teacher assignment. Each equity variable has the potential to become an element in the school counseling program's accountability efforts. At this stage, decision making is based on analyzing the data and determining which indicators (i.e., elements) of school success the school counselors believe that they can have an impact on. Stone and Dahir (2004) provided an example:

> The data revealed (among other important things) that of 50% of your students seeking post secondary education, the majority (34%) came from one particular feeder school where all students were assigned to algebra classes in eighth grade and were supported with mentors and tutors so they would be successful. This feeder middle school placed every student in algebra, a positive practice that could be replicated by other feeder schools. (p. 25)

Step 4: Stakeholders (S) and Unite (U).
At this point, school counselors are encouraged to "identify stakeholders to help and unite to develop an action plan" (Stone & Dahir, 2007, p. 25). This process places school counselors in *leadership* roles because they attempt to identify stakeholders to be involved in teamed efforts

to address selected data elements derived from the disaggregation of school achievement reports and develop action plans. *Collaborating* with others, rather than working in isolation, is advocated. Prospective stakeholders may reside in the schools (e.g., administrators and teachers) or in the community (e.g., parents and business representatives).

Step 5: Results (R).   A reanalysis helps determine whether the goals were met. Reanalysis data can be used to reflect on what worked and what needs to be improved and to determine what goals and activities need to be revised. Stone and Dahir (2007) recommended that, if targeted results are met, set new targets, add new strategies, and replicate what was successful. If the targeted results are not met, make changes to remain focused on student success. Either revise or cancel unsuccessful programs in order to be cost efficient.

Step 6: Educate (E).   This is a vital step in the accountability process. Stone and Dahir (2007) recommended that school counselors disseminate data about changes in the targeted elements to both internal and external stakeholders so they can see the positive impact the school counseling program is having on student success. A MEASURE report card can be used to depict the accomplishments. See appendix D for an example of the report card.

BASIC COMPETENCIES FOR SHARING EVALUATION DATA AND ACHIEVING ACCOUNTABILITY

Presenting Evaluation Data Successfully

The act of collecting evaluative information, although important, is not sufficient in itself. Evaluative information must be shared with others in a manner that leads to understanding. Making evaluative data understandable and informative is primarily the responsibility of school counselors. Therefore, they must be competent in translating evaluative data into meaningful accountability information. This means that school counselors must be able to implement understandable and informative data reporting systems.

Some data reporting systems have been described in the professional counseling literature, and many other adequate systems remain to be developed by creative minds. Although reporting systems differ, they share some basic principles that make them understandable and informative:

- The information is summarized and organized systematically.
- The presentation is clear, concise, and understandable to stakeholders.
- Reports are as brief as possible without omitting valuable information.

A Classic Presentation System.   A classic accountability system that seems to meet these criteria was developed by Krumboltz (1974). Krumboltz's system emphasizes the importance of (a) using agreed-on general counseling goals, (b) measuring outcomes in terms of observable behaviors, (c) stating counseling activities in terms of cost effectiveness rather than activities accomplished, (d) focusing reports on the promotion of effectiveness and self-improvement, (e) recognizing that not every effort is successful but that something positive can be derived from failure, (f) including all users in the designing of accountability systems, and (g) being willing to evaluate and modify systems once they are in place.

When implementing a Krumboltz-style accountability system, users begin by determining general goals for their counseling services—for example, by helping students develop more adaptive and constructive behavior patterns. Next, counselors estimate their hourly pay rate as concisely as possible (e.g., $14.00/hr in the Krumboltz example). As shown in Table 4.4, categories and subcategories organize and present data in the Krumboltz system.

Each general goal is a main category, and two subgoals are established under each main goal. The subgoals are Accomplishment (results-based data) and Cost

Table 4.4
A sample of Krumboltz's suggested accountability plan.

Problem Identification	Accomplishment		Cost		
	Method	Results	Activity	Hours	Dollars
Olive's mother phones: Olive depressed, talking vaguely of suicide, no friends	Analysis of social reinforcers for Olive; social skill training; assigned Olive to help new transfer student	Olive increased frequency of initiating social contacts from 0/month to 4/month; reports having 1 good friend vs. 0; mother reports Olive's depression gone— suicide talk from 1/month before referral to 0/month for 3 consecutive months	Conferences with Olive	38	532
			Conferences with mother	3	42
			Conferences with teachers	2	28
					602
Student X came to me worried about his dependence on mood drugs; requested anonymity	Discussions to find other satisfactions, ways of getting his gang to change	Temporary progress in reducing frequency of drug use offset by relapse each time	Conferences with Student X	25	350
			Conferences with physician	0.5	7
					357

Source: From "An Accountability Model for Counselors" by J. D. Krumboltz, 1974, *Personnel and Guidance Journal, 52,* pp. 639–646. Copyright 1974 by American Counseling Association.

(cost-effectiveness, time-on-task data), which are further divided as shown. Information in the Accomplishment category can take various forms:

- Details about each problem, case, or cluster of like functions, such as specific treatment cases, similar intervention cases, specific prevention programs, and similar prevention programs; identifying names can be replaced with codes that make individuals anonymous
- Brief descriptions of methods, tactics, or strategies used
- Results-based data

The Krumboltz (1974) proposal includes both results-based and time-on-task data and is devoid of perception data. Fortunately, the model is open to reporting perception data. When collected, perception data can be reported in the results-based column. For example, client/student perceptions about the counseling interventions and prevention programs can be collected via surveys. Perception data can also be reported in the outcome column in instances when the general goal and specific problems are designed specifically to address perception data collecting. For example, the general goal might be to learn the perceptions of all stakeholders about the school counseling program, and the specific problems might include measuring the perceptions of current students, teachers, administrators, former students, and parents.

The Krumboltz idea appears to be user friendly while also being compatible with results-based, perception, and time-on-task data reporting. Therefore, it can be used to present comprehensive accountability data that are understandable and informative. It represents a good starting point from which school counselors can depart to additional ideas that seem useful and important.

MEASURE of Success. As presented previously, the last step in Stone and Dahir's (2007) MEASURE system is effectively publicizing the results of the evaluation data for the school counseling program. To help school counselors educate others, they developed a model accountability report card (MEASURE of Success). A sample MEASURE of Success is presented in appendix D. Key components of the document include principal comments, school improvement issues (mission), stakeholders, systematic change, results, and faces behind the data (i.e., anecdotes). This system appears especially useful to those who decide to focus on school improvement/school achievement data.

Stone and Dahir (2007) presented a set of actual MEASUREs of Success that were completed by school counselors in Florida, Indiana, Kentucky, New Jersey, New York, Oregon, and Rhode Island. These completed documents serve as evidence that the system has advocates, is useful, and is perceived as succeeding.

The ASCA Accountability System. The ASCA (2005) also provides formats that can help school counselors present their accountability information, especially if they have adopted the ASCA National Model and are engaged in collecting results-based data and impact on student improvement/achievement data. *Results reports* were designed to provide information about student results data over time. The reports are based on the components of *action plans*. Elements of an action plan are as follows.

- Grade level of students (target groups)
- Content of the delivery program
- ASCA domain/standard (if applicable)
- Identification of program delivery materials
- Projected start and end dates
- Projected number of students affected
- Where the program will be delivered
- A listing of the planned evaluation methods
- Name of contact person

The proposed results report contains information from the action plan such as contact person, target group, materials, content of delivery program, and start and end dates. Process (number of students affected), perception, and results-based data are provided in the report, as well as comments about the implications of the data. An example of the ASCA results report is found in appendix E.

A Portfolio Approach.   Portfolios containing collections of a variety of products that display evidence of one's accomplishments over time can be used by counselors in assembling and storing their evaluation/accountability data (Rhyne-Winkler & Wooten, 1996). The professional literature contains suggestions about what might be included in a portfolio and how it might be constructed. Counselors are free to choose their own approaches should they decide that keeping portfolios is advantageous. Rhyne-Winkler and Wooten offered a comprehensive inventory of recommended components, which included (a) introductory information (e.g., title page, table of contents), (b) program planning materials (e.g., needs assessment findings, time management data), and (c) service/program delivery information (e.g., assessments of individuals; group counseling activities; consulting activities; documentation of coordination, appraisal, and professional activities). Portfolios provide the advantage of being able to store samples of one's accomplishments for presentation when accountability data are requested or when one wants to share the materials with interested parties. Portfolios may be the appropriate way to find and present MEASURE of Success and results reports, especially if they are numerous and supporting data need to be attached to them.

The National Center for School Counselor Outcome Research

http:www.umass.edu/schoolcounseling/.   This Web site appears to be a useful evaluation/accountability tool for school counselors. Among the highlights of the center's offerings are a free software program (EZ Analyze) to help school counselors analyze data, surveys that can be used to assess school program implementation and stakeholder perceptions (e.g., administrators, parents, teachers, counselors, students), school counseling outcome research briefs dating back to 2003 with an option to join the research brief listserv, and information about yearly summer institutes. The mission of the center is to "improve the practice of school counseling by developing the research base that is necessary for responsible and effective practice." We recommend that all readers locate and browse this Web site.

An Alternative: External Reviews.

Schmidt's (1995) recommendation, based on the belief that individual school counselors will seldom design and implement program evaluations despite efforts to assist them, is to employ external reviewers. Advantages of this approach include reduced time for counselors to devote to evaluation/accountability tasks and less demand for counselor expertise in this domain. Schmidt describes two evaluations conducted by external reviewers, one in a comprehensive school system and the other in a more rural school district. The reviewers' responsibilities included on-site visits by a team of consultants and preparation of opinion surveys for students, parents, and teachers. On-site visits consisted of structured interviews of principals, counselors, groups of teachers, the superintendent, and selected central staff personnel.

Schmidt's (1995) report of the evaluations indicates that the external reviews uncovered areas that needed to be improved in both school systems. Evidence that external reviews can be informative and helpful is provided in the report.

Accountability as a Means of Enhancing Public Relations

The evaluation/accountability process provides school counselors with ample opportunities to influence public relations. Of the programs offered by the schools, counseling is usually less well understood by the public than teaching and administering. Consequently, misinformation and misperceptions about the counseling program are more likely to occur. This circumstance challenges school counselors to inform the various stakeholders about their goals, programs, and accomplishments. Notice the assumption that programs with goals are in place before public relations activities are undertaken. Failure to do so entertains the risk of advertising one's shortcomings in advance of attempting to recognize and correct them if they exist.

Strategies for influencing public opinion are numerous. For example, *advisory committees* consisting of cross sections of people from one's school and community provide important feedback for counseling programs and educate these influential members about the intricacies of the program (Fairchild & Seeley, 1995). Another strategy is to hold *accountability conferences* with one's administrators. Such conferences encourage administrators to be actively involved in the accountability process, keep them informed, encourage them to be allies, and enlist their support (Fairchild & Seeley, 1995). Another promising strategy is to prepare a *formal written report* that brings the program's accountability data together into one document that, in turn, can be shared with one's stakeholders. Fairchild and Seeley recommended that, once the report has been prepared and disseminated, a school board presentation and presentations to the teaching faculty be requested. Both meetings provide opportunities to inform important stakeholders and to correct misinformation that has occurred. Fairchild and Seeley cited other opportunities to enhance public relations that can be undertaken as well, including speaking to parent groups, civic organizations, and classrooms of students. Such meetings can focus on accountability data and can be used to share the expertise of the counseling staff through accurate, helpful information-sharing or town meeting formats. Clearly, systematic public relations activities have an important place in the accountability function, and the evaluation data collected by counselors can be the centerpiece of public relations efforts.

Accountability as an Ethical Responsibility

Both the ACA (2005) and ASCA (2004) codes of ethical standards specifically address evaluation and accountability. As a transition from this chapter to the next, which focuses on legal and ethical considerations in professional school counseling, we present an overview of the relevant ethical standards from both codes in Tables 4.5 and 4.6. The standards are presented in full in appendices F and G.

Table 4.5
ACA (2005) ethical standards applicable to evaluation/accountability.

C. Professional Responsibility
C.2.d. Monitor Effectiveness
E. Evaluation, Assessment, and Interpretation
E.1.a. Assessment
E.2.c. Decisions Based on Results
E.3. Informed Consent to Clients
E.3.a. Explanation to Clients
E.3.b. Recipients of Results
E.4. Release of Information to Qualified Professionals
G. Research and Publication
G.1. Research Responsibilities
G.1.a. Use of Human Research Participants
G.2. Rights of Research Participants
G.2.a. Informed Consent in Research
G.2.b. Deception
G.2.c. Student/Supervisee Participation
G.2.d. Client Participation
G.2.e. Confidentiality of Information
G.2.f. Persons Not Capable of Giving Informed Consent
G.2.g. Commitments to Participants
G.2.h. Explanations After Data Collection
G.4. Reporting Results
G.4.a. Accurate Results
G.4.b. Obligation to Report Unfavorable Results
G.4.d. Identity of Participants

Note. ACA = American Counseling Association. Complete text in appendix F.
Source: Data from *ACA Code of Ethics,* by American Counseling Association (ACA), 2005, Alexandria, VA: Author. Used with permission.

Table 4.6
A SCA (2004) ethical standards applicable to evaluation/accountability.

A.9. Evaluation, Assessment, and Interpretation

The professional school counselor:

A.9.a. Adheres to all professional standards regarding selecting, administering, and interpreting assessment measures and only utilizes assessment measures that are within the scope of practice of school counselors.

A.9.d. Provides interpretation of nature, purposes, result and potential impact of assessment/evaluation measures in language the student(s) can understand.

A.9.e. Monitors the use of assessment results and interpretations, and takes reasonable steps to prevent others from misusing information.

A.9.f. Uses caution when utilizing assessment techniques, making evaluations and interpreting the performance of populations not represented in the norm group or on which an instrument is standardized.

A.9.g. Assesses the effectiveness of his/her program in having an impact on students' academic, career, and personal/social development through accountability measures especially examining efforts to close achievement, opportunity, and attainment gaps.

C. Responsibilities to Colleagues and Professional Associations

C. 2. Sharing Information With Other Professionals

The professional school counselor:

C.2.b. Provides professional personnel with accurate, objective, concise and meaningful data necessary to adequately evaluate, counsel and assist the student.

D. Responsibilities to the School and Community

D.1. Responsibilities to the School

The professional school counselor:

D.1.c. Is knowledgeable and supportive of the school's mission and connects his/her program to the school's mission.

D.1.g. Assists in developing . . . (3) a systematic evaluation process for comprehensive, developmental, standards-based school counseling programs, services and personnel. The school counselor is guided by the findings of the evaluation data in planning programs and services.

E. Responsibilities to Self

E.1. Professional Competence

The professional school counselor:

E.1.b. Monitors personal well-being and effectiveness and does not participate in any activity that may lead to inadequate professional services or harm to a student.

F. Responsibilities to the Profession

F.1. Professionalism

The professional school counselor:

F.1.c. Conducts appropriate research and reports findings in a manner consistent with acceptable educational and psychological research practices. The counselor advocates for the protection of the individual student's identity when using data for research or program planning.

Note. ASCA = American School Counselor Association. Complete text in appendix G.

Source: Data from *Ethical Standards for School Counselors,* by American School Counselor Association (ASCA), 2004, Alexandria, VA: Author. Used with permission.

CASE STUDIES

A School District Implements the ASCA National Model for School Counseling Programs

The school counseling program in the Wake County, North Carolina Public School System (WCPSS) adopted the ASCA National Model (ASCA, 2005) to align their program with the county's school improvement plan and promote the academic, career, and personal/social development of all students. In so doing, they present accomplishments in terms of outcomes such as reducing failure rates, increasing Preliminary Scholastic Aptitude Test participation, increasing the number of African Americans who take advanced placement examinations, and receiving high approval rates from students. Readers are invited to view the content of the program at (http://www.genesislight.com/scan21st/model.pdf). Highlights of the report include a rationale for implementation, an action plan for future goals, a definition of the counselor's role, new goals for accountability, an introduction to the ASCA National Model for School Counseling Programs, specific goals and objectives, a plan for individual school counselor participation, and a recognition plan for school counselors. The overall goal is to have 10% of the WCPSS's schools become Recognized ASCA Model Programs schools by 2005.

Protecting a School Counseling Program

Hughes and James (2001) related the case of an elementary school counselor challenged by the decision of the school's site-based decision-making council to increase her classroom guidance time to more than the existing 50%. The reason for the council's decision was to provide more planning time for teachers. More planning time was needed because budget cuts in other areas had reduced collaborative planning time. The school counselor had 5 years of experience and was admittedly deficient in record-keeping, organizational, and accountability procedures. Her goal became explaining the school counselor's various roles and the total value of the school counseling program. She began with data for the previous year (evaluation) and considered ways to present it (accountability).

The counselor sought and received consulting assistance from a counselor educator and the professional literature on program accountability. The counselor decided to focus on time-on-task data to help the site-based council members understand how she used her time and how her time use compared to a national study on counselor time usage. She presented the information graphically, and the council members realized how their decision would reduce the amount of time she would have for individual counseling, group counseling, consultation, and coordination.

The school counselor supported her time-on-task data presentation with a packet of information that included a mission statement, documentation of the grade levels served and topics covered in her prevention programming curriculum, her job description, and the state's professional standards for school counselors. The presentation generated constructive discussion leading to more informed decision making. The outcome was a victory for the status quo, with the council agreeing to find alternative ways to provide teachers with more planning time. For the counselor, this was a preliminary step in a process for which the goal was to further improve her time use so as to serve students better.

In this case, the school counselor benefited from a helpful consultant; useful entries in the professional literature; an open-minded, site-based, decision-making council; support from her principal; and her own willingness to do the work needed to achieve her goals. Note that she was admittedly unprepared at the outset and had to respond reactively rather than proactively. Consequently, it is not surprising that she made the following recommendations to school counselors: (a) keep a collection of references from the professional school counseling literature handy, (b) adopt a personal school counseling model or set of standards, (c) record time spent on each school counseling activity (time-on-task data), and (d) save documents that will inform others about the goals and services of one's school counseling program.

The heroine in this case study was able to accomplish her goals with time-on-task data. Others may need more comprehensive data to accomplish their goals. It is useful to know that accountability goals can be achieved with relatively simple sets of data if they are on target and presented successfully. Also enlightening was her willingness to seek and use the help of consultants and the professional literature as well as her ability to respond to the challenge intellectually—figuring out what needed to be done and how it might be done. Finally, she was willing to admit competency deficits and do something constructive about it, especially learning how and preparing to present her accountability data in a manner that was convincing. Readers should view her as a coping model and learn from her vicariously. She is *any counselor*, an effective model for all school counselors!

FEATURED ACTIVITY: GRADUATE STUDENT PERSPECTIVES ON ACCOUNTABILITY IN SCHOOL COUNSELING

In this chapter, we discuss the need for counselors to evaluate the services they provide as part of their school counseling programs. When elaborating on this need, we point out that evaluation (i.e., gathering information about the attributes of school counseling programs) and accountability (i.e., sharing the results of the evaluation process) complement each other.

When preparing our graduate students to be accountable school counselors, we sometimes hear negative comments such as

> *"I hate statistics, and I'm not good at statistics. What am I to do?"*
> *"Good anecdotes and stories do more to sell a counseling program than statistics."*
> *"The only reason we have to evaluate our work is to satisfy politicians."*
> *"Too much attention to outcomes stifles imagination and creativity!"*

How would you respond to these student comments?

After you read this chapter, go to http://www.genesislight.com/scan21st/ tell_us/ accountability.html and complete the form. With your permission, we will periodically post some of your creative thinking for the world to read.

OTHER SUGGESTED ACTIVITIES

1. Discuss the contention that many school counselors reject accountability activities because of the type of people they are.
2. Analyze the position of evaluation and accountability in the ACA and ASCA ethical standards.
3. Discuss whether there are suitable alternative definitions of the terms *evaluation* and *accountability* to those used in this chapter.

4. Evaluate carefully and in detail the suggestions in this chapter for collecting evaluation data and reporting them for accountability purposes. Do you think the ideas are as good as the authors seem to think they are? Explain your position.
5. Evaluate the WCPSS accountability presentation at http://www.genesislight.com/scan21st/model.pdf.
6. Develop samples of measurable results-based goals and useful perception survey items.
7. Make an inventory of important time-on-task data items across the various functions in a school counseling program.
8. Investigate the feasibility of using commercial computer programs to record and store evaluation data and to organize these data for accountability purposes successfully.
9. Debate the advantages and disadvantages of using accountability data for public relations purposes.
10. Debate the merits of employing external reviewers versus doing one's own evaluation and accountability activities.
11. Go to the SCAN Web site (www.scan21st.com) and propose some ways that this site might help school counselors document and present their professional effectiveness.

CHAPTER 5

Legal and Ethical Responsibilities in School Counseling

Goal: To establish the importance of legal codes and ethical standards in school counseling.

The founder of a college admissions firm recently asked a local high school counselor to work as a consultant with his firm. The firm specializes in helping high school students gain admission to college—and offers programs such as preparing for the Scholastic Achievement Test, finding scholarship money, completing college admission forms, and various other programs related to college admissions. The firm is profitable and is growing rapidly. Its Web site is appealing and attracts a lot of traffic. The firm uses its substantial advertising budget for ads in newspapers and for brief spots on regional radio and television stations. The founder has big dreams for his firm, and in his invitation to the school counselor, he intimated that she could eventually earn a much better living in this business than in the school system.

The school counselor was intrigued by the offer and scheduled a meeting with the firm's founder. The meeting was cordial and to the point. The school counselor's role in the firm was primarily to help in designing orientation programs for parents and students. The school counselor was excited about this opportunity and agreed, during the meeting, to accept a consulting position with the firm. The position offered a generous compensation package that was also attractive to the counselor.

Toward the end of the meeting, the firm's founder suggested to the school counselor that she make other counselors—as well as teachers, parents, and students—aware of her new role with the firm and about the programs that she would be helping to design. After leaving the meeting, the school counselor began to have second thoughts.

What should school counselors do in situations such as this one? What legal and ethical challenges do counselors face regularly as part of their professional lives?

THE IMPORTANCE OF LEGAL AND ETHICAL RESPONSIBILITIES IN BALANCED SCHOOL COUNSELING PROGRAMS

The responsibility for acting in an ethical, law-abiding manner permeates the competencies in a balanced program. That is, school counselors are governed by legal and ethical responsibilities in their roles and functions. The codes of ethics provide guidelines for performing the competencies presented in this textbook. In addition, the concepts and competencies highlighted in the three paradigms presented in previous chapters are influenced by legal and ethical responsibilities, and those who promote the initiatives have taken this into account.

Stone (2005) stated the importance of ethics and law for school counselors well:

School counseling has an inherent moral dimension because of the nature of student/school counselor relationships. Public education involves the exercise of power by one group, educators, over another group, students, and, therefore, educators' work must meet high ethical standards. Educators, especially school counselors, are involved in a particular kind of interpersonal relationship with students, and by virtue of this relationship we have a deeper moral responsibility to our students. (p. 45)

Herlihy and Remley (2001) depicted laws as the "musts" components in our professional behavior. Laws "dictate the minimum standards of behavior that society will tolerate" (p. 71). Ethics depict the "shoulds" of our professional behavior. Ethics "represent the ideals or aspirations of the counseling profession" (p. 71).

Legal Concepts

Each state has its own laws, and new laws continue to be passed as legislators deem necessary. Some laws have a direct influence on school counselors, and counselors

Parental consent is required if a student is under 18 years of age.

need to be familiar with those laws. For instance, Pennsylvania has a statute that states that no school counselor who has acquired information from students in confidence shall be compelled or allowed to disclose that information in legal or governmental proceedings without the student's consent or the consent of the parent or guardian if the student is younger than age 18. This act does not supersede counselors' responsibility to report evidence of child abuse or neglect. Obviously, all school counselors in Pennsylvania should understand the meaning of these two legislative acts.

Legal concepts are operationalized in specific pieces of legislation. For instance, Pennsylvania's statute operationalized the concept of privileged communication. School counselors can become familiar with some important legal concepts before learning the specific laws that operationalize them. Pertinent examples are negligence, malpractice, libel, and slander. Counselors and their stakeholders are served best if knowledge about such important legal concepts is part of the school counselor's basic education. To assist readers, a glossary of the relevant technical terms used in this chapter is presented in Figure 5.1.

Governmental Regulations

State and local governing agencies, in their responsibility to care for and educate children and adolescents, may enact regulations to which professionals under their jurisdiction must conform. Such regulations are usually printed and distributed to affected professionals. Some states, for example, have a regulation that all school districts must have a student record-keeping system approved by the state department of education and that that system must have printed guidelines for all staff members to follow. Examples of local school district regulations are (a) all professional staff members must sign a form when seeking access to individual students' cumulative records, and (b) all

Abuse: The infliction by other than accidental means of physical harm on a body of a child, continued psychological damage, or denial of emotional needs (ASCA, 1988).

Civil liability: The condition of being available, subject, exposed, or open to legal proceedings connected with the private rights of individuals.

Confidentiality: A situation in which one has been entrusted with the secrets or private affairs of another.

Criminal liability: The condition of being subject, exposed, or open to legal proceedings for which punishment is prescribed by law.

Defamation: An act that injures someone's reputation without foundation.

Duty to warn/protect: When a professional has a special relationship with a client and that individual's conduct needs to be controlled, the professional has a duty to act in a manner that protects the client and/or warns foreseeable victims of the client's actions (Gehring, 1982).

Ethical standards: The rules of practice set forth by a profession. Such standards tend to be general and idealistic, seldom answering specific questions for the practitioner (Remley, 1985, p. 181).

Laws: The standards of behavior a society demands of its members. Laws set forth the rights of citizens and usually define minimal acceptable behavior rather than idealized expectations (Remley, 1985, p. 181).

Libel: Words written, printed, or published, in any form other than speech or gestures, that maliciously or damagingly misrepresent.

Malpractice: Improper treatment or action of a client by a professional from neglect, reprehensible ignorance, or with criminal intent.

Mandated reporter: Those required by law (i.e., teachers, counselors, school administrators) to report suspected child abuse immediately. Suspicions are sufficient grounds. Investigation is the domain of others.

Neglect: The failure to provide necessary food, care, clothing, shelter, supervision, or medical attention for a child (ASCA, 1988).

Negligence: The failure to exercise the degree of care that the law requires, under the circumstances, for the protection of the interests of other persons who may be injuriously affected by the lack of such care.

Privileged communication: If an interaction is designated as privileged communication under the law, a judge may not force the professional involved to disclose what was said by a client in an interview (Remley, 1985, p. 184).

Reasonableness and good faith: Criteria used by the courts to judge the conduct of professionals. Was the conduct what a reasonably prudent adult might do under similar circumstances, and was the action clearly for the benefit of the child and the employing entity (Pietrofesa & Vriend, 1971)?

Sexual abuse: Any act or acts involving sexual molestation or exploration, including but not limited to rape, carnal knowledge, sodomy, and unnatural sexual practices (ASCA, 1988).

Slander: Spoken statements that are malicious, false, and defamatory.

Figure 5.1
Glossary of terms.

instances of suspected child abuse and neglect must be reported to the building principal. Most regulations have merit and provide guidance for professionals.

Ethical Standards

Professional groups provide their members with codes of ethics that serve as standards for their behavior. The groups have established standards for several reasons (Van Hoose & Kottler, 1978). First, they are supposed to provide autonomy from governmental regulation and interference by serving as a basis for self-regulation. Second, ethical codes provide behavioral standards for members of a professional group. Third, the codes protect members of the public by providing for their welfare, and protect the professionals by providing guidelines that serve as criteria for judging their actions if individuals sue them for malpractice.

The ethical codes best designed to serve school counselors are the *ACA Code of Ethics* (ACA, 2005) and the ASCA *Ethical Standards for School Counselors* (ASCA, 2004). (Copies of these codes are provided in appendixes F and G, respectively.) Although very useful, ethical standards have limitations. One is that some legal and ethical issues are not addressed by the codes because of changing times, recent legal precedents, and the inability of the codes to cover every possible situation. Ethical codes are primarily reactive, evolving from previous practices and problems. Recognizing the limitations of ethical standards, we recommend that counselors supplement them by keeping up with state and local legislation, reading professional journals for up-to-date information on legal and ethical issues, and seeking advice from other professionals such as attorneys, counselor educators, supervisors, and colleagues. Although limited in their coverage, ethical codes are the best source of criteria for appropriate professional behaviors.

PERTINENT LEGAL CODES AND CONCEPTS

Federal Legislation

Title IX. Known by its full name as Title IX of the Education Amendments of 1972, this legislation prohibits discrimination on the basis of gender by any institution receiving federal funds in any form. Regulated through the U.S. Department of Education, a specific section (45 C.F.R. 586.36) prohibits discrimination on the basis of gender in counseling or guidance of students. In general, this legislation reminds school counselors not to treat children and adolescents of one gender differently than the other in ways that place them at a disadvantage. It provides legal sanctions that support the gender equity principles.

Several potential manifestations of gender discrimination exist in school counseling. One that has received considerable attention is the way standardized tests and information are used in career and educational planning. For example, older interest inventories that restricted young women to considering only the limited range of careers traditionally occupied by women have been changed. School counselors are challenged to be aware of the issues and choices available to all standardized test takers when using interest inventories. Whenever standardized tests or norms are separated by gender, the potential for discrimination exists. Whether discrimination always occurs is less certain.

Title II of the Education Amendments of 1976 (20 U.S.C. 2301–2461).
Title II provides amendments to the Vocational Education Act. According to this legislation, states must draw up plans to ensure equal access to vocational education for both men and women in order to receive funds under the Vocational Education Act. State vocational education agency coordinators must review these plans to ensure men and women are provided equal opportunities in school career counseling. Title II also mandates equal opportunity.

Family Educational Rights and Privacy Act of 1974 (PL 93-380).   Referred to as FERPA or the Buckley Amendment (after the late Senator James Buckley of New York, who sponsored it), the act was designed as a means of restoring parental rights and protecting privacy. FERPA has four major parts. Part I states that federal funds will be denied to any educational institution that prevents authorized access to school records by students who are older than 18 years or by parents of students who are younger than 18 years. When such a request is made, the authorized student or parents must be allowed to inspect the student's entire educational record. However, the school is allowed up to 45 days to comply with such a request.

Part II of FERPA states that parental consent, if a student is younger than 18 years, or the student's consent, if the student is older than 18 years, is required before a student undergoes medical, psychological, or psychiatric examination, testing, or treatment or participates in any school program designed to affect or change the personal behavior or values of a student. This part of FERPA, of course, has implications for many activities included within the realm of the prevention programming described in chapter 8.

Part III forbids the schools to allow any individuals other than those directly involved in the student's education to have access to the records or to any information from the records without written consent of the student, if older than 18 years, or the parent, if the student is younger than 18 years. Some exceptions to this section are discussed later in the chapter.

Part IV of FERPA states that the U.S. Secretary of Health, Education, and Welfare is required to develop regulations to ensure the privacy of students with regard to federally sponsored surveys. Because FERPA was rather quickly developed and passed into law, some basic implementation questions about it confronted confused school officials in the mid-1970s. This situation ushered in a series of amendments and guidelines, the intent of which was to clarify the implementation problems. In December 1974, a "Joint Statement in Explanation of the Buckley/Pell Amendment" was published in the *Congressional Record* (1974). This statement remedied certain omissions in the provisions of the existing law and clarified other provisions that were subject to extensive concern. Several important points from this statement are as follows:

1. FERPA applies only to those programs delegated for administration to the commissioner of education.
2. *Education records* are defined as those records and materials directly related to students that are maintained by a school or one of its agents.
3. Private notes or confidential notes are exempt, provided they are not revealed to another qualified person.

4. Certain law enforcement records are excluded.
5. FERPA does not alter the confidentiality of communications otherwise protected by law.
6. Hearing procedures are to be developed by local school districts.
7. Wherever possible, actual documents are to be shared. When this is not possible, an accurate summary or interpretation is necessary.
8. The federal government will withdraw federal funds from violating or nonconforming schools.
9. Exceptions to the need-for-written-consent requirement for allowing access to information are state and local officials where state laws are more liberal than FERPA, organizations giving entrance or selection examinations, accrediting agencies, parents of students older than 18 years if the students are still dependent according to the Internal Revenue Service, and in cases of health and safety emergencies.

Another clarification appeared in January 1975. This statement clarified the relationship between the institution's right to destroy records and the individual's right to have access to the records. Eligible students or their parents must be granted access to information in the records if said information was in the records when the request was made. If a request for information in a student's records is pending, the institution is not allowed to destroy any such information until after the requesting student or parent has had access to it. When no such requests have been made, institutions do have the right to destroy information in student records unless otherwise forbidden to do so by law. The long-range effect of FERPA has been to encourage institutions to keep and use fewer records than in the past.

Connors (1979) surmised that defamation suits can be filed against people whose comments in the records are deemed libelous by students or parents who have gained access to the records. Although the law is not retroactive before January 1, 1975, the statute of limitations starts when a comment is discovered, rather than when it was written. Thus, since passage of the so-called Buckley Amendment, it has become more important to give careful consideration to the entries placed in student records. Connors recommended that subjective notations such as "Johnny is a cheat" be avoided. Anything that is entered should be stated objectively—for example, "Johnny has been observed copying answers from his neighbor's test paper on 10 different occasions this year." Even objective statements such as this one may be unwise, in Connors's opinion. Perhaps the best protection against defamation suits is to enter no descriptive statements whatsoever into student records.

Legal Concepts

Privileged Communication. A legal responsibility mandated by state codes, privileged communication is a client's right to have prior confidences to certain professionals maintained during legal proceedings. Some states have granted it to school counselors; others have not. Sheeley and Herlihy (1988) reported that, in 20 states, interaction between school counselors and clients had been designated as privileged communication. For example, Pennsylvania mandates that school counselors are required to maintain client confidences during legal proceedings unless requested to disclose that information by their clients or by the parents of their clients if the clients are younger than 18 years. Privileged communication is not extended to instances of suspected child abuse.

Privileged communication legislation mandates that counselors follow the ethical principle of maintaining confidentiality in specific instances—that is, during legal proceedings. Although privileged communication assists school counselors in their efforts to maintain client confidentiality and recognizes their confidences as being as important as those of medical doctors, lawyers, psychologists, and the clergy, the primary purpose of the legislation is to protect clients.

According to Glosoff, Herlihy, and Spence (2000), it is difficult to list general exceptions to privileged communication. This difficulty arises because provisions for privileged communications may be buried in state statutes, each state has its own statutes, and statutes are being modified continually. An exhaustive, yet admittedly incomplete, computerized search by Glosoff et al. (2000) led to their presentation of a matrix of exceptions to privileged communication by states and the District of Columbia. Nine categories of exceptions were found across the 50 states and the District of Columbia. The list includes all professional counselor categories and is not restricted to school counselors. Listed in the order of most to least often found, they are (a) when there is a dispute between the student client and a counselor, (b) when the client raises the issue of mental condition in a court proceeding (e.g., insanity defense, claim of emotional damage), (c) when the student client's condition poses a danger to self and others, (d) child abuse or neglect, (e) knowledge that a client is contemplating commission of a crime, (f) information from court-ordered psychological examinations provided by counselors, (g) when counselors want to participate in the involuntary hospitalization of clients, (h) knowledge that a client has been the victim of a crime, and (i) harm to vulnerable adults (e.g., disabled or institutionalized).

Most instances that require school counselors to testify in court involve abuse or custody cases (Anderson, n.d.). Being informed and prepared is important. Discussions with parents or lawyers who may want a counselor to testify will help determine whether a court appearance is necessary. Reasons for not testifying include having limited information to offer and having several individuals who can provide similar testimony. School counselors may receive subpoenas, which are official court documents and cannot be ignored. Remley and Herlihy (2005) recommended that school counselors consult with and receive advice from an attorney if they have received subpoenas. A counselor should consider several important guidelines if testifying in court: (a) Remember that a school counselor is a licensed or certified educator, and limit comments to facts about what students are doing in school, (b) remember that attributions about the causes of behaviors are in the domain of licensed psychologists and other professionals qualified to assess behavior, (c) review relevant information and check the facts without violating confidentiality, and (d) review and bring pertinent factual data and refer to them as needed when testifying (Anderson, n.d.). It is recommended that counselors withhold their confidential notes unless required to share them. Notes should not be destroyed after a request has been made, and they may be entered into the record if presented. The content of personal notes and how long they should be kept are covered in the record-keeping section of this chapter.

Malpractice and Negligence.

Counselors, like others in the helping professions, may be subjected to charges of malpractice or negligence. Malpractice refers to practices that are outside a professional's training or ability and that result in damage to the recipient of those services—for example, a school counselor recommends or gives medicines or drugs to a client, causing deleterious results. Negligence is a breach of legal duty, or a failure, resulting in damage to a client, to perform acts that are part of the professional's obligation—for example, a school counselor fails to report evidence of child abuse.

Stone (2002) reported two instances where school counselors were embroiled in negligence cases. One case was a suit charging negligence in academic advising (*Sain v. Cedar Rapids Community School District*, 2001), and the second involved a suit alleging negligence in abortion counseling (*Arnold v. Board of Education of Escambia County*, 1989). A careful study of both cases indicates that the school counselors involved were attempting to be advocates for their student clients and believed they were acting in good faith. In the first case, the majority of the Iowa Supreme Court ruled in favor of the plaintiff, stating that "negligent misrepresentation may be applied to the school counselor–student relationship when erroneous advice means a student loses a lucrative scholarship" (Stone, 2002, p. 30). The Court also cautioned that "the ruling should have limited effect as negligent representation is confined to students whose reliance on information is reasonable" (p. 31).

In the latter case, the ruling was in favor of the defendants. The trial court concluded that the students had not been coerced by the principal or the school counselor. Although negligence was not proven in this case, Stone (2002) pointed out that "The question remains: May counselors be held liable for giving abortion advice to pregnant minors?" (p. 33). Stone recommended avoiding referrals to birth control clinics and never taking students to facilities where medical procedures are to occur.

Readers may be wondering what to do. Our best advice is to be well informed about one's legal and ethical responsibilities and to act in good faith. In those rare cases when school counselors are sued for malpractice or negligence, the courts are likely to use the concept of whether the counselor acted in good faith as the criterion for determining guilt or innocence. The concept of *acting in good faith* is based on the principle of using the ethical standards of one's profession as a criterion for making a legal determination. Therefore, school counselors will be judged by the ethical codes of the professional organizations to which they belong or could belong. If, according to the best interpretation of the ethical standards, a counselor acted appropriately, he or she can be judged as having acted in good faith and will likely be cleared of the charges. Knowing whether one is acting in good faith may be a difficult undertaking, however. Accomplishing that goal will be enhanced if school counselors do the following:

- Belong to a professional organization, know its ethical codes, and abide by them.
- Know the relevant state codes and the local board of education regulations and abide by them.
- Know the local school policies and abide by them.
- Develop program policies.
- Develop personal working policies based on knowledge of relevant developmental issues, parental rights, diversity issues, and personal values.

Child Abuse.   All states and the federal government have passed legislation to stop child abuse or neglect. The state codes and regulations have several common ingredients, among which are child protective services agencies, procedures for reporting and investigating child abuse, penalties for abuse and for failing to report it, a toll-free telephone system for anonymously reporting suspected abuse, and designations of certain professionals as mandated reporters. School counselors are usually included among those professionals designated as mandated reporters (Bryant & Milsom, 2005). Although it is clear that child abuse is abhorrent, the signs of abuse are much less clear in some instances. Therefore, the mandate to report child abuse becomes less clear when counselors and their professional colleagues attempt to recognize and report it. According to Remley (1985), many states that require disclosing suspected child abuse fail to clearly define what it is. Remley (1992) also pointed out that although some states specifically note that child abuse must be reported no matter how much time has elapsed since it occurred, many states do not make the time frame clear, leaving it to individuals and the courts to determine how much should be reported. To help readers respond to this challenge, Figure 5.2 presents a suggested set of signs of child abuse, and Figure 5.3 offers suggested steps in the reporting process.

Abuse can include a variety of acts. Included among those acts listed in the professional literature are inadequate supervision that leads to failure of the child to thrive, emotional neglect, abandonment, psychological bullying by classmates, physical abuse (often the easiest to detect), verbal abuse, and sexual abuse or molestation. Sexual

---

Examples of Child Abuse

- Extensive bruises or patterns of bruises
- Burns or burn patterns
- Lacerations, welts, or abrasions
- Injuries inconsistent with information offered
- Sexual abuse
- Emotional disturbances caused by continuous friction in the home, marital discord, or parents who are mentally ill

Examples of Neglect

- Malnourished, ill-clad, dirty, without proper shelter or sleeping arrangements, lacking appropriate health care
- Unattended, lacking appropriate health care
- Ill and lacking essential medical attention
- Irregular/illegal absences from school
- Exploited, overworked
- Lacking essential psychological/emotional nurturance
- Abandonment

Figure 5.2
Signs of child abuse and neglect.

Source: Data from "The School Counselor and Child Abuse/Neglect Prevention," by the American School Counselor Association, 1988, *Elementary School Guidance and Counseling, 22,* pp. 261–263.

- Report suspected cases of child abuse to the building principal immediately; that is, children younger than age 18 who exhibit evidence of serious physical or mental injury not explained by the available medical history as being accidental, or sexual abuse or serious physical neglect, if injury, abuse, or neglect has been caused by the acts or omissions of the child's parents or by a person responsible for the child's welfare.
- Each building principal will designate a person to act in his or her stead when unavailable.
- The principal may want to form a team of consultants with whom to confer (e.g., school nurse, home and school visitor, counselor) before making an oral report to public welfare service representatives. This should be done within 24 hours of the first report.
- It is not the responsibility of the reporter to prove abuse or neglect. Reports must be made in good faith, however.
- Any person willfully failing to report suspected abuse may be subjected to school board disciplinary action.

Figure 5.3
Suggested steps for a school district employee in reporting child abuse.

abuse encompasses a variety of acts, including using children in pornographic films. Mandated reporters are immune from civil or criminal liability in all 50 states and the District of Columbia if they have reported in good faith (Hinson & Fossey, 2000; Kenny, 2001). They may be fined for knowingly failing to report suspected child abuse. Civil or criminal liability should occur only for knowingly making false accusations (Knapp, 1983). For one reason or another, most cases of child abuse go unreported (Crenshaw, Crenshaw, & Lichtenberg, 1995). From a Kentucky survey of elementary and middle school counselors, Wilson, Thomas, and Schuette (1983) concluded that the majority of respondents believed that the problem was more serious elsewhere than in their communities and believed that they were aware of the signs of abuse. Overall, the respondents reported a low incidence of actually reporting child abuse. These findings left several questions: Is relatively little abuse occurring with children and adolescents in the United States? Are counselors and other mandated reporters missing or overlooking the signs of abuse, or are the signs too subtle or hidden to uncover in many cases? Are school counselors trained sufficiently to discover abuse and report it?

In a more recent survey of school counselors in a midwestern state, Bryant and Milsom (2005) found higher reporting rates than in the Wilson et al. (1983) study. They also found that most cases were reported by mandated reporters, elementary school counselors made more reports that middle and secondary school counselors, and counselors in schools with higher percentages of children qualifying for free and reduced lunch were more likely to report abuse. The primary reason given for not reporting was concern that the Department of Human Services would not investigate (follow-up).

Concern about doing something in advance of discovering and treating child abuse that has already occurred led to an increase in systematic prevention efforts.

Adair (2006) reported that reviewers of sexual abuse prevention program evaluations found it difficult to ascertain effectiveness because of methodological problems in the evaluation studies. Adair's review led to the following observations about programs designed to prevent sexual abuse: (a) many different program formats are used; (b) such programs are available in almost all school districts; (c) common topics for programs devised for children are saying no and getting away, telling on adults, body ownership, good touch/bad touch, no secrets, and getting help; (d) little has been reported about programs for adolescents; and (e) almost all prevention programming occurs in schools, overlooking children who are being served by community agencies. Adair recommended that, to be effective, sexual abuse prevention programs should (a) provide information in a manner that will influence behaviors, (b) achieve accurate awareness of one's vulnerability to sexual assault, (c) be of a sufficient length of time to achieve objectives and offer follow-up sessions, (d) be based on up-to-date information about child and adolescent development, (e) be available for children and adolescents, (f) be conducted in collaboration with community organizations that serve children and adolescents, and (g) be carefully evaluated.

Parents and teachers have also been targeted for prevention programming but on a smaller scale (Allsopp & Prosen, 1988; Downing, 1982; Tennant, 1988). The few reported programs targeting parents seem to devote attention to helping them identify the signs of abuse, react in a constructive manner when noticing signs or being informed of abusive acts, and learn ways to educate their children for prevention (Repucci & Haugaard, 1989). Parents Anonymous (PA) represents a form of tertiary prevention for parents who are known and admitted abusers. Organized along the lines of Alcoholics Anonymous, PA meets the needs of some parents. More is needed, according to Post-Kammer (1988), who recommended that one area of need is helping PA members have a better understanding of child development. PA serves as a possible referral source for school counselors. However, not much has been reported about prevention training for teachers either. Such training programs can focus on increased awareness and understanding through content, including information about offenders, current legislation, reporting procedures, and available community resources (Allsopp & Prosen, 1988). Preventive teacher training seems to be an important topic for counselor-led, in-service programming.

Libel, Slander, and Defamation.

Libel is a legal term referring to false statements that are published and bring about hatred, disgrace, ridicule, or contempt toward the individual about whom they are written. *Slander*, also a legal term, refers to verbally communicated statements that have the same results. In civil suits, plaintiffs must prove that damages in the form of *defamation*—an injured reputation—resulted. Historically, the number of such civil cases against counselors has been small. Nevertheless, some counseling duties and functions have the potential for making counselors vulnerable. Sharing standardized test scores over the telephone, telling bystanders about students' grades, and relaying information to third parties about clients when there is no clear obligation to do so are examples of questionable behaviors that could lead to charges of defamation. Also, parents or students may take action over comments in students' cumulative records they deem to be inflammatory. It is also conceivable that information counselors share with colleges, universities, and prospective employers in confidence via recommendations can find its way back to the subjects of the comments and, if viewed as defamatory, lead to civil suits.

Anyone can sue another person but, in so doing, is not guaranteed recovery of damages. Suits, whether won or lost by the plaintiffs, have the potential for causing counselors considerable stress and mental anguish, public embarrassment, and possible financial losses associated with defending themselves if the individuals and school districts do not have sufficient insurance. It is recommended that school counselors carry professional liability insurance. Regardless of insurance, it behooves counselors to be prudent about what they write and say about their charges. This, of course, is also an ethical recommendation.

Several recommendations, if followed, may help counselors minimize the chance of being sued for libel or slander and reduce the probability of the plaintiff recovering damages if a suit does occur. Subjective notations need not be entered in student records, or anywhere else, for that matter. Determine the inquirer's need to know any information before sharing it. For example, in the potentially libelous or slanderous cases cited previously, the need of the person requesting standardized test scores over the telephone to know the desired data can be assessed by acquiring written permission from the individual whose scores are desired, and bystanders by definition have no responsible need to know information about students.

In some instances, determining the need to know is relatively easy. For example, students who plan to matriculate to post–high school educational institutions must usually submit transcripts and letters of recommendation; in doing so, they grant permission to representatives of their high schools, often counselors, to transmit the information and recommendations. The need to know is clear. When some of the same institutions ask questions about the character of students and request narrative evaluations, the need to know is less clear. Exactly what they need to know is left to the respondents to determine.

What to do? With regard to determining the need to know, it seems logical to question the motives behind the request, to predict what will be done with the information, and to understand how that response will affect the student client whose information is being shared. With regard to what to do, one is expected to act in good faith, according to the ethical principles of one's profession. Believing what one is saying or writing is also important. Knowing it is true is even better because truth is an important criterion in civil cases. Report objectively and factually, but some things might be best left unsaid, even objectively (e.g., accusatory statements). Bronner (1998) reported that school counselors are caught between college admissions officers desiring to ensure campus safety and avoid liability for student violence and parents who do not want details of their children's disciplinary problems to ruin their chance of getting into college. Both parties may be more determined than ever to protect their constituencies. A personal guideline of the authors has been to say and write only things that are true and favorable about clients unless there is a clear and imminent danger to themselves or others. If there is not much true and favorable to write in a recommendation about a client, then the brevity may speak for itself. Another option is to refuse the recommendation request.

Unclear Areas.   Desiring to know what to do legally and ethically is a meritorious goal, as is acting responsibly. Yet, efforts to understand what to do sometimes lead to "mixed messages," leaving one unclear about the definition of responsible behavior.

Some areas covered by the concepts of duty to warn and duty to protect are chief among the unclear legal areas with which counselors must grapple. These concepts have been highlighted by prominent court decisions (e.g., *Tarasoff v. Regents of the University of California,* 1976), which focused on concern about warning potential victims of violent behavior. In school settings, the concepts might also be applied to cases of advising minors without parental consent (e.g., providing information about abortions) and cases of suicide (counselors' apparent knowledge of the student's desire to harm him- or herself).

Tarasoff occurred in California during the mid-1970s, and the decision set off a tidal wave of concern and uncertainty across many levels of helping professionals in the United States. In this case, a client informed a psychologist of his intention to kill another individual. Care was taken to commit and confine the client for observation, and the campus police were notified of his stated intentions. He was released after appearing rational and promising to stay away from the individual whose life he had threatened. The psychologist had not warned the intended victim, who was out of the country at the time, or her parents. The client went to her residence and killed her after she arrived home. The courts ruled the therapist and institution in error because there was a foreseeable victim and a duty to warn the victim or her parents. In courts that follow the reasoning of this case, mental health workers will be expected to warn people who have a special relationship with the dangerous person and the intended victim of that person (Gehring, 1982).

Because the *Tarasoff* case occurred in California, its results are not binding elsewhere. Courts in other states, however, may use that case as a precedent for similar decisions, although some states have not adopted the "Tarasoff doctrine" (Herlihy & Remley, 2001). In some decisions in other states, the courts have interpreted similar situations differently. For instance, in North Carolina (*Currie v. United States,* 1986), an employee, while he was in therapy, threatened to kill unspecified coworkers. Subsequently, he did indeed enter the workplace and kill a coworker. The court created what was called the *psychotherapist judgment rule,* in which it refused to allow liability for simple judgment errors in commitment decisions. The therapist had consulted with several colleagues before deciding not to commit the client ("Therapists Bear a Duty," 1987). Clearly, this case differs from *Tarasoff* in that the intended victim was unspecified, and as it was reported, the client had also threatened the therapist. Despite these differences, mental health professionals working with clients who pose a threat to themselves or others or who indicate a disposition toward child abuse should be prepared to report to the proper authorities and to potential victims ("Legal Considerations," 1983).

Writing from his experience as a lawyer to an audience of clinical psychologists, Monahan (1993) offered guidelines for limiting exposure to duty to warn liability. Although the package of recommendations contains entries that are perhaps more extreme than most school counselors require, they provide food for thought:

- Know how to assess client risk, make a real effort to do so thoroughly, and communicate that information to those responsible for making final decisions.
- Have a risk management plan in place (prepare for the few exceptions in advance with a plan for monitoring and managing individuals who may endanger themselves or others).

- Document information received and actions taken. According to Monahan (1993), "It would be an exaggeration to state that in a tort case what is not in the written record does not exist—but not much of an exaggeration" (p. 246). He recommended noting the source of the information, the content, and the date.
- Written policies or guidelines that have been externally reviewed by experienced clinicians and lawyers should be in place, and the staff should receive training about using the guidelines. Compliance with the guidelines should be audited, and forms developed or revised to "prompt and record the actions contemplated by the policy statement" (Monahan, 1993, p. 247).
- If something goes wrong, one can control the damage by relying on the truth and remaining silent publicly when experiencing doubts about one's decisions from the vantage point of hindsight.

Advising minors without parental consent is a particularly unclear area that each counselor needs to investigate. From an ethical standpoint, adherence to the principle of confidentiality usually leads counselors to keep in confidence what minors say during counseling sessions. An example of a troublesome topic held in confidence is knowledge of pregnancy, including the client's planned responses, such as abortion, and the counselor's sharing of information about possible options, including abortion. This has been and continues to be a legal minefield because statutes vary from state to state, as do decisions in court cases, and the national conflict between right-to-life and prochoice supporters promises to lead to more changes in the future. According to Hopkins and Anderson (1990), "counselors are generally free to inform clients of the availability of birth control methods without fear of legal liability and to refer clients to family planning or health clinics for more information" (p. 33). Hopkins and Anderson went on to point out the distinction between providing information and imposing one's own views on a minor client, particularly one who is already pregnant. Additional important information in this domain is that states may regulate the performance of abortions, parents of unmarried pregnant minors may have some rights to know about and consent to an abortion, and physicians are recognized as qualified to provide pregnant women with information and decision-making advice about abortions. Kiselica (1996) offered suggestions for counselors. Helping to clarify confusion about legalities and being advocates on behalf of the clients' legal rights are important ways that counselors can help. Beyond the legal issues, counselors may also be able to provide emotional support and decision-making counseling that includes accurate information. Chapter 9 introduces decision-making counseling.

Because the resolutions of issues in this section are unclear, advice is scarce and conflicting. Two suggestions that have merit are (a) to have policy statements for crises and challenging situations that will guide individual counselors and help others determine whether the counselor acted in good faith (Lawrence & Kurpius, 2000; Monahan, 1993) and (b) to keep proper notes about one's actions and decisions in order to support one's claims if ever called into court or some other formal proceeding (Lawrence & Kurpius, 2000; Monahan, 1993; "Therapists Bear a Duty," 1987).

Most Frequently Reported Legal Issues.   Hermann (2002) surveyed 273 members of the ASCA who were school counselors, using the Legal Issues in Counseling

Survey. The most frequently reported legal issues over the past 12 months, ranked in order of frequency, were as follows: (a) determining whether a client was suicidal (90% of sample; 76% two or more times), (b) determining whether to report suspected child abuse (89% of sample; 74% two or more times), (c) determining whether a client posed a danger to others (73% of sample; 51% two or more times), (d) being pressured to verbally reveal confidential information (51% of sample; 34% two or more times), and (e) clients expressing dissatisfaction with counseling services (42% of sample; 19% two or more times).

Hermann (2002) also inquired about the participants' perceptions of how prepared to respond to the respective legal issues they believed they were. The same five legal issues discussed in the preceding paragraph are presented with the percentage in parentheses of the school counselors who believed that they were well prepared to respond: (a) determining whether a client was suicidal (72%), (b) determining whether to report suspected child abuse (91%), (c) determining whether a client posed a danger to others (63%), (d) being pressured to verbally reveal confidential information (57%), and (e) clients expressing dissatisfaction with counseling services (48%).

It is not surprising that reporting child abuse ranks highest given the explicit mandates found in the state statutes. The legal issues with lower percentages of perceived preparedness seem to fall into a rank ordering according to the severity of complications that can be encountered. For example, the professional literature is replete with checklists to be used when assessing suicide ideation, and suicide ideation is often clearly recognized. However, pressure to reveal confidential information can occur in different ways, and there are no common guidelines for dealing with these requests. This issue, as well as discerning danger to others and client dissatisfaction, may manifest themselves in more subtle, unclear ways.

Two other legal issues that occurred less often in the survey yielded higher percentages of feeling unprepared. Of the sample, 54% felt unprepared to respond to a subpoena to appear as a witness in a legal proceeding, and 22% believed that they were not prepared for being asked to turn over confidential records. These two legal issues were encountered less often than the other five. Therefore, participants, having less experience and perhaps less preparation, felt less well prepared.

It appears as if experience is the best way to prepare for responding to legal issues. Actual experience is one way to address this challenge; however, real-life experiences of this nature are few and far between. The challenges can also be addressed proactively by covertly and overtly simulating what one would do if presented with each of these legal challenges and basing the rehearsed simulations on a thorough study of the relevant professional literature.

ETHICAL RESPONSIBILITIES

American Counseling Association Standards

The ACA published a revised *ACA Code of Ethics* in 2005 (see appendix F). (Also refer to counseling.org/resources/CodeOfEthics/TP/Home/CT2.aspx.) The code has eight major sections: The Counseling Relationship; Confidentiality, Privileged Communication, and Privacy; Professional Responsibility; Relationships With Other

Professionals; Evaluation, Assessment, and Interpretation; Supervision, Training, and Teaching; Research and Publication; and Resolving Ethical Issues. This section of the chapter highlights the parts of the code that are most relevant to school counselors.

Preamble. The preamble states that counselors are expected to consult with other professionals when faced with ethical dilemmas. Because school counselors who are members of the ASCA may also belong to the ACA, school counselors are subject to the codes and standards of both professional organizations.

The Counseling Relationship. Dealing with practices and procedures of individual counseling, group counseling, or both, this section focuses on such matters as client welfare; informed consent; clients served by others; avoiding harm and imposing values; roles and relationships at individual, group, and societal levels; multiple clients; group work; end-of-life care for clients who are terminally ill; fees and bartering; termination and referral; and technology applications.

Confidentiality, Privileged Communication, and Privacy. Confidentiality being a key ethical principle for counselors, this section covers respecting client rights; exceptions; information shared with others; groups and families; clients lacking the capacity to give informed consent; records, research, and training; and consultation. The assumption of confidentiality is a foundation for the counseling, consulting, assessment, and record-keeping functions. It is the foundation for the trust that helps individuals share intimate information with counselors truthfully. Although school counselors have an ethical responsibility to their student clients, they also have a legal responsibility to the parents of minor clients; this can sometimes lead to decision-making dilemmas. As Huey (1986) pointed out, ethical codes do not recommend violating the law. At the same time, Huey cited advice from Corey, Corey, and Callanan (1984) recommending that counselors do not become hamstrung by legal concerns to the point that they become ineffective. No one seems to have a definitive answer about this issue. Most counselors will not want to lose the power to help individuals that confidentiality offers. Therefore, it appears that they will have to deal with the legal ramifications on a case-by-case basis, checking applicable state laws in the process.

Zingaro (1983) provided an example of a case in which a counselor faces this dilemma:

> A child may ask to talk to you about a problem, such as how to get along with a new stepparent. After discussing the child's concern, you arrange a time to meet at a later date. The following day one of the child's parents calls you to ask about the content of your counseling session. It seems obvious from the questions that the parent is aware of some of the issues that you discussed with the child. Would you disclose information that you received from the child with the parent? What would be the effects on the child, parents, and you if you comply with the parent's request? If the child's self-referral is viewed as a step toward autonomy and independence in solving his or her problems, have you handicapped the child's efforts? Would these questions be answered differently if the parent had asked you to speak with his or her child and then asked about the content of your counseling session? (p. 262)

Professional Responsibility.   In this section, matters such as knowledge of standards, professional competence, advertising and soliciting clients, professional qualifications, nondiscrimination, public responsibility, and professional responsibility are covered. Among the components important to school counselors are the emphases on monitoring one's effectiveness, consulting with other professionals about ethical questions and professional practice, keeping current, and representing one's credentials appropriately.

Relationships With Other Professionals.   This section contains important standards about relationships with colleagues, employers, and employees (e.g., confidentiality, personnel selection, harassment) and additional information about consultation.

Evaluation, Assessment, and Interpretation.   As the title implies, this section is devoted to concerns about the use of educational, psychological, and career assessment instruments. Among the specific standards are statements concerning the importance of being competent to use and interpret assessment instruments, providing informed consent to clients, releasing data to qualified professionals, making proper diagnoses of mental disorders, selecting instruments carefully, providing appropriate assessment conditions, recognizing the need for caution in testing because of diversity issues, scoring and interpreting assessments appropriately, keeping tests and assessment data secure, avoiding use of obsolete assessments and outdated results, and engaging in forensic evaluations appropriately. (Readers are challenged to recognize a strong relationship between the standards in this section of the code and the information in chapter 12 of this book.)

Supervision, Training, and Teaching.   This section is of more interest to trainers of school counselors than to school counselors themselves yet has considerable influence on the training of counselors. The standards herein focus on counselor supervision and client welfare; counselor supervision competence; supervisory relationships; supervisor responsibilities; counseling supervision, evaluation, remediation, and endorsement; responsibilities of counselor educators; student welfare; student responsibilities; evaluation and remediation of students; roles and relationships between counselor educators and students; and multicultural diversity competence in counselor education and training programs. The way the standards influence the training of school counselors may influence the direction of the profession throughout the 21st century.

Research and Publication.   Probably of less interest and use to most school counselors than other sections of the code, this section points out that all participants in a research study must be told which information can be shared without affecting the study and that they must be given the opportunity to decide whether to participate. This is referred to as *informed consent.* In addition, the identity of the participants must be disguised when reporting results or making original data available, results reflecting unfavorably on the schools or other vested interests must not be withheld, and agreements to cooperate in research projects imply a responsibility to do so punctually and completely.

Resolving Ethical Issues. The standards in this section admonish counselors to know the *ACA Code of Ethics* thoroughly, to respond to suspected violations appropriately, and to cooperate with ethics committees.

Changes From the 1995* ACA Code of Ethics *and Standards of Practice. One important change is thematic. Kocet (2006) pointed out that

> Scholars in the area of feminist ethics encourage the forming of mutually respectful relationships in the counseling process and seek to recognize the power differential that can exist by handling power in an ethical manner that honors both individuals and relationships and emphasizes care and concern as a central fixture in the therapeutic process. (p. 229)

Kocet continued: "Many of the changes in the 2005 *Code* are designed to integrate this perspective throughout the document, which emphasized the promotion of growth-fostering relationships" (p. 229).

A second thematic change is attention to multicultural and diversity issues. Kocet (2006) stated that "Particular attention was paid to ensure that multicultural and diversity issues were incorporated into key aspects of counseling practice" (p. 230). For example, in Section C.5, nondiscrimination has been expanded to include "spirituality, gender identity, marital status/partnership, language preference . . . or any basis prescribed by law" (p. 230).

New features are (a) a section stating the five main purposes of the code, (b) aspirational introductions at the beginning of each section, (c) a glossary, and (d) an index. The focus on aspirational ethics highlights the potential for "reasonable differences of opinion among counseling professionals and suggests that counselors find and select an ethical decision-making model that best fits their counseling approach and to seek consultation with supervisors and colleagues when faced with an ethical challenge" (Kocet, 2006, p. 229).

Table 5.1 presents a summary of key new areas in the 2005 *Code of Ethics.* The new areas point out ways in which multicultural and diversity issues are infused into the code.

American School Counselor Association Ethical Standards

"Ethical Standards for School Counselors" (ASCA, 2004) in many ways reflects the standards of the ACA code and standards while also presenting issues in a manner recognizing the unique preparation and work settings of school counselors. This can be seen when comparing the ASCA standards in appendix G with the ACA code and standards. The first section entitled Responsibilities to Students includes emphases on informed consent, keeping up to date, avoiding dual relationships, making appropriate referrals, confidentiality, duty to warn, and appropriate use of tests. The second section, Responsibilities to Parents, discusses informed consent for parents, confidentiality, and sensitivity to family issues. The third section, Responsibilities to Colleagues and Professional Associates, deals with such matters as cooperative relationships with faculty, staff, and administration, and appropriate referrals. A fourth section, Responsibilities to the School and Community, deals with standards for protecting the school's mission, personnel, and property, and assisting in the development of school programs and services.

Table 5.1
Key new areas in the 2005 *ACA Code of Ethics*.

Counseling Plans (A.1.c.) Are to be jointly devised by counselors and clients and offer reasonable promise of success.

Potentially Beneficial Interactions (A.5.d.) Stresses the importance of attempting to remedy potential harm to clients from nonprofessional interactions between counselors and clients.

Advocacy (A.6.a.) Counselors examine potential barriers and obstacles that inhibit client access and/or growth and development.

End-of-Life Care for Terminally Ill Clients (A.9.) An entire new section with attention paid to quality of care; counselor competence, choice, and referral; and confidentiality.

Technology Applications (A.12.) Much more comprehensive than previously.

Deceased Clients (B.3.f.) Emphasis is placed on protecting confidentiality within legal requirements of agency policies.

Counselor Incapacitation or Termination of Practice (C.2.h.) A prepared transfer plan should be in place.

Historical and Social Prejudices and Diagnosis of Pathology (E.5.c.) Counselors are expected to recognize these circumstances and their historical impact on diagnosis and treatment.

Multicultural Issues/Diversity in Assessment (E.8.) Stresses recognition of factors about clients that may not be reflected in norms of assessments they are taking.

Innovative Theories and Techniques (F.6.f.) Counselor educators are to define techniques they teach that are without empirical foundation as "unproven" or "developing" and explain potential risks and ethical considerations to students.

Replacing "Subjects" With "Participants" (G.) This change occurs throughout the code and in the professional counseling literature.

Plagiarism (G.5.b.) Presenting another person's work as one's own is unethical.

Conflicts Between Ethics and Laws (H.1.b.) Counselors make their commitment to the code known and attempt to resolve conflicts. When conflicts cannot be worked out, requirements of law, regulations, or other government authority prevail.

Note. ACA = American Counseling Association.

The remaining three sections are Responsibilities to Self, Responsibility to the Profession, and Maintenance of Standards. This last section includes a statement that links the ASCA standards to the code and standards of the ACA.

Although the ACA code is designed for a diverse cross-section of professional counselors and is therefore more broadband in its scope, the ASCA code is primarily for school counselors and is more narrowband in scope. For example, the ACA code uses the word *client*, whereas the ASCA code uses *student*. In truth, the primary recipients of the services of school counseling programs are *student clients*. To decide that the ASCA code is the only code of interest for school counselors because of its primary focus on school counseling would be a mistake because the ACA code, being more comprehensive in nature, covers important ethical matters that are not addressed in the ASCA code (e.g., Research and Publication; Supervision, Training, and Teaching).

Avoiding Ethical Violations

The most logical recommendation for avoiding ethical violations is that counselors be familiar with the codes and continually aware of their ramifications—always employing an ethical mind-set—without being debilitated by reactionary fears of accusations of wrongdoing. Be alert, yet not fearful. DePauw (1986) offered useful guidance for avoiding ethical violations via a timeline for organizing one's thoughts ethically. Users of DePauw's timeline can recognize ethical considerations that are relevant to phases in the counseling relationship. Four phases are addressed in the timeline: initiation, counseling, crisis, and termination.

Initiation. A major consideration relevant to school counselors in the initiation phase of the counseling relationship is that of assessing the client's needs and determining whether one is qualified to be of service. Related to this appropriateness issue is whether the prospective student client may be seeing another professional helper, such as a psychologist or psychiatrist. If this is the case and if the school counselor has determined him- or herself to be an appropriate helper, the student client may have to choose between helpers, negotiate with the school counselor a way to inform the other helper, or seek approval for concurrent counseling. One example is partial referrals, which are described in chapter 10.

Nevertheless, both the ACA (A.1. Welfare of Those Served by Counselors, A.2. Informed Consent in the Counseling Relationship, A.7. Multiple Clients, B.5. Clients Lacking the Capacity to Give Informed Consent) and the ASCA (responsibilities to students, responsibilities to parents) codes of ethics are clear in stating that informed consent is expected for clients and their parents. Kaplan (1996) offered the following analogy:

> Imagine the following scenario: *a person with whom you've had a slight acquaintance comes up to you and insists that they can help you with your problems. However, they will not tell you how they are going to help you, what will be done with the information you provide, who will be told that you are being helped, or the possibilities of what may go wrong if you allow yourself to be helped.* The next thing you hear this person saying is: "relax and tell me your deepest, darkest secrets." (p. 3C)

To meet the spirit of the informed consent expectation, counselors must provide enough information to ensure an informed choice (Kaplan, 1996). Traditionally, school counselors, because of the nature of their work, have not emphasized informed consent as much as counselors and therapists in other settings. Prospective clients are often children and adolescents, and it is not always clear when talking with school-age students in a private or semiprivate setting that a request for counseling services has occurred. To launch into an informed consent explanation at this point could be counterproductive, overwhelming students and causing them to back off or possibly not return, not wanting to be labeled as "needing a shrink."

Because verbal statements may be misunderstood and because offering informed consent in the presence of a prospective client may be problematic, the best approach is probably to have a blanket informed consent form for all parents/guardians and students to sign when students are enrolled in school, keeping the form on file while they are in attendance. What should the informed consent form contain? Kaplan (1996), borrowing from private practitioners, offered a comprehensive approach, suggesting that the consent form might contain (a) the counselor's theoretical framework and treatment approach, (b) a section on confidentiality, (c) the counselor's educational background and training, (d) rules about appointments, (e) session charges and program fees (if appropriate), and (f) an acknowledgment sheet to be signed by the parents/guardians and students.

O'Connor, Plante, and Refvem (1998) offered a less comprehensive approach, a one-page counseling consent form containing (a) the name of the school district and the title of the form, (b) an explanation (e.g., "Counseling services are offered to all students in ____ county. Any parent may withhold consent by checking in front of the specific service and then signing and dating the form. Please return this form to the counseling office by ____. Permission is presumed if this form is not returned."), (c) options to check off or not (e.g., group counseling, individual counseling of more than two sessions, individual nonmandated testing, and referrals—community services or medical), and (d) an acknowledgment section for signatures and dates. Glosoff and Pate (2002) provided additional important advice regarding informed consent. They recommended that school counselors treat informed consent as an ongoing process rather than attempting to address it at the beginning of the helping relationship.

Counseling.   Chief among the ethical considerations during ongoing counseling are confidentiality, consultation, and record keeping. Beyond informing clients about confidentiality, counselors also consider what is confidential and what is not. Certainly, it would be imprudent and inaccurate to inform clients that everything they say is confidential and then not to act accordingly. If counselors are aware of the limitations to confidentiality, such as child abuse, threats to others, and admission of a crime, they will be prepared to respond immediately when those exceptions occur. Being aware and able to respond proactively enhances the chance that making exceptions to the confidentiality principle will not ruin one's relationship with the client and one's reputation among prospective clients.

An awareness of ethical responsibilities will help counselors in determining ways to seek consultation without violating confidentiality or placing consultants in an awkward position. One way to accomplish this is to use hypothetical information. This allows counselors to maintain anonymity for clients while acquiring helpful assistance. As the counseling phases progress, counselors will decide what will be recorded in cumulative files and private case notes. Useful guidelines for record keeping in greater depth appear later in this chapter.

Crises.   Prominent among the crises for which ethical guidance can be given are threats to oneself and others. When threats to oneself (e.g., suicide ideation) occur, counselors must assume responsibility for the client's welfare after carefully determining the seriousness of the threats. DePauw (1986) believed that an open discussion of the counselor's concerns with an accompanying attempt to involve the client in the decision making enhances the chance of voluntary cooperation.

The parameters of the school counselor's ethical duty to warn others when clients threaten others are presented in the Unclear Areas section of this chapter. Although it is usually clear that threats are occurring, it is less clear what to do about them.

DePauw (1986) recommended having contingency plans derived from consulting with informed specialists such as attorneys, psychiatrists, and law enforcement officials.

The following list of possible ingredients of a contingency plan is taken from Sheeley and Herlihy's (1989) guidelines for counseling practice related to duty-to-warn-and-protect issues associated with counseling suicidal clients:

- Know the privileged communication or confidentiality laws in the state where one is employed.
- Keep abreast of related court decisions.
- Communicate the need for related school board policies.
- Develop policy handbooks and ask parents to confirm that they received the materials.
- Circulate descriptions and explanations of the confidentiality principle.
- Encourage students and parents to sign waivers allowing counselors to disclose certain kinds of specified information that is confided during counseling.
- Keep good notes and records.
- Consult with professional peers when in doubt about client assessments and treatments.
- Know a lawyer to contact for legal assistance.
- Know the status of the school district's professional liability insurance coverage plan and have an additional personal liability insurance policy. The ACA and ASCA make this coverage available to their members.

Evidence or suspicion of child abuse is a third ethical crisis area, and mandated reporting is also backed by legal statutes. As is true in cases of threats of suicide, counselors must decide how much to explain to student clients in advance of making a report. The challenge here is to conform with the law while also trying to help and protect the client.

Termination. Two ethical concerns associated with termination are (a) the responsibility to determine whether a counseling relationship is still productive and (b) the decision to submit one's work for review and evaluation. Application of the former concern may lead to a decision to refer. Therefore, one is obligated ethically to know referral sources and to make appropriate referral suggestions. More information on this subject is found in chapter 10. The concept of submitting one's work for review and evaluation may be interpreted as an ethical responsibility to engage in evaluation associated with one's counseling services. Thus, the advocacy of accountability made in chapter 4 has an ethical foundation.

Ethical Multicultural Counseling. The introduction to Section A (The Counseling Relationship) of the ACA *Code of Ethics* provides statements about understanding diverse cultural backgrounds of clients and exploring one's own cultural values, and Standard A.2.c. indicates that counselors "communicate information in ways that are both developmentally and culturally appropriate." The ASCA ethical standards Preamble states: "Each person has the right to respect and dignity as a unique human being and to counseling services without prejudice as to person, character, belief, or practice." Thus, the ethical codes seem to indicate that failure to consider a client's culture(s) may very well be unethical.

Much of what is being written about the application of ethics to multicultural counseling is at a somewhat abstract level. For example, Pedersen (1997), believing that the current ethical codes are derived from a western cultural perspective that emphasizes relativism and absolutism, recommended an approach that can fit different cultural contexts. In addition, LaFromboise, Foster, and James (1996) encouraged consideration for viewing ethical decisions from both a care perspective (emphasis on relationships) and a justice perspective (social contract emphasis).

At a more practical level, LaFromboise et al. (1996) made several recommendations, taken from their review of the professional literature, that may be considered guidelines for ethical multicultural counseling:

- Consider the client's unique frame of reference and personal history. This is consistent with Herring's (1997) synergistic counseling approach.
- Provide the necessary information for informed choices. This includes a treatment plan with alternative intervention methods (e.g., traditional healers) and consideration of potential outcomes with regard to one's family and community.
- Take an activist stance when it appears necessary to protect clients from pathological systems.
- Be aware of the importance of the need to address cultural factors in ethical decision making.

Garcia, Cartwright, Winston, and Borzuchowska (2003) developed a model that they labeled the Transcultural Integrative Ethical Decision-Making Model (TIEDM). Viewing it as an important addition to the ethical decision-making literature, we discuss their model in the next section.

Making Good Ethical Decisions

Although the codes of ethics are indeed comprehensive, the standards are sometimes in conflict with each other, and they may not be specific enough to give individual counselors definitive answers to ethical dilemmas they may encounter. Therefore, the process used to make ethics decisions is important. In proposing the TIEDM, Garcia et al. (2003) considered previous models and evaluated them from a cultural perspective. The models they reviewed include (a) the rational model based on identifying the principles in conflict and using a stepped approach to reaching a rational decision (e.g., identify problem, refer to code of ethics, determine nature and dimensions of dilemma, identify courses of action, assess possible consequences of all options, implement a course of action) (Kitchener, 1984); (b) virtue ethics in which decision makers employ their own wisdom and personal values that shift the focus to the person making the decision rather than the act of making a decision (emphasis is on the influence of one's moral and personal beliefs when making decisions) (Jordan & Meara, 1995); (c) social constructivism (Cottone, 2001), which offers an approach that introduces an interactive decision-making process through which ethical decisions are based on negotiating, consensualizing, and arbitrating (when necessary) with others and thus being guided by social and cultural factors; (d) collaboration (Davis, 1997), which emphasizes a group rather than an individual decision-making perspective (e.g., identify involved parties, define various viewpoints, find a mutually satisfactory solution, implement the individual contributions that are parts of the solution); and (e) an integrative model (Tarvydas, 1998) that combines the morals, beliefs, and experiences of the involved individuals with a rational analysis of the related ethical principals (e.g., become aware of what constitutes an ethical dilemma, use a stepped rational decision-making process, employ personal and contextual values in the decision, consider obstacles to implementing the decision).

The TIEDM model employs the four basic stages from Tarvydas (1998) and adds elements of the Cottone (2001) and Davis (1997) approaches. Multicultural elements have been added to the model. In an effort to keep this presentation from becoming overly abstract to readers, we present highlights of the TIEDM and attempt to apply it to a case study. Readers who want a richer, more comprehensive coverage of the model are referred to Garcia et al. (2003). Important elements of the TIEDM are (a) reflection (i.e., awareness of one's feelings, values, and skills and those of other stakeholders involved in the decision); (b) attention to contextual elements such as team, institutional, policy, society, and cultural factors; (c) consideration of issues and perspectives of all individuals involved; (d) collaboration with all parties who participate in the decision to whatever extent possible; and (e) acceptance of the diverse worldviews of the stakeholders. The four stages of the TIEDM are (a) interpret the situation through awareness and fact finding, (b) formulate an ethical decision, (c) weigh competing nonmoral values and affirm a course of action, and (d) plan and execute the selected course of action.

A case study by Fielstein (1996) is abstracted in the following paragraph, and the TIEDM is applied to it.

One morning, a high school counselor was informed by the principal that a 15-year-old student came to school apparently intoxicated. The student was acting confused and appeared to have alcohol on his breath. The school nurse was not available to ascertain the student's condition, and the student was uncooperative about revealing the causes. As per school policy, the counselor called the student's parents to inform them of what had transpired. The student's grandfather answered the telephone, informed the counselor that the parents were out of town, and behaved in an indifferent manner, apparently not wanting to become involved.

1. *Interpret the situation through awareness and fact finding.*   Our interpretation of the TIEDM suggests that the counselor consider relevant information about the acculturation level and cultural values of the family and the counselor's own multicultural competence when interpreting the situation. For example, the grandfather's apparently indifferent manner may be explained by culture and acculturation factors, and he may have indeed been very interested yet unable to express himself in a manner that the counselor expected from his own cultural perspective. These thoughts are incorporated into a process of considering the welfare and needs of the involved parties, analyzing the dilemma, identifying the ethical and legal relationships to the client and his family, and reviewing the current information in order to understand it as well as possible.

2. *Formulate and ethical decision.*   Next, the counselor attempts to ensure the cultural information acquired in the first stage is considered, estimates whether there is a potential conflict between laws and ethics from a cultural perspective when considering

the impact of the school's policies and procedures, takes inventory of all possible courses of action and how they reflect the cultural worldview of the parties involved, considers the worldview information when weighing the advantages and disadvantages of the possible courses of action, consults with individuals who can shed light on the worldview issues as well as policies and procedures, and chooses a rational course of action that echoes the transcultural analysis and seems ethical. In this case, perhaps the grandfather should be contacted again to better determine how well he understands the circumstances and what his expectations and wishes may be. He may be able to offer important insights to the counselor from a different cultural perspective.

3. *Weigh competing nonmoral values and affirm a course of action.* In the ACA code, Standard B.5.c. states:

> When counseling minor clients or adult clients who lack the capacity to give voluntary consent to release confidential information, counselors seek permission from an appropriate third party to disclose information. In such instances, counselors inform clients consistent with their level of understanding and take culturally appropriate measures to safeguard client confidentiality.

Standard B.2.a. states:

> The general requirement that counselors keep information confidential does not apply when disclosure is required to protect clients or identified others from serious and foreseeable harm or when legal requirements demand that confidential information must be revealed. Counselors consult with other professionals when in doubt as to the validity of an exception. Additional considerations apply when addressing end-of-life issues. *(See A.9.c.)*

How much influence do these standards have on the counselor's decision? Is the counselor's concern about these ethical principles in conflict with supervisors and the family?

4. *Plan and execute the selected course of action.* It appears as if nonmalfeasance, beneficence, and justice are important principles to consider in this instance. The decision seems to require an option that allows the counselor to promote good mental health, do no harm, and be just. Possible options that come to mind are as follows: (a) Inform the principal that it is not a counseling function but rather a discipline problem, (b) keep the student in school under the watchful care of a responsible person until the parents can come to the school, (c) ask the grandfather to come to school to pick up the student and take him home, (d) contact social services for advice and possible help, and (e) let the student sleep it off in the nurse's office and then go to class. *To the reader*: What options other than these come to your mind?

At this stage, the TIEDM suggests that counselors divide the course of action into simple, culturally relevant sequential actions, anticipate and plan countermeasures for barriers to successful implementation of the plan, execute a course of action, gather and document relevant information, and assess the validity of the course of action taken by including both universal and cultural-specific variables. In this scenario, the counselor may have decided to keep the student at school in the nurse's office until the parents could pick him up. In that case, the course of action would be documented and the roles of the counselor, grandparent, school policies and procedures, and any other consultants who were contacted would be included.

Readers are invited to complete the decision-making process independently and to evaluate the process as well.

The decision made in the Fielstein (1996) scenario was to persuade the grandparent to come to school to pick up the student and take him home. It was argued that the school carried out its responsibilities by turning the minor student over to a guardian and that the student's welfare was protected. When originally published, this vignette was not influenced by the TIEDM. Even though the counselor in the scenario believed that the best ethical decision had been made, concerns lingered, among which were not feeling comfortable about leaving the student with the grandparent, not knowing the severity of the condition of the student, and being unsure whether the student would receive appropriate supervision at home. These concerns point out that a decision-making scheme, although a helpful approach, is no guarantee of a 100% foolproof decision. Counselors are challenged to do their best under the circumstances, attempting to act in an ethical manner and seeking informed consultation whenever possible. The TIEDM provides additional structure for attempting to achieve an appropriate decision from a perspective that considers multiple worldviews.

KEEPING GOOD STUDENT RECORDS: A MERGING OF LEGAL AND ETHICAL CODES

School record keeping in the United States can be traced back to the 1820s and 1830s. The original purposes of record keeping seem to have been to certify student enrollment and attendance and to recognize levels of accomplishment (Fischer & Sorenson, 1996). As the schools became more committed to the "whole child" concept, the cumulative record folder became more than an academic record; it became a humanistic document. The cumulative record files are now repositories for a variety of information about students.

A significant development in the arena of student record keeping was the passage of the FERPA. Details about FERPA were presented previously in this chapter.

The FERPA legislation provides specific legal guidelines for student record keeping. The ACA and ASCA codes of ethics provide guidelines, too, including clarification of the differences between confidential records and public records, a caveat to share appropriate information with those who have the right to know it, and instruction about appropriate procedures for transmitting and releasing information to third parties.

FERPA and Codes of Ethics

McGuire and Borowy (1978) insisted that some confidential information typically included in student records was excluded from coverage under the Buckley Amendment. This exception hinges on the purpose or use of the information, rather than on the nature of its content. In their opinion, information obtained solely for the purpose of providing professional and diagnostic services to children is to remain confidential, on the assumption that the information has not been shared with anyone else, including fellow professionals. If it has been shared with anyone, it is no longer confidential.

Prior to the passage of FERPA (PL 93-380), counselors had no guidelines other than ethical codes to use when faced with requests for information that challenged the principle of confidentiality. Such requests, for instance, may have been made by school administrators, school boards, or other persons of authority. PL 93-380 supplements the existing codes of ethics. Better definitions of appropriate counselor behaviors are provided through this union of law and ethics.

Getson and Schweid (1976) offered suggestions for alleviating potential conflicts between PL 93-380 and codes of ethics:

- Purge files of information predating PL 93-380 that would violate students' rights of privacy.
- Remove all information that might be misinterpreted by nonprofessionals.
- Initiate a policy that allows parental review of only those records that are not a threat to client welfare.
- Be sure students are aware of the limits of privacy that exist in a counseling relationship because of parental rights to review student records.
- Make a personal study of the possibility of conflicts between PL 93-380 and the counselor's professional code of ethics.

Developing a Systematic Plan for Collection, Maintenance, and Dissemination of School Records

Guided by ethical standards to take care in record-keeping matters and mandated to engage in certain record-keeping procedures by PL 93-380, school counselors needed ideas for conducting the collection, maintenance, and dissemination of school records in a systematic manner. Into this setting came the Russell Sage Foundation (1970) guidelines, which became the foremost source of ideas for systematizing school record keeping. For example, in Pennsylvania, detailed school record-keeping systems were mandated by the state's department of education in 1976, and the Russell Sage Foundation guidelines were used as the criteria for judging the acceptability of each school district's submitted plan.

Several useful ideas are found in the Russell Sage Foundation guidelines. First, they cover the collection of data in which the distinction between individual and representational (parents' legally elected or appointed representatives) consent is discussed. Second, a useful and important system for categorizing data is given. It can be summarized as follows.

Category A Data.   In this category are the minimum personal data necessary for operation of the education system. Examples are names, addresses, birth dates, and grades. This information is to be maintained perpetually.

Category B Data.   This category includes verified information of clear importance but not absolutely necessary to the school in helping the child or in protecting others. Examples are scores on standardized intelligence tests, aptitude tests, and interest inventories; family background; and systematic teacher ratings. It is recommended that parents be informed periodically of the content of these records and of their right of access to the content. It is also recommended that Category B data be destroyed, or only maintained under conditions of anonymity, after a student leaves school.

Category C Data. Potentially useful data that are primarily timebound to the immediate present are assigned to this category. Examples are legal or clinical findings, personality test results, and unevaluated reports of teachers or counselors. It is recommended that these data be destroyed as soon as their usefulness is ended, unless it is reasonable to transfer them to Category B.

A survey of elementary and middle school counselors in New Hampshire led Merlone (2005) to conclude that there was "confusion and diverse practices regarding the storage, sharing, and destruction of counselors' notes" (p. 372). Ironically, Merlone recommended that the very same Russell Sage Foundation guidelines cited previously provided the best resource for helping counselors become more competent and consistent in their management of student records.

Confidential Data. Any records or notes that are to be kept confidential should be located in the counselor's personal files, rather than in the cumulative records.

Implementing a Record-Keeping System

In a position statement on guidance services made at the time Pennsylvania was mandating detailed record-keeping systems, the Pennsylvania Department of Education (1977) made two useful records maintenance suggestions. First, a school district's record-keeping policies should allow for the retention of information necessary to permit full counseling, referral, and placement services in the years following a student's departure from school. This recommendation will have an important influence on what information is maintained in Category A after a student departs from school. Second, a centrally located storage facility should be established to allow easy access to records for those who have a legitimate interest in them. At the same time, provisions must be made for security against unauthorized use and accidental dissemination of information in student records.

In the same document, the Pennsylvania Department of Education (1977) offered useful advice (heavily influenced by the Russell Sage Foundation guidelines) for administering the record-keeping system:

- The mechanical aspects of record collection, maintenance, security, and dissemination should be handled by the clerical and/or paraprofessional staff under the supervision of the chief school administrator or that administrator's delegate. (In many instances, that authority is delegated to a school counselor.)
- Each school district should have a committee comprised of staff members (instructional, pupil personnel, and administrative), parents, and students that is charged with deciding what information is to be collected and maintained for students' school records.

- The counselor's primary concern and involvement in the area of student records should be to participate with the others listed in the preceding paragraph to determine the content of records and to interpret and apply that content in the education of the student.
- The director of guidance should be responsible for establishing procedures for carrying out the school policy on records.

How involved school counselors are in the school's record-keeping system varies across districts. Certainly, they will keep and handle student records. It is assumed that most counselors will have their own confidential file notes and that they will have to conform to legal codes, ethical guidelines, and local policies when using the cumulative files. Some additional options counselors will not control because they are imposed. Those options include being the person to whom responsibility for administering the record-keeping system has been delegated, serving on the committee that determines what information should be collected and maintained, helping others be better informed through in-service training efforts, and interpreting contents to laypeople when needed. Burky and Childers (1976) offered a good general principle for counselors: Counselors should model behavior displaying their belief in the paramount rights of individuals.

Sources of Ethics Consultation

Guillot-Miller and Partin (2003) provided much of the information for this section in their informative publication.

American School Counselor Association (www.schoolcounselor.org)
- Members may call either 800/306-4722 or 703/683-1619 and will receive consultation from the appropriate person at ASCA headquarters or be referred to the chair of the ASCA ethics committee. The Web site provides links to the ASCA Ethical Standards and position statements such as the following:
  - See "Common Ethical and Legal Concerns of School Counselors," an informational brochure produced by ASCA.
  - See "Doing the Right Thing: Ethics and the Professional School Counselor," an ethics packet produced by the ASCA ethics committee.

American Counseling Association (www.counseling.org)
- Members may call either 800/347-6647 or 703/823-9800 and will be referred to a staff member for consultation.
- The ACA Web site offers the Ethical Code and Standards of Practice and "A Practitioner's Guide to Ethical Decision Making."

National Board for Certified Counselors (www.nbcc.org)
- Counselors certified by the board who call 910/547-0607 will be referred to the ethics officer.
- The Web site includes the NBCC code of ethics and a link to individual state licensure boards.

Additional Web Sites of Potential Usefulness

American Bar Association (www.abanet.org)

National School Boards Association Council of School Attorneys (www.nsba.org/cosa)

American School Board Journal (www.asbj.com/index.html)

Education Law Association (www.educationlaw.org)

Monitor on Psychology, a publication of the American Psychological Association (www.apa.org/monitor/)

U.S. Department of Education (www.ed.gov/index.jsp)

The importance of advocacy is emphasized in a new component of the ACA code (A.6.c.). We turn to that important topic in chapter 6.

FEATURED ACTIVITY: GRADUATE STUDENT PERSPECTIVES ON LEGAL AND ETHICAL ASPECTS OF SCHOOL COUNSELING

 In this chapter, we discuss the legal and ethical aspects of school counseling. One of our graduate students, whose wife is a prominent attorney, suggested that our counselor education program needs a complete course dealing with the legal and ethical aspects of counseling. He and his wife had discussed at length the many difficult and troubling dilemmas school counselors confront involving legal and ethical matters. We acknowledged the worthiness of his suggestion and are considering the development of a course on law and ethics but, of course, have limited faculty resources and face demands for new courses of equal importance.

How would you make the case for a new course on legal and ethical concerns in school counseling? What, in your experience, provides compelling evidence for developing such a course? What other new courses might have equal or higher priority for you?

After you read this chapter, go to http://www.genesislight.com/scan21st/tell_us/legal.html and complete the form. With your permission, we will periodically post some of your creative thinking for the world to read.

OTHER SUGGESTED ACTIVITIES

1. Review your knowledge of state and local legislation relative to counseling.
2. If you do not already have an informed consent statement, develop one. Have your statement critiqued by your instructor, colleagues, and prospective clients.
3. Set up two plans for training teachers to use the record-keeping system appropriately. Have one plan in a group in-service format and the other in a programmed format for self-instruction.
*4. Develop a plan of action for responding to the following legal/ethical challenge:

> An 18-year-old female high school student has left home. Suspecting that the reasons for her leaving may be explained in the young woman's records, one of her parents calls the school counseling office and asks to see the records.

Meanwhile, the young woman has decided to withdraw from school and also requests to see her records. She wants them purged of personal information. Two weeks later, the police call the guidance office for access to the young woman's file during a routine investigation. A prospective employer also calls the guidance office and requests the young woman's IQ score or equivalent information for assistance in making a decision about hiring her.

*5. Answer each of the following true–false questions on the basis of the ACA *Code of Ethics* (ACA, 2005).
   a. Ethical standards are statements of philosophy.
   b. When a member of the ACA accepts employment in a school, he or she accepts the institution's policies.
   c. In a counseling relationship, an ACA member's primary obligation is to the public welfare.
   d. It is inappropriate to continue a counseling relationship with a student client who is involved in counseling or therapy with another professional.
   e. It is unethical to admit failure or inability to be of assistance to a student client.
   f. Explaining to a prospective client the conditions under which the counseling service is being offered at or before entrance into the counseling relationship is essential.
   g. A school counselor can ethically charge a fee for counseling services that clients are entitled to as students.
   h. Unethical behavior by a fellow professional is the responsibility of an ACA member.

*6. Discuss the following cases, using the ethical standards in appendices F and G for guidance. The cases are taken from "An Ethics Quiz for School Counselors" (Huey, Salo, & Fox, 1995). Determine whether you agree (A) or disagree (D) with the counselor's decision in each case, and place the corresponding letter in the blanks:
   a. A group member became very upset and wanted to leave after several members ganged up on her in a vicious verbal attack. The counselor physically barred the sobbing girl from leaving and told her that she must learn to handle conflicts within the group. _____
   b. A counselor self-described his dislike of a new technology as "computer phobia." As part of the school's counseling program, all ninth-grade students were required to use a newly purchased computerized interest inventory. The counselor joked that he was "not sure that he could even turn the machine on" and left the students to themselves "because they were better with computers anyway." _____
   c. As part of an ongoing peer program to assist students in being better able to help their peers with personal concerns, the counselor scheduled regular supervision sessions. Even though the peer helpers were well trained and had not had any problems, the counselor felt an obligation to check in with them. _____
   d. A male counselor refused to close his door when counseling teenage girls, even when requested by students who were emotionally upset. A female colleague believed the counselor was unnecessarily cautious and unethical in not providing the privacy needed by clients. The colleague decided to speak to the counselor to be sure he was aware of his responsibilities. _____

    e. A counselor strongly disliked a particular student assigned to his caseload and found himself distracted by negative feelings every time he saw the student. Despite good faith attempts to change his feelings, the counselor still disliked the student and subsequently referred the student to another counselor. _____

    f. The parents of a sophomore who was having academic problems told the counselor they were going to transfer their son to a private school the next school year. The student loved his current school and was very involved in extracurricular activities. The parents would not reconsider and asked the counselor not to tell their son about the plans. When advising the student about his academic course work for the next year, the counselor was careful not to reveal the parents' plans. _____

7. Go to the SCAN Web site (www.scan21st.com). Discuss some of the ethical and legal issues that might arise from online programs featured at this site.

*Suggested and keyed responses for these activities.

Comments on activity 4: Because the young woman is 18 years old, she must grant written permission for others to see the cumulative (not confidential) records according to the FERPA. There is an exception for her mother if the young woman is a dependent according to the Internal Revenue Service, and the police, depending on state law, should be provided access to the cumulative file information. When sharing information with the mother, the young woman, or the police, school representatives should be present and the documents, or summaries of them, should be shared. The prospective employer will need permission from the young woman or her parent, depending on whether the young woman is a dependent.

Answer key for activity 5: a = true, b = true, c = false, d = true, e = false, f = true, g = false, h = true

Answer key for activity 6: a = D, b = D, c = A, d = A, e = A, f = D

CHAPTER 6

Advocacy in School Counseling

Goal: To recommend a place for advocacy in school counseling and suggest implementation strategies for a balanced program.

Children and adolescents are among the most powerless people in 21st-century society. They can be moved from home to home and school to school with little or no recognition of their needs or rights. The following is an example:

> *Marcus was a 6-year-old boy. He lived in one of the wealthiest suburbs of Denver. He was adopted when he was 5 years old, not long after he appeared on a local television news program that featured children who needed a home. Marcus appeared to be a handsome, strong, healthy youngster during his television appearance, and several callers to the television station requested opportunities to meet Marcus and to consider adopting*

him. An affluent couple in Denver, who had tried unsuccessfully for years to give birth to a child, adopted Marcus and set out to provide a wonderful home for him. Shortly after the adoption, the couple learned that Marcus had a serious disease that would consume much of their time and wealth to manage. The couple, fearing the loss of their wealth and freedom, neglected Marcus and rejected him emotionally. Marcus came to the attention of his school counselor because of the neglect and rejection he faced at home.

What should a school counselor do in a case like this one? How can the counselor advocate for kids like Marcus? What advocacy skills does the counselor need? What dilemmas will school counselors face as they advocate for students? Advocacy is an important role for school counselors; this chapter discusses that role.

THE LEGACY OF ADVOCACY

The Social Reform Movement and School Counseling

As stated in chapter 2, "Guidance first appeared in the schools like any other subject. Guidance had a curriculum, the goals of which evolved from the social reform movements of the late 19th and early 20th centuries. Guidance teachers also sought to have a positive impact on the moral development of their charges." At that time, the need for reform was primarily linked to the negative effects of the Industrial Revolution. The rapid transition from an agrarian to an industrial society in the United States caused some people to find their vocations obsolete, others to be uprooted from familiar surroundings, and still others to be unskilled and powerless employees of powerful and relatively unregulated industrialists.

Aubrey (1977) suggested the process by which social reformers made an impact on the problems when he described the relationship between the social reform movement and vocational guidance:

> The linkage between this movement and vocational guidance was largely built on the issue of the growing exploitation and misuse of human beings. This linkage centering on the two conditions of economic waste and human suffering was to be used time and again as a means of pricking the conscience of the public, especially legislators. Lawmakers, visibly absent among the ranks of social reformers, were forced to be responsive to the persistent and ceaseless cries of social reformers. As a consequence, Congress in 1917 passed the landmark Smith-Hughes Act for secondary vocational education and teacher training. This beginning of enabling legislation was to be strengthened during the next twenty years. (p. 290)

Cremin (cited in Aubrey, 1977) is credited for noting that some reformers viewed the schools as vehicles for improving individuals' lives. Referred to as humanitarians and progressives, these reformers included Horace Mann and John Dewey, who founded the Progressive Education Association. Cremin (1965) was among those who viewed school counselors as the professionals in the schools whose role and functions most epitomized the goals of the progressive movement. In pointing out that Cremin's thought was more of a compliment than a reality, Aubrey observed that the tendency to elevate school counseling idealistically beyond reality reached its zenith with the publication of John Brewer's (1932) *Education as Guidance*. Brewer's point of view and that of the progressives faded during World War II and the postwar years.

The Post–World War II Years

In the years immediately following World War II, the United States found itself among the wealthiest and most powerful of nations. Many social problems of the late 19th and early 20th centuries had abated, and some goals of the reformers had been achieved. School counseling entered a period of rapid expansion following the passage of the NDEA. Much attention was devoted to training new counselors, retraining employed counselors, and developing counselor education programs. The support provided by the NDEA for these efforts was predicated on the assumption that the needs of the United States will be served if its youth are guided into careers that will strengthen the nation in its struggle against communism and keep it strong and prosperous.

The need for social reform still existed. It did not have the high priority in school counseling and in education it had once enjoyed, however, and those who insisted on telling others the right answers, as some early reformers did, were not very popular. An indication of some social problems in the mid-20th century was provided by Wrenn (1962) in *The Counselor in a Changing World*. He cited racial discrimination, occupational restrictions on women, the influence of automation on employment opportunities, increasing divorce rates, and inner-city income and cultural deprivation among the challenges for which new directions in school counseling were needed.

The Call for School Counselors To Be Change Agents

The 1960s and early 1970s were a period of great social unrest in the United States. Exacerbated by a growing confusion over the country's military involvement in Vietnam, many young Americans clashed with their elders over national priorities, social mores, and personal rights and responsibilities. The Vietnam War and the civil rights and women's rights movements were leading factors in the polarization of attitudes. A return to militancy toward social problems developed concurrently with the appearance of individuals whose voices sounded a demanding, uncompromising, and accusing tone.

Contributors to the professional counseling literature during this era encouraged counselors to respond to the conditions proactively. Terms such as *activist, advocacy, social action,* and *change agent* became prominent in the literature (cf. Hansen, 1968; Harris, 1967; Rousseve, 1968; Shaw, 1968; Stewart & Warnath, 1965; Stone & Shertzer, 1963). Clearly, school counselors were being challenged to try to change the circumstances causing various social problems and alleviating the effects. Focusing on the problems of urban America in particular, although also alluding to related problems in rural and suburban areas, Menacker (1974) advocated an interventionist role for school counselors. He argued as follows:

> The most fundamental guidance issue, finally, is the response that guidance ought to take to the concept that the student's out-of-school psychological, social, and physiological environment (food, housing, parents, peers, and so on) are more important determinants of school achievement than anything that occurs inside the school building. (p. 23)

Menacker (1974) insisted that school counselors should respond to "the forces outside the school as those within it and, in so doing, actively support the student" (p. 22). His recommendation placed school counselors idealistically in the role of advocates. Herr (1979) saw this as

> a source of both vulnerability and promise—vulnerability in the sense that many of the problems encountered by school counselors are of long duration of resolution, promise in the sense that the school counselor is a symbol of hopefulness that the school is a caring, humane place that has regard for individual purpose among all students. (p. 11)

Social Advocacy Revisited

Advocacy was not on the front burner in school counseling during the 1980s. Attention to the advocacy concept came primarily from champions for multiculturalism and multicultural counseling competencies in the 1990s. In 1999, the ASCA issued a position statement on multicultural counseling that called for facilitation of student development through an understanding of and appreciation for multiculturalism and diversity. Currently, one can find articles written by advocates for numerous disenfranchised populations in the professional counseling literature, several of which will be cited later in this chapter.

All three of the "best paradigms" for enhancing school counseling highlighted in chapter 2 promote advocacy. In the ASCA National Model for School Counseling Programs (ASCA, 2005), advocacy is one of four themes on which the National Model framework is based. Within the model, school counselors are viewed as uniquely well positioned to serve as advocates for students and families in order to enhance student achievement. The TSCI emphasizes the importance of school counselors advocating for access to rigorous education for all students (House & Hayes, 2002). Access to schoolwide and community data places counselors in a unique position to achieve this goal through efforts such as MEASURE (Stone & Dahir, 2007), which is presented in chapter 4. School counselors are viewed as advocates for school–community collaboration in the School Community–Collaboration Model (Adelman & Taylor, 2002). They are encouraged to take the lead in planning and advocating for less costly, more comprehensive, and more efficient interventions for students and their families.

Kiselica and Robinson (2001) reminded us that advocacy has several synonyms that may be found in the professional literature and that essentially mean the same thing. *Advocacy counseling, social action,* and *social justice* are among the most recent synonyms. Bradley and Lewis (2000) defined advocacy as the act of speaking up or taking action to make environmental changes on behalf of clients. Dinsmore, Chapman, and McCollum (2002) supplemented the definition by pointing out that advocacy can focus on responding on behalf of clients or empowering clients to work on their own behalf. Furthermore, Lee (1998) reminded us that the goal of advocacy in school counseling is to help clients challenge institutional and social barriers that are impediments to academic, career, or personal-social development. Comparing advocacy to the more traditional responsive counseling competencies such as counseling and consulting, Kiselica and Robinson (2001) pointed out that advocating for clients expands the counselor's focus. That is, the focus is expanded from intrapsychic concerns to include responding to extrapsychic forces that may be detrimental to students. Their analysis implies that different competencies may be needed as well.

Furthermore, being advocates for the school counseling profession is also important. The goals for a balanced approach to school counseling presented in chapter 3 included being advocates for all students and for the school counseling profession. Advocacy for the profession can be manifested through individual actions and via participation in and support of professional counseling associations.

CHALLENGES OF THE NEW MILLENNIUM

The Current Litany of Challenges

Two centuries after the beginning of the Industrial Revolution, the United States still faces social problems, and the schools and school counselors are in the midst of those problems. Changing circumstances have caused some traditional problems to decline in importance and new ones to occur, whereas other traditional problems remain pervasive. In the first decade of the 21st century, American society is faced with social issues that are as challenging as ever. The struggle for equality continues for individuals with disabilities, racial and ethnic minority groups, women, senior citizens, homeless individuals and families, immigrants, migrants, drug-addicted babies, AIDS victims, and gays and lesbians. Substance abuse has reached proportions of great magnitude. Drug lords openly vie with public officials for power in some countries, and the staggering value of drugs shipped to and sold in the United States compares favorably with major segments of the federal budget. Alcohol, cigarette, and fast-food manufacturers argue with critics in an effort to protect their investment domains. The environment is threatened by by-products of industrialization, the immense need for energy-producing fuels, and disinterest in recycling waste products. Vulnerable pregnant teenagers are caught between forces advocating and seeking to legislate right-to-life and prochoice viewpoints. Suicide is a national problem among adolescents, especially sexual minority students. The traditional family has declined as the norm, with the children of many single parent, dual-working parent, and disintegrated families left to fend for themselves. AIDS has demanded new views on interpersonal relationships while also creating a new source of stress and uncertainty for young people. Because of rapid changes in the economy, the workplace, and employment opportunities, many Americans have found themselves unemployed after years of employment or underemployed, with a corresponding decline in their standard of living. The same conditions threaten to engulf those young people who, for one reason or another, fail to cope with the expectations of the workplace and condemn themselves to unfulfilling futures living below the economic subsistence level. Statistics on child abuse indicate a problem whose dimensions are more pervasive than once known.

Responding to the Challenges

The litany of problems cited in the previous paragraph can make one feel depressed and overwhelmed. They represent current and future challenges with which society must continue to struggle. The schools and school counselors are in the midst of this struggle; they cannot ignore the problems because individuals affected by the problems attend and will attend the schools. These problems will prevent those children from being successful academically. Like it or not, the schools have become more than a place to impart knowledge. They have become, seemingly more than before, one institution that must help victims or potential victims of debilitating social problems by using both responsive and proactive responses. School counselors have a place in this scene as collaborators with other professional colleagues. School counseling was born in the social reform movement of another era, the legacy lives on, and it will continue to flourish.

In a call for social action in counseling, Lee and Sirch (1994) pointed out that the new millennium will usher in "a more global view of human need and potential" (p. 91). While striving to present their vision of an enlightened world society, Lee and Sirch also recommended two ways the counseling profession may promote their vision through social action, which they refer to as *counseling for an enlightened world society*.

First, counselors must believe in the vision of an enlightened world society and, in so doing, adopt *a sense of social responsibility*. Lee and Sirch (1994) viewed this commitment as manifesting itself in a philosophical commitment to the need for global social change and a willingness to become *social change agents* in the spirit of the models promoted by the activist contributors to the counseling literature of the 1960s and 1970s. Second, counselors are challenged to work with clients from diverse cultural backgrounds, to be able to facilitate client development via traditional intervention and prevention strategies, and to help clients "assess the meaning of life and significant relationships within it" (p. 95).

More recently, Lee (2001) issued a challenge for school counselors as follows:

> [Demographic trends indicate that] as never before, U.S. schools are becoming a social arena where children who represent truly diverse behavioral styles, attitudinal orientations, and value systems have been brought together with one goal—to prepare them for academic, career, and social success in the twenty-first century. (p. 257)

Lee continued by challenging counselors to respond to students representing an expanded set of worldviews to ensure them access to services that promote optimal academic, career, and psychosocial development. Finally, he challenged us to "move beyond the myth of a monolithic society to the reality of cultural diversity" (p. 261).

As was pointed out in chapter 5, advocacy has been highlighted in the 2005 *ACA Code of Ethics* (A.6.a.) within the section on Roles and Relationships at Individual, Group, and Societal Levels. This entry in the code implies that failure to advocate for clients when appropriate is unethical.

In the authors' opinion, the pervasiveness of these social problems and the call for advocacy require school counselors to respond with patience and care. Setting goals and working with others to achieve them is a better strategy than working independently and impulsively to resolve issues. Demanding change may be less palatable to decision makers than leading the way with information and reasoned debate. When singular efforts fail, planning and renewed efforts are needed. These social problems may not be eradicated for a generation or more. Yet, some individuals can be helped.

Many counselors attempting to help many individuals can be very influential. The remainder of this chapter elaborates on advocacy competencies and provides vignettes in which the competencies are demonstrated. We look to author Pat Conroy to support this patience and care theme. In an autobiographical novel about his first year of teaching on an island off the coast of South Carolina, Conroy (a.k.a. "Conrack") reported that he was fired for having been a too demanding advocate for the cultural/ educational enhancement of the children in his class. Efforts on his behalf by those who had supported him had failed, and he had to accept the decision. Reflecting back on the experience, he wrote a book to explain how he had been affected. In the concluding chapter, Conroy (1972/2002) wrote:

> I could be so self-righteous, so inflexible when I thought I was right or that the children had been wronged. I lacked diplomacy and would not compromise. To survive in the future I would have to learn the complex art of . . . that honorable American custom that makes the world go 'round. Survival is the most important thing. As a bona fide . . . , I might lose a measure of self-respect, but I could be teaching and helping kids. As it is, I have enough self-respect to fertilize Yankee Stadium, but I am not doing a thing for anybody. I could probably still be with the Yamacraw kids had I conquered my ego. (p. 289)

A CLOSER LOOK AT ADVOCACY

Popularity of the Intrapsychic Counseling Approach

The popularity of Carl Rogers's nondirective or person-centered approach to counseling in the mid-20th century led to an atmosphere in which most school counselors viewed their role as somewhat clinical in nature. Much emphasis was placed on individual counseling, one-to-one relationships, and counseling interventions. In developmental counseling—the counseling of individuals who were dealing with developmental issues such as selecting courses of study, planning for the future, coping with schoolwork, and getting along with others—many counselors also used client-centered response modes. The fact that client-centered counseling dominated the repertoires of many counselors indicated that they found it effective. Numerous clients were helped by school counselors who were using a predominantly client-centered model or by other models that allowed them to work mainly in their offices, responding to referrals from colleagues and self-referrals by students.

Emergence of an Extrapsychic Counseling Approach

Although effective for some student clients, the intrapsychic counseling model is also a passive, reactive one in which student clients are expected to take responsibility for helping themselves. Therefore, the solutions to problems, choices, and challenges confronting these students are often viewed as being within the grasp of the clients themselves if they can figure out how to solve the problems, make the choices, and meet the challenges successfully. In this approach, school counselors use listening and responding skills to create an accepting and empathic environment for their clients. Clients are helped because they can use that environment to feel understood, to clarify their thoughts and feelings, and to move freely toward decisions or feel better about them-selves and their circumstances. As an alternative method, counselors can share the wis-dom of their experience to offer student clients advice based on the expectation that the clients will be responsible for carrying out that advice. To sum up, in the mid-20th century, most school counselors used helping models drawn primarily from psycho-logical theories that stressed passive verbal interaction and self-directed client activity (Menacker, 1976). It is not a helping model that encourages advocacy, nor is it a train-ing model that produces counselors who are active interventionists. Into this setting came the unrest of the 1960s. With that unrest came dissatisfaction with the accepted counseling models because school counselors seemed too passive and uninvolved and because some clients could not achieve their goals through their own self-directed efforts. Several descriptive terms were used to label different approaches being advo-cated; yet, advocates of these approaches seemed to recommend that school coun-selors become more active, more directive and challenging, and more helpful to individuals confronted by issues whose resolutions were beyond their own self-directed efforts. A sample follows.

Menacker (1974) highlighted the importance of a nontraditional, more active role for school counselors in the urban schools. His position is based on his conclusions that the out-of-school environment of urban students is more important than any-thing that occurs inside the school building and that urban school bureaucracies have inertia and resistance to change, which challenges counselors to adopt an activist, interventionist role to prevent themselves from becoming part of a stifling bureau-cracy. Recommended manifestations of this role include the following:

- Adopting a multiple school counseling program control model in which cen-tral counseling officials, principals, local school counselors, teachers, students, and parent–community representatives are all involved in planning, monitor-ing, implementing, and evaluating the counseling program
- Resisting bureaucratic pressures to achieve maintenance goals and instead advo-cating goals that serve students and promise to improve their circumstances
- Engaging in environmental alteration when such changes seem appropriate, both in the school and in the community as a community resource specialist

In his activist theory, Menacker (1976) advocated a shift away from philosophical underpinnings deeply rooted in psychology and toward a greater emphasis on sociol-ogy, anthropology, and political science. He believes this will bring about increased understanding of the importance of social class and race in schooling, the impact of social change on communities and the schools, the importance of socioeconomic sta-tus, the importance of reference groups, and the effect on learning of the environment outside school. Menacker believes that a pervasive amount of activist philosophy in the approach of school counselors will change their traditional work patterns and their relations with other professionals. New work patterns will include spending more time away from the office and the school interacting with employers, parents, and commu-nity leaders and will lead to different work patterns (e.g., evening and weekend hours). New relations will occur when clients find counselors advocating more assertively for students, sometimes appearing more like attorneys or ombudsmen than mediators.

Implementation of Menacker's (1976) activist theory is founded on the following principles:

1. Direct counselor activity is focused on concrete action that objectively helps students. Activist counselors can achieve empathy through direct, concrete helping activities.
2. There should be mutual client–counselor identification of environmental conditions that may facilitate or retard goals and self-development. Counselors should attempt to capitalize on the positive and to eliminate the negative student client elements.
3. Activist school counseling recognizes the distinction between student client goals and values and those of educational institutions. Thus, rather than always adjusting the student, it may be necessary to acknowledge that the institution is sometimes the pathological element that needs time to adjust or to be adjusted.

Standing out among Menacker's (1976) principles are the ideas that direct helping activities can achieve empathy and that the institution may need to be adjusted. Traditional empathy takes the form of verbal and nonverbal responses by counselors that lead clients to feel understood. One might hypothesize that acts of direct help when help is needed also make clients feel understood. Therefore, empathy might be achieved in ways other than listening and responding passively. Few will claim that the schools are perfect institutions. Yet, the tendency for bureaucratic thinking among school personnel often leads to the expectation that students and parents, even teachers and counselors, must adjust to the system. The traditional goal of verbal counseling has often been to help individuals adjust to the system. Menacker would have counselors attempt to alter the system in those instances when it is the system, and not the student, that seems wrong or pathological and to help students adjust only when it is they who are wrong. Field and Baker (2004) found evidence of a consistent call for advocacy since the 1970s, and the words of Bailey, Getch, and Chen-Hays (2003), published almost 30 years after Menacker's, seem to echo his position: "Students need an advocate who will recognize when student needs are not being heard or met and when they are being squashed emotionally and intellectually by the very system designed to enhance their emotional, physical, and intellectual wellbeing" (p. 420).

Beyond the importance of activist counseling for all students lies the potential for helping disadvantaged students. Sue (1992) summarized the position succinctly:

Evidence continues to accumulate, for instance, that economically and educationally disadvantaged clients may not be oriented toward "talk therapies," that self-disclosure in counseling may be incompatible with cultural values of Asian Americans, Latinos and American Indians, that the sociopolitical atmosphere may dictate against working openly with the counselor, and that some minority clients may benefit from the counselor's active intervention in the system. (p. 14)

In an approach he labeled *synergistic counseling*, Herring (1997a, 1997b) believes that if school counselors are to serve as advocates for culturally different students, they will be challenged to employ a *cultural- and ethnic-specific model*. Herring described synergistic counseling as going beyond eclecticism and the communication skills approaches. The basic themes are that traditional counseling models are incomplete and that school counselors will be more helpful if able to employ counseling strategies that are responsive to students' goals, cultures, and environments. Cultural and environmental factors, as well as psychodynamics, are important in the helping process.

The School Counselor as an Advocate: A Case Study

When interviewing a 17-year-old male student who was having academic difficulties, a rural high school counselor learned that the client had moved away from home and was living in his own apartment. The student was working as many hours as possible after school in a local food market in an effort to earn enough money to support himself. He had too little time for his studies and was often so tired that he overslept or fell asleep in school. The counselor's response was to contact county social services agencies whose services were available to the student. These were services about which the student was uninformed. By contacting the targeted agencies on the student's behalf, the counselor was able to help the client receive assistance that made it possible for him to afford to live alone and finish his high school education. In this case, the counselor recognized the client's needs, knew or found out how they could be met, took the initiative to intercede for a client who was too naive to help himself, and changed the circumstances that were impeding the student's successful academic performance.

Advocacy Behaviors of School Counselors

Field and Baker (2004) reported findings from a study designed to investigate how school counselors define advocacy and what advocacy behaviors they employ. There were nine school counselor participants, and the data were acquired from semistructured interviews and focus groups. The participants defined advocacy as focusing on students, exhibiting specific advocacy behaviors, and going beyond business as usual. They identified several behaviors in their advocacy repertoires, and the first author noted that many of those behaviors "fit within a reactive framework of school counseling or reacting to the individual student after a problem has existed for some time" (p. 62). They concluded: "Other than appealing to people in power, none of these behaviors focus on changing the systems that may be creating or contributing to students' academic, personal, or social problems" (p. 62). This observation mirrored what Baker and Hansen (1972) reported more than 30 years earlier when a national sample of school counselors indicated a preference for helping students help themselves over more active responses.

The findings from these two studies indicate that there may be discrepancies between what those who promote advocacy in school counseling are offering in print and what is actually occurring in the grassroots school counseling programs. That is, it may be easier for individuals to write about the importance of advocacy and challenge professional school counselors to be advocates than it is for the school counseling practitioners to manifest the attributes of being an advocate. There is greater risk and dissonance associated with being an advocate than there is to writing about it. The apparent discrepancy between the importance attributed to advocacy in print and what may actually be occurring in the schools seems to indicate that greater attention should be paid to resolving the challenges associated with being an advocate.

Challenges Associated With Advocacy

Activism has a traditional place in school counseling, along with the more passive, traditional models. Passive and active counseling strategies are different, however, and the special challenges that face counselors who attempt to achieve activist goals are addressed in closing this section. Among these challenges are the possibility of appearing to be an adversary to those one is trying to influence and the real possibility of becoming burned out.

Pyrrhic Victories   In a classic example of a school counselor who demanded that the system do things the way he truly believed it should, Ponzo (1974) reflected on what he learned from his Pyrrhic victory—one in which he achieved his immediate goals but destroyed his relationships with some fellow professionals and part of the community:

> For a host of reasons, systems—human, animal, and social—tend to resist change. The strength of this resistance is dependent on the system's awareness of its need to change, its confidence in its ability to change, and its perception of the entity that proposes to bring the change about. It is prudent as well as necessary for a change agent to consider these factors as part of the change process. In Lincoln I attempted to bring about change without considering those factors. I barged in as if I were asked, wanted, and trusted. I failed to recognize that my "client" was very security conscious and had its borders well guarded. I failed to recognize that I was an outsider looking in. I failed to recognize that much of my behavior created additional barriers to change rather than removing existing ones. (p. 29)

Were he to do it over again, Ponzo would change his strategies, adopting a more diplomatic approach:

- One must understand him- or herself. Your own personality is a strong tool, but it can be administered in dosages that are too heavy.
- One must understand the system. This corresponds to developing a facilitative relationship with a student client. Empathy, warmth, concreteness, and understanding serve to prevent the system (client) from fearing you.
- Learn how the system works. The chances for success increase if one is a consultant who facilitates change rather than a foreign intruder who demands it.
- Noble dreams must be translated into achievable program goals. This will increase the probability of success and decrease the probability of failure and abandonment.

One of Ponzo's (1974) recurring themes is the recommendation to learn the system and then use that knowledge to negotiate differences and initiate new proposals. Counselors will be successful more often if others in the system view them as competent. Counselors are then in a better position to promote competing goals in an appropriately assertive manner and to take positions that are not necessarily popular. The ultimate negotiating goal is to have all sides gain something in the end, with everyone believing that they won something and that the counselor's goals were accomplished.

Burnout An overly literal interpretation of the information about advocacy can lead a counselor to work night and day every day of the week. Few individuals can keep up that pace without burning out. Therefore, the advocacy model, to be effective, must provide for prevention against burnout. Individuals who engage in advocacy need rest and recreation. Some time ago, Gunnings (1978) provided two useful suggestions for preventing burnout and enhancing the effectiveness of advocates. One suggestion is to give school counselors 12-month contracts so they will have time to develop community contacts. A second suggestion is to provide additional funding to reduce the ratio of counselors to students, especially in districts requiring high levels of advocacy. Additional strategies are released time during weekdays for counselors who work evening and weekend hours, periodic sabbatical leaves, and supportive counseling and supervision services for counselors. Counselors are also encouraged to make proactive efforts to prevent becoming burned out. Skovholt (2001) recommended a self-care action plan based on a thorough analysis of one's own other-care–self-care balance and of external factors such as stress at work that may contribute to burnout. Sheffield and Baker (2005) noted proactive approaches that have been used by counselors such as keeping up to date, reading professional books and journals, and attending workshops and conferences.

If the legacy of advocacy is to be kept alive, school counselors who accept the challenge need to be skillful change agents, not martyrs, so advocacy goals can be achieved and clients served. Such counselors need to protect themselves from burnout and to be protected by enlightened supervisors and administrators. Otherwise, they will be used up by the same systems they are trying to help their clients understand and manage; the losses will be great because some will leave the profession, and many will continue to function at a level much less proficient and helpful than they should, cheating both themselves and their clients.

COMPETENCIES FOR ADVOCACY IN SCHOOL COUNSELING

Advocating on Behalf of Student Clients

There are situations in which it seems clear to counselors that students face challenges that lie beyond their coping capacity. These are opportunities to be advocates for our student clients. These are also situations that present significant challenges. What do I do? How do I do it? What are the consequences? Will I place myself or my job at risk? These questions represent a myriad of challenges school counselors who would be advocates on behalf of their student clients will face. In this section, we address the "How do I do it?" question with a set of recommendations taken from recent contributions to the professional literature.

Lee (2001) stated that counselors need to possess cultural awareness, that is, an understanding of the diverse cultural realities of all students. This includes an awareness

New work patterns will include spending more time away from the office and school.

of one's own cultural blind spots. Also required are an awareness of the systemic barriers to quality education that clients face and knowledge of, and competence in, how to challenge the barriers effectively.

Marinoble (1998) suggested that a strategy for challenging systemic barriers successfully is trying to influence school policies, curriculum, and staff development when appropriate. For example, school counselors might lobby for including sexual orientation in the language of nondiscrimination clauses of teacher contracts and school policies about treatment of students and parents, for establishing and enforcing school policies forbidding homosexual slurs and jokes, and for permitting mention of gay and lesbian topics in school publications.

Kiselica and Robinson (2001) highlighted the importance of a capacity for appreciating human suffering and for being able to commit to advocating for those in need. To influence groups that might help students or that may be affecting them negatively, counselors are challenged to understand group change processes. As emphasized by Menacker (1974), organizations or systems (e.g., schools, school systems) sometimes engage in practices or policies that are harmful to students. In advocacy challenges of this nature, Dinsmore, Chapman, and McCollum (2000) recommended being able to (a) ensure that students and their families receive accurate information, (b) serve as a mediator for students and organizations, (c) negotiate with organizations on behalf of students, (d) engage in lobbying efforts on behalf of students, and (e) submit articulate complaints.

Another approach is to try to influence significant others such as colleagues and members of the community by raising the level of discussion (D'Andrea & Daniels, 1997). One such potential discussion topic is racism and how it impedes opportunities for many students to be successful academically.

In closing this section, we share strong words about advocating on behalf of student clients from Kiselica and Robinson (2001): "We are convinced that it is not possible for us as counselors to engage in genuine social action unless we discover a personal moral imperative to serve as a drawing force behind our work" (p. 396).

Advocating for Clients to Work on Their Own Behalf

Helping clients work in their own behalf begins with the basic listening and responding skills presented in chapter 9. Kiselica and Robinson (2001) stressed the importance of being able to listen and respond to clients who need advocates and to help them communicate effectively for themselves. An example would be to help a gay youth who wants to do so to be able to "come out." Arredondo and D'Andrea (2001, 2002) agreed that all communication skills are appropriate in counseling relationships. They stressed that the importance of realizing which skills to use and how to use them may vary across cultural groups. Ethnic and cultural differences across clients highlight the importance of multicultural competence.

This focus on multicultural competence introduces the Multicultural Counseling Standards (Sue, Arredondo, & McDavis, 1992) that are found in appendix H. Designed as guides to interpersonal counseling interactions, the standards define multicultural counseling as "preparation and practices that integrate culture-specific awareness, knowledge and skills into counseling interactions" (Arredondo & D'Andrea, 1995, p. 28) and identify the context as application to "African/Black, Asian, Caucasian/European, Hispanic/Latino, and Native American or indigenous groups which have historically resided in the continental United States and its territories" (p. 28). Note when viewing the standards in appendix H that the major section headings refer to awareness of one's own values and biases, awareness of the client's worldview, and use of culturally appropriate interventions.

These headings allude to the importance of competence based on knowledge and awareness. According to Arredondo and D'Andrea (2002), one cannot apply culturally competent skills without awareness and knowledge, and the process requires lifelong learning; it begins with classes and textbooks and continues with experience and learning from others.

Advocacy Competencies for School Counselors

Trusty and Brown (2005) stated that "Because advocacy cuts across multiple school counseling roles, occurs on multiple levels, and is conceptualized broadly, it is logical to conclude that everything school counselors do is advocacy" (p. 259). Responding to this challenge, Trusty and Brown (2005) offered a way of conceptualizing advocacy to develop advocacy competencies; however, space limitations make it impossible to provide all of their structure. Thus, an overview is presented here.

Three advocacy competency categories have been identified. The categories are dispositions, knowledge, and skills. Within each category, there are several subgroupings. Within the disposition category is advocacy disposition, family/support empowerment disposition, social advocacy disposition, and ethical disposition. For example, school counselors who have an advocacy disposition "Are aware of and embrace their professional advocacy roles. They are autonomous in their thinking and behavior. There is altruistic motivation with the major concern being students' well-being.

Advocates are willing to take risks in helping individual students and groups of students meet their needs" (Trusty & Brown, 2005, p. 260).

The knowledge competencies consist of knowing about resources, parameters (e.g., school policies and procedures), dispute resolution mechanisms (e.g., mediation, conflict resolution), advocacy models, and systems change. Advocacy skills include communicating, collaborating, assessing problems, solving problems, organizing, and taking care of one's self. Trusty and Brown (2005) pointed out that, although advocacy knowledge and skills can be provided through well-designed training programs, dispositions tend to be associated with beliefs and values that individuals acquired before entering training programs. Failure to have or develop advocacy dispositions will probably lead to failure to acquire advocacy skills as well. Therefore, influencing dispositions in the desired direction is an important basic component of acquiring competence as an advocate. Choosing individuals who have basic advocacy dispositions then is an important part of the training program selection process.

Key components of employing advocacy dispositions are autonomy and school climate. If school counselors achieve sufficient autonomy, they are better able to gain self-confidence and form important collaborative relationships with other professionals. If the school climate is a culture of autonomy, the environment is more likely to be democratic, value individual expression and change, and focus on the needs of students. If the school climate is one of conformity, the environment will value the needs of the professionals in the schools over those of the students. To be successful advocates, school counselors are challenged to accept advocacy concepts and possess the knowledge and skills required to be a successful advocate. Potential for success as an advocate is also influenced by one's school climate.

Brown and Trusty (2005) offered a step-by-step model of the advocacy acquisition/ implementation process that proceeds as follows: (a) develop and advocacy disposition, (b) develop advocacy relationships and knowledge, (c) define the advocacy problem, (d) develop advocacy plans, (e) implement advocacy plans, (f) make an evaluation, and (g) celebrate or regroup. This stepped model is similar to the rational approach to ethical decision making presented in chapter 5, the decision-making counseling model in chapter 9, and the collaborative consultation model in chapter 11. An important aspect of the position taken by Brown and Trusty is that there is a rational stepped approach to being an advocate that one can employ after having acquired the appropriate disposition, knowledge, and skills.

The *developmental advocate* role for school counselors proposed by Galassi and Akos (2004) provided a hypothetical application of the proposal by Brown and Trusty (2005). The requisite advocacy *disposition* is a belief that promoting the optimal development of all students is the primary mission of school counselors. The requisite advocacy *knowledge* and *skills* for developmental advocates are composed of (a) learning to be a leader in the school educational community; (b) being able to collaborate with stakeholders (e.g., students, teachers, and administrators) to build developmental supportive learning environments; (c) being able to recommend new strategies for the developmental needs of an increasingly diverse student population; (d) being able to offer proactive educational intervention approaches that help students acquire skills that enhance their academic, career, and personal/social development; and (e) knowing the developmental needs of *today's students*. These components of the developmental advocate model recommended by Galassi and Akos (2004) appear to represent the advocacy competencies highlighted previously and fit within the advocacy acquisition/implementation process proposed by Brown and Trusty (2005) and Trusty and Brown (2005).

EXAMPLES OF ADVOCACY IN SCHOOL COUNSELING

The following examples are a mixture of cases found in the professional literature and others that are hypothetical. We attempt to present a variety of student clients needing advocacy and a variety of approaches to advocacy; yet, we realize that there are numerous other possible examples. The narrative reveals both specific and implied advocacy competencies. Our format is to first provide background about the advocacy challenge. The overview is followed by a narrative summary of the advocate's response and an analysis of the advocacy process involved.

Empowering Her To Be All That She Can Be

Background.   That women have not achieved a status equal to men is a widely accepted and documented proposition. One domain in which these differences have clearly manifested themselves is occupational opportunities (Bartholomew & Schnorr, 1994; Pedersen, 1988). Bartholomew and Schnorr (1994) highlighted the need to enhance the confidence of many young women to enable them to take advantage of career opportunities opening up to them, especially in mathematics and science. The several recommendations Bartholomew and Schnorr offered for responses by counselors add up to a challenge to conceive and implement a broad range of efforts aimed at enhancing the self-esteem of female students so they will view themselves as capable of pursuing expanding career opportunities.

Summary.   When meeting with an 11th-grade female client to discuss her plans for the future, a male counselor asked her what she wanted to be when she graduated from high school. The client, who was a better than average student, stated that she was planning to go to college and to find a major or career field that would not prevent her from being a successful homemaker and having children and a family. When the counselor asked her to elaborate on the criteria for careers that did not prevent her from being a successful homemaker, she responded in a manner that indicated she had considerably restricted her college field and career opportunities.

When the counselor asked her if there were college fields and careers that she might consider pursuing that were not being considered because of her previously stated beliefs, she listed several. The counselor learned that she had been influenced not to consider these fields or careers by her parents and her middle school counselor. They had informed her that she should restrict her options to courses and majors that did not require math and science because girls were not as strong in those disciplines as boys. They also indicated that she should not waste her time in a major or career that was too challenging or required too much of a commitment because she would probably be getting married and raising a family in the not too distant future.

The counselor's advocacy responses were as follows. He provided her with accurate information about the careers of interest to her, about her math and science aptitudes, and about related college majors. He also provided age-appropriate gender equity information for her to read. The information dissemination was accompanied by counseling sessions to help her process the information thoroughly while trying to empower her to make her own decisions. In addition, the counselor volunteered to visit with the student's parents about this concern if she wanted him to and made a note to himself to try to find a way to raise the gender equity consciousness of his middle school counseling colleague.

Analysis.   Much of the activity in this advocacy response occurred in the counselor's office. He recognized the student client's need for someone to empower her to be all that she can be, apparently because he believed in gender equity. He then helped her find and process useful information. Realizing that the student may not be able to deal with her parents alone, the counselor volunteered to help her beyond the confines of his office. Finally, the counselor seemed ready to try to influence the system by approaching the counselor colleague who seemed to be in need of gender equity consciousness raising in an effort to induce change.

An Advocate for the Family in the School

Background.   Exceptional children have a physical, emotional, or intellectual status that places them outside the normal range and therefore causes them to be categorized as having a disability. The welfare of this constituency historically concerned counselors, but they had little direct contact with such children until November 1975. Any question about whether school counselors believed in equity for exceptional children became academic with the passage of PL 94-142, the Education for All Handicapped Children Act, in 1975. This piece of federal legislation made equity for exceptional children mandatory across the United States and challenged school counselors to implement their social activism tradition.

PL 94-142 is specific about what is to be done. One particular ingredient of the law is that all individuals between the ages of 3 and 21 have to be given a free, appropriate public education in some form and setting. That education is to be provided, to some degree, in the same environment with able individuals. This concept is known as *mainstreaming.* Implementation of the mainstreaming concept is specified through annual individualized educational plans (IEPs) that are developed for every child. IEPs must include information about the child's current level of functioning, annual goals, measurable short-term objectives, and an inventory of specific educational services that the child requires. IEPs are drawn up by multidisciplinary teams of teachers, administrators, and pupil service specialists (including counselors) in cooperation with parents. Parents of exceptional children are granted specific due process rights that include the right to independent educational evaluations, the option of requesting hearings by impartial officials, and the inspection of all evaluative records. Chief among the categories of people whose education is governed by PL 94-142 are those children who are deaf, deaf-blind, hard of hearing, mentally retarded, multidisabled, orthopedically impaired, other health impaired, seriously emotionally disturbed, specific learning disabled, speech impaired, and visually impaired.

Passage of the Education of the Handicapped Act Amendments of 1986 (PL 99-457) expanded the mainstreaming concept to working with both the child and the family through individualized family service plans. This legislation calls for school personnel to work closely with the family and the child to identify early intervention services. Greer, Greer, and Woody (1995) stated that PL 99-457 expands the role of counselors in the mainstreaming process.

Concern about programming in schools that seemed to be defeating the principles in PL 94-142 led to enactment of the Education of the Handicapped Act Amendments of 1990 (PL 101-476). PL 101-476 calls for *inclusion*, which means that all students, regardless of the severity of their disability, must be included in all aspects of school life. This vignette is drawn loosely from Hourcade and Parette (1986).

Summary.   A school counselor received a telephone call from the parents of a child with epilepsy who revealed that the child needed an anticonvulsant medicine administered while in school. Unfortunately, unenlightened school personnel resisted responding to the parents' request, and their family physician referred them to the school counselor. The counselor recognized that the family needed an advocate to act as a liaison between them and the school—a champion for their position.

First, the counselor informed the parents that he would try to act as a liaison if they wanted. With their approval, the counselor diplomatically informed the unenlightened school personnel about the student's rights under the applicable federal legislation, the parents' due process rights, and the responsibilities of the school personnel. Upon achieving cooperation from the targeted school personnel, the counselor informed the parents and proceeded to ensure that the student received the requisite anticonvulsant medicine. Coordinating the medication process involved informing/educating all school personnel who were to participate in the process about their responsibilities and roles, arranging the medicine administrations (e.g., times and places, excuses from classes for the student), ensuring the student was cognizant of the system that had been set up, informing the parents about what to expect and their due process rights, keeping notes about important events and agreements in the process, monitoring the process as it occurred, and evaluating the success of the advocacy intervention.

Analysis.   In this vignette, the counselor was appropriately informed about the related legislation while also understanding the student's rights and the school's responsibilities. The counselor also viewed the student's family as part of the client system and realized that they needed help from someone familiar with the school system and personnel. Beyond that, the counselor was willing to take the risk of advocating for them and upsetting the previously uncooperative school personnel. It also appears as if the counselor knew how to approach the school personnel in a manner that got their attention and cooperation. Finally, the counselor was willing and able to coordinate the process once it was initiated.

A Proactive Effort to Expand the Range of Possibilities

Background.   This example is based on a project reported by Vontress (1966). Advocacy is a theme that runs through the multicultural literature (cf. Bailey & Paisley, 2004; Bemak, Chung, & Siroskey-Sabdo, 2005; Casas & Furlong, 1994; Chung, 2005;

Gibbs, 1973; Kopala, Esquivel, & Baptiste, 1994; Luftig, 1983; Rogler, Malgady, Constantino, & Blumenthal, 1987; Ruiz & Padilla, 1977). Pallas, Natriello, and McDill (1989) advocated a role for counselors outside the schools that might be conceived of as a community resource specialist, working with families and communities, helping them learn to use their power and reintegrating them with the schools. Acting in this manner causes a counselor to become known in the community as someone who cares. LaFromboise and Jackson (1996) suggested that doing whatever is possible to help clients control their own lives leads to empowerment—that is, students exerting interpersonal influence, improving performance, and maintaining effective support systems. Vontress (1966) described an all-out attempt to widen the range of possibilities for African American children in a large inner-city school.

Summary. Viewing themselves as advocates for the children in their school, the counselors developed and initiated a plan for a school–community collaboration program. They conducted an analysis of the needs of the students and their families, particularly those needs they were unable to meet through the services their staff could provide. Then, by concentrating on meeting those needs, they initiated a number of intervention strategies such as evening parent conferences, home visits, driving parents to visit colleges, talking to newspaper reporters, making television appearances, meeting with civic leaders, and finding part-time jobs for students. This multifaceted set of interventions consisted of working with students individually and reaching out to several targeted constituencies (e.g., families, the school board, business/community groups).

Analysis. Realizing that they were unable to meet all important needs of their student clients, these counselors were willing to extend their services by engaging in advocacy activities. To accomplish their goals, the counselors were willing and able to engage in activities that might be depicted as public relations and social work. They understood that enriching the current environment and opportunities for their students might have positive long-term benefits for their lives. Their efforts also resulted in the formation of school–community partnerships that had the potential to be continuous.

Advocacy for Sexual Minority Youths

Background. Marinoble (1998) wrote:

> A favorite self-esteem activity among elementary school children involves listening to a story about a "very special person" who can be seen by opening a colorful box. One-by-one the children lift the lid, peer inside, and see their own reflection in a mirror. . . . Most children giggle with glee, pride, or self-consciousness. It is fun, and it encourages children to feel good about the person they see. . . . For some children though, the mirror begins to develop a blind spot—a part of themselves they cannot see or, at best, cannot bring into focus. As these children progress through childhood and adolescence, their schools, families, and communities often collaborate to reinforce the blind spot. The results of this collaboration may range from mild to tragic. The blind spot is homosexuality—a sexual orientation that appears to be natural for approximately 10% of the population. (p. 4)

"Gay adolescents face the same developmental challenges as their heterosexual coun-
terparts, with the added burden of attempting to incorporate a stigmatized sexual
identity" (Fontaine, 1998, p. 13). For some sexual minority youths, the burden may be
too much to bear. Suicide is the number one cause of death among these youths, two
to three times more than among heterosexual youths (Cooley, 1998; Logan &
Williams, 2001; McFarland, 1998). Higher rates of substance abuse, psychiatric treatment, school problems, and running away from home have been documented as well
(Remafedi, 1987; Remafedi, Farrow, & Deisher, 1991). For others, the burden may be
sufficiently challenging to require counseling interventions. Collectively, Black and
Underwood (1998), Cooley (1998), Fontaine (1998), Marinoble (1998), Omizo,
Omizo, and Okamoto (1998), and Savage, Harley, and Nowak (2005) provided an
inventory of burdens that is both impressive and saddening: identity confusion and
conflict, depression, family disruptions, fear of exposure, internalized hostility, peer
relationship problems, self-doubt and low self-esteem, social isolation, unfriendly
environments (e.g., institutional homophobia), powerlessness, and concerns and
doubts about the future. Although heterosexual youths face many of these challenges
as well, some are clearly more applicable to homosexual youths (fear of exposure,
unfriendly environments) or have the potential for being more severe if one has a
homosexual orientation (identity confusion and conflict, family disruptions, peer relationship problems, social isolation, concerns and doubts about the future).

Many sexual minority youths attend schools in which institutionalized homophobia
ranges from outright intolerance to benign neglect. McFarland and DuPuis (2001)
reported about the decisions in three court cases that collectively indicate schools
must ensure safe educational environments for gay and lesbian students. Two examples
of advocacy interventions found in the professional literature are presented here.

Summaries.   Bauman and Sachs-Kapp (1998) provided an example of counselors
helping an alternative high school in Fort Collins, Colorado, manifest its goal to achieve
tolerance toward diversity. The focus of the counselors' efforts was to create schoolwide workshops on a variety of diversity issues, the most controversial of which was
sexual orientation, that were well organized and facilitated by students. The counselors
recruited and trained those students who would lead the workshops. An overview of
the workshops follows.

Student leaders were trained in a for-credit minicourse. Team building, self-
awareness enhancement, demonstrations of effective teaching and facilitating skills,
and practice with constructive feedback were features of the training program. Students
were not required to attend the workshops. An alternative workshop covering fear and
intolerance in more general terms was offered by a popular teacher. A daylong format
involving the entire school was followed. A guest speaker keynoted the workshops
with a presentation that focused on individual humanity being more important than
sexual orientation when dealing with people. Three panels followed, all of which the
students experienced via a rotation format. Guest panel members, chosen by students,
included gay, lesbian, and bisexual individuals (one panel); individuals whose family
members were gays, lesbians, and bisexuals (a second panel); and professional psychologists considered to be experts in human behavior (a third panel). All three panels
were requested by students to focus on the theme *How Hate Hurts*. Following the

panel rotations, small discussion groups, consisting of no more than 10 students and one or two staff members, were facilitated by the trained students. These groups focused on processing the experience and talking about feelings. The leaders followed a structured format they learned during their training. The closing event was an exercise for all in attendance scripted by the counselors and led by a popular teacher. Students who were willing to identify themselves as being gay, lesbian, or bisexual, or as having friends and family members who are (*the targets*), were invited to move silently to the opposite side of the room from the remainder of those present (*the nontargets*).

Ninety-five percent of students opted to participate in the primary program. Follow-up evaluation survey data indicated that, on a 5-point scale, the average rating of the educational value of the workshop was 3.8.

Muller and Hartman (1998) provided suggestions for group counseling, including issues that may be the focus of the group intervention (homophobia, loneliness and isolation, identity issues, alienation from families, suicide, substance abuse). They describe a counseling support group that was conducted in a suburban Maryland public high school. The general goal for this group was to provide an atmosphere for universality, hope, and interpersonal learning. Overt methods for identifying prospective members included placing posters in hallways encouraging sexual minority youths to see a counselor if they wanted to talk about their concerns, posting rainbows and pink triangles around the school with invitations from the counselors, posting antihomophobic slogans in the school counseling area, and the counselors wearing buttons declaring support for sexual minority youths. Teachers known to be trusted by sexual minority youths were informed about the proposed group. Seven students eventually responded and participated. An overview of the group intervention follows.

Two heterosexual female counselors led the group. Both had extensive preparation. Goals for the group counseling process focused on identifying and discussing feelings, developing coping skills, and building a support system. Twenty-five weekly sessions of 45 minutes each were held; meeting times were rotated to prevent students from missing the same class more than once a month. A more detailed description of the content and methods is offered in Muller and Hartman (1998) who stated: "Many sessions were devoted entirely to interpersonal issues which arose in the group. Anger and resentments among members and resulting feedback enriched sessions and became the focus of the group on many occasions" (p. 41).

Analysis.   Both interventions involved groups organized by counselors in their schools. The first group required prevention programming competencies and the second group counseling competencies. Probably speaking for the organizers of both group interventions, the author-counselors in the second intervention pointed out the importance of being aware of their own assumptions and beliefs, and of having the support of their principal in advance of and during the program. They also stated that school system policies on any kind of sexual harassment must be in effect (Muller & Hartman, 1998). Beyond competence, awareness, and acquiring support, the counselors were also risk takers, willing to demonstrate their advocacy for sexual minority youths in a potentially hostile school and community environment. The elements just cited required careful planning by the counselors, who also had to be able to organize and manage the programs efficiently and successfully.

Bully Busting Advocates for Violence Prevention/Intervention

Background.   The following case is hypothetical and based on information presented in Roberts and Morotti (2000) and Hanish and Guerra (2000). School violence has received considerable national attention in recent years, especially in the context of horrific instances where students take the lives of other students and teachers (Sandhu, 2000). Bullying is one manifestation of violence in schools, and, in some recent instances reported in the press, those who took the lives of classmates were bullying victims who responded in a very drastic manner. In our vignette, the counselor views the bully and the bully's target as individuals in need of an advocate.

Summary.   Reports from a few teachers indicate that a middle school eighth-grade boy has been bullying a much smaller, shy, and introverted sixth-grade boy for 2 months since students returned from summer vacation. The counselor's first step was to call in the target, or victim, to get acquainted, establish rapport, and decide when it was appropriate to ask about the bullying. Feeling comfortable with the counselor, the target related a tale of physical and mental abuse that had him both frightened and angry. The counselor immediately indicated that the target student's tale had been believed, that an effort would be made to help him immediately, and that the student was urged to promptly go to the counselor's office if either an act of bullying occurred or he felt like retaliating.

The counselor initiated a plan to work with the target and the bully concurrently. To help the target, the counselor (a) met with the victim to help him process his feelings about the situation and determine proactive strategies for protecting and feeling better about himself; (b) worked with teachers and administrators to make necessary modifications in the school climate to help the victim and reduce the likelihood that the bully would have opportunities to act; and (c) met with the victim's parents to help them process their concerns, determine what they could do to help, and understand that something constructive was being done at the school.

Concurrently, the counselor met with the bully. The first step was to make the contact nonthreatening and listen to what the bully had to say about himself and the situation. Eventually, specific unacceptable behaviors and their possible consequences were described to the bully. The counselor attempted to find opportunities to help the bully achieve increased self-awareness leading to change. Targets for the self-awareness effort were the bully's home environment and the sources of vicarious reinforcement for the bullying behaviors. This led to the counselor working with both the bully and his parents in an effort to induce change. Finally, once the effort was under way, the counselor provided attention, support, and long-term follow-up.

Analysis.   The counselor recognized the need for advocacy—for the victim and the bully—immediately. In addition, the counselor responded quickly, and the response was multifaceted. Interventions involved both the victim and the bully, and they were undertaken concurrently. The multifaceted response involved clients, school personnel, school climate, and parents. The counselor as an advocate achieved collaboration with others and served as a coordinator of the intervention process.

ACHIEVING PROFESSIONAL IDENTITY: ADVOCATING FOR THE SCHOOL COUNSELING PROFESSION

An "Old Ghost"

Confusion and debate about the role of school counselors seem to have accompanied the profession from its beginnings in the early 20th century. More than three decades ago, Shertzer and Stone (1963) referred to role confusion as an "old ghost." The professional literature was then, and is now, sprinkled with articles discussing, lamenting, and offering solutions for role confusion (cf. ASCA, 2005; Carmichael & Calvin, 1970; Gibson & Mitchell, 1981; Hutchinson, Barrick, & Groves, 1986; Knapp & Denny, 1961; Smith, 1955; Stone & Dahir, 2007; Ward, 2005). Although old and timeworn, it remains an important and unresolved issue. Sarbin (1954) likened the importance of being able to define one's role to adjustment of one's individual self-identity.

Haettenschwiller (1971) described counselors as being in a weak or boundary position within the power and status framework of the schools, receiving demands from parents, administrators, and teachers who are able to bestow both positive and negative sanctions. Willower, Hoy, and Eidell (1967) found that school administrators and teachers whose dominant attitudes toward the school environment tended to be custodial, favored maintenance of control or order, and caused humanistic teachers and counselors to remain silent or pay lip service to custodial concerns. School counselors may often find themselves in environments where some of their more influential colleagues and supervisors have beliefs that are contrary to the counselors' preferences and the ideals expressed in their training, possibly leading to role confusion. Despite these negatives, speaking for the TSCI, Reese House stated that school counselors should be attempting to make a difference through advocacy (Ward, 2005).

Enriching the current environment and opportunities for students might have positive long-term benefits for their lives.

Anne Vega/Merrill

A spate of reports about surveys of the school counselor's role appeared in *Journal of Counseling & Development, School Counselor,* and *Elementary School Guidance and Counseling* between 1985 and 1991 (cf. Boser, Poppen, & Thompson, 1988; Gibson, 1990; Helms & Ibrahim, 1985; Hutchinson et al., 1986; Hutchinson & Bottorf, 1986; Hutchinson & Reagan, 1989; Miller, 1989; Moles, 1991; Morse & Russell, 1988; Peer, 1985; Remley & Albright, 1988; Tennyson, Miller, Skovholt, & Williams, 1989; Wilgus & Shelley, 1988). Common themes from those surveys are presented here (Baker, Kessler, Bishop, & Giles, 1993).

Clear, consistent themes emerged. The most common challenges are (a) the role of school counselors is not well defined, (b) student-to-counselor ratios are too high, (c) counselors are engaged in auxiliary work too often, and (d) different stakeholders have conflicting expectations (e.g., students want counselors, parents want consultants, teachers want faculty advocates, principals want administrative assistants). Some unfortunate influences of these challenges are that many students may view counselors as being too busy with paperwork to see them, parents may perceive counselors as ineffective, teachers may distance themselves from counselors, and principals may under- or overvalue counselors for the wrong reasons. Some counselors may acquiesce to these conditions and become minimally effective professionals. Others may become frustrated and leave the profession. Yet others may adjust in a manner that makes them as effective as they can be but less effective than they might be. Johnson (2000) attested to the currency of this situation:

> After decades of struggling through a virtual role-identity crisis, it is time for school counselors to recognize their operational existence by revisiting their stated purpose, functions, and relationship within the system. The new millennium affords transformative opportunities for school counselors to refine their professional identity as highly trained practitioners, whose goal is to facilitate all students to become effective learners through the provision of a contemporary, integrated school counseling program that promotes the achievement of developmentally based competencies across academic, career, and personal-social domains. (p. 32)

The enduring nature of this role confusion indicates that school counselors and counselor educators were not very successful in meeting the challenge during the 20th century. Perhaps professional self-advocacy, the road less traveled, is the approach that needs to be emphasized in the 21st century. Although advocacy directed toward achieving universal recognition of the desired identity for school counselors by individual counselors and counselors within school systems is necessary, it is probably also not sufficient (Baker et al., 1993). A profession that agrees on its mission, role, and functions may be more likely to achieve dramatic change collectively rather than individually. Advocacy for this purpose must occur in each locality *and* collectively, beginning at the grassroots level (Baker, 2001).

A Professional Advocacy Vignette

The following vignette is based on recommendations found in Johnson (2000). Our case describes a group of school counselors who decide to become advocates for their own professional identity.

Summary.   The scenario that we present can conceivably occur anywhere, and it is hoped that it will be carried out in numerous school systems. A group of school counselors within a school system decided to advocate for themselves as primary players in their educational system. Their first step was to conduct internal discussions among themselves and determine a shared, clear vision that consisted of goals and objectives for the program, as well as to define the functions, time, and resources required to achieve them.

This first step was carried out as follows. The counselors conducted a needs assessment—that is, of students, teachers, parents, administrators, and community members. A more detailed coverage of needs assessments is found in chapter 4. The needs assessment data were used to identify goals for their program (e.g., What outcomes do we want to achieve over the next 5 years?). This led to writing a mission statement that reflected their vision for the future, one that can be understood by their stakeholders and used when promoting their cause. Next, they developed a school counseling program plan outlining objectives, activities, services, and expected outcomes across all grade levels. They established a calendar designating what services would be provided and when. The counselors included professional development for themselves within the plan. Going into more detail, the counselors created formal job descriptions for themselves at each level. They invited input from school administrators, union officials, professional organizations, and state legislative and education department representatives. Finally, the counselors selected a strong leader for their unit, someone who could be their advocate throughout the school system. The second step was to determine a strategy for promoting the plan that had been developed. This led to an ongoing public relations campaign designed to inform students, parents, teachers, administrators, the community, and the school board. All components of the plan were systematically integrated. The strategy included (a) presentations about the role of the school counseling program and accountability data about the effects of its services; (b) membership in school–community–based committees and publication of a newsletter for parents and the community that informed readers about program goals, roles, and accomplishments; (c) development of a booklet that informed readers about specific services to special populations; (d) visits to all classrooms in the fall to introduce the counseling program to teachers and students; (e) preparation of an annual accountability report that was distributed to building and central administrators, the school board, and appropriate parent and community groups; (f) invitations to teachers and administrators to visit classroom guidance sessions; (g) arrangements with local service clubs and organizations to offer counselors as speakers on topics related to the mission; (h) development of professional portfolios for each counselor to be made available to the public; and (i) a Web site that provided information about the mission, accountability data, a calendar of school counseling activities, and links for students and the community.

Analysis.   The counselors in this vignette appeared to believe in themselves and the value of their program. They were proactive in their efforts, united as a team, and clear about their goals. They worked their way through a plan to achieve their goals systematically and became advocates for themselves and their profession. Indirectly, they were also advocates for their students, schools, and community, all of whom would become beneficiaries of the accomplishments of the program. The plan was based on an awareness of good practice derived from professional standards. Their strategy for promoting the plan was multifaceted and reached out to their stakeholders. The public relations efforts exposed their important services to the various publics, were enhanced by accountability data, and brought attention to their mission. Because this is a hypothetical vignette, we cannot report on the actual outcomes. We believe that professional advocacy strategies of this nature have excellent potential for successful outcomes.

Achieving Advocacy Goals Through Political Action

We believe that grassroots efforts, such as those depicted in the previous vignette, are necessary for the school counseling profession to enhance itself in the 21st century. In addition, counselor educators and national professional organizations, such as the ASCA and ACA and their affiliates, will benefit from working together. The next generation of school counselors will have to be more active than their predecessors if the counselor role challenge is to be resolved. That resolution will require being active rather than passive in responding to the challenges, being informed, being committed to providing the best possible counseling services, becoming skilled at being successful advocates, and supporting the efforts of national, regional, and state professional counseling associations that are directed toward achieving uniformity and clarity in the school counselor's role.

The ACA provides significant resources for school counselors to use in achieving advocacy goals through political action. The ACA Web site is www.counseling.org. Clicking on Public Policy will pull up the political policy page. The ACA Legislative Action Center provides an inventory of important pending federal legislation with accompanying background about each item. Taking advantage of the opportunity to be an advocate is made easy through recommended content for letters to one's legislators as well as the e-mail addresses of those legislators. In fact, one can use the ACA's recommended model and send an e-mail message from the Web site. Library of Congress Legislative Information has a broad range of data to offer, such as recent legislative actions, texts of bills before Congress, and the Senate and House directories. Links provides access to a number of home pages, including the White House, the U.S. Department of Education, and the National Institute of Mental Health.

Chi Sigma Iota (CSI) (www.csi-net.org) has detailed advocacy ideas in their Professional Advocacy link. It is framed in terms of advocacy for the counseling profession. Information is available about the CSI advocacy themes and training materials, and there are links to other professional associations, including ACA.

Readers will find that state ACA and ASCA divisions also have developed political action programs to encourage members to respond to both federal and state issues. For example, the North Carolina Counseling Association has a government relations committee (www.nccounseling.org) that works closely with ACA and with state psychology, psychiatry, hospital, behavioral health care, marriage and family, social worker, and licensed professional counselors associations, and continues to search for new pathways to inform members and help them achieve advocacy goals.

Achieving Advocacy at the Local Level

Being active in one's community will help school counselors understand the culture of their student clients and identify their support networks. For example, local religious leaders may help school counselors identify previously untapped resources for school–community collaboration. Secular community agencies are also sources of community understanding and advocacy collaboration. Advocacy can become cyclical. When school counselors advocate for their students and communities, the clients and communities in turn may become advocates for the school counselors and their programs. This cyclical advocacy process leads to shared goals and potential for empowering all who are involved. One of the attributes of advocacy is school counselor leadership, a topic that we elaborate on in chapter 7.

FEATURED ACTIVITY: GRADUATE STUDENT PERSPECTIVES ON ADVOCACY IN SCHOOL COUNSELING

In this chapter, we discuss the place of advocacy in school counseling. Some of our students, during their pursuit of graduate degrees, have assumed the role of advocate to improve the university's educational environment for minority students and to improve the university's physical environment for students who are physically challenged. These graduate student advocates have had to ask themselves serious questions before taking on the role of advocate, including who will actually benefit from my advocacy and what risks do I face in assuming this role?

How do you feel about being a student who advocates for improving the educational environment for graduate study? How does this role prepare you for your advocacy role as a school counselor? What are your overall thoughts about advocacy in school counseling?

After you read this chapter, go to http://www.genesislight.com/scan21st/tell_us/advocacy.html and complete the form. With your permission, we will periodically post some of your creative thinking for the world to read.

OTHER SUGGESTED ACTIVITIES

1. Browse through back issues of *ASCA Counselor* or *Counseling Today*, the newsletters of the ASCA and the ACA, respectively; make an inventory of advocacy issues related to its articles.
2. Read several articles in *ASCA Counselor* or *Counseling Today* back issues. Try to determine what, if any, philosophical trends run through the articles that might suggest whether the ASCA and the ACA are consistent in their philosophy.
3. Take an inventory of your personal stance on social problems on the following scale:

   radical . . . . liberal . . . . moderate . . . . conservative . . . . reactionary

   Discuss these views in class.
4. Use the same scale to rate yourself on specific issues.

5. Use the same scale to rate yourself as an advocate.
6. If you have activist leanings, take stock of your chance of being successful versus turning others off or being impatient and undiplomatic. Do you need to make changes, or do you believe that confrontation is the best first option? Support your answer.
7. Organize a discussion among classmates on question 6.
8. Make an inventory of general strategies that counselors might use in the schools to initiate change diplomatically and without being perceived as a threat by the system.
9. Make an inventory of current and future issues in the schools that are most likely to require advocacy to resolve.
10. Debate the merits of Menacker's idea that "activist counselors may achieve empathy through direct, concrete helping activities."
11. Go to the SCAN Web site (www.scan21st.com) and propose some ways that this site might help school counselors become more effective advocates.
12. Brainstorm the following advocacy scenarios with your classmates and instructor.

> You are an elementary school counselor, and a parent of a second-grade student has approached you with the following concern. Her daughter is complaining that her class is boring and that the students who were in her first-grade class last year are in the other second-grade class this year. The teacher is also very strict and sometimes physically disciplines unruly students. The mother looked into the situation and came to the conclusion that the principal, when making room assignments for the current year, got her daughter's name mixed up with another child with a similar name and the two were switched accidentally. Otherwise, the students in the two classes are the same as the previous year. When she shared this observation and concerns about her child's unhappiness in school, the principal denied that a mistake was made and refused to make any changes.
>
> You are a counselor in a comprehensive high school with a large student-to-counselor ratio (700/1). In addition, you are teaching half time in the social studies department and are expected to carry out the same counseling program responsibilities as your full-time school counselor colleagues. These responsibilities include scheduling your students before classes begin and making changes in schedules as needed or requested when school begins and over the duration of the school year, advising the student council and providing oversight for their massive fund-raising scheme each year, supervising the junior and senior proms when your advisees are in those grades, and supervising the student awards program and graduation when your advisees are seniors. The tasks seem overwhelming and impossible for one part-time counselor to do, and it is taking its toll on you both mentally and physically. Quitting is not an option at the present.

CHAPTER 7

Leadership and Collaboration in School Counseling

Goal: To discuss and advocate the role of leadership and collaboration in school counseling and identify leadership and collaboration competencies.

In the mid-1990s, an elementary school counselor in the southeastern United States worked to develop a way for all elementary school counselors in her school system to collaborate with the local senior citizens' center. Her purpose was to help children appreciate the oldest citizens in the community and to give senior citizens an opportunity to contribute some of their wisdom to the children, counselors, and other professionals in the elementary schools.

Among the senior citizens in the community was a former businesswoman who had designed innovative ways for major companies across the United States to exhibit their products and services at conventions around the world. Widowed at an early age, she had raised three children by herself, so she was interested in helping children and parents who were part of single-parent families.

The elementary school counselor was intrigued by the ingenuity and commitment of the former executive. Together they devised a project whereby children working with senior citizens built simple exhibits that provided childrearing tips for single parents and helpful ideas for how children might thrive in a single-parent environment, in particular, how they might contribute to making their families successful.

These exhibits were easy to transport and assemble at their destinations. The exhibits were used at local parent–teacher meetings and at professional meetings across the United States. The senior citizens and the children enjoyed working together in designing materials for the exhibits. Counselors and other professionals in the schools saw and learned from this remarkable collaborative effort. The project was a model for school counselor collaboration with important members of local communities.

Innovative school counselors have, throughout the history of the profession, made important contributions to the evolution of school counseling. These contributions have typically not been publicized or recorded in textbooks. The names of these dedicated counselors have typically remained only in the minds of the children they have served. Nevertheless, the leadership of these creative professionals has contributed much to the profession.

Individuals often enter school counselor preparation programs because they want to work closely with students, parents, and teachers. Seldom do these aspiring counselors consider the leadership skills that are required to build and maintain successful school counseling programs. This chapter focuses on school counselors as leaders and collaborators.

DEMAND FOR LEADERSHIP AND COLLABORATION IN SCHOOL COUNSELING

Leadership

Leadership has not been a traditional function in the repertoire of school counselors. According to Schwallie-Giddis, ter Maat, and Park (2003), the seeds of the current interest in leadership may be traced to the 1980s when school counseling was omitted from the "most quoted and read national publication" about school reform, *A Nation at Risk* (Gardner, 1983). This "real wake-up call" is said to have caused the counseling profession to undertake a number of initiatives that highlighted leadership and collaboration as important components of the school counselor role and functions.

The pathway to the current state of affairs for the ASCA includes the development of National Standards (Campbell & Dahir, 1997) and the National Model (ASCA, 2005). According to Schwallie-Giddis et al. (2003), "Leadership is defined as the ability to lead; the capacity to be a leader. A leader is someone who leads others along the way, one who guides (Morris, 1980)" (p. 171).

The ASCA National Model (ASCA, 2005) highlights leadership as one of four themes. We quote the document as follows:

> **Leadership:** School counselors serve as leaders who are engaged in systemwide change to ensure student success. They help every student gain access to rigorous academic preparation that will lead to greater opportunity and increased academic achievement. Working as leaders, advocates and collaborators, school counselors promote student success by closing the existing achievement gap whenever found among students of color, poor students or underachieving students and their more advantaged peers. School counselors become effective leaders by collaborating with other professionals in the school to influence systemwide changes and implement school reforms. In this way, school counselors have an impact on students, the school, the district, and the state. (p. 24)

Note the mention of systemic change, advocacy, and collaboration—the remaining three ASCA National Model themes. In addition, readers are encouraged to note the emphasis on access to rigorous academic preparation, equal access to academic achievement to close the achievement gap, counselors promoting school success, and involvement in school reform.

The emphases introduced in the previous paragraph mirror those of the TSCI and serve as evidence of the conceptual merger of the ASCA and TSCI paradigms for change. Further evidence is found in the words of TSCI proponent Reese House (Ward, 2005) who stated: "Within the ASCA (American School Counselor Association) Model, advocacy, leadership, and outreach are emphasized. If school counselors could take on this mantle, they would be the leaders needed in the schools to advocate for all students" (p. 34).

While promoting the TSCI, Paisley and Hayes (2003) tied the leadership idea to the ASCA National Standards (ASCA, 2005) by envisioning modern school counselors as leaders who advocate for the academic, career, social, and personal success of all students. Proponents of both TSCI and ASCA paradigms appear to have semi-independently reached the same developmental stage, that is, to promote preparation of school counselors who will be leaders, advocates, collaborators, and systemic change agents.

Although there is little or no outward evidence of collaboration between proponents of the ASCA and TSCI paradigms and those of the school–community collaboration paradigm, it appears as if the constructive work undertaken by the TSCI and the ASCA may also lead toward achieving school–community collaboration goals. Adelman and Taylor (2002) articulated the school–community collaboration goals: "School counselors and all other school personnel concerned must find their way to the leadership tables so that system-wide changes are designed and implemented" (p. 240). The goal is to connect schools, families, and communities (Taylor & Adelman, 2000). As leaders, school counselors will establish collaborations that connect schools with home and community resources. In so doing, considerable effort will be required to link health and human services with the schools.

In this initiative, the leadership emphasis appears to be on linking schools with community services to achieve school–community collaboration. This approach focuses on the perceived need to enhance the services available to students and their families in order to respond to social, emotional, and physical health barriers to student academic success by bringing outside services into better relationships with the schools.

Lewis and Borunda (2006) provided a dimension to leadership that they depicted as *participatory leadership*. In this approach, leadership is spread out among stakeholders democratically. In their own words,

> Participatory leadership emerges from engagement in collaborative efforts to bring about systemic change in specific schools by advocating for and engaging all students in ways in which they are challenged to meet high expectations, provided care and support, and given opportunities to participate in activities they find meaningful. (p. 408)

In this approach, attributes of participatory leaders include (a) drawing on democratic traditions, (b) bringing in and listening to diverse voices, (c) engaging all students in authentic dialogues that help individuals and communities define success for themselves and participate in activities that are meaningful, and (d) discovering outcomes that indicate what "works in helping all students to fulfill their potential in their local schools" (p. 408).

Collaboration

Also, one of National Model (ASCA, 2005) themes, collaboration and teaming is depicted as follows:

> **Collaboration and teaming:** School counselors work with all stakeholders, both inside and outside the school system, to develop and implement responsible educational programs that support the achievement of identified goals for every student. School counselors build effective teams by encouraging genuine collaboration among all school staff to work toward the common goals of equity, access and academic success for every student. (p. 25)

Collaboration appears to be a vehicle through which school counselors achieve leadership goals. The ASCA focus on collaboration emphasizes *working* with all stakeholders; *building* effective teams; *creating* effective working relationships; *understanding and appreciating* contributions of others in achieving educational equity; and *serving* as a vital resource to families, educators, and community agencies.

Keys and Green (2005) defined *collaboration* as "A specific process that occurs among individuals who have come together to solve problems" (p. 362). Keys and Green presented six characteristics that make an interaction collaborative in nature: (a) There is voluntary participation; (b) all involved parties respect each other as equals; (c) the participants have mutual goals; (d) although levels of responsibility may differ, problem-solving is a shared responsibility; (e) tangible (e.g., personnel) and intangible (e.g., knowledge) resources are shared; and (f) accountability for outcomes is shared.

Keys and Green (2005) accurately pointed out that collaboration with outsiders has not been a traditional feature of the public school systems. Consequently, school personnel are challenged to understand that many of their students have environmental and psychosocial problems preventing them from being successful students that school systems are unable to address by themselves. Luongo (2000) cited evidence suggesting that from 30% to 40% of children receiving services from core social institutions such as child welfare, criminal justice, and behavioral health are also in need of special services in the schools.

These circumstances promote a need for collaboration. In the school environments where collaboration with outsiders is the road less traveled, enlightened school counselors may be the professionals who can bring the important stakeholders together to achieve school–community collaboration. Meaningful collaboration may be achieved via intelligent leadership initiatives undertaken by school counselors. Leadership initiatives that lead to successful school–community collaborations bring the leadership and collaboration concepts to life. That is, when the leadership and collaboration concepts are understood and appreciated by school counselors and they engage in successful leading and collaborating, ideas will be translated into action. That is the ultimate goal. Without school counselors who lead and collaborate, leadership and collaboration become inert ideas.

BASIC INGREDIENTS OF LEADERSHIP AND COLLABORATION IN SCHOOL COUNSELING

Are Leaders Born or Made?

This question has been studied for some time, and we do not intend to address it in this edition of the textbook. We are aware that leadership has not traditionally been treated as an important function in the training of school counselors. Indeed, we believe that many individuals who entered school counseling previously did not view themselves as leaders. Otherwise, they may have entered training programs for educational administrators.

There also are conditions in the schools that make leadership a challenge for school counselors. Haettenschwiller (1971) described counselors as being in a weak or boundary position within the power and status framework of the schools, receiving demands from parents, administrators, and teachers who are able to bestow both positive and negative sanctions. Furthermore, school counselors may often find themselves in environments where some of their more influential colleagues and supervisors have beliefs that are contrary to the counselors' preferences and ideals (Willower, Hoy, & Eidell, 1967). This may cause them to be silent or pay lip service to the preferences of their more dominant colleagues.

It seems as if some individuals are by nature and nurture more likely to seek or respond to leadership opportunities successfully. Others may not want to be, or may not be capable of being, good leaders. With regard to school counselors already in the field, perhaps the best thing that can be done is to inform and attempt to motivate them about the importance of leadership and help them if they are so inclined. With regard to future students, counselor educators who believe in the importance of leadership can attempt to select individuals who are willing and able to be leaders, as well as to become competent in all other aspects of the profession. Having done so, they can then provide training opportunities that enhance the potential to be successful leaders.

Perhaps practicum and internship experiences will help. However, it may not be until counseling students are on the job in the real world that they will have the opportunity to emerge as leaders. Then, they will have to be both willing and able.

Understanding Leadership Conceptually

Although relatively uncommon in the school counseling literature, studies of leadership are found elsewhere. Dollarhide (2003) applied important writings about leadership from adult education, management theory, educational administration, and political science to school counseling in a manner that will help readers apply the concept of leadership to practice. Important ingredients of this understanding of leadership are contexts and skills. Borrowing from the work of Bolman and Deal (1997), Dollarhide presented four contexts in which leadership might occur in school counseling. Each leadership context calls for school counselors to engage in corresponding leadership activities and apply requisite skills.

Structural Leadership Context.   According to Dollarhide (2003), the structural leadership context will lead to activities involving the building of effective comprehensive school counseling programs. The structural leadership process will include having a technical mastery of implementation and maintenance strategies. Perceived requisite skills for structural leadership are counseling, consulting, teaching, advocacy, and evaluation/accountability, all of which are common components of graduate school counselor training programs.

Human Resource Leadership Context.   Activities associated with human resource leadership are believing in people and communicating that belief, being visible and accessible, and empowering others. As is the case with structural leadership, the skills associated with human resource leadership (i.e., communicating, empowering, trust building, listening) are traditional components of school counselor training programs.

Political Leadership.   Dollarhide (2003) depicted political leadership as "a more nontraditional role for many counselors [that] may cause . . . anxiety and dissonance" (p. 305). Political leadership activities in school counseling include assessing power distribution in school buildings and districts, building linkages with important stakeholders, persuading, and negotiating. Requisite skills are relatively complex and difficult to teach comprehensively in traditional training programs. Therefore, school counselors may have to acquire and polish political leadership skills associated with negotiation, persuasion, collaboration, and advocacy on the job after completing the training program. Training programs most certainly can begin the process by introducing concepts and basic skills and by motivating trainees to believe in the importance of being successful political leaders.

Symbolic Leadership   The symbolic leadership context draws on "using symbols and metaphors to capture attention, framing experience in meaningful ways for followers, and discovering and communicating a vision" (Dollarhide, 2003, p. 305). This form of leadership focuses importance on relationships with students, families, and communities; articulating and maintaining faith in visions; and inspiring others through effective modeling. The associated skills for symbolic leadership are designing symbols, expressing meaning, inspiring others, and modeling for others. As was stated about political leadership skills, some of the symbolic leadership skills may need to be acquired beyond the training program as school counselors develop professional identities and mature into expert and trustworthy role models.

Viewing a Leadership Vignette Contextually   Excerpts from an example presented by Dollarhide (2003) are presented to enhance understanding. A newly hired school counselor was attempting to develop a comprehensive school counseling program based on the ASCA National Standards (Campbell & Dahir, 1997) in a rural setting where the existing program emphasized scheduling, testing, and discipline. The leadership contexts were used to formulate a change agent strategy.

The first priority was to design a viable program. Reducing inappropriate functions was a second priority. Symbolic and human resource leadership skills were employed initially when the counselor shared a passionate vision about the potential outcomes of her proposed school counseling program with influential stakeholders. Next, structural leadership skills were used to design a viable middle school counseling program. Teachers and parents were consulted. Finally, political leadership was addressed through seeking support from the school principal and establishing an advisory board to help with the design, implementation, and evaluation of the program. Eventually, the counselor weaved all four leadership contexts together into her own leadership style.

The vignette indicates that various leadership contexts may come into play during a leadership episode. Therefore, it behooves school counselors to acquire skills across all four leadership context categories to enhance their effectiveness. Furthermore, a

Are leaders born or made?

David Mager/Pearson Learning Photo Studio

conceptual understanding of the four contexts and their related skills will make school counselors better prepared to achieve leadership goals, such as those presented in this vignette, and analyze the process while engaged in change agent strategies.

COMPETENCIES IN BASIC LEADERSHIP AND COLLABORATION IN SCHOOL COUNSELING

It appears to us that the basic competencies are rather complex combinations of many specific behaviors. We have derived a set of behaviors that seem appropriate for leaders and collaborators. We also believe that these behaviors will be appropriate when used successfully. Using the behaviors successfully depends on a combination of one's genetic proclivities and one's socialization. It is not necessary to exhibit all the following behaviors to be a leader because there are numerous ways one can lead, depending on the circumstances. For example, one person may exhibit leadership qualities by taking charge during the process of developing and implementing a school counseling program. Another individual may demonstrate leadership in more subtle ways, such as being a mediator during a dispute, recruiting volunteers for collaborations, or helping community and school representatives build a sense of community. The following behaviors were taken from the work of Adelman and Taylor (2002), Bemak (2000), Bemak and Cornely (2002), Dahir (2001), Gysbers and Henderson (2000, 2001), Hatch and Bowers (2002), House and Hayes (2002), Keys (2000), and Rowley, Sink, and MacDonald (2002). The order in which they are presented does not reflect an opinion of their importance; rather, we have tried to order them in a manner that makes sense to us. When reading this information, reflect on the position of Chickering and Gameson (1987), who globally describe leadership as being untidy rather than orderly, the art of facilitating one's own growth as well as that of others, and being aware that your presence makes a difference in every situation. A leader in school counseling should be able to

- Cause, lead, implement, and maintain a comprehensive school counseling program.
- Form and lead committees, including chairing committees, planning agendas, and establishing meeting schedules.
- Coordinate the objectives, strategies, and activities of a comprehensive school counseling program.
- Serve as a missionary for the program.
- Develop mechanisms for educating and involving others.
- Develop support systems for yourself and other school counseling personnel.
- Conduct meetings, make commitments for action, form and convene steering committees, form and convene school and community advisory committees, establish work groups, and meet with district administrators and school boards.
- Demonstrate leadership skills as an active member of programs and committees.
- Identify and use complementary skills.

- Mediate conflicts.
- Recognize differences such as race, gender, experience, preferred learning styles, and work roles and use that information to engage in creative problem solving, even though it may involve conflict.
- Recognize opportunities for empowerment.
- Know how work groups operate, especially teams, and how to build effective teams.
- Recruit volunteers to assist in school programs.
- Build a sense of community in the schools.
- Know how to effectively manage school and community bureaucracies.
- Build a consensus and work collaboratively with a broad range of professionals and concerned citizens to achieve a sense of community.
- Keep your fingers on the pulse of the needs of students and on the mission and goals of the school.
- Adopt a systems perspective.
- Facilitate family–school partnerships.
- Break down bureaucratic turf boundaries.
- Work collaboratively with school administrators.
- Bring community services into the schools and coordinate them.
- Develop mutual prevention/intervention programs with community agencies.
- Work closely with other support personnel in the schools (e.g., school psychologists, school social workers, nurses, special educators).
- Support, consult, and work with teachers.
- Collect and share data (e.g., document obstacles to student growth and development).
- Develop a crisis team that is educated in emergency response procedures.
- Inform administrators about the contributions you plan to make rather than asking them what to do.

EXAMPLES OF LEADERSHIP AND COLLABORATION BY SCHOOL COUNSELORS

Transforming the School Culture: An Example of Leadership

This vignette is based on a report by Littrell and Peterson (2001) about an elementary school counselor in Oregon whose goal was to transform the school's culture from one of negativity and high stress to one of problem solving at all levels. The counselor had a vision of a school in which all children were problem solvers. Littrell and Peterson depicted the counselor as having a guiding vision, defined values and beliefs, a willingness to confront the school about her vision, and the ability to clarify how she functions in the system.

We do not know the exact sequence of steps in which the counselor engaged. The following specific acts of leadership were reported by Littrell and Peterson (2001). The counselor adopted a four-step problem-solving model that helped her think systematically. Through a combination of previous experience, meetings, and consultation, she learned about and understood the school climate. Having a vision and knowledge of the school climate, the counselor introduced "a new, but natural and familiar, 'language' that was easy for all to understand—the language of problem solving" (p. 314). For example, she would ask such questions as "What is the problem?" and "What have you tried so far?" Through teaching the language of problem solving, she bonded with students. Eventually, parents picked up the problem-solving language as well.

Eventually, the counselor designed and implemented a developmental curriculum that was based on problem solving. For example, second graders learned 10 ways to solve conflicts. Having established a problem-solving curriculum in classrooms, the counselor also found ways to implement the curriculum content elsewhere (e.g., a problem-solving wheel in the principal's office). In response to numerous referrals by teachers of students who were classroom behavior problems, the counselor created several counseling groups or clubs, beginning with six that were topic focused (e.g., students who get everything done and want to do more and students who need to develop their own unique strengths).

The counselor's systematic approach led to identifying four factors that influenced her individual counseling: (a) accenting client strengths, (b) providing a caring relationship, (c) knowing her counseling theories and techniques, and (d) providing hope. Viewing the entire school as a community, the counselor built partnerships at all levels (e.g., the lunchroom supervisor, the new junior high school counselor, teachers, parents). As a leader, the counselor engaged in advocacy activities such as lobbying legislators to influence policy and mobilizing local merchants to acquire clothing for children who were poor. The report also highlighted the counselor's effectiveness at planning and organizing, her attempts to ensure self-renewal, and an incidence of her efforts being self-sustaining 6 years later.

Littrell and Peterson (2001) concluded their report as follows:

> [She] was not a perfect counselor; however, we chose to study her because her work as a school counselor was exemplary and inspiring. The uniqueness of our model is in the emphasis on the counselor as a person and on the counselor's ability to assess the context and align vision, identity, beliefs/values, capabilities, and behaviors in the interest of creatively conceiving and realizing a programmatic vision. Our hope is that this model helps counselors to be visionary educational leaders. (p. 318)

School-Based Clinicians: An Example of Collaboration

The following vignette was derived from a report by Porter, Epp, and Bryant (2000). The school-based clinicians in the vignette are part of a larger program sponsored by the Community Psychiatry Department of the Johns Hopkins University in Baltimore, Maryland. The Johns Hopkins program partnership includes the departments of social services, juvenile justice, health, and police, and the mental health clinicians include professional counselors, psychologists, arts therapists, and social workers.

Our example took place in an urban high school in which the clinician was a welcome guest because of high incidences of challenging mental health problems. The clinician worked with the difficult mental health cases to allow the school counselors to provide developmental guidance and college counseling services to a broad range of students.

The school's director of guidance implemented a collaborative system that could be established in other schools. She created a school mental health team that consisted of the school counselors, a vice principal, a school nurse, a faculty member, and the school-based clinician. The guidance director chaired the committee and served as coordinator.

The school was referring clients to a clinician from an outside agency that was being paid by Medicaid. Therefore, a system of oversight and referral was needed. According to Porter et al. (2000), the committee was egalitarian, multidisciplinary, and free of turf battles. However, there were a number of challenges from within the school and the community. For example, the magnitude of presenting problems challenged the committee to figure out how to respond within the confines of their resources and not become overwhelmed. Also, some members of the faculty were less than friendly and cooperative, and the committee had to engage in quiet diplomacy in that domain. Occasionally, the committee faced dilemmas about which they were divided (e.g., reporting child abuse) and had to recognize the value of their common mission.

Porter et al. (2000) teased out the following lessons about collaboration that can overcome the potential barriers: (a) use the multidisciplinary team meetings to solve problems and make decisions, (b) ensure cultural sensitivity of clinicians through training, (c) develop a common language across the represented disciplines, (d) develop open and flexible attitudes, and (e) standardize procedures. Porter et al. concluded:

> School counselors are in a unique position to facilitate the collaborative process needed to ensure the provision of comprehensive, accessible mental health services. Collaboration is a major challenge, but when professionals are able to use their varied skills and experiences in a complimentary, collaborative way, they can transcend any barriers. (p. 322)

SCHOOL COUNSELORS AS LEADERS AND COLLABORATORS

Based on a survey of school counselors in South Carolina, Bryan and Holcomb-McCoy (2004) reported that school counselors across all levels indicated that their involvement in school–community–family partnership collaborations was important. We find the potential for school counselors to be leaders and collaborators as just depicted to be exciting. School counseling is a human service career, and school counselors are exposed to numerous situations that challenge their ability to serve all clients who are in need. We believe that leadership and collaboration are avenues through which school counselors can be of greater service to a broad range of clients. Perhaps the most important ingredients are the desire and will to do so.

The structural leadership context introduced in this chapter lists building effective comprehensive school counseling programs as a goal and teaching as one of the competencies. In chapter 8, we focus on the teaching function in school counseling.

Work closely with other support personnel in the schools.

FEATURED ACTIVITY: GRADUATE STUDENT PERSPECTIVES ON LEADERSHIP AND COLLABORATION IN SCHOOL COUNSELING

In this chapter, we discuss leadership and collaboration in school counseling. According to most contemporary paradigms of school counseling, counselors serve as leaders and collaborators who engage in systemwide change to ensure student success. These paradigms suggest that school counselors should help every student gain access to rigorous academic preparation that will lead to greater opportunity and increased academic achievement. Some of our graduate students have argued that taking on the role of leadership toward academic achievement diminishes the primary role of the school counselor in improving the psychological and social well-being of students.

What do you think about the school counselor as a leader and collaborator whose primary goal is to improve educational fulfillment and academic achievement of all students?

After you read this chapter, go to http://www.genesislight.com/scan21st/tell_us/leadership.html and complete the form. With your permission, we will periodically post some of your creative thinking for the world to read.

OTHER SUGGESTED ACTIVITIES

1. Debate the current assumption that school counselors should be leaders.
2. Interview one or more school counselors and ask their opinion about whether they should be leaders.
3. Follow up with the school counselors who believe that they should be leaders, and ask them to provide an inventory of circumstances in which they believe school counselor leadership is needed and appropriate.

4. Study the list of leadership characteristics in this chapter and make a checklist of those with which you agree. Also, check off those you already possess and those you need to acquire.

5. Discuss the interrelationships among leadership, collaboration, and advocacy.

6. Make an inventory of both your leadership strengths and challenges.

7. Working independently or collectively with colleagues, develop a profile of the characteristics of a school counselor who is a good leader.

8. Make an inventory of the risks associated with being a leader as a school counselor. Then, make an inventory of possible ways to prevent or minimize the risks while still being successful.

9. Make an inventory of the disadvantages associated with failing to provide leadership, collaboration, and advocacy as a school counselor. Then, make an inventory of the potential beneficiaries of good school counseling leadership. Finally, compare the two inventories and process your reactions to the comparisons.

10. Discuss the affect you feel when being called to be a leader in the school counseling profession.

11. Brainstorm the following advocacy scenarios with your classmates and instructor.

> You have just graduated from a master's degree program in school counseling, found a job with which you are pleased, been integrated into the school setting, and want to make a contribution to your profession beyond what is being accomplished at your school. Yet, you are not sure what to do. You have landed a new school counseling position and found that the counselors in your school are not very well thought of. They are scapegoats for many of the administration's shortcomings and the objects of many unkind jokes around the school. In addition, the counselors tend to primarily engage in one-to-one counseling on demand and keep to their offices and the office suite all day, more or less avoiding contact with faculty members unless they are approached by them.
>
> Your school counseling colleague has angrily informed you of the problem he is having with local mental health counselors and has stated that he will never refer one of his clients to them again. Previously, he made a referral and never received any feedback from the agency. Upon inquiring about the case, he was informed that they will not tell him anything due to client confidentiality. He wonders whether it is useless to make any referrals to local mental health counselors if they will not help him become better informed to be of service to the referred students when they are in school.

12. Go to the SCAN Web site (www.scan21st.com) and propose some ways that this site might assist school counselors in their roles as leaders and collaborators.

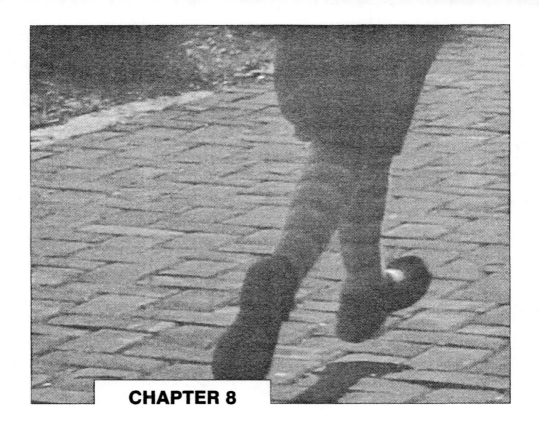

CHAPTER 8

Prevention Programming in School Counseling: Serving All Students Proactively

Goals: To offer evidence of the importance of developmentally appropriate prevention programming, propose basic competencies for proactive prevention programming, and provide examples.

> The Cornish Test of Insanity comprised a sink, a tap of running water, a bucket, and a ladle. The bucket was placed under the tap of running water, and the subject was asked to bail the water out of the bucket with the ladle. If the subject continued to bail without paying some attention to reducing or preventing the flow of water into the pail, he or she was judged to be mentally incompetent. (Morgan & Jackson, 1980, p. 99)

167

We have had many opportunities to hear school counselors discuss their hopes and aspirations for preventive programming in classrooms. The following account from an elementary school counselor is among the most poignant we have heard:

> *I meet with small groups of children every week, giving them an opportunity to discuss their feelings about many aspects of their lives. These groups help the children to feel welcome at school and to know the benefits of self-disclosure and listening. Recently, while discussing the topic "the saddest thing that ever happened to me," a fourth-grade girl reluctantly raised her hand. When I looked toward her, she brought her hand down quickly. She seldom said anything in the group and generally appeared shy and reserved in social situations. Several other youngsters contributed to the group topic before her hand went up again. I looked toward her, and she lowered her hand. Two other members of the group spoke. Her hand went up again and remained up this time. I called on her. She spoke with great care: "The saddest thing I ever saw was my grandfather hanging from a rope in our barn." She had been holding this in for weeks and finally felt trusting enough to share this traumatic experience from her life. She was relieved. I invited her to meet with me later to discuss this matter.*

The flow of problems to counselors' offices can never be reduced unless counselors plan and implement preventive intervention programs. It is not surprising, therefore, that school counselors devote a major portion of their time and effort to preventing the onset of emotional problems in children. In cooperation with teachers, counselors conduct classroom programs that include listening activities and other techniques that are designed to help children (a) feel worthy as persons and as students, (b) recognize their feelings about themselves and about learning, (c) feel comfortable about expressing these feelings openly and honestly, and (d) acquire developmentally appropriate knowledge and coping skills.

DEMAND FOR PREVENTION PROGRAMMING IN SCHOOLS

In chapter 3, we advocated school counseling programs that are balanced between intervention responses and proactive prevention programming. Proactive prevention programming is the mainstay of the prevention function and is pedagogical in nature. The word *pedagogical* identifies these activities because they are primarily instructional; *pedagogics* is the "art, science, or profession of teaching" (*Merriam-Webster's Collegiate Dictionary*, 1998, p. 856). Although pedagogics is seldom associated with counselor education, there is no denying that school counselors engage in instructional or pedagogical activities when delivering many group programs. Many terms label these programs: classroom guidance, group guidance, guidance teaching, developmental guidance, guidance-related courses or units, and wellness programs. This textbook uses the term *proactive prevention programming*. We use this term because it allows us to present a set of pedagogical competencies that are needed to deliver classroom guidance, group guidance, developmental guidance, or any such school counselor program that is pedagogical in nature. The word *proactive* indicates that the activities involved are anticipatory. *Prevention* indicates that the goals are to prevent problems and enhance human development. The word *programming* indicates that the process involves systematically arranging a sequence of intentional applications based on goals and objectives derived from an underlying conceptual rationale. School counselors are challenged to be competent teachers/pedagogues in order to offer proactive prevention programs. Providing a balanced school counseling program seems to require competence as teachers.

The ASCA uses the term *developmental guidance* when referring to proactive prevention programming. Excerpts from its 1978 position statement (reviewed and revised in 1984) on developmental guidance indicate that, aside from differing semantics, the association seems to agree that proactive prevention programming is an important school counseling function:

> Developmental guidance should be an integral part of every school counseling program and be incorporated into the role and function of every school counselor. During recent years a number of counselor educators and school counselors have advanced the proposition that counseling can and should be more proactive and preventive in its focus and more developmental in its content and process.... Developmental guidance is a reaffirmation and actualization of the belief that guidance is for all students and that its purpose is to maximally facilitate personal development.... The program should be systematic, sequential, and comprehensive.... The program should be jointly founded upon developmental psychology, educational psychology, and counseling methodology. (ASCA, n.d., p. 33)

The ASCA National Model with the National Standards therein is the most recent effort of the ASCA to operationalize the developmental guidance concept highlighted here. The ASCA National Model (ASCA, 2005) was introduced in chapter 2. Also introduced was the relationship between the ASCA National Model and the emphasis by Gysbers and Henderson (2000) on a K–12 curriculum for school counselors consisting of "guidance" classes designed to help all students meet the competencies presented in the ASCA National Standards (Campbell & Dahir, 1997).

Stakeholders hope pervasive social and personal problems can be prevented. Childhood and adolescence are opportune times to prevent many problems. Therefore, the school years are an excellent time for programs designed to help children and adolescents get the most out of their school experience and cope better with life's challenges. This is also a good time to identify at-risk individuals and to prevent them from being overwhelmed by the problems they are at risk of experiencing. Proactive prevention programming usually has several common features: It is structured, planned in advance, presented in a group format, and led by individuals working from a predetermined plan.

Many school counselors enter the field with degrees in education and with teaching experience. Traditional counselor education programs are designed to provide them with additional competencies such as counseling and assessment skills. School counseling trainees, however, increasingly come from fields outside education, especially in states that do not require teaching experience as a prerequisite for school counseling certification or licensure. Because these individuals are not trained in pedagogics, it is important to train them as competent instructors and competent counselors. School counseling students, it seems, will benefit from opportunities to become competent at pedagogics during their training in order to provide balanced school counseling services.

Training experiences for school counselors might include opportunities to learn about structured, developmentally appropriate proactive group prevention and intervention programs for students, teachers, and parents, and opportunities to learn skills for presenting and delivering such programs effectively to students representing the students' own and others' worldviews. Counselors planning and presenting structured programs to groups of students will be more successful if they are competent technically—at developing lesson plans and supplementing instruction with activities that are interesting and that complement the instructional goals—as well as competent multiculturally—able to make programs meaningful to individuals representing all worldviews in their schools.

The three best paradigms for enhancing school counseling introduced in chapter 2 advocate the importance of proactive prevention programming competencies. Speaking for the ASCA National Model, Bowers, Hatch, and Schwallie-Giddis (2001) stated that the components should include a guidance curriculum. Furthermore, Gysbers and Henderson (2001) indicated that the curriculum should cover kindergarten through 12th grade and translate the ASCA National Standards (see appendix B) into classroom activities delivered via structured groups. Indeed, the competencies in the ASCA National Standards offer a foundation for proactively designing strategies and producing activities to enhance student achievement and success in academic, career, and personal-social development.

Representing the TSCI, House and Hayes (2002) used the words *planner* and *program developer* as desired competencies for school counselors. The Education Trust hopes to produce school counselors who can promote student achievement through well-articulated developmental school counseling programs. Through these programs, school counselors will teach students how to help themselves via improved organizational, study, and test-taking skills. House and Hayes also promoted school counselor involvement in staff development for school personnel focused on learning how to promote high expectations and standards.

In the school–community collaboration paradigm, part of an interconnected system for meeting the needs of all students is having systems for promoting healthy development and preventing problems (i.e., primary prevention). Examples given are drug and alcohol education, parent involvement, and conflict resolution (Adelman & Taylor, 2002).

PROGRAMMING FOR PREVENTION

Important Initial Conditions

Presenting a plan for prevention programming must have several important initial conditions. First, a school environment in which administrators view teachers and counselors as unique, yet equally important, professionals is essential. Second, participants should understand at the outset that a balanced program is a basic goal. Third, all individuals who influence the counselors' role should understand what prevention means.

The first of these conditions, although important, is somewhat beyond the purview of this book. On the one hand, if not treated as equal to the teachers, counselors will have a difficult time. On the other hand, the balanced program advocated here may help

Edwin R. Gerler, Jr.

Academic achievement can be influenced in a positive direction.

bring about desired changes in administrative attitudes because potential outcomes are visible. The second condition, the goal of a balanced program, has already been addressed. Therefore, we look at ways to help influential individuals understand the meaning of prevention.

The word *prevention* means various things to different people. For instance, the general population longs to have such pervasive problems as AIDS, violence, adolescent suicide, substance abuse, unemployment, and teenage pregnancy prevented, and to have all students be successful academically and in life. This is certainly a tall order and one that creates great expectations. These expectations have led to the identification of students who need intervention responses. Therefore, the public demands prevention, and rightly so. Unfortunately, AIDS, violence, suicide, substance abuse, unemployment, and teenage pregnancy are actually outcomes, the causes of which are varied and subtle. Therefore, planning to prevent any one of those negative outcomes before it occurs is difficult.

Stakeholders also associate some positive or developmental outcomes—such as social skills competence, appropriate assertiveness, multicultural competence, self-esteem, good self-concept, and academic success—with prevention programming. When this is the case, it is hoped and perhaps expected that planned prevention programming will cause the participants to have enhanced social skills, appropriate assertiveness, multicultural competence, greater self-esteem, improved self-concepts, or good grades. Although these appear to be agreeable and important outcomes, the words represent general concepts that beg to be made specific and measurable enough to serve as criteria for prevention programming efforts. That is, programmers need to be able to associate content with identifiable outcomes. These conditions suggest challenges for prevention programmers, who must develop programs with specific activities that lead to measurable outcomes. Thus, the best thing programmers can do to prevent pervasive problems such as adolescent suicide while enhancing the desired personal qualities is to demonstrate a logical connection between their prevention programs and the desired outcomes. For example, many children who learn to cope better with anxiety, communicate better with their peers, understand the features of their developmental stages, and become more assertive when faced with peer pressure are less likely to abuse drugs and more likely to feel good about themselves. The success of such prevention programs may have to be shown simply by participant's acquiring competence and knowledge (ASCA, 2005; Durlak, 1983).

Thus, participants need to demonstrate that they have become more assertive and less anxious or that they have learned information about developmental stages. From these demonstrations, it will have to be assumed that participants are better prepared to cope and less likely to succumb to problem behavior because it is impossible to measure whether something was prevented. We believe that the ASCA National Standards (Campbell & Dahir, 1997) will help school counselors who are attempting to resolve this challenge.

In addition to helping influential people become aware of misperceptions about prevention, it is important to help them understand prevention. Shaw and Goodyear (1984) provided a definition that is both applicable to school settings and generalizable to other situations. It focuses chiefly on primary prevention. Taken in part from Cowen (1982), their definition is as follows:

> It must be group—or mass—rather than individually oriented (even though some of its activities may involve individual contacts). It must have a before-the-fact quality, i.e., be targeted to groups not yet experiencing significant maladjustment (even though they may, because of their life situations or recent experiences, be at risk for such outcomes). It must be intentional, i.e., rest on a solid knowledge-base suggesting the program holds potential for either improving psychological health or preventing maladaptation. School learning problems and behavior problems that contribute to school learning problems are also appropriate targets for primary prevention activities. (Shaw & Goodyear, 1984, p. 444)

Primary prevention programs are designed to help all children and adolescents cope better with the developmental tasks they must face. Some children and adolescents are more vulnerable to life's challenges and are more at risk for trouble. They can be helped with prevention programming, too. In these cases, at-risk children can be identified and offered prevention programming targeted to them specifically. An example is to offer assertiveness training to preteens and young teenagers who are likely to have difficulty resisting peer pressure to participate in substance-abusing behaviors. Such services may also be offered on a one-to-one basis. This form of early efforts to keep small or potential problems from becoming more serious is classified as *secondary prevention* (Shaw, 1973). The term *tertiary prevention* is confusing because in this case the word *prevention* is associated with what are essentially remedial intervention goals. In tertiary prevention, one-to-one and group counseling are used to treat individuals already experiencing problems, to prevent those problems from getting worse, to prevent relapses, and to help resolve the problems (Shaw, 1973). Providing aftercare for adolescents who have returned to school from a temporary sojourn in a drug treatment facility is an example of tertiary prevention that is also part of the responsive counseling intervention function of school counseling. Prevention programming may be designed to reach all students before problems exist or to reach at-risk students before remediation is necessary. In this textbook, primary and secondary prevention are treated globally as prevention.

Stakeholders who influence the counselor's role must understand that major features of prevention programs are the group delivery mode and the intention to help students become better prepared to cope with future events, including developmental tasks. Such stakeholders must also realize that the goal of prevention is to enhance individual development. Understanding this, these stakeholders will probably entertain suggestions for reducing counselor time devoted to intervention and administration and for initiating prevention programming into the regular classroom schedule. Beyond a general understanding of prevention, stakeholders who influence the counselor's role also need information concerning what specifically can be accomplished through prevention programs and how those programs might be implemented.

Intended to address the concerns of counselors who want to achieve program balance through an increasing emphasis on prevention programming, the foregoing information is not meant as a call for eliminating the equally important responsive counseling intervention services that school counselors are expected to provide. As stated previously, the goal is balanced programs. Achieving suitable balance requires a commitment to be informed, organized, systematic, and diplomatic. Responsive counseling interventions are covered in chapter 9.

Going Upstream

Here is a paraphrase of a metaphor sometimes used to support prevention activities: Once upon a time, two people were strolling along a stream and enjoying the scenery when suddenly another person appeared in the stream, struggling to keep from drowning. The two strollers jumped in immediately and saved the struggling individual. No sooner had they accomplished this than another struggling person appeared, and another, and another, and another. As the two rescuers struggled to save as many of the increasingly larger group of unfortunates as they could, the task became more and more hopeless. Suddenly, one of the two rescuers went to the shore and ran upstream. In response to the other's inquiry about what was going on, the person running upstream said, "I'm going to find out who's throwing all these people into the stream" (Shaw, 1973).

The metaphor supports prevention. To achieve the advocated balance between prevention and intervention, some counselors will remain downstream to rescue potential drowning victims, whereas others will go upstream to reduce the number of individuals in need of rescuing. Notice that the word *reduce* is used instead of *eliminate*. It is important to realize that the current state of the art of school counseling is such that, whether the focus is on intervention or prevention, success cannot be predicted in absolute terms. Counselors can provide successful interventions for some clients, and their prevention programs will be more successful for some individuals than for others. A balanced approach combining careful counseling intervention responses and prevention programming has promise for more success than either approach alone because successful prevention programming reduces the need for interventions, and the existence of a complementary intervention thrust provides help for those for whom prevention programming is not enough.

Large-Group Guidance

Large-group guidance is the primary delivery system for prevention programming and developmental curricula (Sears, 2005). The ASCA (1999) listed large-group guidance as one of the four primary school counselor interventions. The remaining three are individual and group counseling (chapter 9), consultation (chapter 11), and coordination (chapter 10). Sears (2005) defined large-group guidance as "an intervention to deliver a curriculum or a series of planned activities to help students anticipate problems before they occur" (p. 190).

BASIC INGREDIENTS OF PREVENTION PROGRAMMING

Point of View

Because large-group guidance is analogous to teaching, it might be argued that the basic ingredients are drawn from the field of education. Education is an applied field, as is counseling, and, like counseling, education has drawn from various disciplines for its foundations. For instance, psychology contributes ideas about human learning, philosophy is the source of ideas about the human condition, and sociology helps educators understand the role of the schools in the greater society. Basic education is also influenced by local, state, and national politics and by applied economics because the schools are primarily supported by taxes. Therefore, when counselors act like teachers and engage in large-group guidance, they are not necessarily mimicking a field that is foreign to them.

The traditional training that counselor education programs impart includes knowledge and competencies that prepare counselors for prevention programming. However, the preparation is often not formalized or specified in traditional counselor education programs. Therefore, the field of education is the source of ideas for formalizing and specifying the ingredients of the prevention programming in counseling. What results is a marriage of ingredients from traditional counseling programs and from education that provides an organizing structure for prevention programming training in counselor education training programs.

This combination may not seem necessary for school counseling students who are experienced teachers with formal training in education. Yet, it is important to remember that teachers are trained to focus on the enhancement of cognitive abilities; in some cases, they learn to divorce thinking about the affective domain from their professional mind-set. Experienced teachers and counselor education students from other disciplines who are being trained as school counselors are challenged to focus on both cognitive and affective domains in their prevention programming. Therefore, there is a place for formalized instruction in prevention programming within counselor education programs.

The competencies to be introduced are valid for all forms of prevention programming. Prevention programming can take different forms depending on the circumstances. For instance, the programming can be direct or indirect. The term *direct programming* indicates that programs are delivered directly to audiences (e.g., the school counselor leads groups designed to help students become better problem solvers). *Indirect programming*, in contrast, indicates that audiences receive programs from third parties (e.g., the school counselor helps classroom teachers prepare for and deliver programs designed to help their students become better problem solvers).

The competencies are also valid for prevention programming that falls within a guidance curriculum or is independent of a curriculum. Some schools and school districts have guidance curriculums. That is, school counselors have their own set of courses (i.e., curriculum) in schools just as the academic disciplines do, and they have their own recognized area of specialization. They have prevention programs based on enhancing specific developmental goals that are sequenced by grade levels. Time for delivering the programs is scheduled by school administrators and recognized by classroom teachers. Essentially, school guidance counseling is accepted as an equally important curriculum and treated accordingly.

Many school counselors work in environments where they do not have guidance curriculums. They arrange to deliver prevention programs via large-group guidance independently of the curriculum by working around the schedule. This requires cooperation from school administrators and teachers and leads to less comprehensive prevention programming than is the case with guidance curriculums. For example, during the fall semester of an academic year, a hypothetical elementary school counselor might present a unit to enhance self-esteem in the classes of kindergarten teachers who want to cooperate and also might provide a study skills program for students who are interested and whose teachers will let them leave the classroom to participate.

Whether prevention programs are delivered via guidance curriculums or by working around the academic curriculums, the programs can be either direct or indirect. Prevention programs can be delivered directly and indirectly in guidance curriculums and in programs that are adapted to the academic curriculum. Whichever of these circumstances may occur, the competencies to be presented remain valid.

Formalizing and Specifying Prevention Programming

Foundations. According to the ASCA (1979), the fruits of prevention programming should be available to all students and should be focused on promoting maximum personal development. Dagley (1987) recommended that these general principles focus school counselor activities devoted to enhancing individual development on distinct goals related to lifelong learning, personal effectiveness, and life roles. Figure 8.1 presents a summary of Dagley's proposal. The goals and outcomes in Figure 8.1 offer

Personal Effectiveness Competencies	Self-Understanding (Identity, Autonomy, Acceptance, Validation)
	Human Relations (respect, empathy, social interest, conflict resolution)
	Health Development (intimacy, leisure, growth stages)
Lifelong Learning Competencies	Communication (reading and writing, listening, expressiveness, assertiveness)
	Information Processing (study and analysis, evaluation, problem solving)
	Personal Enrichment (time management, renewal, change)
Life Roles Competencies	Daily Living (child rearing, consumerism, community involvement)
	Career Planning (values clarification, decision making, planning, goal setting)
	Employability (self-placement, work habits, educational and occupational preparation)

Figure 8.1
Foundations on which prevention programming is based.

Source: "A New Look at Developmental Guidance: The Hearthstone of School Counseling," by J. C. Dagley, 1987, *School Counselor, 35,* p. 103. Copyright 1987 by American Counseling Association.

an inventory of the foundations on which school counselors' prevention programming is based.

Like the counseling function, prevention programming is immersed in a developmental context. The importance of a developmental perspective was discussed in chapter 3. Erikson's theory was presented in chapter 3 to advocate presenting counseling interventions to meet the differing developmental needs of children and adolescents. A summary of Erikson's eight stages of man is presented in Figure 3.1. Another example of the developmental perspective is the work of Havighurst (1972), who identified developmental tasks that must be mastered at various developmental stages in order to achieve happiness and be able to cope with later tasks. Examples of Havighurst's tasks are learning to relate emotionally to family members (infancy and childhood), learning appropriate social roles (middle childhood), and preparing for an economic career (adolescence). The ideas of both Erikson and Havighurst remind us that human development is complex and varied and that individuals develop at different rates, although common themes are found within age groups. Knowledge of human development appears to be an imperative foundation for prevention programming by school counselors.

Thus, prevention programming is often based on developmental theory. That is, the goals and objectives of the programs are designed to achieve outcomes that enhance the development of the recipients and help them meet important developmental tasks. An example is the ASCA National Standards for Students (ASCA, 2005). The

Counselors may coach students while helping them acquire desired skills.

standards are presented in three general clusters: academic development, career development, and personal/social development. The following example indicates how the idea of using developmental theory to identify goals/objectives and competencies that can be acquired and measured in order to achieve the goals/objectives gets played out. Standard A under Academic Development is "Students will acquire the attitudes, knowledge and skills that contribute to effective learning in school and across the life span" (p. 81). Competency A.A3 states: "Achieve School Success" (p. 81). The following indicators are presented under A.A3 to be used to determine if the goal-driven competency is achieved: Take responsibility for their actions; demonstrate the ability to work independently, as well as the ability to work cooperatively with other students; develop a broad range of interests and abilities; demonstrate dependability, productivity and initiative; and share knowledge.

Sears (2005) pointed out that, although developing large-group guidance programs based on developmental theory is useful for primary prevention programming, many students are faced with challenges that block their ability to respond successfully. She stated:

> Having spent considerable time in urban schools, we can attest to the large number of children and youth whose lives are not unfolding in an orderly manner. In fact they are experiencing significant gaps between the demands of their environment and their capacity to cope. These young people need assistance in acquiring the skills needed to cope with or even survive environmental demands such as serious poverty, health-related problems, dysfunctional family situations, and crime-ridden neighborhoods. To expect that a developmental guidance curriculum is going to meet all their needs is not realistic. (p. 193)

Sears's (2005) recommendation was to use large-group guidance interventions to assist at-risk students (i.e., secondary prevention) by helping them learn skills that they should have learned previously at home or in the schools. Designed to replace previously learned dysfunctions responses, these programs focus on such goals as helping at-risk students achieve self-control, manage their anger, and learn to peacefully resolve conflicts. This idea suggests that prevention programming might best consist of two layers. The first layer focuses on all students (primary prevention), and the second layer focuses on at-risk students (secondary prevention) who are unable to take sufficient advantage of the primary prevention programming.

Ingredients. Prevention programming seems to require careful planning. Adherence to specific steps is as important to prevention programming as it is to counseling and consulting interventions. The major steps in prevention programming are planning, delivering, transferring, and evaluating. *Planning* includes assessing the needs of the prospective recipients, setting goals and objectives, researching, and recruiting and selecting participants. *Delivering* includes lesson planning, instructing, demonstrating, and directing. *Transferring* involves providing opportunities for students to transfer their learning to the real world. The ingredients of the delivering component are also important in transferring. *Evaluating* includes assessing, analyzing, and reporting. Together, these ingredients are the basic components of proactive prevention programming.

BASIC COMPETENCIES IN PREVENTION PROGRAMMING

Planning

Assessing Needs. Counselors are encouraged to engage in the measurement and assessment activities that will help them identify the perceived, expressed, and assumed needs of their public. Fall (1994) referred to this first step as asking questions. Direct measurement and assessment of perceived and expressed needs involve counselors in sampling and surveying activities with accompanying skills. Assumed needs can be learned from reading the professional and popular literature. Results of needs assessments may be reported to interested individuals and entities; thus, reporting is an important skill. Needs assessment, whatever the method, sets the stage for setting goals and objectives. More specific coverage of needs assessments is found in chapter 4.

Setting Goals and Objectives. The terms *goal* and *objective* have been used both interchangeably and separately—*goal* meaning a more general purpose, and *objective* meaning the more specific purposes assigned to general goal achievement. Whatever meanings counselors assign to these terms, the requisite skills are constant. Counselors are challenged to translate needs into goals. For instance, if a local needs assessment survey results in a public demand for the school system to do something about the drug abuse problem among teenagers, one goal will be to reduce drug abuse in that group. One objective related to that goal will be to teach adolescents at risk of abusing drugs to respond to peer pressure more assertively. Notice that the example goal and objective are stated in measurable terms. This allows the individuals delivering such programs to assess their ability to achieve the goals and objectives; that is, instances of increased or decreased drug use and acquisition of assertiveness skills can be measured. The results can be offered as evidence of achieving or not achieving the program goals and objectives. Counselors and their publics will be better served if they state their goals and objectives in measurable terms.

Researching.   Having established goals and objectives, counselors may use them to determine the content of their prevention programming. Necessary content may be material with which they are familiar or unfamiliar. When necessary, counselors may have to locate, read, and abstract material from various resources. Therefore, they will benefit from being familiar with available libraries; catalogs of publications, media, and assessment instruments; consultants; relevant professional organizations; and various governmental, service, private, fraternal, and special interest organizations that may have useful information. The Internet has expanded the potential for school counselors to engage in this researching function in the 21st century. There is a limit to the knowledge base that counselors should be expected to have at the outset. In other words, counselors will not be able to deliver all programs for all people on demand. What kinds of prevention programming should counselors be able to deliver initially?

One possibility is that counselors are able to use the competencies they acquired during graduate school. Much of what was learned in counselor education programs can be translated into prevention programming. Some examples are basic interpersonal communication and challenging skills training, decision-making and problem-solving training, peer helper training, teaching individuals to cope with and change irrational thinking, a variety of applications of behavioral rehearsal (e.g., applying for jobs, meeting new people, coping with stressful relationships), self-management training, assertiveness training, relaxation training, career information seeking and information processing, career planning, gaming, cartooning, playing, clarifying and sharing values, support groups, process groups, and parent and teacher groups that focus on any of this content. This is a relatively comprehensive list that can be expanded through research and experience, leaving the impression that counselors can offer much through their prevention programming.

Recruiting and Selecting Participants   On occasion, prevention programming might be offered on a voluntary basis, and counselors will need to recruit volunteers successfully. This involves using information-sharing skills and being able to motivate children and adolescents, as well as being truthful. Circumstances may lead counselors to select possible participants from a pool of volunteers, or counselors may have to determine group membership for individuals in the pool. When engaging in selection activities, counselors again may use their information-sharing skills. For example, they may be challenged to explain their selection decisions to inquiring individuals. In addition, they may use diagnostic and assessment skills to match the right opportunities with the appropriate individuals.

Delivering

Lesson Planning.   Lesson planning involves several important components. The ideas culled from researching can be organized around the goals and objectives of the lesson plan to form a coherent strategy for delivering a program. Lesson plans are organized on a global and unit basis. A global lesson plan covers the entire program, detailing the proposed goals and events sequentially. The events are daily or single-unit lesson plans. Basic ingredients of lesson plans are objectives, materials/resources, identification of the audience, an outline of the planned action steps for presenting the program, identification of information individuals need to participate in the lessons, homework assignments, and evaluation strategies. A sample lesson plan follows.

Lesson Plan for an Anxiety Management Program

Objectives (stated so each objective identifies specific desired outcomes behaviorally that can be measured)
- Participants will be able to generate at least one self-defeating and one self-improving thought without assistance or coaching.
- Participants will contribute to a discussion about applying self-statements to stressful situations in their lives.

Materials/Resources
- Chalkboard and chalk to record information generated during the discussion
- Assertiveness handouts to be distributed as homework for the next lesson

Audience
- Male and female ninth-grade students who have volunteered to participate in the program

Action Steps
- Have participants generate a list of anxiety-provoking situations.
- Review the notion of self-improving thoughts.
- Have participants generate and share one self-defeating and one corresponding self-improving thought for the anxiety-provoking situations they previously listed.
- Discuss how the self-statements may be applied in a stressful situation.
- Distribute assertiveness handouts.
- Introduce assertiveness training and review the important components of appropriate assertive responses by reading the handout aloud.
- Ask participants to read the assertiveness handout and to practice applying coping self-statements in real-life stressful situations as homework.

Evaluation Strategies (parallel to the stated behavioral objectives)
- Participants keep a record of the self-defeating and self-improving thoughts as they occur in their daily experiences.
- Participation is observed during the discussion.

Fall (1994) provided an example of a situation that might require a global plan. A fifth-grade teacher asks an elementary school counselor for assistance with initiating a classroom guidance unit. Goals for the teacher include learning about group membership and developing skills for leading a group. Related objectives might be that the teacher will learn how to include all students in the group activities and how to get the students to work cooperatively in the group activities. Action steps might include providing printed information and helping the teacher understand and process that information. The counselor might follow this by demonstrating the targeted skills and by providing opportunities for the teacher to practice those behaviors via simulations. The counselor offers constructive feedback until the teacher is ready to engage in classroom guidance with the students.

Counselors are also challenged to create environments that ensure their lesson plans will be successful. In a school setting where there is no guidance curriculum, this involves arranging for rooms, adapting or developing the master schedule so targeted individuals can participate, informing administrators and teachers of the program goals and obtaining their cooperation, and securing the cooperation of resource persons such as librarians, speakers and presenters, media coordinators, and custodians—all of whom are vital to the success of the program. Pursuing the example just presented, the counselor might ask the teacher to have the students engage in reading and writing assignments related to the guidance unit. For example, they might be encouraged to write in journals about preassigned topics that coincide with objectives for the guidance unit (Fall, 1994).

Instructing. The term *instructing* as used here refers to behaviors through which people who assume the instructor's role in prevention programming engage in the direct or indirect imparting of information to members of the group. Different forms of direct instructing occur in prevention programming situations. Lecturing, explaining, and reading are prominent examples. Video, audio, film, and graphic media are indirect methods to impart information, as are printed and computer-generated materials. Providing information is an important component of prevention programming, and counselors will be challenged to do this in ways that are interesting and motivating. It seems as if it is as important to prevention programming for counselors to lecture, explain, and read to audiences interestingly as it is for them to listen empathically and to respond facilitatively during responsive counseling interventions. It seems as if it is equally important for counselors to select and prepare media aids and handout materials that are interesting and motivating. Experience indicates that successful instructing leads to a mutually facilitative relationship between the leader and the members of a group, just as successful basic communicating leads to a facilitative counseling relationship. In both instances, acquisition of a facilitative relationship is the foundation for achieving goals successfully.

Demonstrating. Guidance curriculum programs often focus on teaching such skills as communicating with other people more proficiently, making rational decisions, and asserting oneself. In these instances, counselors are challenged to demonstrate the skills adequately. The process is social modeling (Bandura & Jeffery, 1973). Models can be living people, or they can be symbolic—people in films or videos.

Counselors may serve as models themselves, select and train others to serve as models, or develop or locate appropriate symbolic models to provide adequate demonstrations. In addition, counselors will benefit from being familiar with research on modeling to enhance the effectiveness of their demonstrations.

For example, effects are enhanced when there is a similarity between the model and the participants—a model who is coping well, although not perfectly, may be more effective than one who has mastered the skills. Repeated demonstrations are often necessary (Cormier & Nurius, 2003). For example, a counselor might help a teacher by demonstrating how to interact with students when trying to get them to work cooperatively in a group. If the counselor is viewed as a competent, coping model, the probability of helping the teacher is enhanced. Achieving the goal occurs through communicating to the teacher that the counselor is not perfect and does not expect the teacher to be perfect but is performing to the best of his or her ability and appears to the teacher to be providing useful suggestions. Successful demonstrating sets the stage for participants to rehearse the skills. As participants rehearse or practice, counselors direct.

Directing.   Several important behaviors are associated with directing. While helping participants acquire the desired skills, counselors may coach them through the steps and repetitions, provide encouragement, give accurate and useful feedback, determine helpful homework assignments, and discern when the participants have achieved a desirable level of skill or have gone as far as they can to achieve the targeted objectives. Coaching involves instructing and providing cues that help participants determine how they are doing or what to do next. Coaching may be manifested through recommending repeated practices, altering the time devoted to practicing, arranging and rearranging the sequence of practice activities, or offering verbal or physical support (Cormier & Nurius, 2003).

Encouraging is best done via applications of learning principles such as positive reinforcement, withdrawal of reinforcement, and time-outs. Feedback provides participants with information about the quality of their rehearsing efforts. Counselors contribute by providing feedback that helps participants recognize what is desirable and undesirable about their efforts. When offering prevention programs, it is important to dispense feedback judiciously and with as much care and empathy as is provided when engaging in counseling interventions. Keeping up to date on research about feedback is as important as it is for modeling. For example, participants may have opportunities to assess their own performances, verbal assessment may be supplemented with objective assessment, and verbal feedback may contain encouragement and suggestions for improvement (Cormier & Nurius, 2003).

Appropriate homework assignments can help participants acquire the desired skills and knowledge and lay the foundation for developing desirable ideas. Helpful homework also lays the foundation for transfer of training. Counselors can give assignments to teachers (indirect delivery), and teachers or counselors can give assignments to the student participants (direct delivery). Counselors might ask teachers to practice in front of a mirror at home, reading information about leading small, structured groups, and instructing and encouraging students to work cooperatively. Teachers and counselors can ask students who are to be working cooperatively on an activity to distribute components of the activity among themselves voluntarily and set a date for each to have the assigned component ready for sharing and for integrating the components into one joint endeavor. The assignments help the participants engage in constructive, goal-directed activities that, if accomplished successfully, provide evidence that the participants have achieved skills commensurate with the goals of the project.

To be effective at giving homework assignments, counselors may need to explain the purpose and to inform participants about what they are to do, where it is to occur, how often it is to occur, and how it is to be recorded (Cormier & Nurius, 2003). At some time during the rehearsal and homework cycle, counselors will probably need to decide whether participants are achieving targeted levels of accomplishment. If the decision is affirmative, counselors can focus on transfer of training, closure, and evaluation. If the decision is negative, they can determine whether the best alternative is to recycle the participant(s) or to end the training. To make these decisions, counselors will be challenged to assess, diagnose, and make rational decisions. In so doing, counselors may find it necessary to apply the basic and challenging counseling skills as carefully as they do when engaging in counseling interventions.

Transferring

The ultimate goal of prevention programming is transfer or generalization of training to one's natural environment. Goals, training activities, and homework assignments serve us best when they reflect a plan to help participants apply what is being taught to the real world. Procedures for achieving this transfer of training have been identified and discussed previously.

Evaluating

Assessing the effects of all counseling functions is important, and a full chapter in this text is devoted to evaluation and accountability. Here, suffice it to say that evaluating is among the requisite prevention programming skills. In chapter 4, philosophy and method are discussed, along with the importance of determining (a) whether prevention programming objectives have been met, (b) the perceptions of stakeholders concerning prevention programs, and (c) the cost effectiveness of those programs.

EXAMPLES OF PREVENTION PROGRAMMING

In this section, we present information about prevention programs that have been or could be developed. The first group is presented in an abbreviated fashion to add more breadth to this presentation while responding to the contingencies associated with having limited space with which to work. Additional details about the program content and effects are available in the reports cited in the presentation and listed in the references for this chapter.

A second group of programs is presented more comprehensively, each with its own heading. We did this because the problems to be prevented and the areas of human development to be enhanced seem important in these times. As a group, the examples represent the three important domains advocated by the ASCA in the National Model (ASCA, 2005): academic development, career development, and personal/social development.

Overview of Sample Programs

Recognized nationally as an exemplary model, the *Primary Mental Health Project* has spawned related programs in New York and California (Deutsch, 1996). The Los Angeles (California) version, known as the *Primary Prevention Intervention Program (PIP)*, focuses on early identification and prevention of school adjustment difficulties. PIP is a school-based program that engages in systematic screening in kindergarten through third grade, employs trained paraprofessionals supervised by counselors and other mental health professionals, and emphasizes cooperation with local mental health entities. Counselors serve as trainers, consultants, and coordinators. A multimodal individual curriculum programming approach is used to achieve the program's goals.

The *Parent–Teen Empathy Enhancement Process* focuses on stimulating healthy communications among teenagers and their parents (Hawes, 1996). A format of ice breaking, group cohesion formation, interpersonal communication skills enhancement, and learning to discuss important issues with one's parent or teenager is used with groups of volunteers who are either parents or teenagers.

The *School Families Project* is a program designed to help middle school students develop problem-solving skills, decision-making skills, and other life skills without distracting teachers and students from daily school activities (Lawson, McClain, Matlock-Hetzel, Duffy, & Urbanovski, 1997). *School families* consists of one teacher, 20 to 25 students, and four to six community volunteers who meet for 45 minutes, 1 day per week during the school's activity period to engage in group mentoring via a primary prevention perspective.

Berube and Berube (1997) presented a plan for offering a menu of small-group activities in an elementary school served by only one counselor. Following a needs assessment and recruitment of assistance from community resources, the counselor provided a menu that contained leadership training, peer mediation, My Future (career education goals), Special Study Hall (enhanced study environment), Lunch With the Principal (experience her as approachable), Lunch Bunch (forum for discussions with the counselor), a friendship group, Peer Buddies (help special education students interact with peers), Children of Alcoholics (coping focus), and Rainbow Groups (coping with loss).

Two high school counselors met with 9th- through 12th-grade girls once per week for 8 weeks to help participants avoid abusive relationships and understand the effect of such relationships on self-esteem and decision making (Becky & Farren, 1997). Specific sessions focused on providing information about the context of abuse, offering warning signs and risk factors, helping participants understand and prevent date rape, managing conflict, and building interpersonal communication skills.

The *Kwanzaa Group* was established for male African American sixth graders who were underachieving academically and having difficulty controlling their classroom behavior. Participants are taught the seven Kwanzaa principles to instill a positive sense of self and achievement in a Eurocentric education system (Bass & Coleman, 1997). The program is conducted in two phases over a school year. In the first phase, participants are exposed to positive images of the African American culture to facilitate trust in Afrocentric principles. In the second phase, the rites of passage from learning about Kwanzaa principles to applying them are emphasized.

Mosconi and Emmett (2003) reported the effects of a four-part values clarification curriculum. The program was implemented during a high school career exploration elective class. Specific units focused on defining values, identifying and prioritizing values, identifying influences on values, and relating values to future choices and success. The program leaders employed a contemplation and conflict teaching process. Participants were instructed to consider what they believe is true (contemplation) and then to explain their preferences and choices. The dialogue may have created conflict when the participants' preferences and choices were challenged by their peers.

Helping Students Become Self-Regulated Learners

A schematic for helping students become self-regulated, successful learners is offered by Lapan, Kardash, and Turner (2002). Self-regulated learning is "an active, constructive process whereby learners set goals for their learning and then attempt to monitor, regulate, and control their cognition, motivation, and behavior" (Pintrich, 2000). Self-regulated learners can control planning, performing, and completing stages of the learning process and focus on mastering tasks, improving skills, and understanding information. They also use a variety of strategies and tend to attribute poor performance to ineffective strategies rather than inability.

Lapan et al. (2002) elaborated on the value of helping students become more engaged in academics, especially in consideration of national initiatives to help all students be successful learners. Their presentation covers the importance of many of the competencies in a balanced program. In this chapter, we focus on the suggestions that can be translated into prevention programming.

The information presented by Lapan et al. (2002) suggests that school counselors could develop and initiate proactive prevention programs designed to help any student become a self-regulated learner. They offered the following categories of learning strategies that are known to enhance academic performance. The goals of a prevention program would be to teach students these effective learning strategies and to motivate them to use the strategies. The strategies are the ability to (a) separate important from nonessential information, (b) identify main ideas, (c) relate new information to prior knowledge, (d) take effective notes, (e) organize information into useful subsets, (f) monitor whether information is truly understood, and (g) construct internal images that represent the meaning of information studied.

The following tactics for teaching effective learning strategies, recommended by Lapan et al. (2002), could be melded into a prevention program: (a) explain the effective learning strategy to the participants, (b) model/demonstrate the strategy while sharing thoughts aloud, (c) have participants practice the strategy continuously on several important learning tasks, (d) use both covert (e.g., mental imagery) and overt (e.g., physical performance) rehearsals, (e) have students practice with their peers, (f) help participants learn ways to monitor and evaluate their own performance, (g) help students realize concrete benefits of using the strategies, and (h) involve participants in the process of modifying and constructing new strategies.

Teaching Coping Skills

Teaching children and adolescents how to cope successfully with life's various stressors may prepare them for such events in advance of occurrences (primary prevention) or help them manage challenges that are already influencing their lives (secondary prevention). For example, Hains (1992, 1994) reported on the effectiveness of teaching youths to recognize, monitor, and alter stress-arousing or anxiety-provoking thoughts. Romano, Miller, and Nordness (1996) described a stress management and student well-being curriculum for elementary school students that consists of six 45-minute lessons integrated into the fifth- and sixth-grade curriculums, including the importance of physical exercise, good nutrition, focusing and identifying feelings and expressing them positively, communicating well with one's parents, and learning problem-solving skills. Some components of the program engage their parents as well. Deffenbacher, Lynch, Oetting, and Kemper (1996) found that teaching sixth- through eighth-grade students with high anger thresholds to identify anger-provoking situations, acquire specific relaxation skills, and learn how their thoughts influence anger led to increased control of their expressions of anger. The sequential training includes learning to calm down while visualizing anger-provoking situations and replacing the anger-producing thoughts with controlling thoughts that are more calming. Shechtman (2001) demonstrated that prevention goals can be achieved in small groups as well as in large-group interventions. She reported being able to reduce aggressive behaviors and enhance social skills of young children via a small-group counseling intervention.

An example of a coping skills training program is found in Kiselica, Baker, Thomas, and Reedy (1994). Participants in the program were ninth graders enrolled in a guidance class in a rural high school. They met once per week during 60-minute sessions for 8 weeks. The program combines elements of Meichenbaum and Deffenbacher's (1988) stress inoculation training, assertiveness training (Galassi & Galassi, 1977), and progressive muscle relaxation (Bernstein & Borkovec, 1973).

After receiving instruction about stress, stressors, anxiety, and anxiety-related symptoms, participants generate examples of their own anxiety-provoking experiences. Next, participants are taught progressive muscle relaxation through a series of exercises, learning how to transfer the skills to in vivo situations. Then, participants are taught to elicit the relaxation response by repeating a cue word during anxiety-provoking situations. The following step is to teach participants how to identify negative thoughts that lead to self-defeating behaviors and replace them with self-improving thoughts, learning how the process (cognitive restructuring) works. This process is combined with progressive muscle relaxation in practice sessions and in vivo homework. Following discussion of the importance of appropriate assertiveness, participants engage in simulations designed to enhance their assertiveness skills.

Combining cognitive restructuring with progressive muscle relaxation and assertiveness training approaches coping with anxiety arousal from a multimodal perspective. Because the school environment is a source of many anxiety-arousing experiences for children and adolescents, stress inoculation training holds promise for providing coping skills that can be learned and generalized to the real world via proactive primary and secondary prevention programming (Baker, 2001).

Prejudice Prevention

Ponterotto and Pedersen (1993) believed that adolescents, because they are learning to depend on their cognitive skills and are becoming more comfortable with abstract thinking, are at a stage when prejudice prevention may be developmentally appropriate. Concluding that prejudice is caused by stereotypical beliefs that become more important than real people, Ponterotto and Pedersen recommended several exercises designed to increase awareness of ethnic, racial, and cultural identity. An example is the Label Game, the objective of which is to discover how others perceive each participant.

The steps in this exercise are (a) prepare a set of labels containing positive adjectives (e.g., friendly, generous, helpful) and attach one to the forehead or back of each participant so the label cannot be seen by its wearer, (b) have participants mingle while discussing a topic of interest without any additional structure, (c) instruct participants to treat each individual in a manner that reflects the label he or she is wearing, (d) instruct participants not to inform each other about the content of the labels, and (e) instruct each participant to attempt to guess his or her own label before it is removed.

Debriefing includes asking the participants to share with each other how they used feedback from interacting with others to figure out the content of their own labels. They also discuss how it feels to be labeled and treated as if the label were accurate. Components of the exercise are used to introduce such concepts as stereotyping, prejudice, and communication barriers. It is hoped that participants become aware that we do label each other, that there are differences important to each person's identity, and that the differences are not always bad: Diversity is an important reality. The remaining components of the program are designed to help participants engage in meaningful and enjoyable activities that lead to processing important information related to prejudice prevention.

Conflict Resolution

An important response to widespread concern about violence in the schools has been the development and implementation of conflict resolution programming. Attempts to implement conflict resolution programming vary from individual programs to those integrated into the core curriculum of a school system.

Carruthers, Carruthers, Day-Vines, Bostick, and Watson (1996) described the core conflict resolution curriculum in the Wake County, North Carolina Public Schools. The goals are to (a) help make the schools orderly and peaceful, (b) use conflict as an instructional tool, (c) teach participants to generalize what they have learned to future interpersonal interactions, and (d) reinforce the core curriculum goals and objectives. This curriculum has a developmental overlay in which the focus shifts across grade levels to make units relevant to students at different grade levels (e.g., greater emphasis on interpersonal relations in the early grades, conflict resolution in the upper elementary grades, conflict at the middle school level, violence in the high school). Examples of four objectives recommended for specific subjects in the curriculum are as follows:

- *Kindergarten:* The student will dramatize the appropriate behavior when confronted with various warning signs, sounds, and symbols (subject: health living).

- *Second grade:* The student will demonstrate the ability to infer (subject: science).
- *Fourth grade:* The student will propose alternatives to impulsive behavior (subject: healthful living).
- *Seventh grade:* The student will exercise social and interpersonal persuasion (subject: healthful living).

Carruthers et al. provided an inventory of instructional units, goals, and objectives in the appendix to their article.

One popular form of conflict resolution is *peer mediation,* which can be provided as a total school program, as an elective course, or by training selected mediators (Lupton-Smith, Carruthers, Flythe, Goettee, & Modest, 1996). Lupton-Smith et al. described three peer mediation programs, one of which is in a middle school with the in-school suspension coordinator serving as the program coordinator. In the preliminary stage, a core group of school staff members are trained, and the entire staff agrees to refer conflicts between students to mediation before treating them as discipline problems. All sixth graders receive 10 days of conflict resolution instruction in their health classes and are informed about the function of peer mediation in their schools via mini assemblies. Parents are informed at an open house. Selected student mediators receive 20 hours of training that focuses on (a) engaging in self-introspection, (b) considering how to deal with conflict, (c) learning how to use active listening skills in the mediation process, and (d) practicing in simulated sessions. Time is set aside for peer mediation sessions each day in a 30-minute period after lunch known as *teen development time.* Mediation sessions occur in a room adjacent to the coordinator's office with the door between the two rooms left open. Further details and a summary of the mediation steps are found in Lupton-Smith et al. (1996).

The importance of recruiting and selecting a diverse set of peer mediators is highlighted by Day-Vines, Day-Hariston, Carruthers, Wall, and Lupton-Smith (1996). They proposed that, rather than be represented proportionally, all segments of the school's population should be represented equally.

Comprehensive Developmental Guidance

Considerably broader in perspective than the programs just covered, comprehensive developmental guidance programs, as perceived by Gysbers and Henderson (2000), are integrated into the school's curriculum. Primary characteristics of these programs are as follows: They (a) are similar to other programs in education (focused on student outcomes, have activities designed to help students achieve the outcomes, are facilitated by professionally recognized personnel, use curriculum-enhancing resources, and employ student evaluation), (b) are based on developmental principles, (c) represent a full range of guidance services (e.g., assessment, referral, placement, consultation), and (d) involve all school staff members.

The underlying theme or theoretical perspective of the guidance curriculum is *life career development.* "Life career development is defined as self-development over the life span through the integration of the roles, settings, and events in a person's life" (Gysbers & Henderson, 2000, p. 62). Four domains of human growth and development are emphasized in life career development: (a) self-knowledge and interpersonal skills; (b) life roles, settings, and events; (c) life career planning; and (d) basic studies and occupational preparation. The major delivery systems are the school counseling and instructional programs.

Prevention programming is an essential ingredient in comprehensive developmental guidance whether in the school counseling or the instructional program of a school, school district, or state school system. A concrete example, taken from Gysbers and Henderson (2000), is the following curriculum goals for a school district: Students will (a) understand and respect themselves and others; (b) behave responsibly in the school, family, and community; (c) develop decision-making skills; (d) use their educational opportunities well; (e) communicate effectively; and (f) plan and prepare for personally satisfying and socially useful lives. These goals will generate competencies that, in turn, generate educational strategies and materials to support them. For the goal "develop decision-making skills," the recommended competencies are (a) making wise choices, (b) managing change successfully, and (c) solving problems. Subcompetencies for "making wise choices" are (a) awareness of how decisions are made, (b) exploration of use of the process, and (c) implementation of the decision-making process.

More than as a method of implementing the prevention programming concept, Gysbers and Henderson (2000) viewed their idea as a way to reconceptualize school guidance and reform education. Sink and MacDonald (1999) reported that, by 1997, 24 states had plans and 17 others had them in a developmental stage. Not all of them are replicas of the Gysbers and Henderson model. They do, however, represent the basic ideas just presented.

A Model Substance Abuse Prevention Program

Swisher, Bechtel, Henry, Vicary, and Smith (2001) described a substance abuse prevention program that may be integrated into school curriculums under the leadership of school counselors. Adoption of Drug Abuse Training (Project ADAPT) is an initiative funded by the National Institute for Drug Abuse that was instituted and evaluated over a 5-year period prior to publication by Swisher et al. (2001). Project ADAPT employs Botvin's (1998) Life Skills Training concept by helping teachers integrate targeted skills, concepts, and content into their subject matter curriculums. Because teachers are actively involved in the design and delivery of this programming, school counselors are viewed as excellent sources of consultation, modeling, and coaching. For example, Botvin's program includes such activities as group discussions, role-playing, and hands-on activities. School counselors may also contribute by helping teachers find and use developmentally appropriate teaching aids, recruiting capable teachers, and assessing the effects of program implementation. Project ADAPT staff members reported that participating teachers displayed a considerable amount of creativity and initiative.

The goals of Botvin's program are that student participants will (a) learn to resist social pressure to use alcohol, tobacco, and other drugs; (b) develop an enhanced sense of self-direction; (c) be better able to cope with anxiety; (d) acquire improved decision-making skills; (e) improve their basic communication and social skills; (f) acquire increased knowledge about the risks associated with using alcohol, tobacco, and other drugs; and (g) develop healthy beliefs and attitudes consistent with avoiding substance abuse. Swisher et al. (2001) presented a sample lesson plan matrix from a rural middle school that implemented the program. It indicates how specific life skills training components such as decision making, coping with anxiety, and assertiveness are infused/integrated into various curriculums. For example, decision making was approached in geography via a travel exercise in which routes had to be chosen on a map. In earth science, the students considered the pros and cons of space travel. They were taught the steps in personal decision making in a personal development course.

Helping Participants Improve Academic Achievement and School Success Behavior

Based on reviews of research that identified clusters of skills needed for school success, a combined group counseling and group guidance program entitled Student Success Skills was designed for fifth-, sixth-, eighth-, and ninth-grade students (Brigman & Campbell, 2003). This report focuses on the group guidance component. The skills clusters derived from the aforementioned reviews were (a) cognitive and meta cognitive skills such as goal setting, progress monitoring, and memory skills; (b) social skills such as interpersonal skills, social problem solving, listening, and teamwork skills; and (c) self-management skills such as managing attention, motivation, and anger.

The topics for the group guidance program were based on the three skill clusters. The school counselors involved in this program were trained to provide a specifically structured presentation to the participants. Components of a typical presentation were as follows. The first part of a presentation was designed to introduce the topic and stimulate participant motivation to care about the topic. Participants were also asked to share what they already know about the topic. In the second part, school counselors presented information about the specific component to be covered (e.g., goal setting) in a manner that engaged the participants in the process. The third part found the participants applying the information previously presented in small-group discussions. The younger children were divided into pairs. In the final part of a presentation, the participants summarized and set personal goals. In general, the program goals were to have participants reflect on what they did and learned in the sessions and discover ways to transfer that knowledge to the real world.

PREVENTION PROGRAMMING TO ACHIEVE PREVENTION AND DEVELOPMENTAL GOALS: THE CHALLENGE

In a survey of elementary, middle, and high school counselors selected randomly from the membership of the ASCA, Bowman (1987) posed several important questions about the state of "small group guidance and counseling" in basic education. He found that counselors at all levels agree that these are important functions, although high school counselors find them less practical. A variety of topics such as decision making, communication skills and peer helping, self-concept, study skills, career, behavior, and family were identified as having been presented across grade levels with different emphases because of developmental needs. Finding time to engage in prevention programming, coping with resistance from others, and feeling competent in a pedagogical domain were the three categories in which the majority of respondents' professed problems occurred.

It seems clear that counselor education programs face a challenge: helping graduates learn about prevention programming and how to implement prevention programs. School counselors are challenged to know how to plan, deliver, and evaluate such programs; they will also benefit from ideas for coping with the practical challenges of competition for time and space, resistance, and ignorance that are associated with working in school systems. For instance, creative counselors, when attempting to resolve the time challenge, use lunch break groups, form groups of students attending the same study halls, make their groups an option during general activity periods, alternate class periods on a weekly basis to prevent participants from missing the same class every week, and cooperate with teachers to make their prevention programming ideas units in the teachers' classes.

EVALUATING PREVENTION PROGRAMMING: ONE PATHWAY TO ACHIEVING ACCOUNTABILITY

The Challenge of Providing Evidence of Prevention Programming Competence

On the surface, it appears as if evaluating prevention programs or guidance curricula should be a relatively straightforward process. Yet, there is more to consider than what initially comes to mind, making this evaluation and accountability process a considerable challenge. That which initially comes to mind may proceed as follows. Prevention programming is often manifested by delivering programs to participants in large-group settings. The programs are based on previously determined goals and objectives. Therefore, the evaluation will consist of determining whether the goals were achieved by examining or observing the participants at the close of the program.

Unfortunately, following this line of thinking may lead to collecting data that do not conclusively rule out alternative explanations for the results of the end-of-program assessments and observations because methods for controlling the alternative explanations have not been employed. Alternative explanations for the findings are caused by myriad other events in the lives of the participants (e.g., assignments in other classes, reading related materials, learning similar information elsewhere, the effects of one's home environment, natural maturation). These other events may have a concurrent impact while they are involved in the prevention programming.

To control the alternative explanations of the perceived gains found in end-of-program evaluations, professional school counselors will have to use program designs and assessment strategies that are usually beyond their master's-level training and expertise. These evaluation activities may be difficult or impossible to undertake in most K–12 school settings. For example, action research designs that help program evaluators rule out alternative explanations of results-based data will require using control groups that would receive no programming or alternative programming with which the programs to be evaluated (a.k.a. treatment programs) could be compared. These methods are referred to as true experimental or quasiexperimental designs, and they require some form of random assignment of individual participants to groups (true experimental design), individual groups to treatment or control conditions (quasiexperimental design), or individual program presenters to treatment and control conditions. In addition, the results-based data from the respective evaluations must usually be analyzed via inferential statistical models such as analysis of variance.

We suspect that most readers and professional school counselors will find the information presented in the previous paragraph both foreign and overly challenging to understand and implement. Experimental and quasiexperimental research is more often the domain of university faculty members than of professional school counselors.

One way to cope with the challenge of being overwhelmed by these evaluation designs is for professional counselors to work with university faculty members as "effective evaluation teams composed of skilled researchers and school-level practitioners using a variety of salient research methods" (Sink, 2005, p. 11). Although this is an excellent idea that may possibly be implemented somewhere, we believe that most professional school counselors will be unable to participate in such teams either because they do not have sufficient access to skilled researchers or because it will be impossible to implement experimental or quasiexperimental research designs in their settings.

A Proposal for Meeting the Challenge

Distal Data.   Brown and Trusty (2005a) remind us that two kinds of results-based data seem to be employed in the school counseling evaluation/accountability process. One approach is to employ distal results-based data, that is, data that are not directly influenced by prevention programs or by the persons delivering the programs. Examples of using distal data are found when standardized test scores, grades, attendance, and disciplinary referrals are used as results-based data elements to evaluate the impact of specific prevention programming interventions. A variety of influences other than the targeted programs may influence these data. Distal results-based data have a place in the overall accountability process, and prevention programming in general of specific programs may be sited as contributing to distal results-based data.

Proximal Data.   Proximal data are those that are directly targeted by prevention program. We agree with the position taken by Brown and Trusty (2005a) that evaluation of prevention programs should focus on proximal data. This information provides direct evidence of the impact of specific prevention programming efforts on the targeted outcomes. For example, if the objective of a program is to teach participants how to prepare a resume, whether they prepared an acceptable resume during the program is proximal data. This position, however, returns our attention to the challenges associated with using what are essentially experimental research designs that are beyond the expertise of most professional school counselors.

Our Proposal.   We understand that the following proposal will not meet the rigorous standard of experimental research. Yet, we believe that it offers professional school counselors who do not have the experimental approach available to them a way to evaluate their prevention programming interventions in order to provide data that will help achieve accountability to themselves and their stakeholders. We present an overview here, and an example will follow.

Imagine that a school's prevention program has been designed or selected based on the perceived or expressed needs of students. All matters concerning preparation and implementation are in place, and specific goals and objectives have been stated. Results-based data should be collected at the beginning and end of the program.

The most useful results-based data will be that which can be directly measured of observed, that is, participants' assessment of the value of the program and whether they understood or retained the information presented and the skills taught. These results are not unlike those general attributes assessed in typical teacher-led classrooms, and control groups and the like are not required to achieve accountability in teacher-led classrooms.

Prevention programs may have goals and objectives that go beyond achieving participant support for the value of the program and evidence of delivering information and teaching skills successfully. Goals such as influencing self-esteem and achievement motivation and enhancing academic performance (e.g., grades) are worthy yet virtually impossible to employ in our model because they require using the aforementioned experimental conditions to substantiate or rely on distal data.

Although such goals may be stated, we recommend that they be presented as desired outcomes that seem to follow logically if the program intervention is well received by the participants and if the targeted information and skills are presented successfully. Logical assumptions about results can be supported by information drawn from published research. That is, professional counselors can cite the results of published research studies in support of their assumption that the present program may influence targeted attitudes or future behaviors, even though the effects are unable to be measured at the end of the targeted program intervention. This establishes the importance of presenting prevention programming for which there are published results-based studies that support the merits of the targeted program goals and objectives (Brown & Trusty, 2005a). We offer more on this idea later.

An Example.   In the ASCA (2005) National Standards, within the Academic Development domain, Standard B states "Students will complete school with the academic preparation essential to choose from a wide range of substantial post-secondary options, including college" (p. 81). Competency A.B.1. is "Improve Learning." One of the indicators for "Improve Learning" is A.B.1.2. "Learn and apply critical-thinking skills." In our example, a middle school counselor created a 6-week prevention program intervention designed to accomplish the following proximal objectives. Participants will (a) learn the basic principals of critical thinking, (b) apply critical thinking skills in a simulated exercise successfully, and (c) indicate that the intervention program was of value to them. The counselor collected proximal results-based data as follows.

To evaluate the first objective, immediately during the first meeting of the intervention, the participants completed an objective test covering the information about critical thinking that will be presented during the program. The same test was given during the final meeting, and the differences between pre- and posttesting were used to determine whether the objective was achieved.

The second objective was assessed by having the participants engage in a simulated critical thinking exercise following the presentation-related information and a leader demonstration. The simulations were observed and rated on a predetermined performance scale in order to assess whether the second objective was accomplished.

To evaluate the third objective, all participants completed a survey about their attitudes toward the value of the program during both the second and the last sessions. The first survey assessed their expectations after having experienced one session, and the second survey assessed their attitudes on completion of the program. Both surveys provide information about whether the third objective was achieved.

Thus far, our proposal includes focusing on targeting results-based data that can be attributed to a specific intervention (i.e., participants' perceptions of the value of the program, acquisition of information presented, and acquisition of skills taught). These results lend themselves to paper-and-pencil, objectively scored assessments similar to those used by classroom teachers and observations of participants demonstrating competence at skills that were taught. A final component of this proposal is to implement and evaluate the same prevention programming interventions numerous times, and, if possible, in a variety of settings (e.g., different grade levels; Brown & Trusty, 2005b). An accumulation of repeated successful outcomes increases the body of evidence in support of apparently successful prevention program interventions and enhances overall program accountability. This repeated presentation process also reduces concerns over the lack of control groups.

Finding Information About the Effects of Prevention Programs

There are many sources available, and this listing is probably not exhaustive. Therefore, we recommend that individual professional school counselors continuously maintain a vigilant search for information that speaks to the merits of prevention programming interventions before employing them in their own settings, especially if they do not have the resources to conduct experimental action research in their schools.

Internet Resources. The following Web sites may be fruitful. Like all such domains, some of the information presented in not necessarily useful to all individuals. Thus, users are challenged to review the information carefully and selectively.

One potentially useful source is the Society for Prevention Research (http://www.preventionresearch.org/). Click on The Prevention Connection link, then go to Prevention Science Publications. Users will gain access to prevention research in a number of journals such as *Prevention Science, American Journal of Community Psychology,* and *The Journal of Primary Prevention.*

A second potentially useful Web resource is the What Works Clearinghouse (http://www.whatworks.ed.gov). This site requires user patience. On an ongoing basis, the site presents information on studies of educational programs that were screened and identified as effective. Many of these studies are of programs outside the school counseling or prevention domains.

A third source was introduced in chapter 4. Among the services of the Center for School Counseling Outcome Research (http://www.umass.edu/schoolcounseling/) is their publication of school counseling research briefs that provides continuous access to research-based information about school counseling, some of which may focus on prevention programming interventions. For example, Research Brief 2.3, dated April 15, 2004, presents a review of a well-conducted quasiexperimental study by Brigman and Campbell (2003) that provided evidence that a combination of curriculum- and group-based interventions had a positive impact on participants' test scores on a standardized state achievement test. Program content was designed to enhance the participants' cognitive and metacognitive skills, social skills, and self-management skills proven to be related to school success in previous research studies.

Published Literature Reviews.   On occasion, university scholars will collect and review sets of research studies on aspects of prevention programming interventions. The primary interest of these reviewers is usually to assess the merits of the research designs used and to look for important themes about programmatic successes on which to report. Readers who are school counseling practitioners may benefit most from identifying those program interventions that appear to work and determining with whom, and then from locating the sources that more fully describe the specific intervention programs in the reference sections of the reviews. At present, we are aware of only a few such reviews that may be of value to our readers, and, like many journal publications, they may be somewhat dated—not covering more recent research. We list these reviews by author and date herein, and more complete retrieval information is in the reference section of this chapter. They are Baker, Swisher, Nadenichek, and Popowicz (1984); Baker and Taylor (1998); Borders and Drury (1992); and Whiston and Sexton (1998).

Using These Resources Successfully.   The resources we listed previously are the beginning of a multistage process in which professional school counselors are challenged to participate in order to receive the full fruits of their labors. In the first stage, users of the Web sites or readers of the review articles seek and find information about prevention programs that may work. A second stage finds the counselors locating specific sources that have been identified in the first stage and reading them in a quest for information about the particulars of the highlighted programs. A third stage occurs when school counselors develop their own programs based on the information provided in the acquired sources. Delivering and evaluating the programs are the final stages. A quest for useful resources leads one through acquisition, preparation, and delivery stages to a point where evaluation leading to accountability is required to complete the process.

WHAT IF I'M NOT TRAINED AS A TEACHER AND DREAD THE THOUGHT OF LEADING LARGE-GROUP GUIDANCE CLASSES?

This is a real issue for a number of students preparing to become school counselors and among those who are in the school counseling profession. Neuman (2006), who was a family counselor prior to entering the school counseling domain, offers a refreshing approach to coping with the challenge. She stated: "I would dread the thought of doing it. My voice is not loud and classroom management was not my forte. I've had a lot of training to be a counselor, but very little to be a teacher" (p. 5).

To her credit, Neuman (2006) recognized the challenge and decided to try to overcome it. The steps in her quest included (a) thinking of classroom guidance as just a large group (as in group counseling), (b) beginning the sessions by establishing ground rules just as in other groups (e.g., listen, be respectful to the teacher and others, participate), (c) varying the activities, (d) incorporating learning styles and multiple intelligence information into her teaching style (e.g., visual cues to help children remember the lessons), (e) observing other counselors teaching large-group guidance sessions, (f) using appropriate self-disclosure as a part of the lessons (e.g., letting the students know you are not perfect), (g) using the Web and books to find useful materials, (h) knowing the students' needs, (i) making the lessons fun, and (h) continuing to work on her own attitude and presentation skills.

We close this section with the following observations from Neuman (2006): "The students look forward to my lessons and ask me when I'm coming back. Do I still dread the weeks when I teach? Well, not as much as I used to and it's something I'll continue to work on" (p. 5). So, dreading large-group presentations is something that needs to be recognized and worked on over time in order to be able to be a complete school counselor in the 21st century.

From proactive prevention programming for all students, we now turn to responsive counseling interventions for selected students in chapter 9.

FEATURED ACTIVITY: GRADUATE STUDENT PERSPECTIVES ON PREVENTION IN SCHOOL COUNSELING

In this chapter, we discuss prevention in school counseling. One of our counselor education interns in a large, public high school wrote the following in the final report about her internship:

> There were four counselors at my internship school. Each of them were able to lead *SELF BUILDING* sessions for students in about three classrooms during the semester of my internship. I observed some of the sessions; the counselors were well received, and the kids seemed to be very involved in the sessions. Interestingly, many kids were quite self disclosing during the sessions. After one of the best sessions (with a class of seniors about ready to graduate), I asked the counselor who led the session how she felt about leading these kinds of classroom group activities. She responded that she would like to spend most of her time doing prevention and development classes with kids.

What do you think about the counselor's response to the intern?

After you read this chapter, go to http://www.genesislight.com/scan21st/tell_us/prevention.html and complete the form. With your permission, we will periodically post some of your creative thinking for the world to read.

OTHER SUGGESTED ACTIVITIES

1. Take an inventory of prevention programming experiences and competencies you already possess. What additional competencies do you need to be more proficient at prevention programming? Why?

2. Debate one theme of this chapter—for example, prevention programming competence is equally as important in school counseling as is counseling competence.
3. Analyze, discuss, and/or debate the following statement: School counselors do not need to have been classroom teachers to offer prevention programming successfully.
4. Develop a set of lesson plans for a real or imaginary prevention program.
5. Prepare a document explaining how a counselor might convince parents or administrators that prevention programming is a valid school counseling function.
6. Make an inventory of ideas from the "Examples of Prevention Programming" section that are most appealing to you. What are your reasons for selecting these ideas?
7. Critique the merits of the evaluation/accountability proposal made in this chapter.
8. Go to the SCAN Web site (www.scan21st.com). Identify and discuss the challenges of prevention programming on the Internet.

CHAPTER 9

Individual and Group Counseling: Responding to Selected Needs in Schools

Goals: To provide evidence of the demand for counseling interventions from school counselors; to propose a set of basic counseling competencies for a balanced school counseling program.

The many and varied service demands placed on school counselors is best characterized in their own words:

"I was speaking recently with a 12-year-old who watched his mom get sentenced to 5 years in prison for extortion. He said he'd learned a big lesson from his mom: how not to get caught! What is a counselor to do?"

"I was called at 4:00 a.m. on a Sunday to be with a 15-year-old who was about to give birth to her second child. Her grandmother, with whom she lived, sounded completely out of control during the 4:00 a.m. call; so, I went to the hospital. I'm not sure what to do next. This situation seems desperate."

"My principal has a drinking problem. She often misses work on Monday morning and is constantly pestering me to go with her to happy hour on Friday afternoons. How can I ever hope to organize and focus the counseling program at my elementary school when her support for me is based on my accepting her invitations to go drinking?"

"State-mandated, end-of-grade, competency tests have created tremendous anxiety among teachers and parents. Consequently, I'm seeing more and more students who say that they are smart but not good test takers. They are scared to death to fail one of these tests. One student said to me, 'I have forgotten how to add fractions. Will you help me before the test tomorrow?' Which counseling theory is best for dealing with this student?"

"I am leading a group for parents who have adopted children of foreign descent. It is a wonderful group of folks. They are trying to talk me into learning Spanish. I think I will take on the challenge. My counseling could really benefit—and I think my entire counseling program will be stronger if I am able to speak the native language of so many of my students."

"I have been hired as a middle school counselor, but I am only halfway through my master's program in school counseling. I have a provisional license. I am feeling a lot of pressure to finish my program in counselor education and pass the PRAXIS exam. How can I think about and run an effective program at my school when I'm under so much pressure myself?"

This variety of demands requires skills that are learned through preservice preparation and on-the-job experience. This chapter explores some of these demands and the skills required to meet the demands.

DEMAND FOR COUNSELING INTERVENTIONS

The schools are a microcosm of society. Many problems that occur in the greater society also exist in the schools, affecting children and adolescents alike. Current circumstances seem to place increasing responsibility on educators for responding to childhood and adolescent manifestations of society's problems. In some instances, such responsibilities are actually imposed, as was the case with PL 94-142, which mandated that all children with disabilities be accommodated in the mainstream of basic education. Other problems have become the responsibility of the schools simply because they cannot be ignored and, for a variety of reasons, are not successfully treated elsewhere. One way to view this phenomenon is as an imposition, because the primary function of the schools is to impart knowledge. Another way to view the phenomenon is that it is inevitable because the schools as a microcosm of the greater society share responsibility for responding to the problems. Beyond that, it seems illogical to expect the acquisition and use of knowledge to occur for many individuals whose personal and social problems are not treated.

Like the greater society, the schools have experienced varied success in treating personal and social problems. There are many reasons for this, some of which are related to the expertise of the professional staff. Most teachers and principals are not trained to intervene in students' personal and social problems. Specialists in social work, psychology, reading, speech, hearing, and the like are only available part time. Among the full-time professional staff of the schools, the individuals most likely trained to provide interventions for personal and social problems are school counselors. Support for this position is found in the ethical standards of the ASCA (2004) under the heading "Responsibilities to Students": "The school counselor is concerned with the total needs of the student (educational, vocational, *personal*, and *social*)" [italics added]. Therefore, without debating whether this system is fair, it seems obvious that school counselors will be challenged to provide responsive counseling interventions.

The three paradigms presented in chapter 1 state that counseling is an important function for school counselors. In ASCA's (2005) National Model for School Counseling Programs, counseling is considered to be a responsive service. As a responsive service, counseling is viewed from two perspectives (Gysbers & Henderson, 2001). Individual counseling is part of an individual planning process for which the goals are to help students monitor their academic, career, and personal development. Personal counseling is for students who experience problems with relationships, personal con-

Help student clients explore their problem situations and identify their resources.

Mary Hagler/Merrill

cerns, or normal developmental tasks. Most issues addressed in personal counseling will relate to the three domains identified by the ASCA (2005): academic development, career development, and personal/social development.

The TSCI states that counseling remains an important role for school counselors, especially academic counseling for learning and achievement and supporting student success (House & Hayes, 2002). The School–Community Collaboration Model alludes to counseling as a function in systems for care (i.e., treatment of severe and chronic problems such as emergencies and crises) and systems of early intervention (i.e., responding early after the onset of problems; Adelman & Taylor, 2002).

The competencies for counseling in schools, as presented in this textbook, lend themselves to preparing school counselors to function successfully in each initiative just cited. School counselors who possess these competencies will be able to provide individual and personal counseling as defined in the ASCA model, academic counseling, crisis counseling, early interventions, and a host of other categories of important counseling services that are not highlighted in the paradigms.

BASIC INGREDIENTS OF COUNSELING INTERVENTIONS

Point of View

Counseling is essentially a direct service that may be devoted primarily to the responsive treatment intervention goal that was indicated in chapter 3. It is an important function that requires considerable training to learn and develop the requisite skills. It also requires time to acquire the experience necessary for making appropriate decisions during counseling interviews and in case planning. Counseling is at the heart of the responsive treatment intervention function.

The more popular personality and counseling theories on which school counseling is founded were derived from the experiences of psychoanalysts and clinical psychologists (e.g., Sigmund Freud, Alfred Adler, Erik Erikson, Carl Rogers, Albert Ellis) and the research of experimental and social cognitive psychologists (e.g., B. F. Skinner, Albert Bandura). These foundations are useful, but counselor educators and school counselors find themselves translating the information, which is devoted to enhancing long-term psychoanalysis and psychotherapy, into appropriate models for short-term counseling of children and adolescents, most of whom are coping with normal developmental issues.

Historically, the fields of psychoanalysis, psychotherapy, and counseling have endured conflict among disciples of various theoretical camps over which approach is superior. Although differences of opinion still exist, time seems to have diffused some of them. The most common response by less invested persons to such disputes has been to advocate an eclectic approach. Supporters of eclecticism are quick to define what it is and is not. *Eclecticism* is a counselor's systematic, studied, and intelligent assimilation of ideas from differing theoretical perspectives into a personal hybrid that is defensible and identifiable. This individual eclectic theory is then adapted to the specific clientele and setting. Eclecticism is not a random set of acts and thoughts drawn from previous life experiences in response to immediate events.

Eclecticism appears to be the appropriate approach for school counseling. Sue (1992) pointed out that an eclectic approach may also be the path to achieving multicultural competence in one's counseling interventions by becoming culturally flexible:

> In counseling, equal treatment may be discriminatory treatment. And differential treatment is not necessarily preferential. Minority groups want and need equal access and opportunities, which may dictate differential treatment. . . . Counselors must be able to shift their counseling styles to meet not just developmental needs of their clients but also the cultural dimensions. There has to be recognition that no one style of counseling is appropriate for all populations and situations. (p. 14)

In the spirit of Herring's (1997) synergistic model, rather than use counseling interventions universally for all clients, school counselors will make the most appropriate use of the interventions selectively, having taken into account the attributes of individual client characteristics such as ethnicity, environment, culture, and gender. Sue, Ivey, and Pedersen (1996) referred to this as being aware of a *third presence* in counseling relationships: counselor, client, and culture. Readers are encouraged to think about the following hypothetical clients when reading the remainder of this chapter or when identifying their own alternative clients. How would the individual attributes of the following clients influence you in choosing from the menu of basic counseling competencies and strategies and in responding to client resistance or reluctance?

- John is a third-generation Italian American teenager whose close-knit family has recently moved to a metropolitan area of the southeastern United States. The family consists of two parents and six older siblings (three men and three women), all devout Roman Catholics. They own a restaurant, and all family members work in some way in that business.
- Jennifer is a biracial middle school student; she has two younger sisters. Her father is African American, and her mother is Asian American (Thai). The family is currently homeless because of a series of misfortunes that caused both parents to lose good jobs. The family is receiving welfare assistance.
- Brianna is a second grader whose mother is an employed single parent. Brianna just transferred to a new school and is having difficulty making friends because she is considered to be an outsider. Her younger sister has a hearing disability.
- Tomas dropped out of school a year ago because of substance abuse problems. Tomas has returned to school in an effort to graduate and receive his diploma. He belongs to a gang whose negative attitudes about his decisions have caused him to be conflicted.

Because this book is intended to be used for training school counselors, the basic ingredients of eclectic school counseling are presented. It is assumed that school counselors receive training to acquire basic competencies before accepting their first paid counseling positions. What follows, then, are recommended ingredients of the counseling treatment intervention function competencies. It is also assumed that counselors will become lifelong learners after basic training. As lifelong learners, they will surely enhance that basic training through thoughtful analyses of their own counseling experiences, and intelligent applications of information from readings, workshops, conferences, and collegial discussions will enhance the basic competencies.

Foundations

School counselors are challenged to understand several important sets of knowledge to apply basic skills successfully. Such knowledge provides the necessary environment for successful counseling; therefore, these foundation ingredients are addressed first. The list is presented in no particular order. Other writers may identify additional or different foundations:

- Knowledge about human ego defenses, such as rationalization, denial, and intellectualization
- Awareness that the United States is becoming increasingly pluralistic culturally
- Knowledge of the developmental tasks associated with childhood and adolescence
- Knowledge of changing social attitudes and conditions and economic opportunities
- Awareness that the vast majority of student clients need counselors who will help them overcome deficits and learn ways to cope better
- Self-awareness, leading to self-acceptance and a genuine interest in the welfare of all clientele

Types of Responsive Counseling Interventions

Early Identification and Treatment.   Intervention differs from prevention in that it is reactive, rather than proactive, and is offered only to those referred for interventions, rather than to the entire population. *Early identification and treatment* is a phrase that describes the situation of at-risk individuals experiencing a problem or deficit that has not yet overwhelmed them, although they do need individualized help. The following simulations are examples of early identification and treatment cases. The majority of intervention cases with which school counselors work probably fall into this category.

- An elementary school counselor is working with a child who has been disruptive in class. The short-term goal in this case is to help the child learn better ways to gain attention; the long-term goal is to prevent the child from becoming alienated, labeled negatively by teachers, or academically deficient.
- A middle school counselor uses teacher-to-parent progress reports as a means of identifying students at risk of failing courses. On finding those who want assistance and for whom learning or behavioral deficits can be identified, the counselor reaches out to them in an effort to provide individual or possibly small-group counseling interventions that will help them. An intervention will help these students pass their courses and learn more

appropriate or new, more useful behaviors. Over the long term, it is hoped that what was learned or changed will generalize to other challenging situations and that the recipients will have enhanced self-esteem because of their accomplishments.

- At the secondary school level, a counselor who provides an empathic, facilitative relationship for youths experiencing grief over the loss of a loved one or the failure of a friendship may be able to prevent the impact of such experiences from being overwhelming. The immediate goal is to prevent self-deprecating or self-abusive (e.g., suicidal) responses. The long-term goal is that students will not only come to terms with the immediate incapacitating experience but also generalize the accomplishments of that struggle to similar challenges in the future.

Remedial Interventions.   Individuals who need remedial interventions are those with a history of chronic or borderline-chronic maladaptive thoughts and behaviors. Examples are the child who is known to be a school phobic, the adolescent who is or has been addicted to drugs or alcohol, and the chronic truant. These individuals usually represent a relatively small percentage of the total school population but may comprise a substantial portion of the population in some individual schools or districts (e.g., inner-city schools). Yet, they require disproportionately more time per individual than do those receiving prevention and early identification and treatment services. Students who fall within the remedial intervention category represent a small but hard-core segment of the school population, and school counselors are challenged to consider them among the potential recipients of their counseling responses in a balanced counseling program. Suggested approaches for helping those whose needs are within the expertise of school counselors are presented here in chapters 9 and 11. Those who cannot be helped directly may be assisted through intelligent referrals and school–community collaborations, the subject of chapter 10.

Prevention Programming and Responsive Counseling Interventions May Overlap

Although prevention and intervention differ by definition, secondary prevention and early identification and treatment are found in an overlapping region. In the world of school counseling practitioners, this overlap should not matter. Prevention and intervention also differ with respect to the ratio of counselor time spent per student client. Prevention programs are economical in this regard because counselors are able to serve several individuals at once through group activities. Responsive treatment interventions, in contrast, are often delivered on a one-to-one basis, although small-group counseling may be offered to individuals with similar needs and a willingness to share their problems with peers. Multiple one-to-one or small-group counseling sessions are usually required to achieve responsive treatment intervention goals. Therefore, if cost effectiveness is the primary accountability criterion, prevention services are certainly more cost effective than responsive treatment intervention services. Using cost effectiveness as the sole criterion for judging a school counseling program is a mistake, however, because prevention programming will then dominate, and those needing responsive treatment interventions will go underserved and cause unrest. A balanced program serves both predicted and remedial developmental needs, whereas an unbalanced program ignores an important needs area. A balanced counseling program serves all students at all grade levels, responding systematically to the developmental needs of children and adolescents.

Developmental Perspective

The primary means of delivering responsive treatment interventions is through individual and small-group counseling. Counseling is a dynamic, continuous process, and counselors are aided by road maps to help them find their way. On the assumption that all counseling has beginnings and endings—sometimes prematurely—a road map serves as a means of deciding what to do next (e.g., when the student client's goals have been identified) and analyzing the situation when problems occur (e.g., when engaged in helping the client achieve previously established goals and the client suddenly resists). Several such road maps can be found in the professional literature. They often take the form of a stagewise paradigm, appearing developmental, which counseling often is, and linear, which counseling often is not. The comment about the nonlinearity of counseling is important and usually is a disclaimer from authors of stagewise models. One well-known stagewise model applicable to school counseling was developed by Ivey and Ivey (2007).

Ivey and Ivey's (2007) paradigm consists of five stages, which they have subdivided for discussion and increased understanding. Each stage is characterized by goals and related counseling skills. Once familiar with this model or one like it, counselors can use it in making decisions about their own behaviors, analyzing student client needs, and assessing progress in counseling relationships. A summary of the Ivey and Ivey paradigm is presented in Table 9.1.

Table 9.1
The Ivey and Ivey paradigm.

Stage	Goal
I.	Initiate the session—building rapport with and providing structure for the student client
II.	Gather data—listen to the student client's story and search for positive assets
III.	Mutual goal setting for the student client
IV.	Work with student client to explore alternatives, confront incongruities and conflicts, and decide on a constructive action plan
V.	Terminate—help student client generalize and act on action plan

Source: Data from *Intentional Interviewing and Counseling: Facilitating Client Development in a Multicultural Society* (6th ed.) by A. E. Ivey & M. B. Ivey, 2007, Pacific Grove, CA: Thomson/Brooks/Cole.

THE NATURE OF COUNSELING INTERVENTIONS IN SCHOOLS

Unlike the classic therapeutic hour that psychotherapists in private practice or counselors in college and university counseling centers set aside for appointments with clients, school counselors engage in a greater variety of counseling interventions, many of which are brief. In addition, school counselors, due to time or competence limits, are less likely to see student clients for more than one or a few consecutive appointments. Most school counseling interventions are short term rather than long term. Some interventions are short term because the nature of the clients' needs demands nothing else. Others are shortened because a referral is better. More comprehensive information on referrals is provided in chapter 10.

Other factors that impinge on the length of school counseling sessions are (a) the large number of students that each counselor is to serve; (b) little time available for students to see a counselor because of tight academic scheduling; (c) concern about taking students away from their classroom studies for too long; (d) in secondary schools, scheduling periods that are about 40 to 45 minutes in length; and (e) school systems that do not provide activity periods or study halls for students. Faced with having to conduct brief or limited counseling interventions, school counselors are challenged to be efficient. Important to efficiency in brief/limited counseling is being able to establish a working alliance and to determine client goals expeditiously. Equally important is being able to provide the client something of value immediately. Some things of value can be as diverse as feeling understood and receiving something concrete such as valuable information or relief from negative affect (e.g., anxiety). Fortunately, Ivey and Ivey's (2007) helping model lends itself to conducting brief/limited counseling interventions. Being organized from the outset is also important. In the next section, we use the five stages in the Ivey and Ivey paradigm as a foundation for presenting an overview of the basic counseling competencies required of counselors in both individual and small-group counseling.

The information presented in the next section is offered as an overview for readers who may not yet have taken courses in counseling theories and methods, career counseling and development, assessment, prepracticum, and practicum—with the caveat that the information is not intended to be a substitute for, or a primer in, the content of these courses. Indeed, the aforementioned courses will cover these topics more substantively with accompanying opportunities to observe counseling demonstrations and to engage in supervised practice with corresponding constructive feedback. Consider the following information as suggestions for good practice with examples inserted for clarification. Readers are encouraged to revisit this information during or after taking the courses in their training program similar to those generic courses just listed.

STAGE ONE: INITIATING COUNSELING SESSIONS

Responding to Client Aversion to Counseling

Client aversion takes two forms: reluctance and resistance (Doyle, 1992; Ritchie, 1986). Reluctant student clients do not want to be involved in a counseling relationship initially; resistant clients behave in counterproductive ways while involved in the counseling process. Resistance can be a trait or a state in that clients may be resistant throughout the counseling process (trait) or may resist engaging in goal-directed behaviors periodically (state). Reluctance and resistance are natural challenges—part of the counseling process.

Reluctance.   School counselors work in a setting in which they do not always control referrals made to them, and their functions are viewed differently by teachers, administrators, and parents. For example, teachers may refer students to counselors because they are puzzled, baffled, or frustrated by the students' behaviors and want someone to change the students so they will behave as desired in the classroom. Viewing counselors as behavior management specialists or wishing the counselors were such specialists, some teachers refer their troublesome students to counselors. Often, the referred students have not been appropriately prepared for the referral and are reluctant to participate. Administrators sometimes do the same thing; for instance, principals may send misbehaving students to the counselor's office after having administered disciplinary action, expecting the counselor to modify student behavior, validate the principal's disciplinary decisions, or initiate additional discipline. In all these cases, students are likely to be reluctant to visit the counseling office.

Parents sometimes view counselors as their agents in the school, that is, persons who will gather information about their children or who will support the parents' wishes. Viewing counselors as their agents, parents may expect them to initiate interviews with students at the parents' request. In such interviews, students are often reluctant to participate or cooperate. They may be reluctant because they are unfamiliar with counseling or the counselor or because they do not know why they have been summoned to the counseling office. In some of these instances, counselors are faced with students who enter the relationship negatively. When individuals make inappropriate referrals or have unrealistic expectations of counselors, perhaps the best way to cope with the predictably reluctant clients is to find acceptable ways to avoid engaging in such interviews. More is presented on this matter in chapter 10.

Suggestions for coping with reluctance recommend that counselors draw on their basic counseling skills to earn the student's trust and on their challenging skills to explain the counseling relationship and determine student-based goals (information sharing, goal setting). Trust and structure are important in counteracting student reluctance (Ritchie, 1986). The goal is to restructure the relationship to one in which counselors and students work together in mutual understanding to achieve student goals. If, during the process of trying to accomplish this, counselors can replace student reticence, suspiciousness, and defensiveness with trust, they will appear trustworthy and competent to their student clients. Janis (1983) called this "motivating power." Having become what Janis called "referent persons," counselors are able to use their motivating power to challenge student clients to achieve their goals successfully.

Keat (1990a) pointed out that children may often be reluctant at the beginning of counseling relationships because adults initiate the counseling and establish the outcome goals. He recommended that counselors try to convince reluctant children that counselors are special adults who are different from other adults in their lives. Suggestions for employing this idea include (a) demonstrating that counselors have influence over other adults in the children's lives and can effect changes; (b) presenting themselves as adults who can help children by engaging them in activities they find useful, such as learning to relax and cope better with stress, or by giving them therapeutic gifts, such as tape-recorded information or readings; and (c) showing a genuine interest in the children's interests.

Resistance.   Ritchie (1986) believed that the instances of resistance in counseling far outnumber those of reluctance, making it a more pervasive challenge. This seems true because a limited number of reluctant students enter a counselor's life, but all students exhibit resistance at some time. The reasons for resistance vary. Some students do not understand what they are to do, whereas others lack the skills to carry on as expected. Fear of failure and other immobilizing emotions may prevent students from responding. Sometimes students receive more reinforcement for engaging in unproductive behaviors than in productive ones. Sometimes students do not want to admit to needing to change or, if admitting it, do not want to change.

Suggestions for coping with resistance vary because the reasons for resistance vary. Corey, Corey, Callanan, and Russell (1992) and Ritchie (1986) advocated an eclectic approach that can be summed up as using what works best from among available strategies. Cormier and Nurius (2003) offered what might be called a systematic eclecticism (they recommend finding the cause of the resistance and responding accordingly). Causes of resistance may be categorized as being attributable to student client variables (e.g., pessimism, anxiety), environmental variables (e.g., unable to change environment), or counselor or counseling process variables. Inventories of suggestions for coping with resistance present a variety of strategies crossing different theoretical underpinnings and having no absolute guarantees (Corey et al., 1992; Cormier & Nurius, 2003; Cowan & Presbury, 2000; Ritchie, 1986). Consequently, counselors may have to draw on many of their basic skills and creativity when faced with student resistance. What can be stated positively is that counselors are challenged to be prepared because resistance will occur during their careers, manifesting itself in forms ranging from the subtle to the outrageous.

Intentionality

Counselors who have adequate developmental road maps will be able to respond to student clients intentionally. As defined by Ivey and Ivey (2007),

> Intentionality is acting with a sense of capability and deciding from among a range of alternative actions. The intentional individual has more than one action, thought, or behavior to choose from in responding to changing life situations. The intentional individual can generate alternatives in a given situation and approach a problem from different vantage points, using a variety of skills and personal qualities, *adapting styles to suit different individuals and cultures.* (p. 20)

Intentionality is enhanced when counselors possess a repertoire of appropriate behaviors or responses to changing situations and can choose freely from among these options—the epitome of eclecticism. Beyond what may be labeled basic intentionality, Ivey and Ivey (2007) also advocated *cultural intentionality,* a concept they defined as follows: "Cultural intentionality is demonstrated when you are able to have many possible responses to any client issue. Though you may have an excellent personal style, you are able to build on it by expanding your alternatives for responses" (p. 15).

Opening Individual and Group Counseling Sessions

Opening Individual Counseling Sessions. Because the opening influences the remainder of the interview, effectiveness in opening interviews is crucial. Interview openings are of two types. When student clients are self-referred or referred by a third party and their needs are unknown, they are invited to talk. Open invitations beginning with "how," "what," or "tell" will help counselors induce client talk (e.g., "How can I help?" "What brought you here?" "Tell me what I can do for you."). Open invitations to talk encourage student clients to share anything they choose and direct attention to their needs. In so doing, counselors set the stage for listening to the student client's stories and gathering data. Two examples follow:

- A high school student is seated in the office of a school counselor, having made an appointment previously, and the counselor smiles at the student client and asks, "How can I help you today?"
- An elementary school counselor encounters a child who is sobbing and obviously distressed. After helping the child calm down enough to be able to talk, the counselor states, "Tell me what happened."

A second type of counseling interview opening occurs when the counselor requests a meeting with a student, placing the counselor in a position of having to explain the purpose of the meeting. A clear explanation is important. The following suggestions for explaining the purpose of an interview are based on Ivey and Gluckstern's (1974) ideas. First, be effective in self-expression (e.g., appropriate eye contact, body language, verbalizations). Second, share all important information. Third, make the explanation specific and clear. Fourth, verify that the student understands the explanation before proceeding. Two examples follow:

- A middle school counselor has initiated a plan to get acquainted with all students assigned to her, and when inviting each student into the counselor's office, she explains,

  I am trying to get to know my advisees so I can serve them better. Do you have time to visit with me for about a half-hour today? Good, I would like to ask some questions to help us get acquainted. You are not expected to answer them unless you want to do so. Also, feel free to ask me questions that are of interest to you. I'll be asking some questions about your interests, experiences, and goals for the future and sharing some information about the counseling program, while also responding to your questions. Before we begin, do you have any questions about what I just said?

- In an elementary school, a counselor is meeting with an upper elementary school student who has been referred for counseling by her parents, who are concerned about their child's inability to make friends. After making the student welcome, the counselor explains:

If it is OK with you, I would like to talk about friendships. As you know, your parents told me you would like to make some new friends. I hope to be able to help you. Do you want to see what we can do together? Good, I am going to ask some questions about what you do when making friends so I can get a good idea of what is happening. Then, we can think about what else might need to be done for you to be happy about making friends. It may be hard work for both of us. Do you think you understand me?"

Opening Group Counseling Sessions.   Opening individual and group counseling sessions have both similarities and differences. Most group counseling begins after a selection process, so explanations during the first session take the form of a review. Group counseling leaders are better served by giving directions and negotiating rules and expectations. Being believable, thorough, and specific and verifying that members understand are also important when opening group counseling sessions. Explanations, directions, and negotiations are enhanced by exercises designed to get the group off to a good start. An example follows in which the leader of a middle school counseling group—to which the members have been referred for acting-out behaviors in classrooms that have led to in-school suspensions—is negotiating rules, specifically about confidentiality:

"At times, some of us will share information that is private because we believe it is important for the others to know or because we can't help ourselves. I believe that information should be kept in the group and used only for the benefit of the person who shared the information and the other group members. That's called keeping private personal information confidential. I believe that, to be a successful group, we all need to agree that the information shared in our group sessions will be treated as confidential. Is there anything I just said that is confusing or needs to be clarified?"

STAGE TWO: GATHERING DATA BY LISTENING TO THE STUDENTS' STORIES

Basic Attending

One way that counselors convey their desire to understand and help student clients is by their physical behaviors. Physical attending behaviors promote communication and understanding. Egan (2007) offered basic attending behaviors that counselors may use with clients. As a group, these behaviors may be identified by the acronym SOLER, from the first letter of the key words Squarely, Open, Lean, Eye, and Relaxed. These terms are described in the following sections. The SOLER behaviors are important attending behaviors in North American culture and may not have similar positive effects with clients from other cultures. Alternative behaviors may be necessary with clients from other cultures, and counselors are challenged to adjust to such variations in their clientele.

Face the Student Client Squarely.   When the counselor's body is positioned toward the client, psychological contact with the client is heightened. As a result, counselor involvement is communicated.

Adopt an Open Posture.   The counselor's posture during a counseling interview conveys the degree of involvement. Suggestions often state what not to do, rather than what to do. For instance, crossing arms and legs or placing objects such as books, clipboards, and desks between the counselor and the client may lessen the client's perception of counselor involvement. Egan (2007) offered sage advice about these suggestions when he stated that they can be taken literally or metaphorically; that is, crossed legs may not always communicate lack of involvement. Counselors crossing their legs might think about whether that act interferes with communication of involvement with the client.

Lean Forward Slightly.   A forward lean is another posture that conveys involvement. The degree of forward lean serves best when it is a natural reaction to whatever the client is communicating. Egan (2007) pointed out that leaning too far forward and leaning backward are both potentially counterproductive behaviors in that the former may convey too much closeness, whereas the latter may convey disinterest.

Maintain Good Eye Contact.   Counselor involvement is also conveyed via eye contact. Clients who find eye contact with the counselor when seeking a sign of involvement are likely to conclude that the counselor is trying to understand. Staring, of course, is a counterproductive application of this principle because clients will be uncomfortable. Occasionally looking away is acceptable; it is sometimes necessary so counselors can gather their thoughts, and it prevents staring. Looking elsewhere often during the interview, however, conveys disinterest (Egan, 2007). With younger children, adult counselors may have to get down to the children's level to make eye contact by sitting or kneeling on the floor or an object close to the floor.

Try To Be Relatively Relaxed.   Counselors who rigidly conform to the SOLER guidelines will probably make clients uncomfortable and distracted. Counselors who are comfortable with their own behavior are more likely to be natural in their counseling. Only then will they be able to concentrate on their clients. Being relaxed and attentive follows from a genuine interest in the welfare of clients.

Psychological Attending.   Being able to attend to clients psychologically is equally important. Psychological attending manifests itself through listening carefully and focusing on the core or theme of what is being said and felt, and then conveying having done so via verbal responses and physical behaviors.

Observing

An important counseling competency is to be able to observe the nonverbal behavior of clients to better understand what they are feeling internally and expressing verbally. An important component of this process is to identify discrepancies and respond to them appropriately. Nonverbal behavior that may provide important information for counselors includes facial expressions and body language. Verbal behaviors that are important to observe, include key words that may occur often, regardless of whether student clients present information abstractly or concretely, whether issues are attributed to themselves ("I statements") or to others, and whether discrepancies in the stories are shared by the student clients. Counselors are challenged to observe these behaviors and use the awareness of them to help student clients tell their stories successfully (Ivey & Ivey, 2007).

Listening and Responding

The following listening and responding behaviors are considered to be basic components of the successful counselor's repertoire of counseling skills. They are necessary for successful listening and responding and for achieving the goals of the data gathering stage. Whether engaged in individual or group counseling, school counselors are challenged to help student clients explore their problem situations and identify their resources. Several basic counseling or interviewing skills have been recommended for accomplishing the goals associated with successfully initiating counseling relationships. These basic skills remain important throughout all stages of counseling relationships. The basic verbal skills are paraphrasing information, reflecting feelings, clarifying unclear material, summarizing information and feelings, inviting clients to talk, and questioning appropriately.

Paraphrasing Information.   By briefly rephrasing clients' verbal presentations, counselors can help them focus on the content of their messages (Cormier & Nurius, 2003). Therefore, counselors are challenged to be able to restate the information and ideas that clients share. An example of an elementary school counselor paraphrasing the content of a child's verbal message follows:

Student: I don't like school. No one will play with me, and it's not fun. I hate all of them and wish they would move away. Sometimes I don't want to come to school.

Counselor: No one will play with you, and school is not fun.

Reflecting Feelings.   Counselors are also challenged to recognize the affective components in client messages. Sometimes student clients label their feelings, although on other occasions they only imply them by their behavior and statements. Being able to recognize important client feelings and label them (e.g., "You seem frustrated," "That made you happy," "There is sadness in your words") helps clients recognize their feelings and explore them more deeply (Cormier & Nurius, 2003). Continuing with the child who is expressing her dislike of school, a reflection in response to the same student client statement might be:

Counselor: The way the other children treat you hurts your feelings and makes you unhappy.

Clarifying Unclear Material.   Sometimes clients are vague or their messages are unclear; occasionally, counselors just get lost when trying to follow client material. Clarifying vague or missed messages verifies the accuracy of what was heard and encourages client elaborations (Cormier & Nurius, 2003). Such clarification can take the form of questions and paraphrases/reflections or can be in the form of open questions or invitations. An example is based on the unhappy upper elementary school student introduced previously:

Student:	Yes, they hurt my feelings. I wish I could just stay at home. They make me so unhappy that I want to go away.
Counselor:	Please tell me what you mean when you say "I want to go away."

Summarizing Information and Feelings.   Identification and clarification can be enhanced by rephrasing parts of the student client's message, including information and feelings. Summarizing facilitates a client's thinking by tying multiple elements together and identifying themes or patterns (Cormier & Nurius, 2003). A summary of what has been presented thus far about the child client might be as follows:

Counselor:	I think we have gotten off to a good start today. You have shared some important information with me about how bad you feel when being rejected by other children, how much you would like to make friends, and how hopeful you are that we can work together to try to help you be happier.

Inviting Clients to Talk.   Open invitations have been mentioned as being important for beginning counseling interviews. Open questions are also useful for obtaining further information ("Tell me more"), encouraging further client exploration ("How did that affect you?"), eliciting specific examples ("What happened then?"), and motivating the client to continue to communicate ("Could you elaborate on . . . ") when a pause occurs in the interview (Cormier & Nurius, 2003). In the section on clarifying unclear material, the counselor used a "Tell me" open invitation. The counselor could have responded with alternative open invitations and achieved the same goal (e.g., "What does 'I want to go away' mean?" or "Could you elaborate on what you are thinking when saying 'I want to go away'?").

Questioning Appropriately.   All individuals know how to ask closed questions, which require a yes-or-no response. Such questions have a place in counseling if they are used to narrow the topic being discussed ("Is there a reason for that?"), obtain specific information ("Is this decision still important to you?"), identify parameters of a problem ("Have you identified what causes that reaction?"), or focus the interview ("Do you want to talk about your goals?") when necessary (Cormier & Nurius, 2003). Care is recommended, however, when using closed questions to prevent the interview from becoming an interrogation or from coming to a halt. Their use may indicate that the counselor has run out of questions or may lead the client to wait for the next question before responding. Consider the following two hypothetical responses in which closed questions are used. The first is an example of an interrogation and is not recommended; the second is an example of using closed questions that are facilitative:

Student:	Yes, they hurt my feelings. I wish I could just stay at home. They make me so unhappy that I want to go away.
Counselor:	Who hurt your feelings?
Student:	All of those kids.
Counselor:	What kids? Name them for me.
Student:	Amy, James, Sammy, and Alicia.
Counselor:	Have you been staying at home?
Student:	No!
Counselor:	OK, did these children say mean things to you?
Student:	Yes!
Counselor:	Did they hurt you?
Student:	Yes?
Counselor:	Did you tell your parents and your teacher about this?
Student:	Yes!
Counselor:	What do you want me to do about this?
Student:	I don't know.
Counselor:	Can you be more specific?
Student:	Yes, they hurt my feelings. I wish I could just stay at home. They make me so unhappy that I want to go away.
Counselor:	Please tell me what you mean when you say "I want to go away."
Student:	Sometimes I feel like running away or moving away or going to my grandmother's house and living there. Then those kids will be sorry for what they did and I can play with someone who is nice.
Counselor:	So, you have thought about running or moving away. Have you ever run away? (closed question)
Student:	No, I can't do that because I'd miss my mom and dad and it would be scary.

Notice that the closed question received a response similar to that of an open-ended question because it was preceded by a paraphrase ("So, you have thought . . .") and an open invitation to talk ("Please tell me . . ."), both of which created a facilitative atmosphere rather than an interrogative one. The closed question introduced an important element (has the client acted on thoughts of running away?).

Depending on how they are used, questions can be part of basic counseling or challenging responses. If the goal is to elicit in basic counseling, then questions are being used for listening/responding purposes. If the goal is to probe, the questions are being used as challenging skills. The same relationships are true in open invitations.

Integrating the Skills.   The following conversation from a simulated counseling session provides examples of the respective basic verbal listening and responding skills.

An elementary school student is seated in the office of a school counselor. The counselor smiles at the student client and asks, "How can I help you today?" (open-ended question/invitation to talk)

Student:	I don't like school. No one will play with me, and it's not fun. I hate all of them and wish they would move away. Sometimes I don't want to come to school.
Counselor:	No one will play with you and school is not fun (paraphrase), and the way the other children treat you hurts your feelings and makes you unhappy. (reflecting feeling)
Student:	Yes, they hurt my feelings. I wish I could just stay at home. They make me so unhappy that I want to go away.
Counselor:	Please tell me what you mean when you say "I want to go away." (clarifying unclear material)
Student:	Sometimes I feel like running away or moving away or going to my grandmother's house and living there. Then those kids will be sorry for what they did and I can play with someone who is nice.
Counselor:	So, you have thought about running or moving away. (paraphrase) Have you ever run away? (closed question)
Student:	No, I can't do that because I'd miss my mom and dad and it would be scary.

Student client continues to identify and clarify her concerns, and the counselor must close the interview.

Counselor:	I think we have gotten off to a good start today. You have shared some important information with me about how bad you feel when the other children are mean to you, how much you would like to make friends, and how hopeful you are that we can work together to try to help you be happier. (summarizing information and feelings)

During his presentation at the ACA convention, William Glasser (2002) referred to the preceding competencies as "making nice" and stated his belief that anyone who cannot make nice does not belong in the counseling profession. He appeared to allude to a belief that the basic counseling skills are necessary for all counselors in every counseling situation.

STAGE THREE: MUTUAL GOAL SETTING

Through telling their stories, individual student clients and counseling group members learn how to present issues. They may also need help in setting goals. Setting goals is challenging and often requires stronger responses from counselors—responses that are more directive and influential than the ones listed previously. Whereas the previous responses focus on helping student clients understand their own material better, challenging responses evolve from counselor perceptions and are therefore more direct in their influence. Cormier and Nurius (2003) described these as *action responses* because they exert such direct influence on clients. For these reasons, student clients may respond in a negative fashion.

Unproductive client responses such as anger, denial, and attacks on the counselor may set the relationship back, cause a stalemate, or lead to client withdrawal from the counseling relationship. Challenging responses, in contrast, may cause student clients to acquire insights impossible to achieve by themselves, accept responsibility for their behavior, and change their thoughts, behaviors, or both constructively. Because challenging responses are so powerful, they are best used sparingly—only when needed— and skillfully. Rather than single behaviors, as are the previously cited skills (e.g., paraphrasing, reflecting, summarizing), the challenging skills are sets of behaviors that are logically combined to achieve specific goals. Important basic challenging skills include interpretation, self-sharing, confrontation, immediacy, information sharing, and goal setting. A common aspect of the challenging skills is to present them tentatively to allow student clients to negotiate their responses, rather than be forced to defend themselves. Examples of each follow. Ivey and Ivey (2007) used the term *influencing skills* as a synonym for challenging skills.

Interpretation

Also known as *advanced accurate empathy,* interpretation occurs when a counselor challenges a client to think about what is implied rather than stated by the client's words and behaviors. Usually preceded by a paraphrase, reflection, and/or summary of what the client did say, an interpretation is the counselor's hypothesis of what was implied or stated tentatively (e.g., "You decided not to apply to Ivy University. I wonder whether your decision is related to doubts about your ability to succeed at that

Many children and adolescents are confronted with choices.

Anthony Magnacca/Merrill

college."). Successful interpretations evolve from insights acquired by counselors from their clinical experiences and from closely following material presented by the client. When successful, interpretations provide clients either a new view of their material or another explanation for their thoughts and behaviors (Cormier & Nurius, 2003).

Self-Sharing

Also known as *self-disclosure*, self-sharing occurs when counselors share something about themselves with their clients. Usually prompted by a paraphrase, reflection, and/or summary of something about the client, the counselor presents related information and feelings with an attempt to be brief and an invitation for the client to use the information therapeutically (e.g., "You're afraid of flunking out of State University during the first semester and being too embarrassed to face your family. I remember having similar thoughts when trying to decide whether to take this job at Comprehensive High School. I wasn't sure whether the students would accept me, and I had to understand that I might not achieve my goal of working in a high school counseling center if I wasn't willing to take that risk. There seem to be some similarities between your situation and that one of mine."). Successful self-sharing helps student clients learn how to share and discover perspectives they had not considered previously (Egan, 2007). Effectiveness at self-sharing seems to require being selective and not overdoing the sharing by offering material that adds to the student's burden, is too verbose, or causes the roles to shift (i.e., client becomes attentive responder to counselor who is engaging in excessive self-talk).

Confrontation

Confrontation occurs when counselors point out discrepancies, distortions, and conflicts in clients' messages. Best preceded by a summary of the detected discrepancies or distortion, confrontations contain a tentative description of what the counselor has observed as being discrepant, distorted, or conflicting, along with an invitation to think about the counselor's observations (e.g., "You say that not attending college has something to do with your fear of failure, yet you have been able to complete high school when there were trying times for you here."). Confrontations such as this can help student clients consider alternative ways to perceive their issues and become more aware of their discrepancies, distortions, and conflicts (Cormier & Nurius, 2003).

Immediacy

Sometimes referred as *you-and-me talk*, immediacy achieves direct, mutual interactions between counselor and client when the counseling relationship itself is at issue. A counselor's summary of what is interfering with the counseling relationship is followed by a statement of the counselor's feelings about what is occurring and the counselor's goals in bringing attention to the situation. The immediacy response concludes with an invitation to the client to participate in negotiating an amicable resolution. For example, a student client accuses a middle-class European American counselor of overemphasizing concerns about possible academic difficulties as a college student because the student client is African American and from a lower socioeconomic background. The student client wonders whether the counselor is discouraging college attendance because of racist intentions. The counselor responds,

> You think I believe college will be difficult for you because I am White and you are Black and I am a racist, and that both surprises and hurts me. We seem to be in danger of being at odds with each other because you interpreted my comments in a way I did not intend. I apologize for my part in that, and I want to get us back on the right track. Do you think we can resolve this, and if so, do you have any recommendations?

Immediacy serves as a means of engaging clients in mutual assessments of problems in the counselor–client relationship that interfere with progress.

Information Sharing

Information sharing occurs when student clients need information that may challenge them to view circumstances differently. Cormier and Nurius (2003) suggested that this can include the sharing of facts about experiences, events, alternatives, or people. Following a summary of the client's understanding of the information in question, the counselor asks whether the client is aware of, and interested in, additional information. The counselor then shares the information, checking the client's reaction. For example,

> You heard that all freshmen at Ivy University must take calculus and an advanced year of foreign language in the first semester. Are you aware that there is an alternative? . . . No? Would you like to know what it is? . . . Incoming freshmen at Ivy University who do not have the background to take calculus or an advanced year of foreign language are allowed to take other courses appropriate to their high school preparation. How does that affect your thinking?

Information sharing helps clients identify and evaluate alternatives that they were not aware of previously, helps dispel myths that they may harbor, and motivates them to examine issues that they may have been avoiding (Cormier & Nurius, 2003).

Goal Setting

Understanding that most student clients need help in adjusting or coping, learning new and better ways of behaving and thinking, and overcoming deficits in their environment, counselors may view themselves as participants in the counseling process, helping students identify and achieve their goals. Goal setting is at the heart of this participatory relationship between counselors and clients, and counselors are challenged to help student clients find a sense of direction, as well as share the responsibility for clients achieving their goals (Egan, 2007). Several basic counseling intervention skills are involved in the goal-setting process.

Initially, counselors explain the purpose of goal setting; this involves information-sharing skills. The basic verbal responses (paraphrasing and summarizing) will help clients identify and evaluate their options (What are the possible goals?). Basic verbal and challenging skills may be needed to help clients select their goals, clarify them, determine whose goals they really are, decide how to achieve them, and then proceed to achieve them. Helping clients set goals focuses their attention on acting constructively, gets them involved in the helping process, makes them aware of what needs to be accomplished, encourages them to act on their own behalf, and informs them that the counselor is a capable partner in the helping process. A hypothetical interaction between the elementary school counselor and the unhappy student introduced previously provides an example of one of the many approaches counselors might pursue when trying to help clients set goals:

Counselor:	So, we have talked about how bad you feel and how angry you are at the others. Tell me what you want right now.
Student:	I wish they would all disappear in a cloud of smoke!
Counselor:	I can see how that might make you feel better right now. Are you sure that is all you want?
Student:	Well, I wish someone would be nice to me.
Counselor:	Do you think that is something for us to work on—figuring out how to get someone to be nice to you?

The counselor has discovered a possible goal in the client's comments and offered it as a possible goal. At this point, the counselor and client may engage in negotiating whether this would be a viable goal.

STAGE FOUR: WORKING WITH STUDENTS ON A CONSTRUCTIVE ACTION PLAN

In the logic of the five-stage counseling paradigm, initiating the session, gathering data, and mutual goal setting usher in constructive action designed to achieve student client goals. The options available to counselors when helping students act on their goals are far ranging, and many counselors spend their careers trying to learn more about ideas in the counseling literature and to become more accomplished at applying those skills. This book focuses on selected basic action strategies, not all possible action strategies. The strategies presented are suggested because they are appropriate for helping most student clients achieve their goals. Therefore, the suggestions that follow are presented as basic action strategies for the school counselor's repertoire. Some strategies may be more appropriate for counseling children, some more appropriate for counseling adolescents, and others useful for both children and adolescents. When reading the next section, readers are reminded to think about the information on *eclecticism* presented earlier in this chapter.

Readers are also reminded that the purpose of the following information is to provide an overview, rather than to be a substitute for other courses in one's training program. In this section, an overview of action strategies that appear to be useful is presented. Competence in these strategies will come from comprehensive training associated with coursework in one's counselor education training program. After his comments about the necessity of the basic counseling skills (i.e., "making nice") during a more recent ACA convention, William Glasser (2002) stated that the "hard work" follows, that is, helping clients achieve their goals. Each strategy is presented as a way of responding to specific challenges that are common to student clients.

Helping Students Who Need Empathy and Support

Children and adolescents benefit from knowing that someone cares and is trying to understand their circumstances. They respond best to counselors who provide support and understanding by creative and facilitative mutual relationships. These student clients may be experiencing grief, confusion, pain, or apathy, and their goal may be to adjust, understand, or feel accepted. The skills popularly associated with client- or person-centered counseling (Rogers, 1951) are commonly used in supportive counseling. Interestingly, they are the same skills cited previously as the basic verbal counseling responses (e.g., paraphrasing content, reflecting feelings, clarifying unclear material). Thus, in this instance, the action strategy takes the form of continuing counseling responses designed to help students tell their stories in advance of goal setting. What differs is the use of these responses to help clients achieve their goals.

For example, a high school counselor is meeting with a student who is traumatized by the sudden death of a classmate killed in a car accident. Realizing that the student client needs to identify and clarify her feelings, the counselor uses paraphrases, reflections, clarifications, and summaries to provide an empathic atmosphere. Eventually, the counselor learns that the student "just needs someone to talk to." Deciding that needing someone to talk to is the student's immediate goal, the counselor continues to respond in much the same manner as was done initially. That is, the counselor provides a supportive environment for the client to work through and process the thoughts and feelings that led to her seeking help from the counselor.

Helping Students Make Decisions

Many children and adolescents are confronted with choices, and making the best decisions is critically important to them. This is another arena in which counselors can be of service. Counselors are faced with a broad range of client problems that require decision-making assistance. For instance, choices are to be made when seeking a job, selecting a college, or determining whether to pursue a vocational-technical curriculum. Choices are also to be made in the personal-social domain, such as whether to forgive a transgressing peer or to pursue dangerous activities.

When engaging in decision-making counseling as an action strategy, counselors have at their disposal several rational, stepped, decision-making counseling paradigms. As Horan (1979) pointed out, they all have four major components in common; therefore, counselors will be able to follow these paradigms and assist many of their student clients successfully by helping them do the following:

1. Define the problem as involving a decision.
2. Identify the alternative response options (by using basic clarifying and exploring skills).
3. Determine the advantages and disadvantages of each option.
4. Make a tentative choice (by using basic clarifying, exploring, and challenging skills).

Decision-making counseling involves a unique combination of the aforementioned basic responding and challenging skills in a strategy founded on the counselor leading the client through a set of predetermined helping steps. For example, the high school student who was traumatized by the death of a classmate, having processed thoughts and feelings with the help of a supportive counselor, reaches a point of having to decide whether to tell someone about witnessing alcohol abuse by the driver of the car before the accident occurred (the problem is defined as involving a decision). Using the decision-making steps, the counselor helps the student client determine the alternatives (e.g., tell someone, tell no one, have someone else tell). Following identification of the alternatives, the counselor helps the student client consider the advantages and disadvantages of each. For instance, the counselor might say (using an open-ended question): "What are the advantages of telling someone?" Having discussed the advantages, the counselor will then ask, "What are the disadvantages?" After exhaustively discussed the various advantages and disadvantages, the counselor then asks the student which alternative seems to be the best choice. The response may be to make a choice, to not make a choice (which is actually a choice—to do nothing), or to think about the choices further—perhaps acquiring more information or opinions in the process. If more time is needed, the counselor invites the student client to return and continue if desired. If a choice is made, the counselor helps the student make plans for implementing it and returning to meet with the counselor and process the effects. Notice the similarity between this process and that suggested for making ethical decisions in chapter 5.

One prominent application of the decision-making counseling framework that may occur often for school counselors is when working with students who are trying to make career-related decisions. Such decisions include but are not restricted to school-to-school transitions, school-to-work transitions, and school-to-postsecondary education decisions. Examples of questions that may be best approached by the decision-making framework are as follows: What do I want to do when I grow up or after graduation? What courses should I take in high school to prepare me for the transition to work or postsecondary education? To which postsecondary schools should I apply? Which postsecondary school should I select from those that have accepted me? How do I decide what to do about financial aid for postsecondary education?

An important ingredient of the decision-making process is helping student clients acquire and process relevant information that will inform them about the advantages and disadvantages of their options. School counselors are challenged to be aware of the various sources of information that may be available and to find ways to help student clients find that information. It is impossible to know everything that may be important for a variety of clients. Yet, it is possible to acquire and commit to memory information about certain options that are of common interest to many student clients (e.g., admission requirements to local and state postsecondary training institutions), and to be aware of a number of resources that are available in printed materials or on the Web.

Helping students identify useful information and acquire it is an initial step that is enhanced by helping them to process it. That is, once the information is acquired, student clients may also need help making sense of it and putting it to use in the decision-making process. In this phase, counselors use their listening and responding skills to help clients make sense of the information and put it to good use. In some cases during the decision-making process, professional school counselors may be challenged by student clients who are approaching the process irrationally.

Helping Students to Think Rationally

Although humans have the capacity to engage in thinking processes, that capacity is not always used rationally. Some irrational thoughts common among school-age individuals are "People don't like me because my nose is big," "Men who choose careers in nursing are sissies," "The principal is mean because she doesn't smile at me," and "I've got to do what the others are doing or else they won't like me." It is safe to conclude that much irrational thinking occurs during childhood and adolescence and that it often leads to maladaptive responses. Many student clients whom school counselors encounter need help in identifying and coping with their irrational thoughts, and school counselors can use proven strategies to help them.

Rational emotive therapy (RET; Ellis & Dryden, 1997; Ellis, Gordon, Neeman, & Palmer, 1997) provides a system for seeking out irrational beliefs in what clients present and for pointing out the unfortunate consequences of those beliefs. For instance, the counselor working with the African American client discussed previously who believed that the accusation of racism was emotionally rather than factually based might borrow from RET as follows to introduce to the student client the counselor's view of how the situation occurred and to induce mutual discussion.

> Counselor:　So, when I mentioned challenges I thought you would face as a college student, you thought my motives were racist, and that led to your being angry, losing confidence in me, and telling me off.

Basic verbal counseling and challenging responses can be used to help the student become aware of irrational thinking. Counselor–client interactions can be quite challenging, and clients may either recognize their irrational cognitions or leave counseling.

Ellis and others offer systems for teaching clients to think more rationally. *Cognitive self-instruction* is a system for identifying self-defeating thoughts and teaching clients to replace them with coping thoughts (Meichenbaum, 1993, 1994). *Reframing* helps clients learn more rational ways of perceiving situations (Gendlin, 1996). These and other strategies for teaching clients to think more rationally follow the establishment of clients' goals as the acquisition of more rational coping responses. The common ingredients of these strategies are (a) explaining the procedure to the client (information sharing), (b) demonstrating the strategy (serving as a model), (c) helping the client rehearse the new behavior and cognitions (practicing), and (d) encouraging the client to use the skills in the real world (by using basic counseling and challenging skills when encouraging them).

The most challenging aspect of irrational ideation counseling occurs at the beginning: Counselors try to identify the irrational components of the student client's cognitions and the behavioral consequences. Then they may find themselves disputing the student's irrational thinking patterns, which is sometimes very difficult to do. It follows that counselors who are rational thinkers themselves are more likely to help clients think more rationally.

Helping Students to Acquire Coping Skills

Competence Enhancement Counseling. It is not uncommon for school-age clients to set goals successfully and then feel stymied because they do not feel competent to achieve their goals. When these feelings of incompetence are products of inexperience, lack of information, or mild performance anxiety, counselors can help clients enhance or learn the requisite skills. As a result, student clients will be better prepared to cope with the targeted situations and others like them, and they may feel better about themselves for having coped and acquired new or enhanced skills.

Participant modeling, also called *behavioral rehearsal,* is a competence-enhancing counseling strategy for the school counselor's basic action strategies repertoire (Bandura, 1986). The ingredients are modeling, rehearsal with feedback, and transfer of training. The strategy is explained to the client (information sharing), the targeted behavior is demonstrated by a model (observational learning), the client engages in repeated practice sessions—as many as needed—with possible repetitions of the modeling if necessary (basic counseling and challenging skills), and an effort is made to transfer the acquired or enhanced skills to the real world when the client is ready. Among the sample cases that have been presented in this chapter, the elementary school student who is experiencing difficulty in making friends might be helped through friendship training provided by the counselor's employing participant modeling as just described.

Another case that lends itself to behavioral rehearsal is the high school student who, after receiving supportive and decision-making counseling assistance from a counselor following the death of a classmate in a car accident, decides to tell someone about having witnessed alcohol abuse by the driver of the car but is concerned about not being clear and convincing in the presentation. The counselor offers to help the student client feel more confident by employing the participant modeling strategy. After exploring the student client's concerns about telling someone, the counselor helps the client decide who it will be. Counselor and client then determine together how that person might act and how the client should act. Next, counselor and student engage in a series of practice sessions in which the two exchange playing the roles of the student and the person to whom the student is relating the information. When the counselor plays the student's role, modeling occurs; when the client plays the student's role, the counselor provides encouragement and helpful feedback after each rehearsal. Successive approximations are employed until the student client is either ready to carry out the decision or decides to delay action, to not act, or to rethink the alternatives.

Competence enhancement counseling is similar to teaching when counselors engage in participant modeling or behavior rehearsals with student clients. Therefore, counselors are better prepared to be effective if they are familiar with such strategies as induction aids, reinforcing statements, coaching, and arranging the subskills of the targeted behavior into a hierarchy (Cormier & Nurius, 2003).

Assertiveness Counseling. Children and adolescents who are unable to respond to others with appropriate levels of assertiveness are at risk of undesirable consequences that range from feeling unfulfilled (e.g., unable to approach others socially) to being endangered (e.g., unable to resist peer pressure to engage in life-threatening behaviors such as substance abuse or unprotected sexual intercourse). Realizing that there is a fine line between assertiveness and aggressiveness, counselors can help students who are not assertive enough by enabling them to receive compliments, make normal requests of others, express affective feelings such as fondness and displeasure, initiate and maintain conversations, express their legitimate rights, and refuse illegitimate requests—recognize their deficits, establish appropriate goals, and be appropriately assertive (Galassi & Galassi, 1977; Lange & Jakubowski, 1976).

When students engage in maladaptive, nonassertive behaviors, counselors may help them replace those behaviors with adaptive responses. When students have deficits, new behaviors can be taught. As with other instructional counseling intervention strategies, the first step is to explain the purposes and procedures for the training. Second, the counselor teaches student clients how to appraise situations and decide how to behave (information-sharing skills). Third, demonstration and practice with feedback are used to teach the actual assertion skills (observational learning and reinforcement menus). Finally, the skills are implemented in the real world. One of the easiest ways to encourage appropriate assertiveness is to reinforce such behaviors when student clients exhibit them.

In the example of the student client being helped to tell someone about the alcohol abuse of the driver in the car accident through participant modeling, one might conclude that the student client was lacking in assertiveness and may have been helped to be more assertive through competence enhancement counseling. Therefore, it seems appropriate to conclude that although not all participant modeling involves enhancing assertiveness, it is a useful strategy for helping individuals learn to be more assertive.

Self-Management by Student Clients

Counselors have direct influence over their student clients only during periods of direct contact in counseling interviews or group sessions. Interviews and sessions seldom occur more than once per week and often less than that. It is fortunate if counselors spend as much as 45 minutes per week with student clients individually or in groups. Consequently, student clients are on their own most of the time. The influence of counselors may increase when they arrange with third parties to assist in intervention programs. In those cases, however, their influence is indirect.

Because student clients involved in various counseling programs are on their own most of the time, it behooves counselors to introduce a system of self-management to help clients be successful with their interventions. In essence, student clients assume control of their own intervention programs. Counselors remain important partners in the arrangement, however, because they introduce the self-management system and because they receive dependable information about client progress. Therefore, counselors assume indirect control over the intervention program, with the self-management system serving as the third party. More work by the client may occur between counseling sessions than during them. This is good because much more time is devoted to the intervention program than if client action is restricted to the counseling sessions.

Self-management programs require workable systems that are taught to clients. Appropriate homework assignments provide clear explanations (information sharing), teach clients how to carry them out (pedagogical skills), and assess client success with self-management activities (e.g., self-evaluation, standard setting, self-reinforcement, self-monitoring, stimulus control; Cormier & Nurius, 2003). An interesting secondary effect of self-management activities is that clients often experience more success than they might have otherwise simply because they pay more attention to the targeted behaviors.

In an example of self-management programming (self-monitoring) for a middle school student, a counselor and the student have agreed that academic performance in school may improve if the student becomes involved in a self-managed schoolwork program. To initiate the program, the counselor explains to the student how it works:

Counselor: I think the best way to do this is for you to set aside 2 hours for homework each evening and to write down on the chart I am giving you what you need to accomplish (goals), what you accomplish (outcomes), and how you feel about it (opinions) without spending too much time doing the record keeping. The chart is like a weekly and monthly calendar, and you can see how things are progressing. What do you think?

Student: Sounds good to me.

Counselor: OK! Now let's decide when you will start, and set up a series of meetings between the two of us to analyze how you are doing and determine what to do next.

Helping Students Who Do Not Express Themselves Well Verbally

Verbal interactions between counselors and their clients are not the only way to achieve counseling goals; in fact, nonverbal strategies may be better in some cases. Although the following strategies all include some verbal material and interactions, they are classified here as nonverbal because of the special importance of nonverbal material and activities.

Play therapy offers counselors an avenue into the world of young children that is less successfully traveled through verbalizations. Counselors are able to use play therapy to learn what children are thinking. Here, counselors can communicate with children indirectly by using basic counseling skills to inquire about the play activities. Understanding the play therapy process and having at one's disposal the necessary space or, at least, equipment is imperative (e.g., toys, games, materials; Keat, 1990b). Barlow, Strother, and Landreth (1985) recommended that teachers and principals be aware of the goals and benefits of play therapy to make them more understanding partners in the helping process.

O'Connor (1991) believed that play therapy can be adapted for children at all levels of functioning. Children at higher levels will find the treatment more cognitive than experiential. Therefore, it is important to have a sense of a child's level of cognitive development before initiating play therapy activities. When done well, play therapy provides an opportunity for children to have a new understanding with corresponding response options. Further information is available in the following sources: O'Connor and Schaefer (1994) provided a menu of theoretical approaches to play therapy (e.g.,

Adlerian, time-limited, cognitive-behavioral); ideas for adapting play therapy to adolescent clients; and descriptions of several play therapy techniques. Schaefer and Cangelosi (1993) offered recommendations for a wide variety of play therapy techniques (e.g., using puppets, sand play, water play, using food, finger painting, checkers or chess, and Nintendo games). Ideas for using play therapy in concert with specific presenting problems are suggested by Landreth, Homeyer, Glover, and Sweeney (1996; e.g., abuse and neglect, aggression and acting out, attachment difficulties, grief, reading difficulties, social adjustment). For more on play therapy, see Landreth (2002) and the Web site for the Center for Play Therapy at the University of North Texas (http://www.coe.unt.edu/cpt/).

Kahn (1999) believed that art therapy is an effective medium for counseling adolescents in several important ways by helping them with developmental tasks such as individuation and separation from their families. This is accomplished by aiding them to achieve control over their expressions, stimulate their creativity, have pleasurable experiences, and employ media options that reflect personal and age group symbols and metaphors. She also believed that school counselors can establish art stations in their offices, using a variety of materials, each selected for specific reasons (e.g., felt-tip markers can be used quickly and are relatively easy to control). Stressing that counselors do not need to be artistically talented themselves, Kahn pointed out that the process should be planned, normalized, and explained to parents, teachers, and administrators. She also stressed the importance of informing students that they are engaged in a communication process rather than a talent show and of maintaining the confidentiality of the artwork done by students—it is not for exhibition. Kahn closed with the presentation of a stagewise art therapy case with a high school junior who returned to school following alcohol abuse rehabilitation. In the last seven sessions, the client was able to summarize insights acquired about the role of alcohol in his schooling and interpersonal relationships coupled with a record free of alcohol-related or disciplinary actions.

Other physical activities in which clients can engage therapeutically are drawing and writing. Whereas drawing is useful for children and adolescents, writing is probably more useful with adolescents and possibly older children. These activities provide alternative avenues for student clients to express themselves and may also be therapeutic action stage strategies. The process will be enhanced by counselors who can explain the strategies, help clients carry them out, and help them find meaning in their drawings and writings.

Film, video, audio, and printed media are also nonverbal resources that counselors can employ as action strategies for children and adolescents. Again, counselors are challenged to be able to explain the purposes and procedures involved in these strategies, help their student clients carry them out, and help them find meaning in the messages. Knowing where to find media sources that are appropriate for specific client needs (e.g., grief, substance abuse, divorce) is a challenge. It behooves counselors to use media sources to enhance their intervention repertoires, and they may learn about media resources through catalogs, advertisements, annotated bibliographies, and journals. The April 1987 issue of *Elementary School Guidance and Counseling* has several articles on counseling with expressive arts ("Special Issue on Counseling With Expressive Arts," 1987). Included are articles on using play therapy, computer art, writing, drama, music, puppets, sand play, and poetry. See also Cochran (1996) and Fall (1994, 1997).

Helping Students Via a Brief Counseling Process

Models for brief counseling have appeared in the school counseling literature recently (Bruce, 1995; Littrell, 1998; Murphy, 1997). Bruce (1995) described a brief counseling approach that is time limited by design, rather than by default. Essential components of this approach are (a) a strong working alliance between counselors and students, (b) affirmation and use of student strengths and resources, (c) high levels of counselor and student client affective and behavioral involvement, and (d) establishment of clear, concrete goals. Synonyms for brief counseling include *solution-focused counseling, brief solution-focused counseling, and brief solution-oriented interviewing and counseling.* Murphy (1994, 1997), referring to the approach as solution-focused counseling, believed that counselors should focus on increasing their student clients' existing success, rather than on trying to eliminate problems. In this approach, counselors help students identify exceptions and encourage them to engage in the exceptions more often. An example follows:

> A middle school counselor is seeing a female student whose presenting problem is stated vaguely as wanting to be more successful academically. The counselor quickly helps the client assess the problem in concrete terms. In this hypothetical case, the student and the counselor agree that academic success involves her doing her homework more consistently and correctly and then getting higher grades. Next, the counselor helps the student client identify solutions to the problem that the client attempted previously, looking for exceptions (specific circumstances in which the presenting problem does not occur or occurs with less intensity; Murphy, 1994). The student client indicates that when she takes her schoolwork home and completes it in a quiet environment and in a timely manner, she seems to be more successful. The counselor then helps the client determine short-term goals that are concrete, achievable, and measurable, establishing a deadline for achieving the goals. With the counselor's assistance, the hypothetical student client decides that she wants to get her homework done successfully for the next month with the hope of improving her grades. They agree that the student will set aside a specific amount of time each evening to complete her homework in a quiet place at home.

The student now has control of her own solution, and measurable, achievable goals have been established. This plan could conceivably have been accomplished in one counseling session. Follow-up sessions are in order to determine how well the student is doing and whether the goals need to be revisited. Murphy (1997) referred to these as "booster sessions." Counselors use their social influence to help students own and maintain their accomplishments. Another feature of the approach is the possibility that the effects of the intervention strategy will generalize to other aspects of the student client's life. Bruce and Hopper (1997), LaFountain, Garner, and Eliason (1996), and Murphy (1997) reported research that provides some empirical support for the claims of proponents of this approach, indicating that it has promise for school counseling in both individual and group counseling relationships.

One criticism of the brief counseling approach is that building a counselor–client relationship or working alliance based on empathy may be overlooked in an attempt to move quickly to goal setting. Aware of this concern, Ivey and Ivey (2007) demonstrated that all five stages in their helping model can be incorporated into the brief counseling process. It there are instances in which school counselors fail to establish rapport with clients successfully yet are able to provide concrete assistance, one might argue that providing concrete assistance is a form of empathy as Menacker (1976) proposed in his theory of activist guidance.

Helping Students Via Small-Group Counseling

Sometimes a group mode is the most effective vehicle for achieving intervention goals. Group counseling has advantages over individual counseling. Krieg (1988) pointed out that group members may keep fellow members honest, preventing them from manipulating counselors as easily as they might during individual sessions. Dinkmeyer (1969) suggested that group relationships are more realistic than individual relationships between adult counselors and children or adolescents. When counselors can observe social interactions in a group setting, peers may serve as role models and provide feedback, student clients have opportunities to help their peers, and student clients may become aware that they are not alone in their circumstances.

Group counseling differs from group guidance (i.e., prevention programming), group therapy, and sensitivity training. The distinctions are important considerations for school counselors. Two basic differences between group guidance and group counseling are the roles of the leaders and the goals of the groups. Group guidance goals are determined by the leaders and are usually instructive and preventive in nature. The role of the leader is pedagogical, instructing, informing, directing, and leading. Group counseling goals are determined by the needs of the members, and the role of the leader is therapeutic, using counseling skills to help members of the group achieve individual and common goals. Group counseling is appropriate for the schools and is within the scope of the school counselor's training. The members are usually volunteers who are functioning normally and are possibly at risk. Topics are personal, often related to normal developmental concerns, and are shared by the members. Desired outcomes include greater self-understanding, self-acceptance, and resolution of targeted concerns.

The basic individual counseling and challenging skills are important ingredients of group counseling. Counselors also use skills more specific to group counseling, such as forming groups, teaching members about group processes, understanding the finer points of the small-group process contrasted with individual counseling, and mediating between and among members. Group counseling is not without challenges. Scheduling time for counseling groups in the schools is more difficult than scheduling individual counseling sessions. The difficulty of bringing groups of students together for counseling is compounded by the need to find student volunteers who share the same goals and can be scheduled together. When working in groups, many counselors find that maintaining a leadership role is more difficult than working with individuals. Maintaining confidentiality is more challenging in small counseling groups because several individuals might breach it, rather than only two.

Group counseling appears to be more cost effective than individual counseling, and sometimes that may be true. More important, group counseling may be the most successful strategy for school counselors to use in helping some student clients.

Therefore, it appears to be an important part of the school counselor's repertoire. An example of a group counseling intervention for elementary school children points out that successful group counseling has many features that are often not recognized by casual observers (Corey & Corey, 1997):

> Students ranging in age from 6 to 11 years were referred to group counseling by a principal, their teachers, and the school nurse. The students were experiencing a host of problems that, in turn, influenced their academic performance. The counselor's goal was to alleviate school problems and prevent arrested development by helping the students cope with underlying problems. She hoped to identify maladaptive behaviors, teach the students to express their emotions constructively, and provide an atmosphere where they could express their emotions freely while understanding that problems are caused by the way they act on feelings, rather than by the feelings themselves. Important ingredients of the counseling process were as follows:
>
> - The counselor worked with the students individually and in small groups.
> - The students received tutoring from empathic tutors concurrently with the counseling.
> - The students and their parents agreed to participate only after informed consent sessions.
> - The counselor had continuous meetings with parents, teachers, the school nurse, school psychologists, and the principal throughout the helping process.
> - The counselor engaged in social action activities as needed to help the students and their families receive clothing, food, money, and special services.
>
> Several groups were formed. Those deemed most successful consisted of three to five students of the same age and gender. In forming the groups, which were open to new members at any time, the counselor attempted to combine withdrawn and outgoing students and to keep together students experiencing similar problems. The typical group met twice per week for 30 to 60 minutes. Students could leave a session before it ended, although they were encouraged to stay. A termination date was set in advance, and the students were prepared for termination as it approached.
>
> Activities designed to help the students express their emotions safely included role-playing, play therapy, acting out special situations, painting, finishing stories started by the leader, puppet shows, playing music, and dancing. Most students manifested observable behavior changes. The leader commented that although the group provided an excellent setting for the students to learn and practice relational skills, the individual counseling provided opportunities to pay attention to each student and to develop a trusting relationship.

Hoag and Burlingame (1997) reported encouraging findings from a metaanalytic review of group counseling studies that had been published between 1974 and 1997. Fifty-six studies were included in the review. Most studies (approximately 74%) occurred in schools, 20% involved school counselors as leaders, and 25% involved mixtures of school counselors and other school professionals (e.g., school psychologists, school social workers). The overall effects were labeled as *moderate*; however, there was a wide range of effectiveness across the 56 studies. Disruptive behavior, anxiety, adjustment to divorce, cognitive performance, social skills, and self-esteem were among the outcomes that appeared to be targeted successfully in the counseling groups. Two demographic variables were influenced differently. In the socioeconomic status category, middle-class students received more from group counseling than working-class students generally. Regarding settings, group counseling conducted in clinics was more successful than in schools.

Helping Students Experiencing Crises

Although not labeled as such, school counseling offices are often viewed as drop-in counseling centers. Some students never drop in and have to be invited. Others make appointments. Some drop in to see whether a counselor is available. Emergencies or crises occur in the schools, as well as in the greater society. Some emergencies are handled in the main office, by nurses, or by other staff members. Students in crisis also find their way to the counseling office, and it behooves counselors to have crisis counseling skills in their intervention repertoire. For example, students grieving over the suicide of a classmate may be overwhelmed. Others who have just had a traumatic experience (e.g., a physical beating, taunts and insults from peers, a broken relationship, a rejection letter from a prospective college or employer, receipt of disappointingly low scores on a college entrance exam) may panic. In these cases and others like them, counselors do not have the advantage of making appointments or opening the interviews in a relatively calm working atmosphere.

Crisis counseling is an immediate, time-limited treatment process. Clients are clearly unable to employ the usual coping mechanisms, and counselors do not have time to move patiently through the usual counseling steps. Because clients in crisis are extremely amenable to being assisted, counselors who act quickly and appropriately can be helpful. Even in crisis situations, counselors can follow potential helping stages (Caplan, 1961). First, the counselor can assess how effectively the student is functioning and whether an immediate referral is necessary (e.g., determine whether the student needs psychiatry services). Second, if an immediate referral is not needed, the counselor can help the student cope with powerful affect, accept that affect, and find out the causes of the affect (use basic counseling skills). Third, some sort of immediate resolution or plan to resolve the problem is negotiated with the student (use basic counseling and challenging skills). Next, after determining whether it is appropriate for the student to be allowed to leave (e.g., determine whether the student is expressing suicide ideation) or whether the student wants to end the interview, the counselor will determine whether termination, referral, or an appointment is warranted.

What has been suggested about crisis counseling thus far is clearly within the basic intervention repertoire of school counselors. Interestingly, school counselors cannot choose whether to include crisis counseling in their intervention repertoires. Crises will seek them out, and they will be expected to respond successfully. Therefore, it is important for their students' welfare and their own reputations that school counselors be prepared to respond to crises. A strategy that counselors may employ to be prepared for crises is to conduct controlled simulations of possible crisis interventions, following them with analyses of their performances to rectify problems encountered during the simulations.

Roberts (1995) provided an example of how a small, rural school system that was prepared in advance responded to a crisis. A 14-year-old student with a long, troubled history took his life 3 weeks after classes had dismissed for summer vacation. Although the school had a crisis prevention-intervention team, it was not prepared to respond during the summer. Under the circumstances, the school counselor collected accurate information about the event, contacted team members who could be located to ensure they knew the facts and could dispel rumors, and received commitments from some of them to volunteer to hold conferences with students they had contact with in the community. Most of the immediate postvention responsibilities were handled by the counselor, the principal, and the school secretary.

The school served as the center for communications about the facts of the suicide, information about the funeral; and so on. Care was taken to protect the family's privacy and to prevent speculation and rumors. Telephone calls were answered and messages returned. The counselor scheduled supportive interviews with students and others in need (e.g., nurses in the hospital emergency room) on request. Members of the deceased student's peer group and their parents were contacted to provide support and to encourage the parents to provide support as well. Home visits were made to these students to provide immediate assistance, inform them about sources of help in the future, and assess their emotional stability. Local media outlets were requested to handle the matter tactfully. The school was kept open to assist students and adults from early morning until late at night for 5 days following the suicide.

Long-range postvention continued throughout the summer and into the next school year. For example, all faculty members were briefed at the first teachers' meeting, faculty members experiencing guilt were seen by the counselor, and the student's peer group members were monitored for 18 months.

Recognizing the importance of helping counselors respond to crises successfully, the ACA created "Responding to Tragedy" resources on its Web site in 2001. See www.counseling.org.

STAGE FIVE: TERMINATE AND HELP STUDENT CLIENTS GENERALIZE AND ACT ON THEIR ACTION PLANS

Individual and group counseling relationships are analogous to lives in that they have beginnings and endings. The endings may be good because the student clients are ready, they may be difficult because the clients are resistant, or they may be bad because they occur prematurely. Ward (1984) recommended that termination be viewed as one of several stages in the counseling process. Indirectly supporting the termination-as-a-stage concept, Krieg (1988) advocated devoting 10% of the life of a group to termination.

Cummings (1986) suggested that therapy and counseling can be thought of as analogous to medicine without adopting the medical treatment model. He thought that the ending of a counseling relationship is considered an interruption rather than a termination. Physicians treat patients for problems (e.g., the flu), and when the treatments are completed, the physician–patient relationship is interrupted. The relationship may be reactivated to treat different or recurring problems (e.g., headaches). The relationship is therefore continuous, with intermittent contacts when needed. If responsive counseling interventions are viewed similarly, then termination will not be treated as a permanent event. School counselors are encouraged to view termination as an interruption in the counseling process.

The basic counseling and challenging skills are important as counselors engage in terminating or interrupting individual and group counseling relationships. These skills provide an appropriate climate for carrying out the activities required to accomplish the following goals:

- Evaluating student client readiness
- Resolving affective issues between students and counselors or among group members
- Maximizing transfer of training to the real world
- Enhancing student client self-reliance and confidence
- Coping with and responding to premature terminations
- Enhancing the prospects of student clients being able to cope successfully after the terminations
- Making successful referrals when needed
- Ensuring that student clients are aware of their counselors' availability after the terminations (Corey et al., 1992; Ward, 1984)

Achieving these goals is challenging because the issues are varied and because student clients respond differently to the circumstances associated with termination/ interruption. School counselors can achieve the goals eclectically, using what works from their repertoire of skills.

Although counseling interventions are conceivably available to all students, and counselors are employed to serve all student clients to the best of their ability, as Yalom (1975) pointed out, the matching of interventions, counselors, and student clients is less than perfect. Freedom to terminate or interrupt is an important option because it is a source of protection for the student client. Although counseling interventions in the schools are imperfect, counselors can increase the probability of positive interventions by having a desire to serve and help their student clients and by being knowledgeable about and skillful at counseling. School counselors have the freedom to choose whether to do everything in their power to provide effective counseling interventions.

EVALUATING INDIVIDUAL AND GROUP COUNSELING

The Challenge of Providing Evidence of Counseling Intervention Competence

In chapter 8, we pointed out the challenges associated with evaluating prevention programs and offered a proposal for professional school counselors. Individual and small-group counseling present challenges of both a similar and a different nature. We discuss those challenges briefly, and then offer a proposal for evaluating individual and small-group counseling.

Evaluating the impact of small-group counseling poses the same challenges related to evaluating prevention groups that we presented in chapter 8 (i.e., alternate explanations, control groups). In addition, members of small counseling groups may be attempting to resolve somewhat dissimilar issues, and their goals will differ.

To evaluate one's individual counseling efforts requires a strategy that treats each case independently of the others, and this approach at first glance probably seems overwhelmingly difficult to manage and report. In addition, the process and content of individual and small counseling sessions is subject to ethical confidentiality standards. So, how do school counselors evaluate counseling interventions and demystify for stakeholders what goes on behind the closed doors of the counseling suites?

A Proposal for Meeting the Challenge

A Case-by-Case Approach.   We propose that each student client or member of a small counseling group be considered an independent counseling intervention and evaluated accordingly. Our proposal is based on the following assumptions. Each student client has a specific goal, or specific goals, that will be targeted mutually by the counselor and client prior to determining how to achieve the goals. Progress toward achieving the goals can be measured over time. This second assumption is more elusive in some cases than in others because not all counseling goals are equally measurable. Therefore, not all counseling interventions will lend themselves to this approach. Yet, enough interventions may qualify to allow professional counselors using this approach to provide sufficient evaluation data about their individual counseling interventions in order to be accountable to stakeholders in this domain. Continuing with our assumptions, confidentiality can be maintained by assigning pseudonyms or numbers to each intervention case when reporting the findings.

Our proposal is based on a research approach referred to as single-case experimental designs (Heppner, Kivlighan, & Wampold, 1999). The common characteristics of single-case designs are (a) mutually specify the counseling intervention goals so counselor and student clients are in agreement and working together to achieve them, (b) identify objectively scored behaviors or measures of goal attainment that student clients can use successfully and which provide meaningful data for record keeping, (c) collect assessments of the behavior and goal attainment measure over time segments that are appropriate for the targeted goals (e.g., hours, days, weeks, months), and (d) establish baseline data on the behavior and goal attainment measures before attempting to institute a plan or program to achieve the goals. We offer an example to help readers understand the process.

A Case Example.   Liu and Baker (1993) reported the progress of efforts to help a 4-year-old Chinese girl who was experiencing culture shock when attending a day care center at a large American university. The child's progress in response to a counselor's friendship training program was charted graphically. Figure 9.1 depicts the child's progress at achieving the targeted outcome behaviors—increased verbal contacts with peers—graphically. The evaluation design, known as ABA, is one of several single-case designs that can be used to plot the progress of individual student clients (Barlow & Herson, 1984). In this case, A represents the time when no intervention occurs, and B represents the time when the intervention is in progress. Thus, the first A phase allows a counselor to collect baseline data, the B phase provides information about a student client's progress during the intervention, and the second A phase offers data depicting the client's progress after the intervention is completed. In this case, client progress is

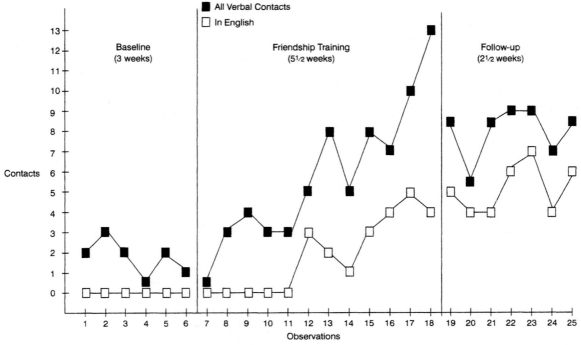

Figure 9.1
Number of self-initiated verbal contacts.

Source: From "Enhancing Cultural Adaptation Through Friendship Training," by Y. C. Liu and S. B. Baker, 1993, *Elementary School Guidance and Counseling, 28,* p. 97. Copyright 1993 by American Counseling Association.

visible and relatively easy to determine. The process itself is also relatively easy. A key factor in using this approach is being able to identify outcomes that lend themselves to observing and counting behaviors. When working with cases of this nature, the single-case design is useful for school counselors. From an accountability perspective, counselors can present graphic representations from several cases, with student clients' identity protected, as evidence of effectiveness (i.e., accountability). This offers promise for counselors who feel nagged by criticisms that no one knows what is being done that is worthwhile behind the closed doors to their counseling sessions.

Collect Case Data in a Portfolio. We suggest that school counselors use the AB single-case design to evaluate their counseling interventions. This requires data collection during a baseline phase and during the intervention. That would be the first A and the B components in the Figure 9.1 presentation. We further suggest that professional school counselors use this approach as often as they can. From an accountability perspective, a set of graphic representations such as is depicted in Figure 9.1 can be collected and presented in a portfolio format as part of an accountability dossier. In addition to being a useful accountability strategy, this evaluation approach has promise

Table 9.2
Examples of behaviors and attitudes that can be assessed in single-case designs.

Assess Changes in Academic Performance Behaviors Over Time (Counselors and Student Clients Keep Records of Changes in the Following Behaviors)
   Grades or grade-point averages
   Rate of homework completion
   Increased time devoted to homework/studies
   Decrease in wasted time
   Increased attendance
Assess Ratings of Targeted Attitudes/Perceptions Over Time (Counselors and Student Clients Keep Records of Changes in Ratings on a Scale of 1 [low] to 10 [high])
   How do you feel about your relationships with other students today?
   How do you rate your friendships today?
   How do you rate the decision you made today?
   How do your rate your relationship with _____ today?
   How do you rate the relationship with your math teacher today?

---

for helping clients better manage their progress toward goal attainment and offers counselors data for working with specific student clients more efficiently and effectively. Table 9.2 suggests how behaviors and goals that do not lend themselves to clearly defined behaviors can be assessed. The behaviors provided are one set that can be used if appropriate. Other behaviors will be peculiar to individual cases. However, the process remains constant; that is, the mutual goals set by counselors and student clients focus on trying to either increase or decrease the targeted behaviors.

Targeted counseling intervention goals that do not lend themselves to identifying behaviors that can be reduced or increased over time can be assessed by easily employed goal attainment scales. When employing goal attainment scales, student clients rate their perceptions/attitudes on a scale with low and high dimensions (e.g., "On a scale of 1 [low] to 10 [high], how do you rate yourself on what we accomplished today [how you feel today, how close we are to making an achievable decision, etc.])?

Importance of Self-Monitoring by Student Clients.   Students involved in individual and small-group counseling spend significantly more time away from sessions with counselors than they do in the sessions. Therefore, establishing systems for helping student clients monitor their progress toward achieving targeted counseling goals when away from their schools and their school counselors is an important component in their successfully achieving targeted counseling goals. Cormier and Nurius (2003) point out that the mere act of paying attention to one's counseling goals through self-monitoring activities encourages the clients toward achieving their goals. We recommend that counselors bring this idea to the attention of their student clients and help them set up systems for conducting the self-monitoring process. Unfortunately, if counselors merely suggest that their student clients engage in this activity without helping them set it up, the probability that no self-monitoring will occur are considerable. To help readers understand how self-monitoring forms can be constructed, we have included an example in Figure 9.2. The self-monitoring form is for the middle school student who wants to enhance his/her academic performance. This student was introduced in the section "Self-Management of Student Clients."

Weekly Homework Record   Name_____

Date	Start Time	End Time	Goals	Outcomes	Feelings

Figure 9.2
Sample self-monitoring form.

Source: From S. B. Baker & E. R. Gerler, Jr., with permission.

School counselors are capable of helping numerous students who are experiencing personal developmental challenges through individual and group counseling interventions. Preparation for engaging in responsive counseling interventions successfully is a component of counselor education training programs. We have also pointed out that the individual and small-group counseling process is amenable to evaluation strategies that can lead to achieving accountability in this domain. Unfortunately, some students are unable to be successful in school because they manifest problems that are beyond the training and scope of what school counselors can respond to effectively. Chapter 10 is devoted to presenting ideas for helping these students.

FEATURED ACTIVITY: GRADUATE STUDENT PERSPECTIVES ON INDIVIDUAL AND GROUP COUNSELING IN SCHOOLS

In this chapter, we discuss individual and group counseling in schools. Counselor education graduate students often have differing abilities and interests related to counseling interventions. Recently, we heard a student comment that she became a counselor education student primarily because of her interest in working individually with students. She was surprised to learn in her first school counseling course that some school counselors spend more time doing group interventions than individual interventions. She wondered what her future as a school counselor would be like. Would she be able to fulfill her desire to work individually with students, or would she be spending more time in group work? Also, how much control would she have in making decisions about the interventions (individual or group) to use as a school counselor?

What do you think about counseling interventions in schools? How do counselors choose which interventions to employ?

After you read this chapter, go to http://www.genesislight.com/scan21st/tell_us/intervention.html and complete the form. With your permission, we will periodically post some of your creative thinking for the world to read.

OTHER SUGGESTED ACTIVITIES

1. Analyze a counseling model in terms of the following:
   a. Basic steps
   b. Basic competencies
   c. Multicultural potential
2. Make an inventory of responsive counseling intervention competencies that are new to you and learn more about them.
3. From the responsive counseling intervention competencies suggested in this chapter, select those that you think are debatable and debate their merits.
4. Analyze, discuss, and/or debate the intent of the following statement: "School counselors have neither the credentials nor the training required to provide therapy, but they can offer therapeutic counseling."
5. Discuss or debate the merits of eclecticism and multicultural competence in school counseling.

6. Among the various competencies cited in the chapter, identify those that are important or mostly important for counselors working in the elementary, middle, and secondary schools; identify those that are universal across all three levels. Which list is the largest? Why do you think it is the largest?

7. Compare the suggested basic competencies in this chapter with those taught in the curriculum in your own training program. Analyze your findings.

8. Evaluate the concept that the freedom to terminate counseling is an important protection for clients.

9. Watch a film or a televised talk show and analyze the differences among conversing, interviewing, and counseling.

10. Discuss the merits of brief, solution-focused counseling.

11. Debate the merits of the recommendations for evaluating individual and small-group counseling presented in this chapter.

12. Go to the SCAN Web site (www.scan21st.com). Submit a recommendation for how the Internet might be used to enhance school counseling interventions.

CHAPTER 10

Referral and Coordination in School Counseling

Goals: To explain the unique circumstances of the referral and coordination functions in school counseling. To propose competencies for counselor-initiated referrals and a system for managing referrals to school counselors. To highlight the place of coordination in the referral process.

Manuela, a 7-year-old, lived in New Jersey with her mother and her grandfather. She was increasingly absent from school. When teachers questioned her about her absence, Manuela responded simply that her grandfather was very sick. Manuela said she had to care for him when her mother was not at home. She would then lower her eyes and walk away quickly. One teacher, suspicious that something was wrong, asked the school counselor to speak with Manuela. Noticing that Manuela had tears in her eyes when she spoke about her home situation, the counselor immediately contacted social services to explore outside help for Manuela. Social services discovered that Manuela's grandfather had recently died and that her mother had moved to Baltimore for a job, promising to return for Manuela as soon as she found a suitable place to live in Baltimore. In short, 7-year-old Manuela was living by herself in New Jersey. Social services placed Manuela in foster care, and the school counselor worked with various professionals to find additional help and support for Manuela. The process to help Manuela required much coordination and diligence to avoid having Manuela's case lost in a sea of bureaucracy.

School counselors are frequently called on to refer and coordinate difficult cases such as that of Manuela. This chapter examines the skills and processes involved in these efforts.

DEMAND FOR REFERRAL AND COORDINATION IN SCHOOL COUNSELING

In previous chapters, a case was made for balanced school counseling programs consisting of equally important responsive counseling intervention and proactive prevention emphases in a balanced, comprehensive school counseling programs. Counseling, prevention programming, and consulting were presented as important competencies in a balanced program. All professionals are limited in expertise and time; they refer clients to others whose services are more appropriate. In addition, school counselors receive referrals from other professionals who are also limited in expertise and time. Consequently, school counselors are challenged to have the skills to make referrals, manage the referrals they receive, coordinate the process once referrals have been made or accepted, and collaborate with important service providers beyond the school settings. Referring and coordinating are functions that fit within a broader school counselor role concept that appears to be increasingly important. Atkinson and Juntunen (1994) used the label *school–home–community liaison* for this role. As liaisons, school counselors work with students, parents, and members of the community to identify and use valuable human services inside and outside the school system that meet both remedial and enhancement goals for students, and they coordinate the acquisition and use of the services, acting at times like brokers.

Collaboration between the schools and their communities seems to be increasingly important. Students are faced with problems that require comprehensive services, many of which are beyond the capacities of the services the schools can provide. Hobbs and Collison (1995) found evidence that collaboration between the schools and local agencies (in their study, youth services teams in four communities in Oregon) is increasing. They believe that school counselors need to reassess their role in the context of the community rather than the school and to develop or enhance collaboration skills. Downing, Pierce, and Woodruff (1993) pictured this collaboration in the context of developing networks among the community's professional helpers inside and outside the schools, a challenging yet potentially fruitful undertaking.

One focus of this chapter is on two types of referrals. They are treated separately and referred to as either counselor-initiated referrals or referrals to counselors. Because counseling is a human services profession, it is important that counselors help student clients receive needed services. At times, the needed services are beyond the scope and setting of school counseling. In such cases, school counselors help clients through a referral process. Referrals are made to other professionals or sources of help; these are known as counselor-initiated referrals. Prospective referees are encouraged to use the school's counseling services voluntarily and, in so doing, to understand the goals and limitations of those services. At other times, school professionals (e.g., teachers, administrators) and individuals outside the schools who are interested in students' welfare (e.g., parents) look to counselors as a source of help for their students/children and make referrals to counselors. This process works best when the prospective referees clearly understand the counselors' range of competencies. All parties are served best when school counselors inform others about their services and efficiently manage the referrals they receive.

Spokespersons for the three school counseling paradigms introduced in chapter 2 cite the importance of appropriate referrals and helpful coordination of the referral process. In the ASCA's National Model for School Counseling Programs, referral is depicted as a responsive service through which school counselors seek help for students from professional resources in and out of the school when necessary (ASCA, 2003). The National Standards highlight the potential for making referrals that provide needed assistance to students and their families in the academic development, career development, and personal/social domains. The TSCI places importance on the role of school counselors as brokers of services for parents and students from community and school system resources. To accomplish this goal, school counselors are challenged to understand and appreciate the contributions that these significant others can make (House & Hayes, 2002). Referring and coordinating seem to be subsumed under a somewhat broader context referred to as collaboration in the School–Community Collaboration Model (Adelman & Taylor, 2002). The citations attributed to Hobbs and Collison (1995) and Downing et al. (1993) offered a hint of what this broader context means. These school–community collaboration writers pointed out the importance of collaborating cooperatively with community resources to make needed services available to students and their families in a systematic manner.

SCHOOL COUNSELOR-INITIATED REFERRALS

Point of View

In the *ACA Code of Ethics* (ACA, 2005) and in the ASCA *Ethical Standards for School Counselors* (ASCA, 2004), referrals are presented as a mandate to do what is in the client's best interests:

> If counselors determine an inability to be of professional assistance to clients, they avoid entering or immediately terminate a counseling relationship. Counselors are knowledgeable about referral resources and suggest appropriate alternatives. If clients decline the suggested referral, counselors should discontinue the relationship. (ACA, 2005, Section A.11, paragraph b)

> The professional school counselor: a. Makes referrals when necessary or appropriate to outside resources. Appropriate referral necessitates informing both parents/guardians and students of applicable resources and making proper plans for transitions with minimal interruption of services. Students maintain the right to discontinue counseling relationships at any time. (ASCA, 2004, A.5)

Two delicate issues that counselors face in the referral process are the related possibilities of referring student clients prematurely and of treating them too long. On the one hand, busy counselors may wrongly view referral as a way to divest themselves of part of their counseling burden. Then referral sources become repositories for excess workloads. The motives behind such referrals are primarily selfish. Premature referrals may also result from counselors' feelings of inadequacy, low risk-taking thresholds, or failure to appreciate their own ability. Although counselors' intentions may be honorable, the outcomes are still premature referrals.

On the other hand, counselors may continue working with student clients too long for selfish reasons, such as a need to feel responsible for curing their clients. This mistaken motivation serves the needs of the counselors, rather than those of the students. Counselors may also work with student clients too long for altruistic reasons, as when students convince them that no one else can help or refuse to be referred. Kimmerling (1993) referred to deciding when to refer a client as "when saying no is the right thing to do" (p. 5).

Shertzer and Stone (1981) offered suggestions for resolving these referral fallacies. First, counselors realize that referral is not merely a technique they use when operating a clearinghouse. Second, they understand that referrals are not limited to emergencies. Many emergencies can be averted by timely referrals. Third, referrals are not admissions of failure. Instead, they are intelligent decisions to provide the best possible assistance to student clients.

When approaching the referral decision, counselors are forced to look within themselves and beyond their work settings to ask several important questions. These questions draw on evaluations of their competencies, the competencies of their referral sources, and their own motives. Assessing one's competencies realistically can be difficult and painful. Although counselors are the main sources of information about their own competencies, respected colleagues can provide wise counsel.

Knowing the competencies of potential referral sources requires careful intelligence gathering. Sources of information are numerous, and using them requires considerable effort. Information can be acquired through cooperative research with colleagues. Categories of important information that counselors might acquire about referees are offered by Weinrach (1984), who suggests that referees can make the referral process more mutual by demystifying it. Important information that Weinrach recommends counselors and clients should know about referees includes their qualifications, expertise, and orientation; intake procedures, fee structures, and scheduling methods; whether the services are publicly or privately provided; follow-up procedures; and general attitudes toward clients.

Motives can be controlled if counselors hold their clients' welfare above their own needs. This is continuous because client cases change and counselors grow in experience and competence. In all, the decision process requires honest introspection and a willingness to spend time and energy gathering information.

Knowing the competencies of potential referral sources requires careful intelligence gathering.

A unique aspect of the referral function in school counseling is that most student clients are minors. Therefore, the referral process is complicated by the need for parental knowledge and cooperation. At times, all seems well until the students' parents or guardians become involved. Parents may be the source of students' attitudes that lead to ignoring or rejecting referral suggestions, and usually parents cannot be forced to respond as desired. On other occasions, students who are minors may themselves make the referral process extremely difficult. They may not, want their parents or guardians to know about the issues leading to referral suggestions, or they may ignore or reject referral suggestions. Children and adolescents are less likely than adults to understand the referral process and to be objective about it.

School counselors face the additional challenge of working with parents or guardians through their children, often without authority to require desired responses. Because of this two-tiered decision-making situation, school counselors are challenged to be more adept at making referrals than many other helping professionals. They also face the dilemma of deciding whether to continue counseling clients who fail to accept referral suggestions or to discontinue the relationships. Discontinuing counseling services under these circumstances is ethically acceptable. Yet, failing to respond to referral suggestions may be caused by parental attitudes, leaving students caught in the middle and counselors struggling to determine whether their own services are better than none.

Another challenge for school counselors is managed care. Many families may be insured by health maintenance organizations or preferred provider organizations, which place restrictions on one's freedom to choose service providers. Therefore, even though student clients and their parents are cooperative, their insurance may not cover the services being recommended or the services can only be provided by a restricted group of preferred or contracted providers. Counselors will then be challenged to become aware of a larger cohort of approved providers across various organizations serving their student clients' families.

Foundations

Counselor-initiated referring and coordinating beg for a systematic approach. A system helps counselors know in advance what to do and makes the process more efficient for everyone. The process is more likely to progress effectively, and student clients are more likely to be treated appropriately. The five-stage helping model adapted from Ivey and Ivey (2007) for counseling is also applicable to referring and coordinating. The five stages can be expressed as initiating, gathering data, mutually setting goals, working on a constructive action plan, and terminating. The following suggested competencies are woven into the fabric of these stages. They are culled from several sources in the professional literature (cf. Amatea & Fabrick, 1984; Baker, 1973; Bobele & Conran, 1988; Downing, 1985; Weinrach, 1984).

BASIC COMPETENCIES FOR SCHOOL COUNSELOR-INITIATED REFERRALS

Initiating and Gathering Data

Counselors are challenged to know themselves and their referral sources—to evaluate realistically their own competencies and those of other referral sources. Beyond that, counselors who have sufficient knowledge about their student clients make educated decisions about referral sources. The basic counseling competencies are again paramount because most referrals begin as counseling or consulting relationships. An example follows:

A high school teacher refers a student to a high school counselor after witnessing a noticeable change in the student's affect indicating that the student seemed depressed. The student responds to the counselor's invitation to have an interview. The counselor explains that the teacher is concerned about the student's welfare and has asked for help to be provided if needed. The student agrees that things are not good and agrees to talk with the counselor. Beginning the relationship as if it were a potential counseling intervention, the counselor asks the client to talk about the presenting problem and the feelings associated with it. Using the basic responsive counseling intervention skills, the counselor helps the client try to identify and clarify the problem and concludes that the student seems quite depressed and is also at a loss to offer specific reasons for the depressed affect.

Mutually Setting Goals

Bringing a counseling relationship to the point where goals are established helps counselors determine whether a referral is needed. Thus, the basic influencing skills are also part of the referral process. Because many student clients and their parents do not necessarily think they need specialized help outside the school system, counselors may have to use influencing skills to challenge them to consider and accept a referral suggestion (e.g., advanced accurate empathy, confrontation, information sharing, immediacy). An example follows:

> The case of the depressed high school student moves to the goal-setting stage when the counselor, after having met with the client for two sessions to identify and clarify the situation, concludes that the student client is deeply depressed, seemingly unable to identify causes, and apparently in need of help that is beyond the scope of the counselor's expertise. The counselor indicates to the student client that the best source of help may be a referral to a clinician in private practice (e.g., psychologist, psychiatrist).

Counselor:	We have talked extensively about how miserable you seem to feel, and you have indicated a desire to get some relief. I agree that you need and should get some relief, and I also think that the best way to get relief is to see a professional who is a specialist and who can devote the amount of time needed to help you in a setting that is more private than being seen here at school.
Student:	I don't know. That sounds expensive, and I don't know if my parents will agree to it. Besides, I don't want people to think I am crazy and have to see a "shrink."
Counselor:	So, you are concerned about the cost and what people will think, perhaps what you think about yourself as well [advanced accurate empathy]. Are you familiar with the services of Wellsprings?
Student;	No! What do they do?
Counselor:	They may be able to help you without it being too expensive and without you thinking of yourself as needing to see a "shrink." Do you want to know more?
Student:	Yes!

The counselor then proceeds to provide accurate information about Wellsprings [information sharing]. After sharing the information, the counselor asks, "Well, what do you think?"

Student:	I don't know, it sounds pretty involved to me. I don't think I will have enough time, and my parents will probably object to my going there.

Counselor: It sounds involved, and you worry about what your parents will say. However, you have indicated to me that things are really bad and you have to get some help, and I have pointed out that the kind of help you seem to need is not really available here in school, leading me to suggest Wellsprings. We can explore other alternatives, but before we do, I'm wondering if you need to think first about how badly you want help and whether you and your parents are willing to make the commitment needed to take that first step. I want to help you, but I also think you need to take a good look at what you have just been saying. What do you think? [confrontation]

In the foregoing interaction, the counselor employed three influencing responses: advanced accurate empathy, information sharing, and confrontation. All are presented caringly and tentatively in the hope that the student client will accept a referral suggestion to achieve expressed goals.

Working on a Constructive Action Plan and Terminating

Sometimes, counseling relationships move into the working stage before a referral suggestion is considered, or the act of referring becomes the constructive action stage of the helping relationship. In either case, where and how to refer become the basic referring objectives, and how to coordinate a successful referral becomes the third basic action strategy objective. Referring and coordinating competencies are devoted to responding to those questions.

Where to Refer Student Clients.   Deciding where to refer student clients requires knowing a variety of referral sources. Acquisition of such information demands investigative skills, using time and energy to locate and evaluate telephone books and the Internet, attending meetings of professional organizations, conferring with colleagues, interviewing potential service providers, and evaluating advertisements. School counselors may also have opportunities to acquire useful information from service organizations. Hollis and Hollis (1965) suggested that awareness includes identification of sources, a working knowledge of their services, knowledge of ways to use the services, and development of reciprocal services. Figure 10.1 lists various referral sources with which school counselors in any community might develop referral agreements.

Multiculturally aware counselors will develop resource lists of "educational and community support services to meet the socioeconomic and cultural needs of culturally diverse students and their families" (ASCA, 1989, p. 322). Recognizing the importance of cultural sensitivity in the referral process, Atkinson and Juntunen (1994) recommended that counselors be familiar with services offered in ethnically diverse communities. They also suggest that referrals can be traditional—that is, to remediate problems—and can be made to enhance the development of students from diverse backgrounds. In the latter instance, the coordinating function comes into play as counselors refer students to such programs as Big Brothers Big Sisters and

Local Volunteer Organizations

Churches—Clergy
Counseling Services
Emergency Financial Assistance
Health Councils
Hospitals
Information Services

Job Placement Services
Medical Societies
Nursing Services
Parents Without Partners
Planned Parenthood Association
Private Schools

Rape Crisis Centers
Referral Services
Runaway Hotlines
Sheltered Workshops
Thrift Shops

Government Agencies and Services

Bureau of Employment Security
Bureau of Special Health
    Services
Bureau of Vocational
    Rehabilitation
Child Welfare League of America
Child Welfare Services
Civil Service Commission
Community Action

County Board of Assistance
County Health Services
Department of Agriculture
Department of Consumer
    Services
Department of Human Services
Department of Public Welfare
Family Planning Centers
Foster Home Care

Home Health Services
Human Relations Commission
Mental Health/Mental
    Retardation
State Department of Health
State Hospitals
State Schools
Upward Bound
Youth Service Bureau

National Nonprofit Organizations

Alanon
Alateen
Alcoholics Anonymous
Altrusa International
American Association
    of University Women
American Bar Association
American Cancer Society
American Heart Association
American Red Cross
Catholic Social Services
Chamber of Commerce

Easter Seal Society
Economic Opportunity
    Commission
Goodwill
Junior Chamber of Commerce
Lions Club International
Lutheran Social Services
March of Dimes Foundation
Narcotics Anonymous
National Association for the
    Advancement of Colored
    People

National Association of Business
    and Professional Women
National Federation of the Blind
National Runaway Hotline
Optimist International
Rotary International
Salvation Army
Society for Crippled Children
Young Men's Christian
    Association (YMCA)
Young Women's Christian
    Association (YWCA)

School District Services

Administrators
Adult Education
Counseling Colleagues
Intermediate Service Units

School Nurses
School Psychologists
School Social Workers
Speech and Hearing Specialists

Teachers
Other Pupil Personnel
    Specialists

Proprietary Services

Attorneys
Boarding Houses
Chiropractors
Clinical Psychologists
Counseling Psychologists
Counselors

Employment Agencies
Nurses
Occupational Therapists
Opticians
Optometrists
Osteopaths

Physical Therapists
Physicians
Preparatory Schools
Professional Resume Services
Psychiatrists

Figure 10.1
Potential referral resources available to school counselors.

children's workshops and to such organized, sponsored athletic programs as Little League baseball that may enhance their development. Although those recommendations are from writers whose focus is on serving ethnic minority students, the ideas are useful for, and applicable to, serving all students. Examples of referrals made to enhance development are as follows:

A middle school counselor pursuing the school–home–community liaison role engages in the following related activities as part of his or her overall functioning as a school counselor during 1 week.

- The counselor coordinates arrangements for a group of students to visit nearby colleges and technical schools.
- The counselor, in conjunction with cooperating local employers, arranges for part-time work for several students who are borderline delinquents.
- The counselor recommends a Big Brother to an 11-year-old male student and coordinates a meeting between the student and a volunteer recommended by the Big Brother organization.
- A female student who has been attending an after school drama workshop because the counselor recommended and arranged it stops by the office and reports that she is enjoying the activity.

After adequate information has been gathered, a system for storing and retrieving it is necessary. Options include personal memory and filing systems. In this age of computers, the information can be stored relatively easily. Simplicity of organization and efficient retrieval are mandatory, so new information can be added, old information updated, and existing information accessed easily.

Counselors are challenged to be willing to serve as reciprocal referral sources. It seems logical that counselors do for others that which others request them to do. To implement a reciprocal arrangement, formal or semiformal agreements can make both parties aware of the services each is prepared to deliver to the other on request.

Carrying the idea of organization a step farther, a follow-up system can be considered. Among the benefits is the acquisition of helpful information about the student clients and the referral service. The follow-up can contain information from both parties covered in the referral service agreement. One example of a reciprocal feedback proposal follows:

A school counselor successfully arranges for a referral of a student client to Dr. X. Per their agreement, Dr. X supplies the counselor with appropriate information about the client after acquiring signed permissions from the client or the client's parents. The counselor expects this feedback from Dr. X and will seek it out if necessary. (paraphrased from Baker, 1973)

Because clients are the most important parties in the referral process, follow-up data from them are a valuable source of information about the adequacy of referral services. Some sort of client survey is suggested. Important questions can be incorporated into these surveys by using any one of several available formats. Here are some areas that client survey questions should cover:

- The student client's level of satisfaction with the counselor's manner when making the referral suggestion
- The accuracy of the counselor's description of these referral services to the student
- The student client's level of satisfaction with the helper's services
- The student client's perception of the competence of the new helper
- The client's level of satisfaction with the new helper or the combination of original and referred helpers (Baker, 1973)

Such surveys measure client satisfaction perceptions about the referral services. A more comprehensive evaluation of the referral services also includes procedures for acquiring results-based data derived from referral objectives and time-on-task data that determine cost effectiveness of the referral services.

These follow-up procedures, including the survey, fall into the coordinating domain. As such, counselors are attempting to ensure success for referrals and to assess the success of the referring and coordinating efforts.

How to Refer Clients.   Perhaps the most important facet of the referral process is the referral suggestion. Brammer, Abrego, and Shostrom (1993) believed that the way the referral suggestion is introduced and explained has considerable influence on the chance for success. Two challenges confront counselors when suggesting referrals:

1. Clients may feel abandoned or rejected by the suggestion.
2. Clients may reject the suggestion.

Responding to the first challenge requires sensitivity and good communication skills. The second challenge requires resilience and persistence; if rejected, counselors are challenged to keep seeking answers to the challenges.

To avoid confusion when referrals are made, counselors determine whether referrals are partial or complete. A *partial referral* results in the continuation of the original counseling relationship, with supplementary services being provided by the referral source. For instance, after arranging for a referral physical examination and pregnancy test, the counselor meets with the young woman again to discuss her possible alternatives once the medical results are known. A *complete referral* is just what the term implies: The client is referred to another helper, and the counselor who made the referral completely disassociates from the case unless approached for consultation by the referee with client permission.

Carey, Black, and Neider (1978) proposed a plan for increasing the success of referral suggestions. They believed that client expectations about complete referrals are seldom fulfilled. Thus, partial referrals are likely to be the best choice in many cases. They suggested looking at the problem from the client's point of view, which is often a troubled one. They concluded that two variables, client motivation and confidence, have a strong effect on the success of any referral. Both variables can be influenced strongly by counselors. Carey et al. offered the following suggestions for increasing student client motivation and confidence:

- Eliminate some student client dilemmas by recommending partial referrals. This should increase client motivation.
- Know your referral sources well. Counselors who do are less likely to project ambiguity to student clients.
- Communicate appropriate and important information about student clients to the referral sources. Telling clients that you have done this provides an additional safeguard and increases student client motivation and confidence in the referral.
- Give specific information about cost, time, location, and so on to student clients to help make their decision easier.
- When necessary, help student clients by becoming active in the referral process. This may require making direct contact with referral sources to arrange for appointments or accompanying or transporting clients to appointments.

These suggestions can be implemented by school counselors. Becoming active in the referral process to the point of arranging appointments and providing transportation, however, gets counselors into the arena of legal and ethical decisions. It also raises the issue of whether such acts are within the school policies where one is employed. Deciding to accompany or transport minor clients is predicated on thorough consideration of ethical standards, legal precedents, insurance liability, and school district policies. A more thorough presentation of legal and ethical issues is offered in chapter 5.

It is virtually impossible to develop a foolproof, cookbook-type method for making referral suggestions. The following suggestions may increase the chances of success. When reading and processing them, reflect on the hypothetical case about a depressed high school student presented previously in this chapter and how well the counselor followed the suggestions made here. Those suggestions that offer ideas that will be incorporated during the implementation of the constructive action strategies stage are accompanied by extensions of the counselor–client interactions introduced previously in the chapter.

1. *Assess a student client's readiness carefully before making the suggestion.* In so doing, attempt to determine the psychological and emotional climate. It is important to know the student client's ability to cope not only with making the decision but also with the implications of making such a suggestion. In the hypothetical case of the depressed high school student, the counselor first explored the student's presenting problem and the client's assets and assessed his or her own capabilities before introducing the referral suggestion.

2. *Treat the student client as you would like to be treated.* Consider the following questions and their implications (Baker, 1973):

Would [the student] want the counselor to be attentive and nonthreatening? Objective and factual? Completely honest? Partially honest? Should the counselor "sell" the referral service, or does the student client want an objective evalua-tion with a choice of optional resources? Does the client want the counselor to assist with the arrangements, or would he or she rather do it alone?

3. *Whenever possible, discuss the potential referral with prospective referees before making the referral suggestion* **(Weinrach, 1984).** This can be accomplished without divulging confidential information. Counselors can describe the specifics without mentioning identifying information, or they can present case information hypothetically. After selecting potential referees, informing them about the case, and deciding to make the referral suggestion, communicate confidence in the student (Bobele & Conran, 1988). The way the counselor introduced the idea of making a referral to Wellsprings indicates a familiarity with its services that predates the inter-view with the student.

4. *Be able to explain that the referral suggestion is congruent with the student client's goals and why the referee will be better able to meet those goals* **(Downing, 1985).** Avoid implying that problem severity is the main reason for the referral. Doing so may lead clients to think negatively about themselves. Allow ample time for pre-senting and discussing the referral suggestion with the student client. Offer specific information about names, orientations of referees, fees, and procedures. Communicate an interest in knowing how the referral fared for the student—to the point of arranging follow-up meetings and providing support (Downing, 1985). The hypothetical case is continued as follows:

Student:	(in response to the counselor's confrontation) I guess you are right. I do need to do something about this situation because it seems to be getting worse instead of better. But it's so hard. I don't have any energy, and it seems over-whelming to go to that place and start telling my story all over again.
Counselor:	You realize something needs to be done, yet there seems to be no energy, making it appear almost impossible. Perhaps knowing that I can be of some help in the process and will be here for you even though you are seeing someone out-side the school may help. What do you think?
Student:	You'll help me and will see me, too? How?
Counselor:	Before you do anything, I'll see to it that you and your mother receive all the information needed to better know the people at Wellsprings, what they do, how they operate their services, and how much it may cost. I'll also help your mother make an appointment if she wants. Also, I'll work with you here at the school in cooperation with whomever you are working with at Wellsprings. That is usually the way it is done. It makes the whole process run more smoothly when someone here at the school coordinates these arrange-ments. So, what do you think about that?

Student:	It sounds good, but I haven't really told my mother about how bad I feel or about seeing you. Will you help me tell her?
Counselor:	Yes! Let's explore how we can do that.

5. *When client and parental permissions are granted, cooperate with referees by providing helpful information when it is requested* (**Amatea & Fabrick, 1984**).

6. Parental resistance to a referral suggestion may be natural because problems involving their children threaten family systems and may seem to reflect badly on the core of the parents' being. They want to protect their family systems. Counselors may have to *use challenging/influencing skills to persuade resistant parents of the seriousness of the problem.* Amatea and Fabrick (1984) recommended, as one approach, that the counselor hold back on tentativeness and assume the stance of an authoritative expert. The hypothetical case continues after the counselor has helped the student client tell the parents about the referral and the counselor and client have explained what has transpired thus far:

Parent:	As you know, I am a single parent, and this all sounds to me like it could be very expensive. I don't know if my insurance will cover this, and I'm also not sure it is as serious as you say. Can't my child just shake it off and straighten things out with your help and mine?
Counselor:	You have doubts, and that is a reasonable response. I agree that your child has the capacity to get better and that both of us can be helpful. However, I also believe that additional help is needed, both in terms of time and expertise, and that help is available at Wellsprings. Before thinking about the cost, let's think about the effect this situation is having on your child and what the human costs will be if sufficient help is not provided. What are your thoughts about that?
Parent:	Well, I like the idea of you helping us get information before making a decision. What do we do now?
Counselor:	I think we should ask your child to explain just how serious it is and then look carefully at the options, and if seeing someone at Wellsprings turns out to be part of the plan, we need to gather information that will answer your questions. Then, I hope you'll be ready for a decision. I'll try to help you as much as I can, whatever the decision.

7. *Give careful consideration to the arrangements for the first meeting and for follow-up procedures.* A successfully accomplished referral suggestion can be damaged severely by expecting the student client to make the next move (Baker, 1973). Experts are divided on this issue. Some think that student clients should initiate contacting referees (Amatea & Fabrick, 1984), others think that referees should initiate contacts (in this case, family therapists; Bobele & Conran, 1988) and others suggest that counselors

should be willing to help student clients and parents initiate contacts (Baker, 1973; Downing, 1985). The natural compromise is for counselors to be prepared to use all three approaches because circumstances will dictate which is best. Some student clients are independent, whereas others need help with making arrangements. Be sure to deal with this part of the referring/coordinating process carefully and conscientiously. What do the circumstances dictate in our hypothetical case?

8. *Engage in this process with an awareness of the implications involved when entering into the referral process with student clients and referees who represent different worldviews* (e.g., gender differences, different cultural backgrounds). This concern leads to being able to take cultural differences and levels of tolerance into consideration when trying to select referees for student clients.

9. *Understand that referrals are only one step in the counseling process.* They are not the end of the helping relationship. For example, the counselor in the hypothetical case running through this chapter may make arrangements for a partial referral in which the student client continues to see the counselor while seeing a helper at Wellsprings, and the counselor serves as a coordinator of services the student client is receiving in and out of school.

How to Coordinate a Successful Referral.

Where referring ends and coordinating begins is somewhat unclear. In our hypothetical case, it may be argued that the coordinating process begins when the school counselor volunteers to participate in the process of bringing the clients and referees together. It makes no difference whether referrals are partial or complete. Coordinating remains important in either approach. Important coordinating competencies include being able to (a) keep track of whether clients and referees met, (b) submit all information and materials that are needed by the referee, (c) help the client while not interfering with the work of the referee if the referral is partial, (d) serve as a consultant to the referee when necessary, and (e) evaluate the effects of the referral. What follows is an application of these recommendations to the hypothetical case running through this section of the chapter.

> Soon after the referral was made, the school counselor checks with the student and finds out that a relationship with a therapist at Wellsprings has been successfully initiated. At the request of the referee at Wellsprings, and with the approval of the parent, the counselor provides pertinent information about the student from the cumulative records without violating confidentiality. Next, the counselor meets with the client periodically to address issues that are appropriate and have been recommended by the referee at Wellsprings. As the helping process continues, the referee contacts the school counselor for consultation about the case, and the counselor responds cooperatively. Finally, when appropriate, the counselor gathers information from the client, parent, and referee that will help determine the effectiveness of the referral. In addition, the data are used to find ways to improve the process.

Clearly, making a good referral and coordinating it successfully require considerable thinking and conscientious organizing. To ignore the importance of devoting the necessary thought and effort to this task is to flirt with the danger of reducing the effectiveness of the school counseling program.

The information presented here recommends preferred practices. Data collected from a sample of 149 Ohio school counselors and analyzed by Ritchie and Partin (1994) provided evidence of differences between the recommendations and the realities of professional practice, leaving room for improvement. Included in their summary are the following comments:

> Our findings indicate that school counselors are faced with a host of concerns. . . . Emotional concerns, family concerns, alcoholism, drug abuse, and suspected child abuse were the concerns most frequently referred. . . . Although counselors claimed to be familiar with referral resources in their school, . . . they were less familiar with referral resources outside of school. . . . Many counselors expressed a need for more formal training in ethical referral practices. (p. 270)

School–Community Collaboration.   School counselors are able to accomplish only so much through a coordination process such as that described previously. The school–community collaboration paradigm introduced in chapter 2 and developed further in chapter 7 highlights the importance of establishing working alliances with community resources to deliver the many services students and their families need to enhance student readiness for academic achievement. Keys and Bemak (1997) encouraged school counselors to view themselves as leaders in a process of integrating their programs within a broader system of community services. Adelman and Taylor (2002) indicated that schools will not be able to address current barriers to learning without working collaboratively with community-based organizations and families. The primary steps in this process for school counselors are (a) accepting the collaboration concept as having merit; (b) influencing counselor, administrator, and teacher colleagues about the merits of the idea,; (c) identifying relevant community services; (d) influencing community services representatives of the merits of the idea, (e) creating a grand implementation design in collaboration with other stakeholders; (f) working with significant stakeholders to implement the design; (g) establishing your role within the design (e.g., coordination); and (h) monitoring the process (i.e., evaluation and accountability). Readers are encouraged to look into the description of an attempt at school–community collaboration in Porter, Epp, and Bryant (2000). Their story generally describes a successful collaboration process. Yet, there were challenges to overcome.

MANIFESTATIONS OF SCHOOL COUNSELOR-INITIATED REFERRING AND COORDINATING

The School Counselor as a Referral Service Coordinator

Referral service coordinating encompasses a blend of counseling, consulting, and referral services. Taken from DeVoe and McClam (1982), the following is a summary of proposed phases of referral service coordinating with examples of their implementation in the case of Brenda, a student with many overwhelming problems.

After establishing counseling relationships leading to awareness of goals and priorities, counselors may determine what information about a case is needed, collect critical information, organize it, and assess it to identify problems and goals. DeVoe and McClam (1982) called this the *information retrieval phase*. Brenda is a young woman experiencing failure in school, abuse of drugs, possible child abuse, and possible pregnancy. Information about her perception of her problems is acquired via an accepting, participatory counseling relationship. In addition, physicians, teachers, school psychologists, social workers, and neighbors are asked for information that can help identify Brenda's needs. In some instances, those questioned are referees in partial referrals.

After receiving the information, counselors may determine how their own expertise can meet client needs and where referrals are needed. Evaluating one's professional capability, making appropriate referrals, establishing a timeline, and determining follow-up procedures comprise the *information assessment phase*. With Brenda, the counselor realizes that some problems are beyond her own expertise and/or require more time and attention than she can offer. She then pursues a plan of joint, cooperative actions, setting up the information assessment phase.

While continuing to offer legitimate counseling services, the counselor acts as a coordinator of referral services. As coordinator, the counselor orchestrates the referral process and mobilizes the referral services by making referrals and devising plans for communications among referral services. In so doing, the counselor acts as an advocate for Brenda, ensuring that she does not get lost in the system. As the professional who is providing direct, caregiving services to Brenda in school, the counselor occupies the most strategic position for coordinating the helping services, including

Being a referee for other professionals and parents can be a source of professional satisfaction.

following up on referral services and incorporating them with the direct services when appropriate.

DeVoe and McClam (1982) viewed referral service coordination as a way for school counselors to alleviate concerns about not being able to meet their student clients' needs while also providing a more comprehensive set of services. Effective referral service coordination results in more effective counseling interventions. In the referral service coordination scenario described, the counselor used referrals as one means of helping the student client while serving as a liaison between the various persons and agencies involved in providing services for Brenda.

School Counselors and Student Assistance Programs

Designed for At-Risk Students. Student assistance programs (SAPs) are approaches that the schools use to reach out to and help a variety of at-risk students. SAPs are helpful to school counselors because they bring into play sources of help, in responding to the challenges at-risk students present, that are more systematic and comprehensive than individual counselors are usually able to be when working independently with at-risk students and trying to make referrals.

Modeled on the concept of the employee assistance programs (EAPs) established in business and industry, SAPs are designed to identify high-risk students experiencing decreased productivity (declining academic performance) because of chemical abuse and other suspected mental health problems. Identification is followed by intervention and referral to appropriate community services. An aftercare component is provided to support those returning to school after having received counseling intervention services. One important distinction between EAPs and SAPs is that EAPs provide adult employees with voluntary participation and an option to resign; SAPs, in contrast, often demand that adolescent students participate or face expulsion (Roman, 1989). This circumstance occurs because the school differs from the workplace.

The school atmosphere favors acceptance of referral suggestions, although it is also more subject to abuse and exploitation unless great care is exercised. Because of legitimate national concern about chemical abuse and prevention of mental health problems, SAPs became increasingly popular in the late 1980s. As Roman (1989) pointed out, the rapid transfer of the core technology from the workplace (EAPs) to the school (SAPs) posed both advantages and disadvantages. High-risk adolescents and the school personnel trying to help them gain the advantages because SAPs offer additional systematic opportunities for help. Inconsistency of services is one disadvantage, however, because there is no national consensus on the definition of SAPs.

Three approaches to organizing SAPs have emerged (Borris, 1988). Some SAPs follow an externally based model, in which a specialized staff is available for services outside the school. Others have employed an internally based model, in which a specialized staff is available for services inside the school. Because it is the most common and cost-effective model, a third approach, the core team idea, is described in detail here.

Core Team Student Assistant Programs. Core team members are trained to screen, refer, intervene with, and support dysfunctional students. Diversity in team membership is recommended to represent all kinds of school personnel and to provide a variety of pathways to discovering potential student clients. Therefore, central office and building administrators, teachers, counselors, nurses, school psychologists, and other specialists are members of core teams. Certified providers outside the school district can give specialized training, usually short term and intense, to core team members. The training often includes a knowledge base about SAPs, group process, chemical dependency and the disease concept, suicide prevention/intervention, symptoms of mental illness, theories of adolescent development, treatment recovery, continuity of care, and action planning. Some of these topics are similar to the basic training programs of school counselors. Simulations and rehearsals of confrontations with targeted adolescents and their parents/guardians are often included in the training. Having been trained themselves, core team members, in turn, provide training to other school personnel through in-service programs. Such faculty in-service training creates an informed and helpful professional staff supportive of the core team.

Core teams network with referral sources just as counselors do as part of their liaison function. In this instance, the networking involves a team of professionals that includes counselors, rather than counselors acting independently. Identification of at-risk students can therefore involve all professional school personnel because of the pyramid-like nature of core teams and the in-service training of others. Self-referrals and referrals from peers, parents, and others are welcomed. When at-risk students are identified, the core teams are responsible for investigating the referrals and meeting with the students and their parents/guardians if further action is deemed appropriate.

Informing and involving parents/guardians varies from school to school; the nature of such contacts seems to be independent rather than a universal policy. Meetings with parents are informational in that the core teams share their findings and recommendations. The meetings may also be confrontational because of the possibility of denial and resistance from the students and/or their families. In these situations, school systems are often empowered to threaten suspension as a form of caring coercion if cooperation is not achieved. This occasional resorting to coercion may cause school counselors to be concerned about students' perceptions of them. This issue has not yet been resolved beyond the individual decision-making level.

Recommended intervention plans vary because of differing circumstances where SAPs exist. When appropriate services are provided outside the schools, core teams are responsible for assessing the readiness of returning students and for providing aftercare services. When necessary services are not readily available, which is the case in many communities, or targeted families cannot afford the services, or both, core teams may have to devise alternative intervention programs. Sometimes such alternative services are provided by school personnel and are offered in the schools during or after the school day.

The nature of the problem also affects where students receive help. Students with discipline and attendance problems might receive help in the school, whereas students with substance abuse problems require more specialized help off-site. In some instances, counselors are among the staff professionals with competencies that enable them to serve as referees and referral recommenders. For example, Zubrod (1992) described a situation where a school counselor provided ongoing counseling groups for students referred to the school's SAP. In this case, the counselor was able to help many participants achieve improved mental health, and all who indicated substance abuse problems reported change in a positive direction. Confidence in the viability of the group counseling program, which was high at the outset, continued throughout.

Aftercare is another challenge facing core teams. A system must be established and monitored for accepting the referred student back in school or for determining whether problem behaviors have been changed successfully. Beyond that, support is needed to prevent or detect relapses or both. Aftercare seems to be natural for counselors as part of their responsive counseling intervention function (i.e., tertiary prevention). One way school counselors provide aftercare for these students is through ongoing counseling groups that returning students can join to process things in a safe environment while trying to adapt to having returned to the school after a substantial absence (e.g., Zubrod, 1992).

SAPs offer counselors an exceptionally useful adjunct to their referral services, whether they are members of core teams or are making referrals to core teams or to external and internal experts. Advantages include the team concept, the targeting of dysfunctional behaviors by informed staff members, and the comprehensive and systematic nature of the program.

SAPs are designed to identify, inform, and refer many more students than counselors can independently under their less formalized referral services. To ensure appropriate counselor involvement in SAPs, Zimman and Cox (1989) made several recommendations:

- The program should be mandated by the school's administration to avoid turf battles between counselors and teachers.
- Services within the SAPs should be spelled out clearly to avoid confusion over what is to be referred internally (e.g., to counselors) and what is to be referred externally.
- Coordinators should be designated in a manner that conveys the broadest possible ownership of the program.
- The headquarters of the SAP program should be located in an office near but not within the counseling or administrative offices to give the program separate status.
- Responsibilities of all professionals should be clarified in advance.
- Allowances should be made for individual differences among counselors and grade-level differences among students when implementing the program.

A relatively recent idea, SAPs have already had a significant influence on the basic education scene. Designed originally to serve high school adolescents, SAPs were gradually being implemented in junior high, middle, and elementary schools.

REFERRALS TO SCHOOL COUNSELORS

Referrals From Other Professionals and Parents

Being a referee for other professionals and parents can be a source of both professional satisfaction and frustration. Satisfaction is achieved from knowing that coworkers and parents know and appreciate one's efforts. Frustration occurs when the process is misunderstood, expectations are unrealistic, and referrals are made inappropriately. Consider, for example, the following hypothetical and real cases:

- Tina's mother, Mrs. Jones, calls the counselor and requests an interview. In the interview, the counselor learns that Mrs. Jones is terribly worried about Tina's behavior in and out of school. She requests help from the counselor to find out what is wrong and perhaps bring about a cure.
- Gene has just arrived in the counselor's office. He has been brought by Ms. Smith, the principal, who finds Gene's behavior reprehensible. The principal requests that the counselor straighten Gene out and hints at more drastic methods if this does not work.
- Taking a survey of teacher-initiated referrals during 1 week of school, a counselor creates the following list: six cases of students fighting, four cases of classroom acting out, two cases of smoking, and one case of inappropriately affectionate behavior in the hallways.
- Analysis of 313 referral documents and findings from focus group interviews with 10 elementary school teachers led Jackson and White (2000) to conclude that many teachers tend to view referrals from the perspective of a medical model. That is, many teachers assume that children are not responsible for their problems. Therefore, they attribute responsibility to the referees (i.e., school counselors), expecting them to solve the problem for the child (and possibly for the teacher as well).

These four frustrating scenarios demonstrate some pitfalls awaiting counselors who respond to referrals indiscriminately. Indeed, these cases dictate the challenge to organize the system by which referrals are made to counselors. The examples offer several ideas about how this aspect of the referral service can be organized. The ideas are organized around three basic questions: Who is my client? What is the proper referral procedure? and What is a legitimate referral?

Who Is My Client?   Mrs. Jones's request places the counselor in a dilemma from which there is no escape if the counselor attempts to serve her and her daughter at the same time. Initially, Mrs. Jones requests to be the client, but it is her daughter who is to receive the direct intervention. If the counselor initiates a counseling relationship with Tina, Tina will become a client. Then, from an ethical perspective (and legally in some states), Mrs. Jones can no longer be a client because whatever Tina shares with the counselor becomes confidential and the counselor cannot share it with Tina's mother without Tina's permission. If the counselor decides to accept Mrs. Jones as a client, then consultation is in order. Then, Tina is the client and Mrs. Jones is the consultee. A more detailed coverage of consultation is presented in chapter 11. With Mrs. Jones as the client, the counselor's services to Tina are indirect; that is, the counselor helps Tina by consulting with Mrs. Jones, who works directly with Tina. When Mrs. Jones's goals become clear to the counselor, it is time to clarify the issues and negotiate which client to serve directly. A third option is to work out a system for serving both clients if an understanding of mutually acceptable goals can be achieved. Mrs. Jones's request indicates a misunderstanding of the counseling services and naïveté about counseling ethics, problems counselors handle systematically or individually on a case-by-case basis.

What Is the Proper Referral Procedure?

Ms. Smith, the principal, expects the counselor to cure Gene quickly and dramatically. This appears to be a manifestation of the medical model belief reported previously from Jackson and White (2000). The counselor is challenged to clarify for Ms. Smith what are and what are not legitimate expectations (referrals). Among other things, clarification involves requesting information from Ms. Smith about what transpired before the referral, what behavioral goals Ms. Smith has for Gene, and what outcomes he expects. In fairness to the counselor, this information will be the content of negotiations with Ms. Smith. This is also a "Who is my client?" situation because it is not Gene who initiated the request for a responsive counseling intervention. Smith wants an intervention to change Gene's behaviors. As is the case with Mrs. Jones and Tina, the "Who is my client?" question needs to be resolved quickly.

Ms. Smith essentially commands the counselor to perform a service. In this case, the counselor is not forewarned, availability of the counselor's services is assumed, and outcome expectations are vague. Such a situation underscores the need for communication with superiors and colleagues to establish a clearly defined referral system. Diplomacy is in order, leading to a systematic plan wherein the needs of all parties are being served, and both the principal and the counselor believe they are winners.

What Is a Legitimate Referral?

The two hypothetical cases and the findings by Jackson and White (2000) required thought about whether counselor involvement in the interventions is appropriate. Neither Tina nor Gene asks the counselor for help. The list of reasons for the referrals demands that one ask whether demonstrations of affection or smoking in school are counseling problems or matters of rules and mores that should be regulated by either administrators or community consensus. The findings from the Jackson and White study indicate that expectations of teachers and others may be inappropriate when making referrals, placing school counselors in no-win situations. This raises two questions: How do the counselors help teachers and other referees understand that all involved parties, including students and teachers, are potentially involved in achieving solutions to problems that cause referrals? and Do school counselors view themselves as miracle workers or super counselors who can fix all problems referred to them, or do they understand that all players, including teachers, students, and parents, are involved in helping students realize their potential?

Another issue is the fact that all the referrals involved some form of acting out. No referral involved a student who exhibited symptoms of being overly passive or withdrawn. This narrowness of focus in recognizing problems indicates that members of the school staff do not seem to be aware of a broader range of potential problems. The situation offers an opportunity to design an in-service presentation for other members of the faculty and staff.

A report by Wagner (1976) offers food for thought about referral patterns of elementary school teachers. Teachers were invited to make referrals to groups that help students enhance personal problem-solving skills. Data from the teachers' responses showed that they consistently recommended more boys than girls for this kind of help. This finding led Wagner to hypothesize that girls' problems in adjusting to home and school are more difficult to observe from their school-related attitudes and behaviors than boys' are and that perhaps expectations of boys in elementary school need further investigation. The latter hypothesis was based on Wagner's observation that, in general, boys are encouraged to be independent, active, and mobile but that exhibiting these behaviors in classrooms often leads to teacher distress and disciplinary referrals.

- *Are Referrals Being Made When Making Them Would Be Appropriate?* Another serious problem is the absence of referrals to the school counselor. Some colleagues and parents are apathetic or poorly informed. This suggests that counselors need to establish systems for receiving referrals and to make those systems known. Ingredients of any system are bound to differ among communities, schools, and counseling goals. Despite such differences, some basic suggestions are relevant to most school districts:
- Distribute information about the services that school counselors provide (e.g., counseling, consulting, information).
- Include examples of how those services are carried out (what kind of counseling is offered and the outcomes to expect).
- Make public a referral system, explaining the process for making referrals to counselors and providing necessary forms. Make the system simple, efficient, and multiculturally appropriate.
- Include procedures for providing feedback to referral sources.
- Explain the policy regarding confidentiality.
- Look for opportunities to explain the system. Do so proactively (e.g., faculty meetings, in-service programs, distributive materials).

Referrals From Students

Much of the preceding discussion of referrals from professionals and parents also holds true for students. They, too, have misperceptions and unrealistic expectations, and sometimes they are apathetic. They seldom refer a peer, although occasionally they do. Among those students who refer peers are those trained to be peer helpers. Ingredients of the counselor-initiated referrals described at the beginning of this chapter can be part of the training programs for peer helpers. More on training peer helpers is found in chapter 11.

In most instances, referrals from students are self-referrals, and counselors are challenged to present themselves to students clearly while also living up to realistic expectations. In their efforts to enhance the probability of student self-referrals, counselors face several difficult challenges. Park and Williams (1986) listed the following negative expectations that make reaching some students more difficult:

- Adults are persons who give information to students, talking *to* them rather than *with* them.
- Adults give advice, and students view their own role as captive listeners who are forced to accept adult solutions.
- Adults respond critically and tell students how they should feel when students try to express feelings, leading to the conclusion that disclosing feelings is a risky business.

- Adults can be punitive; they have the power to make students feel shame or guilt over mistakes.
- Adults do not treat information about students confidentially. Often, they share it with other people, which sometimes leads to punitive responses.

Obviously, faced with these unflattering perspectives, counselors are truly challenged to prove that they are special adults who are dedicated to helping students and who are different from other adults.

Revisiting Wagner's (1976) study provides further food for thought about student self-referrals. It is less likely that boys who hypothetically might have been referred by teachers will refer themselves. It is also more likely that girls who hypothetically might have been referred by teachers will refer themselves for help. This indicates that boys who need help may be the least likely students to refer themselves. Elementary school boys and girls, however, refer themselves at about an equal ratio, evidence that not all boys are reticent about referring themselves.

What to do? Realize that not all students need to refer themselves for counseling services. They want to be able to avail themselves of these services if needed. When school counseling is not perceived positively and accurately by students, there are insufficient self-referrals. Insufficient student self-referrals diminish the impact of a counseling program or at least result in an unbalanced program. A proactive stance leads to counselors providing information about their programs to students in a manner that is simple, truthful, and in the students' vernacular. Park and Williams (1986) offered an interesting suggestion for implementing this idea. Applying the principles of social modeling, they exposed elementary school students to live or filmed performances of children modeling behaviors they wanted the students to learn. The targeted behaviors included social skills needed to initiate contacts with adults. Demonstrated were situations in which initiating contacts would be appropriate, showing how the models coped with the anxiety and reluctance associated with approaching adults.

Another idea is offered by LaFountain (1983), who asked elementary school children to complete information-gathering graphic checklists during her weekly classroom visits. One of the checklists is the Smiley-Frowney Face Sheet, on which children in kindergarten and first and second grades are asked to make an X on the face that best depicts their feelings about school, friends, and family. Six faces, ranging from teary eyed to openly smiling, are presented for each of the three categories. The reverse side of the paper is used for writing news to the counselor. A second graphic checklist is the Feelometer, which LaFountain used in third through sixth grades. Thermometers with scales ranging from *Very Unhappy* to *Very Happy* are located beside each of three questions asking how students are feeling about school, friends, and family. The Feelometer also contains boxes that can be checked by children who want to see the counselor. In a space on the reverse side, children can write messages to the counselor. The information is used for reaching out to children proactively and as a resource for referrals.

Student self-referrals occur more often if they are easy to make. Students desire to know that their counselors maintain confidentiality. Counselors who are visible and appear to students as adults who talk with them, participate in the decision-making process as equals, empathize with feelings, and accept individual differences are more likely to receive student self-referrals. To repeat the admonition made earlier in this chapter: Ignoring the importance of devoting the necessary thought and effort to this task is flirting with the danger of reducing the effectiveness of the counseling program.

FEATURED ACTIVITY: GRADUATE STUDENT PERSPECTIVES ON REFERRAL AND COORDINATION IN SCHOOL COUNSELING

In this chapter, we discuss referral and coordination in school counseling. Collaboration between schools and their communities is becoming increasingly important. Before entering graduate programs in school counseling many students gain both volunteer and paid work experience in community agencies.

What experiences, if any, have you had in working with community agencies? What have these experiences taught you about collaboration between school counselors and professionals who work in social services and related community agencies? What important, creative thoughts do you have about referral and coordination in school counseling?

After you read this chapter, go to http://www.genesislight.com/scan21st/tell_us/referral.html and complete the form. With your permission, we will periodically post some of your creative thinking for the world to read.

OTHER SUGGESTED ACTIVITIES

1. Using the criteria suggested in this chapter, evaluate the referral services in the institution where you are employed and/or where you attended school for counselor-initiated referrals and for referrals to counselors.
2. Using the results of the previous activity, develop a proposal for improving the referral services.
3. List the referral sources you use. Check those with which you have reciprocal relationships. Make a different mark by those about which you have adequate knowledge. What do the results tell you? Are these sources appropriate for serving a multiculturally diverse population?
4. Add possible referral sources to your list.
5. Brainstorm ideas for enhancing the image of counseling among children and adolescents, and suggest ways to implement them. What are the underlying principles for your ideas?
6. Cooperatively generate a list of referral sources that can be used to enhance student client development.
7. Create a presentation to the faculty and administrators of a hypothetical school in which one is presenting a detailed overview of the preferred process for making referrals to the school counselor.
8. Create a school–community collaboration plan for a hypothetical school system or for a system with which you are familiar.
9. Go to the SCAN Web site (www.scan21st.com) and propose some ways that this Web site might assist school counselors in developing referral sources.

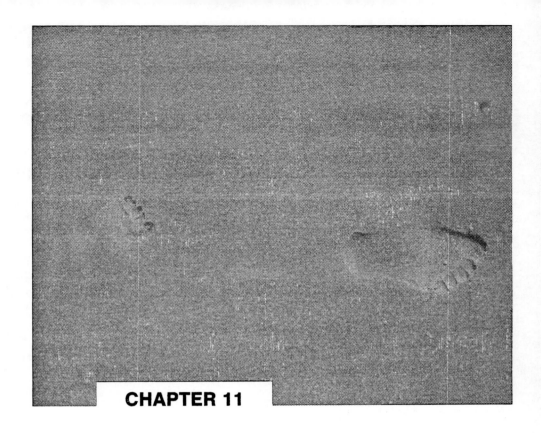

CHAPTER 11

School Counselor Consulting: A Bridge Between Prevention and Intervention

Goals: To introduce a specific consultation role for school counselors and to cite the similarities and differences between consultation and other school counseling functions while proposing basic competencies and training recommendations.

The following case led a school counselor to begin a series of consultations with a student's parents and his physical education (PE) teacher:

> *Joel is a sixth-grade boy who recently transferred to a new school. He does not know any of the other students well. In fact, most of the school's students come from affluent neighborhoods, and Joel is unable to understand their carefree attitudes about money. They seem to be able to afford everything they want—new sneakers, MP3 players, video games, and bikes. Joel has tried to find ways of fitting in but nothing seem to work. Going to school in the morning is a frightening prospect for him.*
>
> *One thing that has earned him a negative reputation is him a inability to succeed at athletics. He has never been "sports oriented" and is somewhat overweight. He worries constantly about going to PE class. He especially worries during the math class immediately prior to PE.*
>
> *Joel is particularly uncomfortable in PE class because every so often in the locker room, certain students will single him out and hide his PE uniform. As a result, Joel gets a zero grade for that day. One day Joel becomes so angered by the taunting that he retaliates, physically attacking another student. The PE teacher kicks Joel out of class, and he and the assistant principal report Joel's behavior to his parents.*

Students often exhibit behaviors and describe feelings that require the school counselor to consult with parents and teachers as a way of alleviating the presenting problems and of preventing the occurrence of future problems. This chapter presents the school counselor as a consultant.

DEMAND FOR CONSULTING IN SCHOOL COUNSELING

Definitions of *consultation* abound in the professional literature; a perusal of them leads to the conclusion that the differences are largely varying degrees of comprehensiveness. When consultation is treated as a topic or process, the definitions are quite comprehensive. When consultation is treated as a competency, the definition is more narrow and compact (cf. Brack, Jones, Smith, White, & Brack, 1993; Dougherty, 1990; Kurpius, Fuqua, & Rozecki, 1993; Mendoza, 1993; Rockwood, 1993; Ross, 1993). Dougherty (1990) offered a useful, comprehensive definition: "Consultation is a process in which a human services professional assists a consultee with a work-related (or caretaking-related) problem with a client system, with the goal of helping both the consultee and the client system in some specified way" (p. 8).

School Counselor Consulting

Dougherty's (1990) definition introduced three terms that are important to a discussion of consulting: *human services professional, consultee,* and *client system.* In this chapter, the human services professional is referred to as a consultant, and the client system is referred to as a student client. Consultation involves three parties, two of whom are working together to serve a third. The two working together are a consultant and a consultee; the recipient of their efforts is the client. At times, multiple consultants, consultees, or clients may be involved in the consultation process. For example, a school counselor (consultant) is consulted by two parents (consultees) about helping their child (client) be more successful in school. When the school counselor and the parents agree to work together, a consulting relationship develops in which the school counselor (consultant) works with the parents (consultees) to find ways to help their child (client). The school counselor's interactions with the child are most likely to be indirect. That is, the school counselor directly assists and interacts with others (e.g., parents, teachers) who are working directly with the child. Therefore, the school counselor might be depicted as working behind the scenes. These circumstances describe *school counselor consulting*.

In most consulting relationships, consultants will help consultees by sharing their expertise. Consultees, in turn, will use that help in their work with student clients who receive the help. Thus, a prime feature of school counselor consulting is that the school counselor participates in the helping process as a helper whose influence on the student client is indirect and whose influence on the consultee is direct.

An Example of School Counselor Consulting

Students in our training program engage in consulting relationships while enrolled in their school counseling internships, and they are required to report and analyze one of those consultation experiences. The following excerpt of school counseling consultation is taken from a report by Coleman (2006). References are made within parentheses to the different consultation modes, which are presented in detail later in this chapter.

The school counselor intern formed a close relationship with a first-year English teacher. Like many first-year teachers, she was given exceptionally tough classes, and she struggled with classroom management and discipline. Having once been in the teacher's shoes as a classroom teacher who struggled with the same challenges, the intern quickly formed a close bond with the teacher, and they met often to discuss the students and strategies the teacher could use to maintain order in her classroom (initiation mode).

One case involved two girls who were involved in an extremely disruptive dispute. The case first came to the intern's attention when the teacher became worried about the content of an intercepted note from one girl to the other while in class. The teacher asked the intern to talk to the girls (provision mode). After talking to the girls and resolving part of the problem (mediation mode), the intern realized that the hostilities were likely to resurface in class. Shortly thereafter, continued whispering and name-calling occurred, and the intern met with the teacher to brainstorm solutions (collaboration mode).

Although the dispute originally involved only two girls, the entire classroom was now involved, causing a disruption in the teacher's instruction time. The intern met with the teacher to plan an intervention (collaboration mode). One goal that resulted was to find ways the teacher could deal with the problem without further disrupting class time. The strategy to reach this goal was for the teacher to periodically contact the girls' parents to update them on any undesirable behaviors, and the students knew of this plan. As a result, some of the disruptive behaviors decreased.

Another goal was to get the girls to coexist peacefully for 90 minutes while in class. The intern recommended that the teacher give the girls ground rules for classroom behavior (prescription mode). The intern worked with the teacher to determine the rules and consequences for breaking these rules (collaboration mode). The teacher believed that her meeting with the girls to discuss the ground rules had a positive impact on how they interacted outwardly.

A goal the teacher established was to avoid singling the girls out in class and making them believe that she was picking on them. A zero tolerance policy was established for all instances of talking, whispering, and note passing, regardless of who the culprits were. By being able to consistently enforce this policy in her classroom, the teacher began to feel more confident. The goal and strategy were the teacher's ideas, and the intern provided support through positive verbal reinforcement.

By the end of the grading period, the two girls seemed to have put their differences aside, and classroom disruptions were minimal. The intern, when reflecting on this consultation experience, shared the following observations:

> The main thing I learned from this particular consultation relationship was how little I had to do to be helpful. I did offer some suggestions and insight, but mainly I served as a person who the teacher felt comfortable coming to discuss her concerns and frustrations as well as someone who could provide an outsiders' perspective. Additionally, I learned that the real expert in many consultation relationships is the classroom teacher; after all they are the ones who are in the classrooms day after day, and the ones who observe the students regularly and are the ones who ultimately have to employ the strategies. (Coleman, 2006, p. 3)

A Brief Historical Overview

Counselors have probably always provided consultation; however, a formalized consulting function has been an important part of the school counselor's repertoire only since the late 1970s. Earlier, the proposal that professionals branch out from one-to-one relationships to work with caregivers who, in turn, work with clients was popularized in the mental health field (Caplan, 1959). School counseling was one helping profession that incorporated the idea because the large student-to-counselor ratios in virtually every school district made more effective use of counselor time appealing. Consultation is one way counselors can use their skills to influence many people (Gerler, 1992). The fact that consultation is an important function in counseling today and in the future is confirmed by the appearance of special issues of counseling journals devoted solely to consultation (Dougherty, 1992; Kurpius & Fuqua, 1993a, 1993b) and by the specific attention devoted to it as a "basic intervention" emphasized in the role statement for school counselors advocated by the ASCA (n.d.):

> The counselor as a consultant helps people to be more effective in working with others. Consultation helps individuals think through problems and concerns, acquire more knowledge and skill, and become more objective and self-confident. This intervention can take place in individual or group conferences, or through self-development activities. (p. 23)

Although the idea has gained momentum and acceptance, the meaning of consultation has been less clear. There is no universal definition of consultation (Kurpius & Fuqua, 1993a). Various helping fields have differing versions of the ingredients of consulting, and consulting behaviors are based more on trial-and-error activities than on theory (Bardon, 1985; Gallessich, 1985). The lack of theory does not need to be as unsettling for school counselors as it is for counselor educators because the peculiar environment in which school counselors work creates a relatively specific consultation role for school counselor consulting.

School counselors work in the schools, where the natural recipients of consulting services are students, teachers, administrators, parents, and occasionally others in the school district. For example, school counselors might consult with civic leaders who want to establish a scholarship program for local students or with members of a local service club who want to establish a system for recruiting American Field Service volunteers. Natural circumstances related to daily activities in school systems create situations in which individuals need consultation, and counselors can often provide the needed assistance. Counselors respond to teachers working with challenging students and/or planning units about which counselors have topical knowledge or implementation ideas. The first example involves a counseling intervention response and the second a prevention programming response, indicating that consultation services are important to both responsive counseling intervention and proactive prevention programming domains. School counselors do not need to create a consulting service—one already exists. Counselors who understand what exists can improve on it.

Evidence of School Counselor Consulting

Because consultation is important in both counseling interventions and prevention programming, it is a vital ingredient in the comprehensive balanced program concept introduced in chapter 3. Our position is supported by the ASCA National Model, in which consultation is presented as one of the four components of a comprehensive school counseling program (ASCA, 2005). Excerpts from the professional literature indicate that school counselors are, in fact, engaging in consulting activities; the activities most often reported involve consulting with teachers as consultees and students as the indirect recipients of the counselors' consulting services.

The most common reports of school counselors consulting with teachers involve teachers receiving assistance with students who exhibit challenging behaviors. Through excerpts of a consultation dialogue between an elementary school counselor and a teacher, Keat (1974) demonstrated that assistance provided by the counselor included empathy, additional ideas, support, confirmation, and recommendations. Dowd and Moerings (1975) reported a case in which an eighth grader's underachievement and social isolation were alleviated when a counselor consulted with three of the student's teachers and developed a treatment strategy. Off-task behaviors having a detrimental effect on the academic performance of six male and female sixth graders were reduced by modifications in the encouraging behaviors of teachers in consulting relationships (Rathvon, 1990). In a case in which the extent of the teacher's problem was unclear, Osterweil (1987) offered suggestions for achieving clarity and eventually suggested a treatment plan. Viewing teachers as information gatherers and hypothesis formers, Bauer and Sapona (1988) recommended that counselors have the expertise to help with students who exhibit challenging behaviors. Offering support for school counselor consulting, Bundy and Poppen (1986) reported that significant improvements in student behavior, adjustment, or achievement were found in 77% of the consultation studies they reviewed.

Strein and French (1984) pointed out that counselors are also an important consultation source for teachers in helping them foster affective growth in students. Therefore, counselors as consultants are seen as people who not only can help solve or treat existing problems but also can also offer assistance with proactive prevention program planning. Taking the prevention concept a step farther, Robinson and Wilson (1987) stated that counselor involvement in human relations training groups can be conceived of as a form of consultation. Teachers of second and fifth graders in 13 elementary schools received 25 hours of human relations training that led to overall improvements in their skills. Robinson and Wilson also reported evidence suggesting that teachers who learn to be more effective communicators may, in turn, enhance the academic achievements and self-concepts of their students.

Parents may also find value in the consultation services of school counselors. Purkey and Schmidt (1982) suggested that school counselors can help parents enhance their children's growth by adopting an invitational approach to family living. Purkey and Schmidt's ideas are practical and easily adopted and can be conveyed to parents in several relatively easy ways. Myrick (1977) also stated that parent consultation is a potentially important function for school counselors, especially elementary school counselors, because of the important role of parents in child development. He also noted, however, debate among various writers about the cost effectiveness of taking time away from other functions to engage in consultations with parents. Mullis and Edwards (2001) suggested that, if school counselors view concerns expressed by parents through a family systems lens, they can help parents plan interventions that may be successful in a time-efficient manner. We present more about this consulting approach later in the chapter.

Smaby, Peterson, Bergmann, Bacig, and Swearingen (1990) may have identified an approach to parental consultation that is cost effective. They described school-based, comprehensive, community suicide prevention and intervention programs in northeastern Minnesota in which school counselors serve as members of community intervention teams. Including teachers, social workers, community mental health workers, law enforcement officials, members of the clergy, and students, the teams developed and presented workshops and trained personnel from participating schools who, in turn, trained others in their respective schools, agencies, and communities. Most of the consultation offered to parents by these school counselors was indirect, which allowed them to help more people than direct service consultation in this instance.

Mathias (1992) stated that "there is a myriad of interventions available to the [school counselor] consultant" (p. 191). She provided several examples, including listening to parent and teacher concerns about children and adolescents and helping them explore alternative ways to address those concerns, developing and locating helpful printed materials that can be distributed to parents and teachers, working with school librarians to develop bibliotherapy sections in the school library, participating in child study teams with other school professionals, and serving on committees designed to improve the school as a system.

School Counselor Consulting in the Three Paradigms

The importance of consulting is highlighted in the three paradigms for enhancing school counseling that were introduced in chapter 2. In the ASCA's (2005) National

Model, consulting is an important responsive service just as counseling is. Gysbers and Henderson (2001) depicted consulting as being dedicated to helping students manage and resolve personal/social, educational, and career concerns. Representing the TSCI, House and Hayes (2002) viewed consulting as an important function for helping parents enroll their children in academic courses that will lead to attending college and teaching them how to make formal requests to school officials successfully. They also thought that school counselors can help educators resolve issues that involve the schools and their communities through consultation. Adelman and Taylor (2002) viewed consultation as part of an interconnected system for meeting students' needs via the School–Community Collaboration Model. More specifically, conflict resolution (a.k.a. mediation) is presented as a primary prevention strategy, and dropout and family support are seen as early intervention components.

BASIC INGREDIENTS OF SCHOOL COUNSELOR CONSULTING

Although less voluminous, the consultation literature, like the counseling literature, offers several recommendations about how consulting may be conducted. As is the case with the basic counseling skills, the competencies of consulting are atheoretical; they can be learned, developed, and incorporated into the behavioral repertoire, and they can be applied according to one's own theoretical persuasion. Two major themes stand out in these positions: modes and steps or stages. *Consulting modes* are the methods individuals use or the ways they behave when engaging in consulting services. *Consulting steps* or stages are the sequential behaviors in which individuals engage when carrying out any of the consulting modes. Because steps and stages depend on modes, modes are discussed first here.

School Counselor Consulting Modes

Kurpius (1978) suggested four modes that school counselors might use, each of which leads to different attitudes and behaviors and therefore requires different competencies. The following material extends Kurpius's ideas and also reflects thoughts expressed by Gallessich (1985).

We have added a fifth mode (mediation) to the four modes identified by Kurpius (1978). All five consulting modes are available to school counselors, and they are not mutually exclusive. It is likely that some modes are more prevalent among practicing counselors and in counselor education training programs. It is also likely that some are preferred by counselors or are recommended by counselor educators more than others. When reading this section, reflect on how the modes were used in the example presented previously in this chapter from Coleman (2006).

Prescription Mode. As consultants, school counselors may provide intervention plans or aid in the selection of intervention strategies for predetermined problems. When doing so, consultants investigate and diagnose the circumstances, negotiating strategies and people to implement them. This is an indirect service. An example of the prescription mode is a case in which an elementary school counselor (consultant) helps a frustrated teacher (consultee) establish a plan for a token economy program designed to enhance students' (clients') on-task behaviors and to reduce their acting-out behaviors. One-to-one consultation sessions with the teacher are accompanied by classroom observations by the counselor, who then analyzes students' behaviors prior to suggesting an intervention plan that the teacher may implement in the classroom. In this mode, the counselor suggests (i.e., prescribes) a plan for the teacher.

Provision Mode.   At times, school counselors as consultants provide direct services to clients because consultees lack time, interest, or competence. When doing so, counselors draw on competencies used in responsive counseling interventions and proactive prevention programming. This differs from basic counseling or prevention programming because the assistance is initiated by a consulting relationship. An example of the provision mode might occur from the same concerns that led to the prescription consultation example in the preceding paragraph. In an alternate scenario, the teacher may be unable to initiate the recommended (i.e., prescribed) plan or may have tried unsuccessfully to do so. As a provision-mode consultant, the counselor could enter the classroom as a substitute or collaborator and implement the proposed token economy program to the students (clients). In this example, the counselor (consultant) serves as a model for the teacher (consultee), who will still have to become involved eventually because the program will take time to complete. If the program necessitates only one class session and the counselor replaces the teacher, the provided consultation services completely eliminate active participation by the teacher.

Initiation Mode.   School counselors as consultants may contact prospective consultees proactively after having recognized and studied a problem, offering their consulting services. Depending on the nature of the problem, the consulting services may be either direct or indirect. An example of the initiation mode is a case in which a high school counselor responds to a first-year teacher who makes many disciplinary referrals to the assistant principal's office, appears unhappy when with colleagues, and is heard making comments about leaving the school district or the profession. The counselor (consultant) responds by inviting the teacher (consultee) to meet and talk, taking the opportunity to mention the events and offering to help the teacher resolve the problem. In this example, the consultation mode can then become prescriptive, provisional, collaborative, or a combination there of. A happier, more confident teacher may make fewer disciplinary referrals and serve the students (clients) better. The Coleman (2006) example began as initiation and expanded to provision, mediation, collaboration, and prescription.

Collaboration Mode.   As consultants, school counselors may respond to requests from consultees by engaging in mutual efforts to understand the problem, devise an action plan, and implement it. The services are usually indirect. A case of collaborative consulting will occur if the high school teacher (consultee) who has classroom management problems agrees that help is needed and engages in a joint problem-solving relationship with the counselor (consultant). They might engage in such collaborative activities as defining the problem clearly, identifying alternative solutions, selecting mutually agreeable strategies, and figuring out ways to implement them. Their ultimate goal is to discover ideas that, when implemented, will help the teacher be more effective with the students (clients). This stepped counseling process is similar to the one used in the decision-making counseling strategy presented in chapter 9.

Mediation Mode.   As consultants, school counselors may respond to requests from two or more consultees to help them accomplish an agreement or a reconciliation by serving as facilitators for the consultees. The resultant consultation services are direct. Mediation consulting may occur whenever two people or groups become locked in mutual disagreements and seemingly unresolvable differences of opinion. Antagonists may be teacher versus student, student versus parent, student versus student, or administrator versus student. If all sides agree, counselors can mediate by serving as intermediaries. An example is for a counselor (consultant) to help a teacher (consultee) having discipline problems work out differences with a student (client) angered by being sent to the principal's office. The mediating counselor can meet with both parties to help them share their explanations and try to achieve a mutual understanding and an improved relationship leading to a settlement of their differences. In so doing, the counselor might make suggestions but will never dictate resolutions to the disputing parties. It is also important that both the teacher and the student believe that the counselor is a fair, impartial mediator. That mediation has become an important consulting mode is seen in the attention paid to conflict resolution in the counseling literature (Messing, 1993).

A companion of mediation as consultation mode for school counselors is for counselors to train students to be peer mediators for fellow students. In this process, school counselors serve as trainers and supervisors. Theberge and Karan (2004) highlighted factors that may inhibit success in peer mediation and offered suggestions for strengthening these programs.

School Counselor Consulting Steps or Stages

Several writers deserve credit for helping counselors by spelling out important steps or stages to be considered when delivering consulting services (Bauer & Sapona, 1988; Brown, Wyne, Blackburn, & Powell, 1979; Dustin & Ehly, 1984; Kurpius, 1978; Myrick, 1977; Stum, 1982; Umansky & Holloway, 1984). They have more commonalities than differences. Essentially, their ideas fit into the five stages of Ivey and Ivey's (2007) helping paradigm presented in Table 9.1 (see chapter 9). Briefly, those stages are (a) initiating consulting sessions, (b) gathering data by listening to the consultees' stories, (c) setting goals with consultees mutually, (d) working with consultees on constructive action plans, and (e) terminating and helping consultees generalize and act on their action plans. The same five stages were previously presented for organizing and implementing responsive counseling interventions and are also advocated in conjunction with organizing and implementing consulting interventions. Therefore, the task of implementing the systems for both counseling and consulting interventions is easier because the systems are alike. An example follows:

Reflect on the two parents (consultees) who approached a counselor (consultant) for consultation about ways to help their child (the student client) become more successful in school (as described in the opening section of this chapter). The mode for this consulting relationship is collaboration. Implementing the first two of Ivey and Ivey's (2007) stages (initiate the session and listen to the consultees' story), the counselor/consultant uses basic interviewing skills to help the parents (consultees) tell their story, identify related affect, and discover resources available to them. Next, the counselor/consultant helps the consultees set goals based on a mutual understanding of the problem (Ivey and Ivey's third stage). Having agreed on what seemingly needs to be done, the consultant works with the consultees to identify strategies that can be employed to try to reach the goals that were established and to devise plans for implementing the strategies (Ivey and Ivey's fourth and fifth stages).

BASIC COMPETENCIES FOR SCHOOL COUNSELOR CONSULTING

The nature of school counseling itself places counselors in a position as prospective consultants. Because opportunities for consulting may present themselves from at least five modes, the school counselor is challenged to be a versatile consultant, able to be the provider, the mediator, or the initiator. The five modes can be further categorized as representing either direct or indirect services. The basic skills of a comprehensive consulting model are presented here in the context of Ivey and Ivey's five stages. Fortunately, consulting does not require a completely independent set of competencies. Instead, many of the counseling and some of the prevention programming competencies are simply applied in a different context. Research by Lin, Kelly, and Nelson (1996) indicated that many verbal behaviors are common to counseling and consulting interactions. The importance of being multiculturally competent—sensitive to the worldviews of consultees and their clients—remains as important as it is in counseling interventions and prevention programming. Because counseling and consulting competencies are similar, we find that school counseling students sometimes get confused and cannot tell the difference. So, we challenge readers to peruse this information carefully in order to discern the different nuances clearly.

Initiate Consultation and Listen to the Consultees' Stories

Opening Consulting Interviews.   Most often, consulting relationships are initiated by individuals who are seeking consulting assistance. In such cases, counselors draw on the same skills used when beginning responsive counseling relationships with student clients—open invitations that encourage consultee sharing, identifying, and clarifying. When counselors initiate consulting relationships, clear explanations of the invitation and proposal are necessary, just as they are in counseling interviews initiated by counselors. For example, a counselor will respond with an open invitation to talk with a consultee as the elementary school teacher did who approached a counselor for help out of frustration with students' acting-out behaviors. Horton and Brown's (1990) review of research on the importance of interpersonal skills led them to conclude that successful clinical consultants establish facilitative relationships with their consultees. Therefore, the counselor's initial consulting goal is to find out what the teacher wants. The counselor who approached the high school teacher having disciplinary difficulties in the Initiation Mode section of this chapter is an example of a prospective consulting relationship that needs to begin with an explanation. Having initiated the meeting, the counselor provides the teacher with an explanation of what appears to be occurring and how the counselor as a consultant might help the teacher.

Identifying the Presenting Problem and Preparing Consultees for Consultation.

After opening the consulting interview successfully, counselors will invite prospective consultees to share their presenting or targeted (initiation mode) problems and establish a facilitative working alliance in the process. In this process, consultees can be encouraged to share pertinent information about themselves (e.g., experiences, feelings, perceived level of competence to resolve the current problem, motives, initial goals), student clients (e.g., culture, age, gender, maturity, behaviors), interactions between clients and consultees (e.g., communications, behaviors, affect, attitudes, antecedents, reactions), and the context in which the interactions occurred (e.g., physical setting, contemporaries, peers, relationships, expectations, distractions, challenges). This process is similar to opening counseling interviews. Therefore, providing the core facilitative conditions, attending physically, and using the basic verbal counseling responses are as important to consulting as they are to counseling interventions.

While prospective consultees respond to invitations to share pertinent information about presenting problems, consulting counselors determine which mode is suggested by the circumstances and whether the consultees are ready, willing to proceed, and able to provide professional assistance. Then counselors are in a position to negotiate their roles and explain their own understanding of the presenting problems and the consultees' motives. Being clear with consultees about one's role as a consultant is important at the outset and remains important throughout the consultation process. Consequently, when providing consulting services, counselors make sure they and their consultees agree about expectations. More emphatically, it is recommended that, early in the consulting process, counselors periodically assess whether the expectations of all parties match and ensure that counselors renegotiate and reiterate those expectations as necessary. One of the many reasons for doing this is that consultees sometimes have hidden agendas. For example, the teacher who expressed a desire for help in coping with a misbehaving student may also harbor a desire to punish that student. Another reason for assessing the consulting relationship periodically is that consultees sometimes misunderstand or misinterpret initial explanations. For example, in cases where consultants perceive their roles as mediators and the consultees expect arbitration, the consultees may be disappointed that the consultants do not dictate a solution.

Agreeing to Consult, Defining the Problem, and Exploring Possible Solutions.

At some point in the identifying and clarifying process, a decision to consult must be made. Assuming the decision is affirmative, the parties engage in further definition of the problem and exploration of possible solutions. Basic challenging skills (e.g., information sharing, immediacy, confrontation) and the basic counseling competencies will be as useful at this time as they are in counseling relationships. This step in the consulting relationship is similar to identifying alternative response options in the decision-making counseling strategy presented in chapter 9. Consultants and consultees can brainstorm hypotheses about the problem and possible solutions. This is especially appropriate when counselors are using the initiation and collaboration consulting modes. In brainstorming, the idea is to identify as many solutions or hypotheses as possible without engaging in analyses of the ideas—a follow-up task. In the prescription mode, consultants explain the details of their treatment plans and brainstorm or negotiate who will implement them. In the provision and mediation

The consultant works with consultees to identify strategies that can be employed.

modes, consultants may either brainstorm ideas about possible strategies or inform consultees about what they will do as they carry out their consulting services.

Exploring solutions leads to evaluating alternatives once they have been identified. Osterweil (1987) recommended using reasonability, workability, and motivation as criteria for evaluating potential solutions. Additional information about problem antecedents, consequences, and participant responses may be required before conclusions can be made and may require research by consultants and consultees (Umansky & Holloway, 1984). One important skill in this instance is to observe clients in natural settings unobtrusively and concurrently collect relevant data. After that has been done, the stage is set for establishing goals.

Recall again the case of the parents who desire more success for their child in school. After finding out the parents' goals, the counselor suggests that the goals be considered tentative until there is an opportunity to collect baseline data about how well the child is currently doing in school. An important means of collecting data will be for the counselor (consultant) to observe the child in classroom settings and/or to ask the child's teacher to provide information based on observations. Observations are supplemented by data from standardized tests and performance on tasks and assignments in the classroom. After data are collected, the parents and counselor meet to continue solidifying goals and determining constructive action strategies.

Mutually Setting Goals With Consultees

As it is in counseling, goal setting is the heart of consulting because consulting, like counseling, is a participatory helping relationship. Counselors as consultants help consultees find a sense of direction and share the responsibility of achieving their own goals. The same counseling skills that are important for goal setting in counseling relationships remain important in consulting relationships. Helping consultees set goals focuses their attention on acting constructively, involves them in the helping process either directly or indirectly, makes them aware of what needs to be accomplished, encourages them to act on their own behalf or on behalf of their student clients, and informs them that school counselors are capable partners in the consulting process.

For example, the counselor and the parents in the continuing hypothetical case, after having perused the data from observations and records, decide that two goals will suffice for the time being. They will remain open to reviewing the goals, revising them, and possibly changing them. The two goals are to convince the child's teacher to help by employing some strategies designed to keep the child on task when attention deficits occur and to have the parents set aside time each evening to discuss schoolwork with the child and to provide encouragement and, if necessary, appropriate assistance. The counselor agrees to approach the teacher, seek cooperation, and provide instruction. The counselor also helps the parents carefully define and, if necessary, rehearse their interactions with their child. Systems for monitoring the child's progress are determined, and a plan for meeting again to discuss the case is established.

Basic Action Strategies for School Counselor Consulting

As discussed in chapter 9, counselors can choose among numerous strategies to achieve consulting goals. Therefore, the strategies presented here are those that seem most appropriate for school counselors in the majority of their consulting cases. Additions may occur with experience and in response to the peculiarities of one's professional setting.

Basic Strategies for Reaching Consulting Goals. Most action strategies important for achieving counseling goals, presented in chapter 9, are also important in achieving consulting goals. Settings and applications may differ, but the importance of the skills remains constant. The empathy and support counseling strategy will prove useful in all consulting modes because of the importance of the basic counseling skills throughout the consulting process.

In all five consulting modes, consultees may need help with making decisions. Consequently, decision-making counseling is another action stage strategy applicable to both counseling and consulting services. All the modes may also be approached via the brief counseling model. Other basic counseling service action strategies vary in their applicability to the five consulting modes. All the strategies seem applicable in the provision mode. Table 11.1 provides a summary of this discussion.

Assertiveness, group, and crisis counseling seem applicable only in the provision mode, whereas counseling for rational thinking seems applicable in both the provision and the mediation modes. Competence enhancement counseling seems applicable in the prescription, provision, initiation, and collaboration modes. Self-management and nonverbal counseling seem appropriate for the prescription, provision, initiation, and collaboration modes. The foregoing categorizations are logical but arbitrary, and it may be that the applications are broader or more limited than indicated here. Much depends on the individual counselor providing the consulting. The most important theme is that the basic action strategies are applicable to both counseling and consulting services.

Table 11.1
Applicability of counseling strategies to consultation modes.

Counseling Strategies	Consultation Modes				
	Prescription	Provision	Initiation	Collaboration	Mediation
Empathy and support	Yes	Yes	Yes	Yes	Yes
Decision making	Yes	Yes	Yes	Yes	Yes
Brief counseling	Yes				
Competence enhancement	Yes	Yes	Yes	Yes	
Self-management	Yes	Yes	Yes	Yes	
Nonverbal	Yes	Yes	Yes	Yes	
Rational thinking		Yes			Yes
Assertiveness		Yes			
Group		Yes			
Crisis		Yes			

Consulting to Enhance Child and Adolescent Development.   In the prescription, initiation, and collaboration modes, school counselors may find themselves trying to help consultees understand and use knowledge about human development to intervene appropriately. Parents, teachers, and administrators are sometimes at a loss to match expectations with maturational differences. Counselors who are knowledgeable about developmental expectations at various age levels and about individual differences within all age levels are in a position to help colleagues and parents understand the behaviors of their students and children more intelligently and make decisions about whether to respond accordingly. When the decision to respond is made in consultation with counselors, helpful interventions can be developed. The key assumption here is that school counselors who offer consultation to enhance child and adolescent development are indeed knowledgeable about the topic. The hypothetical case running throughout this chapter of the parents who want to help their child become more successful in school is an example of child development consulting.

Consulting With Teachers to Enhance Classroom Management.   It is not unusual for counselors working in the prescription, initiation, or collaboration consulting modes to be assisting with management of student classroom behaviors, especially at the elementary and perhaps middle school levels. In these cases, specific undesirable behaviors such as acting out, aggressiveness, and withdrawal can be targeted through teacher/consultee reports and consultant observations. Counselors can introduce teacher/consultees to the importance of recognizing and collecting baseline data to have benchmarks about the presenting behaviors against which efforts to induce changes can be compared.

In general, classroom management consulting involves implementing behavior modification principles. Therefore, counselors responding to requests for such consultation are challenged to be versed in these basic principles. The principles are summarized in the following list and can be shared with teacher/consultees:

- Behavior is learned when it is reinforced consistently.
- Specific behaviors that require acceleration or deceleration can be identified and the child's strengths emphasized.
- When engaging in behavior modification activities, small gains are to be anticipated initially.
- Consequences of behavior must be meaningful to the student.
- Consequences, rewards, or punishments are more meaningful if they follow the behavior immediately.
- Reinforcement may be physical or social.
- Purposes and goals should be clear.
- The target behavior should be the best one for the particular student.
- The aim of behavior control should be self-control. (Center for Studies of Child and Family Mental Health Principles, cited in Keat, 1974, p. 165)

These principles are applied to changing targeted behaviors. To help teacher/consultees achieve desired behavior changes, counselors may select from among several available behavior modification strategies. The most applicable strategies are response differentiation, fading, shaping, chaining, token systems, contingency management, and time-out procedures. Finally, counselors help teacher/consultees keep sufficient records for evaluating progress toward achieving desired objectives. (Evaluation involves assessment skills, a topic covered more comprehensively in chapter 12.) That part of the hypothetical case in this chapter in which the teacher is being asked to enhance the student client's on-task behavior in class is an example of classroom management consultation. For instance, one strategy the teacher may use is shaping (e.g., gently reminding the student to pay attention to the desired task when off task, reinforcing on-task behavior with praise when noticed, generally paying attention to on and off-task behavior).

Consulting With Individuals to Enhance Their Understanding of Schools as Organizations.

Schools operate according to organizational principles. Sometimes this is manifested pathologically, or individual applications of and responses to these principles are pathological. Similar circumstances occur in organizations outside the school, and the effects may be manifested in the school. Organizational pathologies and pathological responses to organizations may lead to situations in which counselors engage in prescription, initiation, or collaboration consulting services. For example, students, parents, or teachers need assistance determining how to respond to school regulations they perceive as being repressive or unreasonable, such as dress codes and tardiness criteria. As with classroom management consulting, this form of consultation often takes the form of sharing knowledge with consultees that will empower them to behave more effectively.

To be effective at helping individuals in this way, it behooves counselors to understand the schools as organizations. Examples of information that may help counselors in this role are knowing how well educated staff members are and how liberal or conservative they are regarding new ideas and innovations. Better educated and secure professionals are more open to innovations (Brown et al., 1979). It is also useful to know whether the school's decision-making structure is centralized or decentralized because centralized power tends to retard innovation, whereas distribution of decision making among groups seems to encourage it. It follows that counselors who are familiar with the balance of power in the school system are more likely to know how to influence it positively. Identifying the most influential stakeholders inside and outside the organization helps a counselor understand the sources of authority and influence. All others have little or no authority or influence unless they find ways to influence the decision makers (Haettenschwiller, 1970). Under these circumstances, most counselors, teachers, and students find that diplomacy and subtlety are the best avenues to effect influence.

In summary, counselors engaging in organizational consultation help consultees translate noble dreams into achievable goals that will increase the probability of success and decrease the probability of failure and abandonment (Ponzo, 1974). Acting as consultants, counselors can help consultees understand how the system works and establish action plans that seem to have the best chances of succeeding. At times, consulting counselors are proactive and serve as advocates for their consultees (e.g., representing student consultees or joining them in meetings with administrators). At other times, the assistance will be indirect (e.g., preparing student consultees for meetings with administrators through structured behavior rehearsals). Of course, the prospect of redesigning the strategy for additional follow-up efforts is necessary because no plan can be a guaranteed success. An understanding of the organization also helps counselors when offering consultation through in-service programs and when helping colleagues plan curriculum programs. A hypothetical example of organizational consultation follows:

> In a high school setting, the administration (principal and assistants) arbitrarily dictated a student dress code to which some have strong objections. Several students ask to meet with a counselor to air their complaints about the new code and to ask for help. The counselor believes that the administrators have the right to determine policies; she also thinks that the students seem to have some legitimate complaints about the code. These beliefs lead to the counselor offering to serve as a consultant (collaborative mode) to the students to help them try to achieve their goals. Initially, the counselor helps the students identify and clarify their position and the affect associated with it. Next, using knowledge of the school as a system, the counselor helps the students devise a strategy that demonstrates respect for the office of the principal, awareness of the lines of authority in the school system, and conformity with their goals. Having agreed on a strategy, the counselor helps the students prepare to implement it and develops a follow-up strategy for dealing with the range of possible responses from the school's administrators. For example, the counselor may help the students prepare to deliver to the principal an inventory of their objections to the dress code in a manner that is respectful, yet appropriately assertive, after advising them on behaviors that seem to have the best potential for success. Follow-up activities will depend on the administration's response. Whether the administrators are conciliatory and willing to negotiate or steadfast in defending their position, the counselor remains available to consult with the students about the process, outcomes, and appropriate next steps.

Consulting to Achieve Successful Mediation.   In the mediation mode, counselors respond directly to requests from two or more consultees to facilitate a mutual agreement or reconciliation. For example, two students who have been feuding and fighting over issues they are unable to resolve agree to meet with a counselor to work out an amicable settlement. Initially, the consultees must understand the assumptions on which mediation is founded: The mediator is not expected to dictate a resolution, the consultees agree to declare a truce during mediation, the mediator facilitates communications between the disputing parties, the disputing parties listen to each other's views, the disputing parties agree that their goal is to achieve a mutually agreeable resolution, and mediation is completed successfully when the disputing parties achieve a mutually agreeable solution.

Counselors who understand and accept the assumptions on which mediation is founded will be quite capable of serving as mediation consultants. The basic counseling and influencing skills coupled with knowledge about interpersonal communications are the requisite skills for mediation consultation. Beyond that, counselors can draw on experience, previous formal knowledge, and familiarity with the schools to help mediation consultees. The following example introduces the use of mediation as a consulting strategy in conflict resolution. In a hypothetical case of conflict resolution, the counselor acts as a mediator in a student–teacher dispute with cultural diversity overtones:

The participants in the simulation are an African American male counselor (the consultant), a European American female teacher (the consultee), and a 13-year-old African American female student (the client). Their middle school is located in a middle-class

The mediator facilitates communications between disputing parties.

area of a predominantly European American community. The student is a client of the counselor's whom he has counseled previously regarding school adjustment and academic performance. One class (English) that has been discussed in their counseling sessions is taught by the consultee, and the student has mentioned disliking the teacher as a reason for not performing well in the class, without specifically elaborating on reasons. After about 40% of the school year passes, the teacher approaches the counselor for consultation about getting the student, who appears to be stubbornly refusing to complete assignments, to complete her schoolwork. The consultation relationship opens in the collaboration mode.

Counselor (consultant)–teacher (consultee) discussions lead to defining the problem as student stubbornness, and they agree that the first step is that the counselor meet with the student to share the teacher's concern and position and try to determine whether the student can be persuaded to do her schoolwork. Before proceeding, the counselor makes sure that both the student and the teacher know of his previous relationships with each of them to avoid complications associated with having dual professional relationships (Dougherty, 1992). During the interview with the counselor, the student refuses to do any more homework than she is doing because she is passing the course; she also accuses the teacher of being racist, without providing specific examples of racist behaviors.

The counselor suggests a meeting between the student and the teacher, with him present to serve as a mediator. They agree, although the student is not very hopeful in her comments when doing so. The counselor, as a consultant, has introduced the mediation mode. During the meeting, both the student and the teacher, despite the counselor's best efforts to explain how mediation works, behave as if the purpose of the meeting is to have the counselor take their side against the adversary. The student openly accuses the teacher of being a racist and refuses to change her study behaviors, again citing her impression that she is passing. The teacher, while recognizing that the student is passing, tries to point out the folly of the student's actions and encourages her to try harder. Surprised by the accusation of racism, she denies it and defends herself as anything but a racist while also saying things that indicate her potential cultural insensitivity. The counselor, acting as a mediator, lets the interactions occur while trying to help both parties clarify their positions and understand each other's. In addition, the counselor attempts to keep the parties focused on trying to resolve the conflict.

Within a week, the counselor, who believes that the mediation session went quite badly, checks with the teacher and the student to find out how things are progressing. To his surprise, he learns from the teacher that the student is turning in assignments and is not behaving belligerently in class. He learns from the student that the teacher's attitude has changed and is more acceptable. There are several possible explanations for why the conflict seems to be resolved. Perhaps the most important observation is that the counselor, using his mediation skills, provided an atmosphere in which the adversaries could find ways to communicate what worked best for them.

Responding to Consultee Reluctance and Resistance.

When attempting to initiate consulting, counselors may encounter reluctance from prospective consultees. The same competencies used for coping with reluctance when initiating counseling relationships are important when initiating consulting relationships. Because prescription, provision, collaboration, and mediation consulting relationships are usually initiated by consultees, resistance is more common than reluctance in consulting relationships.

Resistance to consulting is similar to resistance to counseling. Therefore, the requisite competencies are similar. As with counseling, consulting relationships have such variables as individual personalities, different settings, and previous experiences that influence the counselor's responses to resistance and whether those responses work. In summary, when consulting, counselors may encounter reluctance and resistance just as they do when counseling, and the repertoire of possible responses is the same.

Closing Consulting Relationships. The similarity between counseling and consulting relationships includes the closing phase. The same competencies are important in both. Evaluating consulting relationships is as important as evaluating responsive counseling interventions and proactive prevention programming. Readers are referred to the Evaluating Individual and Group Counseling section of chapter 9, in which a strategy for evaluating counseling interventions is presented. We believe the same strategy can be applied to consulting interventions.

EXAMPLES OF CONSULTING IN SCHOOL COUNSELING

Planned Periodic Consulting in an Elementary School Setting

This example and those that follow are paraphrased from reports about consultation activities of school counselors that appeared in the professional literature or are derived from the professional experience of the authors. In the first example, Fall (1995) described a *periodic planned consultation* idea between school counselors and teachers. With the knowledge and support of the principal, the counselor schedules 1-hour meetings every 10 weeks (three times a year) with each teacher to whom the counselor is responsible. Each consultation meeting may have its own topics. For example, determining the accuracy of student placement, assessing whether students' needs are being met, and asking how well the entire classroom is functioning may be topics for the first meeting.

Fall (1995) recommended a set of five steps that may be followed in each planned consultation. In the first step, the counselor observes the classroom for 30 minutes prior to the consultation meeting. Goals of the observation are acquiring background for understanding concerns the teacher may have; identifying classroom and teacher strengths; and noticing student behavior, particularly potential problem behaviors (e.g., appear withdrawn and unfocused). The second step consists of beginning the consultation session with positive comments from the observation step (e.g., "Your class worked well in groups. I was impressed by the way you let the students express themselves."). The goal of this interaction is to pave the way for accurate, nondefensive communication by being nonjudgmental and respectful.

During the third step, the counselor (consultant) employs reflective listening skills while the teacher is invited to share information about the entire classroom and specific students, including problems. This is followed by the counselor helping the teacher explore possible solutions. An excerpt from a hypothetical interaction follows:

Counselor:	It sounds like Ivy's behaviors are distracting the class and keeping her from being successful academically.
Teacher:	Some days are better than others. Mondays seem to be the worst.
Counselor:	That may be important. How does she do in subject areas?
Teacher:	She's OK when she pays attention. I've tried many things, and nothing seems to work unless I keep on her. I don't have time to do that.
Counselor:	Unquestionably, this has exasperated you. It appears as if attention from you works.
Teacher:	I hadn't thought of that, but I think you're right. (Fall, 1995)

The fourth step consists of exploring possible interventions for identified problems. Fall (1995) recommended doing this jointly, similar to the mutual counselor–consultee interaction presented in the collaboration mode described previously in this chapter. This approach increases potential for identifying a host of possible solutions and for creating a good working alliance between the counselor (consultant) and teacher (consultee). The fifth step finds the counselor summing up what has been accomplished and making plans, jointly with the teacher, to follow up on plans for action that have been generated.

Gang Mediation in a Middle School

Tabish and Orell (1996) described a middle school gang intervention program for which the goal is to allow gang-involved youths to confront issues with rivals in a safe area where respect is maintained. To achieve this goal, Washington Middle School in Albuquerque, New Mexico, initiated peer and formal mediation in 1990. Peer mediation is for two rival gang members; formal mediation is for two or more rival gangs. Trained student mediators provide the peer mediation. The school's gang interventionist or selected outside mediators perform the formal mediations between rival gangs. An overview of the formal mediation process is provided:

Initially, the interventionist meets with the rival gangs in a small assembly to explain the purpose, roles, and process. Participation is voluntary; however, it should be noted that the school's administration has made it known that negative gang behaviors will not be tolerated in the school. Each gang selects two representatives and an alternate to negotiate on their behalf. One to 3 hours per day for 3 to 5 days are devoted to the process. They meet in a room selected to provide a formal, serious atmosphere. The following rules are posted in the room: All parties must (a) try to solve the problem; (b) refrain from name calling and putting others down, (c) show respect by not interrupting each other; (d) be honest; (e) avoid using weapons, threats, and intimidating behaviors; and (f) maintain confidentiality. There is an agenda, and a list of gang members is distributed. The formalities are seen as indicating to the participants that the atmosphere is mature and serious. The mediation process itself is a form of social modeling that will help the participants generalize the process to other problems.

The process consists of four meetings. The introductory events just described occur during the first meeting. Establishing an atmosphere of mutual trust and understanding while allowing all parties to share their feelings and views is the focus of the second meeting. Witnesses may be called in to clarify the problem. Solutions to the problem are identified during the third meeting, using a brainstorming approach. Adjournment occurs only after an agreement is reached by all parties. The fourth meeting is devoted to reviewing and confirming the agreement. Follow-up meetings with representatives of both gangs in attendance or with each gang separately are held to evaluate the agreement and acquire signatures missed earlier.

The preceding information describes mediation provided by a trained professional consultant who could be a school counselor using the collaborative mode. An atmosphere of respect for each student was promoted.

Supervising Peer Counselors in a Secondary School Setting

A high school counselor trained student volunteers to help their peers meet with the peer counselors on a regular basis to provide them with support and supervision. The following scenario represents a hypothetical supervisory relationship. The counselor supervisor is the consultant, the student peer counselor is the consultee, and the students whom she is helping are the clients:

The counselor-supervisor opens a supervision meeting with an open-ended question or open invitation to the peer counselor to share whatever concerns her most. The peer counselor describes the circumstances of a case that are particularly challenging for her. The client is a student who sought out the peer counselor for help because she is failing her mathematics course, having relationship problems with a boyfriend, and experiencing pressure from her parents about her schoolwork and the relationship. She believes that her parents have unrealistic academic expectations and should not try to influence her choice of boyfriends.

After helping the peer counselor tell her story and clarify the facts, the counselor consultant invites her to share her feelings about the case. The peer counselor wonders aloud whether she is competent enough to deal with the issues the student client has presented. The counselor/consultant agrees that this may be a genuine concern and asks the peer helper what options she has considered, offering to help brainstorm them (collaboration mode). The brainstorming session leads the counselor/supervisor (consultant) to conclude that the peer helper (consultee) may be able to help the student client in some ways but is not the appropriate person to respond to all the issues that were presented. The supervisor-consultant then offers suggestions for the peer helper to consider (initiation mode).

The consultant offers the following recommendations for the consultee to consider (prescription mode): (a) Meet with the student client again and ask whether she is interested in receiving tutoring for her mathematics difficulties. If she is, the peer helper can then make the necessary arrangements for her to receive that help. (b) Inform the student client that she (the peer counselor) discussed the case with the consultant/supervisor, who, in turn, recommends that the student client see one of the school's professional counselors about the relationship and parental issues, indicating that the counselor/supervisor is willing to receive the referral. Following discussion of the merits of the recommendations, the peer counselor agrees to the plan. After attempting to carry out the agreed-on strategy, the consultee will report what transpired with the student client to the supervisor/consultant, and together they will determine what to do next.

The hypothetical consulting relationship transpired across the five stages described earlier in the chapter, and the consultant used several consulting modes in the process. Switching modes is not uncommon. As presented herein, the modes are primarily means of classifying, studying, and understanding different ways to engage in consultation.

Solution-Focused School Consultation

Kahn (2000) used a middle school setting to provide an example of solution-focused school consultation. Kahn emphasized that school counselors (consultants) should help consultees (e.g., teachers or parents) to set goals that they can control rather than assessing their success in terms of student client change. Kahn's approach is for the school counselor as consultant to begin with an orientation to solution-focused consulting and help the consultee to identify strengths and resources and set initial goals. In a case illustration, the school counselor (consultant) begins with an invitation to the teacher (consultee) to share what she hoped to accomplish in the first consulting session. The teacher reveals her frustration with a literature/language class. The counselor's response focuses on the teacher's recent accomplishments (e.g., started an afterschool study hall and tailored her curriculum to students). After the teacher remembers that she has experienced success, the counselor restates the problem positively ("Let's see what we can do to help you feel like you are staying afloat"; p. 252). The counselor follows with a request for a survey of what has been happening in the teacher's class.

The teacher then describes a class out of her control and a specific student who takes over the class, sabotaging her lesson plans. The (counselor) consultant briefly responds by asking how the teacher will know when things are better for the troublesome student. When the teacher responds, the counselor attempts to help her be specific and use concrete terms (i.e., "When he's tuned in" becomes "He wouldn't disrupt my class"; Kahn, 2000, p. 252). Next, the counselor asks the teacher how she will feel when the student is "tuned in." The teacher lists several positive outcomes. At this point, the goals have been established.

Having established goals early in the consultation process, the counselor proceeds to seek solutions that will be acceptable to the consultee. The process begins with the counselor helping the teacher remember occasions when the troublesome student was not troublesome. This is followed by an analysis of the circumstances that led to his not being troublesome (e.g., "shorten his task . . . ask him what he needs during breaks between tasks"; Kahn, 2000, p. 252). The counselor then asks: "What do you need to do to make it happen again?" (p. 253). When the teacher states that she should reinitiate the procedures that once worked, the counselor/consultant gives her immediate positive verbal reinforcement. The counselor then recommends that the teacher evaluate the effects of her efforts ("So, if Jon is a four this week, what will have to happen for him to be a five by our next meeting?"; p. 253 [principle: incremental changes will cause a rippling effect]). The counselor closes the session by recommending that the teacher think about how she can react differently to the troublesome student and perhaps change their relationship before the next consultation session.

Kahn (2000) stressed that the solution-focused approach can be conducted in one or a few sessions, focuses on the future, uses the consultee's strengths as resources, and is collaborative in nature. The primary steps in the process, as just demonstrated, are (a) perform initial structuring, (b) establish goals for consultation, (c) examine previously attempted solutions and exceptions, (d) help the consultee find a solution, and (e) summarize goals and praise the consultant for past successes. As presented, the model seems user friendly for school counselors as consultants and their consultees.

CONSULTATION: A NATURAL FUNCTION FOR SCHOOL COUNSELORS

Consulting is a widely accepted counseling function. It is not as clearly understood as responsive counseling interventions and proactive prevention programming and varies across settings. Natural circumstances in the schools provide school counselors with a relatively specific consultation role that can manifest itself in several modes. Many students, teachers, administrators, and parents view counselors as being in a relatively neutral position in the schools and as possessing competencies that can be shared in consulting relationships. Therefore, being available for, and sought out by, others for consultation assistance is a natural function for school counselors. They are strategically located in the schools as people who might be trusted to serve as consultants via the various consulting modes introduced in this chapter. School counselors who recognize the interrelationships between consulting and other important school counseling functions can appreciate the unique qualities of consultation activities and recognize opportunities to consult in an organized fashion.

FEATURED ACTIVITY: GRADUATE STUDENT PERSPECTIVES ON CONSULTATION IN SCHOOL COUNSELING

In this chapter, we discuss consultation in school counseling. One of our new graduate students told us that she became interested in school counseling because of the changes that occurred in her childhood family after a school counselor consulted with her stepfather. Her stepfather apparently had no idea how to overcome the animosity he was creating as part of his new family; the counselor worked with him to improve his interactions at home, particularly with the new children he was trying to parent.

How do counselors make a difference in their roles as consultants? How can counselors improve their effectiveness as consultants? Tell us what you think.

After you read this chapter, go to http://www.genesislight.com/scan21st/tell_us/consultation.html and complete the form. With your permission, we will periodically post some of your creative thinking for the world to read.

OTHER SUGGESTED ACTIVITIES

1. Debate the position taken in this chapter that school settings naturally determine the parameters of consulting for school counselors.
2. Take an inventory of the competencies taught in your core counseling methods course that are applicable to consulting.

3. Review the five consulting modes presented in this chapter; determine which ones you would be comfortable providing and which do not appeal to you.
4. Analyze, discuss, and/or debate the following statement: "Courses in school counselor training programs devoted only to consultation are unnecessary because there is so much in common between counseling and consulting."
5. List ways that consulting assignments can be incorporated into your field internship or practicum.
6. Debate the merits of the basic consulting action strategies mentioned in this chapter. Which ones seem appropriate to you and which do not? What are the reasons for your decisions?
7. Analyze the conflict resolution mediation consulting simulation (the simulation in which a female student believed that her teacher was a racist) in this chapter from the perspective of critiquing the (counselor) consultant's actions and trying to hypothesize possible explanations for the outcomes.
8. After having read the Examples of Consulting in School Counseling section, what new thoughts about consultation occurred to you?
9. Discuss or debate how the modes and stages of consultation presented in this chapter fit into a multicultural perspective of helping diverse consultees and clients with varied worldviews. Are they sufficient, or do they need to be altered in some way?
10. Go to the SCAN Web site (www.scan21st.com) and explain how this site might assist school counselors in their consulting roles.

CHAPTER 12

Assessment in School Counseling

Goals: To describe the strategic role of counselors in the total assessment services of the schools. To identify basic competencies for fulfilling associated responsibilities.

We recently had an opportunity to hear a school counselor voice a concern expressed frequently in schools:

> *I have little time to do what I really need to do to help students with all the other things going on in their lives. The emphasis on testing has also created new problems for kids. I spend many hours visiting with parents who are concerned about whether their children will pass the required tests at the end of the year. The children also worry. I can*

hardly believe how many cases of test anxiety I handle. Children feel as if their lives will be total failures if they don't make a passing mark on end-of-grade tests.

Sometimes the problem seems especially complicated. I recently listened to Brett, a kindergartner, crying about his older sister, a fourth grader. His sister, Rhonda, was told (by her stepfather) that she could not go along on the family summer vacation unless she passed her end-of-grade reading test. Brett didn't care whether Rhonda passed the test; he just wanted her along on the family vacation. Brett said that he wanted his stepfather to stay at home during the summer vacation—not Rhonda.

I am at a loss to know how to handle all of this. What can I do?

School counselors have always been concerned about their role in testing. The profession has seen a lively debate over the years about this very matter. This chapter addresses some of the many issues school counselors face as they consider their roles in testing and assessment.

DEMAND FOR ASSESSMENT IN SCHOOL COUNSELING

The term *assessment* is used here instead of the more traditional term *testing* because the scope of these activities has now expanded from the exclusive use of standardized tests to the inclusion of nonstandardized methods. Therefore, *assessment* more accurately represents the comprehensive nature of the activities. Assessment activities are a wide range of strategies, including standardized testing, used to gather information about students that is useful in individual and institutional decision making.

Historical Roots

The demand for assessment in school counseling is wrapped up in the history of standardized testing and the demand for testing in society and in education. Scholarly activities by psychologists in Western Europe and later in the United States during the late 19th and early 20th centuries led to the development of efforts to assess individual differences and, in so doing, to employ methods that were scientifically rigorous (orderly, accurate, and reproducible). The work was conducted in laboratories and universities by such individuals as Wilhelm Wundt, Sir Francis Galton, James T. Cattell, Edward L. Thorndike, and Charles Spearman, all of whom eventually became recognized as pioneers of the testing and assessment movement (Linden & Linden, 1968).

Primarily a scholarly enterprise conducted without much fanfare and with only limited applications, standardized assessment received a major boost in popularity during World War I when a committee of scholars developed group tests of intelligence, known as Army Alpha and Beta, to help the military determine which recruits were fit for service. In the period following World War I, scholarly assessment ideas were applied on a much larger scale, and testing became a business. Several factors were at work: massive immigration to the United States at the turn of the century, industrialization and urbanization of what had been primarily a rural society, and legislation to protect children from industrial usury and to enhance their educational opportunities, which led to a changing educational philosophy—away from exclusivity and toward mass education.

Becoming a Big Business

The growth in the number of children attending school and the need to assimilate immigrants into American society created an environment where standardized assessment flourished. The availability of tests that could be administered to groups of schoolchildren and that could provide information about individual differences, as well as individual and group achievement, helped make standardized testing a big business. Test results were used primarily for institutional decision making, such as for classifying students into instructional tracks and for comparing the academic achievement of a particular school's students with achievements from national samples. These purposes for using standardized tests in the schools became traditional uses that are as important now as they were a century ago, helping make such testing a multimillion-dollar business.

Concurrently, vocational guidance professionals, influenced by the publication of Parsons's book *Choosing a Vocation* (1909), were able to use standardized tests as one source of dependable information for individuals attempting to make occupational choices. As noted in chapter 2, the influence of vocational guidance on the schools was minimal at that time. The psychological testing movement eventually led to tests being used as important school guidance tools, primarily for trying to predict academic and occupational success. By the late 1930s, test scores, particularly from aptitude tests and interest inventories, had become a major component of vocational guidance in the schools, and prediction of future performance in education or work was the primary purpose for using them.

Becoming Identified With the School's Testing Programs

The demand for standardized tests was further enhanced by the NDEA of 1958. The NDEA influenced the growth of school counseling significantly by drawing attention to the need for effective guidance of students who are gifted and talented, and by infusing large sums of money into the schools in an effort to improve guidance and instruction. One outcome was an increase in the purchase and use of standardized tests in the schools. School districts received federal funds to buy tests to identify students who are gifted. Another outcome was to highlight the importance of assessment as a school counseling function. Traditional uses of standardized tests to make institutional placement and curriculum decisions continued, and school counselors found that they had become associated with the schools' testing programs. Consequently, it was common for school counselors to use tests in guidance and counseling, as well as to participate in and direct programs designed to gather information for placing, tracking, and monitoring the performance of local students on achievement tests. This occurred particularly often in elementary schools, where counselors were often assigned responsibility for coordinating testing services. In addition, counselors had become responsible for arranging students' access to entrance testing for postsecondary education and to placement testing for transitions from school to work. In the minds of many administrators and classroom teachers, school counseling and testing became synonymous.

In the years after the popularization of standardized assessment, widespread use led to abuses and to concerns about inherent biases. Warnings and criticisms in scholarly writings and in popular publications led to technical improvements in tests and their accompanying explanatory materials, to the publication of standards for tests and testing applications, and to improvements in the training of users. Yet, the continued growth of applications and the increase in users were so great that further abuses were inevitable.

The Failed Marriage Metaphor

In the early 1970s, Goldman (1972) attracted the attention of counseling professionals and test publishers to this issue. Describing the relationship between tests and counseling as analogous to a failed marriage, Goldman suggested that most tests were developed for selection purposes and that, although useful for such institutional decisions in the military services, business and industry, and colleges and universities, they were of little use in one-to-one or small-group counseling because the predictive validity of the tests was too low. He also pointed out that the same tests were even less useful for disadvantaged populations, noting that most counselors lacked the skills needed to derive whatever limited value the tests do have to offer. He concluded with a recommendation for reducing the use of tests in counseling and for limiting test interpretations to highly qualified specialists.

Goldman's (1972) statements came amidst criticisms that were leveled at standardized testing and test corporations and that called for moratoriums on testing. These criticisms included allegations of racial and gender bias in the tests, invasion of privacy by the testing procedures, and declining performances on college entrance examinations. Spurred, in part, by these criticisms, as well as by improvements naturally generated by corporate competition and scholarly research, changes occurred. In the early 1980s, a group of scholars examining the years since Goldman's failed marriage analogy made the following observations:

- Counselors are increasingly privy to nonstandardized assessment instruments that emphasize process over outcomes (Zytowski, 1982).
- Publishers are producing standardized instruments accompanied by computer-generated counseling information, which changes the emphasis from using tests for predicting to using them as tools in a self-discovery/future potential exploratory process.
- Major problems are still associated with using standardized assessment instruments with disadvantaged populations (Goldman, 1982).

Survey data indicated a trend away from using maximum performance tests measuring achievement, intelligence, and aptitude, and toward using typical performance instruments measuring interests, attitudes, and personality attributes. This trend indicated a need for even greater counselor sophistication than was the case when Goldman leveled his criticism in the early 1970s (Zytowski & Warman, 1982). A concurrent survey indicated that testing was important in most schools and that career guidance was the primary purpose for using tests in counseling (Engen, Lamb, & Prediger, 1982).

In 1994, *Measurement and Evaluation in Counseling and Development* published another scholarly discussion of Goldman's (1972) marriage metaphor. Bradley (1994), Goldman (1994), Prediger (1994), and Zytowski (1994) agreed that the reductionistic scientific view of using a statistical regression model to make predictions from test scores, especially ability measures such as the SAT and the American College Test (ACT), was outdated. Both Prediger (1994) and Zytowski (1994) believed that a discriminant model in which membership or similarity to people in groups when blended or applied to estimates of one's potential is more useful and is the wave of the future for using tests in counseling. An example of this model is to use data from interest inventories such as the Strong Interest Inventory to indicate to clients how similar or dissimilar their expressed interests are when compared with those of successful, employed women and men representing several work categories or groups (e.g., teachers, psychologists, physicists). In the model, counselors will help individuals process the discriminant data in combination with self-assessments and other information about their abilities when making decisions about how to use the assessment data to understand themselves and to make plans for their lives. Goldman (1994) continued to believe that standardized tests have limited usefulness for counselors and that perhaps 10% possess the requisite skills and attitudes to use them properly. He believed the remaining 90% should use qualitative assessment techniques such as card sorts, simulations, and observations that require no statistical or psychometric sophistication.

Concerns About Cultural Sensitivity in Assessment

Additional comments were expressed by individuals possessing concerns about culturally sensitive assessment. For example, Facundo, Nuttal, and Walton (1994) pointed out that, in many cases, the people conducting cognitive, academic, personality, and social functioning assessments are of different national, ethnic, racial, or social class backgrounds from the children being assessed. Referring to this phenomenon as "cross-cultural assessment," Facundo et al., focusing primarily on the challenges of assessing Latino children, believed in what appears to be an eclectic, culturally sensitive approach that includes the following:

1. Establishing rapport with the families and making them feel comfortable in the school environment
2. Using assessment instruments that are appropriate for the populations being served
3. Writing culturally sensitive assessment reports

Reporting on the RACE 2002 conference at Arizona State University, Arredondo and D'Andrea (2002) addressed the issue of whether current assessments are culturally informed. One presenter stated that, because the standardized testing industry will not self-destruct, cultural experts must voice their collective perspectives. Ideas presented at the RACE 2002 conference included (a) increasing the representation of minority groups in standardization studies, (b) developing and applying ethnic specific assessment processes, (c) using qualitative approaches and methods to learn more about the influence of cultural background and socialization processes on gaining access to educational and vocational opportunities and being successful, and

(d) approaching assessment from a culturally informed perspective. The tone and nature of the presentations indicate that cultural experts believe much improvement is needed to overcome the disadvantages such groups as African Americans and Latinos experience when taking many standardized tests. The cultural experts appear to know much more about what is wrong than what to do to correct it. Overcoming cultural biases in testing is among the greatest challenges we all face as educators and counselors.

Recent Information About How School Counselors Are Involved in Assessment

Giordano, Schwiebert, and Brotherton (1997) surveyed approximately 120 school counselors in Illinois and found that even though counselors reported believing in the usefulness of a wide range of assessment instruments (intelligence tests, personality inventories, substance abuse instruments, eating disorder inventories, depression assessments, achievement tests, and interest inventories), they actually tended to use a narrower range. The assessment instruments used most often were primarily achievement tests and interest inventories. The five highest ranked instruments according to use were the Wechsler Intelligence Scale for Children–Revised (WISC-R), Career Orientation Placement and Evaluation Survey/Career Abilities Placement Survey/Career Occupational Preference Survey (COPES/CAPS/COPS), SAT, Myers-Briggs Type Indicator, and Career Assessment Inventory. The WISC-R is usually administered for diagnostic purposes, such as placement in special education programs and identification of students who are gifted. Clinical, counseling, and school psychologists usually administer the tests. The SAT is administered at designated testing centers under the auspices of the College Board, and postsecondary education institutions use the scores for admissions decisions. The remaining three instruments are typical performance measures of personality types and interests used to help middle and secondary school students learn more about themselves in the career guidance and counseling process (i.e., a self-discovery process).

Ekstrom, Elmore, Schafer, Trotter, and Webster (2004) reported findings from a survey of a random sample of 179 ASCA members who indicated they were school counselors. This survey focused on a list of 39 assessment activities in which they might engage. The following activities were selected as those in which 80% or more of the respondents engaged: (a) referring students to other professionals for additional testing when appropriate (98%); (b) interpreting scores from tests/assessments and using the information in counseling (91%); (c) reading about and being aware of ethical issues in assessment (86%); (d) reading about and being aware of current issues involving multicultural assessment, the assessment of students with disabilities, and the assessment of language minorities (84%); (e) synthesizing and integrating test and nontest data to make decisions about individuals (84%); (f) reading a variety of professional literature on topics such as the use of testing and assessment in school counseling and career counseling research (84%); (g) communicating and interpreting test/assessment information to parents (81%); (h) communicating and interpreting test/assessment information to teachers, school administrators, and other professionals (80%); and (i) helping teachers use assessments and assessment information (80%).

Our first impression was that these data indicated that the school counselors in this sample were engaging in legitimate testing/assessment activities for which they should have been trained and that we believe fall within the assessment role for school counselors. However, there was a host of other legitimate activities in which smaller numbers of counselors indicated they participated. So, the cup is half full and half empty. Ekstrom et al. (2004) concluded that many schools may not be using their school counselors' expertise and training effectively. Thus, they highlighted the need for school counselors to enhance their competencies through professional development opportunities.

Blacher, Murray-Ward, and Ullendahl (2005) reported survey findings based in part on questions similar to those asked in the Giordano et al. (1997) survey. That is, they inquired about how often the respondents used standardized assessment techniques. In addition, they inquired about frequency of using nonstandardized assessment techniques and about how adequate the assessment training was perceived to be. Respondents were 203 members of the California School Counselor Association. About 50% were secondary school counselors, 30% in middle schools, 14% in elementary schools, and 6% not designated.

The techniques reported as being used most often were observation of students and structured student interviews, both of which are nonstandardized techniques. Blacher et al. (2005) did not find this surprising because many components of the training of school counselors focus on acquisition of these skills. The researchers wondered why the respondents were "so infrequently engaged in career assessments, made little use of teacher- or counselor-completed rating scales, were rarely involved in their school's assessment program logistics, and utilized few career, academic, achievement, and social skill resources" (p. 341). Concern about relatively low ratings of the respondents' preparation for assessment was also expressed. Clearly, many of the respondents in this study did not feel more than adequately trained and did not engage in many of the assessment functions on which traditional assessment training is focused.

School Counselors and High-Stakes Testing

President Bush's No Child Left Behind initiative includes yearly achievement testing, a feature that places increased emphasis on the use of standardized tests for educational accountability purposes. Hayes (2001) reported that the instruments are selected by states and local school districts, and standards are supposed to be flexible enough for current state standards to be acceptable. The apparent early popularity of the initiative indicated that public confidence in standardized test data was as strong as or stronger than it was previously. Some have referred to this initiative as ushering in a "high-stakes" testing era (Hayes, 2001).

School counseling leaders and school counselors predicted that the brunt of the additional work required to implement the No Child Left Behind testing mandate in the schools would fall on school counselors. These school counseling representatives, as well as leaders in the Association for Assessment in Counseling and the testing industry, also pointed out how important it is for school counselors, teachers, and administrators to have appropriate levels of sophistication and skills to ensure that tests and test-generated data are used appropriately (Hayes, 2001).

School counselors are in a strategic position to promote responsible use of tests.

One example of the high-stakes testing phenomenon manifested by the No Child Left Behind testing mandate is the North Carolina ABCs of Public Education. As suggested previously, the emphasis is on "basics, high education standards, and local control of schools" (North Carolina Department of Public Instruction, 1999). The tests are administered to elementary, middle, and high school students and consist of end-of-grade reading, mathematics, and writing tests in grades 3 to 8 and end-of-course tests in some high schools. The tests are based on the state-mandated North Carolina Standard Course of Study curriculum, and schools are classified according to state test performances in categories ranging from schools of excellence to low-performing schools. The "stakes" involved in this testing program range from incentive bonuses for licensed staff members to failure to be promoted for students and loss of jobs for some school administrators.

From surveys completed by 282 North Carolina school counselors, Brown, Galassi, and Akos (2004) reported that

> Eighty percent or more of the respondents reported that they or another counselor served as the school's testing coordinator and that this function consumed a considerable percentage of their time. So, it appears as if the assumption by school administrators following the NDEA legislation 40 years ago that school counselors should be involved in all of the school's testing programs is still prominent in the mind of twenty-first century school administrators. Although the counselors noted some positive effects of the high-stakes testing program, they overwhelmingly reported that it negatively impacted their ability to provide services and their relationships with students, teachers, and administrators. (p. 31)

A surprising finding was that a very small percentage of the respondents recommended that their schools acquire a separate testing coordinator. One possible explanation is that there is a feeling of powerlessness—unable to influence the situation and therefore resigned to it. This led Brown et al. (2004) to recommend major advocacy efforts by state and national professional organizations.

An example of state advocacy for school counselors occurred in North Carolina in 2006, when the State Board of Education was in the process of revising the job description for school counselors and there was recommendation that test coordination be written into that description. The North Carolina School Counselor Association initiated an effort to have members contact the board to inform them about the folly of the testing coordinator proposal. The first author of this textbook responded to the call for advocacy with the following letter to selected members of the board (excerpts presented here):

> I understand that the Board of Education is in the process of updating the job description for school counselors in North Carolina and am encouraging you and your colleagues to ensure that the job description conforms with the Standards for Preparation of School Counselors prepared by the NC Department of Public Instruction in 2005. These are times when those of us who have responsibility as caretakers for the basic education process in North Carolina are challenged to be careful about how our decisions affect the students in our schools.
>
> The Standards for Preparation of School Counselors state: "The school counselor has primary responsibility for leadership in the development, implementation, and evaluation of a comprehensive school counseling program. Such a program consists of individual and group counseling, classroom/large group guidance, individual and group consultation, assessment, career development, collaboration and advocacy, program evaluation, preventive, remedial, and responsive services to address academic achievement, career development, and personal/social development of students."
>
> Therefore, it seems important for you and your colleagues to ensure that there are not components in the job description that appear to be detrimental to school counselor efforts to achieve these goals. In my opinion, establishing test coordination as a part of the school counselor's job description will be detrimental. This is an administrative function and will take too much of the counselor's time away from the functions they were trained to perform.
>
> I have observed that enlightened school systems assign the test coordinator responsibilities to assistant principals or others hired specifically for that function. Unfortunately, the school systems most likely to use their school counselors as testing coordinators are also the one's that can least afford to reduce the time that school counselors are available to meet the needs of students.

The revised job description did not include test coordination, making the advocacy efforts successful at that level. Of course, it remains to be seen if individual school administrators are influenced accordingly. When advocacy efforts are initiated, we think one important strategy is to point out discrepancies between what school counselors are trained to do via state or nationally mandated training program content and the assignments given to school counselors that are beyond the guidelines and that may also interfere with implementation of the mandated guidelines.

What Is the Appropriate Assessment Role for School Counselors?

Assessment remains an important school counseling function, and providing useful assessment services has become even more difficult. Whether school counselors are up to the challenge is unknown. Complicating matters further for counselors, the mid-1980s ushered in an era of general educational criticism and demands for reform, leading to recommendations for minimum competency tests not only for students graduating from high school but also for adults receiving teaching certificates or holding their teaching positions. Such recommendations implied a widespread belief that standardized tests can precisely identify competence and incompetence, indicating that the general public, politicians, and some educators were as naive as their predecessors in the 1920s.

Surrounded by a charged environment in which students, teachers, administrators, parents, and the general public expect much of but know little about formal and informal assessment tools, counselors walk a tightrope between understanding the limited data those instruments provide and helping individuals use those data successfully. Refusing to participate in the assessment services does not seem to be an option for most school counselors. In fact, many counselors are routinely drawn into performing noncounseling assessment services such as becoming testing coordinators in a high-stakes testing environment. If refusing to participate is not an option, helpful participation demands competence. Much is expected, less can probably be delivered, and school counselors are challenged to understand what they are doing to educate consumers about realistic expectations and to deliver services that meet reformulated expectations.

Positions Taken by the Best Currently Available School Counseling Paradigms

The ASCA National Model.   In the ASCA National Model (ASCA, 2005), appraisal (also known as assessment) is a process for which the goal is helping students carry out the individual planning process. Through data from a variety of assessment activities, students receive help in interpreting their abilities, interests, skills, and achievements (Gysbers & Henderson, 2001). In addition, Dahir (2001) stressed the importance of using measurable indicators to determine whether students experience achievement in academic, career, and personal-social development. In the first context, assessment is viewed as a process tool for helping students make informed decisions about their futures. In the second context, assessment is viewed as an accountability tool. A more detailed coverage of accountability is presented in chapter 4.

The Transforming School Counseling Initiative.   In the TSCI, school counselors are viewed as having a unique, strategic, schoolwide perspective that can be used to help students become successful academically. This perspective includes quantitative and qualitative data (e.g., students' cumulative files, reports about whole school and individual student academic successes and failures, student course placement information, course-taking patterns, teacher characteristics, parental contacts with the school, status of community resources). House and Hayes (2002) believed school counselors can use these data to promote and effect systematic change and teach students to help themselves (e.g., improved test taking, organizational, and study skills). House and Hayes appear to present assessment as a process for collecting data to be used by school counselors in a leadership role. We cover leadership more thoroughly in chapter 7.

The School–Community Collaboration Model.   The role of assessment in the School–Community Collaboration Model was not specifically mentioned in the material we read. However, we deduced that it was important in this model because the interconnected system for meeting the needs of all students presented in Adelman and Taylor (2002) includes an early identification and treatment component. Logic indicates that early identification and treatment require diagnostic data that would be derived from assessment processes. Thus, assessment is presented in a diagnostic light in this model—more about diagnostic assessment later in this chapter. We believe that Adelman and Taylor would expand the assessment function beyond diagnosis if presented with a direct question to that effect.

A Proposed Role for School Counselors in Assessment

What should the role of school counselors be in the assessment function? We believe that the primary role of school counselors in the assessment function is to acquire basic competencies that will allow them to help students and colleagues in a variety of ways that fall within the range of their role as school counselors. Table 12.1 presents an inventory of functions that we believe are important components of the assessment role. Ekstrom et al. (2004) was a helpful resource for identifying these functions.

Table 12.1
Important assessment functions for school counselors.

- Selecting, developing/adapting, and administering standardized and nonstandardized assessment instruments/techniques for academic, career, and personal/social counseling and for program evaluation purposes
- Interpreting assessment data to individual students and groups of students for academic, career, and personal/social self-understanding and decision making
- Making modifications in assessment techniques to meet the special needs of students with disabilities
- Communicating clearly with parents, teachers, and administrators about assessment data
- Understanding when to refer students for diagnostic assessments
- Understanding assessment-based diagnostic reports by psychologists and other professional diagnosticians
- Being able to use measurement and statistical information graphically to explain assessment data to individuals and groups
- Being able to develop, administer, and interpret needs assessment and program evaluation instruments
- Being able to use computer technology to process and manage assessment information
- Being able to develop and manage a plan for selecting and administering a school counseling assessment program
- Helping students to be better test takers and overcome test anxiety
- Keeping up to date on current assessment issues and being able to evaluate one's own assessment competence
- Being aware of the legal and ethical standards that are associated with assessment
- Being an advocate for ethical assessment-related behavior by colleagues

In the remainder of this chapter, we present an overview of many of the assessment competencies that are important for school counselors to possess to address the assessment role. Those competencies that are associated with program evaluation and accountability have already been covered in chapter 4. Readers are challenged to understand that this information is an introductory survey rather than comprehensive coverage. More comprehensive coverage of this information will occur in specific courses in tests and measurement, research and assessment, and statistics.

BASIC ASSESSMENT COMPETENCIES IN SCHOOL COUNSELING

The authors believe that the only legitimate assessment functions for school counselors are those used to achieve counseling goals. *Counseling* is defined globally here and includes all school counselor functions—prevention programming, consulting, referring and coordinating, providing information, enhancing transitions, advocating, leading and collaborating, counseling students, and being accountable. Unfortunately, this is a challenging stance in light of the long-standing tradition of having counselors involved in virtually all group assessments that occur in the schools. A strong coalition of students, teachers, administrators, and stakeholders believe that school counseling and assessment are synonymous.

The following information is meant to be an overview of, and not a substitute for, a comprehensive tests and measurement course. Readers are encouraged to seek general understanding and not be taken aback by technical terms with which they are not familiar. Readers are also encouraged to review this material while enrolled in, or after having completed, their tests and measurement, assessment, appraisal, or statistics courses.

Assessment for Enhancing Student Development

Helping individuals with academic, career, and personal/social decision making is one legitimate use of assessment services in school counseling. Many standardized and nonstandardized assessment tools are designed to help individuals acquire information about themselves that can be combined with information from other sources when making academic, career, and personal/social decisions. In many instances, decision making will be enhanced by individuals who can help the decision makers travel the road more successfully. School counselors are qualified by their specialized training to provide this assistance. A useful term for the process is *individual self-exploration*. School counselors can use standardized and nonstandardized assessment tools in conjunction with their own responsive counseling intervention and proactive prevention programming skills to enhance the self-exploration of individual clients.

Standardized measures of interests and aptitudes can be used in self-exploration. Examples of standardized interest measures useful with high school students are the Self-Directed Search (Psychological Assessment Resources) and the Strong Interest Inventory (Consulting Psychologists' Press). At the junior high, middle, and upper elementary school levels, the Harrington-O'Shea Career Decision-Making System (American Guidance Services) and the COPSystem (CAPS, COPS, and COPES; EdITS) may be useful. All measures can be used for the same general purpose—helping individuals acquire information that may be used in making informed decisions. These measurement tools are designed to serve adolescents and children at different developmental stages.

Examples of standardized, group aptitude test batteries for high school students are the Career Planning Survey (ACT) and the Armed Services Vocational Aptitude Battery (U.S. Department of Defense). The Career Planning Survey may also be useful with junior high and middle school students. Aptitude testing below these levels is not recommended because the attributes being measured have not developed sufficiently in children, and the norms are not useful. Profiles, computerized printouts, and graphic report forms that can be helpful in the exploratory process are generated for many of these instruments.

Some publishers have designed programs for converting data from standardized sources (e.g., interest inventories, aptitude tests) and nonstandardized sources (e.g., grades, self-reported experiences) into comprehensive counseling tools to be used to achieve self-exploration goals. One such conversion is the Career Planning Program (American College Testing Service), which is designed to help adolescents organize their thoughts about decisions related to professional and technical careers. Others have included assessment components in computerized career guidance programs, allowing users to generate data from assessment instruments built into the programs or to enter relevant data from assessments taken independently of the computer programs. See The Career Key Web site (http://www.careerkey.org/english). The trend in the direction of developing and publishing assessment tools designed to enhance individual self-exploration is definitely a turn in the right direction. As these instruments and ideas become more sophisticated and are designed to serve increasingly younger consumers, the challenge to get meaning out of them increases. Most children and adolescents need help making sense of the information generated by these instruments. Therefore, school counselors are challenged to make themselves capable of helping their student clients. To do this, they are challenged to make sense of the output generated by these advanced assessment tools and to transmit that understanding to their student clients. An example follows:

> Middle school counselors conducting a career exploration program (prevention programming) include having students complete an age-appropriate interest inventory as part of the program. They also acquire the students' latest general aptitude test scores from their files. In a segment of the program, the counselors explain the meaning of the scores and the purpose of the measures to the students collectively. The students then work on assignments designed to have them incorporate the test data with other information about themselves and try to integrate the information into a meaningful set of information about themselves. This activity is followed by another group presentation on future planning, which is then followed up by individual counseling sessions in which a counselor helps each student process what they have learned and find out whether they understand the meaning of the assessment data correctly. During the counseling sessions, students are encouraged to share how the data affect their self-perceptions and future plans.

Assessment for Diagnosing Student Status

Using assessment tools for diagnostic purposes seems to be a common role in elementary school counseling. It is also a legitimate assessment role in secondary school counseling. Elementary school counselors often work with children too young for the kind of self-exploration previously described. They more commonly use assessment tools to appraise individual children for diagnostic purposes. Specific purposes include diagnosis as a prelude to counseling, as part of consultation, and as part of referral and coordination services. Whatever the diagnostic assessment goals, Keat (1974) recommended that the questions be relevant and that constructive action follow the assessments.

Counseling services offered to elementary school children are often therapeutic in nature. Therefore, diagnostic assessment is an important precursor to implementing intervention strategies. Elementary school counselors who apply a counseling model similar to the multimodal approach advocated by Keat (1990) and others use assessment tools and strategies as part of the gathering data stage of the responsive counseling relationship, mixing data collecting with relationship establishing.

Because children are less able to engage in semi independent reconstruction of irrational cognitions and in self-management of their treatment programs, more collaboration among adults significant in their lives is required than is usually the case with adolescent and adult clients. The need for collaboration when helping children leads to consulting relationships. Elementary school counselors often consult with teachers and parents in joint efforts to help individual children. Assessment data commonly serve as the foundation for therapeutic plans devised by counselors in cooperation with parents and teachers.

Recommendations that children be referred for specialized services are often based on assessment information acquired by counselors. The assessment data are usually collected in response to referrals made by colleagues or parents to counselors. Consequently, school counselors, acting as professionals who are both providers and recipients of referrals, need to assess situations and targeted individuals to respond usefully.

Diagnostic assessment expectations of school counselors should be within their range of expertise. Unless they have received specialized training, school counselors do not have the same expertise as school psychologists; clinical and counseling psychologists; or reading, speech, and hearing specialists. In many instances, these specialists can be called on for assessment assistance, although delays may occur before referral requests can be honored.

What is the range of diagnostic assessment expertise of school counselors? The following assessment strategies seem important enough to be part of the basic training of school counselors, particularly elementary school counselors:

- *Taking case histories:* being able to collect accurate descriptive data from records, reports, and interviews of significant others about a variety of important topics as diverse as statistical information and relationships
- *Observing and diagnosing behavior:* being able to observe targeted individuals unobtrusively, organize one's observations, and report them diagnostically
- *Performing individual assessment:* being able to select and administer standardized and nonstandardized instruments usable within the confines of one's

training and to report the results accurately (e.g., using objectively scored intelligence and achievement screening tests as preliminary estimates of academic potential and achievement)

• *Acquiring sociometric data:* being able to survey classrooms of students and compile the results meaningfully (e.g., in sociograms)

It seems as if secondary school counselors should also be able to take case histories, give individual tests, and, to a lesser extent, observe and diagnose behavior and acquire sociometric data. As do elementary school counselors, secondary school counselors use diagnostic assessment services in support of counseling and consulting relationships and as part of the referral and coordination, advocacy, leadership, and collaboration functions.

External Assessment Expectations

As part of the transition function, secondary school counselors help students acquire information about, and make arrangements for, various tests required for entrance into institutions of higher education, the military service, and some job placements. Examples are the SAT, the Armed Services Vocational Aptitude Battery, and the General Aptitude Test Battery. In addition, individual students need help understanding the results of these tests, deciding what to do, and knowing what kinds of decisions institutional personnel and prospective employers make on the basis of the test results. These tests are referred to as external because entities outside the school system create the demand for students to take them. School personnel assume the responsibility for helping students gain access to higher education, military, and employment opportunities by creating clearinghouses for information and by serving as support personnel for the testing corporations and prospective educators and employers. Support takes the form of distributing information, giving tests, submitting completed test results, interpreting the results, and helping students process the information. This is another legitimate assessment component. For example, counselors in many high schools take the responsibility for making the PSAT available to students. This requires those counselors to announce the availability of the testing program and its purpose, identify students who want to take the test, be responsible for the test-taking logistics, send the completed answer sheets to the Educational Testing Service, distribute the results on their return, and help students process their results.

Leadership in Promoting Responsible Use of Standardized Tests in Assessment

Although assessment has been an important function of basic education for some time, many administrators, teachers, and counselors are not very well informed about tests, measurement, and related ethical positions. As the professionals on the school staff probably most knowledgeable in these areas—as well as those usually responsible for most assessment functions—school counselors are in a strategic position to promote responsible use of tests among their colleagues.

Test users face many challenges. Traditional challenges include determining whether the decision to test is correct, selecting the appropriate tests, administering the tests, scoring the tests accurately, and interpreting or communicating the results. Additional challenges have evolved from the knowledge that test content and norms reflect existing inequalities in U.S. society (Castenell & Castenell, 1988; Miller-Jones, 1989) and from the fact that testing can now be computerized efficiently, which raises concerns about confidentiality (Sampson, 1983; Wood, 1984).

As advocates for the responsible use of standardized tests, school counselors can strive to promote positive assessment environments. Assuming that individuals who abuse tests do so out of ignorance rather than guile, counselors can use an educational strategy. Many abuses can be corrected if all users become better informed. This is certainly something school counselors are capable of achieving.

Talbutt (1983) suggested resources that counselors can employ to help colleagues become responsible users of tests. He recommended that school counselors become knowledgeable about regulations and guidelines of local and state boards of education. They should also be aware of the ethical standards of the counseling profession (see chapter 5). Other resources are relevant publications such as The *Code of Fair Testing Practices in Education* (Joint Committee on Testing Practices, 1988) and *Competencies in Assessment and Evaluation for School Counselors* (Joint Committee of American School Counselor Association, 2001). Counselors are challenged to keep up to date by perusing journals for relevant information and by attending appropriate sessions at professional meetings.

Talbutt's (1983) recommendations call for informed counselors to transmit useful information to colleagues. The appropriate application of one's acquired knowledge is action. Therefore, school counselors can be models of responsible test use. Counselors who are viewed by their colleagues as competent and responsible may serve as models of appropriate behavior. They are more likely to influence the attitudes and behaviors of their colleagues positively than are counselors who are not desirable models.

Knowledge About Principles of Measurement

Lacking basic knowledge of measurement principles, test users are navigating without compasses. They know they are going somewhere, but they do not know where or how to get there. Test users who lack basic knowledge about measurement may harm the individuals they are trying to serve. Those individuals would have best received no service at all. Unfortunately, most people whose use of tests is coupled with misinformation about measurement are not aware of that shortcoming or do not realize how crucial their behavior can be.

What should school counselors know about measurement? This is a difficult domain to master, and, unfortunately, it often ranks low in the minds of many counseling students. In addition, measurement can appear complex if taught in a manner that befuddles counseling students and/or if taught by instructors who cannot apply it to using tests in counseling. Beginning school counselors are not expected to know all the intricacies of measurement at the outset of their careers. They are encouraged to increase their knowledge after their graduate-level training. Following is an attempt to identify a set of important assessment competencies. This information cannot replace the knowledge acquired from courses in descriptive statistics, measurement, and assessment. A goal of these subsections is to give relevance to the large body of information presented in such courses.

Scales and Scoring Systems. All standardized and some nonstandardized assessment instruments have scales and scoring systems that report individual and group results. School counselors are challenged to be familiar with these systems in order to understand the results correctly and to help others understand and use the results appropriately. The following simulation supports the contention that counselors serve students better if they understand the scales and scoring systems of various assessment instruments:

> *Simulation:* All students in the elementary schools of a school district participate in an annual achievement testing program. Standardized achievement tests are given in each grade to compare the average scores of the school district with national norms, to evaluate teachers, to locate content areas that need to be improved, and to identify students who need remedial or advanced work. One of the scales used by the test publisher is known as *grade equivalents.* Individual scores on specific content area subtests are reported as grade levels with corresponding months above and below the first month in that grade level. For instance, Jafar, a fourth-grade student, received scores of Second Grade—Third Month, Second Grade—Fifth Month, Second Grade—Tenth Month, and Third Grade—First Month on the language, reading, arithmetic, and social studies subtests, respectively. Jamilah, also a fourth-grade student, receives scores of Sixth Grade—Seventh Month, Sixth Grade—Eighth Month, Sixth Grade—Tenth Month, and Seventh Grade—First Month on the same subtests. In addition, approximately half of the fourth-grade class had average scores below Fourth Grade—First Month.
>
> The following false conclusions were made about this information by otherwise intelligent and well-meaning persons. Jafar's teacher entertained thoughts of recommending that he be given second-grade materials to study as part of a remedial program. Jamilah's parents considered requesting that she be advanced to sixth grade. The principal was upset to learn that half of the fourth grade was below grade level on the tests. Why were these false conclusions made, and what were the reasons for making them?
>
> Jafar's teacher, Jamilah's parents, and the school principal, not knowing the scoring system on which grade equivalent scales are based, interpreted the words literally and came to apparently logical conclusions. Counselors are challenged not to make such conclusions. Their job is to understand the scales and scoring systems used in various assessment programs and to help others avoid such errors. Detailed information about grade equivalents can be presented as part of well-designed and comprehensive courses on assessment, including information about measurement systems.
>
> Briefly, Jafar's teacher and Jamilah's parents made conclusions without knowing that Jafar's and Jamilah's test results had only been compared with those of other fourth graders. They had not been compared with second, third, sixth, or seventh graders. The grade equivalents in Jafar's case indicated that he is well below average fourth graders. Jamilah is well above average. On grade-equivalent scales, test publishers use grade levels higher and lower than the one of interest—in this case, fourth grade—for scores outside the 10 months of the

school year. Therefore, Fifth Grade—First Month follows Fourth Grade—Tenth Month and Third Grade—Tenth Month precedes Fourth Grade—First Month, even though the scale is used exclusively for fourth graders.

The school principal did not realize that the average score for fourth graders should identify them as being where they were when they took the test—which was the Fourth Grade—First Month. If they achieve average performance on the tests, they will be at that point. Those who score below the middle will have third- or lower-grade equivalents. If the class has a normally distributed group of fourth-grade students, about half of them will have scores below the average or middle of the distribution of scores. Therefore, it is to be expected that a substantial number of students have grade equivalents below Fourth Grade—First Month. The fact that half of the students are below grade level merely means that half of them are below the middle or average score.

This example shows only a few of the many problems that can occur when assessment data are misunderstood. Scales and scoring systems represent an important technology about which school counselors are challenged to be sophisticated. It appears as if minimum competence should include knowledge about the following:

- The different kinds of scales (nominal, ordinal, interval, and ratio) and their properties
- The scoring systems derived from the basic scales used in psychological and educational assessment (e.g., standard scores, percentile ranks)
- The standard normal distribution and its properties—leading to an understanding of the role of norms in assessment
- Sampling theory for selecting test items and establishing norms or reference groups
- Basic descriptive statistics (e.g., measures of central tendency, such as means, medians, and modes; measures of dispersion from the center of a distribution, such as standard deviations and ranges)

Reliability and Validity.   Simply stated, *validity* means that assessment tools should achieve the goals they are designed to achieve. Validity also means that tests should be used appropriately. *Reliability* means that the assessment tools perform consistently. The following simulation highlights the importance of counselors being knowledgeable about these measurement principles:

Simulation: Middle and junior high school students are given a vocational interest inventory as part of a career exploration unit. One purpose of the inventory is to provide food for thought—to suggest careers about which participants might acquire further information because they demonstrated higher interest in them than most other individuals of their age and gender. Jana brought her results home and announced that they indicated she should be an artist. Jarek filed his results and discovered them 3 years later when planning for life after high school. He used the results to begin a search for information about careers appropriate for him to pursue.

Both Jana and Jarek used the results of their interest inventories inappropriately because they knew nothing about validity and reliability. That is to be expected in most instances. Therefore, school counselors are challenged to prevent these situations as often as possible. Jana misinterpreted the purpose of the inventory and ascribed a degree of certainty to the results that was not intended by the test publisher or by the individuals who designed the career exploration program. She invalidated the results by assuming that they identified a specific career for her when, in fact, the inventory was designed to compare her interests with those of others of her age and sex.

Jarek created a reliability problem when he assumed that the results were useful 3 years later. Because of the dramatic changes that occur in individuals as they mature from childhood through adolescence, it was likely that Jarek's interests had changed in 3 years and that his later responses would be quite different from the earlier ones. The reliability of interest inventories over a period of 3 years is limited—not in every case, but certainly in many cases. Jarek would have been served better by the results of an inventory taken concurrently with his career search activities, and a school counselor who understood reliability principles would have been able to provide Jarek with helpful information in that regard.

Reliability and validity are important concepts; minimally, a school counselor should know the following:

- Classic reliability theory, including the concepts of true scores and observed scores
- Methods for estimating reliability used by test publishers, such as the test–retest, parallel forms, split halves, and internal consistencies strategies
- Basic statistical procedures used when reporting most reliability and some validity estimates (correlation analyses and correlation coefficients)
- Methods used by test publishers for estimating validity (content validity, construct validity, predictive validity, and concurrent validity)
- Procedures used to translate reliability and validity data into counseling information (e.g., standard error of measurement, standard error of estimate, expectancy tables)

Knowledge About Standardized Tests

Standardized tests vary in their designs and purposes. It is important to understand their differences, limitations, and purposes. One way to make sense of the information is to categorize it. One system for categorizing standardized tests is according to the purpose. Standardized tests used by school counselors usually fall into one of the following five purpose categories: intelligence, aptitude, achievement, interests, and personality.

Intelligence Tests.   Intelligence tests are designed to provide a general or global measure of academic potential. That academic potential is usually expressed by a single score. The score is expressed as an intelligence quotient (IQ) with a scale score attached to it. For example, Emily's IQ of 115 indicates that her intelligence ranks 15 points higher than the average of 100. Among the most common uses of intelligence tests are determining which individuals should be placed in special education or gifted programs and classifying students for grouped or tracked academic programs in the schools.

Aptitude Tests.   Also designed to provide information about individual potential, aptitude tests are more specific than intelligence tests. They are designed to identify specific attributes or aptitudes, such as verbal, mechanical, artistic, musical, numerical, and spatial. Some aptitude tests address only one aptitude; others cover several, providing a profile of aptitude scores. An example of the latter approach is the General Aptitude Test Battery (published by the U.S. Employment Service). This test provides scores for 12 subtests or aptitudes. Some aptitude tests are used in predicting future performance and therefore support the decisions of personnel and admissions workers in business and industry, military services, or colleges and universities. Other aptitude tests help individuals acquire information about their capabilities to use in a process of educational and career decision making.

Achievement Tests.   Designed to find out what individuals have learned up to the time they are tested, achievement tests are used to evaluate curriculum efforts in the schools. Individual students, teachers, schools, and communities may be evaluated by achievement testing results. Performances by local students are compared collectively to national standards. The national standards are usually the results of a sampling of schools and students from across the country at each grade level. Achievement tests cover important academic areas such as language arts, reading, arithmetic, social studies, and science. In addition to being compared to national norms, individual scores may also be used diagnostically to identify academic deficiencies and initiate remedial instructional programming. For instance, in the simulation presented previously, Jafar had relatively low grade-equivalent scores on the language, reading, arithmetic, and social studies subtests of an achievement test battery. That information could be used in designing a remedial instructional program. The North Carolina ABCs tests described earlier in this chapter are achievement tests created for a specific purpose in North Carolina. When Garrison Keillor refers to the children in Lake Wobegon as being above average, he is probably referring to their performance on achievement tests.

Interest Inventories.   These instruments are most often used to initiate career exploration activities. Therefore, they are primarily counseling tools. Individuals are usually asked to rate the attractiveness of activities in some manner. Examples of such activities are persuading others of the merits of one's point of view, meeting new people, and working out solutions to arithmetic problems. Two approaches are used in designing interest inventories. One compares the respondents' answers with answers of other individuals of their own age and gender, providing information about the strength of their interests in comparison with their peers (i.e., normative data). The second approach compares the respondents' answers with those of individuals successful in specific occupations. The basis of this approach is that people of similar interests are more

Counselors can incorporate test interpretations into the counseling process.

likely to find success in similar careers. This is the discriminant information advocated by Prediger (1994) and Zytowski (1994) in comments about the state of the marriage between tests and counseling earlier in this chapter. Interest inventory results are often very comprehensive and require careful interpretations to avoid misunderstandings.

Personality Measures.   These instruments provide information about individual emotional, motivational, interpersonal, and attitudinal characteristics (Anastasi, 1997). In psychiatry, clinical psychology, and counseling psychology, they may help develop or determine clinical diagnoses, as well as help individuals better understand themselves and their thoughts and actions—a common use in education. In business, industry, and the military, personality measures are sometimes used to make selection decisions.

A variety of such instruments are published, representing several different methods of test development. Some have questions and scoring systems based on particular personality theories, whereas others are developed through statistical procedures that provide useful scoring systems. An example of the statistical approach, instruments developed from factor analyses provide information about individual placement along bipolar scales. Such scales include trust versus defensiveness, activity versus lack of energy, and masculinity versus femininity. A second example is criterion-referenced keying, which provides the kind of information referred to previously in the section on interest inventories—comparing the answers of respondents with those of specific categories of other people. As with interest inventories, results of personality measures are often comprehensive and demand care in interpretation.

A second system for categorizing standardized tests is according to the type of motivation respondents are expected to have when taking the tests. Two motivational categories can be determined: maximum performance and typical performance.

Motivation for Maximum Performance.   On intelligence, aptitude, and achievement tests, the questions have right or wrong answers, and those who use the test results require accurate estimates of the respondents' capabilities. Therefore, respondents need to be motivated to do their best when answering items on these assessment instruments.

Motivation for Typical Performance.   Interest inventories and personality measures do not have questions for which there are right or wrong answers. All answers have meaning according to the scales or keys developed for the instruments. Therefore, it is important that respondents be truthful when answering the questions. This requires the individuals to take the test in a frame of mind that is usual or typical of them at times when they are not responding to the test.

Knowledge About Nonstandardized Assessment Strategies

Goldman (1972) declared that standardized tests, representing a quantitative approach, failed to live up to their promise as counseling tools. He suggested that qualitative strategies may contribute more to counseling than standardized tests (Goldman, 1982, 1994). Qualitative strategies are not standardized; they are devoid of cumbersome and confusing statistical data; the instruments are readily adapted to different age groups, reading levels, and settings; and their administration involves counseling—or at least has implications for decision making, problem solving, and planning—a more active role for clients, Goldman (1982, 1990, 1994) claimed. He continued by suggesting several nonstandardized strategies for acquiring qualitative assessment data in counseling, two of which—work samples and observation—are elaborated on here.

Work Samples.   Work samples provide an alternative to aptitude testing. They are most useful for individuals who have a disability or who are gifted. Standardized tests are either too difficult for such individuals or too simple. In either case, work samples provide more comprehensive information. In general, work sampling involves analyzing important components of a task that occur in specific jobs or activities. The analysis is used to develop a simulation of the task. For example, it is possible to simulate the basic tasks of repairing watches. Clients can be carefully observed as they attempt to follow the steps in the instructions. They can be timed, their behaviors noted, and their ability to perform the skills assessed. The information may be used diagnostically, educationally, or for selection purposes. Most schools cannot afford to develop or purchase work samples. However, they are available at many vocational rehabilitation services. Counselors may be able to use the referrals to make them available to some clients. Kapes and Whitfield's *A Counselor's Guide to Career Assessment Instruments* (2002) is a good source of information about specific commercial work samples.

Observation.   Goldman (1990) defined *qualitative observation* as collecting comments and impressions. Quantitative observation entails translating observations into standardized scoring systems or counting the number of times specific behaviors occur. Collecting comments can take the form of asking elementary school teachers to share comments about students in their classrooms. This might be done to verify observations of others or to acquire narrative information about student behaviors. The information may be used diagnostically to plan counseling interventions or to determine the effects of interventions already under way. Collecting impressions through observations might occur through work shadowing. For example, children and adolescents can accompany working adults as they proceed through all or part of their days at work and can formulate impressions of the jobs while they do so.

The multimodal approach to counseling and therapy offers a system for using observation in the process of assessing a client's current level of functioning (diagnosis) and proceeding to develop intervention plans. The multimodal approach is founded on the principles of comprehensiveness and eclecticism. The diagnoses are to be broad based according to a predetermined plan and the interventions selected from a wide spectrum of strategies that work. Two plans for organizing diagnostic information have been popularized in the counseling and therapy literature. Each suggests several categories of information to acquire when making diagnostic assessments through interviews, observations, and instrumental data gathering. The categories help counselors organize their findings and suggest information that should be collected. Assessments are not restricted to presenting problems. All categories should be investigated, even though no suggestions of problems in those areas have been reported. This procedure implements the comprehensiveness principle.

Lazarus's (1976) plan is identified by the acronym BASIC ID, and Keat's (1990) plan has a HELPING acronym. The categories in the BASIC ID plan are

B = Behavior
A = Affect
S = Sensation
I = Imagery
C = Cognition
I = Interpersonal relationships
D = Drugs/diet

The HELPING plan categories are

H = Health
E = Emotions/feelings
L = Learning/school
P = Personal relationships
I = Imagination/interests
N = Need to know/think
G = Guidance of acts, behaviors, and consequences

Table 12.2 contains a summary of the findings of a multimodal assessment and plans for the subsequent treatment. The BASIC ID was used, and the client was a 16-year-old female high school sophomore. The case study by Seligman (1981), too long to present

Table 12.2
Findings from a multimodal assessment.

Modality	Problem	Treatment
Behavior	Excessive eating, weight gain	Participation in weight control program
	Circumscribed range of activities	Behavioral rehearsal; defining and planning pleasurable activities
Affect	Negative self-statements	Nonreinforcement; positive self-talk assignments
	Depression, suicidal feelings	Increasing experiences providing positive reinforcement
	Expression of anger	Role-playing
Sensation	Loneliness, emptiness	Relationship building; communication skills
	Lack of positive sensory experiences	Sensate focusing; planned pleasurable experiences
	Feelings of being bloated, obese	Diet, exercise
	Headaches, stomachaches	Relaxation, improved eating habits
Imagery	Tension	Relaxation
Cognition	Image of self as grossly overweight	Thought-stopping
	Suicidal fantasies	Thought-stopping; rational self-talk
	Poor study habits	Study skills training; assertiveness training
	Lack of educational and occupational information	Career counseling, including assessment and information giving
	Irrational beliefs; irrational self-talk	Corrective self-talk; rational disputation
Interpersonal relations	Sexual misinformation	Sex education; bibliotherapy
	Fears of social situations	Behavioral rehearsal
	Competitiveness with female peers	Group counseling
	Inconsistent relationships with parents	Family conferences; role-playing; attending weight control sessions with mother
Drugs/diet	Poor dietary habits	Involvement in weight reduction program
	Excessive smoking, some solitary drinking	Self-administered behavior modification program; jogging

Source: From "Multimodal Behavior Therapy: A Case Study of a High School Student" by L. Seligman, 1981, *School Counselor, 28,* pp. 255–256. Copyright 1981 by American Counseling Association. No further reproduction authorized without written permission of the American Counseling Association.

here, provides an interesting example of applying the multimodal idea. Case studies involving child clients may be found in Keat (1990). Not all treatment plans are initiated at once, but several can be under way concurrently because categories of information about clients are interdependent.

Nonstandardized assessment strategies lend themselves to the goals of culturally sensitive assessment because counselors are better able to accommodate linguistic challenges and to determine stages of acculturation when engaged in nonstandardized assessment activities (Facundo et al., 1994). Despite these advantages, the challenges of engaging in cross-cultural assessments exist, with the need for being fair and sensitive remaining.

Knowledge About Managing School Testing Programs

When school counselors are given full or partial responsibility for school testing programs, they are faced with a challenge to be good managers. How to meet that challenge is an administrative question, and the contingencies that influence the system used will be affected by the views and practices of school and district administrators, as well as by a host of other factors that make setting up a system situation specific. Setting up a system is, however, imperative. What follows is an inventory of important factors to be considered when establishing a system for managing a school testing program:

- A budget for purchasing tests and supplies is needed, in addition to a system for making purchases and accounting for expenditures.
- The program is founded on goals. The goals can define the reasons why tests are used, what information is desired from the test results, and how that information is used effectively.
- The specific responsibilities of school counselors in the testing program are explicated. In addition, the roles and responsibilities of administrators, teachers, and support personnel are clearly defined.
- Testing practices conform to professional ethical standards and other established principles for using tests. Counselors can serve as monitors of testing practices in their schools and can educate their colleagues proactively.
- Advisory committees can be established to help determine testing policies, monitor test uses, and educate various stakeholders about testing and assessment.

Knowledge About Assessment Issues

School counselors knowledgeable about basic measurement principles understand the different sides in issues involving assessment services. Basic knowledge about measurement will be more useful if counselors are also familiar with the viewpoints of the protagonists. A combination of knowing what the protagonists believe and the basics about measurement will allow counselors to explain the issues and to help their clientele draw objective conclusions. For example, knowledge about the principles associated with normal distributions will help counselors lead others away from stereotyping members of different racial groups.

To elaborate on the example, it has not been uncommon for people to assume that the mean or average difference between European Americans and African Americans

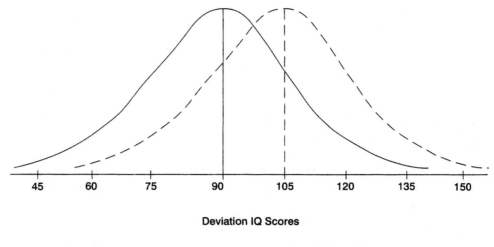

Deviation IQ Scores

— **Group A Distribution** Mean = 90; – 3 Standard
Deviations = 45; + 3 Standard Deviations = 135

— **Group B Distribution** Mean = 105; – 3 Standard
Deviations = 60; + 3 Standard Deviations = 150

Figure 12.1
Differences within and between groups when attributes are distributed normally.

on standardized intelligence tests indicates that European Americans are more intelligent than African Americans because the average for European Americans is higher. Accurate knowledge of normal distributions, however, makes one realize that greater differences are found within groups than between groups. Figure 12.1 demonstrates that many African Americans have higher intelligence test scores than many European Americans, even though the average score for European Americans is higher. This indicates that individual members of a group should not be stereotyped or labeled according to the statistically average group member. Rather, all members of a group are individuals with their own combinations of attributes. Intelligence test data about individuals can be used to determine where one ranks in a group, and different groupings can be established (e.g., gender groups, racial groups, age groups).

Following is an inventory of several issues that are important because they are about assessment uses and abuses that touch the lives of children and adolescents. They rank high among the assessment issues important for school counselors to understand.

Using Standardized Tests Leads to Invasion of Privacy. Those who feel this way about tests generally object to item content or to required assessments. More specifically, critics have raised the following objections:

- Selected items on personality tests, when taken out of context, seem outrageous.
- Attitude surveys may present questions to individuals that are upsetting or request information about behaviors that some parents do not want their children to consider.

- Results of some tests may be kept in computer banks by institutions or agencies whose motives are questionable.
- Some schools require all students to take targeted tests.

Counselors are in a strategic position to provide information, offer support, or serve as consultants, depending on the demands of the situation. For instance, concerns about the meanings of individual test items may be alleviated if people understand the purpose of the questions in the context of the entire test. Concerns about test content and required participation may be alleviated by recommending that participation be voluntary and that the decision whether to participate be preceded by an opportunity to learn the purposes of the testing program and the tests in question.

An example of how test content can lead to the problems just cited occurred in Pennsylvania during the 1970s when the schools were required to administer a battery of tests called the Educational Quality Assessment (EQA) program. The EQA was designed to provide information about achievement and attitudes across the school districts. This, in turn, was used to make comparisons to a set of state standards. Reports were issued to school districts, indicating the areas in which they were deficient and those in which they were doing well. The tests were given at specified points from elementary through the high school grades. Some parents objected to having their children answer specific attitudinal questions and filed civil suits. One objectionable question was "Have you ever used marijuana?" Those who objected did not want the idea of using marijuana even suggested to their children. Eventually, participation in the program was made voluntary.

Standardized Tests Are Biased, and Their Use Furthers Discrimination Against Some People.   These objections surround the use of tests for classification and selection, and for helping individuals choose careers. Specifically, it is believed that African Americans, Hispanics, members of other minority racial and ethnic groups, women, people with disabilities, and individuals from economically disadvantaged backgrounds are, on average, less likely than others to appear desirable on standardized tests used to select who goes where to college, who is placed in special education and accelerated K–12 basic education trackings, who gets jobs, and who gets scholarships. In addition, some believe that women are encouraged to consider a more limited range of career possibilities than are men when aptitude tests with separate gender scores and interest inventories that present limited choices are used in career counseling.

School counselors who are well informed about this issue are in a position to provide assistance in several ways. They can inform students, parents, and colleagues that some test scores reflect educational and social shortcomings that need to be identified and corrected. They can act as advocates for students' rights when they have evidence that results of tests used by the school system are leading to decisions that unfairly place some students at a disadvantage. They can be careful and discriminating when selecting tests to be used in career counseling. When the alleged bias is attributable to the use of external tests such as the SAT, counselors can try to help students find alternative ways to enhance their desirability or to achieve their goals. Counselors can act as advocates for individuals with disabilities by establishing opportunities for alternative testing arrangements (e.g., arranging special environments for dyslexic students so they have more time to complete the tests and opportunities to ask questions to clarify material that confuses them).

Some Assessment Issues Create a Stressful Environment in Schools While Not Necessarily Influencing Clients Directly. Concern over declining entrance exam scores and pressure to pass end-of-course or end-of-grade tests are examples of issues that may influence students indirectly. Since the 1960s, concern over declining performance on college entrance exams has created puzzlement over the causes of the declines, as well as criticisms of teachers. The declining averages and other negative impressions of the nation's schools have led to an erosion of confidence in the competence of teaching professionals.

School counselors can help students, parents, and colleagues put the highly publicized declining entrance exam scores issue in perspective by informing them about the history of the issue and the fact that it is a phenomenon that also leaves the experts puzzled. That is, explanations are as diverse as outdated norms, birth order, and family sizes. In addition, concerned individuals can be informed that other measures of student performance should be considered, such as standardized achievement tests. If the entrance exam scores indicate problems, there are constructive ways to respond. Examples are enhancing and altering the curriculum, teaching students to be more proficient test takers, and changing the anxious atmosphere sometimes associated with the college selection process to make it more rational.

End-of-course and end-of-grade tests for students have created a highly charged atmosphere in states where they have been used and recommended. School counselors can help students become better test takers through testwiseness training and cope with inordinate test anxiety. *Testwiseness* involves knowledge of the characteristics and formats of tests that allows individuals to achieve scores reflecting their true capacities not influenced by the structure of the test (Millman, Bishop, & Ebel, 1965). Performance tests have right and wrong answers and are the kind of standardized selection examinations most commonly used. Testwiseness can be taught; such training includes instruction in developing strategies for time use, error avoidance, guessing, deductive reasoning, test constructor intent consideration, and cue using (Sarnacki, 1979). Brown (1982) offered a testwiseness program for children that appears to be a modification of the principles published in Sarnacki's (1979) review. Brown's (1982) suggestions reflect an awareness of developmental differences and focus on enhancing familiarity with tests, learning how to answer test items, and using time efficiently.

Test anxiety is the tendency of individuals to respond to the stress associated with testing situations with worried, negative, self-centered ideation (Spielberger, Anton, & Bedell, 1976). This results in lowered performances. A considerable body of research on test anxiety has been generated, and no single or simple cure has been found. Some individuals can be helped by enhancing their testwiseness. For others, test anxiety is a complicated phobic response. School counselors are challenged to be able to prevent some test anxiety by making students more skillful and knowledgeable test takers. Others, for whom more help is needed, can be identified and referred to clinical or counseling specialists. Some cases of test anxiety can be treated by school counselors who are familiar with strategies that are sometimes successful (e.g., cognitive self-instruction, stress inoculation, systematic desensitization). Some individuals can be helped through direct intervention, and others through referrals: School counselors can identify all individuals who require help in order to begin the process of getting it for them.

Test anxiety prevention can be approached via prevention programming. Cognitive self-instruction and stress inoculation are coping skills that can be used to prevent test anxiety and a host of other thinking-related anxieties. Test anxiety can be treated as the sole focus of such groups or as one of several foci. Group interventions designed to teach coping skills can be offered from upper elementary through high school levels. One example, cited in the professional school counseling literature, is summarized here: Wilkinson (1990) recommended that elementary school counselors offer minilectures and classroom guidance programs to help children overcome test anxiety. Wilkinson suggested that students be helped to realize when they engage in negative self-talk. Examples of negative self-talk are "I can't ever finish on time" and "My parents will hate me if I fail." Students can be taught to replace such negative self-talk with positive thoughts. This strategy is known as *cognitive self-instruction*, and it is based on the principle that one cannot have two competing thoughts concurrently. The positive thoughts are used to interrupt and replace the negative thoughts. Wilkinson also recommended helping children improve time management and study techniques to reduce the probability that the reasons for having test anxiety are legitimate.

Knowledge About Selecting and Administering Assessment Instruments

The reasons for counselors to become involved in the selection of assessment tools and strategies are varied. One reason is to select instruments to be used for institutional decision making, such as group intelligence and achievement tests. A second reason is to select diagnostic instruments and strategies, such as quick intelligence tests, case study outlines, and observation recording strategies, to support one's counseling activities. A third reason is to select tests that individual student clients can take when trying to make educational and career decisions.

When school counselors are involved in the process of selecting tests for institutional decision-making purposes, they can draw on their knowledge about basic measurement principles and testing issues to make significant contributions to the selection process. The basic ingredient of this selection process is a systematic approach, including specifications of goals and inquiries about the technical and practical attributes of the various tests being considered. Counselors will also contribute by suggesting that those involved in the selection process read certain appropriate test reviews that have been published. Useful sources of test reviews are the *Mental Measurement Yearbooks* and *Tests in Print* (see http://www.unl.edu/buros/) and *A Counselor's Guide to Career Assessment Instruments* (Kapes & Whitfield, 2002). The same approach can be used by individual counselors when selecting instruments and techniques that are to be used diagnostically. In addition, they can consult with colleagues and mentors for their ideas.

When school counselors engage in selecting tests for individual decision making, degree of client involvement becomes an issue. School counselors know about tests and have more life experience than their student clients. Yet, clients, being involved in a decision-making method, seem to need to share the responsibility for selecting the tests. Counselors can provide information about tests that they can interpret competently and use their decision-making counseling skills to help student clients choose the tests in the clients' best interests. With this process, test selection becomes part of the counseling process, rather than an adjunct activity.

Good test administration is essentially having concern for accuracy and caring for the test takers. Test publishers provide explicit instructions that must be followed by those who administer the tests to enhance the validity of the outcomes. Testing environments are best when test takers are comfortable and are allowed to do their best. A good principle for test administrators to follow is to create a testing environment similar to one in which they would be willing to participate.

The challenges of test administration are expanded when students take tests on the Internet (Sampson, 2000). On the one hand, distance barriers are broken down when individuals can take tests via the Internet rather than traveling to test sites. On the other hand, there is increased potential for circumstances that detract from the standardized conditions that should be found at any test site.

Knowledge About Communicating Assessment Information Accurately

Test interpretations in counseling might be described as efforts by counselors to help test takers make sense out of the results and process the information to use it constructively. Test interpretation, like the test selection process, is best accomplished by making it part of the counseling process, rather than an adjunct activity. Therefore, counselors can incorporate test interpretations into the counseling process. To accomplish this, counselors blend their knowledge of basic measurement principles with their counseling competencies. The following presentation suggests how the blending might occur.

If one is viewing test interpretation as part of the decision-making counseling process, the first step or goal is to establish a mutually acceptable working relationship between the counselor and the student client. These attitudes and competencies are described in chapter 9. Beyond that, the reasons for taking the test are made clear to all involved, and the counselors are aware of their student clients' expectations. Unrealistic or misinformed expectations may need to be challenged immediately, and unmet expectations will need to be addressed eventually. Judicial use of basic communication skills will help counselors learn about student clients' expectations.

Relationship development and expectation assessment set the stage for disseminating the information if the student is ready and interested. The information is often technical and sometimes comprehensive, leaving counselors with the challenge of keeping it from overwhelming and confusing the student client. In meeting this challenge, counselors will share their technical knowledge about tests and measurement while remembering their communication skills. They will translate technical terms into words and phrases understandable to the student and not use those terms directly with the student client unless necessary. For example, students seldom need to know what methods were used to estimate the reliability or validity of a test. They can be helped to understand the concept of the standard error of measurement without being introduced to the term *standard error of measurement* or to the formula for estimating it. The developmental stage of students will also serve as a guide to what technical information they can process. Certainly, children need to be treated differently than high school adolescents.

Graphic aids such as publisher-generated profiles provide visual assistance to counselors and student clients. The counselor can help students by making sure they are able to see the aids clearly and understand them. Computerized printouts from test publishers or from the Internet can also be very helpful, providing printed and graphic interpretive information. Many students will need help with the computer-generated printouts because such reports often provide more information than student clients can process successfully and may include information students do not understand.

Because the information dissemination segment of the test interpretation process contains so much that needs to be shared and explained, there is a danger of too much counselor and too little client involvement in the process. Counselor overactivity and student passivity can be avoided through the use of counseling skills. The counselor can draw student clients into the information dissemination process by asking them to summarize at strategic points, to answer questions that will inform the counselor how well they understand the information, and to explain results in their own words after having observed counselor demonstrations. It may also help to incorporate segments of client data processing into the dissemination process. Getting student clients involved in the information dissemination process should be primary in counselors' minds and within their range of basic skills.

Student processing of the information leads to a continuation of the decision-making process, completing the test interpreting component. Basic counseling skills can be used to invite student clients to begin processing the information. For example, a counselor might ask, "What are your thoughts about these test results?" after sharing the appropriate information. Student processing can lead the counseling relationship in several directions, such as decision-making counseling and support counseling. Accurate communication of assessment information requires attitudes and skills that are commensurate with good counseling. The ingredient that differentiates these interpretations from other counseling endeavors is the technical information generated by the assessments that begs to be translated clearly in order to be useful. As Goldman (1971) implied, competent counselors can bridge the gap between the assessment data and constructive client use of those data.

The following simulation is an abbreviated example of a test interpretation interview. The student, Ned, is an eighth grader who took an aptitudes test as an assignment in a career planning unit led by the counselor, Ms. Bigelow (prevention programming with an assessment component). The purpose of the testing is to use data from the test to help Ned and his classmates think about future plans and, more immediately, make course selections for ninth grade. Ned is having difficulty understanding the information on the profile of scores provided by the test publisher and seeks out Ms. Bigelow for assistance:

Ms. Bigelow (B):	Hello, Ned, what can I do for you?
Ned (N):	Hi! Ms. Bigelow, I'm having trouble understanding these test scores. Can you help me?
B:	I certainly will try. Tell me what you think you know about the scores and what you hope to learn from them.
N:	Well, I hope to find out what I want to do when I grow up and what courses I should take next year—and I'm not sure what I know about the scores.

B: Okay! You would like to use the information to make plans for the future, and it appears as if you are really confused about the scores. Should we begin with them?

N: Yes! I'm really confused about all the numbers and graphs.

B: They can be confusing for many people. In fact, it took me a while as an adult student in graduate school to feel that I understood the information well enough to explain it to others. Let's look at the profile sheet you have together. Okay?

N: Yes.

B: Some of the information can be read. For example, the name of the test, the names of the subtests, and descriptions of each subtest and what it's supposed to measure. Are you experiencing any difficulty understanding that part of the profile?

N: No. I don't think so. It seems clear right now.

B: Okay! Let's look at the graphic and numerical parts. There seem to be two kinds of numerical scores—percentile ranks and standard scores—and there are shaded areas on each graph, about an inch in length, above and below where your scores fall on the scale. Do you see all that?

N: Yes. I see them but am not sure how to use them.

B: Let's choose a place to start because several subtests and different kinds of scores are reported. Do you have a preference?

N: Not especially. Let's start with the numerical section. That seems to be my worst score, and I don't like math very much. Yet, my dad says that I'll need to take a lot of math to get along well in the world.

B: Okay! Let's look at your math score on the profile. Do you understand percentile ranks?

N: I don't know. Does that mean the percentage of questions I got right?

B: Not exactly, but that is a conclusion many people make when first experiencing percentile ranks because the word *percentile* is used. Actually, your performance on the test is being compared to the performances of a large group of people your age who already took the test, and the percentile rank informs us how you compared to that group. Does that make sense?

N: I think so.

B: So, on the numerical section the number of questions you answered correctly was equal to or higher than 40% of the

	people in that comparison group, which is labeled as a norms group. However, 60% of the norms group had higher scores on the test than you did. Does that help?
N:	I think so.
B:	Well, let's check you out by looking at the verbal section next. Why don't you explain to me what it means so I can check out how well you understand that information.
N:	My score on the verbal section is at the 80th percentile, which means my score is higher than 80% of the norms group.
B:	That's pretty good! What percentage of the norms group scored higher than you did?
N:	Twenty percent.
B:	Correct. You seem to understand it quite well now.

Note: At this time, the counselor may explain the nuance about Ned's score actually being equal to or higher than those in the norms group. The counselor may also explain the concept of standard error of measurement and how it is applied. Having taken care of these matters, the counselor may then make sure the student is able to engage in the same process without prompting on the remaining subtest scores on the test. The simulation resumes after these procedures have been completed:

B:	Well, you seem to have a better understanding now. At least, that is the way it appears to me because you are now able to explain to me what the scores mean. Do you have any more questions about the scores?
N:	No. I think I understand them better now. Thanks!
B:	Good! Now, earlier in our interview you mentioned some things that I believe it would be important to discuss further. One is that you hope the scores will help you decide what to do when you grow up. Another is that you hope they will tell you what courses to take next year. Yet another comment was that you believe math is your weak academic area and that your father believes you should continue taking math courses because they are important for getting along in the world. Finally, I think we should talk about your reaction to your performance on the test; that is, how do you feel about your scores? Those seem to be some important issues we probably should discuss further. Would you like to do that?
N:	Okay. That's something I wanted to talk about, too, and I was hoping the test scores would be helpful.
B:	Fine. If it is OK with you, tell me what you think the test scores should be able to do for you. . . .

Ms. Bigelow has helped Ned understand the scoring system of the test further by involving him in the process and providing him with information he can understand. She has also identified issues that need to be addressed further as part of the counseling process. Several tracks are possible at this point, all of which may be interwoven: (a) clarifying Ned's too narrow perception about the usefulness of the test scores, (b) processing his thoughts about his father's beliefs and their influence on him, (c) thinking more about career planning, (d) helping Ned plan his course of studies for ninth grade, and (e) processing negative affect derived from his performance on the test.

The simulation presents one of many possible scenarios involving the application of assessment to counseling. In this case, the assessment was part of a prevention programming effort. The counselor provided a direct service in response to a request for assistance from the student client. Basic counseling and assessment skills were combined to help the client, and the test interpretation opened the door to further counseling with the client. It appeared as if the counselor was sufficiently competent to explain the technical information associated with standardized testing in a manner that the client could comprehend, and she involved him in the process while doing so. Competent counselors can bridge the gap between assessment data and constructive client use of those data.

Knowledge About Ethical Responsibilities in the Assessment Process

Both the ACA and the ASCA codes offer ethical guidance for using tests in counseling. Section E of the *ACA Code of Ethics* provides considerable guidance for counselors. Examples are (a) counselors are to recognize the limits of their competence (E.2.a.) and are responsible for the appropriate application, scoring, interpretation, and use of assessment instruments (E.2.b.); (b) counselors are cautious when selecting tests for culturally diverse populations (E.6.c.); (c) counselors administer tests under the same conditions that were established in their standardization (E.7.a.); (d) counselors indicate any reservations they have about test validity or reliability when reporting results (E.9.a.); and (e) counselors do not use data or test results that are obsolete or outdated (E.11.). For greater detail, see appendix F.

The ASCA ethical standards include a section devoted to evaluation, assessment, and interpretation (A.9.). See appendix G. Ending this chapter on an ethical note seems appropriate. All functions within the school counselor's assessment role are in some way guided by professional ethical standards.

FEATURED ACTIVITY: GRADUATE STUDENT PERSPECTIVES ON CONSULTATION IN SCHOOL COUNSELING

In this chapter, we discuss assessment in school counseling. One of our counselor education interns wrote the following in his journal during the sixth week of his school counseling internship:

I have always heard that school counselors spend an inordinate amount of time with testing at school. My internship supervisor convinced the administration at her school that there was a need for a testing coordinator. The coordinator who

*was hired happens to be a licensed school counselor, but the coordinator's work
has freed up the other counselors to do what counselors are supposed to do!*

What roles should school counselors play in assessment? How can counselors improve their effectiveness by rethinking what they do in assessment? Tell us what you think.

After you read this chapter, go to http://www.genesislight.com/scan21st/tell_us/ assessment.html and complete the form. With your permission, we will periodically post some of your creative thinking for the world to read.

OTHER SUGGESTED ACTIVITIES

1. Take an inventory of testing and assessment abuses of which you are aware. Suggest possible solutions for each abuse. Share your observations with colleagues, and discuss the similarities and differences.
2. Make an inventory of tests you feel competent to interpret at this time. Add to the list those tests you plan to become competent to interpret in the near future.
3. Make an inventory of nonstandardized assessment techniques you feel competent to use, and add to the list those you plan to become competent with in the near future.
4. Debate the merits of the following statement: "The only legitimate assessment services are those used to achieve counseling goals."
5. In light of what you know about the use of tests in school counseling today, what is your response to Goldman's claim that the marriage between tests and counseling has failed?
6. Discuss the merits of computerized and Internet testing, and what the role of counselors should be.
7. Compare your thoughts with the authors' ideas about the basics in measurement that all school counselors should possess. Which expectations are the greatest? Why do you think this is so?
8. Which, if any, assessment issues presented in this chapter have influenced your life? Have they been resolved? If so, how? If not, did you acquire any information that might lead to a resolution?
9. Make an inventory of the tests that are mandated in the state where you currently reside or work. What is your impression of this condition?
10. Analyze the performance of the counselor in the test interpretation simulation from a counseling skills perspective. What were her strengths? What are your recommendations for improving her performance?
11. What are the high-stakes testing circumstances in the state where your program resides? Do any of the advocacy and prevention recommendations within this chapter appear helpful for school counselors in your state?
12. Go to the scan Web site (www.scan21st.com) and propose some ways that this site might assist school counselors in their various assessment functions.

CHAPTER 13

Inventing a School Counseling Program Online

Goals: To provide an opportunity for readers to apply the information presented in Chapters 1 to 12 and the appendices to a hypothetical real world situation, to achieve integration of information and transfer of knowledge, and to use the Internet as a means of inventing and sharing programmatic ideas.

INTRODUCTION

In the mid-1990s, we began to experiment with teaching some of our counselor education units of instruction online. Our first attempts were hit and miss, and our students often viewed these online activities as frustrating and as a distraction from what they wanted from counselor education classes, namely, face-to-face instruction and considerable interpersonal activity in class. Now, 10 years later, we typically receive 5 to 10 calls per month wondering if our counselor education degree program is online and available to students throughout the United States. We even receive e-mails from international students inquiring whether they can participate in our degree program online. To date, we do not offer our complete program online; however, many of our counselor education courses are Internet assisted, and it is possible that we will soon offer several courses completely online.

Although there are many important questions about the effectiveness of counselor education online, it is increasingly apparent that as interactive tools on the Internet improve, online preparation of counselors becomes increasingly possible. The online activities at the end of each chapter show that we regard the Internet as an important means for giving graduate students and practicing school counselors increased opportunities to share their views about counseling with each other and with the world.

In the previous 12 chapters, however, we have largely presented *our* ideas about the important ingredients of a balanced comprehensive school counseling program and have incorporated the guidance of highly regarded and nationally recognized models of school counseling. Each chapter has its own goals, and the information is presented categorically according to important themes (e.g., accountability) or functions (e.g., prevention programming). You have been left to integrate the parts (e.g., legal and ethical considerations) into a whole (i.e., a school counseling program). To help

you achieve transfer of training and accomplish integration of the information (as well as to give you the opportunity to challenge us and be creative), this chapter is yours to write. This chapter is a living, ever-changing document, a collection of ideas from counselor education graduate students and from school counselors around the world. This collection of ideas appears on the School Counseling Activities Network for the 21st Century Web site at www.scan21st.com.

You may produce your contributions to this chapter as part of a guided exercise that is featured at http://www.genesislight.com/scan21st/newdirections/.

When you get to this site, click on step 1 and follow the directions to making your contributions to what school counseling can become in the 21st century.

STEP 1—INVENTING A SCHOOL COUNSELING PROGRAM

Step 1 is your opportunity to begin to invent a school counseling program from your own ingenuity. As you read the first 12 chapters of this textbook, you had the opportunity to provide your reactions to the topics covered. During this process, you have undoubtedly wondered how school counselors might do things better, more efficiently, and with more significant results. As you read the material in the first 12 chapters, you may also have wondered if the "real" world of school counseling resembles what is presented in the national models and paradigms discussed in this textbook. You now have a chance to contribute your own ideas about school counseling beginning here in step 1. Begin by writing your ideas about what you would like your school counseling program to be. You may write your ideas using your favorite word processing program (e.g., Microsoft Word) or simply by jotting notes on scratch pads. Eventually you will be sharing your thoughts electronically,

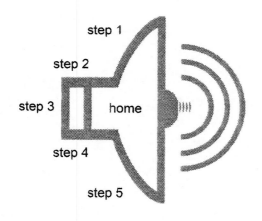

Step 1 - - Inventing a School Counseling Program

We want to give you the opportunity to create the foundation for an innovative school counseling program. You will walk yourself through five steps - - the last step will be an opportunity to share your ideas with school counselors all over the world. Completing all five steps may take two or three weeks (or longer). Take your time. Invention takes patience - - not easy for most of us in a fast-paced, electronic world.

Here in step 1 we suggest that you open your favorite word processing program (for example, microsoft word) and begin to write ideas about what you want your school counseling program to be. Some of you may prefer to write your ideas on a scratch pad or in a journal instead of using a word processing program. You may also want to write your ideas over the period of a few days.

Exercise your imagination. Be inventive. Write your ideas as they come to you. Please do not discard anything you write - - whether you write your ideas electronically or on paper.

Keep all your ideas together in a convenient place.

When you are reasonably (not perfectly) satisfied with the ideas you have written, move to step 2.

but some of you may prefer to begin writing your thoughts the old-fashioned way, using paper and pencil. Whatever your preference for getting your thoughts down, feel free to exercise your imagination. Be creative—and please do not discard any of the ideas you write. Some ideas that, at first, may seem useless may turn out, in the end, to be some of the most interesting and useful.

When you are reasonably (not perfectly) satisfied with the ideas you have accumulated, move to step 2.

STEP 2—SUMMARIZING YOUR EARLY IDEAS

Now it is time for you to collect your ideas and summarize them. By the way, you may easily get the impression in graduate school and elsewhere that documents with lots of words are the most valuable instruments for making progress in the field of school counseling. We take the opposite point of view and encourage you to use words parsimoniously. We recommend that you look over the school counseling ideas you have accumulated and summarize them in only 1 or 2 pages of text. Believe it or not, it is usually more difficult to convey your thoughts in 2 pages than to convey them in 20 pages. Most decision makers, however, simply have no time to read 20 pages of ideas; therefore, we suggest that you use words wisely and precisely. Present your school counseling program in no more than 2 pages of text, thinking creatively along the way.

When you are reasonably (not perfectly) satisfied with the ideas you have accumulated, move to step 3.

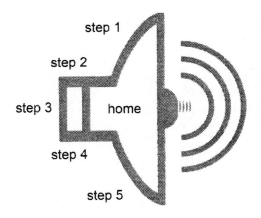

Step 2 - - Summarizing Your Early Ideas

Bring together all the school counseling ideas you have written. Open your favorite word processing program. Try to summarize all your ideas into one or two pages of text. Some folks believe that lots of words are important. In this exercise, lots of words get in the way. We want you to summarize your thoughts clearly and concisely. (By the way, please do not discard any of the draft ideas you wrote on scratch pads or in your journal. You may want to refer to them later.)

Remember to continue to exercise your imagination as you summarize your programmatic ideas. Your inventive thoughts may contribute exciting new ways of helping students.

After you have completed your summary in one or two pages, print it. Read it. Let it sit for a day or two and read it again. Revise it if you like.

When you are reasonably (not perfectly) satisfied with the summary of your ideas, move to step 3.

STEP 3—REALITY TESTING YOUR IDEAS

Now that you have summarized your inventive ideas about what you want a school counseling program to be, give it a reality check. Ask these questions about your program ideas:

1. How will my program enhance the academic, career, and personal/social development of students? If your program does not focus on one or more of these areas, why not?
2. Which aspects of your program meet developmental needs of students? Which aspects are preventive? Which aspects of your program are simply focused on responding to students' needs?
3. How will you collaborate within your school, school system, and larger community to implement your school counseling program?
4. How will you evaluate your program?

Be thoughtful and patient as you ask these questions about your programmatic ideas. You may want to write some of your responses to these questions. Remember, a large accumulation of words often distracts from clear expression. Keep your reactions to these four questions brief and to the point.

When you are reasonably (not perfectly) satisfied that you have put your ideas through the test of reality, move to step 4.

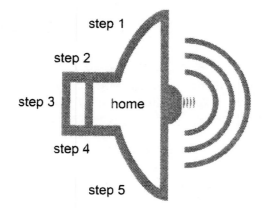

Step 3 - - Reality Testing Your Ideas

Now that you have summarized your inventive ideas about what you want a school counseling program to be, give it a reality check. Ask these questions about your program ideas:

1. How will my program enhance the academic, career, and personal/social development of students? If your program does not focus on one or more of these areas, why not?

2. Which aspects of your program meet developmental needs of students? Which aspects are preventive? Which aspects of your program are simply focused on responding to students' needs?

3. How will you collaborate within your school, school system, and larger community to implement your school counseling program?

4. How will you evaluate your program?

Be thoughtful and patient as you ask these questions about your programmatic ideas. You may want to write some of your responses to these questions.

When you are reasonably (not perfectly) satisfied that you have put your ideas through the test of reality, move to step 4.

STEP 4—REVISING YOUR IDEAS

After you have thoughtfully and patiently checked the first summary of your ideas against the reality of counseling in today's schools, think carefully about how you want to revise the original one- to two-page document you wrote. As you think about revising your early ideas, consider also how you might best attract attention to your ideas. Many counselor education graduate students and practicing school counselors around the world will be sharing their ideas here. How can you increase the chances that we will pay attention to your ideas? Think hard before you revise your ideas to share with the world.

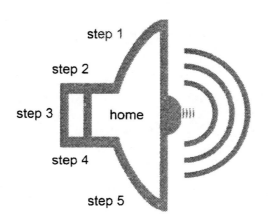

Step 4 · · Revising Your Ideas

After you have thoughtfully and patiently checked the first summary of your ideas against the reality of counseling in today's schools, think carefully about how you want to revise the original one to two page document you wrote.

Once again, open your favorite word processing program and begin revising your original ideas. Remember few words are better than many words. Express yourself simply (to the point), energetically, and creatively. Your revised document should be no more than one or two pages long.

Print your new document. Read it. Put it aside for a day or two. Read it again. Revise it if you wish.

When you are reasonably (not perfectly) satisfied with the revised document you have created, we invite you to share it with the world. Move to step 5.

Once again, use your favorite word processing program to revise your original ideas. Remember, few words are better than many words. Express yourself simply (to the point), energetically, and creatively. Your revised document should be no more than one or two pages long.

Print your new document. Read it. Put it aside for a day or two. Read it again. Revise it if you want.

When you are reasonably (not perfectly) satisfied with your revised document, we invite you to share it with the world. Move to step 5.

STEP 5—SHARING YOUR IDEAS WITH THE WORLD

You have taken the opportunity to create the foundation for an innovative school counseling program. As you have progressed through the five steps in this effort, you have been freed to think creatively and openly about what you would like school coun-

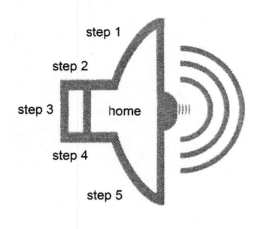

seling to be. You have now shared your ideas with school counselors around the world. If you want to see the ideas of other school counselors go to the School Counseling Activities Network for the 21st Century Web site at http://www.genesislight. com/scan21st.

The ideas on this site have also become part of a living chapter, "Inventing a School Counseling Program Online," in the following textbook: Baker, S. B., & Gerler, E. R. (2008). *School counseling for the twenty-first century* (5th ed.). Upper Saddle River, NJ: Merrill/Prentice Hall.

Counselor education graduate students and practicing school counselors around the world will read and learn from the ideas you have contributed here. Keep the ideas coming. Continue to create and contribute your programmatic ideas online. We welcome them!

CHAPTER 14

Beyond the Training Program: A School Counseling Career

Goals: To offer suggestions for enhancing the professional identity and well-being of school counselors and to discuss future prospects for school counselors.

We heard the following testimonial from a school counselor whose experience in the profession spanned 35 years:

> *I have been a school counselor for 35 years. As I reflect on my years in counseling, I realize that I could not have chosen a better, more rewarding career for myself. Students I have counseled have attended fine universities and distinguished themselves in*

prominent careers. I have seen some of my favorite students graduate, join the military, go off to war, and then return to my office years later to reflect on the horrors they had seen or to grieve about the physical scars they suffered in battle. I have helped adolescent girls, raising children by themselves, struggle to complete the courses needed to graduate from high school. I have listened to African American youngsters—devalued by teachers—as they struggle to prove their worth in an unfriendly academic environment. I have been awakened on several nights by phone calls from parents who were trying to cope with the loss of a child in an automobile accident. I have sat with teachers, ready to leave their profession, because they no longer could tolerate the disrespect they experienced in the classroom. I have watched gifted young artists express themselves through painting and music. I have helped a fine athlete overcome his alcohol abuse and obtain a scholarship to a small college that valued his talent. I have found so many friends among teachers and parents who were willing to listen when I was confused and troubled in the work I had chosen for myself. I am retiring next year. I am glad to have found a profession that embraced me for who I am.

BEYOND THE TRAINING PROGRAM

Our theme in this section of the chapter is that, upon completing their training, graduates are challenged to keep motivated and current as professional school counselors. Five studies published by the ASCA and ACES journals in 2005 and 2006 support this theme. All five studies employed multiple-regression statistical analyses that provided information about how strong relationships between predictors and estimated outcomes (i.e., criteria) seem to be. Four studies had national samples, and the one with the largest sample had participants from the state of Florida. In all, the five studies sampled 2,851 school counselors. The estimated outcomes or criteria included role incongruence and ambiguity (Culbreth, Scarborough, Banks-Johnson, & Solomon, 2005), emotional exhaustion and personal accomplishment (Butler & Constantine, 2005), overall job satisfaction and stress (Rayle, 2006), career satisfaction and commitment, (Baggerly & Osborn, 2006), and job and life satisfaction (Bryant & Constantine, 2006).

The important predictors of these criteria were perceiving high self-efficacy, experiencing high levels of personal accomplishment, mattering to others, being positively perceived by others, having appropriate job duties, possessing the ability to manage multiple life roles in their lives effectively, experiencing low levels of emotional exhaustion, and receiving district and peer supervision. Negative predictors were role conflict and stress. The research team conducted its investigations independently, so the terminology used is peculiar to the measures the team employed. It appears as if the best summary of the overall findings is that school counselors are more likely to feel good about themselves and their work if their job duties conform with their training, they are regarded highly for their professional competence, they can manage their professional and personal responsibilities effectively, they are able to keep current professionally, and they believe they can be competent and effective professionally.

Thus, we now turn to recommendations for achieving these outcomes. They are presented as ideas about keeping motivated and keeping current.

Keeping Motivated

Burnout is a widely used label for a broad range of symptoms leading to losing the interest or competence to perform one's job effectively. It is something to be avoided. No one wants to be burned out. Yet, many professionals receive the label. Without getting overly diagnostic, several challenges cause school counselors to experience burnout. One challenge may be the stress associated with counselors trying to be all things to all people while having too little control over their professional identity. Principals who treat counselors like administrative assistants, teachers who are unhappy with class enrollments, parents who blame counselors because their children fail to get accepted to a preferred college, students who cannot be successfully helped, student-to-counselor ratios that are too large to manage, and insufficient administrative support are but a few additional examples. Low status in the professional hierarchy, insufficient budgetary support and resources, low pay, professional isolation, loss of competence and confidence, and personal problems are also examples of stressors faced by school counselors. Using the Counselor Occupational Stress Inventory, Moracco, Butcke, and McEwen (1984) documented the causes of stress among a sample of 361 ASCA members. Their analysis led to an observation that occupational stress seems to be a multidimensional concept. The dimensions they identify in their factor analysis are lack of decision-making authority, financial stress (small rewards), nonprofessional duties, job overload, and dissatisfying professional relationships with teachers and principals. Behannon (1996) assembled comments from several counseling professionals that, in summary, pointed out that the nature of their work makes school counselors at high risk of burning out.

The purpose of this discourse is not to lament these problems because school counselors are not the only individuals who experience such stressors and suffer from burnout. Rather, they are presented as challenges. Individually and collectively, school counselors are challenged to accept stressors as a fact of life and do everything within their power to prevent themselves from burning out by treating the symptoms quickly and appropriately when they occur. As can be determined from the sampling of causes listed previously, school counselors have many stressors with which to cope. Some can be managed individually or in cooperation with colleagues, and support from larger bodies, such as professional organizations and legislatures, and from enlightened individuals with sufficient influence to cause change. What can individual counselors do to prevent burnout? The authors' belief is that keeping motivated and current are strategies within the control of each counselor that have promise for self-enhancement and burnout prevention.

The theme of this presentation on keeping motivated is "Be proactive." We are challenged to take the responsibility for motivating ourselves. Many strategies for implementing this idea exist. Following is a presentation of goals, not to be considered a listing of strategies. Strategies are varied, numerous, and do not work universally. Readers can more easily respond to suggested goals, determining whether they are personally appropriate and deciding on their own strategies for implementing them. In a book aptly entitled *A Survival Guide for the Secondary School Counselor*, Hitchner and Tifft-Hitchner (1987) suggested establishing consulting alliances with colleagues to find sanity in numbers and leaving the emotions associated with problems at work so

Working school counselors form peer supervision groups similar to those they experienced as graduate students.

they do not interfere with one's home life. Both are commendable goals that may be accomplished differently by individual counselors.

The suggestions mentioned previously focus on internal sources and resources. However, an important external motivational source is one's salary and the corresponding effect on income and lifestyle. The good news in this domain as we go to press is that the median annual earnings of school counselors in 2004, as reported by the U.S. Department of Labor Statistics, was $51,160, and that figure was higher than for junior college counselors; counselors employed by colleges, universities, and professional schools; individual and family counselors; and vocational rehabilitation counselors (ACA, 2006). Although there are a number of contingencies that may affect the lower median salaries in the other counseling fields that do not influence the salaries of school counselors, the fact remains that, on average, school counselors seem to be the best paid category.

Cognitive Health.   One arena over which individuals have potential control is their own thoughts. Self-acceptance is an important goal and is founded on the belief that one is doing her or his best and making decisions in good faith. A belief in having acted in good faith allows individuals to accept constructive criticism as challenging rather than as damning. Recognizing irrational and self-defeating thoughts may prevent corresponding irrational ideation and self-defeating behaviors. The same tactics that counselors use to recognize and treat irrational ideation experienced by student clients can be applied to themselves. The investigations by Butler and Constantine (2005) and Rayle (2006) pointed out the perceived importance of self-esteem and mattering to others in the workplace, respectively.

Dollarhide and Saginak (2003) highlighted the importance of achieving personal mental health through balancing external reality and internal needs. They also stressed the importance of finding one's spiritual or moral center, that is, an awareness of our own morals and values, and by extension, those of our student clients. They challenged school counselors to understand when they have done their best, realizing that student clients are empowered to choose their own responses to efforts to help them, and to be able to let them make their decisions while taking responsibility for the consequences.

Physical Health.   A second arena over which individuals have potential control is their physical health. Some symptoms of stress can be treated and prevented physically. Relaxed individuals with healthful diets are less likely to experience burnout. The health sciences offer numerous suggestions for achieving and maintaining good physical health. Physical health will make individuals better able to cope with stress while also causing them to think about themselves more positively. Some symptoms of stress can be treated successfully by such physical responses as deep diaphragmatic breathing and progressive muscle relaxation. These treatments may be even more effective if used in conjunction with cognitive strategies for coping with irrational and self-defeating ideation (Cormier & Nurius, 2003).

Healthy Interactions.   A third arena over which control can be achieved is interactions with others. The environment includes other people. Achieving appropriate assertiveness is an important goal for coping with others. Individuals are challenged to achieve direct or open, honest, and appropriate expressions of their affectionate or oppositional feelings, preferences, needs, and opinions (Fitch, Newby, Ballestero, & Marshall, 2001; Galassi & Galassi, 1977). Appropriate assertiveness means that one is able to give and receive compliments; make requests; express liking, love, and affection; initiate and maintain conversations; express one's legitimate rights; refuse requests; and express justified annoyance, displeasure, and anger. Performing these behaviors successfully will improve the working environment of school counselors. A pleasant, sufficiently spacious, private, and appropriately heated and ventilated physical environment can also work wonders. Counselors can achieve some of these goals on their own, whereas other goals may require assertive action.

Rayle's (2006) investigation points out the importance that school counselors hold for believing that what they do professionally matters to others. Counselors who understand the goals and expectations of other individuals in their environment are better able to develop ways to cope with them successfully. For example, teachers may expect counselors, as coprofessionals, to take their side in disputes with students, rather than approach disputes as student advocates; principals, who have broad definitions of their own jobs, may define counselors' jobs similarly; and parents may view counselors as individuals who will readily share information with them about their children, regardless of whether the information is confidential. Some combination of creative thinking, appropriate assertiveness, and diplomacy is required to cope with these and other misperceived expectations and to keep from being worn down by them. Having confidence in one's ability to be a successful professional school counselor is related to career satisfaction (Baggerly & Osborn, 2006). These feelings of self-efficacy are important ingredients in the process of achieving healthy interactions with others and demonstrate the relationship between good cognitive health and healthy interactions with stakeholders.

Reasonable Workload. Student-to-counselor ratios are determined predominantly by the financial condition of the school district and secondarily by the perceived worth of the guidance program (Shaw, 1973). Universal ratios are difficult to dictate because of individual differences associated with the severity of student problems, amount of available secretarial and clerical assistance, curriculum options, and referral support. In a time of a generally perceived need for good counseling, when it was believed that the United States was threatened by Soviet technological advances, Conant (1959) recommended 250 to 300 students to each counselor. This was probably a compromise between providing high-quality counseling services and what was economically feasible for school districts. As reported by Peters (1978), the Education Task Force of the 1971 White House Conference on Youth recommended a ratio of 50 to 1 throughout elementary and secondary schools. Peters himself recommended 200 to 1, again as a compromise.

In *A Nation at Risk: The Imperative for Educational Reform*, reported by the National Commission on Excellence in Education in 1983, no mention was made of school counseling (Hitchner & Tifft-Hitchner, 1987). This report and others like it emphasize the importance of improving the knowledge and work habits of Americans to cope with the economic challenges from political allies in the Far East and Western Europe. Consequently, attention was devoted to the cognitive domain. The theme is to produce better-educated and disciplined citizens. Although the report is useful, with important goals, it falls short because it does not also recognize the affective needs of students.

These affective needs are likely to grow. Figures from the 1980 U.S. Census led to projections that one third of the population in the United States would be either African American or Hispanic by 2020. Historically, children of poverty have come primarily from minority groups. Women are increasingly entering the labor force; 50% of the labor force in 1985 were women. The number of single-parent homes and latchkey children is increasing dramatically, and drop-out rates, already significant in some areas of the United States, promise to become even more problematic (Hitchner & Tifft-Hitchner, 1987). Poverty, minority status, having a working mother, and coming from a single-parent family are highly correlated with school failure (William T. Grant Foundation Commission on Work, Family and Citizenship, 1988). School failure leads to dropping out or to floundering within the system. The Grant Commission views these individuals, "the forgotten half," as being in danger of not finding places for themselves in the economic system. In addition, individuals from these highly vulnerable groups who are capable of benefiting from the opportunities associated with receiving a higher education are not likely to receive adequate precollege guidance (College Entrance Examination Board, 1986).

The preceding findings lead one to conclude that an emphasis placed solely on improving the environment for cognitive development is insufficient for the United States to meet the economic challenges of the 21st century. This was highlighted in earlier chapters by referring to the work of Adelman and Taylor (2002). Counseling programs with better proactive and responsive counseling responses, in conjunction with improved instruction, are crucial, and they go hand in hand (Dahir, 2001; Gysbers & Henderson, 2000). Better counseling programs are linked to lower student-to-counselor ratios, especially where the most vulnerable students are attending the schools. Exactly what the ratios should be is a moot question. They must be decreased for counselors to be more effective and to perceive themselves as such. The challenge probably has to be met collectively through efforts of national professional organizations. Currently, "the ASCA recommends a ratio of 1/100 (ideal) to 1/300 (maximum) to implement a standards-based, comprehensive developmental school counseling program" (Campbell & Dahir, 1997, p. 13). As we go to press, the current ACA and ASCA recommendation is 250 to 1.

Enhanced Competence.   Becoming a licensed professional counselor (LPC) is an opportunity available to counselors in most states. Being an LPC is not a requisite for certification/licensure as a school counselor. Therefore, many counselors have this option as a way of keeping current and motivated. Although LPC requirements may vary from state to state, becoming an LPC usually requires having one's credentials reviewed, passing an examination (e.g., the National Counseling Examination), and providing evidence of postgraduate coursework and/or clinical supervision. These are activities that help one become and remain current. They may also lead to a sense of personal accomplishment, add to one's perceived professional stature, and provide an opportunity for economic enhancement (e.g., private counseling practice or consultation services).

In a survey of 267 members of the ASCA who were school counselors, Page, Pietrzak, and Sutton (2001) found that 29% were receiving peer clinical supervision, and 57% wanted to receive it. Those expressing a preference for peer clinical supervision expressed a desire that it be provided by school counselors who were trained to provide supervision. Data from the investigations by Baggerly and Osborn (2006) and Culbreth et al. (2005) also express the perceived importance of supervision to school counselors.

Sutton and Page (1994) and Agnew, Vaught, Getz, and Fortune (2000) reported on the advantages of peer supervision activities as a way to keep motivated. Working school counselors form peer supervision groups similar in nature to those they experienced in counseling and internship practicums while graduate students. Agnew et al. found that counselors who participated in a peer group clinical supervision program experienced improved professional relationships, believed they had increased the opportunities to learn counseling skills and techniques, and experienced an increased sense of professionalism. The report also stressed the importance of administrative support, training in clinical supervision, adequate funding, and adequate time in making the activity successful.

In the 21st century, it appears as if most professional school counselors feel comfortable using computer technology such as e-mail and the Internet (Carlson, Portman, & Bartlett, 2006). Yet, most have probably only scratched the surface of enhancing their competence in this domain. Continued exposure and experience will increase usage and the prospects for using various forms of useful software.

Keeping Current

At mid-20th century, one axiom stated in counselor training programs was that there will be jobs in the future that do not exist today. That turned out to be true, accurately depicting the rapid changes in the second half of the 20th century and indicating a continuation of the same circumstances in the early 21st century. Rapidly changing times feature increasing educational and technological developments. Consequently, matriculating from the most up-to-date and comprehensive counselor training program may still leave a graduate's preparation dated within a decade unless an effort is made to keep current with new developments—an effort to seek self-renewal (Baker, 1981). Walz and Benjamin (1978) suggested that self-renewal be viewed from two perspectives. The first perspective defines self-renewal as updating and streamlining previously acquired skills and knowledge to ensure that one knows what has been learned and adds new ideas to old approaches. From the second perspective, counselors can use self-renewal to acquire techniques, ideas, and skills they never had before, making them even more versatile. Thus, whether keeping current involves refurbishing the old model or developing a new hybrid, the need for self-renewal is a real and constant issue confronting school counselors.

Counselors are challenged to keep current and to achieve continuous self-renewal. This can be done in many ways, some creative and some traditional. Among the traditional ways to keep current are attending workshops; enrolling in university and college courses via on-site or distance learning; reading professional journals, books, and reports; listening to audio and observing visual media; attending professional conferences and conventions; and teaching—that is, sharing one's knowledge and skills with others. Creative responses are determined by the ideas each counselor generates individually. For instance, those who have access to the information highway provided by the Internet may find exploring the Web an opportunity to gain useful information and mastering the Internet an interesting challenge.

When self-renewal activities require time away from work or travel and tuition expenses, school counselors are encouraged to demonstrate to their administrators that what they are doing meets the school's goals and objectives (Hatch, 2001). In this way, the efforts are more likely to receive moral and perhaps financial support.

The National Board for Certified Counselors (NBCC) provides an opportunity for counselors to keep current while engaging in a certification process. The NBCC certifies counselors who pass NBCC examinations, referring to them as national certified counselors. Among the certificates is that for national certified school counselor. Preparation for the examinations and involvement in NBCC-approved workshops and continuing education programs are examples of ways to keep current that have been sponsored by professional counseling associations such as the ACA and ASCA. They are designed to meet the needs of practicing counselors.

Membership in professional associations such as the ACA and ASCA and their regional and state affiliates provides a number of avenues for keeping current. Those opportunities include published newsletters and professional journals, electronic newsletters, comprehensive Web sites, and professional conferences/conventions. A visit to one or more of these Web sites can be quite illuminating to individuals motivated to self-renewal through keeping current.

Of all the challenges to the professional identity of school counselors, keeping current may be the one most within the power of individual counselors to achieve. No less important than the others, it is a goal that can be achieved at any time. Perhaps it should be the first goal set by graduates of counselor training programs. The trainers, having done their best to make students up to date when they complete training, pass to their students the responsibility for keeping the torch of knowledge lit. Students, in turn, by keeping the flame burning, make themselves valuable to their stakeholders throughout their years of service.

BEYOND THE PRESENT: WHAT DOES THE FUTURE HOLD FOR SCHOOL COUNSELORS?

Clearly, school counseling has changed considerably since the beginning of the 20th century, and the role of school counselors lacks the clarity of either teachers or principals. Unfortunately, one feature of the changing role has been an apparent process of expansion of the functions within the role without corresponding attempts to remove established functions to make room for new ones—an additive effect (Lambie & Williamson, 2004).

Unfortunately, a point/counterpoint presentation in the June 2006 issue of *Counseling Today* depicted the role-seeking process for school counselors in an either–or light. Anderson and Perryman (2006) were presented as spokespersons for mental health expert role: "The school counselor is quite possibly the only mental health professional in the school and perhaps the community uniquely equipped to recognize and refer students for specialized needs. . . . This ultimately enhances the

School counselors have new perspective on the future.

academic success rates because problems are treated" (p. 14). Presenting the other perspective, Tejada (2006) stated: "The first word in our job title is 'school.' Often, the best way for school counselors to help children succeed academically and socially is to address the academic and social needs of large groups of children" (p. 14).

One of the characteristics of this form of print debate is that the proponents of each point of view are not interacting face to face. And we are uncertain about whether they read each other's point of view before stating their own. One consequence of this form of debate is that the differing proponents are unable to locate and negotiate points of agreement and separate them from their major differences. Thus, a careful reading of the presentations may lead one to conclude that the supposed differences are a mirage due to differing terminology or focusing on small, albeit disparate, parts of the big picture.

Our belief is that both points of view presented in that debate are valid, yet limited, and represent components within a larger comprehensive balanced school counseling program such as that described and promoted in this textbook. Although there is most certainly role confusion present today—the *Old Ghost* (Shertzer & Stone, 1963) cited in chapter 3—there appears to be evidence that school counselors are regarded highly by stakeholders and that progress is being made toward resolving the role problems and enhancing the profession.

Evidence of stakeholder regard is presented in studies reported by Amatea and Clark (2005) and Zalaquett (2005). The former study was qualitative in nature with a small sample (N = 26 school administrators), yet yielding *richer data*. Amatea and Clark (2005) reported that four distinctive role emphases for school counselors were preferred: (a) innovative school leader (see chapter 7), (b) collaborative case consultant (see school–community collaboration), (c) responsive direct service provider (see chapter 9), and (d) administrative team player (see noncounseling functions in chapter 1). Three of the role emphases fit within the roles promoted in this textbook and within the three promising paradigms presented in earlier chapters (e.g., the ASCA National Model, the TSCI, and the School–Community Collaboration Model). The administrative team player data provides evidence that there is still work to achieve with stakeholders.

The participants in Zalaquett's (2005) survey study were 500 principals in Florida. These stakeholders had high regard for their school counselors and expressed confidence in their positive impact on student academic, behavioral, and mental health development. Zalaquett noted that expressions of confidence in academic, behavioral, and mental health domains were a confirmation of the ASCA National Model (ASCA, 2005).

In the remainder of this chapter, we offer our evidence of what we perceive are the initiatives that have the best potential for responding school counselor role confusion and enhancing the profession's development. They are (a) meeting the need for leadership, (b) meeting the need for collaboration, (c) achieving licensure portability, and (d) promoting the utility of the ASCA National Model.

Meeting the Need for Leadership

In chapter 7, we explored the role of leadership in school counseling and cited what seem to be important competencies school counselors should develop and acquire as leaders. This challenge for leadership seems pervasive; that is, it is needed at all levels of the profession—from the school to the national level. The school counseling profession appears to be redefining its identity in the early 21st century (Kaffenberger, Murphy, & Bemak, 2006). Challenges causing this redefinition process include school reform emphases on closing the achievement gap and financial challenges leading to budget cuts in some school systems. We agree with the conclusion stated by Kaffenberger et al. that "It is essential that the leaders of the school counseling field shape the discussion which involves a number of critical issues that will define the future direction of school counseling" (p. 288). Readers may remember that attention to the importance of leadership has been attributed to both the ASCA National Model and the TSCI in previous chapters.

In our opinion, although the challenges may change with time, a leadership structure for meeting the challenges is needed. Such a structure needs grassroots support and coordination at various levels such as local school districts, county and state professional organizations, and regional and state organizations. Currently, existing professional organizations such as the ASCA, the ACA, and the ACES and their local, state, and regional affiliates seem to be the best vehicles for accomplishing this goal. If a structure is in place and ongoing, challenges requiring professional leadership can be better addressed as they occur.

Kaffenberg et al. (2006) described an apparently successful example of achieving leadership structure in the northern Virginia area. The collaboration included professional school counselors and counselor educators, and was influenced by national professional organizations. The accomplishments of the northern Virginia School Counseling Leadership Team (SCLT) were quite impressive (e.g., reinstatement of a permanent school counseling position in the Virginia State Department of Education, revision of the Virginia school counselor standards, a series of workshops and summit meetings for school counselors and guidance directors). Kaffenberg et al. provided information about how the SCLT was formed that should be instructive to others seeking ideas for achieving leadership structure. Highlights of the recommendations for forming collaborative leadership teams are (a) including a comprehensive range of stakeholders among the team members; (b) identifying leaders of the team who can manage logistical details, lead meetings, mediate individual differences, balance the interests of all participants, and serve as spokespersons for the team; (c) identifying short- and long-term goals; (d) spreading the influence of the team via a variety of training formats; and (e) achieving accountability through regular and consistent evaluations.

Accepting the importance of a leadership role at all levels of the school counseling profession and working to achieve leadership structure is one of our recommendations for readers of this text. This goal can be achieved both individually through one's behaviors as a professional school counselor and collectively in cooperation with other school counselors, and by supporting professional associations that work to advance the school counseling profession and serve students better.

Meeting the Need for Collaboration

Also a component of chapter 7, collaboration is closely associated with leadership. Therefore, the content of this section is presented and interactive with that of the previous section on leadership. The same circumstances that demand leadership currently and in the future will promote the need for collaboration from the grassroots to the national levels of the school counseling profession. Recognition of the value of collaboration is especially important in the personal/social development domain of students directly. As was pointed out previously (e.g., chapter 2), many students are unable to take advantage of opportunities for achieving academic success, if opportunities are available, because of mitigating circumstances that interfere with their being successful in school (e.g., poverty, mental health challenges, substance abuse, broken homes, truancy). The School–Community Collaboration Model was introduced in chapter 2 as a vehicle for attempting to address this challenge. Underlying principles are that academic achievement/development cannot be achieved for some students until personal/social obstacles in their lives are addressed successfully and that most school systems do not have the sufficient resources to achieve this goal from within the system. The School–Community Collaboration concept stresses the importance of forming collaborations between schools and their communities to better address these challenges. The School–Community Collaboration literature suggests a number of ways that the collaboration concept can be implemented and what the outcomes have been where such collaborations have occurred (Adelman & Taylor, 2002).

We believe that collaboration thrust, particularly between schools and community support services, is an important goal for the future enhancement of the school counseling profession and those whom we serve. A basic part of the challenge is to convince local administrators that the concept is viable, that school counselors can be leaders and players in the collaboration process, and that turf issues that may occur between school and community personnel will need to be resolved (Brown, Dahlbeck, & Sparkman-Barnes, 2006). The various parties who need to cooperate to achieve collaboration goals may be more likely to engage in a mutually cooperative manner if they concurrently accept the principle of focusing on the development of the whole child in order to deal with the complicated process students who have in-school and out-of-school lives (Walsh & Galassi, 2002).

Working to build a foundation for collaboration in one's local school system that will make it acceptable to stakeholders is one way that beginning school counselors can work to achieve this goal. Obviously, there is much to do beyond this first step, and successful collaborative relationships will probably result from a series of steps taken by those who are trying to achieve this goal. Success may also require going back to the drawing board and retracing one's steps at times. Although the need for collaboration may be national in nature, in our opinion the foundation for achieving this goal successfully is located in each local school district where collaborations unique to those schools and communities will have to be forged.

Achieving Licensure Portability

PSCs and LPCs have usually met the licensure/certification requirements for a specific state upon finishing their training programs, passing requisite examinations, and submitting various documents attesting to their legitimacy of their preparation. Unfortunately, there are no reciprocity agreements among the states. Therefore, PSCs and LPCs are often limited in their ability to move beyond the state of original licensure without engaging in a time-consuming, frustrating, and expensive process of being licensed in another state. At first glance, this seems to be a problem associated with the counselors who need or want to move elsewhere and prospective employers in some locales who are facing professional personnel shortages. Events associated with the massive destruction caused by the Hurricane Katrina in 2005 pointed out that another class of victims of the delays caused by lack of the portability of counselor credentials is those prospective clients who are in great need of immediate help. Yet, that help cannot be made readily available until the credentials of individuals who may be willing to travel across state lines to respond to an emergency have been approved.

We are believers in a national registry for PSCs and LPCs that would be the ultimate portability plan. There are national standards in place that could be adopted by all states if the parties involved were willing to do so. Unfortunately, this is a domain rife with concerns about turf issues and influenced by local and state politics. So, the national registry is currently a goal unlikely to be soon achieved.

Fortunately, a step in the desired direction began in 2006. Mascari (2006) and Kennedy (2006) reported progress achieved toward a second path to portability, that is, a credential data bank known as the National Credential Registry (NCR). While states continue to maintain their own regulations, the second path concept is an attempt to streamline the process of presenting one's credentials to states beyond the origin of one's licensure. The NCR concept is a national credentials database. For an initial fee and a yearly maintenance fee, participants can submit their credentials to the database, and the database will submit copies of the original documents to cooperating state licensure/certification boards on request of the participants. The perceived advantage of the database is that it lessens the time one has to invest in the portability process when an opportunity to seek employment or volunteer services out of one's licensure jurisdiction occurs. Participant requests can be honored immediately. Readers are urged to compare this process to asking all entities that must provide required evidence each time such assistance is needed and to also consider that, in some instances, former supervisors may have moved, retired, or passed away.

Based on what we know of the NCR, readers are encouraged to investigate it thoroughly and consider enrolling. At the time the Kennedy (2006) and Mascari (2006) reports were published, 20 states had agreed to participate, but the negotiations were somewhat secretive in nature. The entity in charge of the process is the American Association of State Counseling Boards and their Web site seems to be the best source of current information (www.aascb.org).

The Utility of the ASCA National Model

The ASCA National Model (ASCA, 2005) was introduced early in this text and has been mentioned in relation to a variety of topics throughout the succeeding chapters. Because the ASCA National Model is so well developed, comprehensively presented, and thoroughly supported in the school counseling profession and beyond, we believe that it is currently the best idea for enhancing the school counseling profession. Important reasons for our support are as follows:

- It attempts to define the role of school counselors.
- There is a comprehensive emphasis on meeting the developmental needs of students across academic, career, and personal/social domains.

- The standards-based focus emphasizes the importance of school counselors being accountable for setting and achieving goals and objectives and having a positive influence on students.
- The model has a historical connection to the existing knowledge base in counseling and education, and it was developed in cooperation with individuals who have been important contributors to the profession's development for decades.
- Although there seems to be a greater emphasis on proactive prevention and large-group guidance related curricular programming than on responsive services and individual and small-group counseling in the model, it still has the elements of a balanced program within the framework.
- Important concepts such as leadership, advocacy, and collaboration are emphasized.
- There is an emphasis on working within school systems for constructive change.
- There is advocacy of a system for managing and delivering services within school counseling programs.
- There is some empirical evidence that school counselors across the United States support the model (Foster, Young, & Hermann, 2005).
- The ASCA has a system in place for promoting and recognizing implementation of the model (Sparks, Johnson, & Lewis, 2005).
- The ASCA is establishing a National School Counseling Research Center (Sabella, 2006).

While lauding the potential influence the ASCA National Model may have on enhancing the school counseling profession, we also believe that it is probably an imperfect paradigm. Readers are encouraged to view the model as analogous to a theory. In this analogy, the ASCA National Model seems to be a presentation of principles that appear to be plausible to the presenters (e.g., preventive in design, developmental in nature, and an integral part of the total educational program). The principles are based on both scientific knowledge and informed ideals or plausible hypotheses. For example, although the ASCA National Standards that are part of the National Model appear to be plausible, they have not been supported empirically to any great extent as far as we know. And, as Galassi and Akos (2004) pointed out, the ASCA National Standards "Do not explicitly draw on current developmental theory and research. As such, these standards propose outcomes for academic, personal/social, and career development, but they do not address development by level; rather, they only articulate content areas that should be addressed" (p. 148).

Keys, Bemak, and Lockhart (1998) pointed out that the model's "primary prevention focus may be too broad, causing programs to be less sensitive to the differences in needs presented by at-risk youth" (p. 382). They believed that many primary prevention programs (i.e., the National Model focus) do not meet the needs of at-risk students sufficiently. Keys et al. promoted an additional focus on secondary and tertiary prevention programs that does not seem to be part of the current ASCA National Model. They believed that these secondary and tertiary prevention programs should emphasize responsive services that have greater depth than the model recommends, recognize that individual change is a function of school-based strategies *and* changes in the environments of at-risk youth, realize that individual school systems cannot themselves provide the broad range of services at-risk students need, and recognize that needs assessments should focus on the situation in the schools rather than the needs. It appears as if the expectations offered by Keys et al. suggest that the National Model may need to be expanded to incorporate ideas from, or similar to, the School–Community Collaboration Model.

Furthermore, although theories may appear comprehensive, theorists may have overlooked important elements of the domain of interest. For example, Foster, Young, and Hermann (2005) pointed out that school counselor competencies have yet to be defined within the ASCA National Model. This seems to be an important area for the ASCA to address in the future. Ironically, we emphasize what appear to us as the important school counselor competencies throughout our presentation of a balanced school counseling program in this textbook—perhaps another presentation analogous to a theory. In addition, although advocacy is one of the principles stated within the ASCA National Model, it does not appear to directly address multicultural competence, an appreciation for diversity, and advocacy for social justice.

If readers accept our theory analogy, what should they do next? We believe that theories are to be tested rather than accepted without debate. Therefore, readers are encouraged to familiarize themselves thoroughly with the ASCA National Model and all activities being generated in conjunction with it. Some school counselors will have to become participants in the implementation process because their school districts have adopted it. Others will be able to decide whether to promote the National Model in their school systems, wait and watch what develops, or reject it.

Based on the ASCA's professed interest in evaluation leading to accountability, those who participate in the process of implementing the National Model will have opportunities to test it in real world settings. We believe that testing the National Model is a good idea. If some of the principles appear to be invalid, a purpose of the evaluation/accountability process is to use the evaluation data to reconsider and revise ideas, goals, and practices, if necessary.

The ASCA National Model has the support of some individuals whose promotion of the paradigm may appear similar to selling a product. These behaviors are probably necessary to get the attention of grassroots school counseling professionals and provide opportunities for the model to be adopted and tested. We believe that widespread adoption and testing of the model is the best thing that can happen. We also believe that the findings from cumulative attempts to test the model will lead to further attempts to improve it. As the process of testing, analyzing, and improving the model grows, we believe the outcomes will be the most productive efforts to enhance the school counseling profession and corresponding services to students that will occur in the foreseeable future.

Closing Thoughts

Our position on the future of school counseling thus stated, we close with a comment about competencies, a subject highlighted throughout this textbook. As stated previously, we believe that the competencies presented here are generic to any model for school counseling. We also believe that these competencies will remain important. Therefore, we encourage all school counseling students and school counselors to be skillful across these competency domains. Whatever the circumstances may be, competent, flexible school counselors are better positioned to provide high-quality services to their stakeholders and make their programs relevant than are those who are inadequately competent and inflexible. This appears to be one important way that each school counselor can have an impact on his or her own future.

FEATURED ACTIVITY: GRADUATE STUDENT PERSPECTIVES ON A CAREER IN SCHOOL COUNSELING

In this chapter, we discuss a career in school counseling. As counselor educators, we have many opportunities to listen to our students' ideas about a career in school counseling. Students who are enrolled in internships often have the idealism that they held early in their graduate study challenged by the realities of everyday life in schools. One school counseling intern recently wrote:

> I want to do so much when I work with students at my internship site; however, I don't seem to have the time to do what I want to do. I guess I hoped to change the world when I started my counselor education program. Now, I'm not so sure about how much I'll be able to accomplish. My supervisor, a terrific counselor, encourages me to be optimistic—and I really am trying. But, the question I face every afternoon when I leave my internship school is "how am I going to have a positive influence on students' lives?"

How are you going to have a positive influence on students' lives through a career in school counseling? Tell us what you think.

After you read this chapter, go to http://www.genesislight.com/scan21st/tell_us/counselingcareer.html and complete the form. With your permission, we will periodically post some of your creative thinking for the world to read.

OTHER SUGGESTED ACTIVITIES

1. Discuss the merits, limits, and cautions associated with computer-assisted counseling and using the Internet in school counseling.
2. Independently establish a plan for keeping current, and then share your ideas with others.
3. Discuss the merits of the various attempts in this chapter to predict or influence the future of school counseling.
4. Go to the scan Web site (www.scan21st.com) and propose some ways that this site might help communicate the appeal of a career in school counseling.

Standards for School Counseling Programs

In addition to the common core curricular experiences outlined in Section II.K, the following curricular experiences and demonstrated knowledge and skills are required of all students in the program.

A. Foundations of School Counseling

1. history, philosophy, and current trends in school counseling and educational systems;

2. relationship of the school counseling program to the academic and student services program in the school;

3. role, function, and professional identity of the school counselor in relation to the roles of other professional and support personnel in the school;

4. strategies of leadership designed to enhance the learning environment of schools;

5. knowledge of the school setting, environment, and pre-K–12 curriculum;

6. current issues, policies, laws, and legislation relevant to school counseling;

7. the role of racial, ethnic, and cultural heritage, nationality, socioeconomic status, family structure, age, gender, sexual orientation, religious and spiritual beliefs, occupation, physical and mental status, and equity issues in school counseling;

8. knowledge and understanding of community, environmental, and institutional opportunities that enhance, as well as barriers that impede student academic, career, and personal/social success and overall development;

9. knowledge and application of current and emerging technology in education and school counseling to assist students, families, and educators in using resources that promote informed academic, career, and personal/social choices; and

Source: From Council for the Accreditation of Counseling and Related Educational Programs (CACREP), 2001, Alexandria, VA: Author. Used with permission. © 2001 by the Council for the Accreditation of Counseling and Related Educational Programs.

10. ethical and legal considerations related specifically to the practice of school counseling (e.g., the ACA Code of Ethics and the ASCA Ethical Standards for School Counselors).

B. Contextual Dimensions of School Counseling

Studies that provide an understanding of the coordination of counseling program components as they relate to the total school community, including all of the following:

1. advocacy for all students and for effective school counseling programs;

2. coordination, collaboration, referral, and team-building efforts with teachers, parents, support personnel, and community resources to promote program objectives and facilitate successful student development and achievement of all students;

3. integration of the school counseling program into the total school curriculum by systematically providing information and skills training to assist pre-K–12 students in maximizing their academic, career, and personal/social development;

4. promotion of the use of counseling and guidance activities and programs by the total school community to enhance a positive school climate;

5. methods of planning for and presenting school counseling-related educational programs to administrators, teachers, parents, and the community;

6. methods of planning, developing, implementing, monitoring, and evaluating comprehensive developmental counseling programs; and

7. knowledge of prevention and crisis intervention strategies.

C. Knowledge and Skill Requirements for School Counselors

1. Program Development, Implementation, and Evaluation

a. use, management, analysis, and presentation of data from school-based information (e.g., standardized testing, grades, enrollment, attendance, retention, placement), surveys, interviews, focus groups, and needs assessments to improve student outcomes;

b. design, implementation, monitoring, and evaluation of comprehensive developmental school counseling programs (e.g., the ASCA National Standards for School Counseling Programs) including an awareness of various systems that affect students, school, and home;

c. implementation and evaluation of specific strategies that meet program goals and objectives;

d. identification of student academic, career, and personal/social competencies and the implementation of processes and activities to assist students in achieving these competencies;

e. preparation of an action plan and school counseling calendar that reflect appropriate time commitments and priorities in a comprehensive developmental school counseling program;

f. strategies for seeking and securing alternative funding for program expansion; and

g. use of technology in the design, implementation, monitoring, and evaluation of a comprehensive school counseling program.

2.   Counseling and Guidance

a. individual and small-group counseling approaches that promote school success, through academic, career, and personal/social development for all;

b. individual, group, and classroom guidance approaches systematically designed to assist all students with academic, career, and personal/social development;

c. approaches to peer facilitation, including peer helper, peer tutor, and peer mediation programs;

d. issues that may affect the development and functioning of students (e.g., abuse, violence, eating disorders, attention deficit hyperactivity disorder, childhood depression and suicide)

e. developmental approaches to assist all students and parents at points of educational transition (e.g., home to elementary school, elementary to middle to high school, high school to postsecondary education and career options);

f. constructive partnerships with parents, guardians, families, and communities in order to promote each student's academic, career, and personal/social success;

g. systems theories and relationships among and between community systems, family systems, and school systems, and how they interact to influence the students and affect each system; and

h. approaches to recognizing and assisting children and adolescents who may use alcohol or other drugs or who may reside in a home where substance abuse occurs.

3.   Consultation

a. strategies to promote, develop, and enhance effective teamwork within the school and larger community;

b. theories, models, and processes of consultation and change with teachers, administrators, other school personnel, parents, community groups, agencies, and students as appropriate;

c. strategies and methods of working with parents, guardians, families, and communities to empower them to act on behalf of their children; and

d. knowledge and skills in conducting programs that are designed to enhance students' academic, social, emotional, career, and other developmental needs.

D. Clinical Instruction

For the School Counseling Program, the 600 clock hour internship (Standard III.H) occurs in a school counseling setting, under the supervision of a site supervisor as defined by Section III, Standard C.1-2. The requirement includes a minimum of 240 direct service clock hours.

The program must clearly define and measure the outcomes expected of interns, using appropriate professional resources that address Standards A, B, and C (School Counseling Programs).

Lesson Outlines for Succeeding in School

Section 1, Models of Success, helps make students aware of successful people and how they achieved their success. The section helps students be aware that they will experience failures in school and elsewhere and that failure often aids learning. Here are some of the topics covered in Section 1:

A. The need for children to be aware of successful people

B. Examples of successful people (Sally Ride, astronaut; Michael Jordan, athlete; John Hope Franklin, historian; Bill Gates, computer expert) and what they have in common

C. What it takes to be successful

D. Why success in school is not always possible

E. How occasional failures aid learning

F. How success and failure in school will affect students' lives in the future

G. How to achieve success in school

Section 2, Being Comfortable in School, helps students view the classroom as an enjoyable and comfortable place to be. Although effective learning climates involve some tension and anxiety, students should be comfortable at school and not regularly experience feelings that lead to school avoidance. Students need to learn how to cope with feelings of anxiety about school and should occasionally participate in games and other activities that are intended to be relaxing and to create a calm classroom environment. Although physical exercise, proper diet, and adequate sleep contribute to children being comfortable at school, teachers and children sometimes need to discuss how to relax and feel comfortable. Here are some of the topics covered in Section 2:

A. Stress and relaxation

B. Why and how different people relax

C. What might cause students to be nervous or anxious at school

D. What it means to be relaxed at school

E. Methods of relaxation that students can practice in the classroom and elsewhere

F. How teachers can help students be comfortable at school

Section 3, Being Responsible in School, helps students see the importance of putting work ahead of play and the value of acting responsibly in their relations with peers, teachers, and family. Because students are easily distracted from behaving responsibly, they need to receive instruction and participate in discussions about responsibility. Students may learn much about responsibility from observing respected adults and peers behaving responsibly. Students need to consider the good feelings and beneficial outcomes associated with acting responsibly. Here are some of the topics covered in Section 3:

A. A definition of responsibility in terms of self and others

B. How children can learn the meaning of responsibility through observing responsible people at home and elsewhere

C. The importance of taking roles that require responsible behavior

D. What it means to behave responsibly at school

E. The effects of being responsible at school

F. Responsibility and students' future lives

G. How students can encourage each other to be responsible

Section 4, Listening in School, helps students understand that academic responsibility requires attentive listening in the classroom. Teachers often model effective listening skills and encourage students to practice these skills. Here are some of the topics covered in Section 4:

A. Why responsible behavior at school requires listening

B. How listening pays off at school and elsewhere

C. Skills needed for effective listening

D. How listening among students can be improved in the classroom

E. How teachers improve listening among students

Section 5, Asking for Help in School, associates listening with the need for students to ask for help when they do not understand what they hear. Many students do not ask questions due to their fears of being put down by adults or being made fun of by peers. These students need to understand that learners are not passive; they are instead quick to ask questions and to seek out information. Here are some of the topics covered in Section 5:

A. How listening and asking for help are complementary

B. Why students may be afraid to ask for help

C. Ways for students to overcome their fears about asking for help

D. Positive results from asking for help

E. How students may improve their abilities to ask for help

Section 6, Improving at School, helps students become aware of their academic strengths and weaknesses. Students need to ask themselves such questions as "What subjects am I good at?" and "What subjects do I need to improve in?" It is especially important for students to understand their academic strengths. Often students are deterred from academic progress by focusing solely on their failures. If students are aware of their academic strengths, they are more willing and able to work toward improving weak areas. Here are some of the topics covered in Section 6:

A. What students need to know about their strengths and weaknesses to improve at school

B. Why it is important for students to focus on their academic strong points

C. An overview of study skills needed for academic improvement

D. How teachers can help students monitor improvement in schoolwork

E. How students benefit by seeing themselves improve academically

F. How students may help each other focus on academic improvement

Section 7, Cooperating With Peers, considers the importance of peer relationships and examines the need

for students to cooperate at school. Some educators and researchers have concluded that nearly all instruction should occur within a cooperative environment. Some, in fact, have specifically recommended peer tutoring and cross-age tutoring as avenues to promoting both cooperation and achievement. Although competition often motivates students and promotes their academic success, students need to recognize that cooperation often results in satisfying and important academic successes. Here are some of the topics covered in Section 7:

A. The importance of friendship in the lives of students

B. How relations with peers may affect academic success

C. The importance of cooperative learning in the classroom

D. The value of peer and cross-age tutoring

E. Helping students focus on ways to help each other at school

Section 8, Cooperating With Teachers, discusses the importance of empathy between teachers and students. Teacher expectations of students, for example, is a major influence on achievement. Students perceived as low in ability and high in effort receive more positive feedback than high ability–high effort students. Similarly, pupils believed to be low in ability and low in effort receive more positive feedback than high ability–low effort students. It is essential, therefore, that teachers and students make every effort to understand each other and that students learn to show initiative in developing cooperative working relations with teachers. Here are some of the topics covered in Section 8:

A. The importance of empathy, genuineness, and positive regard between students and teachers

B. The role of self-disclosure in creating a cooperative environment in the classroom

C. How students can help teachers be more effective

D. Specific avenues of cooperation between teachers and students

Section 9, The Bright Side of School, helps students focus on pleasant aspects of school life. Because negative discussions about school are prevalent among students, this section provides an unusual opportunity for considering the positive side. Focusing on the positive aspects of school should be at least a start in fostering positive attitudes toward school and ultimately in reducing truancy and numbers of school dropouts. Students who do not like school, especially to the point of being truant, are unlikely to experience academic success. Here are some of the topics covered in Section 9:

A. The value of a positive attitude toward school

B. What factors contribute to a student's attitude toward school

C. An overview of positive aspects of school life

D. How students can work to improve their view of school

E. Helping students focus on the bright side of school

Section 10, The Bright Side of Me, focuses on helping students feel good about themselves. Most educators acknowledge that children benefit academically from high self-esteem. Teachers need to concentrate on bolstering the self-image of children, recognizing the strong relationship between self-image and achievement. Here are some of the topics covered in Section 10:

A. An overview of the relationship between self-image and student achievement

B. Factors that affect a student's self-image

C. How school contributes to a student's self-image

D. A classroom environment that promotes positive self-image

Key Components of the National Standards for School Counseling Programs

American School Counselor Association

INTRODUCTION

All students growing up in America face the usual challenges of coping with everyday problems. In addition, societal challenges in expectations, values, and behavioral norms create confusion for students and the adults who guide them. Added to this are children who have been abused or neglected, who are frustrated with the cycle of personal and academic failure, who have a disability that requires special support or attention, who are substance abusers, who engage in sexual activity, who feel worthless, and who are homeless.

Coupled with these societal challenges is the national standards movement, the current educational reform agenda that focuses on raising expectations for teaching and learning. Many students face emotional, physical, social, and economic barriers that inhibit successful learning. What mechanisms exist to ensure that these barriers to academic success will be eliminated? School counselors are actively committed to helping students understand that the choices they make will affect their future educational and career options. Students are constantly reminded that academic success is the key to opening the door of opportunity. The school counseling program is the foundation of school success.

How do we, the school counselor community, reach these students, touch their lives, and help them

Source: This appendix was written by Chari A. Campbell, Ph.D., University of South Florida; and Carol A. Dahir, Ed.D., Nassau BOCES, Westbury, New York.

Source: Standards from "The National Standards for School Counseling Programs" (pp. coversheet, 1, 2, 9–11, 17–31), by American School Counselor Association, 1998, Alexandria, VA: Author. Copyright 1998 by American School Counselor Association.

find ways to achieve the skills and knowledge needed for success in the 21st century? We begin by guaranteeing that all children receive the services of a credentialed or certified school counselor who delivers a school counseling program that is comprehensive in scope and developmental in nature. The school counseling program affects specific skills and learning opportunities through academic, career, and personal/social development experiences in a proactive and preventive manner for all students.

How will the National Standards for School Counseling Programs help? Standards are a public statement of what students should know and be able to do as a result of participating in a school counseling program. Standards represent what a school counseling program should contain, serve as an organizational tool to identify and prioritize the elements of a quality school counseling program, and ensure equitable access to school counseling programs for all students. Adopting and implementing national standards will change the way school counseling programs are designed and delivered throughout the United States.

Accountability is the key to determining the success of school counseling programs. Decisions at the building and system levels will be needed to determine the degree to which students have acquired the skills and knowledge defined by the standards. Aligning school counseling programs with national standards requires a rethinking of priorities, time, resources, and outcomes. A school counseling program based on national standards necessitates the involvement of the entire school community to integrate academic, career, and personal/social development of students into the mission of each school. Measurable success resulting from this effort can be documented by an increased number of students completing school with the academic preparation, career awareness, and personal/social growth essential to choose from a wide range of substantial postsecondary options, including college.

For years, school reform initiatives have been enacted in the name of achieving excellence in education. Since the late 1980s, leaders in the counseling profession have called for a revitalization and transformation in school counseling programs. Organizations that have an interest in the work of school counselors, such as the ACT, College Board, and National Association of College Admissions Counselors (NACAC), have advocated the reorganization of school counseling programs to meet the needs of all students. Historically, the professional association, the ASCA, has established positions and goals for the profession in statements that guide the practitioner in implementation. More specifically, the ASCA has published role definitions, a program philosophy, and monographs that speak to the role of guidance and counseling in the educational system. Until now, however, this effort had not been supported by a national focus on a design or framework for program development and delivery.

The current movement to design national standards and world-class benchmarks in the academic disciplines ensures that all graduates of our high schools and postsecondary institutions can compete in a global economy. The challenge lies in providing all students with conditions for learning to help them achieve the expectations of rigorous academic standards. Effective school counseling programs ensure that all students have equal access to quality academic programs and the needed support in academic, career, and personal/social development to meet the demands of these challenges.

The ASCA's decision to participate in this educational reform agenda through the development of national standards for school counseling programs offers an opportunity for the school counseling profession to implement the goals deemed important by the profession, to promote its mission in educational reform, and to ensure that all students have an opportunity to participate in a school counseling program as part of the learning experience.

DOCUMENT OVERVIEW

The National Standards for School Counseling Programs is organized in the following manner:

The first chapter of this document defines standards and provides the ASCA's rationale for the development of the National Standards for School Counseling Programs. It also outlines the process the ASCA used to develop standards for school counseling programs.

The second chapter provides a brief overview of the history of the school counseling profession and defines the school counseling program. The goals of the school counseling program are outlined, and the major components of the program are described, along with the benefits that may be derived by its constituencies.

The third chapter outlines the standards for each student development area: academic, career, and personal/social. The standards are followed by a list of student competencies that define the specific knowledge, attitudes, and skills students should obtain or demonstrate as a result of participating in a school counseling program.

The fourth chapter focuses on the initial stages of implementation and evaluation for a standards-based school counseling program. Sample activities of standards into practice are presented.

DEFINITION OF A SCHOOL COUNSELING PROGRAM

A comprehensive school counseling program is developmental and systematic in nature, sequential, clearly defined, and accountable. It is jointly founded on developmental psychology, educational philosophy, and counseling methodology (ASCA, 1994). The school counseling program is integral to the educational enterprise, is proactive and preventive in its focus, and assists students in acquiring and using lifelong learning skills. More specifically, school counseling programs employ strategies to enhance academics, provide career awareness, develop employment readiness, encourage self-awareness, foster interpersonal communication skills, and impart life success skills for all students.

The school counseling program has characteristics similar to other educational programs, including a scope and sequence, student outcomes or competencies, activities and processes to assist students in achieving these outcomes, professionally credentialed personnel, materials and resources, and accountability methods.

School counseling programs are developed by design, focusing on needs, interests, and issues related to the various stages of student growth. Included are objectives, activities, special services, and expected outcomes, with an emphasis on helping students learn more effectively and efficiently. The commitment is to individual uniqueness and the maximum development in three major areas: academic, career, and personal/social (ASCA, 1990).

Most school counselors agree that their skills, time, and energy should be focused on direct services to students. School counseling programs and the role of the school counselor should be determined by the educational, career, and personal developmental needs of students. The comprehensive school counseling program places the counselor in a key position to identify the issues that affect student learning and achievement. The school counselor is at the core of school planning, school programs, and school environment.

The school counselor is not the counseling program. The school counselor and the school counseling program use a collaborative model as their foundation. Counselors do not work alone; all educators play a role in creating an environment that promotes the achievement of identified student goals and outcomes. The counselor facilitates communication and establishes linkages for the benefit of students, with teaching staff, administration, families, student service personnel, agencies, business, and other members of the community. School success depends on the cooperation and support of the entire faculty, staff, and student services personnel.

As student advocates, school counselors are committed to participate as members of the educational team. They consult and collaborate with teachers, administrators, and parents to assist students in being successful academically, vocationally, and personally. School counselors are recognized as indispensable partners of the instructional staff in the development of good citizens and leaders. As schools and communities initiate and establish partnerships to address common concerns, it is important that these efforts are implemented in a manner that facilitates the educational process and the full use of school and other community resources on behalf of students and their families.

Our educational system is being challenged by the growing needs of today's students and the rising expectations of society. Some students attend school with emotional, physical, and interpersonal barriers to learning as a result of societal and other factors. All students, however, require systematic support for their development. Therefore, in a comprehensive school counseling program, less emphasis is placed on crisis-oriented services. The emphasis is on development for all students. An effective school counseling program begins when students enter the school system and continues as they progress through the educational process. School counseling is an integral part of the total educational enterprise.

Our nation is rich in multicultural diversity. Effective school counseling programs and trained staff reflect and are responsive to the diversity in our schools and communities. Effective school counseling programs serve all students and acknowledge that diversity and individual differences are valuable. Programs and staff ensure that communication is open and that the community is represented and involved as counseling programs are developed and implemented. Counseling programs help ensure equal opportunity for all students to participate fully in the educational process.

The school counseling model supports and is compatible with *GOALS 2000* (1994). The School to Work Opportunities Act (1994), the Elementary Counseling Demonstration Act (1995), the *Children's Defense Fund Report* (1990), the Secretary's Commission on Achieving Necessary Skills (U.S. Department of Labor, 1991), and the *National Career Development Guidelines* (NOICC, 1989) support the school counseling program and acknowledge the role of the school counselor as essential to student success.

THE GOAL OF SCHOOL COUNSELING PROGRAMS

The primary goal of the school counseling program is to promote and enhance *student learning* through the three broad and interrelated areas of *student development*. Each area of student development encompasses a variety of desired student learning competencies, which, in turn, is composed of specific knowledge, attitudes, and skills that form the foundation of the developmental school counseling program. The three areas of student development are (a) academic development, (b) career development, and (c) personal/social development. Recognizing that all children do not develop in a linear fashion according to a certain timetable, the overlap among grade levels (elementary, middle school/junior high, and high school) is intentional. The school counseling program reflects the progression of student development throughout the pre-K through 12 experience. It is understood that mastery of basic skills facilitates the mastery of higher-order skills in each area of development. The school counselor uses a variety of strategies, activities, delivery methods, and resources to promote the desired student development. The school counselor's responsibilities include the design, organization, implementation, and coordination of the program.

NATIONAL STANDARDS FOR SCHOOL COUNSELING PROGRAMS

Overview

The purpose of a counseling program in a school setting is to promote and enhance the training process. To that end, the school counseling program facilitates student development in three broad areas: academic development, career development, and personal/social development.

The standards for each content area are intended to provide guidance and direction for states, school systems, and individual schools to develop quality and effective school counseling programs. The emphasis is on success for all students, not only those students who are motivated, supported, and ready to learn. The school counseling program based on national standards enables all students to achieve success in school and to develop into contributing members of society.

School success requires that students make successful transitions from elementary school to middle/junior high school to high school. Graduates from high school have acquired the attitudes, skills, and knowledge essential to the competitive workplace of the 21st century.

A school counseling program based on national standards provides the elements for all students to achieve success in school. School counselors continuously assess their students' needs to identify barriers and obstacles that may be hindering success, and they also advocate for programmatic efforts to eliminate these barriers.

Each standard is followed by a list of student competencies that articulate desired student learning outcomes. Student competencies define the specific knowledge, attitudes, and skills that students should obtain or demonstrate as a result of participating in a school counseling program. These listings are not meant to be all inclusive, nor is any individual program expected to include all competencies in the school counseling program. The competencies offer a foundation for what a standards-based program should address and deliver. These can be used as a basis to develop measurable indicators of student performance.

The program standards for academic development guide the school counseling program to implement strategies and activities to support and maximize each student's ability to learn.

Academic development includes acquiring skills, attitudes, and knowledge that contribute to effective learning in school and across the life span; employing strategies to achieve success in school; and understanding the relationship of academics to the work world and to life at home and in the community. Academic development standards and competencies support the premise that all students meet or exceed the local, state, and national academic standards.

The purpose of a counseling program in a school setting is to promote and enhance the learning process.

The program standards for career development guide the school counseling program to provide the foundation for the acquisition of skills, attitudes, and knowledge that enable students to make a successful transition from school to the world of work and from job to job across the life span.

Career development includes employing strategies to achieve future career success and job satisfaction, as well as fostering the understanding of the relationship among personal qualities, education and training, and the work world. Career development standards and competencies ensure that students develop career goals as a result of participation in a comprehensive plan of career awareness, exploration, and preparation activities.

The program standards for personal/social development guide the school counseling program to provide the foundation for personal and social growth as students progress through school and into adulthood.

Personal/social development contributes to academic and career success. Personal/social development includes the acquisition of skills, attitudes, and knowledge that help students understand and respect self and others, acquire effective interpersonal skills, understand safety and survival skills, and develop into contributing members of society. Personal/social development standards and competencies ensure that students have learned to negotiate their way successfully and safely in the increasingly complex and diverse world of the 21st century.

National Standards for School Counseling Programs

I. Academic Development

Standards in this area guide the school counseling program to implement strategies and activities to support and enable the student to experience academic success, maximize learning through commitment, produce high-quality work, and be prepared for a full range of options and opportunities after high school.

The academic development area includes the acquisition of skills in decision making, problem solving and goal setting, critical thinking, logical reasoning, and interpersonal communication and the application of these skills to academic achievement.

The school counseling program enables all students to achieve success in school and to develop into contributing members of our society.

Standard A: Students will acquire the attitudes, knowledge, and skills that contribute to effective learning in school and across the life span.

Student Competencies: Improve academic self-concept, acquire skills for improving learning, and achieve school success.

Standard B: Students will complete school with the academic preparation essential to choose from a wide range of substantial post-secondary options, including college.

Student Competencies: Improve learning and plan to achieve goals.

Standard C: Students will understand the relationship of academics to the work world and to life at home and in the community.

Student Competencies: Relate school to life experiences.

II. Career Development

Standards in this area guide the school counseling program to implement strategies and activities to support and enable the student to develop a positive attitude toward work and to develop the necessary skills to make a successful transition from school to the work world and from job to job across the life career span. Also, standards in this area help students understand the relationship between success in school and future success in the world of work. Career development standards reflect the recommendations of the Secretary's Commission of Achieving Necessary Skills (SCANS; 1991) and the content of the *National Career Development Guidelines* (NOICC, 1989).

The school counseling program enables all students to achieve success in school and to develop into contributing members of our society.

Standard A: Students will acquire the skills to investigate the work world in relation to knowledge of self and to make informed career decisions.

Student Competencies: Develop career awareness and develop employment readiness.

Standard B: Students will employ strategies to achieve future career goals with success and satisfaction.

Student Competencies: Acquire career information and identify career goals.

Standard C: Students will understand the relationship among personal qualities, education, training, and the work world.

Student Competencies: Acquire knowledge to achieve career goals and apply skills to achieve career goals.

III. Personal/Social Development

Standards in the personal/social area guide the school counseling program to implement strategies and activities to support and maximize each student's personal growth and enhance the educational and career development of the student.

The school counseling program enables all students to achieve success in school and to develop into contributing members of our society.

Standard A: Students will acquire the knowledge, attitudes, and interpersonal skills to help them understand and respect self and others.

Student Competencies: Acquire self-knowledge and acquire interpersonal skills.

Standard B: Students will make decisions, set goals, and take necessary action to achieve goals.

Student Competencies: Self-knowledge applications.

Standard C: Students will understand safety and survival skills.

Student Competencies: Acquire personal safety skills.

Note: In the complete document containing the ASCA National Standards, each student competency is followed by a listing of desired student outcomes. There is not enough space herein to list all of them.

Presidential High School: MEASURE of Success

Presidential High School: MEASURE of Success
  Principal: Elsie Davis
  Enrollment: 2112
  Counselors: Timothy Bishop, Gray Howell, Katie Handel, and Amanda Riemer

Principal's Comments

Preparing students to choose from a wide array of options after high school is part of our district's mission of academic success for every student. Our counselors worked very hard this year to impact the school board's desire to improve the postsecondary going rate for every student. They looked at the important data elements that contribute to improving our student's futures and used their leadership, advocacy, teaming, and collaboration skills to make a positive difference. .

School Improvement Issues

Postsecondary going rate is 50%.
Underrepresented students do not transition to a wide variety of options after high school.

Stakeholders

Parents: Assisted in establishing a tutoring program; created a phone chain to call parents to remind them of important school events.
Community: Assisted in establishing a mentoring program; ran evening and Saturday programs with school personnel for parents and students on raising aspirations. homework help, technology awareness.
Volunteers: Participated in training delivered by financial aid officers on the Free Application for Federal Student Aid (FAFSA); worked with individual students on the power of financial aid to impact their future.
Business Partners: Assisted in establishing a mentoring program. Provided site visits to their businesses. Helped organize and participate in career fairs.

Systemic Changes

Measurable results showed how the school counseling program worked to increase the postsecondary going rate through a whole school and community effort to impact the instructional program.

Results

Comparative Changes in Postsecondary Rates

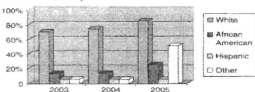

Percentages of Students by Ethnicity Accepted to Postsecondary Institutions

2005 Data Summary

Ethnicity	No. of Seniors	% of Seniors	% to Post-secondary	No. to Post-secondary
Caucasian	150	59%	82%	123
African American	50	20%	22%	10
Hispanic	45	19%	15%	8
Other	4	2%	50%	2

Faces Behind the Data

A parent approached her child's school counselor at the end of the graduation ceremony: "I didn't think my child's dream of going to college was going to happen this year. I am recently divorced and did not realize that financial aid would be available. Thank you for keeping after both of us to fill out the FAFSA so that it wasn't too late to get some help."

NOTE: The Educate step in MEASURE has been adapted with permission from the Student Personnel Accountability Report Card sponsored by the California Department of Education and Los Angeles County Office of Education.

XYZ Closing the Gap Results Report

APPENDIX

XYZ SCHOOL DISTRICT

XYZ Closing the Gap Results Report

Year _____

Counselor	Target Group	Standards, Competencies, Indicators Addressed	Type of Service Delivered In What Manner?	Start Date End Date	PROCESS DATA (Number of students affected)	PERCEPTION DATA (Pre and post test competency attainment or student data)*	RESULTS DATA (How did the student change as a result of the lesson?)*	Implications (What do the data tell you?)
Berry	8th Grade: 64 students in danger of being retained at the end of Trimester 1	Standard A Competency A2 & A3 Indicator A:A2.1 & A:A3.1	Academic Counseling Groups Peer Mentoring	Sept 2002 June 2003	64	*Immediate* 99% correct on post-test knowledge of promotion information.	*Intermediate* 46 (72%) demonstrated improvement in GPA from Trimester 1 to Trimester 3. *Long term* 85% of at risk students showed improvement in GPA from Trimester 1 to Trimester 2.	Excellent academic improvement. Re-evaluate the curriculum used. Participants in the academic support groups may need further encouragement from other resources such as adult mentors.

*Attach data, examples and documentation

Principal's signature _____   Date _____   Prepared by _____

Source: From *The ASCA National Model: A framework for school counseling programs,* 2nd ed., by American School Counselor Association (ASCA), 2005, Alexandria, VA: Author. Used with permission.

ACA Code of Ethics

PREAMBLE

The American Counseling Association is an educational, scientific, and professional organization whose members work in a variety of settings and serve in multiple capacities. ACA members are dedicated to the enhancement of human development throughout the life span. Association members recognize diversity and embrace a cross-cultural approach in support of the worth, dignity, potential, and uniqueness of people within their social and cultural contexts.

Professional values are an important way of living out an ethical commitment. Values inform principles. Inherently held values that guide our behaviors or exceed prescribed behaviors are deeply ingrained in the counselor and developed out of personal dedication, rather than the mandatory requirement of an external organization.

PURPOSE

The *ACA Code of Ethics* serves five main purposes:

1. The *Code* enables the association to clarify to current and future members, and to those served by members, the nature of the ethical responsibilities held in common by its members.
2. The *Code* helps support the mission of the association.
3. The *Code* establishes principles that define ethical behavior and best practices of association members.
4. The *Code* serves as an ethical guide designed to assist members in constructing a professional course of action that best serves those utilizing

Source: Reprinted from *ACA Code of Ethics* 2005. © 2005 The American Counseling Association. Reprinted with permission. No further reproduction authorized without written permission from the American Counseling Association.

counseling services and best promotes the values of the counseling profession.
5. The *Code* serves as the basis for processing of ethical complaints and inquiries initiated against members of the association.

The *ACA Code of Ethics* contains eight main sections that address the following areas:

Section A:	The Counseling Relationship
Section B:	Confidentiality, Privileged Communication, and Privacy
Section C:	Professional Responsibility
Section D:	Relationships With Other Professionals
Section E:	Evaluation, Assessment, and Interpretation
Section F:	Supervision, Training, and Teaching
Section G:	Research and Publication
Section H:	Resolving Ethical Issues

Each section of the *ACA Code of Ethics* begins with an Introduction. The introductions to each section discuss what counselors should aspire to with regard to ethical behavior and responsibility. The Introduction helps set the tone for that particular section and provides a starting point that invites reflection on the ethical mandates contained in each part of the *ACA Code of Ethics*.

When counselors are faced with ethical dilemmas that are difficult to resolve, they are expected to engage in a carefully considered ethical decision-making process. Reasonable differences of opinion can and do exist among counselors with respect to the ways in which values, ethical principles, and ethical standards would be applied when they conflict. While there is no specific ethical decision-making model that is most effective, counselors are expected to be familiar with a credible model of decision making that can bear public scrutiny and its application.

Through a chosen ethical decision-making process and evaluation of the context of the situation, counselors are empowered to make decisions that help expand the capacity of people to grow and develop.

A brief glossary is given to provide readers with a concise description of some of the terms used in the *ACA Code of Ethics.*

SECTION A

The Counseling Relationship

Introduction

Counselors encourage client growth and development in ways that foster the interest and welfare of clients and promote formation of healthy relationships. Counselors actively attempt to understand the diverse cultural backgrounds of the clients they serve. Counselors also explore their own cultural identities and how these affect their values and beliefs about the counseling process.

Counselors are encouraged to contribute to society by devoting a portion of their professional activity to services for which there is little or no financial return (pro bono publico).

A.1. Welfare of Those Served by Counselors

A.1.a. Primary Responsibility
The primary responsibility of counselors is to respect the dignity and to promote the welfare of clients.

A.1.b. Records
Counselors maintain records necessary for rendering professional services to their clients and as required by laws, regulations, or agency or institution procedures. Counselors include sufficient and timely documentation in their client records to facilitate the delivery and continuity of needed services. Counselors take reasonable steps to ensure that documentation in records accurately reflects client progress and services provided. If errors are made in client records, counselors take steps to properly note the correction of such errors according to agency or institutional policies. *(See A.12.g.7., B.6., B.6.g., G.2.J.)*

A.1.c. Counseling Plans
Counselors and their clients work jointly in devising integrated counseling plans that offer reasonable promise of success and are consistent with abilities and circumstances of clients. Counselors and clients regularly review counseling plans to assess their continued viability and effectiveness, respecting the freedom of choice of clients. *(See A.2.a., A.2.d., A.12.g.)*

A.1.d. Support Network Involvement
Counselors recognize that support networks hold various meanings in the lives of clients and consider enlisting the support, understanding, and involvement of others (e.g., religious/spiritual/community leaders, family members, friends) as positive resources, when appropriate, with client consent.

A.1.e. Employment Needs
Counselors work with their clients considering employment in jobs that are consistent with the overall abilities, vocational limitations, physical restrictions, general temperament, interest and aptitude patterns, social skills, education, general qualifications, and other relevant characteristics and needs of clients. When appropriate, counselors appropriately trained in career development will assist in the placement of clients in positions that are consistent with the interest, culture, and the welfare of clients, employers, and/or the public.

A.2. Informed Consent in the Counseling Relationship

(See A.12.g., B.5., B.6.b., E.3., E.13.b., F.l.c., G.2.a.)

A.2.a. Informed Consent
Clients have the freedom to choose whether to enter into or remain in a counseling relationship and need adequate information about the counseling process and the counselor. Counselors have an obligation to review in writing and verbally with clients the rights and responsibilities of both the counselor and the client. Informed consent is an ongoing part of the counseling process, and counselors appropriately document discussions of informed consent throughout the counseling relationship.

A.2.b. Types of Information Needed
Counselors explicitly explain to clients the nature of all services provided. They inform clients about issues such as, but not limited to, the following: the purposes, goals, techniques, procedures, limitations, potential risks, and benefits of services; the counselor's qualifications, credentials, and relevant experience; continuation of services upon the incapacitation or death of a counselor; and other pertinent information. Counselors take steps to ensure that clients understand the implications of diagnosis, the intended use of tests and reports, fees, and billing arrangements. Clients have the right to confidentiality and to be provided with an explanation of its limitations (including how supervisors and/or treatment team professionals are involved); to obtain clear information about their records; to participate in the ongoing counseling plans; and to refuse any services or modality change and to be advised of the consequences of such refusal.

A.2.c. Developmental and Cultural Sensitivity
Counselors communicate information in ways that are both developmentally and culturally appropriate. Counselors use clear and understandable language when discussing issues related to informed consent. When clients have difficulty understanding the language used by counselors, they provide necessary services (e.g., arranging for a qualified interpreter or

translator) to ensure comprehension by clients. In collaboration with clients, counselors consider cultural implications of informed consent procedures and, where possible, counselors adjust their practices accordingly.

A.2.d. Inability to Give Consent

When counseling minors or persons unable to give voluntary consent, counselors seek the assent of clients to services, and include them in decision making as appropriate. Counselors recognize the need to balance the ethical rights of clients to make choices, their capacity to give consent or assent to receive services, and parental or familial legal rights and responsibilities to protect these clients and make decisions on their behalf.

A.3. Clients Served by Others

When counselors learn that their clients are in a professional relationship with another mental health professional, they request release from clients to inform the other professionals and strive to establish positive and collaborative professional relationships.

A.4. Avoiding Harm and Imposing Values

A.4.a. Avoiding Harm

Counselors act to avoid harming their clients, trainees, and research participants and to minimize or to remedy unavoidable or unanticipated harm.

A.4.b. Personal Values

Counselors are aware of their own values, attitudes, beliefs, and behaviors and avoid imposing values that are inconsistent with counseling goals. Counselors respect the diversity of clients, trainees, and research participants.

A.5. Roles and Relationships With Clients

(See F.3., F.10., G.3.)

A.5.a. Current Clients

Sexual or romantic counselor–client interactions or relationships with current clients, their romantic partners, or their family members are prohibited.

A.5.b. Former Clients

Sexual or romantic counselor–client interactions or relationships with former clients, their romantic partners, or their family members are prohibited for a period of 5 years following the last professional contact. Counselors, before engaging in sexual or romantic interactions or relationships with clients, their romantic partners, or client family members after 5 years following the last professional contact, demonstrate forethought and document (in written form) whether the interactions or relationship can be viewed as exploitive in some way and/or whether there is still potential to harm the former client; in cases of potential exploitation and/or harm, the counselor avoids entering such an interaction or relationship.

A.5.c. Nonprofessional Interactions or Relationships (Other Than Sexual or Romantic Interactions or Relationships)

Counselor–client nonprofessional relationships with clients, former clients, their romantic partners, or their family members should be avoided, except when the interaction is potentially beneficial to the client. *(See A.5.d.)*

A.5.d. Potentially Beneficial Interactions

When a counselor–client nonprofessional interaction with a client or former client may be potentially beneficial to the client or former client, the counselor must document in case records, prior to the interaction (when feasible), the rationale for such an interaction, the potential benefit, and anticipated consequences for the client or former client and other individuals significantly involved with the client or former client. Such interactions should be initiated with appropriate client consent. Where unintentional harm occurs to the client or former client, or to an individual significantly involved with the client or former client, due to the nonprofessional interaction, the counselor must show evidence of an attempt to remedy such harm. Examples of potentially beneficial interactions include, but are not limited to, attending a formal ceremony (e.g., a wedding/commitment ceremony or graduation); purchasing a service or product provided by a client or former client (excepting unrestricted bartering); hospital visits to an ill family member; mutual membership in a professional association, organization, or community. *(See A.5.c.)*

A.5.e. Role Changes in the Professional Relationship

When a counselor changes a role from the original or most recent contracted relationship, he or she obtains informed consent from the client and explains the right of the client to refuse services related to the change. Examples of role changes include

1. changing from individual to relationship or family counseling, or vice versa;
2. changing from a nonforensic evaluative role to a therapeutic role, or vice versa;
3. changing from a counselor to a researcher role (i.e., enlisting clients as research participants), or vice versa; and
4. changing from a counselor to a mediator role, or vice versa.

Clients must be fully informed of any anticipated consequences (e.g., financial, legal, personal, or therapeutic) of counselor role changes.

A.6. Roles and Relationships at Individual, Group, Institutional, and Societal Levels

A.6.a. Advocacy

When appropriate, counselors advocate at individual, group, institutional, and societal levels to examine potential barriers and obstacles that inhibit access and/or the growth and development of clients.

A.6.b. Confidentiality and Advocacy

Counselors obtain client consent prior to engaging in advocacy efforts on behalf of an identifiable client to improve the provision of services and to work toward removal of systemic barriers or obstacles that inhibit client access, growth, and development.

A.7. Multiple Clients

When a counselor agrees to provide counseling services to two or more persons who have a relationship, the counselor clarifies at the outset which person or persons are clients and the nature of the relationships the counselor will have with each involved person. If it becomes apparent that the counselor may be called upon to perform potentially conflicting roles, the counselor will clarify, adjust, or withdraw from roles appropriately. *(See A.8.a., B.4.)*

A.8. Group Work

(See B.4.a.)

A.8.a. Screening

Counselors screen prospective group counseling/therapy participants. To the extent possible, counselors select members whose needs and goals are compatible with goals of the group, who will not impede the group process, and whose well-being will not be jeopardized by the group experience.

A.8.b. Protecting Clients

In a group setting, counselors take reasonable precautions to protect clients from physical, emotional, or psychological trauma.

A.9. End-of-Life Care for Terminally Ill Clients

A.9.a. Quality of Care

Counselors strive to take measures that enable clients

1. to obtain high-quality end-of-life care for their physical, emotional, social, and spiritual needs;
2. to exercise the highest degree of self-determination possible;
3. to be given every opportunity possible to engage in informed decision making regarding their end-of-life care; and
4. to receive complete and adequate assessment regarding their ability to make competent, rational decisions on their own behalf from a mental health professional who is experienced in end-of-life care practice.

A.9.b. Counselor Competence, Choice, and Referral

Recognizing the personal, moral, and competence issues related to end-of-life decisions, counselors may choose to work or not work with terminally ill clients who wish to explore their end-of-life options. Counselors provide appropriate referral information to ensure that clients receive the necessary help.

A.9.c. Confidentiality

Counselors who provide services to terminally ill individuals who are considering hastening their own deaths have the option of breaking or not breaking confidentiality, depending on applicable laws and the specific circumstances of the situation and after seeking consultation or supervision from appropriate professional and legal parties. *(See B.5.c., B.7.c.)*

A.10. Fees and Bartering

A.10.a. Accepting Fees From Agency Clients

Counselors refuse a private fee or other remuneration for rendering services to persons who are entitled to such services through the counselor's employing agency or institution. The policies of a particular agency may make explicit provisions for agency clients to receive counseling services from members of its staff in private practice. In such instances, the clients must be informed of other options open to them should they seek private counseling services.

A.10.b. Establishing Fees

In establishing fees for professional counseling services, counselors consider the financial status of clients and locality. In the event that the established fee structure is inappropriate for a client, counselors assist clients in attempting to find comparable services of acceptable cost.

A.10.c. Nonpayment of Fees

If counselors intend to use collection agencies or take legal measures to collect fees from clients who do not pay for services as agreed upon, they first inform clients of intended actions and offer clients the opportunity to make payment.

A.10.d. Bartering

Counselors may barter only if the relationship is not exploitive or harmful and does not place the counselor in an unfair advantage, if the client requests it, and if such arrangements are an accepted practice among professionals in the community. Counselors consider the cultural implications of bartering and discuss relevant concerns with clients and document such agreements in a clear written contract.

A.10.e. Receiving Gifts

Counselors understand the challenges of accepting gifts from clients and recognize that in some cultures, small gifts are a token of respect and showing gratitude. When determining whether or not to accept a gift from clients, counselors take into account the therapeutic relationship, the monetary value of the gift, a client's motivation for giving the gift, and the counselor's motivation for wanting or declining the gift.

A.11. Termination and Referral

A.11.a. Abandonment Prohibited

Counselors do not abandon or neglect clients in counseling. Counselors assist in making appropriate arrangements for the continuation of treatment, when necessary, during interruptions such as vacations, illness, and following termination.

A.11.b. Inability to Assist Clients

If counselors determine an inability to be of professional assistance to clients, they avoid entering or continuing counseling relationships. Counselors are knowledgeable about culturally and clinically appropriate referral resources and suggest these alternatives. If clients decline the suggested referrals, counselors should discontinue the relationship.

A.11.c. Appropriate Termination

Counselors terminate a counseling relationship when it becomes reasonably apparent that the client no longer needs assistance, is not likely to benefit, or is being harmed by continued counseling. Counselors may terminate counseling when in jeopardy of harm by the client, or another person with whom the client has a relationship, or when clients do not pay fees as agreed upon. Counselors provide pretermination counseling and recommend other service providers when necessary.

A.11.d. Appropriate Transfer of Services

When counselors transfer or refer clients to other practitioners, they ensure that appropriate clinical and administrative processes are completed and open communication is maintained with both clients and practitioners.

A.12. Technology Applications

A.12.a. Benefits and Limitations

Counselors inform clients of the benefits and limitations of using information technology applications in the counseling process and in business/billing procedures. Such technologies include but are not limited to computer hardware and sofware, telephones, the World Wide Web, the Internet, online assessment instruments, and other communication devices.

A.12.b. Technology-Assisted Services

When providing technology-assisted distance counseling services, counselors determine that clients are intellectually, emotionally, and physically capable of using the application and that the application is appropriate for the needs of clients.

A.12.c. Inappropriate Services

When technology-assisted distance counseling services are deemed inappropriate by the counselor or client, counselors consider delivering services face to face.

A.12.d. Access

Counselors provide reasonable access to computer applications when providing technology-assisted distance counseling services.

A.12.e. Laws and Statutes

Counselors ensure that the use of technology does not violate the laws of any local, state, national, or international entity and observe all relevant statutes.

A.12.f. Assistance

Counselors seek business, legal, and technical assistance when using technology applications, particularly when the use of such applications crosses state or national boundaries.

A.12.g. Technology and Informed Consent

As part of the process of establishing informed consent, counselors do the following:

1. Address issues related to the difficulty of maintaining the confidentiality of electronically transmitted communications.
2. Inform clients of all colleagues, supervisors, and employees, such as Informational Technology (IT) administrators, who might have authorized or unauthorized access to electronic transmissions.
3. Urge clients to be aware of all authorized or unauthorized users including family members and fellow employees who have access to any technology clients may use in the counseling process.
4. Inform clients of pertinent legal rights and limitations governing the practice of a profession over state lines or international boundaries.
5. Use encrypted Web sites and e-mail communications to help ensure confidentiality when possible.
6. When the use of encryption is not possible, counselors notify clients of this fact and limit electronic transmissions to general communications that are not client specific.
7. Inform clients if and for how long archival storage of transaction records are maintained.
8. Discuss the possibility of technology failure and alternate methods of service delivery.
9. Inform clients of emergency procedures, such as calling 911 or a local crisis hotline, when the counselor is not available.
10. Discuss time zone differences, local customs, and cultural or language differences that might impact service delivery.
11. Inform clients when technology-assisted distance counseling services are not covered by insurance. (See A.2.)

A.12.h. Sites on the World Wide Web

Counselors maintaining sites on the World Wide Web (the Internet) do the following:

1. Regularly check that electronic links are working and professionally appropriate.
2. Establish ways clients can contact the counselor in case of technology failure.
3. Provide electronic links to relevant state licensure and professional certification boards to protect consumer rights and facilitate addressing ethical concerns.
4. Establish a method for verifying client identity.
5. Obtain the written consent of the legal guardian or other authorized legal representative prior to rendering services in the event the client is a minor child, an adult who is legally incompetent, or an adult incapable of giving informed consent.
6. Strive to provide a site that is accessible to persons with disabilities.

7. Strive to provide translation capabilities for clients who have a different primary language while also addressing the imperfect nature of such translations.
8. Assist clients in determining the validity and reliability of information found on the World Wide Web and other technology applications.

Section B

Confidentiality, Privileged Communication, and Privacy

Introduction

Counselors recognize that trust is a cornerstone of the counseling relationship. Counselors aspire to earn the trust of clients by creating an ongoing partnership, establishing and upholding appropriate boundaries, and maintaining confidentiality. Counselors communicate the parameters of confidentiality in a culturally competent manner.

B.1. Respecting Client Rights

B.1.a. Multicultural/Diversity Considerations
Counselors maintain awareness and sensitivity regarding cultural meanings of confidentiality and privacy. Counselors respect differing views toward disclosure of information. Counselors hold ongoing discussions with clients as to how, when, and with whom information is to be shared.

B.1.b. Respect for Privacy
Counselors respect client rights to privacy. Counselors solicit private information from clients only when it is beneficial to the counseling process.

B.1.c. Respect for Confidentiality
Counselors do not share confidential information without client consent or without sound legal or ethical justification.

B.1.d. Explanation of Limitations
At initiation and throughout the counseling process, counselors inform clients of the limitations of confidentiality and seek to identify foreseeable situations in which confidentiality must be breached. *(See A.2.b.)*

B.2. Exceptions

B.2.a. Danger and Legal Requirements
The general requirement that counselors keep information confidential does not apply when disclosure is required to protect clients or identified others from serious and foreseeable harm or when legal requirements demand that confidential information must be revealed. Counselors consult with other professionals when in doubt as to the validity of an exception. Additional considerations apply when addressing end-of-life issues. *(See A.9.c.)*

B.2.b. Contagious, Life-Threatening Diseases
When clients disclose that they have a disease commonly known to be both communicable and life threatening, counselors

may be justified in disclosing information to identifiable third parties, if they are known to be at demonstrable and high risk of contracting the disease. Prior to making a disclosure, counselors confirm that there is such a diagnosis and assess the intent of clients to inform the third parties about their disease or to engage in any behaviors that may be harmful to an identifiable third party.

B.2.c. Court-Ordered Disclosure
When subpoenaed to release confidential or privileged information without a client's permission, counselors obtain written, informed consent from the client or take steps to prohibit the disclosure or have it limited as narrowly as possible due to potential harm to the client or counseling relationship.

B.2.d. Minimal Disclosure
To the extent possible, clients are informed before confidential information is disclosed and are involved in the disclosure decision-making process. When circumstances require the disclosure of confidential information, only essential information is revealed.

B.3. Information Shared With Others

B.3.a. Subordinates
Counselors make every effort to ensure that privacy and confidentiality of clients are maintained by subordinates, including employees, supervisees, students, clerical assistants, and volunteers. *(See F.1.c.)*

B.3.b. Treatment Teams
When client treatment involves a continued review or participation by a treatment team, the client will be informed of the team's existence and composition, information being shared, and the purposes of sharing such information.

B.3.c. Confidential Settings
Counselors discuss confidential information only in settings in which they can reasonably ensure client privacy.

B.3.d. Third-Party Payers
Counselors disclose information to third-party payers only when clients have authorized such disclosure.

B.3.e. Transmitting Confidential Information
Counselors take precautions to ensure the confidentiality of information transmitted through the use of computers, electronic mail, facsimile machines, telephones, voicemail, answering machines, and other electronic or computer technology. *(See A.12.g.)*

B.3.f. Deceased Clients
Counselors protect the confidentiality of deceased clients, consistent with legal requirements and agency or setting policies.

B.4. Groups and Families

B.4.a. Group Work
In group work, counselors clearly explain the importance and parameters of confidentiality for the specific group being entered.

B.4.b. Couples and Family Counseling

In couples and family counseling, counselors clearly define who is considered "the client" and discuss expectations and limitations of confidentiality. Counselors seek agreement and document in writing such agreement among all involved parties having capacity to give consent concerning each individual's right to confidentiality and any obligation to preserve the confidentiality of information known.

B.5. Clients Lacking Capacity to Give Informed Consent

B.5.a. Responsibility to Clients

When counseling minor clients or adult clients who lack the capacity to give voluntary, informed consent, counselors protect the confidentiality of information received in the counseling relationship as specified by federal and state laws, written policies, and applicable ethical standards.

B.5.b. Responsibility to Parents and Legal Guardians

Counselors inform parents and legal guardians about the role of counselors and the confidential nature of the counseling relationship. Counselors are sensitive to the cultural diversity of families and respect the inherent rights and responsibilities of parents/guardians over the welfare of their children/charges according to law. Counselors work to establish, as appropriate, collaborative relationships with parents/guardians to best serve clients.

B.5.c. Release of Confidential Information

When counseling minor clients or adult clients who lack the capacity to give voluntary consent to release confidential information, counselors seek permission from an appropriate third party to disclose information. In such instances, counselors inform clients consistent with their level of understanding and take culturally appropriate measures to safeguard client confidentiality.

B.6. Records

B.6.a. Confidentiality of Records

Counselors ensure that records are kept in a secure location and that only authorized persons have access to records.

B.6.b. Permission to Record

Counselors obtain permission from clients prior to recording sessions through electronic or other means.

B.6.c. Permission to Observe

Counselors obtain permission from clients prior to observing counseling sessions, reviewing session transcripts, or viewing recordings of sessions with supervisors, faculty, peers, or others within the training environment.

B.6.d. Client Access

Counselors provide reasonable access to records and copies of records when requested by competent clients. Counselors limit the access of clients to their records, or portions of their records, only when there is compelling evidence that such access would cause harm to the client. Counselors document the request of clients and the rationale for withholding some or all of the record in the files of clients. In situations involving multiple clients, counselors provide individual clients with only those parts of records that related directly to them and do not include confidential information related to any other client.

B.6.e. Assistance With Records

When clients request access to their records, counselors provide assistance and consultation in interpreting counseling records.

B.6.f. Disclosure or Transfer

Unless exceptions to confidentiality exist, counselors obtain written permission from clients to disclose or transfer records to legitimate third parties. Steps are taken to ensure that receivers of counseling records are sensitive to their confidential nature. *(See A.3., E.4.)*

B.6.g. Storage and Disposal After Termination

Counselors store records following termination of services to ensure reasonable future access, maintain records in accordance with state and federal statutes governing records, and dispose of client records and other sensitive materials in a manner that protects client confidentiality. When records are of an artistic nature, counselors obtain client (or guardian) consent with regard to handling of such records or documents. *(See A.1.b.)*

B.6.h. Reasonable Precautions

Counselors take reasonable precautions to protect client confidentiality in the event of the counselor's termination of practice, incapacity, or death. *(See C.2.h.)*

B.7. Research and Training

B.7.a. Institutional Approval

When institutional approval is required, counselors provide accurate information about their research proposals and obtain approval prior to conducting their research. They conduct research in accordance with the approved research protocol.

B.7.b. Adherence to Guidelines

Counselors are responsible for understanding and adhering to state, federal, agency, or institutional policies or applicable guidelines regarding confidentiality in their research practices.

B.7.c. Confidentiality of Information Obtained in Research

Violations of participant privacy and confidentiality are risks of participation in research involving human participants. Investigators maintain all research records in a secure manner. They explain to participants the risks of violations of privacy and confidentiality and disclose to participants any limits of confidentiality that reasonably can be expected. Regardless of the degree to which confidentiality will be maintained, investigators must disclose to participants any limits of confidentiality that reasonably can be expected. *(See G.2.e.)*

B.7.d. Disclosure of Research Information

Counselors do not disclose confidential information that reasonably could lead to the identification of a research participant unless they have obtained the prior consent of the person. Use of data derived from counseling relationships for purposes of training, research, or publication is confined to content that is disguised to ensure the anonymity of the individuals involved. *(See G.2.a., G.2.d.)*

B.7.e. Agreement for Identification
Identification of clients, students, or supervisees in a presentation or publication is permissible only when they have reviewed the material and agreed to its presentation or publication. *(See G.4.d.)*

B.8. Consultation

B.8.a. Agreements
When acting as consultants, counselors seek agreements among all parties involved concerning each individual's rights to confidentiality, the obligation of each individual to preserve confidential information, and the limits of confidentiality of information shared by others.

B.8.b. Respect for Privacy
Information obtained in a consulting relationship is discussed for professional purposes only with persons directly involved with the case. Written and oral reports present only data germane to the purposes of the consultation, and every effort is made to protect client identity and to avoid undue invasion of privacy.

B.8.c. Disclosure of Confidential Information
When consulting with colleagues, counselors do not disclose confidential information that reasonably could lead to the identification of a client or other person or organization with whom they have a confidential relationship unless they have obtained the prior consent of the person or organization or the disclosure cannot be avoided. They disclose information only to the extent necessary to achieve the purposes of the consultation. *(See D.2.d.)*

SECTION C
Professional Responsibility

Introduction

Counselors aspire to open, honest, and accurate communication in dealing with the public and other professionals. They practice in a non-discriminatory manner within the boundaries of professional and personal competence and have a responsibility to abide by the *ACA Code of Ethics*. Counselors actively participate in local, state, and national associations that foster the development and improvement of counseling. Counselors advocate to promote change at the individual, group, institutional, and societal levels that improves the quality of life for individuals and groups and remove potential barriers to the provision or access of appropriate services being offered. Counselors have a responsibility to the public to engage in counseling practices that are based on rigorous research methodologies. In addition, counselors engage in self-care activities to maintain and promote their emotional, physical, mental, and spiritual well-being to best meet their professional responsibilities.

C.1. Knowledge of Standards

Counselors have a responsibility to read, understand, and follow the *ACA Code of Ethics* and adhere to applicable laws and regulations.

C.2. Professional Competence

C.2.a. Boundaries of Competence
Counselors practice only within the boundaries of their competence, based on their education, training, supervised experience, state and national professional credentials, and appropriate professional experience. Counselors gain knowledge, personal awareness, sensitivity, and skills pertinent to working with a diverse client population. *(See A.9.b., C.4.e., E.2., E.2., F.11.b.)*

C.2.b. New Specialty Areas of Practice
Counselors practice in specialty areas new to them only after appropriate education, training, and supervised experience. While developing skills in new specialty areas, counselors take steps to ensure the competence of their work and to protect others from possible harm. *(See F.6.f.)*

C.2.c. Qualified for Employment
Counselors accept employment only for positions for which they are qualified by education, training, supervised experience, state and national professional credentials, and appropriate professional experience. Counselors hire for professional counseling positions only individuals who are qualified and competent for those positions.

C.2.d. Monitor Effectiveness
Counselors continually monitor their effectiveness as professionals and take steps to improve when necessary. Counselors in private practice take reasonable steps to seek peer supervision as needed to evaluate their efficacy as counselors.

C.2.e. Consultation on Ethical Obligations
Counselors take reasonable steps to consult with other counselors or related professionals when they have questions regarding their ethical obligations or professional practice.

C.2.f. Continuing Education
Counselors recognize the need for continuing education to acquire and maintain a reasonable level of awareness of current scientific and professional information in their fields of activity. They take steps to maintain competence in the skills they use, are open to new procedures, and keep current with the diverse populations and specific populations with whom they work.

C.2.g. Impairment
Counselors are alert to the signs of impairment from their own physical, mental, or emotional problems and refrain from offering or providing professional services when such impairment is likely to harm a client or others. They seek assistance

for problems that reach the level of professional impairment, and, if necessary, they limit, suspend, or terminate their professional responsibilities until such time it is determined that they may safely resume their work. Counselors assist colleagues or supervisors in recognizing their own professional impairment and provide consultation and assistance when warranted with colleagues or supervisors showing signs of impairment and intervene as appropriate to prevent imminent harm to clients. *(See A.11.b., F.8.b.)*

C.2.b. Counselor Incapacitation or Termination of Practice

When counselors leave a practice, they follow a prepared plan for transfer of clients and files. Counselors prepare and disseminate to an identified colleague or "records custodian" a plan for the transfer of clients and files in the case of their incapacitation, death, or termination of practice.

C.3. Advertising and Soliciting Clients

C.3.a. Accurate Advertising

When advertising or otherwise representing their services to the public, counselors identify their credentials in an accurate manner that is not false, misleading, deceptive, or fraudulent.

C.3.b. Testimonials

Counselors who use testimonials do not solicit them from current clients nor former clients nor any other persons who may be vulnerable to undue influence.

C.3.c. Statements by Others

Counselors make reasonable efforts to ensure that statements made by others about them or the profession of counseling are accurate.

C.3.d. Recruiting Through Employment

Counselors do not use their places of employment or institutional affiliation to recruit or gain clients, supervisees, or consultees for their private practices.

C.3.e. Products and Training Advertisements

Counselors who develop products related to their profession or conduct workshops or training events ensure that the advertisements concerning these products or events are accurate and disclose adequate information for consumers to make informed choices. *(See C.6.d.)*

C.3.f. Promoting to Those Served

Counselors do not use counseling, teaching, training, or supervisory relationships to promote their products or training events in a manner that is deceptive or would exert undue influence on individuals who may be vulnerable. However, counselor educators may adopt textbooks they have authored for instructional purposes.

C.4. Professional Qualifications

C.4.a. Accurate Representation

Counselors claim or imply only professional qualifications actually completed and correct any known misrepresentations of their qualifications by others. Counselors truthfully represent the qualifications of their professional colleagues. Counselors clearly distinguish between paid and volunteer work experience and accurately describe their continuing education and specialized training. *(See C.2.a.)*

C.4.b. Credentials

Counselors claim only licenses or certifications that are current and in good standing.

C.4.c. Educational Degrees

Counselors clearly differentiate between earned and honorary degrees.

C.4.d. Implying Doctoral-Level Competence

Counselors clearly state their highest earned degree in counseling or closely related field. Counselors do not imply doctoral-level competence when only possessing a master's degree in counseling or a related field by referring to themselves as "Dr." in a counseling context when their doctorate is not in counseling or a related field.

C.4.e. Program Accreditation Status

Counselors clearly state the accreditation status of their degree programs at the time the degree was earned.

C.4.f. Professional Membership

Counselors clearly differentiate between current, active memberships and former memberships in associations. Members of the American Counseling Association must clearly differentiate between professional membership, which implies the possession of at least a master's degree in counseling, and regular membership, which is open to individuals whose interests and activities are consistent with those of ACA but are not qualified for professional membership.

C.5. Nondiscrimination

Counselors do not condone or engage in discrimination based on age, culture, disability, ethnicity, race, religion/spirituality, gender, gender identity, sexual orientation, marital status/partnership, language preference, socioeconomic status, or any basis proscribed by law. Counselors do not discriminate against clients, students, employees, supervisees, or research participants in a manner that has a negative impact on these persons.

C.6. Public Responsibility

C.6.a. Sexual Harassment

Counselors do not engage in or condone sexual harassment. Sexual harassment is defined as sexual solicitation, physical advances, or verbal or nonverbal conduct that is sexual in nature, that occurs in connection with professional activities or roles, and that either

1. is unwelcome, is offensive, or creates a hostile workplace or learning environment, and counselors know or are told this; or
2. is sufficiently severe or intense to be perceived as harassment to a reasonable person in the context in which the behavior occurred.

Sexual harassment can consist of a single intense or severe act or multiple persistent or pervasive acts.

C.6.b. Reports to Third Parties
Counselors are accurate, honest, and objective in reporting their professional activities and judgments to appropriate third parties, including courts, health insurance companies, those who are the recipients of evaluation reports, and others. *(See B.3., E.4.)*

C.6.c. Media Presentations
When counselors provide advice or comment by means of public lectures, demonstrations, radio or television programs, prerecorded tapes, technology-based applications, printed articles, mailed material, or other media, they take reasonable precautions to ensure that

1. the statements are based on appropriate professional counseling literature and practice,
2. the statements are otherwise consistent with the *ACA Code of Ethics,* and
3. the recipients of the information are not encouraged to infer that a professional counseling relationship has been established.

C.6.d. Exploitation of Others
Counselors do not exploit others in their professional relationships. *(See C.3.e.)*

C.6.e. Scientific Bases for Treatment Modalities
Counselors use techniques/procedures/modalities that are grounded in theory and/or have an empirical or scientific foundation. Counselors who do not must define the techniques/procedures as "unproven" or "developing" and explain the potential risks and ethical considerations of using such techniques/procedures and take steps to protect clients from possible harm. *(See A.4.a., E.5.c., E.5.d.)*

C.7. Responsibility to Other Professionals

C.7.a. Personal Public Statements
When making personal statements in a public context, counselors clarify that they are speaking from their personal perspectives and that they are not speaking on behalf of all counselors or the profession.

SECTION D
Relationships With Other Professionals

Introduction

Professional counselors recognize that the quality of their interactions with colleagues can influence the quality of services provided to clients. They work to become knowledgeable about colleagues within and outside the field of counseling.

Counselors develop positive working relationships and systems of communication with colleagues to enhance services to clients.

D.1. Relationships With Colleagues, Employers, and Employees

D.1.a. Different Approaches
Counselors are respectful of approaches to counseling services that differ from their own. Counselors are respectful of traditions and practices of other professional groups with which they work.

D.1.b. Forming Relationships
Counselors work to develop and strengthen interdisciplinary relations with colleagues from other disciplines to best serve clients.

D.1.c. Interdisciplinary Teamwork
Counselors who are members of interdisciplinary teams delivering multifaceted services to clients keep the focus on how to best serve the clients. They participate in and contribute to decisions that affect the well-being of clients by drawing on the perspectives, values, and experiences of the counseling profession and those of colleagues from other disciplines. *(See A.1.a.)*

D.1.d. Confidentiality
When counselors are required by law, institutional policy, or extraordinary circumstances to serve in more than one role in judicial or administrative proceedings, they clarify role expectations and the parameters of confidentiality with their colleagues. *(See B.1.c., B.1.d., B.2.c., B.2.d., B.3.b.)*

D.1.e. Establishing Professional and Ethical Obligations
Counselors who are members of interdisciplinary teams clarify professional and ethical obligations of the team as a whole and of its individual members. When a team decision raises ethical concerns, counselors first attempt to resolve the concern within the team. If they cannot reach resolution among team members, counselors pursue other avenues to address their concerns consistent with client well-being.

D.1.f. Personnel Selection and Assignment
Counselors select competent staff and assign responsibilities compatible with their skills and experiences.

D.1.g. Employer Policies
The acceptance of employment in an agency or institution implies that counselors are in agreement with its general policies and principles. Counselors strive to reach agreement with employers as to acceptable standards of conduct that allow for changes in institutional policy conducive to the growth and development of clients.

D.1.h. Negative Conditions
Counselors alert their employers of inappropriate policies and practices. They attempt to effect changes in such policies or procedures through constructive action within the organization.

When such policies are potentially disruptive or damaging to clients or may limit the effectiveness of services provided and change cannot be effected, counselors take appropriate further action. Such action may include referral to appropriate certification, accreditation, or state licensure organizations, or voluntary termination of employment.

D.1.i. Protection From Punitive Action
Counselors take care not to harass or dismiss an employee who has acted in a responsible and ethical manner to expose inappropriate employer policies or practices.

D.2. Consultation

D.2.a. Consultant Competency
Counselors take reasonable steps to ensure that they have the appropriate resources and competencies when providing consultation services. Counselors provide appropriate referral resources when requested or needed. *(See C.2.a.)*

D.2.b. Understanding Consultees
When providing consultation, counselors attempt to develop with their consultees a clear understanding of problem definition, goals for change, and predicted consequences of interventions selected.

D.2.c. Consultant Goals
The consulting relationship is one in which consultee adaptability and growth toward self-direction are consistently encouraged and cultivated.

D.2.d. Informed Consent in Consultation
When providing consultation, counselors have an obligation to review, in writing and verbally, the rights and responsibilities of both counselors and consultees. Counselors use clear and understandable language to inform all parties involved about the purpose of the services to be provided, relevant costs, potential risks and benefits, and the limits of confidentiality. Working in conjunction with the consultee, counselors attempt to develop a clear definition of the problem, goals for change, and predicted consequences of interventions that are culturally responsive and appropriate to the needs of consultees. *(See A.2.a., A.2.b.)*

SECTION E
Evaluation, Assessment, and Interpretation

Introduction

Counselors use assessment instruments as one component of the counseling process, taking into account the client personal and cultural context. Counselors promote the well-being of individual clients or groups of clients by developing and using appropriate educational, psychological, and career assessment instruments.

E.1. General

E.1.a. Assessment
The primary purpose of educational, psychological, and career assessment is to provide measurements that are valid and reliable in either comparative or absolute terms. These include, but are not limited to, measurements of ability, personality, interest, intelligence, achievement, and performance. Counselors recognize the need to interpret the statements in this section as applying to both quantitative and qualitative assessments.

E.1.b. Client Welfare
Counselors do not misuse assessment results and interpretations, and they take reasonable steps to prevent others from misusing the information these techniques provide. They respect the client's right to know the results, the interpretations made, and the bases for counselors' conclusions and recommendations.

E.2. Competence to Use and Interpret Assessment Instruments

E.2.a. Limits of Competence
Counselors utilize only those testing and assessment services for which they have been trained and are competent. Counselors using technology-assisted test interpretations are trained in the construct being measured and the specific instrument being used prior to using its technology-based application. Counselors take reasonable measures to ensure the proper use of psychological and career assessment techniques by persons under their supervision. *(See A. 12.)*

E.2.b. Appropriate Use
Counselors are responsible for the appropriate application, scoring, interpretation, and use of assessment instruments relevant to the needs of the client, whether they score and interpret such assessments themselves or use technology or other services.

E.2.c. Decisions Based on Results
Counselors responsible for decisions involving individuals or policies that are based on assessment results have a thorough understanding of educational, psychological, and career measurement, including validation criteria, assessment research, and guidelines for assessment development and use.

E.3. Informed Consent in Assessment

E.3.a. Explanation to Clients
Prior to assessment, counselors explain the nature and purposes of assessment and the specific use of results by potential recipients. The explanation will be given in the language of the client (or other legally authorized person on behalf of the client), unless an explicit exception has been agreed upon in advance. Counselors consider the client's personal or cultural context, the level of the client's understanding of the results, and the impact of the results on the client. *(See A.2., A.12.g., F.1.c.)*

E.3.b. Recipients of Results

Counselors consider the examinee's welfare, explicit understandings, and prior agreements in determining who receives the assessment results. Counselors include accurate and appropriate interpretations with any release of individual or group assessment results. *(See B.2.c., B.5.)*

E.4. Release of Data to Qualified Professionals

Counselors release assessment data in which the client is identified only with the consent of the client or the client's legal representative. Such data are released only to persons recognized by counselors as qualified to interpret the data. *(See B.1., B.3., B.6.b.)*

E.5. Diagnosis of Mental Disorders

E.5.a. Proper Diagnosis

Counselors take special care to provide proper diagnosis of mental disorders. Assessment techniques (including personal interview) used to determine client care (e.g., locus of treatment, type of treatment, or recommended follow-up) are carefully selected and appropriately used.

E.5.b. Cultural Sensitivity

Counselors recognize that culture affects the manner in which clients' problems are defined. Clients' socio-economic and cultural experiences are considered when diagnosing mental disorders. *(See A.2.c.)*

E.5.c. Historical and Social Prejudices in the Diagnosis of Pathology

Counselors recognize historical and social prejudices in the misdiagnosis and pathologizing of certain individuals and groups and the role of mental health professionals in perpetuating these prejudices through diagnosis and treatment.

E.5.d. Refraining From Diagnosis

Counselors may refrain from making and/or reporting a diagnosis if they believe it would cause harm to the client or others.

E.6. Instrument Selection

E.6.a. Appropriateness of Instruments

Counselors carefully consider the validity, reliability, psychometric limitations, and appropriateness of instruments when selecting assessments.

E.6.b. Referral Information

If a client is referred to a third party for assessment, the counselor provides specific referral questions and sufficient objective data about the client to ensure that appropriate assessment instruments are utilized. *(See A.9.b., B.3.)*

E.6.c. Culturally Diverse Populations

Counselors are cautious when selecting assessments for culturally diverse populations to avoid the use of instruments that lack appropriate psychometric properties for the client population. *(See A.2.c., E.5.b.)*

E.7. Conditions of Assessment Administration

(See A.12.b., A.12.d.)

E.7.a. Administration Conditions

Counselors administer assessments under the same conditions that were established in their standardization. When assessments are not administered under standard conditions, as may be necessary to accommodate clients with disabilities, or when unusual behavior or irregularities occur during the administration, those conditions are noted in interpretation, and the results may be designated as invalid or of questionable validity.

E.7.b. Technological Administration

Counselors ensure that administration programs function properly and provide clients with accurate results when technological or other electronic methods are used for assessment administration.

E.7.c. Unsupervised Assessments

Unless the assessment instrument is designed, intended, and validated for self-administration and/or scoring, counselors do not permit inadequately supervised use.

E.7.d. Disclosure of Favorable Conditions

Prior to administration of assessments, conditions that produce most favorable assessment results are made known to the examinee.

E.8. Multicultural Issues/Diversity in Assessment

Counselors use with caution assessment techniques that were normed on populations other than that of the client. Counselors recognize the effects of age, color, culture, disability, ethnic group, gender, race, language preference, religion, spirituality, sexual orientation, and socioeconomic status on test administration and interpretation, and place test results in proper perspective with other relevant factors. *(See A.2.c., E.5.b.)*

E.9. Scoring and Interpretation of Assessments

E.9.a. Reporting

In reporting assessment results, counselors indicate reservations that exist regarding validity or reliability due to circumstances of the assessment or the inappropriateness of the norms for the person tested.

E.9.b. Research Instruments

Counselors exercise caution when interpreting the results of research instruments not having sufficient technical data to support respondent results. The specific purposes for the use of such instruments are stated explicitly to the examinee.

E.9.c. Assessment Services

Counselors who provide assessment scoring and interpretation services to support the assessment process confirm the validity of such interpretations. They accurately describe the purpose, norms, validity, reliability, and applications of the procedures and any special qualifications applicable to their use. The public offering of an automated test interpretations service is considered a professional-to-professional consultation. The formal responsibility of the consultant is to the consultee, but the ultimate and overriding responsibility is to the client. *(See D.2.)*

E.10. Assessment Security

Counselors maintain the integrity and security of tests and other assessment techniques consistent with legal and contractual obligations. Counselors do not appropriate, reproduce, or modify published assessments or parts thereof without acknowledgment and permission from the publisher.

E.11. Obsolete Assessments and Outdated Results

Counselors do not use data or results from assessments that are obsolete or outdated for the current purpose. Counselors make every effort to prevent the misuse of obsolete measures and assessment data by others.

E.12. Assessment Construction

Counselors use established scientific procedures, relevant standards, and current professional knowledge for assessment design in the development, publication, and utilization of educational and psychological assessment techniques.

E.13. Forensic Evaluation: Evaluation for Legal Proceedings

E.13.a. Primary Obligations
When providing forensic evaluations, the primary obligation of counselors is to produce objective findings that can be substantiated based on information and techniques appropriate to the evaluation, which may include examination of the individual and/or review of records. Counselors are entitled to form professional opinions based on their professional knowledge and expertise that can be supported by the data gathered in evaluations. Counselors will define the limits of their reports or testimony, especially when an examination of the individual has not been conducted.

E.13.b. Consent for Evaluation
Individuals being evaluated are informed in writing that the relationship is for the purposes of an evaluation and is not counseling in nature, and entities or individuals who will receive the evaluation report are identified. Written consent to be evaluated is obtained from those being evaluated unless a court orders evaluations to be conducted without the written consent of individuals being evaluated. When children or vulnerable adults are being evaluated, informed written consent is obtained from a parent or guardian.

E.13.c. Client Evaluation Prohibited
Counselors do not evaluate individuals for forensic purposes they currently counsel or individuals they have counseled in the past. Counselors do not accept as counseling clients individuals

they are evaluating or individuals they have evaluated in the past for forensic purposes.

E.13.d. Avoid Potentially Harmful Relationships
Counselors who provide forensic evaluations avoid potentially harmful professional or personal relationships with family members, romantic partners, and close friends of individuals they are evaluating or have evaluated in the past.

SECTION F
Supervision, Training, and Teaching
Introduction

Counselors aspire to foster meaningful and respectful professional relationships and to maintain appropriate boundaries with supervisees and students. Counselors have theoretical and pedagogical foundations for their work and aim to be fair, accurate, and honest in their assessments of counselors-in-training.

F.1. Counselor Supervision and Client Welfare

F.1.a. Client Welfare
A primary obligation of counseling supervisors is to monitor the services provided by other counselors or counselors-in-training. Counseling supervisors monitor client welfare and supervisee clinical performance and professional development. To fulfill these obligations, supervisors meet regularly with supervisees to review case notes, samples of clinical work, or live observations. Supervisees have a responsibility to understand and follow the *ACA Code of Ethics.*

F.1.b. Counselor Credentials
Counseling supervisors work to ensure that clients are aware of the qualifications of the supervisees who render services to the clients. *(See A.2.b.)*

F.1.c. Informed Consent and Client Rights
Supervisors make supervisees aware of client rights including the protection of client privacy and confidentiality in the counseling relationship. Supervisees provide clients with professional disclosure information and inform them of how the supervision process influences the limits of confidentiality. Supervisees make clients aware of who will have access to records of the counseling relationship and how these records will be used. *(See A.2.b., B.1.d.)*

F.2. Counselor Supervision Competence

F.2.a. Supervisor Preparation
Prior to offering clinical supervision services, counselors are trained in supervision methods and techniques. Counselors who offer clinical supervision services regularly pursue continuing education activities including both counseling and supervision topics and skills. *(See C.2.a., C.2.f.)*

F.2.b. Multicultural Issues/Diversity in Supervision
Counseling supervisors are aware of and address the role of multiculturalism/diversity in the supervisory relationship.

F.3. Supervisory Relationships

F.3.a. Relationship Boundaries With Supervisees
Counseling supervisors clearly define and maintain ethical professional, personal, and social relationships with their supervisees. Counseling supervisors avoid nonprofessional relationships with current supervisees. If supervisors must assume other professional roles (e.g., clinical and administrative supervisor, instructor) with supervisees, they work to minimize potential conflicts and explain to supervisees the expectations and responsibilities associated with each role. They do not engage in any form of nonprofessional interaction that may compromise the supervisory relationship.

F.3.b. Sexual Relationships
Sexual or romantic interactions or relationships with current supervisees are prohibited.

F.3.c. Sexual Harassment
Counseling supervisors do not condone or subject supervisees to sexual harassment. *(See C.6.a.)*

F.3.d. Close Relatives and Friends
Counseling supervisors avoid accepting close relatives, romantic partners, or friends as supervisees.

F.3.e. Potentially Beneficial Relationships
Counseling supervisors are aware of the power differential in their relationships with supervisees. If they believe nonprofessional relationships with a supervisee may be potentially beneficial to the supervisee, they take precautions similar to those taken by counselors when working with clients. Examples of potentially beneficial interactions or relationships include attending a formal ceremony; hospital visits; providing support during a stressful event; or mutual membership in a professional association, organization, or community. Counseling supervisors engage in open discussions with supervisees when they consider entering into relationships with them outside of their roles as clinical and/or administrative supervisors. Before engaging in nonprofessional relationships, supervisors discuss with supervisees and document the rationale for such interactions, potential benefits or drawbacks, and anticipated consequences for the supervisee. Supervisors clarify the specific nature and limitations of the additional role(s) they will have with the supervisee.

F.4. Supervisor Responsibilities

F.4.a. Informed Consent for Supervision
Supervisors are responsible for incorporating into their supervision the principles of informed consent and participation. Supervisors inform supervisees of the policies and procedures to which they are to adhere and the mechanisms for due process appeal of individual supervisory actions.

F.4.b. Emergencies and Absences
Supervisors establish and communicate to supervisees procedures for contacting them or, in their absence, alternative on-call supervisors to assist in handling crises.

F.4.c. Standards for Supervisees
Supervisors make their supervisees aware of professional and ethical standards and legal responsibilities. Supervisors of post-degree counselors encourage these counselors to adhere to professional standards of practice. *(See C.1.)*

F.4.d. Termination of the Supervisory Relationship
Supervisors or supervisees have the right to terminate the supervisory relationship with adequate notice. Reasons for withdrawal are provided to the other party. When cultural, clinical, or professional issues are crucial to the viability of the supervisory relationship, both parties make efforts to resolve differences. When termination is warranted, supervisors make appropriate referrals to possible alternative supervisors.

F.5. Counseling Supervision Evaluation, Remediation, and Endorsement

F.5.a. Evaluation
Supervisors document and provide supervisees with ongoing performance appraisal and evaluation feedback and schedule periodic formal evaluative sessions throughout the supervisory relationship.

F.5.b. Limitations
Through ongoing evaluation and appraisal, supervisors are aware of the limitations of supervisees that might impede performance. Supervisors assist supervisees in securing remedial assistance when needed. They recommend dismissal from training programs, applied counseling settings, or state or voluntary professional credentialing processes when those supervisees are unable to provide competent professional services. Supervisors seek consultation and document their decisions to dismiss or refer supervisees for assistance. They ensure that supervisees are aware of options available to them to address such decisions. *(See C.2.g.)*

F.5.c. Counseling for Supervisees
If supervisees request counseling, supervisors provide them with acceptable referrals. Counselors do not provide counseling services to supervisees. Supervisors address interpersonal competencies in terms of the impact of these issues on clients, the supervisory relationship, and professional functioning. *(See F.3.a.)*

F.5.d. Endorsement
Supervisors endorse supervisees for certification, licensure, employment, or completion of an academic or training program only when they believe supervisees are qualified for the endorsement. Regardless of qualifications, supervisors do not endorse supervisees whom they believe to be impaired in any way that would interfere with the performance of the duties associated with the endorsement.

F.6. Responsibilities of Counselor Educators

F.6.a. Counselor Educators
Counselor educators who are responsible for developing, implementing, and supervising educational programs are skilled as teachers and practitioners. They are knowledgeable regarding the ethical, legal, and regulatory aspects of the profession, are skilled in applying that knowledge, and make students and supervisees aware of their responsibilities. Counselor educators conduct counselor education and training programs in an ethical manner and serve as role models for professional behavior. *(See C.1., C.2.a., C.2.c.)*

F.6.b. Infusing Multicultural Issues/Diversity
Counselor educators infuse material related to multiculturalism/diversity into all courses and workshops for the development of professional counselors.

F.6.c. Integration of Study and Practice
Counselor educators establish education and training programs that integrate academic study and supervised practice.

F.6.d. Teaching Ethics
Counselor educators make students and supervisees aware of the ethical responsibilities and standards of the profession and the ethical responsibilities of students to the profession. Counselor educators infuse ethical considerations throughout the curriculum. *(See C.1.)*

F.6.e. Peer Relationships
Counselor educators make every effort to ensure that the rights of peers are not compromised when students or supervisees lead counseling groups or provide clinical supervision. Counselor educators take steps to ensure that students and supervisees understand they have the same ethical obligations as counselor educators, trainers, and supervisors.

F.6.f. Innovative Theories and Techniques
When counselor educators teach counseling techniques/procedures that are innovative, without an empirical foundation, or without a well-grounded theoretical foundation, they define the counseling techniques/procedures as "unproven" or "developing" and explain to students the potential risks and ethical considerations of using such techniques/procedures.

F.6.g. Field Placements
Counselor educators develop clear policies within their training programs regarding field placement and other clinical experiences. Counselor educators provide clearly stated roles and responsibilities for the student or supervisee, the site supervisor, and the program supervisor. They confirm that site supervisors are qualified to provide supervision and inform site supervisors of their professional and ethical responsibilities in this role.

F.6.h. Professional Disclosure
Before initiating counseling services, counselors-in-training disclose their status as students and explain how this status affects the limits of confidentiality. Counselor educators ensure that the clients at field placements are aware of the services rendered and the qualifications of the students and supervisees rendering those services. Students and supervisees obtain client permission before they use any information concerning the counseling relationship in the training process. *(See A.2.b.)*

F.7. Student Welfare

F.7.a. Orientation
Counselor educators recognize that orientation is a developmental process that continues throughout the educational and clinical training of students. Counseling faculty provide prospective students with information about the counselor education program's expectations:

1. the type and level of skill and knowledge acquisition required for successful completion of the training;
2. program training goals, objectives, and mission, and subject matter to be covered;
3. bases for evaluation;
4. training components that encourage self-growth or self-disclosure as part of the training process;
5. the type of supervision settings and requirements of the sites for required clinical field experiences;
6. student and supervisee evaluation and dismissal policies and procedures; and
7. up-to-date employment prospects for graduates.

F.7.b. Self-Growth Experiences
Counselor education programs delineate requirements for self-disclosure or self-growth experiences in their admission and program materials. Counselor educators use professional judgment when designing training experiences they conduct that require student and supervisee self-growth or self-disclosure. Students and supervisees are made aware of the ramifications their self-disclosure may have when counselors whose primary role as teacher, trainer, or supervisor requires acting on ethical obligations to the profession. Evaluative components of experiential training experiences explicitly delineate predetermined academic standards that are separate and do not depend on the student's level of self-disclosure. Counselor educators may require trainees to seek professional help to address any personal concerns that may be affecting their competency.

F.8. Student Responsibilities

F.8.a. Standards for Students
Counselors-in-training have a responsibility to understand and follow the *ACA Code of Ethics* and adhere to applicable laws, regulatory policies, and rules and policies governing professional staff behavior at the agency or placement setting. Students have the same obligation to clients as those required of professional counselors. *(See C.1., H.1.)*

F.8.b. Impairment

Counselors-in-training refrain from offering or providing counseling services when their physical, mental, or emotional problems are likely to harm a client or others. They are alert to the signs of impairment, seek assistance for problems, and notify their program supervisors when they are aware that they are unable to effectively provide services. In addition, they seek appropriate professional services for themselves to remediate the problems that are interfering with their ability to provide services toothers. *(See A.1., C.2.d., C.2.g.)*

F.9. Evaluation and Remediation of Students

F.9.a. Evaluation

Counselors clearly state to students, prior to and throughout the training program, the levels of competency expected, appraisal methods, and timing of evaluations for both didactic and clinical competencies. Counselor educators provide students with ongoing performance appraisal and evaluation feedback throughout the training program.

F.9.b. Limitations

Counselor educators, throughout ongoing evaluation and appraisal, are aware of and address the inability of some students to achieve counseling competencies that might impede performance. Counselor educators

1. assist students in securing reme dial assistance when needed,
2. seek professional consultation and document their decision to dismiss or refer students for assistance, and
3. ensure that students have re course in a timely manner to address decisions to require them to seek assistance or to dismiss them and provide students with due process according to institutional policies and procedures. *(See C.2.g.)*

F.9.c. Counseling for Students

If students request counseling or if counseling services are required as part of a remediation process, counselor educators provide acceptable referrals.

F.10. Roles and Relationships Between Counselor Educators and Students

F.10.a. Sexual or Romantic Relationships

Sexual or romantic interactions or relationships with current students are prohibited.

F.10.b. Sexual Harassment

Counselor educators do not condone or subject students to sexual harassment. *(See C.6.a.)*

F.10.c. Relationships With Former Students

Counselor educators are aware of the power differential in the relationship between faculty and students. Faculty members foster open discussions with former students when considering engaging in a social, sexual, or other intimate relationship. Faculty members discuss with the former student how their former relationship may affect the change in relationship.

F.10.d. Nonprofessional Relationships

Counselor educators avoid nonpro-fessional or ongoing professional relationships with students in which there is a risk of potential harm to the student or that may compromise the training experience or grades assigned. In addition, counselor educators do not accept any form of professional services, fees, commissions, reimbursement, or remuneration from a site for student or supervisee placement.

F.10.e. Counseling Services

Counselor educators do not serve as counselors to current students unless this is a brief role associated with a training experience.

F.10.f. Potentially Beneficial Relationships

Counselor educators are aware of the power differential in the relationship between faculty and students. If they believe a nonprofessional relationship with a student may be potentially beneficial to the student, they take precautions similar to those taken by counselors when working with clients. Examples of potentially beneficial interactions or relationships include, but are not limited to, attending a formal ceremony; hospital visits; providing support during a stressful event; or mutual membership in a professional association, organization, or community. Counselor educators engage in open discussions with students when they consider entering into relationships with students outside of their roles as teachers and supervisors. They discuss with students the rationale for such interactions, the potential benefits and drawbacks, and the anticipated consequences for the student. Educators clarify the specific nature and limitations of the additional role(s) they will have with the student prior to engaging in a nonprofessional relationship. Nonprofessional relationships with students should be time-limited and initiated with student consent.

F.11. Multicultural/Diversity Competence in Counselor Education and Training Programs

F.11.a. Faculty Diversity

Counselor educators are committed to recruiting and retaining a diverse faculty.

F.11.b. Student Diversity

Counselor educators actively attempt to recruit and retain a diverse student body. Counselor educators demonstrate commitment to multicultural/diversity competence by recognizing and valuing diverse cultures and types of abilities students bring to the training experience. Counselor educators provide appropriate accommodations that enhance and support diverse student well-being and academic performance.

F.11.c. Multicultural/Diversity Competence

Counselor educators actively infuse multicultural/diversity competency in their training and supervision practices. They actively train students to gain awareness, knowledge, and skills in the competencies of multicultural practice. Counselor educators include case examples, role-plays, discussion questions, and other classroom activities that promote and represent various cultural perspectives.

SECTION G
Research and Publication

Introduction

Counselors who conduct research are encouraged to contribute to the knowledge base of the profession and promote a clearer understanding of the conditions that lead to a healthy and more just society. Counselors support efforts of researchers by participating fully and willingly whenever possible. Counselors minimize bias and respect diversity in designing and implementing research programs.

G.1. Research Responsibilities

G.1.a. Use of Human Research Participants
Counselors plan, design, conduct, and report research in a manner that is consistent with pertinent ethical principles, federal and state laws, host institutional regulations, and scientific standards governing research with human research participants.

G.1.b. Deviation From Standard Practice
Counselors seek consultation and observe stringent safeguards to protect the rights of research participants when a research problem suggests a deviation from standard or acceptable practices.

G.1.c. Independent Researchers
When independent researchers do not have access to an Institutional Review Board (IRB), they should consult with researchers who are familiar with IRB procedures to provide appropriate safeguards.

G.1.d. Precautions to Avoid Injury
Counselors who conduct research with human participants are responsible for the welfare of participants throughout the research process and should take reasonable precautions to avoid causing injurious psychological, emotional, physical, or social effects to participants.

G.1.e. Principal Researcher Responsibility
The ultimate responsibility for ethical research practice lies with the principal researcher. All others involved in the research activities share ethical obligations and responsibility for their own actions.

G.1.f. Minimal Interference
Counselors take reasonable precautions to avoid causing disruptions in the lives of research participants that could be caused by their involvement in research.

G.1.g. Multicultural/Diversity Considerations in Research
When appropriate to research goals, counselors are sensitive to incorporating research procedures that take into account cultural considerations. They seek consultation when appropriate.

G.2. Rights of Research Participants

(See A.2, A.7.)

G.2.a. Informed Consent in Research
Individuals have the right to consent to become research participants. In seeking consent, counselors use language that

1. accurately explains the purpose and procedures to be followed,
2. identifies any procedures that are experimental or relatively untried,
3. describes any attendant discom forts and risks,
4. describes any benefits or changes in individuals or organizations that might be reasonably expected,
5. discloses appropriate alternative procedures that would be advan tageous for participants,
6. offers to answer any inquiries concerning the procedures,
7. describes any limitations on confidentiality,
8. describes the format and potential target audiences for the dissemina tion of research findings, and
9. instructs participants that they are free to withdraw their consent and to discontinue participation in the project at any time without penalty.

G.2.b. Deception
Counselors do not conduct research involving deception unless alternative procedures are not feasible and the prospective value of the research justifies the deception. If such deception has the potential to cause physical or emotional harm to research participants, the research is not conducted, regardless of prospective value. When the methodological requirements of a study necessitate concealment or deception, the investigator explains the reasons for this action as soon as possible during the debriefing.

G.2.c. Student/Supervisee Participation
Researchers who involve students or supervisees in research make clear to them that the decision regarding whether or not to participate in research activities does not affect one's academic standing or supervisory relationship. Students or supervisees who choose not to participate in educational research are provided with an appropriate alternative to fulfill their academic or clinical requirements.

G.2.d. Client Participation
Counselors conducting research involving clients make clear in the informed consent process that clients are free to choose whether or not to participate in research activities. Counselors take necessary precautions to protect clients from adverse consequences of declining or withdrawing from participation.

G.2.e. Confidentiality of Information
Information obtained about research participants during the course of an investigation is confidential. When the possibility exists that others may obtain access to such information, ethical research practice requires that the possibility, together with the plans for protecting confidentiality, be explained to participants as a part of the procedure for obtaining informed consent.

G.2.f. Persons Not Capable of Giving Informed Consent

When a person is not capable of giving informed consent, counselors provide an appropriate explanation to, obtain agreement for participation from, and obtain the appropriate consent of a legally authorized person.

G.2.g. Commitments to Participants

Counselors take reasonable measures to honor all commitments to research participants. *(See A.2.c.)*

G.2.h. Explanations After Data Collection

After data are collected, counselors provide participants with full clarification of the nature of the study to remove any misconceptions participants might have regarding the research. Where scientific or human values justify delaying or withholding information, counselors take reasonable measures to avoid causing harm.

G.2.i. Informing Sponsors

Counselors inform sponsors, institutions, and publication channels regarding research procedures and outcomes. Counselors ensure that appropriate bodies and authorities are given pertinent information and acknowledgment.

G.2.j. Disposal of Research Documents and Records

Within a reasonable period of time following the completion of a research project or study, counselors take steps to destroy records or documents (audio, video, digital, and written) containing confidential data or information that identifies research participants. When records are of an artistic nature, researchers obtain participant consent with regard to handling of such records or documents. *(See B.4.a, B.4.g.)*

G.3. Relationships With Research Participants (When Research Involves Intensive or Extended Interactions)

G.3.a. Nonprofessional Relationships

Nonprofessional relationships with research participants should be avoided.

G.3.b. Relationships With Research Participants

Sexual or romantic counselor-research participant interactions or relationships with current research participants are prohibited.

G.3.c. Sexual Harassment and Research Participants

Researchers do not condone or subject research participants to sexual harassment.

G.3.d. Potentially Beneficial Interactions

When a nonprofessional interaction between the researcher and the research participant may be potentially beneficial, the researcher must document, prior to the interaction (when feasible), the rationale for such an interaction, the potential benefit, and anticipated consequences for the research participant. Such interactions should be initiated with appropriate consent of the research participant. Where unintentional harm occurs to the research participant due to the nonprofessional interaction, the researcher must show evidence of an attempt to remedy such harm.

G.4. Reporting Results

G.4.a. Accurate Results

Counselors plan, conduct, and report research accurately. They provide thorough discussions of the limitations of their data and alternative hypotheses. Counselors do not engage in misleading or fraudulent research, distort data, misrepresent data, or deliberately bias their results. They explicitly mention all variables and conditions known to the investigator that may have affected the outcome of a study or the interpretation of data. They describe the extent to which results are applicable for diverse populations.

G.4.b. Obligation to Report Unfavorable Results

Counselors report the results of any research of professional value. Results that reflect unfavorably on institutions, programs, services, prevailing opinions, or vested interests are not withheld.

G.4.c. Reporting Errors

If counselors discover significant errors in their published research, they take reasonable steps to correct such errors in a correction erratum, or through other appropriate publication means.

G.4.d. Identity of Participants

Counselors who supply data, aid in the research of another person, report research results, or make original data available take due care to disguise the identity of respective participants in the absence of specific authorization from the participants to do otherwise. In situations where participants self-identify their involvement in research studies, researchers take active steps to ensure that data are adapted/changed to protect the identity and welfare of all parties and that discussion of results does not cause harm to participants.

G.4.e. Replication Studies

Counselors are obligated to make available sufficient original research data to qualified professionals who may wish to replicate the study.

G.5. Publication

G.5.a. Recognizing Contributions

When conducting and reporting research, counselors are familiar with and give recognition to previous work on the topic, observe copyright laws, and give full credit to those to whom credit is due.

G.5.b. Plagiarism

Counselors do not plagiarize; that is, they do not present another person's work as their own work.

G.5.c. Review/Republication of Data or Ideas

Counselors fully acknowledge and make editorial reviewers aware of prior publication of ideas or data where such ideas or data are submitted for review or publication.

G.5.d. Contributors

Counselors give credit through joint authorship, acknowledgment, footnote statements, or other appropriate means to those who have contributed significantly to research or concept development in accordance with such contributions. The principal contributor is listed first, and minor technical or professional contributions are acknowledged in notes or introductory statements.

G.4.e. Agreement of Contributors
Counselors who conduct joint research with colleagues or students/supervisees establish agreements in advance regarding allocation of tasks, publication credit, and types of acknowledgment that will be received.

G.5.f. Student Research
For articles that are substantially based on students' course papers, projects, dissertations or theses, and on which students have been the primary contributors, they are listed as principal authors.

G.5.g. Duplicate Submission
Counselors submit manuscripts for consideration to only one journal at a time. Manuscripts that are published in whole or in substantial part in another journal or published work are not submitted for publication without acknowledgment and permission from the previous publication.

G.5.h. Professional Review
Counselors who review material submitted for publication, research, or other scholarly purposes respect the confidentiality and proprietary rights of those who submitted it. Counselors use care to make publication decisions based on valid and defensible standards. Counselors review article submissions in a timely manner and based on their scope and competency in research methodologies. Counselors who serve as reviewers at the request of editors or publishers make every effort to only review materials that are within their scope of competency and use care to avoid personal biases.

Section H
Resolving Ethical Issues

Introduction

Counselors behave in a legal, ethical, and moral manner in the conduct of their professional work. They are aware that client protection and trust in the profession depend on a high level of professional conduct. They hold other counselors to the same standards and are willing to take appropriate action to ensure that these standards are upheld.

Counselors strive to resolve ethical dilemmas with direct and open communication among all parties involved and seek consultation with colleagues and supervisors when necessary. Counselors incorporate ethical practice into their daily professional work. They engage in ongoing professional development regarding current topics in ethical and legal issues in counseling.

H.1. Standards and the Law
(See F.9.a.)

H.1.a. Knowledge
Counselors understand the *ACA Code of Ethics* and other applicable ethics codes from other professional organizations or from certification and licensure bodies of which they are members. Lack of knowledge or misunderstanding of an ethical responsibility is not a defense against a charge of unethical conduct.

H.1.b. Conflicts Between Ethics and Laws
If ethical responsibilities conflict with law, regulations, or other governing legal authority, counselors make known their commitment to the *ACA Code of Ethics* and take steps to resolve the conflict. If the conflict cannot be resolved by such means, counselors may adhere to the requirements of law, regulations, or other governing legal authority.

H.2. Suspected Violations

H.2.a. Ethical Behavior Expected
Counselors expect colleagues to adhere to the *ACA Code of Ethics.* When counselors possess knowledge that raises doubts as to whether another counselor is acting in an ethical manner, they take appropriate action. *(See H.2.b., H.2.c.)*

H.2.b. Informal Resolution
When counselors have reason to believe that another counselor is violating or has violated an ethical standard, they attempt first to resolve the issue informally with the other counselor if feasible, provided such action does not violate confidentiality rights that may be involved.

H.2.c. Reporting Ethical Violations
If an apparent violation has substantially harmed, or is likely to substantially harm, a person or organization and is not appropriate for informal resolution or is not resolved properly, counselors take further action appropriate to the situation. Such action might include referral to state or national committees on professional ethics, voluntary national certification bodies, state licensing boards, or to the appropriate institutional authorities. This standard does not apply when an intervention would violate confidentiality rights or when counselors have been retained to review the work of another counselor whose professional conduct is in question.

H.2.d. Consultation
When uncertain as to whether a particular situation or course of action may be in violation of the *ACA Code of Ethics,* counselors consult with other counselors who are knowledgeable about ethics and the *ACA Code of Ethics,* with colleagues, or with appropriate authorities.

H.2.e. Organizational Conflicts
If the demands of an organization with which counselors are affiliated pose a conflict with the *ACA Code of Ethics,* counselors specify the nature of such conflicts and express to their supervisors or other responsible officials their commitment to

the *ACA Code of Ethics.* When possible, counselors work toward change within the organization to allow full adherence to the *ACA Code of Ethics.* In doing so, they address any confidentiality issues.

H.2.f. Unwarranted Complaints
Counselors do not initiate, participate in, or encourage the filing of ethics complaints that are made with reckless disregard or willful ignorance of facts that would disprove the allegation.

H.2.g. Unfair Discrimination Against Complainants and Respondents
Counselors do not deny persons employment, advancement, admission to academic or other programs, tenure, or promotion based solely upon their having made or their being the subject of an ethics complaint. This does not preclude taking action based upon the outcome of such proceedings or considering other appropriate information.

H.3. Cooperation With Ethics Committees
Counselors assist in the process of enforcing the *ACA Code of Ethics.* Counselors cooperate with investigations, proceedings, and requirements of the ACA Ethics Committee or ethics committees of other duly constituted associations or boards having jurisdiction over those charged with a violation. Counselors are familiar with the *ACA Policy and Procedures for Processing Complaints of Ethical Violations* and use it as a reference for assisting in the enforcement of the *ACA Code of Ethics.*

Ethical Standards for School Counselors

ASCA's Ethical Standards for School Counselors were adopted by the ASCA Delegate Assembly, March 19, 1984, revised March 27, 1992, June 25, 1998 and June 26, 2004.

PREAMBLE

The American School Counselor Association (ASCA) is a professional organization whose members are certified/licensed in school counseling with unique qualifications and skills to address the academic, personal/social and career development needs of all students. Professional school counselors are advocates, leaders, collaborators and consultants who create opportunities for equity in access and success in educational opportunities by connecting their programs to the mission of schools and subscribing to the following tenets of professional responsibility:

• Each person has the right to be respected, be treated with dignity and have access to a comprehensive school counseling program that advocates for and affirms all students from diverse populations regardless of ethnic/racial status, age, economic status, special needs, English as a second language or other language group, immigration status, sexual orientation, gender, gender identity/expression, family type, religious/spiritual identity and appearance.

• Each person has the right to receive the information and support needed to move toward self-direction and self-development and affirmation within one's group identities, with special care being given to students who have historically not received adequate educational services: students of color, low socio-economic students, students with disabilities and students with nondominant language backgrounds.

• Each person has the right to understand the full magnitude and meaning of his/her educational choices and how those choices will affect future opportunities.

• Each person has the right to privacy and thereby the right to expect the counselor-student relationship to comply with all laws, policies and ethical standards pertaining to confidentiality in the school setting.

In this document, ASCA specifies the principles of ethical behavior necessary to maintain the high standards of integrity, leadership and professionalism among its members. The Ethical Standards for School Counselors were developed to clarify the nature of ethical responsibilities held in common by school counseling professionals. The purposes of this document are to:

• Serve as a guide for the ethical practices of all professional school counselors regardless of level, area, population served or membership in this professional association;

• Provide self-appraisal and peer evaluations regarding counselor responsibilities to students, parents/guardians, colleagues and professional associates, schools, communities and the counseling profession; and

• Inform those served by the school counselor of acceptable counselor practices and expected professional behavior.

A.1. Responsibilities to Students

The professional school counselor:

A. Has a primary obligation to the student, who is to be treated with respect as a unique individual.

B. Is concerned with the educational, academic, career, personal and social needs and encourages the maximum development of every student.

C. Respects the student's values and beliefs and does not impose the counselor's personal values.

D. Is knowledgeable of laws, regulations and policies relating to students and strives to protect and inform students regarding their rights.

A.2. Confidentiality

The professional school counselor:

A. Informs students of the purposes, goals, techniques and rules of procedure under which they may receive counseling at or before the time when the counseling relationship is entered. Disclosure notice includes the limits of confidentiality such as the possible necessity for consulting with other professionals, privileged communication, and legal or authoritative restraints. The meaning and limits of confidentiality are defined in developmentally appropriate terms to students.

B. Keeps information confidential unless disclosure is required to prevent clear and imminent danger to the student or others or when legal requirements demand that confidential information be revealed. Counselors will consult with appropriate professionals when in doubt as to the validity of an exception.

C. In absence of state legislation expressly forbidding disclosure, considers the ethical responsibility to provide information to an identified third party who, by his/her relationship with the student, is at a high risk of contracting a disease that is commonly known to be communicable and fatal. Disclosure requires satisfaction of all of the following conditions:

- Student identifies partner or the partner is highly identifiable
- Counselor recommends the student notify partner and refrain from further high-risk behavior
- Student refuses
- Counselor informs the student of the intent to notify the partner
- Counselor seeks legal consultation as to the legalities of informing the partner

D. Requests of the court that disclosure not be required when the release of confidential information may potentially harm a student or the counseling relationship.

E. Protects the confidentiality of students' records and releases personal data in accordance with prescribed laws and school policies. Student information stored and transmitted electronically is treated with the same care as traditional student records.

F. Protects the confidentiality of information received in the counseling relationship as specified by federal and state laws, written policies and applicable ethical standards. Such information is only to be revealed to others with the informed consent of the student, consistent with the counselor's ethical obligation.

G. Recognizes his/her primary obligation for confidentiality is to the student but balances that obligation with an understanding of the legal and inherent rights of parents/guardians to be the guiding voice in their children's lives.

A.3. Counseling Plans

The professional school counselor:

A. Provides students with a comprehensive school counseling program that includes a strong emphasis on working jointly with all students to develop academic and career goals.

B. Advocates for counseling plans supporting students right to choose from the wide array of options when they leave secondary education. Such plans will be regularly reviewed to update students regarding critical information they need to make informed decisions.

A.4. Dual Relationships

The professional school counselor:

A. Avoids dual relationships that might impair his/her objectivity and increase the risk of harm to the student (e.g., counseling one's family members, close friends or associates). If a dual relationship is unavoidable, the counselor is responsible for taking action to eliminate or reduce the potential for harm. Such safeguards might include informed consent, consultation, supervision and documentation.

B. Avoids dual relationships with school personnel that might infringe on the integrity of the counselor/student relationship check.

A.5. Appropriate Referrals

The professional school counselor:

A. Makes referrals when necessary or appropriate to outside resources. Appropriate referrals may necessitate informing both parents/guardians and students of applicable resources and making proper plans for transitions with minimal interruption of services. Students retain the right to discontinue the counseling relationship at any time.

A.6. Group Work

The professional school counselor:

A. Screens prospective group members and maintains an awareness of participants' needs and goals in relation to the goals of the group. The counselor takes reasonable precautions to protect members from physical and psychological harm resulting from interaction within the group.

B. Notifies parents/guardians and staff of group participation if the counselor deems it appropriate and if consistent with school board policy or practice.

C. Establishes clear expectations in the group setting and clearly states that confidentiality in group counseling cannot be guaranteed. Given the developmental and chronological ages of minors in schools, the counselor recognizes the tenuous nature of confidentiality for minors renders some topics inappropriate for group work in a school setting.

D. Follows up with group members and documents proceedings as appropriate.

A.7. Danger to Self or Others

The professional school counselor:

A. Informs parents/guardians or appropriate authorities when the student's condition indicates a clear and imminent danger to the student or others. This is to be done after careful deliberation and, where possible, after consultation with other counseling professionals.

B. Will attempt to minimize threat to a student and may choose to 1) inform the student of actions to be taken, 2) involve the student in a three-way communication with parents/guardians when breaching confidentiality or 3) allow the student to have input as to how and to whom the breach will be made.

A.8. Student Records

The professional school counselor:

A. Maintains and secures records necessary for rendering professional services to the student as required by laws, regulations, institutional procedures and confidentiality guidelines.

B. Keeps sole-possession records separate from students' educational records in keeping with state laws.

C. Recognizes the limits of sole-possession records and understands these records are a memory aid for the creator and in absence of privilege communication may

be subpoenaed and may become educational records when they 1) are shared with others in verbal or written form, 2) include information other than professional opinion or personal observations and/or 3) are made accessible to others.

D. Establishes a reasonable timeline for purging sole-possession records or case notes. Suggested guidelines include shredding sole possession records when the student transitions to the next level, transfers to another school or graduates. Careful discretion and deliberation should be applied before destroying sole-possession records that may be needed by a court of law such as notes on child abuse, suicide, sexual harassment or violence.

A.9. Evaluation, Assessment and Interpretation

The professional school counselor:

A. Adheres to all professional standards regarding selecting, administering and interpreting assessment measures and only utilizes assessment measures that are within the scope of practice for school counselors.

B. Seeks specialized training regarding the use of electronically based testing programs in administering, scoring and interpreting that may differ from that required in more traditional assessments.

C. Considers confidentiality issues when utilizing evaluative or assessment instruments and electronically based programs.

D. Provides interpretation of the nature, purposes, results and potential impact of assessment/evaluation measures in language the student(s) can understand.

E. Monitors the use of assessment results and interpretations, and takes reasonable steps to prevent others from misusing the information.

F. Uses caution when utilizing assessment techniques, making evaluations and interpreting the performance of populations not represented in the norm group on which an instrument is standardized.

G. Assesses the effectiveness of his/her program in having an impact on students' academic, career and personal/social development through accountability measures especially examining efforts to close achievement, opportunity and attainment gaps.

A.10. Technology

The professional school counselor:

A. Promotes the benefits of and clarifies the limitations of various appropriate technological applications.

The counselor promotes technological applications (1) that are appropriate for the student's individual needs, (2) that the student understands how to use and (3) for which follow-up counseling assistance is provided.

B. Advocates for equal access to technology for all students, especially those historically underserved.

C. Takes appropriate and reasonable measures for maintaining confidentiality of student information and educational records stored or transmitted over electronic media including although not limited to fax, electronic mail and instant messaging.

D. While working with students on a computer or similar technology, takes reasonable and appropriate measures to protect students from objectionable and/or harmful online material.

E. Who is engaged in the delivery of services involving technologies such as the telephone, videoconferencing and the Internet takes responsible steps to protect students and others from harm.

A.11. Student Peer Support Program

The professional school counselor:

Has unique responsibilities when working with student-assistance programs. The school counselor is responsible for the welfare of students participating in peer-to-peer programs under his/her direction.

B. Responsibilities to Parents/ Guardians

B.1. Parent Rights and Responsibilities

The professional school counselor:

A. Respects the rights and responsibilities of parents/guardians for their children and endeavors to establish, as appropriate, a collaborative relationship with parents/guardians to facilitate the student's maximum development.

B. Adheres to laws, local guidelines and ethical standards of practice when assisting parents/guardians experiencing family difficulties that interfere with the student's effectiveness and welfare.

C. Respects the confidentiality of parents/guardians.

D. Is sensitive to diversity among families and recognizes that all parents/guardians, custodial and noncustodial, are vested with certain rights and responsibilities for the welfare of their children by virtue of their role and according to law.

B.2. Parents/Guardians and Confidentiality

The professional school counselor:

A. Informs parents/guardians of the counselor's role with emphasis on the confidential nature of the counseling relationship between the counselor and student.

B. Recognizes that working with minors in a school setting may require counselors to collaborate with students' parents/guardians.

C. Provides parents/guardians with accurate, comprehensive and relevant information in an objective and caring manner, as is appropriate and consistent with ethical responsibilities to the student.

D. Makes reasonable efforts to honor the wishes of parents/guardians concerning information regarding the student, and in cases of divorce or separation exercises a good-faith effort to keep both parents informed with regard to critical information with the exception of a court order.

C. Responsibilities to Colleagues and Professional Associates

C.1. Professional Relationships

The professional school counselor:

A. Establishes and maintains professional relationships with faculty, staff and administration to facilitate an optimum counseling program.

B. Treats colleagues with professional respect, courtesy and fairness. The qualifications, views and findings of colleagues are represented to accurately reflect the image of competent professionals.

C. Is aware of and utilizes related professionals, organizations and other resources to whom the student may be referred.

C.2. Sharing Information with Other Professionals

The professional school counselor:

A. Promotes awareness and adherence to appropriate guidelines regarding confidentiality, the distinction between public and private information and staff consultation.

B. Provides professional personnel with accurate, objective, concise and meaningful data necessary to adequately evaluate, counsel and assist the student.

C. If a student is receiving services from another counselor or other mental health professional, the counselor, with student and/or parent/guardian consent, will inform the other professional and develop clear agreements to avoid confusion and conflict for the student.

D. Is knowledgeable about release of information and parental rights in sharing information.

D. RESPONSIBILITIES TO THE SCHOOL AND COMMUNITY

D.1. Responsibilities to the School

The professional school counselor:

A. Supports and protects the educational program against any infringement not in students' best interest.

B. Informs appropriate officials in accordance with school policy of conditions that may be potentially disruptive or damaging to the school's mission, personnel and property while honoring the confidentiality between the student and counselor.

C. Is knowledgeable and supportive of the school's mission and connects his/her program to the school's mission.

D. Delineates and promotes the counselor's role and function in meeting the needs of those served. Counselors will notify appropriate officials of conditions that may limit or curtail their effectiveness in providing programs and services.

E. Accepts employment only for positions for which he/she is qualified by education, training, supervised experience, state and national professional credentials and appropriate professional experience.

F. Advocates that administrators hire only qualified and competent individuals for professional counseling positions.

G. Assists in developing: (1) curricular and environmental conditions appropriate for the school and community, (2) educational procedures and programs to meet students' developmental needs and (3) a systematic evaluation process for comprehensive, developmental, standards-based school counseling programs, services and personnel. The counselor is guided by the findings of the evaluation data in planning programs and services.

D.2. Responsibility to the Community

The professional school counselor:

A. Collaborates with agencies, organizations and individuals in the community in the best interest of students and without regard to personal reward or remuneration.

B. Extends his/her influence and opportunity to deliver a comprehensive school counseling program to all students by collaborating with community resources for student success.

E. RESPONSIBILITIES TO SELF

E.1. Professional Competence

The professional school counselor:

A. Functions within the boundaries of individual professional competence and accepts responsibility for the consequences of his/her actions.

B. Monitors personal well-being and effectiveness and does not participate in any activity that may lead to inadequate professional services or harm to a student.

C. Strives through personal initiative to maintain professional competence including technological literacy and to keep abreast of professional information. Professional and personal growth are ongoing throughout the counselor's career.

E.2. Diversity

The professional school counselor:

A. Affirms the diversity of students, staff and families.

B. Expands and develops awareness of his/her own attitudes and beliefs affecting cultural values and biases and strives to attain cultural competence.

C. Possesses knowledge and understanding about how oppression, racism, discrimination and stereotyping affects her/him personally and professionally.

D. Acquires educational, consultation and training experiences to improve awareness, knowledge, skills and effectiveness in working with diverse populations: ethnic/racial status, age, economic status, special needs, ESL or ELL, immigration status, sexual orientation, gender, gender identity/expression, family type, religious/spiritual identity and appearance.

F. RESPONSIBILITIES TO THE PROFESSION

F.1. Professionalism

The professional school counselor:

A. Accepts the policies and procedures for handling ethical violations as a result of maintaining membership in the American School Counselor Association.

B. Conducts herself/himself in such a manner as to advance individual ethical practice and the profession.

C. Conducts appropriate research and report findings in a manner consistent with acceptable educational and psychological research practices. The counselor advocates for the protection of the individual student's identity when using data for research or program planning.

D. Adheres to ethical standards of the profession, other official policy statements, such as ASCA's position statements, role statement and the ASCA National Model, and relevant statutes established by federal, state and local governments, and when these are in conflict works responsibly for change.

E. Clearly distinguishes between statements and actions made as a private individual and those made as a representative of the school counseling profession.

F. Does not use his/her professional position to recruit or gain clients, consultees for his/her private practice or to seek and receive unjustified personal gains, unfair advantage, inappropriate relationships or unearned goods or services.

F.2. Contribution to the Profession

The professional school counselor:

A. Actively participates in local, state and national associations fostering the development and improvement of school counseling.

B. Contributes to the development of the profession through the sharing of skills, ideas and expertise with colleagues.

C. Provides support and mentoring to novice professionals.

G. MAINTENANCE OF STANDARDS

Ethical behavior among professional school counselors, association members and nonmembers, is expected at all times. When there exists serious doubt as to the ethical behavior of colleagues or if counselors are forced to work in situations or abide by policies that do not reflect the standards as outlined in these Ethical Standards for School Counselors, the counselor is obligated to take appropriate action to rectify the condition. The following procedure may serve as a guide:

1. The counselor should consult confidentially with a professional colleague to discuss the nature of a complaint to see if the professional colleague views the situation as an ethical violation.

2. When feasible, the counselor should directly approach the colleague whose behavior is in question to discuss the complaint and seek resolution.

3. If resolution is not forthcoming at the personal level, the counselor shall utilize the channels established within the school, school district, the state school counseling association and ASCA's Ethics Committee.

4. If the matter still remains unresolved, referral for review and appropriate action should be made to the Ethics Committees in the following sequence:

state school counselor association
American School Counselor Association

5. The ASCA Ethics Committee is responsible for:

• educating and consulting with the membership regarding ethical standards
• periodically reviewing and recommending changes in code
• receiving and processing questions to clarify the application of such standards; Questions must be submitted in writing to the ASCA Ethics chair.
• handling complaints of alleged violations of the ethical standards. At the national level, complaints should be submitted in writing to the ASCA Ethics Committee, c/o the Executive Director, American School Counselor Association, 1101 King St., Suite 625, Alexandria, VA 22314.

Multicultural Counseling Standards

I. COUNSELOR AWARENESS OF OWN CULTURAL VALUES AND BIASES

A. Attitudes and Beliefs

1. Culturally skilled counselors have moved from being culturally unaware to being aware of and sensitive to their own cultural heritage and to valuing and respecting differences.

2. Culturally skilled counselors are aware of how their own cultural backgrounds and experiences and attitudes, values, and biases influence psychological processes.

3. Culturally skilled counselors are able to recognize the limits of their competencies and expertise.

4. Culturally skilled counselors are comfortable with differences that exist between themselves and clients in terms of race, ethnicity, culture, and beliefs.

B. Knowledge

1. Culturally skilled counselors have specific knowledge about their own racial and cultural heritage and how it personally and professionally affects their definitions of normality-abnormality and the process of counseling.

2. Culturally skilled counselors possess knowledge and understanding about how oppression, racism, discrimination, and stereotyping affect them personally and in their work. This allows them to acknowledge their own racist attitudes, beliefs, and feelings. Although

Source: From "Multicultural Competencies/Standards: A Pressing Need," by D. W. Sue, P. Arredondo, and R. J. McDavis, 1992, *Journal of Counseling & Development, 70,* pp. 485–486. Copyright 1992 by the American Counseling Association. Reprinted with permission.

this standard applies to all groups, for White counselors it may mean that they understand how they may have directly or indirectly benefited from individual, institutional, and cultural racism (White identity development models).

3. Culturally skilled counselors possess knowledge about their social impact on others. They are knowledgeable about communication style differences, how their style may clash or foster the counseling process with minority clients, and how to anticipate the impact it may have on others.

C. Skills

1. Culturally skilled counselors seek out educational, consultative, and training experience to improve their understanding and effectiveness in working with culturally different populations. Being able to recognize the limits of their competencies, they (a) seek consultation, (b) seek further training or education, (c) refer out to more qualified individuals or resources, or (d) engage in a combination of these.

2. Culturally skilled counselors are constantly seeking to understand themselves as racial and cultural beings and are actively seeking a nonracist identity.

II. COUNSELOR AWARENESS OF CLIENT'S WORLDVIEW

A. Attitudes and Beliefs

1. Culturally skilled counselors are aware of their negative emotional reactions toward other racial and ethnic groups that may prove detrimental to their clients in counseling. They are willing to contrast their own beliefs and attitudes with those of their culturally different clients in a nonjudgmental fashion.

2. Culturally skilled counselors are aware of their stereotypes and preconceived notions that they may hold toward other racial and ethnic minority groups.

B. Knowledge

1. Culturally skilled counselors possess specific knowledge and information about the particular group they are working with. They are aware of the life experiences, cultural heritage, and historical background of their culturally different clients. This particular competency is strongly linked to the "minority identity development models" available in the literature.

2. Culturally skilled counselors understand how race, culture, ethnicity, and so forth may affect personality formation, vocational choices, manifestation of psychological disorders, help-seeking behavior, and the appropriateness or inappropriateness of counseling approaches.

3. Culturally skilled counselors understand and have knowledge about sociopolitical influences that impinge upon the life of racial and ethnic minorities. Immigration issues, poverty, racism, stereotyping, and powerlessness all leave major scars that may influence the counseling process.

C. Skills

1. Culturally skilled counselors should familiarize themselves with relevant research and the latest findings regarding mental disorders of various ethnic and racial groups. They should actively seek out educational experiences that foster their knowledge, understanding, and cross-cultural skills.

2. Culturally skilled counselors become actively involved with minority individuals outside of the counseling setting (community events, social and political functions, celebrations, friendships, neighborhood groups, and so forth) so that their perspective of minorities is more than an academic or helping exercise.

III. CULTURALLY APPROPRIATE INTERVENTION STRATEGIES

A. Attitudes and Beliefs

1. Culturally skilled counselors respect clients' religious and/or spiritual beliefs and values, including attributions and taboos, because they affect worldview, psychosocial functioning, and expressions of distress.

2. Culturally skilled counselors respect indigenous helping practices and respect minority community intrinsic help-giving networks.

3. Culturally skilled counselors value bilingualism and do not view another language as an impediment to counseling (monolingualism may be the culprit).

B. Knowledge

1. Culturally skilled counselors have a clear and explicit knowledge and understanding of the generic characteristics of counseling and therapy (culture bound, class bound, and monolingual) and how they may clash with the cultural values of various minority groups.

2. Culturally skilled counselors are aware of institutional barriers that prevent minorities from using mental health services.

3. Culturally skilled counselors have knowledge of the potential bias in assessment instruments and use procedures and interpret findings keeping in mind the cultural and linguistic characteristics of clients.

4. Culturally skilled counselors have knowledge of minority family structures, hierarchies, values, and beliefs. They are knowledgeable about the community characteristics and the resources in the community as well as the family.

5. Culturally skilled counselors should be aware of relevant discriminatory practices at the social and community level that may be affecting the psychological welfare of the population being served.

C. Skills

1. Culturally skilled counselors are able to engage in a variety of verbal and nonverbal helping responses. They are able to *send* and *receive* both *verbal* and *nonverbal* messages *accurately* and *appropriately*. They are not tied down to only one method or approach to helping but recognize that helping styles and approaches may be culture bound. When they sense that their helping style is limited and potentially inappropriate, they can anticipate and ameliorate its negative impact.

2. Culturally skilled counselors are able to exercise institutional intervention skills on behalf of their clients. They can help clients determine whether a "problem" stems from racism or bias in others (the concept of health paranoia) so that clients do not inappropriately personalize problems.

3. Culturally skilled counselors are not adverse to seeking consultation with traditional healers and religious and spiritual leaders and practitioners in the treatment of culturally different clients when appropriate.

4. Culturally skilled counselors take responsibility for interacting in the language requested by the client and, if not feasible, make appropriate referral. A serious problem arises when the linguistic skills of a counselor do not match the language of the client. This being the case, counselors should (a) seek a translator with cultural knowledge and appropriate professional background and (b) refer to a knowledgeable and competent bilingual counselor.

5. Culturally skilled counselors have training and expertise in the use of traditional assessment and testing instruments. They not only understand the technical aspects of the instruments but are also aware of the cultural limitations. This allows them to use test instruments for the welfare of the diverse clients.

6. Culturally skilled counselors should attend to as well as work to eliminate biases, prejudices, and discriminatory practices. They should be cognizant of sociopolitical contexts in conducting evaluation and providing interventions, and should develop sensitivity to issues of oppression, sexism, elitism, and racism.

7. Culturally skilled counselors take responsibility in educating their clients to the processes of psychological intervention, such as goals, expectations, legal rights, and the counselor's orientation.

REFERENCES

Adair, J. (2006). The efficacy of sexual violence prevention programs: Implications for counselors. *Journal of School Violence, 5*(2), 87–97.

Adelman, H. S., & Taylor, L. (2002). School counselors and school reform: New directions. *Professional School Counseling, 5*, 238–248.

Agnew, T., Vaught, C. C., Getz, H. G., & Fortune, J. (2000). Peer group clinical supervision program fosters confidence and professionalism. *Professional School Counseling, 4*, 6–12.

Alexander, C. M., Kruczek, T., Zagelbaum, A., & Ramirez, M. C. (2003). A review of the school counseling literature for themes evolving from the Educational Trust Initiative. *Professional School Counseling, 7*, 29–34.

Allsopp, A., & Prosen, S. (1988). Teacher reactions to a child sexual abuse training program. *Elementary School Guidance and Counseling, 22*, 299–305.

Amatea, E. S., & Clark, M. A. (2005). Changing schools, changing counselors: A qualitative study of school administrators' conceptions of the school counselor role. *Professional School Counseling, 9*, 16–27.

Amatea, E. S., & Fabrick, F. (1984). Moving a family into therapy: Critical referral issues for the school counselor. *School Counselor, 31*, 285–294.

American Association for Counseling and Development (AACD). (1991). *Special issue: Multiculturalism as a fourth force in counseling.* Alexandria, VA: Author.

American Counseling Association (ACA). (2005). *Code of ethics.* Alexandria, VA: Author.

American Counseling Association (ACA). (2006). By the numbers: Annual earnings of counselors. *Counseling Today, 49*(3), 3.

American Personnel and Guidance Association (APGA). (1969). *The elementary school counselor in today's schools.* Washington, DC: Author.

American School Counselor Association (ASCA). (1979, April 1). A new look at developmental guidance. *ASCA Counselor, 16*, 2–3, 11–12.

American School Counselor Association (ASCA). (1988). The school counselor and child abuse/neglect prevention. *Elementary School Guidance and Counseling, 22*, 216–263.

American School Counselor Association (ASCA). (1989). American School Counselor Association statement: Cross/multicultural counseling. *Elementary School Guidance and Counseling, 23*, 322–323.

American School Counselor Association (ASCA). (1990). Role statement: The school counselor. *ASCA guide to membership resources.* Alexandria, VA: Author.

American School Counselor Association (ASCA). (1996). *School counseling legislation: Elementary and Secondary Education Act (ESEA).* Alexandria, VA: Author.

American School Counselor Association (ASCA). (1999). *Role statement: The school counselor.* Alexandria, VA: Author.

American School Counselor Association (ASCA). (2003). *The ASCA national model: A framework for school counseling programs.* Alexandria, VA: Author.

American School Counselor Association (ASCA). (2004). 2004 ASCA RAMP schools announced! *ASCA School Counselor, 41*(6), 32–33.

American School Counselor Association (ASCA). (2004). *Ethical standards for school counselors.* Alexandria, VA: Author.

American School Counselor Association (ASCA). (2005). *The ASCA National Model: A framework for school counseling programs* (2nd ed.), Alexandria, VA: Author.

American School Counselor Association (ASCA). (n.d.). *Guide to membership resources.* Alexandria, VA: Author.

Anastasi, A. (1997). *Psychological testing.* (7th ed). Upper Saddle River, NJ: Prentice Hall.

Anderson, L., & Perryman, K. (2006). School counselors are uniquely qualified as mental health experts. *Counseling Today, 42*(8), 14.

Anderson, R. F. (n.d.). *Counselors going to court.* Unpublished paper, Wake County, North Carolina Public Schools, Raleigh.

Arnold v. Board of Education of Escambia County, 880 F.2d 305 (Alabama 1989).

Arredondo, P., & D'Andrea, M. (1995, September). AMCD approves multicultural counseling competency standards. *Counseling Today*, pp. 28–29, 32.

Arredondo, P., & D'Andrea, M. (2001, April). Changing paradigms in organizations. *Counseling Today, 38*, 44.

Arredondo, P., & D'Andrea, M. (2002, March). Are assessments culturally informed? *Counseling Today, 28*, 32.

Arredondo, P., & D'Andrea, M. (2002, June). What do culturally competent practices look like? *Counseling Today, 28*, 32.

Astramovich, R. L., & Holden, J. M. (2002). Attitudes of American School Counselor Association members toward utilizing paraprofessionals in school counseling. *Professional School Counseling 5*, 203–210.

Atkinson, D. R., & Juntunen, C. L. (1994). School counselors and school psychologists as school–home–community liaisons in ethnically diverse schools. In P. Pedersen & J. C. Carey (Eds.), *Multicultural counseling in schools* (pp. 103–120). Boston: Allyn & Bacon.

Aubrey, R. E. (1977). Historical development of guidance and counseling and implications for the future. *Personnel and Guidance Journal, 55*, 288–295.

Baggerly, J., & Osborn, D. (2006). School counselors' career satisfaction and commitment: Correlates and predictors. *Professional School Counseling, 9*, 197–205.

Bailey, D. F., Getch, Y. Q., & Chen-Hayes, S. (2003). Professional school counselors as social and academic advocates. In B. T. Erford (Ed.), *Transforming the school counseling profession* (pp. 411–434). Upper Saddle River, NJ.: Merrill-Prentice Hall.

Bailey, D. F., & Paisley, P. O. (2004). Developing and nurturing excellence in African American male adolescents. *Journal of Counseling and Development, 82*, 10–17.

Baker, S. B. (1973). Referrals: Who? when? where? how? *Pennsylvania Personnel and Guidance Journal, 1*, 19–23.

Baker, S. B. (1981). *School counselor's handbook: A guide for professional growth and development.* Boston: Allyn & Bacon.

Baker, S. B. (1982). Free school counselors from gatekeeping and custodial tasks. *National Association of Secondary School Principals Bulletin, 66*, 110–112.

Baker, S. B. (1994). Mandatory teaching experience for school counselors: An impediment to uniform certification standards for school counselors. *Counselor Education and Supervision, 33*, 314–326.

Baker, S. B. (2001). Coping skills training for adolescents: Applying cognitive behavioral principles to psychoeducational groups. *Journal for Specialists in Group Work, 26*, 219–227.

Baker, S. B. (2001). Reflections on forty years in the counseling profession: Is the glass half full or half empty? *Professional School Counseling, 5*, 75–83.

Baker, S. B., & Gerler, S. B. (2001). Counseling in schools. In D. Locke, J. E. Myers, & E. L. Herr (Eds.), *The handbook of counseling* (pp. 289–318). Thousand Oaks, CA: Sage.

Baker, S. B., & Hansen, J. C. (1972). School counselor attitudes on a status quo—Change agent measurement scale. *School Counselor, 19*, 243–248.

Baker, S. B., Kessler, B. L., Bishop, R. M., & Giles, G. N. (1993). *School counselor role: A proposal for ridding the profession of an "old ghost."* Unpublished manuscript, The Pennsylvania State University, University Park.

Baker, S. B., Swisher, J. D., Nadenichek, P., & Popowicz, C. L. (1984). Measured effects of primary prevention. *Personnel and Guidance Journal, 62*, 459–463.

Baker, S. B., & Taylor, J. G. (1998). Effects of career education interventions: A meta-analysis. *Career Development Quarterly, 46*, 376–385.

Bandura, A. (1986). *Social foundations of thought and action: A social cognitive theory.* Upper Saddle River, NJ: Prentice Hall.

Bandura, A., & Jeffery, R. W. (1973). Roles of symbolic coding and rehearsal processes in observational learning. *Journal of Personality and Social Psychology, 26*, 122–130.

Barber, B. (1965). Some problems in the sociology of a profession. In K. S. Lynn (Ed.), *Professions in America.* Boston: Houghton Mifflin.

Bardon, J. I. (1985). On the verge of a breakthrough. *Counseling Psychologist, 13*(3), 355–362.

Barlow, D. H., & Herson, M. (1984). *Single-case experimental designs: Strategies for studying behavior changes* (2nd ed.). New York: Pergamon Press.

Barlow, K., Strother, J., & Landreth, G. (1985). Child-centered play therapy: Nancy from baldness to curls. *School Counselor, 32*, 347–356.

Bartholomew, C. G., & Schnorr, D. L. (1994). Gender equity: Suggestions for broadening career options of female students. *School Counselor, 41*, 245–256.

Bass, C. K., & Coleman, H. L. K. (1997). Enhancing the cultural identity of early adolescent male African Americans. *Professional School Counseling, 1*(2), 48–51.

Bauer, A. M., & Sapona, R. H. (1988). Facilitation and problem solving: A framework for collaboration between counselors and teachers. *Elementary School Guidance and Counseling, 23,* 5–9.

Bauman, S., & Sachs-Kapp, P. (1998). A school takes a stand: Promotion of sexual orientation workshops by counselors. *Professional School Counseling, 1*(3), 42–45.

Becky, D., & Farren, P. M. (1997). Teaching students how to understand and avoid abusive relationships. *School Counselor, 44,* 303–308.

Beers, C. (1908). *A mind that found itself.* New York: Longmans Green.

Behannon, M. (1996). Overworked and under stress. *Counseling Today, 39*(2), 17.

Bellotti v. Baird, 443 U.S. 622 (1979).

Bemak, F. (2000). Transforming the role of the counselor to provide leadership in educational reform through collaboration. *Professional School Counseling, 3,* 323–331.

Bemak, F., Chung, R. C., & Siroskey-Sabdo, L. A., (2005). Empowerment groups for academic success: An innovative approach to prevent high school failure of at-risk urban African American girls. *Professional School Counseling, 5,* 377–389.

Bemak, F., & Cornely, L. (2002). The SAFI model as a critical link between marginalized families and schools: A literature review and strategies for school counselors. *Journal of Counseling & Development, 5,* 322–331.

Bernstein, D. A., & Borkovec, T. D. (1973). *Progressive relaxation training.* Champaign, IL: Research Press.

Berube, E., & Berube, L. (1997). Offering a menu of small-group opportunities in response to students' expressed needs by drawing on school and community resources. *School Counselor, 44,* 294–302.

Black, J., & Underwood, J. (1998). Young, female, and gay: Lesbian students and the school environment. *Professional School Counseling, 1*(3), 15–20.

Blacher, J. H., Murray-Ward, M., & Ullendahl, G. E. (2005). School counselors and student assessment. *Professional School Counseling, 8,* 337–343.

Bobele, M., & Conran, T. J. (1988). Referrals for family therapy: Pitfalls and guidelines. *Elementary School Guidance and Counseling, 22,* 192–198.

Bolman, L. B., & Deal, T. E. (1997). *Reframing organizations: Artistry, choice, and leadership* (2nd ed.). San Francisco: Jossey-Bass.

Borders, D. L., & Drury, R. D. (1992). Comprehensive school counseling programs: A review for policy makers and practitioners. *Journal of Counseling and Development, 70,* 487–498.

Borders, L. D. (2002). School counseling in the twenty-first century: Personal and professional reflections. *Professional School Counseling, 5,* 180–185.

Borders, L. D., & Drury, S. M. (1992). Comprehensive school counseling programs: A review for policy makers and practitioners. *Journal of Counseling and Development, 70,* 487–498.

Borris, A. F. (1988). Organizational models. *Student Assistance Journal, 1,* 31–33.

Boser, J. A., Poppen, W. A., & Thompson, C. L. (1988). Elementary school guidance evaluation: A reflection of student–counselor ratio. *School Counselor, 36,* 125–135.

Botvin, G. J. (1998). *Life skills training: Promoting health and personal development.* Princeton, NJ: Princeton Health Press.

Bowers, J., Hatch, T., & Schwallie-Giddis, P. (2001, September–October). The brain storm. *ASCA Counselor,* 17–18.

Bowman, R. P. (1987). Small-group guidance and counseling in schools: A national survey of counselors. *School Counselor, 34,* 250–262.

Brack, G., Jones, E. S., Smith, R. M., White, J., & Brack, C. J. (1993). A primer on consultation theory: Building a flexible worldview. *Journal of Counseling & Development, 71,* 619–628.

Bradley, R. (1994). Tests and counseling: Did we ever become partners? *Measurement and Evaluation in Counseling and Development, 26,* 224–226.

Bradley, L., & Lewis, J. (2000). Introduction. In J. Lewis & L. Bradley (Eds.), *Advocacy in counseling: Counselors, client & community* (pp. 3–4). Greensboro, NC: ERIC Clearinghouse on Counseling and Student Services.

Brammer, L. M., Abrego, P. J., & Shostrom, E. L. (1993). *Therapeutic counseling and psychotherapy* (6th ed.). Upper Saddle River, NJ: Prentice Hall.

Brewer, J. M. (1932). *Education as guidance.* New York: Macmillan.

Brigman, G., & Campbell, C. (2003). Helping students improve academic achievement and school success behavior. *Professional School Counseling, 7,* 91–98.

Bronner, E. (1998, March 14). Guidance counselors fearful of litigation. *The News & Observer,* p. 12A.

Brown, C., Dahlbeck, D. T., & Sparkman-Barnes, L. (2006). Collaborative relationships: School counselors and non-school mental health professionals working together to improve the mental health needs of students. *Professional School Counseling, 9,* 332–335.

Brown, D., & Trusty, J. (2005a). School counselors, comprehensive school counseling programs, and academic achievement: Are school counselors promising more than they can deliver? *Professional School Counseling, 9,* 1–8.

Brown, D., & Trusty, J. (2005b). The ASCA National Model, accountability, and establishing causal links between school counselors' activities and student outcomes. *Professional School Counseling, 9,* 13–15.

Brown, D., & Trusty, J. (2005c). *Designing and leading comprehensive school counseling programs: Promoting student competence and meeting student needs.* Belmont, CA: Thomson, Brooks/Cole.

Brown, D., Galassi, J. P., & Akos, P. (2004). School counselors' perceptions of the impact of high-stakes testing. *Professional School Counseling, 8,* 31–39.

Brown, D. (1982). Increasing test-wiseness in children. *Elementary School Guidance and Counseling, 16,* 180–186.

Brown, D., Wyne, M. D., Blackburn, J. E., & Powell, W. C. (1979). *Consultation: Strategy for improving education.* Boston: Allyn & Bacon.

Brown, G. I. (1971). *Human teaching for human learning: An introduction to confluent education.* New York: Viking.

Bruce, M. A. (1995). Brief counseling: An effective model for change. *School Counselor, 42,* 353–363.

Bruce, M. A., & Hopper, G. C. (1997). Brief counseling versus traditional counseling: A comparison of effectiveness. *School Counselor, 44,* 171–184.

Bryan, J., & Holcomb-McCoy, C. (2004). School counselors' perceptions of their involvement in school–family–community partnerships. *Professional School Counseling, 7,* 162–171.

Bryant, J., & Milsom, A. (2005). Child abuse reporting by school counselors. *Professional School Counseling, 9,* 63–71.

Bryant, R. M., & Constantine, M. G. (2006). Multiple role balance, job satisfaction, and life satisfaction in women school counselors. *Professional School Counseling, 9,* 265–271.

Bundy, M. L., & Poppen, W. A. (1986). School counselors' effectiveness as consultants: A research review. *Elementary School Guidance and Counseling, 29,* 215–222.

Burky, W. D., & Childers, J. H., Jr. (1976). Buckley Amendment: Focus on a professional dilemma. *School Counselor, 23,* 162–164.

Butler, S. K., & Constantine, M. G. (2005). Collective self-esteem and burnout in professional school counselors. *Professional School Counseling, 9,* 55–62.

Campbell, C. A., & Dahir, C. A. (1997). *Sharing the vision: The National Standards for School Counseling Programs.* Alexandria, VA: American School Counseling Association Press.

Caplan, G. (1959). *Concepts of mental health and consultation.* Washington, DC: U.S. Department of Health, Education and Welfare, Children's Bureau.

Caplan, G. (1961). *An approach to community mental health.* New York: Grune & Stratton.

Carey, A. R., Black, K. J., & Neider, G. G. (1978). Upping the odds on the referral gamble. *School Counselor, 25,* 186–190.

Carl D. Perkins Vocational and Applied Technology Education Act, 20 U.S.C. & 2301 (1984).

Carlson, L. A., Portman, T. A. A., & Bartlett, J. R. (2006). Professional school counselors' approaches to technology. *Professional School Counseling, 9,* 252–256.

Carmichael, L., & Calvin, L. (1970). Functions selected by school counselors. *School Counselor, 17,* 280–285.

Carruthers, W. L., Carruthers, B. J. B., Day-Vines, N. L., Bostick, D., & Watson, D. C. (1996). Conflict resolution as a curriculum: A definition, description, and process for integration in core curricula. *School Counselor, 43,* 345–373.

Casas, J. M., & Furlong, M. J. (1994). School counselors as advocates for increased Hispanic parent participation in schools. In P. Pedersen & J. C. Carey (Eds.), *Multicultural counseling in schools: A practical handbook* (pp. 121–156). Boston: Allyn & Bacon.

Castenell, L. A., Jr., & Castenell, M. E. (1988). Norm-referenced testing and low-income Blacks. *Journal of Counseling & Development, 67,* 205–206.

Cecil, J. H. (1990). Interdivisional task force on school counseling. *ACES Spectrum, 50*(4), 3–4.

Chickering, A., & Gameson, Z. (1987). Principles for good practices in undergraduate education. *AAHE Bulletin, 39,* 3–7.`

Chung, R. C. (2005). Women, human rights, and counseling: Crossing international boundaries. *Journal of Counseling and Development, 83,* 262–268.

Clark, M. A., & Amatea, E. (2004). Teacher perceptions of expectations of school counselor contributions: Implications for program planning and training. *Professional School Counseling, 8,* 132–140.

Cochran, J. L. (1996). Using play and art therapy to help culturally diverse students overcome barriers to school success. *School Counselor, 43,* 287–298.

Coleman, H. K. L. (1995). Cultural factors and the counseling process: Implications for school counselors. *School Counselor, 42,* 180–185.

Coleman, S. (2006). *Consultation reflection.* Unpublished manuscript, North Carolina State University, Raleigh.

College Board. (1986). *Keeping the options open— Recommendations: Final report of the Commission on Precollege Guidance and Counseling.* New York: College Entrance Examination Board.

College Entrance Examination Board. (1986). *Keeping the options open: An overview.* New York: Author.

Conant, J. B. (1959). *The American high school today.* New York: McGraw-Hill.

Congressional Record (120–S21487, daily edition, December 13, 1974). Joint statement in explanation of the Buckley/Pell Amendment. Washington, DC: Government Printing Office.

Connors, E. T. (1979). *Student discipline and the law.* Bloomington, IN: Phi Delta Kappa Foundation.

Conroy, P. (1972/2002). *The water is wide.* New York: Bantam Books.

Cook, D. W. (1989). Systematic needs assessment: A primer. *Journal of Counseling & Development, 67,* 462–464.

Cooley, J. J. (1998). Gay and lesbian adolescents: Presenting problems and the counselor's role. *Professional School Counseling, 1*(3), 30–34.

Corey, G., Corey, M. S., & Callanan, P. (1984). *Issues and ethics in the helping professions* (2nd ed.). Monterey, CA: Brooks/Cole.

Corey, G., Corey, M. S., Callanan, P., & Russell, J. M. (1992). *Group techniques* (2nd ed.). Pacific Grove, CA: Brooks/Cole.

Corey, M. S., & Corey, G. (1997). *Groups: Process and practice* (6th ed.). Pacific Grove, CA: Brooks/Cole.

Cormier, S., & Nurius, P. S. (2003). *Interviewing strategies for helpers: Fundamental skills and cognitive behavioral interventions* (4th ed.). Pacific Grove, CA: Brooks/Cole.

Cottone, R. R. (2001). A social constructivism model of ethical decision making in counseling. *Journal of Counseling & Development, 90,* 39–45.

Council for the Accreditation of Counseling and Related Educational Programs (CACREP). (2001). *CACREP accreditation manual.* Alexandria, VA: Author.

Cowan, E. W., & Presbury, J. H. (2000). Meeting client resistance and reactance with reverence. *Journal of Counseling & Development, 78,* 411–419.

Cowen, E. L. (1982). Primary prevention research: Barriers, needs, and opportunities. *Journal of Primary Prevention, 2,* 131–137.

Cremin, L. A. (1965). The progressive heritage of the guidance movement. In R. L. Mosher, R. E. Carle, & C. D. Kehas (Eds.), *Guidance: An examination* (pp. 3–12). New York: Harcourt, Brace & World.

Crenshaw, W., Crenshaw, L., & Lichtenberg, J. (1995). When educators confront child abuse: An analysis of the decision to report. *Child Abuse & Neglect, 19,* 1095–1113.

Culbreth, J. R., Scarborough, J. L., Banks-Johnson, A., & Solomon, S. (2005). Role stress among practicing school counselors. *Counselor Education and Supervision, 45,* 58–71.

Cummings, N. A. (1986). The dismantling of our health system. *American Psychologist, 41,* 426–431.

Currie v. United States, 644 E Supp. 1074 (N.C., 1986).

D'Andrea, M., & Daniels, J. (1997). Continuing the discussion about racism: A reaction by D'Andrea and Daniels. *ACES Spectrum, 58*(2), 8–9.

Dagley, J. C. (1987). A new look at developmental guidance: The hearthstone of school counseling. *School Counselor, 35,* 102–109.

Dahir, C. (1997). National Standards for School Counseling Programs: A pathway to excellence. *ASCA Counselor, 35*(2), 11.

Dahir, C. (2001). The National Standards for School Counseling Programs: Development and implementation. *Professional School Counseling, 4,* 320–327.

Dahir, C. (2004). Supporting a nation of learners: The role of school counseling in educational reform. *Journal of Counseling and Development, 82,* 344–353.

Davis, A. H. (1997). The ethics of caring: A collaborative approach to resolving ethical dilemmas. *Journal of Applied Rehabilitation Counseling, 28,* 36–41.

Day-Vines, N. L., Day-Hariston, B. O., Carruthers, W. L., Wall, J. A., & Lupton-Smith, H. (1996). Conflict resolution: The value of diversity in the recruitment, selection, and training of peer mediators. *School Counselor, 43,* 392–410.

Deffenbacher, J. L., Lynch, R. S., Oetting, E. R., & Kemper, C. C. (1996). Anger reduction in early adolescents. *Journal of Counseling Psychology, 43,* 149–157.

DePauw, M. E. (1986). Avoiding ethical violations: A timeline perspective for individual counseling. *Journal of Counseling & Development, 64,* 303–305.

Deutsch, J. (1996). Primary intervention program makes a big difference for the ordinary kid. *ASCA Counselor, 34*(2), 15–16.

DeVoe, M. W., & McClam, T. (1982). Service coordination: The school counselor. *School Counselor, 35,* 95–101.

Dinkmeyer, D. (1967). Elementary school guidance and the classroom teacher. *Elementary School Guidance and Counseling, 1,* 15–26.

Dinkmeyer, D. (1969). Group counseling theory and techniques. *School Counselor, 17,* 148–152.

Dinsmore, J. A., Chapman, A., & McCollum, V. J. C. (2000, March). *Client advocacy and social justice: Strategies for developing trainee competence.* Paper presented at the annual conference of the American Counseling Association, Washington, DC.

Dinsmore, J. A., Chapman, A., & McCollum, V. J. C. (2002, March). *Client advocacy and social justice: Strategies for developing trainee competence.* Paper presented at the annual conference of the American Counseling Association, New Orleans, LA.

Dobbins, J. E., & Skillings, J. H. (1991). The utility of race labeling in understanding cultural identity: A conceptual tool for the social science practitioner. *Journal of Counseling & Development, 70,* 37–44.

Dollarhide, C. T. (2003). School counselors as program leaders: Applying leadership contexts to school counseling. *Professional School Counseling, 6,* 304–309.

Dollarhide, C. T., & Saginak, K. A. (2003). *School counseling in the secondary school: A comprehensive process and program.* Boston: Allyn & Bacon.

Dorlak, J. A. (1983). Social problem-solving as a primary prevention strategy. In R. D. Felner, L. A. Jason, J. N. Morltsuga, & S. S. Farber (Eds.), *Preventive psychology: Theory, research, and practice* (pp. 31–48). New York: Pergamon.

Dougherty, A. M. (1990). *Consultation: Practice and perspectives.* Pacific Grove, CA: Brooks/Cole.

Dougherty, A. M. (1992). School consultation in the 1990s. *Elementary School Guidance and Counseling, 26,* 163–164.

Dowd, E. T., & Moerings, B. J. (1975). The underachiever and teacher consultation: A case study. *School Counselor, 22,* 263–266.

Downing, C. J. (1982). Parent support groups to prevent child abuse. *Elementary School Guidance and Counseling, 17,* 119–124.

Downing, C. J. (1985). Referrals that work. *School Counselor, 32,* 242–246.

Downing, J., Pierce, K. A., & Woodruff, P. (1993). A community network for helping families. *School Counselor, 41,* 102–108.

Doyle, R. E. (1992). *Essential skills and strategies in the helping process.* Pacific Grove, CA: Brooks/Cole.

Dustin, R., & Ehly, S. (1984). Skills for effective consultation. *School Counselor, 32,* 23–29.

Dykeman, C. (1995). The privatization of school counseling. *School Counselor, 43,* 29–34.

Education Amendments of 1972, Title IX, 7 U.S.C. § 301 (1972).

Education Amendments of 1976, Title II, 20 U.S.C. §§ 2301-2461 (1976).

Education for All Handicapped Children Act of 1975, Pub. L. 94-142, 89 Stat. 773 (1975).

Education of the Handicapped Act Amendments of 1986, Pub. L. 99-457, 100 Stat. 1145 (1986).

Education of the Handicapped Act Amendments of 1990, Pub. L. 101-476, 104 Stat. 1103 (1990).

Education Trust. (1997). *Working definition of school counseling.* Washington, DC: Author.

Egan, G. (2007). *The skilled helper: A problem-management and opportunity development approach to helping* (8th ed.). Belmont, CA: Thomson Higher Education.

Ekstrom, R. B., Elmore, P. B., Schafer, W. D., Trotter, T. V., & Webster, B. (2004). A survey of assessment and evaluation activities of school counselors. *Professional School Counseling, 8,* 24–30.

Elementary and Secondary Education Act (ESEA) of 1965, Pub. L. 89–10, as added Pub. L. 103–382, title I, § 101, 108 Stat. 3519 (20 U.S.C. 6301 *et seq.*) (1994).

Elementary School Counseling Demonstration Act (ESCDA) of the Elementary and Secondary Education Act, 20 U.S.C. § 3161 (1992).

Ellis, A., & Dryden, W. (1997). *The practice of rational emotive behavior therapy* (2nd ed.). New York: Springer.

Ellis, A., Gordon, J., Neeman, M., & Palmer, S. (1997). *Stress counseling: A rational emotive behavior approach.* Herndon, VA: Cassell.

Engen, H. B., Lamb, R. R., & Prediger, D. H. (1982). Are secondary schools still using standardized tests? *Personnel and Guidance Journal, 60,* 287–290.

Erikson, E. H. (1963). *Childhood and society* (2nd ed.). New York: Norton.

Ewing, D. B. (1975). Direct from Minnesota—E. G. Williamson. *Personnel and Guidance Journal, 54,* 78–87.

Facundo, A., Nuttal, E. V., & Walton, J. (1994). Culturally sensitive assessment in schools. In P. Pedersen & J. C. Carey (Eds.), *Multicultural counseling in schools: A practical handbook* (pp. 225–238). Boston: Allyn & Bacon.

Fairchild, T. N., & Seeley, T. J. (1995). Accountability strategies for school counselors: A baker's dozen. *School Counselor, 42,* 377–392.

Fall, M. (1994). Developing curriculum expertise. A helpful tool for school counselors. *School Counselor, 42,* 92–99.

Fall, M. (1994). Self-efficacy: An additional dimension in play therapy. *International Journal of Play Therapy, 3,* 21–32.

Fall, M. (1995). Planning for consultation: An aid for the elementary school counselor. *School Counselor, 43,* 151–156.

Fall, M. (1997). From stages to categories: A study of children's play. *International Journal of Play Therapy, 6,* 1–21.

Family Educational Rights and Privacy Act, 20 U.S.C. §§ 1221nt., 1232g (1974).

Field, J. E., & Baker, S. B. (2004). Defining and examining school counselor advocacy. *Professional School Counseling, 8,* 56–63.

Fielstein, L. L. (1996). Case study 12: Ensuring a student's welfare. In B. Herlihy & G. Corey (Eds.), *ACA ethical standards casebook* (5th ed., pp. 248–250). Alexandria, VA: American Counseling Association.

Fischer, L., & Sorenson, G. P. (1996). *School law for counselors, psychologists, and social workers* (3rd ed.). New York: Longman.

Fitch, T., Newby, E., Ballestero, V., & Marshall, J. L. (2001). Future school administrators' perceptions of the school counselors' role. *Counselor Education and Supervision, 41,* 89–99.

Fontaine, J. H.(1998). Evidencinganeed:Schoolcounselors'experienceswithgayandlesbianstudents. *ProfessionalSchoolCounseling,1*(3),8–14.

Foster, L. H., Young, J. S., & Hermann, M. (2005). The work activities of professional school counselors: Are the National Standards being addressed? *Professional School Counseling, 8,* 313–321.

Galassi, J. P., & Akos, P. (2004). Developmental advocacy: Twenty-first century school counseling.

Journal of Counseling and Development, 82, 146–157.

Galassi, M. D., & Galassi, J. P. (1977). *Assert yourself! How to be your own person.* New York: Human Sciences Press.

Gallessich, J. (1985). Toward a meta-theory of consultation. *Counseling Psychologist, 13*(3), 336–354.

Garcia, J. G., Cartwright, B., Winston, S. M., & Borzuchowska, B. (2003). A transcultural integrative model for ethical decision making counseling. *Journal of Counseling and Development, 81,* 268–277.

Gardner, D. (1983). *A nation at risk: The imperative for educational reform.* Report of the National Commission on Excellence in Education. Washington, DC: Government Printing Office.

Gehring, D. C. (1982). The counselor's "duty to warn." *Personnel and Guidance Journal, 61,* 208–210.

Gendlin, E. T. (1996). *Focusing oriented psychotherapy: A manual of experiential methods.* New York: Guilford.

George-Barden Vocational Education Act, 20 U.S.C. § 1241 (1996).

Gerler, E. R. (1990). Children's success in school: Collaborative research among counselors, supervisors, and counselor educators. *Elementary School Guidance and Counseling, 25,* 64–71.

Gerler, E. R. (2001). *Succeeding in school.* Retrieved January 20, 2007, from http: $word$.com/web $word$.

Gerler, E. R., & Anderson, R. F. (1986). The effects of classroom guidance on children's success in school. *Journal of Counseling and Development, 65,* 78–81.

Gerler, E. R., Drew, N. S., & Mohr, P. (1990). Succeeding in middle school: A multimodal approach. *Elementary School Guidance and Counseling, 24,* 263–271.

Gerler, E. R., & Herndon, E. (1993). Learning how to succeed academically in middle school. *Elementary School Guidance and Counseling, 27,* 186–197.

Gerler, E. R., Jr. (1992). Consultation and school counseling. *Elementary School Guidance and Counseling, 26,* 162.

Gerler, E. R., Jr. (Ed.). (1987). Counseling with expressive arts [special issue]. *Elementary School Guidance and Counseling, 21*(4).

Getson, R., & Schweid, R. (1976). School counselors and the Buckley Amendment—Ethical standards squeeze. *School Counselor, 24,* 56–58.

Gibbs, J. T. (1973). Black students/White university: Different expectations. *Personnel and Guidance Journal, 51,* 463–470.

Gibson, R. L. (1990). Teachers' opinions of high school guidance and counseling programs: Then and now. *School Counselor, 37,* 248–255.

Gibson, R. L., & Mitchell, M. H. (1981). *Introduction to guidance.* New York: Macmillan.

Gilligan, C. (1982). *In a different voice.* Cambridge, MA: Harvard University Press.

Giordano, F. G., Schwiebert, V. L., & Brotherton, D. L. (1997). School counselors' perceptions of the usefulness of standardized tests, frequency of their use, and assessment training needs. *School Counselor, 44,* 198–205.

Glasser, W. (2002, March). Program presented at the annual convention of the American Counseling Association, New Orleans, LA.

Glosoff, H. L., & Pate, R. H., Jr. (2002). Privacy and confidentiality in school counseling. *Professional School Counseling, 6,* 20–27.

Glosoff, H. L., Herlihy, B., & Spence, E. B. (2000). Privileged communication and the counselor-client relationship. *Journal of Counseling & Development, 78,* 454–462.

Goals 2000: Educate America Act, 20 U.S.C § 5801 (1994).

Goetz, B. (1997). School enrollment to hit all time high. *Counseling Today, 40*(4), 12.

Goldman, L. (1971). *Using tests in counseling* (2nd ed.). New York: Appleton-Century-Crofts.

Goldman, L. (1972). Tests and counseling: The marriage that failed. *Measurement and Evaluation in Guidance, 4,* 213–220.

Goldman, L. (1982). Assessment in counseling: A better way. *Measurement and Evaluation in Guidance, 15,* 70–73.

Goldman, L. (1990). Qualitative assessment. *Counseling Psychologist, 18*(2), 205–213.

Goldman, L. (1994). The marriage is over . . . for most of us. *Measurement and Evaluation in Counseling and Development, 26,* 217–218.

Green, A., & Keys, S. (2001). Expanding the developmental school counseling paradigm: Meeting the needs of the 21st century student. *Professional School Counseling, 5,* 84–95.

Greenwood, E. (1957). Attributes of a profession. *Social Work, 2,* 45–55.

Greer, B. B., Greer, J. G., & Woody, D. E. (1995). The inclusion movement and its impact on counselors. *School Counselor, 43,* 24–132.

Guerra, P. (1998). Revamping school counselor education: The DeWitt Wallace Reader's Digest Fund. *Counseling Today, 40*(8), 19, 36.

Guillot-Miller, L., & Partin, P. W. (2003). Web-based resources for legal and ethical issues in school counseling. *Professional School Counseling, 7,* 52–57.

Gunnings, T. S. (1978). Guidance and counseling in special settings. In *The status of guidance and counseling in the nation's schools* (pp. 147–156). Washington, DC: American Personnel and Guidance Association.

Gysbers, N. C. (2001). School guidance and counseling in the 21st century: Remember the past into the future. *Professional School Counseling, 5,* 96–105.

Gysbers, N. C. (2004). Comprehensive guidance and counseling programs: The evolution of accountability. *Professional School Counseling, 8,* 1–14.

Gysbers, N. C., & Henderson, P. (2000). *Developing and managing your school guidance program* (3rd ed.). Alexandria, VA: American Association for Counseling and Development.

Gysbers, N. C., & Henderson, P. (2001). Comprehensive guidance and counseling programs: A rich history and a bright future. *Professional School Counseling, 4,* 246–256.

Haettenschwiller, D. L. (1970). Control of the counselor's role. *Journal of Counseling Psychology, 17,* 437–442.

Haettenschwiller, D. L. (1971). Counseling Black college students in special programs. *Personnel and Guidance Journal, 50,* 29–36.

Hains, A. A. (1992). Comparison of cognitive-behavioral stress management techniques with adolescent boys. *Journal of Counseling & Development, 70,* 600–605.

Hains, A. A. (1994). The effectiveness of a school-based, cognitive-behavioral stress management program with adolescents reporting high and low levels of emotional arousal. *School Counselor, 42,* 114–125.

Hanish, L. D., & Guerra, N. G. (2000). Children who get victimized at school: What is known? What can be done? *Professional School Counseling, 4,* 113–119.

Hansen, L. S. (1968). Are we change agents? *School Counselor, 15,* 245–246.

Harris, P. R. (1967). Guidance and counseling: Where it's been—Where it's going. *School Counselor, 15,* 10–15.

Hatch, T. (2001, September/October). Challenges of professional development. *ASCA School Counselor, 9–12.*

Hatch, T., & Bowers, J. (2002, May–June). The block to build on. *ASCA Counselor*, 13–17.

Havighurst, R. J. (1972). *Human development and education*. New York: Longman Green.

Hayes, L. (2001, September). Testing, 1-2-3. *Counseling Today*, 8–9.

Hawes, D. J. (1996). Who knows who best? A program to stimulate parent–teen interaction. *School Counselor, 44*, 115–121.

Helms, B. J., & Ibrahim, F. A. (1985). A comparison of counselor and parent perceptions of the role and function of secondary school counselors. *School Counselor, 32*, 266–274.

Helms, J. E. (1995). An update of Helms's white and people of color racial identity models. In J. G. Ponteroto, J. M. Casas, L. A. Suzuki, & C. M. Alexander (Eds.), *Handbook of multicultural counseling* (pp. 181–198). Thousand Oaks, CA: Sage.

Heppner, P. P., Kivlighan, D. M., Jr., & Wampold, B. E. (1999). *Research design in counseling* (2nd ed.). Belmont, CA: Wadsworth.

Herlihy, B., & Remley, T. P. (2001). Legal and ethical challenges. In D. C. Locke, J. E. Myers, & E. L. Herr (Eds.), *The handbook of counseling* (pp. 69–89). Thousand Oaks, CA: Sage.

Hermann, M. A. (2002). A study of legal issues encountered by school counselors and perceptions of their preparedness to respond to legal challenges. *Professional School Counseling, 6*, 12–19.

Herr, E. L. (1979). *Guidance and counseling in the schools: Perspectives on the past, present, and future*. Falls Church, VA: American Personnel and Guidance Association.

Herr, E. L. (1985). AACD: An association committed to unity through diversity. *Journal of Counseling & Development, 63*, 395–404.

Herr, E. L. (2001). The impact of national policies, economics, and school reform on comprehensive guidance programs. *Professional School Counseling, 4*, 236–245.

Herr, E. L. (2002, April). School reform and perspectives on the role of school counselors: A century of proposals for change. *Professional School Counseling, 5*, 220–234.

Herr, E. L., & Cramer, S. G. (1987). *Controversies in the mental health professions*. Muncie, IN: Accelerated Development.

Herring, R. D. (1997a). *Counseling diverse and ethnic youth: Synergistic strategies and interventions for school counselors*. Ft. Worth, TX: Harcourt Brace College.

Herring, R. D. (1997b). *Multicultural counseling in schools: A synergistic approach*. Alexandria, VA: American Counseling Association.

Hinson, J., & Fossey, R. (2000). Child abuse: What teachers in the 90s know, think, and do. *Journal of Education for Students Placed at Risk, 5*, 251–266.

Hitchner, K. W., & Tifft-Hitchner, A. (1987). *A survival guide for the secondary school counselor*. West Nyack, NY: Center for Applied Research in Education.

Hoag, M. J., & Burlingame, G. M. (1997). Evaluating the effectiveness of child and adolescent group treatment. *Journal of Clinical Child Psychology, 26*, 234–246.

Hobbs, B. B., & Collison, B. (1995). School–community agency collaboration: Implications for school counselors. *School Counselor, 43*, 58–65.

Holland, J. L. (1997). *Making vocational choices: A theory of vocational personalities and work environments* (3rd ed.). Odessa, FL: Professional Assessment Resources.

Hollis, J. W., & Hollis, L. U. (1965). *Organizing for effective guidance*. Chicago: Science Research Associates.

Hopkins, B. R., & Anderson, B. S. (1990). *The counselor and the law*. Alexandria, VA: American Association for Counseling and Development.

Horan, J. J. (1979). *Counseling for effective decision making*. North Scituate, MA: Duxbury.

Horton, G. E., & Brown, D. (1990). The importance of interpersonal skills in consultee-centered consultation. *Journal of Counseling & Development, 68*, 423–426.

Hoskins, R. G., & Rosenthal, N. R. (1983). Microcomputer-assisted guidance scheduling for career information programs. *Vocational Guidance Quarterly, 32*, 122–124.

Hourcade, J. J., & Parette, H. P., Jr. (1986). Students with epilepsy: Counseling implications for the hidden handicapped. *School Counselor, 33*, 279–285.

House, R. M., & Hayes, R. L. (2002). School counselors: Becoming key players in school reform. *Professional School Counseling, 5*, 249–256.

House, R. M., & Martin, P. (1998). Advocating for better futures for all students: A new vision for school counselors. *Education, 119*, 284–291.

Hoyt, K. B., Evans, R. N., Mackin, E. F., & Mangum, G. L. (1974). *Career education: What is it and how to do it* (2nd ed.). Salt Lake City: Olympus.

Huey, W. C. (1986). Ethical concerns in school counseling. *Journal of Counseling & Development, 64*, 321–322.

Huey, W. C., Salo, M. M., & Fox, R. W. (1995). An ethics quiz for school counselors. *School Counselor, 42,* 393–398.

Hughes, D. K., & James, S. H. (2001). Using accountability data to protect a school counseling program: One counselor's experience. *Professional School Counseling, 4,* 306–309.

Hutchinson, R. L., Barrick, A. L., & Groves, M. (1986). Functions of secondary school counselors in the schools: Ideal and real. *School Counselor, 34,* 87–91.

Hutchinson, R. L., & Bottorf, R. L. (1986). Selected high school counseling services: 1986 Student assessment. *School Counselor, 53,* 350–354.

Hutchinson, R. L., & Reagan, C. A. (1989). Problems for which seniors would seek help from school counselors. *School Counselor, 36,* 271–279.

Ibrahim, F. A. (1991). Contribution of cultural worldview to generic counseling and development. *Journal of Counseling & Development, 70,* 13–19.

Ivey, A. E., & Gluckstern, N. (1974). *Basic attending skills: Leader and participants manual.* North Amherst, MA: Microtraining

Ivey, A. E., & Ivey, M. B. (2007). *Intentional interviewing and counseling: Facilitating client development in a multicultural society* (6th ed.). Pacific Grove, CA: Thomson, Brooks/Cole.

Jackson, S. A., & White, J. (2000). Referrals to the school counselor: A qualitative study. *Professional School Counseling, 3,* 277–286.

Janis, I. L. (1983). The role of social support in adherence to stressful decisions. *American Psychologist, 38,* 143–160.

Johnson, L. S. (2000). Promoting professional identity in an era of educational reform. *Professional School Counseling, 4,* 31–40.

Johnson, S., & Johnson, C. D. (2003). Results-based guidance: A systems approach to student support programs. *Professional School Counseling, 6,* 180–185.

Joint Committee of the American School Counselor Association and the Association for Assessment in Counseling. (2001). Competencies in assessment and evaluation for school counselors. In G. R. Walz & J. C. Bleuer (Eds.), *Assessment issues and challenges for the millennium* (pp. 95–100). Greensboro, NC: ERIC Counseling and Student Services Clearing House.

Joint Committee on Testing Practices. (1988). *Code of fair testing practices in education.* Washington, DC: Author.

Jordan, A. E., & Meara, N. M. (1995). Ethics and professional practice of psychologists: The role of virtue and principles. In D.N. Bershoff (Ed.), *Ethical conflicts in psychology* (pp. 135–141). Washington, DC: American Psychological Association.

Josselson, R. (1987). *Finding herself: Pathways to identity development in women.* San Francisco: Jossey-Bass.

Kaffenberger, C. J., Murphy, S., & Bemak, F. (2006). School Counseling Leadership Team: A statewide collaborative model to transform school counseling. *Professional School Counseling, 9,* 288–294.

Kahn, B. B. (1999). Art therapy with adolescents: Making it work for school counselors. *Professional School Counseling, 2,* 291–298.

Kahn, B. B. (2000). A model of solution-focused consultation for school counselors. *Professional School Counseling, 3,* 248–254.

Kapes, J. T., & Whitfield, E. A. (Eds.). 2002. *A counselor's guide to career assessment instruments* (4th ed.). Alexandria, VA: National Career Development Association.

Kaplan, D. M. (1996). *Developing an informed consent brochure for secondary students: All about ASCA membership.* Alexandria, VA: American School Counselor Association.

Keat, D. B. (1974). *Fundamentals of child counseling.* Boston: Houghton Mifflin.

Keat, D. B. (1990). *Child multimodal therapy.* Norwood, NJ: Ablex.

Keat, D. B. (1990a). Change in child multimodal counseling. *Elementary School Guidance and Counseling, 24,* 248–262.

Keat, D. B. (1990b). *Child multimodal therapy.* Norwood, NJ: Ablex.

Kelly, F. R., Jr., & Ferguson, D. G. (1984). Elementary school guidance needs assessment: A field-tested model. *Elementary School Guidance and Counseling, 18,* 176–180.

Kennedy, A. (2006). Licensure portability update announced at convention. *Counseling Today, 48*(11), 8, 23.

Kenny, M. C. (2001). Child abuse reporting: Teacher's perceived deterrents. *Child Abuse and Neglect, 25,* 81–92.

Keys, S. G. (2000). Living the collaborative role: Voices from the field. *Professional School Counseling, 3,* 332–338.

Keys, S. G., & Bemak, F. (1997). School-family-community linked services: A school counseling role for changing times. *School Counselor, 44,* 255–263.

Keys, S. G., Bemak, F., & Lockhart, E. J. (1998). Transforming school counseling to meet the mental health needs of at-risk youth. *Journal of Counseling & Development, 76,* 381–388.

Keys, S. G., & Green, A. (2005). Enhancing developmental school counseling programs through collaboration. In C. Sink (Ed.), *Contemporary school counseling: Theory, research, and practice* (pp. 390–405). Boston: Lahaska Press/Houghton Mifflin.

Kimmerling, G. F. (1993). When saying no is the right thing to do. *American Counselor, 2,* 5–6.

Kiselica, M. S. (1996). Legal issues in abortion counseling with adolescents. *ASCA Counselor, 33*(4), 1.

Kiselica, M. S., Baker, S. B., Thomas, R. N., & Reedy, S. (1994). Effects of stress inoculation training on anxiety, stress, and academic performance among adolescents. *Journal of Counseling Psychology, 41,* 335–342.

Kiselica, M. S., & Robinson, M. (2001). Bringing advocacy counseling to life: The history, issues, and human dramas of social justice. *Journal of Counseling & Development, 79,* 387–397.

Kitchener, K. S. (1984). Intuition, critical evaluation, and ethical principles: The foundation for ethical decisions in counseling psychology. *The Counseling Psychologist, 12,* 43–55.

Knapp, D. L., & Denny, E. W. (1961). The counselor's responsibility in role definition. *Personnel and Guidance Journal, 40,* 48–50.

Knapp, S. (1983). Counselor liability to report child abuse. *Elementary School Guidance and Counseling, 17,* 177–179.

Kocet, M. M. (2006). Ethical challenges in a complex world: Highlights of the 2005 *ACA Code of Ethics. Journal of Counseling & Development, 84,* 228–234.

Kopala, M., Esquivel, G., & Baptiste, L. (1994). Counseling approaches for immigrant children: Facilitating the acculturative process. *School Counselor, 41,* 352–359.

Krieg, E. J. (1988). *Group leadership training and supervision manual for adolescent group counseling in schools* (3rd ed.). Muncie, IN: Accelerated Development.

Krumboltz, J. D. (1974). An accountability model for counselors. *Personnel and Guidance Journal, 52,* 639–646.

Kuranz, M. (2002). Cultivating student potential. *Professional School Counseling, 5,* 172-179.

Kurpius, D. J. (1978). Consultation theory and process: An integrated model. *Personnel and Guidance Journal, 56,* 335–338.

Kurpius, D. J., & Fuqua, D. R. (1993a). Consultation I: Conceptual, structural, and operational dimensions. *Journal of Counseling & Development, 71,* 596–708.

Kurpius, D. J., & Fuqua, D. R. (1993b). Consultation II: Prevention, preparation, and key issues. *Journal of Counseling & Development, 72,* 115–198.

Kurpius, D. J., Fuqua, D. R., & Rozecki, T. (1993). The consulting process: A multidimensional approach. *Journal of Counseling & Development, 71,* 601–606.

LaFountain, R. (1983). Referrals. *Elementary School Guidance and Counseling, 17,* 226–230.

LaFountain, R. M., Garner, N. E., & Eliason, G. T. (1996). Solution-focused counseling groups: A key for school counselors. *School Counselor, 43,* 256–266.

LaFromboise, T. D., Foster, S., & James, A. (1996). Ethics in multicultural counseling. In P. B. Pedersen, J. G. Draguns, W. J. Lonner, & J. E. Trimble (Eds.), *Counseling across cultures* (4th ed., pp. 47–72). Thousand Oaks, CA: Sage.

LaFromboise, T., & Jackson, M. (1996). MCT theory and Native American populations. In D. W. Sue, A. E. Ivey, & P. B. Pedersen (Eds.), *A theory of multicultural counseling and therapy* (pp. 192–203). Pacific Grove, CA: Brooks/Cole.

Lambie, G. W., & Williamson, L. L. (2004). The challenge to change from guidance counseling to professional school counseling. *Professional School Counseling, 8,* 124–131.

Landreth, G. L. (2002). *Play therapy: The art of relationships* (2nd ed.). New York: Brunner-Routledge.

Landreth, G. L., Homeyer, L. E., Glover, G., & Sweeney, D. S. (1996). *Play therapy interventions with children's problems.* Northvale, NJ: Jason Aronson.

Lange, A., & Jakubowski, P. (1976). *Responsible assertive behavior.* Champaign, IL: Research Press.

Lapan, R. T., Gysbers, N. C., & Sun, Y. (1997). The impact of more fully implemented guidance programs on the school experiences of high school students: A statewide evaluation study. *Journal of Counseling & Development, 75,* 292–302.

Lapan, R. T., Kardash, C. M., & Turner, S. (2002). Empowering students to become self-regulated learners. *Professional School Counseling, 5,* 257–265.

Lawrence, G., & Kurpius, S. E. R. (2000). Legal and ethical issues involved when counseling minors in nonschool settings. *Journal of Counseling & Development, 78,* 130–136.

Lawson, D. M., McClain, A. L., Matlock-Hetzel, S., Duffy, M., & Urbanovski, R. (1997). School families: Implementation and evaluation of a middle school prevention program. *Journal of Counseling & Development, 76,* 82–89.

Lazarus, A. A. (1976). Multimodal assessment. In A. A. Lazarus (Ed.), *Multimodal behavior therapy* (pp. 25–47). New York: Springer.

Lee, C. C. (1998). Counselors as agents for social change. In C. C. Lee & G. R. Walz (Eds.), *Social action: A mandate for counselors* (pp. 3–16). Alexandria, VA: American Counseling Association.

Lee, C. C. (2001). Culturally responsive school counselors and programs: Addressing the needs of all students. *Professional School Counseling, 4,* 257–262.

Lee, C. C., & Sirch, M. L. (1994). Counseling in an enlightened society: Values for a new millennium. *Counseling and Values, 38,* 90–97.

Lee, R. S. (1993). Learning how to succeed academically in middle school. *Elementary School Guidance and Counseling, 27,* 163–171.

Legal considerations should not shape clinical decisions, seminar told. (1983, July 6). *Mental Health Reports,* pp. 7–8.

Lewis, R. L., & Borunda, R. (2006). Lived stories: Participatory leadership in school counseling. *Journal of Counseling and Development, 84,* 406–413.

Lin, M., Kelly, K. R., & Nelson, R. C. (1996). A comparative analysis of the interpersonal process in school-based counseling and consultation. *Journal of Counseling Psychology, 43,* 389–393.

Linden, K. W., & Linden, J. D. (1968). *Modern mental measurement: A historical perspective.* Boston: Houghton Mifflin.

Littrell, J. M. (1998). *Brief counseling in action.* New York: Norton.

Littrell, J. M., & Peterson, J. S. (2001). Transforming the school culture: A model based on an exemplary counselor. *Professional School Counseling, 4,* 310–319.

Liu, Y. C., & Baker, S. B. (1993). Enhancing cultural adaptation through friendship training. *Elementary School Guidance and Counseling, 18,* 92–103.

Locke, D. C., Myers, J. E., & Herr, E. L. (2001). Counseling and the future. In D. C. Locke, J. E. Myers, & E. L. Herr (Eds.), *The handbook of counseling* (pp. 683–691). Thousand Oaks, CA: Sage.

Logan, C., & Williams, C. B. (2001, April). Ethical issues in counseling gay youth. *Counseling Today,* 41–42.

Luftig, R. L. (1983). Effects of schooling on the self-concept of Native American students. *School Counselor, 30,* 251–260.

Luongo, P. F. (2000). Partnering child welfare, juvenile justice, and behavioral health with schools. *Professional School Counseling, 3,* 308–313.

Lupton-Smith, H., Carruthers, W. L., Flythe, R., Goettee, E., & Modest, K. H. (1996). Conflict resolution as peer mediation: Programs for elementary, middle, and high school students. *School Counselor, 43,* 149–157.

Marinoble, R. M. (1998). A blind spot in the mirror. *Professional School Counseling, 1*(3), 4–7.

Mascari, J. B. (2006). AASCB and ACA partner to develop licensing portability. *Counseling Today, 48*(9), 12.

Maslow, A. H. (1954). *Motivation and personality.* New York: Harper.

Mathias, C. E. (1992). Touching the lives of children: Consultative interventions that work. *Elementary School Guidance and Counseling, 26,* 190–201.

McCullough, L. (1994). Challenges to guidance programs: How to prevent and handle them. *Guidepost, 36*(8), 1, 12.

McFarland, W. P. (1998). Gay, lesbian, and bisexual student suicide. *Professional School Counseling, 1*(3), 26–29.

McFarland, W. P., & DuPuis, M. (2001). The legal duty to protect gay and lesbian students from violence in school. *Professional School Counseling, 4,* 171–179.

McGuire, J. M., & Borowy, T. D. (1978). Confidentiality and the Buckley/Pell Amendment: Ethical and legal considerations for counselors. *Personnel and Guidance Journal, 56,* 554–557.

Meichenbaum, D. H. (1993). Stress inoculation training: A 20-year update. In P. M. Lehrer & R. L. Woolfolk (Eds.), *Principles and practices of stress management* (2nd ed., pp. 373–406). New York: Guilford.

Meichenbaum, D. H. (1994). *A clinical handbook: Practical therapist manual for assessing and treating adults with post-traumatic stress disorders.* Waterloo, Ontario, Canada: Institute Press.

Meichenbaum, D. H., & Deffenbacher, J. L. (1988). Stress inoculation training. *Counseling Psychologist, 16,* 69–89.

Menacker, J. (1974). *Vitalizing guidance in urban schools.* New York: Dodd, Mead.

Menacker, J. (1976). Toward a theory of activist guidance. *Personnel and Guidance Journal, 54,* 318–321.

Mendoza, D. W. (1993). A review of Gerald Caplan's *Theory and Practice of Mental Health Consultation. Journal of Counseling & Development, 71,* 629–635.

Merlone, L. (2005). Record keeping and the school counselor. *Professional School Counseling, 8,* 372–376.

Merriam-Webster's collegiate dictionary (10th ed.). (1998). Springfield, MA: Merriam-Webster.

Messing, J. K. (1993). Mediation: An intervention strategy for counselors. *Journal of Counseling & Development, 72,* 67–72.

Miller, G. D. (1989). What roles and functions do elementary school counselors have? *Elementary School Guidance and Counseling, 24,* 77–88.

Miller-Jones, D. (1989). Culture and testing. *American Psychologist, 40,* 360–366.

Millman, J., Bishop, C. H., & Ebel, R. (1965). An analysis of test-wiseness. *Educational and Psychological Measurement, 25,* 707–726.

Moles, O. C. (1991). Guidance programs in American high schools: A descriptive portrait. *School Counselor, 38,* 163–177.

Monahan, J. (1993). Limiting therapist exposure to *Tarasoff* liability. *American Psychologist, 48,* 242–250.

Moracco, J. C., Butcke, P. G., & McEwen, M. K. (1984). Measuring stress in school counselors: Some research findings and implications. *School Counselor, 32,* 110–118.

Morgan, C., & Jackson, W. (1980). Guidance as a curriculum. *Elementary School Guidance and Counseling, 15,* 99–103.

Morrissey, M. (1996). The baby boom echo generation: Ready or not, here it comes. *Counseling Today, 39*(6), 1, 6, 8.

Morse, C. L., & Russell, T. (1988). How elementary counselors see their role: An empirical study. *Elementary School Guidance and Counseling, 23,* 54–62.

Mosconi, J., & Emmett, J. (2003). Effects of a values clarification curriculum on high school students' definition of success. *Professional School Counseling, 7,* 68–78.

Mosher, R. L., & Sprinthall, N. A. (1970). Psychological education in secondary schools: A program to promote individual and human development. *American Psychologist, 25,* 911–924.

Muller, L. E., & Hartman, J. (1998). Group counseling for sexual minority youth. *Professional School Counseling, 1*(3), 38–41.

Mullis, F., & Edwards, D. (2001). Consulting with parents: Applying family systems concepts and techniques. *Professional School Counseling, 5,* 116–123.

Murphy, J. J. (1994). Working with what works: A solution-focused approach to school behavior problems. *School Counselor, 42,* 59–72.

Murphy, J. J. (1997). *Solution-focused counseling in middle and high schools.* Alexandria, VA: American Counseling Association.

Myrick, R. D. (1977). *Consultation as a counselor intervention.* Washington, DC: American School Counselor Association.

Myrick, R. D. (2003). Accountability: Counselors count. *Professional School Counseling, 6,* 174–179.

National Defense Education Act, 20 U.S.C. §§ 15aaa–15ggg, 401–403 (1958).

Neukrug, E. S., Barr, C. G., Hoffman, L. R., & Kaplan, L. S. (1993). Developmental counseling and guidance: A model for use in your school. *School Counselor, 40,* 356–362.

Neuman, N. (2006, Winter). Classroom guidance doesn't have to be a chore. *North Carolina School Counselor Association News,* 5.

No Child Left Behind (PL 107-110)

No Child Left Behind Act, 20 U.S.C. § 6301 (2001).

North Carolina Department of Public Instruction. (1999). *The ABCs of public education.* Raleigh: Author.

Nuttal, E. V., Webber, J. J., & Sanchez, W. (1996). MCT theory and implications for training. In D. W. Sue, A. E. Ivey, & P. B. Pedersen (Eds.), *A theory of multicultural counseling and therapy* (pp. 123–138). Pacific Grove, CA: Brooks/Cole.

O'Connor, K. J. (1991). *The play therapy primer: An integration of theories and techniques.* New York: John Wiley.

O'Connor, K. J., & Schaefer, C. E. (Eds.). (1994). *Handbook of play therapy: Vol. 2. Advances and innovations.* New York: John Wiley.

O'Connor, K., Plante, J., & Refvem, J. (1998, March). *Parental consent and the school counselor.* Poster session presented at the annual meeting of the North Carolina Counseling Association, Chapel Hill.

Olson, M. J., & Allen, D. N. (1993). Principals' perceptions of the effectiveness of school counselors with and without teaching experience. *Counselor Education and Supervision, 33,* 10–21.

Omizo, M. M., Omizo, S. A., & Okamoto, C. M. (1998). Gay and lesbian adolescents: A phenomenological study. *Professional School Counseling, 1*(3), 35–37.

Osterweil, Z. O. (1987). A structured process of problem definition in school consultation. *School Counselor, 34*, 245–252.

Page, B. J., Pietrzak, D. R., & Sutton, J. W., Jr. (2001). National survey of school counselor supervision. *Counselor Education and Supervision, 41*, 142–150.

Paisley, P. O., & Borders, D. L. (1995). School counseling: An evolving specialty. *Journal of Counseling and Development, 74*, 150–153.

Paisley, P. O., & Hayes, R. L. (2003). School counseling in the academic domain: Transformations in preparation and practice. *Professional School Counseling, 6*, 198–205.

Paisley, P. O., & McMahon, H. G. (2001). School counseling for the 21st century: Challenges and opportunities. *Professional School Counseling, 5*, 106–115.

Pallas, A. M., Natriello, G., & McDill, E. L. (1989). The changing nature of the disadvantaged population: Current dimensions and future trends. *Educational Researcher, 18*(5), 16–22.

Park, W. D., & Williams, G. T. (1986). Encouraging elementary children to refer themselves for counseling. *Elementary School Guidance and Counseling, 21*, 8–14.

Parsons, F. (1909). *Choosing a vocation.* Boston: Houghton Mifflin.

Parten, M. (1966). *Surveys, polls, and samples: Practical procedures.* New York: Cooper Square.

Pedersen, J. S. (1988). Constraining influences on the vocational guidance of girls from 1910 to 1930. *Career Development Quarterly, 36*, 325–336.

Pedersen, P. B. (1997). *Culture-centered counseling interventions: Striving for accuracy.* Thousand Oaks, CA: Sage.

Peer, G. G. (1985). The status of secondary school guidance: A national survey. *School Counselor, 32*, 181–189.

Pennsylvania Department of Education. (1977). *Guidance services in Pennsylvania: Position statement.* Harrisburg: Author.

Perusse, R., Goodenough, G. E., Donegan, J., & Jones, C. (2004). Perceptions of school counselors and principals about the National Standards for School Counseling Programs and the Transforming School Counseling Initiative. *Professional School Counseling, 7*, 182–191.

Perusse, R., Goodnough, G. E., & Noel, D. (2000, March). *What school counselors need to know, what counselor educators need to teach.* Paper presented at the annual meeting of the American Counseling Association, Washington, DC.

Peters, D. (1978). The practice of counseling in the secondary school. In *The status of guidance and counseling in the nation's schools* (pp. 81–100). Washington, DC: American Personnel and Guidance Association.

Peterson, J., Goodman, R., Keller, T., & McCauley, J. (2004). Teachers and non-teachers as school counselors: Reflections on the internship experience. *Professional School Counseling, 7*, 246–255.

Pietrofesa, J. J., & Vriend, J. (1971). *The school counselor as a professional.* Itasca, IL: F. E. Peacock.

Pintrich, P. R. (2000). The role of goal orientation in self-regulated learning. In M. Boekaerts, P. R. Pintrich, & M. Zeidner (Eds.), *Handbook of self-regulation* (pp. 452–502). New York: Academic.

Pitch, T., Newby, E., Ballestero, V., & Marshall, J. L. (2001). Furture school administrators' perceptions of the school counselors' role. *Counselor Education and Supervision, 41*, 89–99.

Ponterotto, J. G., & Pedersen, P. B. (1993). *Preventing prejudice: A guide for counselors and educators.* Newbury Park, CA: Sage.

Ponzo, Z. (1974). A counselor and change: Reminiscence and resolutions. *Personnel and Guidance Journal, 53*, 27–32.

Porter, G., Epp, L., & Bryant, S. (2000). Collaboration among school mental health professionals: A necessity not a luxury. *Professional School Counseling, 3*, 315–322.

Post-Kammer, P. (1988). Effectiveness of Parents Anonymous in reducing child abuse. *School Counselor, 35*, 337–342.

Powers, S. I., Hauser, S. T., & Kilner, L. A. (1989). Adolescent mental health. *American Psychologist, 44*, 200–208.

Prediger, D. J. (1994). Tests and counseling: The marriage that prevailed. *Measurement and Evaluation in Counseling and Development, 26*, 227–234.

Proctor, W. (1925). *Educational and vocational guidance: A consideration of guidance as it relates to all of the essential activities of life.* Boston: Houghton Mifflin.

Purkey, W. W., & Schmidt, J. J. (1982). Ways to be an inviting parent: Suggestions for the counselor-consultant. *Elementary School Guidance and Counseling, 17*, 94–99.

Rathvon, N. W. (1990). The effects of encouragement on off-task behavior and academic productivity. *Elementary School Guidance and Counseling, 24*, 189–199.

Rayle, A. D. (2006). Do school counselors matter? Mattering as a moderator between job stress and job satisfaction. *Professional School Counseling, 9,* 223–230.

Remafedi, G. (1987). Adolescent homosexuality: Psychosocial and medical implications. *Pediatrics, 79,* 331–337.

Remafedi, G., Farrow, J. A., & Deisher, R. W. (1991). Risk factors in attempted suicide in gay and bisexual youth. *Pediatrics, 87,* 869–875.

Remley, T. P., Jr. (1985). The law and ethical practices in elementary and middle schools. *Elementary School Guidance and Counseling, 19,* 181–189.

Remley, T. P., Jr. (1992). How much record keeping is enough? *American Counselor, 1,* 31–33.

Remley, T. P., Jr., & Albright, P. L. (1988). Expectations for middle school counselors: Views of students, teachers, principals, and parents. *School Counselor, 35,* 290–296.

Remley, T. P., Jr., & Herlihy, B. (2005). *Ethical, legal, and professional issues in counseling* (2nd ed.). Upper Saddle River, NJ: Pearson-Merrill-Prentice Hall.

Repucci, N. D., & Haugaard, J. J. (1989). Prevention of child sexual abuse. *American Psychologist, 44,* 1266–1275.

Rhyne-Winkler, M. C., & Wooten, H. R. (1996). The school counselor portfolio: Professional development and accountability. *School Counselor, 44,* 146–150.

Ritchie, M. H. (1986). Counseling the involuntary client. *Journal of Counseling & Development, 64,* 516–518.

Ritchie, M. H., & Partin, R. L. (1994). Referral practices of school counselors. *School Counselor, 41,* 263–272.

Roberts, W. B., Jr. (1995). Postvention and psychological autopsy in the suicide of a 14-year-old public school student. *School Counselor, 42,* 322, 330.

Roberts, W. B., Jr., Coursol, D. H., & Morotti, A. A. (1997). Chief school administrators' perceptions of professional school counselors on measures of employability in Minnesota. *School Counselor, 44,* 280–287.

Roberts, W. B., Jr., & Morotti, A. A. (2000). The bully as victim: Understanding bully behaviors to increase the effectiveness of interventions in the bully–victim dyad. *Professional School Counseling, 4,* 148–155.

Robinson, E. H., & Wilson, E. S. (1987). Counselor-led human relations training as a consultation strategy. *Elementary School Guidance and Counseling, 22,* 124–131.

Rockwell, P. J., & Rothney, J. W. M. (1961). Some ideas of pioneers in the guidance movement. *Personnel and Guidance Journal, 11,* 34–39.

Rockwood, G. G. (1993). Edgar Schein's process versus content consultation models. *Journal of Counseling & Development, 71,* 636–638.

Rogers, C. R. (1942). *Counseling and psychotherapy.* Boston: Houghton Mifflin.

Rogers, C. R. (1951). *Client-centered therapy.* Boston: Houghton Mifflin.

Rogers, C. R. (1961). *On becoming a person.* Boston: Houghton Mifflin.

Rogler, L. H., Malgady, R. G., Constantino, G., & Blumenthal, R. (1987). What do culturally sensitive mental health services mean? The case of Hispanics. *American Psychologist, 42,* 565–570.

Roman, P. M. (1989). Perils, payoffs of technology transfer. *Employee Assistance, 1,* 16–17.

Romano, J. L., Miller, J. P., & Nordness, A. (1996). Stress and well-being in the elementary school: A classroom curriculum. *School Counselor, 43,* 268–276.

Ross, G. J. (1993). Peter Block's flawless consulting and homunculus theory: Within each person is a perfect consultant. *Journal of Counseling & Development, 71,* 639–641.

Rousseve, R. J. (1968). The role of the counselor in a free society. *School Counselor, 16,* 6–10.

Rowley, W. J., Sink, C. A., & MacDonald, G. (2002). An experiential and systemic approach to encourage collaboration and community building. *Professional School Counseling, 5,* 360–365.

Rowley, W. J., Stroh, H. R., & Sink, C. A. (2005). Comprehensive guidance and counseling program's use of guidance curricula materials: A survey of national trends. *Professional School Counseling, 8,* 296–304.

Ruiz, R. A., & Padilla, A. M. (1977). Counseling Latinos. *Personnel and Guidance Journal, 55,* 401–408.

Russell Sage Foundation. (1970). *Guidelines for the collection, maintenance, and dissemination of pupil records.* Hartford, CT: Author.

Sabella, R. A. (2006). The ASCA National Counseling Research Center: A brief history and agenda. *Professional School Counseling, 9,* 412–415.

Sain v. Cedar Rapids Community School District, 626 N.W.2d 115 (Iowa 2001).

Sampson, J. P., Jr. (1983). Computer-assisted testing and assessment: Current status and implications for the future. *Measurement and Evaluation in Guidance, 15,* 293–299.

Sampson, J. P. Jr. (2000). Using the Internet to enhance testing in counseling. *Journal of Counseling & Development, 78,* 348–356.

Samuelson, R. J. (2005, June 27). Time to toss in the textbook. *Newsweek, CXLV*(26), 39.

Sandhu, D. S. (2000). Foreward. *Professional School Counseling, 4,* iv.

Sarbin, T. R. (1954). Role theory. In G. Lindzey (Ed.), *Handbook of social psychology.* London: Addison-Wesley.

Sarnacki, R. (1979). An examination of test-wiseness in the cognitive test domain. *Review of Educational Research, 49,* 252–279.

Savage, T. A., Harley, D. A., & Nowak, T. M. (2005). Applying social empowerment strategies as tools for self-advocacy in counseling lesbian and gay male clients. *Journal of Counseling and Development, 83,* 131-137.

Schaefer, C. E., & Cangelosi, D. M. (Eds.). (1993). *Play therapy techniques.* Northvale, NJ: Jason Aronson.

Schmidt, G. (1986). Idea exchange: Guidance program evaluation. *Elementary School Guidance and Counseling, 20,* 225–227.

Schmidt, J. J. (1995). Assessing school counseling programs through external reviews. *School Counselor, 43,* 114–122.

Schmidt, J. J. (2003). *Counseling in schools: Essential services and comprehensive programs.* Boston: Allyn & Bacon.

School-to-Work Opportunities Act, 20 U.S.C § 6101 (1994).

Schwallie-Giddis, P., ter Maat, M., & Park, M. (2003). Initiating leadership by implementing the ASCA National Model. *Professional School Counseling, 6,* 170–173.

Sears, S. (2005). Large group guidance: Curriculum development and instruction. In C. A. Sink (Ed.), *Contemporary school counseling: Theory, research, and practice* (pp. 189–213). Boston: Lahaska Press/Houghton Mifflin.

Sears, S. J., & Granello, D. H. (2002). School counseling now and in the future. *Professional School Counseling, 5,* 164–171.

Seem, S. (2002, April). Accreditation makes counselors strong. *Counseling Today, 7.*

Seligman, L. (1981). Multimodal behavior therapy: A case study of a high school student. *School Counselor, 28,* 249–256.

Shaw, M. C. (1968). *The function of theory in guidance programs. Guidance Monograph Series I.* Boston: Houghton Mifflin.

Shaw, M. C. (1973). *School guidance systems: Objectives, functions, evaluation, and change.* Boston: Houghton Mifflin.

Shaw, M. C., & Goodyear, R. K. (1984). Introduction to the special issue on primary prevention. *Personnel and Guidance Journal, 62,* 444–445.

Shechtman, Z. (2001). Prevention groups for angry and aggressive children. *Journal for Specialists in Group Work, 26,* 228–226.

Sheeley, V. L., & Herlihy, B. (1988). Privileged communication in schools and counseling: Status update. In W. C. Huey & T. P. Remley, Jr. (Eds.), *Ethical and legal issues in school counseling* (pp. 85–92). Alexandria, VA: American Association for Counseling and Development.

Sheeley, V. L., & Herlihy, B. (1989). Counseling suicidal teens: A duty to warn and protect. *School Counselor, 37,* 89–97.

Sheffield, D. S., & Baker, S. B. (2005). Themes from retrospective interviews of school counselors who experienced burnout. *Hecettepe University Journal of Education, 29,* 177–186.

Shertzer, B., & Stone, S. (1963). The school counselor and his publics: A problem in role definitions. *Personnel and Guidance Journal, 41,* 687–693.

Shertzer, B., & Stone, S. C. (1981). *Fundamentals of guidance* (4th ed.). Boston: Houghton Mifflin.

Sink, C. (2002). In search of the profession's finest hour: A critique of four views of 21st century school counseling. *Professional School Counseling, 5,* 156–164.

Sink, C. A. (2005). Comprehensive school counseling programs and academic achievement—A rejoinder to Brown and Trusty. *Professional School Counseling, 9,* 9–14.

Sink, C. A., & MacDonald, G. (1998). The status of comprehensive guidance and counseling in the United States. *Professional School Counseling, 2,* 88–94.

Skovholt, T. M. (2001). *The resilient practitioner: Burnout prevention and self-care strategies for counselors, therapists, teachers, and health professionals.* Boston: Allyn and Bacon.

Smaby, M. H., Peterson, T. L., Bergmann, P. E., Bacig, K. L. Z., & Swearingen, S. (1990). School-based community intervention: The school counselor as lead consultant for suicide prevention and intervention programs. *Elementary School Guidance and Counseling, 37,* 370–377.

Smith, G. E. (1955). *Counseling in the secondary school.* New York: Macmillan.

Smith, S. L., Crutchfield, L. B., & Culbretn, J. R. (2001). Teaching experience for school counselors: Counselor educator's perceptions. *Professional School Counseling, 4,* 216–228.

Smith-Hughes Vocational Education Act, 20 U.S.C. §§ 11–15, 16–28 (1917).

Sparks, E., Johnson, J., & Lewis, R. (2005). Re-forming the role of school counselor. *ASCA School Counselor, 42*(5), 10–15.

Speight, S. L., Myers, L. J., Cox, C. I., & Highlen, P. S. (1991). A redefinition of multicultural counseling. *Journal of Counseling & Development, 70,* 29–36.

Spielberger, C. D., Anton, W. D., & Bedell, J. (1976). The nature and treatment of test anxiety. In M. Zuckerman & C. D. Spielberger (Eds.), *Emotions and anxiety* (pp: 317–341). Mahwah, NJ: Lawrence Erlbaum.

Stamm, M. L., & Nissman, D. (1971). *New dimensions in elementary guidance.* New York: Richards Rosen Press.

Stewart, L. H., & Warnath, C. F. (1965). *The counselor and society.* Boston: Houghton Mifflin.

Stone, C. (2002). Negligence in academic advising and abortion counseling: Courts rulings and implications. *Professional School Counseling, 6,* 28–35.

Stone, C. (2005). Ethics and law for school counselors. *ASCA School Counselor, 42*(6), 44–49.

Stone, C., & House, R. (2002, May–June). Train the trainers program transform school counselors. *ASCA Counselor,* 20–21.

Stone, C. B., & Dahir, C. A. (2007). *School counselor accountability: A MEASURE of student success* (2nd ed.). Upper Saddle River, NJ: Pearson-Merrill-Prentice Hall.

Stone, S. C., & Shertzer, B. (1963). The militant counselor. *Personnel and Guidance Journal, 42,* 342–347.

Strein, W., & French, J. L. (1984). Teacher consultation in the affective domain: A survey of expert opinion. *School Counselor, 31,* 339–344.

Stringer, E., & Dwyer, R. (2005). *Action research in human services.* Upper Saddle River, NJ: Pearson-Merrill-Prentice Hall.

Stum, D. L. (1982). DIRECT: A consultation skills training model. *Personnel and Guidance Journal, 60,* 296–301.

Sue, D. W. (1992). The challenge of multiculturalism: The road less traveled. *American Counselor, 1,* 7–14.

Sue, D. W., Arredondo, P., & McDavis, R. J. (1992). Multicultural competencies/standards: A pressing need. *Journal of Counseling & Development, 70,* 477–486.

Sue, D. W., Ivey, A. E., & Pedersen, P. B. (1996). *A theory of multicultural counseling and therapy.* Pacific Grove, CA: Brooks/Cole.

Super, D. E. (1953). APGA: Promise and performance. *Personnel and Guidance Journal, 31,* 496–799.

Sutton, J. M., Jr., & Page, B. J. (1994). Post-degree clinical supervision of counselors. *School Counselor, 42,* 32–39.

Swisher, J. D., Bechtel, L., Henry, K. L., Vicary, J. R., & Smith, E. (2001). A model substance abuse prevention program. In D. C. Locke, J. E. Myers, & E. L. Herr (Eds.), *The handbook of counseling* (pp. 551–560). Thousand Oaks, CA: Sage.

Talbutt, L. C. (1983). The counselor and testing: Some legal concerns. *School Counselor, 30,* 245–250.

Tabish, K. R., & Orell, L. H. (1996). RESPECT: Gang mediation at Albuquerque, New Mexico's Washington Middle School. *School Counselor, 44,* 65–70.

Tarasoff v. Regents of the University of California, 551 p. 2nd 334 (California, 1976).

Tarvydas, V. M. (1998). Ethical decision-making processes. In R. R. Cottone & V. M. Tavrydas (Eds.), *Ethical and professional issues in counseling* (pp. 144–154). Upper Saddle River, NJ: Prentice Hall.

Taylor, L., & Adelman, H. S. (2000). Connecting schools, families, and communities. *Professional School Counseling, 3,* 298–307.

Tejada, L. (2006). The first word in our job description is 'school.' *Counseling Today, 48*(8), 14–15.

Tennant, C. G. (1988). Preventive sexual abuse programs: Problems and possibilities. *Elementary School Guidance and Counseling, 23,* 48–53.

Tennyson, W. W., Miller, G. D., Skovholt, T. G., & Williams, R. C. (1989). Secondary school counselors: What do they do? Why is it important? *School Counselor, 36,* 253–259.

Tennyson, W. W., Miller, G. D., Skovholt, G. G., & Williams, R. C. (1989). How they view their role: A survey of counselors in different secondary schools. *Journal of Counseling & Development, 67,* 399–403.

Theberge, S. K., & Karan, O. (2004). Six factors inhibiting the use of peer mediation in a junior high school. *Professional School Counseling, 7,* 283–290.

Therapists bear a duty to commit, says U.S. district court judge. (1987). *Mental Health Law Reporter,* pp. 4–5.

Thompson, D. W., Loesch, L. C., & Saraphine, A. E. (2003). Development of an instrument to assess the counseling needs of elementary school students. *Professional School Counseling, 7,* 35–39.

Trusty, J., & Brown, D. (2005). Advocacy competencies for professional school counselors. *Professional School Counseling, 8*, 259–265.

Umansky, D. L., & Holloway, E. L. (1984). The counselor as consultant: From model to practice. *School Counselor, 31*, 329–338.

Urbaniak, J. (2000, September). The ESCDA battle. *Counseling Today*, 18.

Van Hoose, W. H., & Kottler, J. (1978). *Ethical and legal issues in counseling and psychotherapy*. San Francisco: Jossey-Bass.

Vontress, C. (1966). *Counseling the culturally different adolescent: A school community approach*. Moravia, NY: Chronicle Guidance Publications.

Wagner, C. A. (1976). Referral patterns of children and teachers for group counseling. *Personnel and Guidance Journal, 55*, 90–93.

Walsh, M. E., & Galassi, J. P. (2002). An Introduction: Counseling psychologists and schools. *The Counseling Psychologist, 30*, 675–681.

Walz, G. R., & Benjamin, L. (1978). Professional development and competency. In *The status of guidance and counseling in the nation's schools* (pp. 127–136). Washington, DC: American Personnel and Guidance Association.

Ward, C. C. (2005). Social advocacy and professional identity: An interview with Reese M. House. *Counseling Today, 48*(1), 34–35.

Ward, D. E. (1984). Termination of individual counseling: Concepts and strategies. *Journal of Counseling & Development, 63*, 21–25.

Weinrach, S. G. (1984). Toward improved referral making: Mutuality between the counselor and the psychologist. *School Counselor, 32*, 89–96.

Westbrook, S. D., & Sedlacek, W. E. (1991). Forty years of using labels to communicate about nontraditional students: Does it help or hurt? *Journal of Counseling & Development, 70*, 20–28.

Whiston, S. C. (2002). Response to the past, present, and future of school counseling: Raising some issues. *Professional School Counseling, 5*, 148–155.

Whiston, S. C., & Sexton, T. (1998). A review of school counseling outcome research. *Journal of Counseling and Development, 76*, 412–426.

Wilgus, E., & Shelley, V. (1988). The role of the elementary school counselor: Teacher perceptions, expectations, and actual functions. *School Counselor, 35*, 259–266.

Wilkinson, C.M. (1990). Techniques for overcoming test anxiety. *Elementary School Guidance and Counseling, 24*, 234–237.

William T. Grant Foundation Commission on Work, Family and Citizenship. (1988). *The forgotten half: Non-college youth in America: An interim report on the school-to-work transition*. Washington, DC: Author.

Williamson, E. G. (1950). *Counseling adolescents*. New York: McGraw-Hill.

Williamson, E. G., & Darley, J. G. (1937). *Student personnel work: An outline of clinical procedures*. New York: McGraw-Hill.

Willower, D. J., Hoy, W. K., & Eidell, T. L. (1967). The counselor and the school as a social organization. *Personnel and Guidance Journal, 46*, 228–234.

Wilson, J., Thomas, D., & Schuette, L. (1983). Survey of counselors on identifying and reporting cases of child abuse. *School Counselor, 30*, 299–305.

Wood, S. (1984). Computer use in testing and assessment. *Journal of Counseling & Development, 63*, 177–179.

Wrenn, C. G. (1962). *The counselor in a changing world*. Washington, DC: American Personnel and Guidance Association.

Yalom, I. D. (1975). *The theory and practice of group psychotherapy* (2nd ed.). New York: Basic Books.

Zaccaria, J. (1969). *Approaches to guidance in contemporary education*. Scranton, PA: International Textbook.

Zalaquett, C. P. (2005). Principals' perceptions of elementary school counselors' role and functions. *Professional School Counseling, 8*, 451–457.

Zimman, R. N., & Cox, V. (1989). The role of guidance counselors. *Student Assistance Journal, 1*, 22–24.

Zingaro, J. (1983). Confidentiality: To tell or not to tell. *Elementary School Guidance and Counseling, 17*, 261–267.

Zubrod, A. R. (1992). The influence of group social skills development on attitudes and behaviors of at-risk adolescents. *Dissertation Abstracts International, 53–11A*, p. 3856. (University Microfilms No. AA19236928)

Zytowski, D. G. (1982). Assessment in the counseling process for the 1980s. *Measurement and Evaluation in Guidance, 15*, 15–21.

Zytowski, D. G. (1994). Tests and counseling: We are still married and living in discriminant analysis. *Measurement and Evaluation in Counseling and Development, 26*, 219–223.

Zytowski, D. G., & Warman, R. E. (1982). The changing use of tests in counseling. *Measurement and Evaluation in Guidance, 15*, 147–152.